Keynes's *Economic Consequences* *of the Peace* after 100 Years

The Economic Consequences of the Peace is one of the most famous books in the history of economic thought. It is also one of the most polemical. Published as a response to what Keynes saw as the grave errors of the Treaty of Versailles, the book predicted that war reparations and other harsh terms imposed on Germany would lead to its collapse, which in turn would lead to devastating consequences for Europe and the wider world. We now know these predictions to have been all too accurate. Keynes's *Economic Consequences of the Peace* after 100 Years brings together an international team of experts to assess the legacy of Keynes's best-selling work. It compiles a series of wide-ranging chapters, exploring the varied influence of his ideas and policy contributions. Written in an accessible style, it recovers the importance of this history and examines the continued relevance of Keynes's controversial book.

PATRICIA CLAVIN is Professor of Modern History at Oxford University and a Professorial Fellow of Worcester College. She won the British Academy Medal for her landmark work on the League of Nations and the history of political economy after 1918. She is a Fellow of the British Academy, a Foreign Member of the Norwegian Academy of Science and Letters, and serves on the editorial board of the journal *Past & Present*.

GIANCARLO CORSETTI is the Pierre Werner Chair and Professor of Economics at the European University Institute. He previously taught at Cambridge University, where he was director of the Cambridge-INET Institute. He is a leading scholar in international economics and open-economy macro-economics with contributions on currency, financial and sovereign debt crises, and monetary and fiscal policy. He has been a long-serving consultant at the European Central Bank and the Bank of England, and a regular visiting professor in central banks and international institutions. He is a fellow of the British Academy.

MAURICE OBSTFELD is the C. Fred Bergsten Senior Fellow at the Peterson Institute for International Economics and the Class of 1958 Professor of Economics Emeritus at the University of California, Berkeley. From 2015 through 2018, he served as Economic Counsellor and Director of Research at the International Monetary Fund. During 2014 and 2015, he was a member of President Obama's Council of Economic Advisers. Prior to joining the economics department at Berkeley, he held faculty appointments at Columbia and the University of Pennsylvania, as well as a visiting appointment at Harvard.

ADAM TOOZE is Professor of History at Columbia University. He teaches and researches widely in the fields of twentieth-century and contemporary history. His books have won the Leverhulme Prize fellowship, the H-Soz-Kult Historisches Buch Prize, the Longman History Today Prize, the Wolfson Prize, and the *Los Angeles Times* History Prize. He was shortlisted for the Kirkus, Duff Cooper, and Hessell-Tiltman prizes, and his books have featured in the book-of-the-year lists of the *Financial Times*, *Los Angeles Times*, *Kirkus Reviews*, *Foreign Affairs*, and *The Economist*.

Keynes's *Economic Consequences of the Peace* after 100 Years

Polemics and Policy

Edited by

PATRICIA CLAVIN
University of Oxford

GIANCARLO CORSETTI
European University Institute

MAURICE OBSTFELD
Peterson Institute for International Economics

ADAM TOOZE
Columbia University

with

CATHERINE PINER
Harvard Business School

CAMBRIDGE
UNIVERSITY PRESS

Shaftesbury Road, Cambridge CB2 8EA, United Kingdom

One Liberty Plaza, 20th Floor, New York, NY 10006, USA

477 Williamstown Road, Port Melbourne, VIC 3207, Australia

314–321, 3rd Floor, Plot 3, Splendor Forum, Jasola District Centre, New Delhi – 110025, India

103 Penang Road, #05–06/07, Visioncrest Commercial, Singapore 238467

Cambridge University Press is part of Cambridge University Press & Assessment, a department of the University of Cambridge.

We share the University's mission to contribute to society through the pursuit of education, learning and research at the highest international levels of excellence.

www.cambridge.org
Information on this title: www.cambridge.org/9781009407519

DOI: 10.1017/9781009407540

First published 2023

Printed in the United Kingdom by CPI Group Ltd, Croydon CR0 4YY

A catalogue record for this publication is available from the British Library

Library of Congress Cataloging-in-Publication Data
Names: Clavin, Patricia, editor. | Corsetti, Giancarlo, editor. | Obstfeld, Maurice, editor. | Tooze, Adam, editor.
Title: Keynes's economic consequences of the peace after 100 years : polemics and policy / edited by Patricia Clavin, University of Oxford, Giancarlo Corsetti, European University Institute, Maurice Obstfeld, Peterson Institute for International Economics, Adam Tooze, Columbia University, New York.
Description: 1 Edition. | New York : Cambridge University Press, [2023] | Includes bibliographical references and index.
Identifiers: LCCN 2023020459 (print) | LCCN 2023020460 (ebook) | ISBN 9781009407519 (hardback) | ISBN 9781009407540 (ebook)
Subjects: LCSH: Keynes, John Maynard, 1883–1946. Economic consequences of the peace. | Treaty of Versailles (1919 June 28) | World War, 1914–1918 – Economic aspects. | Economic history – 1918– | Keynesian economics.
Classification: LCC HC57 .K4255 2023 (print) | LCC HC57 (ebook) | DDC 940.3142–dc23/eng/20230501
LC record available at https://lccn.loc.gov/2023020459
LC ebook record available at https://lccn.loc.gov/2023020460

ISBN 978-1-009-40751-9 Hardback

Contents

The plates will be found between pages [238] and [239].

Plates

Figures

Tables

Contributors

OLIVIER ACCOMINOTTI is Professor of Economic History at the London School of Economics and Political Science and a Research Fellow at the Centre for Economic Policy Research.

JONATHAN BOFF is Reader in History at the University of Birmingham and has written widely on the First World War and on strategy.

MICHAEL D. BORDO is the Board of Governors Professor of Economics and director of the Center for Monetary and Financial History at Rutgers University.

ELISE S. BREZIS is Professor of Economics at Bar-Ilan University and is the head of the Aharon Meir Center for Banking and Economic Policy. She is also the director of the Macro Forum in Israel and is the laureate of the 2020 Elinor Ostrom prize.

BENNY CARLSON is Professor Emeritus in Economic History at the Lund University School of Economics and Management.

JAGJIT S. CHADHA is the Director of the National Institute of Economic and Social Research (NIESR).

DAVID CHAMBERS is the Invesco Professor in Finance and Co-Director of the Centre for Endowment Asset Management at the Judge Business School, Cambridge University. He is also a Research Fellow of the Centre for Economic Policy Research and a Fellow of Clare College, Cambridge.

PETER CLARKE is Emeritus Professor of Modern British History at Cambridge University.

PATRICIA CLAVIN, FRHistS, FBA, is Professor of Modern History at the University of Oxford and a Professorial Fellow of Worcester College, Oxford.

GIANCARLO CORSETTI, FBA, is Pierre Werner Chair and Professor of Economics at the European University Institute.

MICHAEL COX is Professor Emeritus of International Relations at the London School of Economics and Political Science and Director of LSE IDEAS.

MADELEINE LYNCH DUNGY is a researcher in the Fate of Nations Research Group for the Global History and Political Economy of Natural Resources at the Norwegian University of Science and Technology.

MAX HARRIS is a senior fellow at the Wharton Initiative on Financial Policy and Regulation.

SIMON HINRICHSEN runs sovereign debt investments in emerging markets for a Danish labour pension fund and is an external associate professor at the University of Copenhagen.

HAROLD JAMES is the Claude and Lore Kelly Professor in European Studies at Princeton University, Professor of History and International Affairs at Princeton's School for Public and International Affairs, and an official historian of the International Monetary Fund.

LARS JONUNG is Professor Emeritus in Economics at Lund University.

ANDREW KOGER graduated with high honours in History from Princeton University with a concentration in economic history and the history of emerging markets.

JASON LENNARD is an Assistant Professor at the London School of Economics and Political Science, a research affiliate at the Centre for Economic Policy Research, and a research associate at the Economic Statistics Centre of Excellence.

JAMES ASHLEY MORRISON is Assistant Professor in the Department of International Relations at the London School of Economics and Political Science.

MAURICE OBSTFELD is the C. Fred Bergsten Senior Fellow at the Peterson Institute for International Economics and the Class of 1958 Professor of Economics Emeritus at the University of California, Berkeley.

EYÜP ÖZVEREN is currently an independent scholar. He was previously full professor at the Department of Economics, Middle East Technical University.

GUILHERME SAMPAIO is an intellectual historian and research fellow in the ECOINT project at the European University Institute.

CATHERINE R. SCHENK is Professor of Economic and Social History at the University of Oxford.

SOLOMOS SOLOMOU is a professor in the Faculty of Economics, Cambridge University, and a Fellow of Peterhouse.

CATHERINE PINER is a research associate at Harvard Business School.

RYLAND THOMAS is a senior technical advisor at the Bank of England. He is currently the curator of the Bank of England's historical macroeconomic database and the ESCoE UK historical data repository. He also chairs the Historical and Monetary Financial Statistics network hosted at the Bank for International Settlements (BIS).

ADAM TOOZE holds the Shelby Cullom Davis chair of History at Columbia University and serves as Director of the European Institute at Columbia.

DAVID VINES is Emeritus Professor of Economics and Emeritus Fellow of Balliol College at Oxford University, Director of the Ethics and Economics Programme at the Institute for New Economic Thinking in the Oxford Martin School and a Research Fellow at the Centre of Economic Policy Research.

Preface

This volume collects contributions to a conference marking the centenary of John Maynard Keynes's *The Economic Consequences of the Peace*. The conference took place in September 2019 at King's College, Cambridge, an institution with which Keynes was closely associated throughout his adult life. Keynes's book is rightly celebrated as a brilliant piece of advocacy by one of the twentieth century's pre-eminent economists. It instantly gave Keynes worldwide fame, igniting controversies that have endured to the present. What explains the lasting relevance of a work seemingly so laser-focused on the issues of its day? The book made an accurate prophecy of the repercussions of a "Carthaginian peace" while offering a prescient plea for the type of global economic co-operation that later informed key aspects of reconstruction after World War II – including the Bretton Woods institutions (which Keynes helped to design) and the Marshall Plan. But the book has remained so relevant because, despite the undoubted progress in global co-operation made after World War II, Keynes's central theme of myopic nationalism versus peaceful economic integration has not been definitively resolved in favour of the latter. Indeed, the text has an accentuated resonance now, given growing ethno-nationalism, the fraying of traditional alliances, emerging threats to the global commons, heightened geopolitical tensions, and attacks on the multilateral institutions that have supported economic and financial globalisation since 1945.

When the participants convened in Cambridge in September 2019, the world was still feeling the protracted effects of the Global Financial Crisis, which were political as well as economic. They had no idea that only a few months later a global pandemic would emerge, comparable to the great influenza that raged as statesmen negotiated the Treaty of Versailles and while Keynes penned his critique. And when the editors of the present volume reconvened to assemble the chapters and write the overview chapter that opens this volume (periodically consulting over Zoom), they did not know that a Russian invasion of Ukraine was coming, with all of its direct human cost and global economic repercussions. These tragic events, still unfolding, further underscore the present-day relevance of the issues Keynes raised in 1919, but they do so in a world where war has the capacity to be much more destructive. Future debates about the causes of geopolitical revanchism will reference the cases of Germany in the 1930s and Russia in the 2020s, no doubt citing Keynes's arguments in the *Economic Consequences.*

This volume opens with an introductory chapter by the editors reviewing the last hundred years from the perspective of the lasting influence of Keynes's ideas and evolving views on economics, policy, and international institutions. A central thesis is the durable relevance of the factors Keynes saw as crucial in 1919. Then, the chapter by Michael Cox explores the multifaceted origins of Keynes's classic and its influence on contemporary debates. Several chapters exploring the intellectual reception of the *Economic Consequences* follow. Peter Clarke adds historical discipline to critical assessments of Keynes's contribution. Benny Carlson and Lars Jonung offer a compelling account of the multi-layered and rich interactions between Keynes and leading Swedish economists, unveiling reciprocal intellectual influence as well as the relevance of these interactions in shaping public opinion in Sweden. Guilherme Sampaio sketches a balanced picture of the public debate on the *Economic Consequences* in France, where views and analyses differed profoundly – therein reflecting opposing assessments of the merits and the costs of the Treaty. Harold James and Andrew Koger contrast Keynes's critique of Versailles, rooted in the rarefied intellectual milieu of Cambridge, with the art of sophisticated multilateral diplomacy dominating in Paris and the pragmatic financial market-oriented thinking prevailing in Amsterdam.

The next group of chapters explores how the ideas that grew out of the *Economic Consequences* have influenced economic theory, practice, and policy. The chapter by Simon Hinrichsen brings Keynes's analysis to bear on the historical experience of reparations through a comparative analysis of fifteen case studies between 1915 and today. Olivier Accominotti, David Chambers, and James Ashley Morrison explore the extent to which Keynes's analysis and policy experience guided his portfolio choices and investments in foreign currencies. Elise Brezis reads Keynes's analysis of reparations through the lens of a political economy model built around three key elements featured in the introduction of his book: the opposing interests of the elite and the working class, the notion of national sovereignty or identity, and the international political system. Eyüp Özveren weaves a fascinating tapestry of events that plausibly link the Turkish translation of the *Economic Consequences* by a prisoner of war in Malta to the likely influence of Keynes's ideas and work in Turkey's later economic and foreign policies. Madeleine Dungy leads us through Keynes's evolving advice and analysis on free trade versus protection in the interwar period, balancing his aspirations for multilateralism against national stabilization concerns. In his chapter, Max Harris offers a novel and informative account of the workings and achievements of the Tripartite Agreement of 1936, through which monetary authorities took the lead in pursuing an effective form of cross-border co-operation. These pathways foreshadowed the more comprehensive post-war construction of Keynes and Harry Dexter White. The long-standing question of the effects of tariffs on inflation, and their potential role in helping the United Kingdom counter the global deflationary shock in the 1930s, is reconsidered in the study by Jagjit Chadha, Solomos Solomou, and Ryland Thomas. Here again, the theme touches on the trade-off between economic integration and the imperative that national governments pursue domestic prosperity.

Turning to Keynes's long-run influence on international economic relations, Michael Bordo and Catherine Schenk revisit the turning points in the evolution of the global economic and monetary system, and in international co-operation. They do so from the perspective of Keynes's analytical views on the possibility of achieving lasting, stable, and reliable arrangements. David Vines reads the *Economic Consequences* as a key stepping stone in Keynes's development and overarching contribution as a theorist, challenging a conventional wisdom that downplays the analytical economic content of his 1919 book. Jonathan Boff concludes the volume with an exploration of the cultural and intellectual ramifications of Keynes's critique of the peace of Versailles, as evidenced in the post-war popular perception of the war.

We hope that this rich array of contributions gives a flavour of the extraordinarily intensive and productive interdisciplinary exchange during the conference. The final editing of the book obviously benefited from the ideas and discussions in all the sessions, and especially during the concluding policy panel. In that session, moderated by

Adam Tooze, Edward Carr (*The Economist*), Stanley Fischer (Senior Adviser, BlackRock), Cecilia Skingsley (Sveriges Riksbank), and Geoff Mann (Simon Fraser University) led an insightful, provocative, and critical discussion of how Keynes's analysis resonates in today's troubled world. A video of the panel discussion, as well as other information about the King's College conference, can be found at https://ecp .econ.cam.ac.uk/

This book is intended as a reference for researchers and practitioners in economics, history, international law, sociology, political science, and international relations. It is conceived as a concerted reflection on the terrible events and the underlying factors that a hundred years ago undermined decades of unprecedented economic globalization, destroyed empires, and redefined the balance of power among regions and countries. As such, it also speaks to a wider audience for whom the worrisome unfolding of current events sparks an appetite to explore the lessons of history.

The post-war multilateral system was successful for a long while on its initial terms, but it did not prove fully adequate to counter evolving threats to financial stability, global health, climate, and collective security. The world's response to Russia's actions of March 2022 has been uneven – notably owing to the important exception of China and the ambivalent position of parts of the Global South. Those events may still admit the possibility of a more unified response to other threats, a response that encompasses actions taken autonomously by the private sector as well as by governments. Technology sometimes can help. Unlike in the cases of earlier war crimes that the dark history of the twentieth century brought in sad abundance, the fact that nearly everyone carries a video camera nowadays may be more conducive to a unified global resolve to do better. The non-unanimous, but still very high, degree of consensus in recent Group of Twenty communiqués gives some grounds for hope on key collective action challenges that require international co-operation. We still have work to do, and the world's capacity to prosper depends on our achieving co-operation in areas where national incentives align, despite commercial and geopolitical tensions.

Acknowledgements

The proposal for an *Economic Consequences* centenary conference originally emerged as a high-profile initiative of Cambridge INET, now transitioned into the Janeway Institute at Cambridge University. Special thanks go to the managers of the Institute, Patrick Bolton and Bill Janeway in particular, for supporting the plan for a conference favouring intense interdisciplinary discussion. The Banca d'Italia, Bank of England, and Sveriges Riksbank offered both generous financial support and strong encouragement to pursue the conference project, testifying to the longevity and lasting policy relevance of the themes that Keynes raised in his book. In line with its interdisciplinary nature, the organisation of the conference relied on the active involvement of the Cambridge Public Policy Strategic Research Initiative and the ESRC Centre for Macroeconomics, both providing financial support and key suggestions on topics and themes.

The success of the conference owes much to the intellectual and factual contributions of the Organizing Committee, including Gareth Austin and David Howarth at Cambridge University, Michael Kumhof from the Bank of England, Eugenio Gaiotti from the Banca d'Italia, and Jesper Lindé from the Sveriges Riksbank. We also thank Soumaya Keynes for valuable help and advice.

The dedication and commitment of Anne Hitchin and Marion Reusch, administrators of Cambridge INET (at the time of its transition to become the Janeway Institute in Cambridge), were essential for a conference on such a scale to run smoothly. A celebration of the book in Cambridge could not be hosted but in King's College, which generously gave participants the opportunity to familiarize themselves with Keynes's rooms, the Keynes archives, and all the other spaces in the college where Keynes lived and worked. Special thanks go to the Master of King's, Professor Michael Proctor, as well as to King's senior archivist Dr Patricia McGuire, who opened the Keynes archives to us.

We were lucky to be joined in the effort by Director Clare Trowell and the fantastic staff of the Marshall Library, who relentlessly promoted the conference among students and researchers at the University and elsewhere. The Marshall Library organized exhibits showing the early edition of the book as well as the proofreading pages with original comments by Keynes; ran a blog shedding light on intriguing and informative aspects of the production process of the *Economic Consequences*, as well as in the contemporary debate on it; and co-hosted with the Marshall Society a student competition for an essay on the book.

Finally, we are especially thankful to the Keynes Fund at Cambridge University, for supporting the publication of the conference proceedings.

From Day One of this project, throughout all of the different publication phases, Catherine Piner was the enthusiastic and most effective organizer, blog contributor, archive researcher, and text co-editor. Her input was invaluable and essential in bringing this volume to completion.

P.C., G.C., M.O, A.T.
May 2023

1 | *Lessons of Keynes's* Economic Consequences *in a Turbulent Century*

PATRICIA CLAVIN, GIANCARLO CORSETTI,
MAURICE OBSTFELD, AND ADAM TOOZE

The community of nations is badly positioned to meet the existential challenges it faces. The first two decades of the twenty-first century generated economic and political dilemmas that in many ways resemble those the world faced in 1919. As then, disunity provides a weak basis for providing key global public goods and countering collective global threats. For all the subsequent controversy over its facts, analysis, and style – even its geopolitical repercussions – John Maynard Keynes's book, *The Economic Consequences of the Peace*, stands as a prescient warning. A piece of history-writing, and history-making, the book painted a picture of what happens when enlightened multilateralism gives way to national rivalry and inward-looking electoral calculation. These lessons need to be taken to heart today. The stakes for humanity are higher than ever before.

Keynes correctly predicted the drift of the following decades, even if he was "right for the wrong reasons," as the historian Charles Maier put it. In many ways, we live with the repercussions of 1919 to this day. In this chapter, we review the arc of experience since 1919 from the perspective of Keynes's influence and his changing understanding of economics, politics, and geopolitics during a tumultuous historical period. At decisive moments that punctuated this past century, international economic, financial, and political relations took on particular architectures embodied in specific international institutions and legal treaties. Accompanying these constructions of "global order" was the development of international modes of governance that connected policymakers with advisers. Notable hinge points include the Paris Peace Conference of 1919, the Bretton Woods agreement of 1944, and the end of the Cold War and reunification of Germany three decades ago. There are other key evolutions, particularly the collapse of the Bretton Woods system and the re-emergence of China as a global force in the late 1970s, alongside the deregulation

1

of financial markets, the emergence of neoliberalism, and the resulting shock waves. Through it all, Keynes, as an economist, a political thinker, an adviser, a government actor, and a general intellectual
lodestar – as in 1919 – remained a potent factor.

Setting Keynes within this century-long context draws out the dangers of binary thinking in relation to the year 1919 and his influential
text. Historians and economists often present momentous years such as
1919, 1929, 1945, or 1971 as pivot points when the world is made, or
unmade. This approach sets up a false dichotomy that contrasts a crisis – or shock – with an imagined prior stability when economic relations
and global politics were in a supposed state of equilibrium. Reflecting
on the century since *The Economic Consequences of the Peace* draws
out that the world did not abruptly swing from one side to the other –
from stability and peace to war and depression. Rather, in the past,
as now, the world experienced periods, and occasionally decades, of
turbulence. Sometimes that turbulence led to new forms of economic
thinking, as well as to multilateral cooperation that sought to moderate
the choppy waves for the good of states, market actors, and civil society
(see, e.g., Papadia and Välimäki 2018). But as the history of Keynes and
his 1919 text also exemplifies, the lines between these moments of crisis
and the emergence of new paradigms were far from direct.

Putting Keynes at the centre of our analysis not only highlights
questions about him and his role, but also points to broader questions
about the turbulent world he knew and its evolution since his death in
the spring of 1946. How should we judge Keynes's varied contributions: as the expert, the government adviser, the public intellectual,
the gadfly? How should we evaluate the ways his experience in 1919
shaped his subsequent professional trajectory? And what explains the
persistent influence of his ideas and his personal example? That influence grew from his activities and his writings, notably including the
Economic Consequences, but it reached far beyond his considerable
policy contributions. The role of the expert in shaping policy is a question about Keynes himself, but also, by extension, concerns the roles of
academics and advisers. These experts include those Keynes described
as "defunct academic scribblers," but as importantly scholars, scientists, journalists, and others who, already in Keynes's day, functioned
as public intellectuals, actively seeking influence over government
policies (and, sometimes, financial support from vested interests). In
the realm of macroeconomics, Keynes's ideas became dominant, as
both inspiration and target, helping to define the political landscape

of the past century. While its specific merits and shortcomings remain contested, *The Economic Consequences of the Peace* is undeniably a seminal document of the twentieth century. The worldview it set out and the intellectual process it catalysed have been essential ingredients in the unfolding of history since 1919.

Global Order on the Eve of World War I

The global order upended by World War I was one of empires in which laissez-faire capitalism prevailed but was increasingly questioned. Before 1914, new political forces – populism, nationalism, socialist, organized labour, and communist parties – arose to challenge capitalist norms and practices in the major European metropoles of Britain, France, Germany, Austria-Hungary, Italy, Spain, and Russia. There were also rising tensions between empires that played out globally. The declining fortunes of the Ottoman Empire and imperial Spain fanned rivalries over territory, for example. The crumbling of Ottoman authority became salient to the world in 1875 when the empire defaulted on its public debt to European creditors. By the late nineteenth century, Tunisia was a French colony, Egypt a British protectorate, and by the dawn of the twentieth century, Bulgaria and Romania gained independence. If this set the scene for new geopolitical arrangements in Eurasia and North Africa, the US victory in the 1898 Spanish-American naval war fought in the Caribbean and Pacific confirmed that a new ordering was also underway in American and world relations.

Spain lost the last remnants of its overseas empire in a defeat that triggered a fierce debate about the decline of Catholicism as a global force in ways that also tainted French, Italian, and Austro-Hungarian authority. In 1905, rising Japan defeated Orthodox Russia in war and a domestic revolution shook the Tsarist regime. Protestant values and Anglo-Saxon empires, by contrast, seemed ascendant. Following the Spanish-American war, the United States gained island possessions that were strategically important to its navy, in particular, with US interests now spanning the world. Controversial at home, globally these territorial acquisitions signalled a US interest in expansion that completed its move from a former colony to a leading naval imperial power, with economic and political ambitions to match. Rivalry with Japan was only a matter of time.

Momentous changes in the global balance of power were readily evident also at the heart of Europe. If ethno-nationalist claims were challenging the coherence of the Ottoman and Austro-Hungarian empires, they fuelled the ambitions of the recently unified German and Italian states. German, and notably Prussian, supremacy was measured in economic terms, and often related to military capacity. Like the United States, Germany enjoyed rich natural endowments of hard and soft commodities such as coal, iron ore, and grains that stressed the link between territory, economic strength, and military power in ways that were profoundly consequential for international politics before and after 1914.

More specifically, the German empire challenged the norms and practices of laissez-faire, notably in relation to trade. The onset of a global depression in 1873 triggered a move to greater trade protection, with free trading Britain increasingly an outlier in Western trade policy. The newly unified German state, in contrast, assumed a more central role. In 1902, Germany passed a tariff increase to take effect in 1906 as an opening bid for a series of trade negotiations. Many of its trade partners responded by introducing higher *tarifs de combat* as a basis for negotiations. By 1905, Germany had signed treaties with Russia, Italy, Belgium, Austria-Hungary, Serbia, and Switzerland. These were bilateral deals but contained concessions automatically extended to all third parties with most-favoured nation status. Some regarded the German approach as a future model for world economic relations, others as dangerous gamesmanship that risked tariff wars, especially as not all *tarifs de combat* were cancelled in subsequent trade treaties (see Dietzel 1903; Bairoch 1989).

Britain and the United States, the two countries that were the decisive players in shaping the new economic order after 1918, played relatively modest roles in the European system of trade treaties before 1914. Britain had no protective tariffs, and, thus, few bargaining chips. The United States had high tariffs, but the executive branch of its government had few powers to negotiate them down with trade treaties. The two countries did not forget their experience of European protectionism. It shaped Woodrow Wilson's decision to include free trade in his January 1918 Fourteen Points. These, in turn, formed the basis of the Armistice negotiated in November 1918 and of Anglo-American determination to force Germany, Austria, and Hungary to move to free trade in peace negotiations in 1919. As shown in the chapter by Madeleine Dungy, these changes drew comment and interest from Keynes.

Before 1914, British, French, and US power and authority in shaping global order, defined by the arrangement of relations between states, markets, and civil society, lay much more in their importance in the international financial system. Particularly central were their roles as international creditors and in the fixed exchange mechanism, the gold standard, which they dominated. The gold standard network comprised a group of the world's most prosperous countries, with Britain at the centre, which offered access to major markets of the world without the disruption of currency fluctuations. It facilitated international capital movements by reducing exchange rate risk. It was assumed that the rules governing the gold standard meant it was difficult for governments and financiers to manipulate money for their own ends, and the system was associated with an increased standard of living in the countries that adopted it. Major belligerents in World War I switched from silver or bimetallic currencies to gold in the last quarter of the nineteenth century: Germany in 1872, France in 1878, the United States in 1879, and Japan and Russia in 1897 (Meissner 2005). These developments – like free trade – were associated with international cooperation and harmony. Membership was contingent, however, and could be suspended in a crisis. And no crisis came bigger than World War I.

War and Peacemaking

The war meant free trade, too, was readily abandoned, notably by Britain. The move was central to British military strategy. The British government orchestrated a blockade against the Central Powers. The Allied blockade was designed to prevent all goods, including food and agricultural supplies as well as more overt war materiel, from entering Germany, Austria-Hungary, Bulgaria, and Turkey. Britain also implemented a series of political, bureaucratic, military, and naval manoeuvres to convince neutral countries to cease trading with the Central powers. The operations of the blockade created a network of administrative bodies that underpinned Allied relations, and greatly increased the need for economic and statistical expertise.[1] The blockade unleashed other contradictory impulses as its operations both

---

[1] The classic studies of the blockade's operation are Bell (1937) and Marder (1961). Lambert (2012) has recently re-energized scholarly debates regarding the importance of economic warfare and the blockade to the course and outcome of war. For an incisive and extended critique of Lambert's argument, see Coogan (2015). Mulder (2022) offers a comprehensive account of the role of economic sanctions in the 1914–1945 period.

helped globalize the war and break up global markets that had become increasingly integrated and specialized in the preceding century.[2] Nor did the blockade end with the war in November 1918. It remained in force until the conclusion of peace negotiations in Paris the following year, with catastrophic effects on commodity supplies, notably food desperately needed for the civilian populations across Central and Eastern Europe (M. E. Cox 2019).

At the same time, the war increased Western European dependency on US commodity markets, notably in relation to foodstuffs, and on US capital in ways that had a transformative effect on the global economy and international relations. Nor did this dependence end with the Armistice in November 1918. Under the direction of future Secretary of Commerce and Republican President Herbert Hoover, the United States took the lead in organizing aid, notably food and medical supplies, to war-shattered Europe (Riley 2017). By February 1922, allied debts to the United States amounted $10,512 million. France alone owed $3,555 million and Britain $4,427 million. Each, in turn, had loaned money to its imperial allies. The net effect did more than transform the United States from a debtor to a creditor nation; it was now the world's banker.

America's role in the world economy was transformed, a change matched, in the first instance at least, by President Wilson's ambition in international relations. His plan for a new intergovernmental organization, the League of Nations, signalled a momentous break with the nineteenth-century notion that a "balance of power" would pacify the European continent and prevent its military domination by a single state or group of powers. After 1919, there was an attempt to establish procedural rules on which stable and legitimate cooperation would depend.

Power politics remained inherent to the work of the League, although economists and historians too often ignore a step that contemporaries in 1919 found radical: in founding the League, the Paris peacemakers multilateralized the practice of international relations at a stroke. It proved difficult to negotiate multilateral arrangements such as the 1936 Tripartite stabilization pact within the League, partly because

---

[2] In these circumstances, globalization did not disappear, but it was transformed to meet the imperatives of the global war economy (see Tooze and Fertik 2014).

the United States failed to join (though it regularly sent experts to its conferences and meetings).[3] At the same time, the legal norms and practices developed by the League were foundational for new institutions of global governance founded in 1945 (Clavin 2013). By 1989, the move from bilateral treaties to a multilateral world order seemed a given, but the unfolding history of the twenty-first century suggests that one can take neither multilateralism, nor the institutional bodies that support it, for granted (Ruggie 1993).

Although Keynes did not engage directly with the League project, he was involved in a number of related initiatives. Notably, at one point, he hoped to pin the credit-raising initiatives tracked in the chapter by Harold James and Andrew Koger to the League's coat tails.[4] In *The Economic Consequences of the Peace*, Keynes stressed the systemic breakdown at the heart of Europe that peacemakers missed because of their fixation with the politics of ethno-nationalism and territorial carve-ups.[5] As he would put it later, "The Wilsonian dogma, which exalts the divisions of race and nationality above the bonds of trade and culture, and guarantees frontiers but not happiness, is deeply embedded in the conception of the League of Nations as at present constituted" (Keynes 1922, p. 14). The principle of self-determination inspired many, but disappointed more, when it became clear that it would apply only to white, Western populations and in often contradictory ways. If it reunited ethnic Poles who had fought on different sides of the war in a new Polish republic, it also banned union between ethnic Germans of the former Austria-Hungary and the new Weimar Republic. Victorious nationalists, such as Thomas Masaryk, the highly respected Slovak president of the new Czechoslovak republic, may have portrayed the new states in Eastern Europe as a victory against the "Caesarism" of Europe's former empires. Yet, Czechoslovakia was not alone among the new states in harbouring its own imperial ambitions (Lemmen 2021, pp. 343–362).

Keynes's cynical view of Wilsonian idealism was understandable. While dismantling the empires of the losers, the global order instituted

---

[3] On the Tripartite Agreement, see the chapter by Max Harris.
[4] Keynes to Florence Keynes, April 17, 1919, and Austen Chamberlain to Lloyd George, April 17, 1919, in Johnson and Moggridge (1978, pp. 428–436).
[5] See the chapter by Elise Brezis on the role of new balance of power relationships in steering domestic political consensus, especially workers' attitudes, on the pursuit of national sovereignty.

in Paris reasserted the imperial rights of the victors. In 1919, the British Empire reached its greatest territorial extent. Britain, under the mandatory regime of the League of Nations, took charge of territories such as Palestine, Transjordan, and Iraq (Pedersen 2015 and the essays in "AHR Reflections: One Hundred Years of Mandates." *American Historical Review* 124 (December 2019): 1673–1731). At the same time, British Dominions became sovereign members of the League with Australia and New Zealand also gaining mandatory authority in the Pacific (Duffy 2019). The United States, too, toyed with the idea of mandatory authority.

Keynes was famously more animated, however, on the financial settlement and its implications. The chapters by Peter Clarke, Michael Cox, and Guilherme Sampaio touch on the long-running and well-known controversy over Germany's ability to pay the magnitude of indemnity that seemed probable after the peace conference.[6] More broadly, Keynes feared that reparations, legitimated by the Allies' insistence on a legal war guilt clause, would combine with other demands flowing from the Treaty to embitter international relations going forward, especially within Europe. The Treaty would also promote economic fragmentation. In Keynes's words, it would "impair yet further, when it might have restored, the delicate, complicated organisation, already shaken and broken by war, through which alone the European peoples can employ themselves and live" (1919, pp. 1–2).

But there were also the sins of omission. In a passage foreshadowing similar challenges that would arise a quarter century later in 1945, Keynes wrote:

The Treaty includes no provisions for the economic rehabilitation of Europe,—nothing to make the defeated Central Empires into good neighbours, nothing to stabilise the new States of Europe, nothing to reclaim Russia; nor does it promote in any way a compact of economic solidarity amongst the Allies themselves; no arrangement was reached at Paris for restoring the disordered finances of France and Italy, or to adjust the systems of the Old World and the New.... It is an extraordinary fact that the fundamental eco-

---

[6] Simon Hinrichsen's chapter elucidates the debate through a novel comparative analysis of fifteen episodes of enforced war reparations between 1800 and today. Keynes had a broad view of possible harmful economic effects of reparations on Germany, including what economists now call the debt overhang effect (Keynes 1919, p. 217).

nomic problem of a Europe starving and disintegrating before their eyes, was the one question in which it was impossible to arouse the interest of [Clemenceau, Lloyd George, Wilson, and Orlando]. (Keynes 1919, p. 211)

For Keynes (1919, p. 274n), "Hoover was the only man who emerged from the ordeal of Paris with an enhanced reputation … his eyes steadily fixed on the true and essential facts of the European situation." This was because he sought to address the economic and social challenges posed by the warlike conditions of the peace. Wilson, in contrast, was puritanical and out of touch. Between 1918 and 1923, revolution, civil war, and episodes of ethnic cleansing killed another four million people across Central and Eastern Europe, a figure higher than the combined figure of war casualties of Britain, France, and the United States (Gerwarth and Horne 2012).

At the same time, immigrant access to North America, a main escape route for oppressed and unemployed Europeans before the war, contracted. In Canada, 1919 amendments to the Immigration Act expanded the grounds for denial of entry and deportation. In the United States, the reaction was more far-reaching. The US Immigration Act of 1917 introduced a literacy test for immigrants; the 1921 Emergency Quota Act placed numerical limits on immigration; while the 1924 Johnson-Reed National Origins Act aimed to restrict overall immigration and freeze America's racial composition through a national origins quota formula based on immigrant population percentages as of 1890.[7] US *external* immigration restrictions could not address a second migration-based cause of cultural tensions within the United States – the large-scale *internal* movement of southern Blacks to the North. The years after World War I saw a national resurgence of the Ku Klux Klan and widespread violence against Blacks, including the deadly Tulsa massacre of 1921 (Tooze 2014).

Riven by ethnic, racial, and class tensions, employment concerns, and fears of socialist subversion, the United States was in no position to deliver global public goods. The US Senate's final rejection of the Versailles Treaty in 1920 and, with it, US membership in the League

---

[7] The 1924 act also excluded Asians. The US Congress modified its provisions in the McCarran-Walter Immigration and Nationality Act of 1952 (which Congress passed over President Truman's veto), but nationality quotas heavily favouring north-western Europeans remained in place until they were effectively loosened in the 1965 Hart-Celler Immigration and Nationality Act.

of Nations was just one consequence of the country's domestic political disarray.

Keynes's Influence in Private and Public

Keynes was a young man when he took up his role as an adviser to the UK Treasury. His efforts to shape the Treaty terms in the face of countervailing political realities proved fruitless. Michael Cox's chapter outlines how Keynes authored two detailed memoranda on the indemnity issue in 1918 and further memoranda in Paris, finally proposing what he called a "grand scheme" to ease the logjam of reparations and inter-Allied debt, while providing Germany (and other defeated powers) some financial support for domestic reconstruction. His proposal was not taken up, and his warnings against the Versailles Treaty were not heeded. Ultimately, reparations went largely unpaid, and the Treaty terms and *sequelae* served as a potent prod to nationalistic resentment within Germany. Having failed to move official opinion within the UK government, Keynes decided to go public with his views. The decision provoked a mixed reaction at the time, and heated historical debate ever since. Maier (2009) judges that Keynes's book was "brilliant, unfair, wrongheaded, destructive perhaps in its consequences … but right for the wrong reasons." Kindleberger's (1973, p. 39) view is more even-handed:

Keynes's brilliant polemic … may have been distorting in many respects; self-confirming in its contention that if the Germans heard a reasonable argument to the effect that they could not pay, they would not; and devastatingly encouraging to American isolationists in its attacks on President Wilson as an incompetent invalid; but it was surely right in thinking it useful to cancel war debts, set a small figure for reparations … and clear the issue off the international agenda.

One might add that Keynes was most unfair in his treatment of Clemenceau, who, far from being a reactionary, had more claim to the mantle of radicalism than Wilson, Lloyd George, or Keynes himself. It was the government of Republican France that pushed for a peace that was not merely more punitive, but also provided a more robust international security order.

With its widespread notoriety, Keynes's book threw a shadow over the League of Nations. It also empowered isolationists in the United

States, who helped block that key country's participation and who remained influential in the subsequent two decades. Some even claim the book created a degree of international sympathy for Germany's revanchist claims in the 1930s (Peter 2015). The Canadian economist and past president of the American Economic Association, Jacob Viner, expressed this view in 1947, drawing out how the "war guilt" clause became tied to the public's memory of the French invasion of the Ruhr, the hyperinflation, and the suffering these episodes inflicted on ordinary Germans. The result was a psychological complex that shaped policy for the worse (Viner 1947):

[T]he guilt complex toward Germany and toward the Treaty of Versailles, which Keynes helped to establish in England and America; the grossly unfair caricature of the personality, the character, and the intellect of Woodrow Wilson, which is the most widely remembered part of his book on the Peace; his exaggerated account of the greed and intransigence of the French and of their obsession with a security bogy – these ... contributed their weight to easing the path to world hegemony for a resurgent and reparations-free Nazi Germany.

The issues Keynes raised in his book, his decision to publish his privately expressed official advice, and his provocative language remain controversial. Arguably Keynes was politically naïve if he expected that going public with his arguments would win the day when his attempts to influence policy from within the councils of government had not. Perhaps he believed too much in people power. After all, expectations of self-determination were also cruelly dashed. Perhaps Keynes had overlooked the fact that if positive ideas on economic policy are to move from concept into practice, they must dovetail with the political and social imperatives of the times.[8] It was a trap that would ensnare many other economists in subsequent years.

---

[8] As MacMillan (2018) observes: "Keynes would have preferred that the economist ran things, writing in 1922: 'He is a better and wiser governor than the general or the diplomatist or the oratorical lawyer.' Perhaps, but what he was suggesting was not politically feasible in 1919, in the aftermath of one of the worst wars Europe had ever experienced. Looking back from the vantage point of a century later we know how badly Europe and the world were going to fare, but we have to remember that the peacemakers did not have free rein." Keynes himself acknowledged the political constraints of 1919 in the early 1920s (Tooze 2014, p. 295). He went on in Keynes (1922) both to clarify and to defend his earlier analysis, while proposing a new scheme to end the debt overhang entangling America and Europe, which he did not think private sector initiatives could solve.

There was another side to the balance sheet. *The Economic Consequences of the Peace* gave Keynes instant worldwide fame. It launched his career as a "public intellectual" in economics and as a perennial government adviser. He was not alone in trying to influence policy through lectures, popular writings, and the press. In the United States, Irving Fisher, like Keynes a proponent of managed money, wrote in non-specialist outlets on topics beyond economics, including public health, eugenics, and the League of Nations (which he supported; see Dimand 2013). The chapter by Benny Carlson and Lars Jonung highlights the energetic involvement of Swedish university professors in public economic discourse. These public-facing scholars included Gustav Cassel, whose systemic critique of the gold standard was prescient, and Knut Wicksell, a key Keynesian interlocutor who argued that his chief obligation was the education of the Swedish people. In Britain, William Beveridge, Henry Clay, G. D. H. Cole, Walter Layton (editor of *The Economist*), and A. C. Pigou were among many other economists who sought to take economic science to a wider audience in order to influence views beyond academia.

Keynes took these activities to a higher level. Backhouse and Bateman (2013, p. 70) recount that in writing the *Economic Consequences*, Keynes was so confident his book would find a ready market he underwrote the publishing costs himself. Macmillan thereby acted as his agent, giving him control of the book's price and its print run. He published all his subsequent books the same way, helping to make journalism his principal income source. As Michael Cox notes in his chapter, Keynes even contracted with the trades-union-affiliated Labour Research Department to bring out a very successful low-priced edition of the *Economic Consequences*.[9]

An early example of Keynes's entrepreneurship – and the immense convening power that came because of his intellectual firepower, connections, and fame – was his editorship of a series of twelve *Manchester Guardian* reconstruction supplements that appeared between April 1922 and January 1923. These assembled contributions by Keynes

---

[9] In the blog series that the Marshall Library at Cambridge University devoted to the centennial of the *Economic Consequences*, Catherine Piner analyzes Keynes's correspondence around the publication date, highlighting the "unanticipated enormity of the response" to the book. See http://marshlib .blogspot.com/2019/05/the-economic-consequences-of-peace-by.html

himself (forming the basis for his classic *Tract on Monetary Reform*) and an international cast of distinguished contributors including Hjalmar Schacht, Walter Lippmann, John H. Williams, Luigi Einaudi, Lord Asquith, Ramsay MacDonald, Cassel, Pigou, and Fisher (Skidelsky 1992 p. 103; Backhouse and Bateman 2013).[10] Keynes established a pathway to a "business model" for the social scientist as public intellectual.[11]

Since World War II, business models similar to that of Keynes have powered public advocacy by economists of diverse view ranging from Milton Friedman on the Right to Paul Krugman on the Left, sometimes with consequential results.[12]

A World Restored?

Wilson's Fourteen Points proclaimed, "There shall be free trade between the countries who accept the peace." Subsequently, Part I, Article 23(e) of the Treaty of Versailles enjoined members of the League of Nations to "make provision to secure and maintain freedom of communications and of transit and equitable treatment for the commerce of all Members of the League." Wilson's proclamation and the Paris treaties established free trade as a supporting pillar of the coming global economic order. In 1919, Keynes explicitly embraced the goal of free trade, because he feared that "nationalism and private interest" would join forces to turn political into economic frontiers (Keynes 1919 p. 91). Indeed, he proposed a European Free Trade Union under the auspices of the League.

---

[10] The *Guardian* newspaper offers the flavour of these at www.theguardian .com/business/from-the-archive-blog/2020/mar/04/reconstruction-in-europe-keynes-guardian-guide-1922

[11] Keynes's influence as a public intellectual may well have been unusually far reaching, though hard to demonstrate. The chapter by Jonathan Boff argues that the *Economic Consequences* helped shape the collective memory of the Great War in Britain and elsewhere. The chapter by Eyüp Özveren presents a fascinating account of how the book shaped the minds of key political figures in Turkey, helping to determine the country's treaty re-negotiations and subsequent foreign policy. Even in France where anti-German sentiment remained especially intense throughout the inter-war period, a non-negligible segment of public opinion sympathized with Keynes's arguments in the *Economic Consequences*, as Sampaio recounts in his chapter.

[12] Fourcade (2009, pp. 178–181) notes that in Britain, alignment between economic writers and the press has long been especially strong, and she discusses some hypotheses about the reasons for this relationship.

The negotiators at Versailles also assumed implicitly that the world order starting in 1919, like the pre-war order, would be reconstructed on the monetary basis of an international gold standard (Eichengreen 2019, p. 7) – although, as Keynes pointed out, no explicit plan for the complementary goals of stabilizing currencies and public finances was agreed on at the peace conference. Only a few years later in his *Tract on Monetary Reform*, Keynes characterized gold as a "barbarous relic" (Keynes 1923, p. 172). Later, he fiercely opposed sterling's 1925 return to gold at the pre-war parity. Nonetheless, as of 1919, in line with prevailing opinion at the time, Keynes did not yet reject the implicit assumption of an eventual return to gold. (The Cunliffe Committee had recommended this route for Britain in 1918.[13]) Keynes would not be prepared to urge a definitive rift between sterling and gold until just before the UK government's withdrawal from gold convertibility in September 1931 (Irwin 2014, p. 217).[14]

The attempt to reboot the post–World War I global economy along pre-1914 lines was only partially successful.[15] The system was an unsustainable, turbulent, and short-lived construction (James 2001). An initial post-war rebuilding boom led to sharp price rises (notably in America and Britain), analogous to those that accompanied economic reopening in 2021 following the COVID-19 lockdowns. But boom turned to bust, and consumer prices fell sharply in 1921, notwithstanding a global boom in commodity prices. The latter was short lived. World agricultural prices dropped as farmlands in Europe returned to production. Figure 1.1 shows the trajectory of US and UK consumer price levels (eloquently encapsulating key features of

---

[13] Late in 1920, he told a Cambridge lecture audience, "There is a great deal to be said against gold, but nearly all the more significant and scientific arrangements depend on confidence in governments. The advantage of the gold standard is the convention behind it that it is … disgraceful to tamper with gold" (Skidelsky 1992, p. 45). Later in the same lecture series, however, Keynes recommended that sterling's return to gold occur at a depreciated parity, not the pre-war parity.

[14] See also Temin (1989, p. 15). The chapter by Olivier Accominotti, David Chambers, and James Ashley Morrison (Chapter 8) builds an illuminating bridge between Keynes's analysis of post-war monetary issues and his activity as a foreign-exchange investor between August 1919 and February 1920.

[15] The chapter by Michael Bordo and Catherine Schenk provides a complementary chronicle of the international monetary system since 1919, focusing on systemic aspects of international policy cooperation.

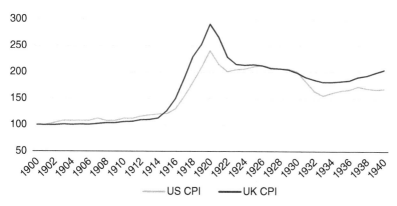

Figure 1.1 US and UK consumer price levels, 1900–1940 (1900 = 100)
Source: US data: www.minneapolisfed.org/about-us/monetary-policy/inflation-calculator/consumer-price-index-1800-;
UK data: Constructed from annual inflation data reported at https://fred.stlouisfed.org/series/CPIIUKA

Anglo-American inter-war macroeconomic history). The price-level collapse left the United Kingdom with a persistent legacy of double-digit unemployment, helping to convince Keynes that deflation was even more dangerous than the inflation he had warned against in the *Economic Consequences*.[16]

The United States restored gold convertibility in June 1919. Thereafter, numerous European countries returned to gold either at the 1913 parities – for example, Sweden (in 1922), Australia, the United Kingdom, the Netherlands (all in 1925), and Canada (in 1926) – or at depreciated parities – famously France (in 1926), but also Belgium (in 1926) and Italy (in 1927). Germany returned after a monetary reform in November 1923, whereas Japan waited until December 1930 to return at the pre-war parity, shortly before the gold standard's collapse. In his missions to Latin America and other countries such as Poland, Princeton professor Edwin Kemmerer lobbied effectively for monetary reforms and the gold exchange standard during the 1920s. Figure 1.2 shows the historical course of

---

[16] The chapter by Jagjit Chadha, Jason Lennard, Solomos Solomou, and Ryland Thomas (Chapter 13) brings a novel high-frequency dataset to bear on the question of whether high tariffs and devaluation in the 1930s helped counteract UK deflation by raising import prices.

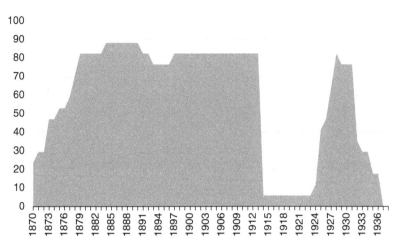

Figure 1.2 Number of countries pegged to gold
Source: Jordà, Schularick, and Taylor (2017). www.macrohistory.net/database/.

gold standard adherence, notably the rush to return in the 1920s. The Versailles aspiration of free trade fared less well. The League of Nations attempted to effect multilateral trade negotiations, but trade deals remained bilateral, and numerous countries declined either to roll back or to freeze existing tariffs. New quotas and tariffs were widely levied, culminating in the US Smoot-Hawley Tariff Act in 1930 (Kindleberger 1973, pp. 77–78).

The 1920s also saw a resurgence of what modern economists would call the "global financial cycle" as capital flows revived and asset prices soared, supported in part by an accommodative Federal Reserve policy stance. In 1924, the Dawes Plan saw French forces leave the Ruhr region, and it set a schedule for German reparation payments. The scheme floated collateralized bonds in world markets to help Germany pay. Kindleberger (1973, p. 38) argues that "More than anything else, [the Dawes loan] was the spark that ignited foreign lending from New York, first to Germany, and shortly thereafter to Latin America and much of the rest of Europe." Figure 1.3 shows net foreign capital flows into the sample of twenty-six debtor countries for which Reinhart, Reinhart, and Trebesch (2016) have assembled data. Only the pattern of commodity prices after mid-decade failed to conform to the typical pattern of a global financial cycle – an ominous signal when primary

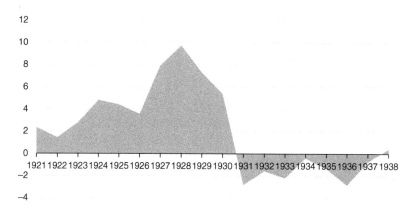

Figure 1.3 Total net capital inflows into 26 debtor economies (percent of UK GDP)
Source: Reinhart, Reinhart, and Trebesch (2016).

producing countries were borrowing heavily. Much of this foreign lending ended in tears, as did the global growth boom of 1925–1929. After 1931, the international gold standard quickly unravelled under the pressure of global depression, currency crises, and bank failures. Centrally implicated were systemic flaws in the international payments system, best explained at the time by Cassel, although the issue was only partially addressed in the later architecture of the Bretton Woods system.[17]

Reparations were not a direct cause of collapse, but through their political as much as economic effects, they acted as a constant irritant and destabilizer. As Kindleberger (1973, p. 39) puts it, "together with war debts they complicated and corrupted the international economy at every stage of the 1920s." Germany's balance of payments was severely lopsided, setting it up for a savage sudden stop in 1930 and making it vulnerable to bank runs in 1931.

Out of the debates launched by Keynes's *Economic Consequences of the Peace*, key parts of modern international macroeconomics were born. The celebrated 1929 exchange in the *Economic Journal* between Keynes (the journal's editor) and the Swedish economist Bertil Ohlin

[17] See Irwin (2014), who notes Keynes's endorsement of Cassel's gold standard critique.

grew directly out of the book and opened a controversy that remains central for open-economy theory and policy.[18]

Keynes claimed that Germany's need to transfer reparations payments abroad would require it to have a larger trade surplus. However, to market additional exports abroad, Germany would need to lower export prices, creating a loss in her terms of trade that would add to the real economic pain of reparations. Ohlin denied the necessity of this outcome. The transfer would reduce German income but would augment recipients' incomes equally. If those countries raised their overall spending as much as Germans cut theirs, and at the margin spent the same proportion on German goods as Germans did, there need be no change in relative prices in equilibrium.

The "transfer problem" at issue in the Keynes–Ohlin debate remains a central focus of research and policy debate. It is a question about the basic nature of countries' external adjustment processes and, by implication, about the need for exchange rate movements to preserve full employment as domestic and foreign demand fluctuate. In his chapter, David Vines argues that as of 1929, not yet having the intellectual apparatus of his *General Theory* at hand, Keynes was unable to frame a rigorous counterargument to Ohlin. The argument would have been that German and foreign expenditure patterns might be skewed at the margin toward their own products, and that Germany would cut its spending more than transfer recipients raised theirs if its residents had higher marginal propensities to consume out of income.

Although Ohlin was the more accomplished theorist as of 1929, subsequent analysis and experience suggest that Keynes's intuition was correct as a practical matter. Paul Samuelson (1946, p. 195) concluded that "If it can be said that [Keynes] was right in his reparations-transfer controversy with Ohlin, it is in part for the wrong reasons – reasons which in terms of his later system are seen to be classical as compared to the arguments of Ohlin." Similarly, Krugman (1991, p. 19) judged, "[W]hile Keynes may have been wrong in theory, he was right in practice." The British economist John Williamson (1991, p. 243) dismissed the outcome Ohlin suggested as an "immaculate transfer." As

---

[18] The chapter by Carlson and Jonung also discusses the Keynes–Ohlin dialogue, as does Mundell (2002). Some French economists, notably Jacques Rueff, also weighed in to criticize Keynes on the issue (see Sampaio's chapter). Rueff attacked Keynes's economics repeatedly over the following decades.

always, Keynes was concerned, not with what *may* happen, but with what *will* happen.[19] Keynes's realistic judgment would later underlie the structure of the Bretton Woods international monetary system, as Vines details in his chapter.

Inter-war Multilateralism

Central to Keynes's argument in 1919 was the underlying insight that a sustainable peace would be impossible without going beyond gold and free trade to create the preconditions for shared prosperity, social security, and social cohesion. Jan Christiaan Smuts, an author of the League of Nations covenant who grew to be close to Keynes at the peace conference, painted a bleak view of Europe after the war: "We witness the collapse of the whole political and economic fabric of Central and Eastern Europe. Unemployment, starvation, anarchy, war, disease, despair stalk the land" (Clavin 2020, p. 2). Addressing a broad range of potential social ills motivated much of the League's inter-war work on a range of economic and social issues. The same sense of social crisis permeated Keynes's polemic. As Maier (2009) puts it:

The greatest damage the war had inflicted was not on French and Belgian territories, but on the hitherto docile acceptance of class inequality. Could the Europeans and the Americans (who were being asked to cancel their financial claims as well) not understand a venerable civilization was at stake? We must read [Keynes's] text finally not as just a statistical argument about realistic peace-making but as a warning about the social and cultural order. Here is where Keynes's critique proved prophetic.

Keynes's mother Florence and his sister Margaret played important roles in steering his thinking toward a more capacious

---

[19] The turn of phrase is adapted from Deardorff (1987). While Krugman (1991) strongly endorsed Keynes's conclusion, Krugman (1989) showed theoretically how the export prices of a fast-growing economy need *not* fall if its growth takes the form of completely new products (a case of higher supply as opposed to lower domestic demand). In the same framework, however, Corsetti, Martin, and Pesenti (2013) show that while entry of new products may reduce the need for a fall in the market price of exports, entry adds a different form of secondary burden to a transfer of income to foreigners: it harms consumption and employment. Welfare therefore deteriorates substantially, even though changes in the terms of trade and relative labour costs are contained, suggesting that Keynes was correct in practice after all (if again for the wrong reasons).

conceptualization of security. Both were very active in the Women's International League for Peace and Freedom (WILPF) and its landmark campaign, led by Eglantyne Jebb and Dorothy Buxton, to "Save the Children" that created the nongovernmental organization with the same name. (Margaret was a close friend of Jebb's.) Both before and after Keynes was in Paris, his mother wrote to him repeatedly regarding what she described as "famine conditions" in Central Europe. Her views undoubtedly helped to shape her son's decision to resign from the peace delegation, as well as his take on the failings of the peace.[20]

Save the Children, the NGO founded in 1919, is one example of the type of global movement that began to spring up in the late nineteenth century to foster international cooperation on a range of issues, including health, culture, peace, and communications (including the landmark Universal Postal Union) – see Ikenberry (2020, Chapter 3). Despite the crippling absence of official US political engagement (though hundreds of Americans would participate in its work as experts), the League of Nations pursued initiatives in many of these areas.[21] While superficial perceptions of the period label the League as a "failure," it played a key role as a locus for international diplomacy and the dissemination of information. Moreover, the precedents it established created a "muscle memory" – physically embodied in its cadre of international civil servants – that would be reactivated across a range of more robust post–World War II institutions. Crucially, these did have full US political support.

---

[20] Private papers of John Maynard Keynes, Kings College Cambridge (hereafter, JMK), JMK PP/45/168/9/159, Florence Keynes to John Maynard Keynes, March 6, 1919. Only his response is published. See Johnson and Moggridge (1978, p. 428). The WILPF grew out of the International Committee of Women for Permanent Peace, headed by Jane Addams, which denounced the terms of the Versailles Treaty in 1919 prior to changing the organization's name and moving its headquarters to Geneva for proximity to the planned League of Nations. Over the inter-war years, the WILPF cooperated in a number of League of Nations' social and humanitarian initiatives, including in the areas of refugees, disarmament, and multilateral cooperation over aviation. Two WILPF leaders won Nobel Prizes for Peace: Addams (in 1931) and Emily Greene Balch (in 1946). Balch was the first woman economist ever to win a Nobel Prize (Dimand 2011). Jonung (2022) explores the deliberations in 1922, 1923, and 1924 over a possible Peace Prize for Keynes for the *Economic Consequences*.

[21] In 1924, the League adopted the Declaration of the Rights of the Child, drafted by Jebb.

One key arena of inter-war multilateralism was global public health. Recent experience with COVID-19 has revived popular consciousness of the last great global pandemic, the 1918–1919 influenza plague. Though eclipsed in much historical writing by the dramatic political events of those years, the H1N1 virus (avian influenza) killed tens of millions worldwide and likely more than three million in Europe. Many of those at the Paris peace conference contracted the "Paris Cold," including Clemenceau, Lloyd George, Wilson, and Keynes himself, Keynes falling quite ill with a possible secondary bacterial infection as well (Carter 2020, p. 64). Flu was not the only epidemic disease that preoccupied the peacemakers. At the time, contemporaries were as – if not more – preoccupied by the risks of typhus and tuberculosis (TB). In 1920, TB caused one in every four deaths in Vienna. Poor nutrition and living conditions were behind death rates so high they rivalled those of the fourteenth-century Black Death (Rosenfeld 1931). The disintegration of European empires highlights three causes of morbidity that are evident in the COVID-19 pandemic too: population density and poverty, along with mobility. Revolution, civil war, and nation-building drove mass population displacement at the same time as Central European armies did not so much demobilize as disintegrate. The legacy of disease may have helped to disrupt inter-war politics.[22]

Building on earlier international health conventions (see Cooper 1989; Fidler 2001), the League created its Health Committee in 1923, the precursor to the World Health Organization, and in 1924 sponsored what is now called the World Organisation for Animal Health. Moreover, the inter-war period saw the conclusion of ten international treaties relating to human infectious diseases, covering specialized issues extending from dengue fever to venereal disease among sailors. In general, the continuing warlike conditions in Europe after 1918 obliged the League to undertake a range of other activities that moved beyond health, covering refugees, transportation, and communication.

Economic and financial questions came to be a major arena for League activity, even though – perhaps surprisingly – the United States and the Allies did not plan for it to have competencies in this sphere.

---

[22] See Blickle (2020) on the predictive power of influenza mortality for subsequent German voting patterns.

Albeit indirectly, Keynes did help to make the case. With League help, Austria stabilized its currency and returned to gold. In the process, the League transformed its Provisional Economic and Financial Committee, which would take on the status of a permanent "specialist organization" of the League (Clavin 2013, p. 16). The Economic and Financial Organization (EFO) went on to play myriad roles, employing some of the most storied theoretical, empirical, and policy economists of the twentieth century. These functions ranged from surveillance of member countries to the systematic collection, publication, and analysis of global economic data. In 1928, the EFO helped organize the Gold Delegation that assessed the performance of the global gold standard (Clavin and Wessels 2004), and it provided support for the first-ever global economic conferences in the 1920s and 1930s. These included the fateful London Conference of 1933, which famously failed to stabilize exchange rates after the US devaluation. The organization also sponsored Ragnar Nurkse's (1944) classic study of inter-war currency experience, setting out the EFO view of recent international macroeconomic history. Its intent was to influence the framing of the new Bretton Woods institutions – and it did. Today, the activities of the International Monetary Fund and the World Bank mirror many of EFO's functions.

Rebuilding after World War II: Lessons Learned

The plan for a United Nations organization, this time with US participation, was announced at Dumbarton Oaks in Washington D.C. in October 1944. Two of the United Nations' key economic agencies – the International Monetary Fund and the World Bank – had been agreed earlier that year in Bretton Woods, following a protracted bilateral negotiation between Keynes, leading for the UK Treasury, and Harry Dexter White, leading the US Treasury team. Despite the rapidly changing power-political character of these states' relations, and their place in the world, the patterns of diplomacy were remarkably similar to 1919. These Anglo-American initiatives became part of a broader post-war settlement that would promote the rebuilding of war-shattered countries, including western Germany and Japan, and a revival of global trade.

Unlike 1918, however, 1945 was not a unipolar moment. Whereas in 1918, the Russians had been knocked out of the war, leaving the coalition of the British Empire, France, and the United States to dictate terms, in 1945 the victory over Germany was even more complete, and within the United Nations coalition, the Western powers were pitted against the Soviet Union. In the aftermath, each side pursued its own vision of economic and political development, domestically and on the global stage.

Eichengreen (2007) describes the first twenty-five years after World War II as a "golden age" for the West European economies, under-pinned in part by a "neocorporatist bargain" in which wage restraint by workers augmented profits that in turn were devoted to investment. The arrangement recalls Keynes's (1919) account of pre–World War growth. He put it down to the "psychology of society" which had channelled high profits into capital accumulation and growth largely because labour was powerless rather than self-restrained. Japan staged its own economic miracle, based on far-reaching industrial policy and government-sponsored credit expansion. Aggregate demand due to the Korean War gave an early fillip to growth everywhere, but espe-cially in Japan with its key position as a regional supplier.

In contrast to 1919, this time multilateral institution building flourished, backed in both the US and Soviet spheres of influence by hard-power security agreements. Achievements included rounds of multilateral trade liberalization under the General Agreement on Tariffs and Trade (GATT): GATT negotiations reached their high-water mark in 1994 with the establishment of the World Trade Organization, an institution envisaged by Keynes during World War II but rejected by the United States in 1950. The GATT helped global trade to revive in the quarter century after the war under the stabilized exchange rates mandated in the IMF Articles of Agreement, and sup-ported by the latter's provisions for the restoration of national curren-cies' convertibility for current account transactions.

The United Nations organization, the intergovernmental heir to the League, also resurrected League-created bodies. UNESCO, for exam-ple, succeeded the League's International Committee on Intellectual Cooperation in 1945, and the World Health Organization (WHO) of 1948 built on its Health Committee (as noted earlier). The UN also cre-ated new agencies, beyond the IMF and World Bank linked to Keynes, such as the Food and Agriculture Organization (founded in1945), which absorbed the independent International Institute of Agriculture created in 1905. The crowning achievement of post–World War II international health efforts was the eradication of smallpox globally by 1979, the result of more than two decades of effort requiring close collaboration by Cold War adversaries working through the WHO (Cooper 1989; Carroll 2016). The case of global public health well illustrates, however, that as the number of specialist global institutions proliferated alongside a growing number of NGOS, the challenges of coordination and cooperation among them grew. Such frictions often went unaddressed because, as in 1944–1945, social and health questions appeared to be second-order priorities compared with hard security and financial stability.

Indeed, in 2020, the COVID-19 pandemic revealed that international cooperation on public health remained much too limited to meet current challenges, despite advances in institutional infrastructure and remarkable scientific progress. Keynes – or perhaps more likely his mother and sister – would argue that future global pandemic diseases remain a fundamental threat to peace and security within, as well as between, societies. As in 1919, a highly contagious virus killed millions across the world, with more set to die if the international community continued to respond in a disjointed fashion to a truly global threat.

It is tempting to credit Keynes's warnings of 1919 for the comparative success of post–World War II arrangements. But it is hard to draw straight lines from *The Economic Consequences of the Peace* to the post-1945 settlement. A multitude of other factors was in play, notwithstanding Keynes's important personal contributions in the financial sphere.

In 1945, Allied sentiment and policy toward the defeated Germany was, if anything (and understandably), more hostile after the second great war than after the first. In academic circles, Étienne Mantoux's *The Carthaginian Peace, or the Economic Consequences of Mr. Keynes* was a well-received economic and political critique that warned of the perils of treating Germany too leniently after World War II. (The book appeared posthumously at the start of 1946, its author having died in action only days before the end of the war.) More generally, as of the first half of the 1940s, the prevailing opinion of the Versailles Treaty was not that it had been too harsh, but that it had failed to neuter Germany decisively enough to prevent its industrial resurgence and a new, deadlier, conflict.

Initial proposals to deindustrialize Germany after the war reflected this mind-set. In late 1943, the Allies agreed in principle that Germany and its allies should pay some form of reparations.[23] Famously, Treasury Secretary Henry Morgenthau Jr.'s 1944 memo, *Suggested Post-Surrender Program for Germany*, included, among other provisions, partitioning a diminished Germany, turning the Ruhr into an international zone, and stripping German territory of its industries (by removing plant and equipment and destroying mines). President Roosevelt distanced himself from the plan only after opposition from his own State and War departments, as well as from the British government, which feared the wider repercussions for Europe's recovery. FDR was also warned that knowledge of the plan had strengthened German resistance in the field.

But the plan's general spirit survived. Immediately after the German surrender in May 1945, President Truman authorized a policy that prohibited US occupation forces from taking any steps to restore or maintain the German economy. Slightly more than two months later, at the Potsdam Conference, Truman, Churchill, and Stalin agreed to divide Germany into occupation zones. They agreed to strip it of resource-rich territories, including industrial Upper Silesia, impose reparations (by seizing industrial equipment and other assets), dismantle industry potentially capable of producing military goods, and take measures that would ensure Germans' standard of living would be no greater than the European average. The problem of German ethnic minorities across Eastern Europe, which had upset the peace after 1919, was resolved after 1945 by the ruthless transfer of between 12 and 14 million Germans above all from the territories of Poland and Czechoslovakia. It was the largest forced transfer of population in European history. At least 500,000 died in the process. Unlike after World War I, there was little sympathy for German suffering on the Allied side and no protest from Keynes.

As far as reparations were concerned, a total of $20 billion was set, to be paid in kind. Priority was given to Poland and the Soviet Union. Early in 1946, the Allies' first Level of Industry Plan set out a concrete plan to cap German industrial capacity at half the 1938 level through the destruction of 1,500 manufacturing establishments. Meanwhile, France occupied the coal-rich Saar, although the Americans and

---

[23] US officials consulted Keynes on the issue, "[y]et the man who had pronounced so famously in 1919 was now very reluctant to be drawn on the lessons of history" (Clavin 2013, p. 320).

Britons thwarted French attempts to control the Ruhr's coal and steel industry by establishing the International Authority for the Ruhr. French goals were in line with the Monnet Plan of 1946, which sought to transform France into Europe's leader in heavy industry on the back of the two contested German regions.[24] It was circumstances rather than any lessons of history read from *The Economic Consequences of the Peace* that prompted a change of strategy on the part of the Americans, British, and (more reluctantly) the French.

By the end of 1947, the United States led a change in the punitive approach toward German industrial rehabilitation owing to three principal factors. First, with the German economy disabled, the costs to Allied (and especially US) taxpayers of the German occupation were high, mounting, and ultimately difficult to sustain. The territories of what would now comprise "Germany" needed to become self-supporting. Second, it was becoming evident that the engine of German capital goods exports would be necessary for a broad-based European recovery. Third, the emerging Cold War split placed a premium on Western European recovery and cohesion and hardened the unwillingness of the Western powers to see Soviet demands for reparations satisfied from "their" zones of Germany.

After World War I, partition of Germany had never seriously been considered. Clemenceau considered the aggressive mutation of German nationalism in the nineteenth century – in no small part due to the violence of Napoleonic imperialism – as tragic, but he took unification to be irreversible. After World War II, there were no such qualms. By 1948, as an effect of Western–Soviet conflict, the partition of Germany was an accomplished fact.

The three western occupation zones were amalgamated over 1947–1948, and a new currency, the Deutsche Mark, was introduced. In April 1948, the US-sponsored Marshall Plan commenced operations – another reflection of the imperative to support European economic

---

[24] Monnet attended the Paris peace conference and in 1919 became deputy secretary-general of the League, a post he occupied until 1922. He played a key role much later in inspiring the Schuman Plan for the European Coal and Steel Community, which superseded the early post-war arrangements for the Ruhr, removed output ceilings in key German industrial sectors, and set Europe on the path to the current European Union. However, the emergence of the Schuman Plan owed much to American pressure (Berger and Ritschl 1995, pp. 216–219).

recovery as a bulwark against Communism. The Marshall Plan was less about the monetary resources the United States provided to Europe than about US efforts to leverage Marshall aid in the interest of European economic integration and cooperation. These were viewed as necessary conditions for western economic and political security in the light of the Soviet threat (Berger and Ritschl 1995; Eichengreen 2010). The western economic interventions triggered the Soviet blockade of Berlin in June 1948 – and a sharp escalation of East–West tensions.

These economic initiatives echoed arguments Keynes had made in 1919, but not because western policymakers consciously channelled the *Economic Consequences*. It was because Keynes's vision of the requirements for Europe's return to prosperity had been fundamentally correct after World War I and remained so after World War II.[25] How could Europe after World War I return to prosperity on the back of a disabled German economy, when, prior to the war, Germany was "a central support [of] the rest of the European economic system," enjoying an "overwhelming" economic interdependence with her neighbours?[26] The goal should be to "make possible the renewal of hope and enterprise within her territory" and "permit the continuance of Germany's industrial life" (Keynes 1919, pp. 248–249). In the later 1940s, the aim of policymakers became to remake the economy of Western Europe, not according to the fragmented inter-war model, but as a rump of the pre-1914 allocation of activity, implying that a revived western Germany would need to play a driving role.

Perhaps ironically, the volte-face on US policy towards Germany owed much more to Herbert Hoover than to Keynes – the same Hoover of whom Keynes had written glowingly after Versailles, but who presided over the US slide into depression a decade later. Recognizing Hoover's success in organizing aid to Europe after the previous war, President Truman invited him to tour Europe again in 1947, and specifically to make recommendations on the humanitarian and economic crisis in Germany and Austria. The third of his three reports, dated March 18, 1947, contained this warning:

---

[25] George F. Kennan, an architect of the Marshall Plan at the US State Department, wrote in later life that the major influence on his initial thinking about the shape of post–World War II Europe was not Keynes but Bainville (1920), which was written as a counterpoint to the *Economic Consequences* (Kennan 1998).

[26] Keynes (1919, p. 14).

There is only one path to recovery in Europe. That is production. The whole economy of Europe is intertwined with [the] German economy through the exchange of raw materials and manufactured goods. The productivity of Europe cannot be restored without the restoration of Germany as a contributor to that productivity.[27]

Hoover had made similar arguments after World War I, and Keynes quotes him extensively and with approval in chapter VI of the *Economic Consequences*. This time, Hoover's vision, backed by the United States' preponderant power, won the day.

In one indirect and incidental way, Keynes's contribution to the post-war monetary system may have accelerated US understanding of the need to fortify all of Western Europe against Soviet designs. Early in 1946, while serving as deputy head of the US mission in Moscow, George Kennan received a request from the US Treasury to explain the USSR's refusal to join the Bretton Woods institutions (despite having been party to the negotiations creating them). This refusal surprised some in Washington, who naively expected the Soviets to embrace the Keynes–White vision of multilateral economic governance despite the facts unfolding on the ground in Europe, the Middle East, and Asia. Shortly thereafter, Kennan on February 22, 1946, composed and sent to the State Department his influential "long telegram" on the inevitability of Soviet hostility to the West (Kennan 1967, p. 293).[28] Soviet rejection of Keynes's handiwork thereby marked a key moment in the opening of the Cold War.

---

[27] The *New York Times* published a complete report text, available at https://timesmachine.nytimes.com/timesmachine/1947/03/24/issue.html. Hoover also noted that "[E]ntirely aside from any humanitarian and political aspects, policies which will restore productivity in Germany and exports with which to buy their food and relieve [the monetary] drain upon us are of primary importance." In his report, Hoover identified the "major mistake of Versailles" as the failure to demilitarize Germany effectively and permanently. Yet, he believed demilitarization could be accomplished consistently with German economic prosperity.

[28] The components of the former USSR eventually joined the IMF over 1992–1993. In his authoritative biography of Kennan, Gaddis (2011, p. 216) denies that the Treasury request was the catalyst for the telegram (despite what Kennan recounts in his own memoirs). Regardless of these details, the Soviet attitude toward the Bretton Woods institutions was one of several indications of coming tensions. If one reads the long telegram today (as reproduced in Kennan 1967), the continuity of the subversive methods Kennan describes with current tactics of "asymmetric warfare" is striking.

The last act in the drama of German foreign indebtedness was the London Debt Agreement (LDA) of 1953 (Tooze 2011). An Anglo-French pact to pressure the United States into cancelling its war debts had the effect of enabling Germany to wriggle out of its World War I reparations bill, but Germany still had obligations connected with the Dawes and Young loans (which grew out of those reparations). It also owed monies because of private cross-border loans made to German businesses and government bodies during the inter-war period, as well as assistance extended to Germany after World War II (including a portion of the Marshall aid). The LDA terms were relatively lenient, with the United States forgiving $2 billion in German debt and Germany paying at best half of what it owed (Guinnane 2015). As with the earlier reconstruction initiatives, the motivations for this generosity were to bind Germany into the western democratic alliance and to resist Communism through prosperity. Galofré-Vilà et al. (2019) argue that the LDA powerfully catalysed German growth through multiple channels.

Despite some efforts to anticipate the problem, the international community was ill equipped in the late 1940s to deal with one of the most salient products of the war: refugees. Fears regarding population displacement and concerns over the scale of the implied material needs made questions over population movement and support a focus of international planning by the Allied powers after the United States entered World War II. These concerns led to the creation of the United Nations Relief and Rehabilitation Administration (UNRRA). League of Nations officials based in the United States helped to inform this work, drawing on their knowledge of events after 1918. Then, the implosion of the Austro-Hungarian and Ottoman empires, border adjustments, and the creation of new nation states and mandates in central, southern, and eastern Europe, in North Africa, and in the Middle East triggered significant population movements. These crisscrossed with demobilized soldiers returning home. Among the largest refugee flows was the population of Magyars who left Romania for the defeated, new republic of Hungary, their number joined by Bulgarians expelled from western Thrace. The continuing armed conflict after 1918 – civil war in Russia, the Polish–Soviet War, and the Greek-Turkish War in 1921–1922 – found its echo in bitter civil wars in Greece after 1945 and partisan violence in the Baltic states. Conflict along the frontier of Poland and Ukraine ended only in 1955. In 1945, the magnitude of population displacement in Europe as "peace" came outstripped that of 1918 by a large margin, almost defying contemporaries' imaginations. Some twenty-three million people were uprooted in the final stages of World War II owing to border changes, repatriations, and population transfers that followed the Allied deal at Potsdam (Gatrell 2013; Reinisch and White 2011).

Keynes and the Achievement of Bretton Woods

Keynes's *The General Theory of Employment Interest and Money* (1936) was a work of closed-economy theorizing, as Vines's chapter reminds us. The book sought to explain how a largely autarkic economy operating as an insular unit could pull itself out of depression. By the early 1930s, Keynes had come to believe that the political stability of democratic capitalism depended on each government's ability to satisfy its citizens' legitimate demands for economic security. The primacy of this national objective meant jettisoning laissez-faire principles, including unimpeded international trade and capital movements, when necessary.[29] However, Keynes did not favour autarky per se and did not view his prescriptions for domestic stabilization as being inconsistent with a degree of international economic integration. Instead, he recognized that countries could reap benefits from international interdependence and need not fall into policy conflicts as a result, provided they also had macroeconomic tools sufficient to ensure domestic economic stability. As *The General Theory* (p. 382) put it:

[I]f nations can learn to provide themselves with full employment by their domestic policy ... there need be no important forces calculated to set the interest of one country against that of its neighbours. There would still be room for the international division of labour and for international lending in appropriate conditions.

In June 1940, Keynes returned to the UK Treasury as an adviser – this time, not as a brilliant but relatively unknown 31-year-old, but as the world's most renowned economist. By then he had an influential following among economists in the United States (Carter 2020), including at the US Treasury. (Indeed, it was the Depression and World

---

[29] On Keynes's views, see Obstfeld (2021).

War II that cemented the influence of economists at treasuries in both America and Britain, in part owing to Keynes's ideas about government's role in the economy; see Ikenberry 1992.) As early as 1941, he began to consider post-war international economic arrangements. Key elements of his approach were to provide international liquidity and to channel countries' nationalistic pursuit of prosperity away from the international conflicts that beggar-thy-neighbour policies caused. Allied negotiations over the post-war monetary system, most importantly the bilateral negotiations between the United States and the United Kingdom, began in 1942 and culminated in the July 1944 Bretton Woods agreement.

The Bretton Woods compromise between the United States and the United Kingdom envisioned a world economy with fixed exchange rates and two inclusive international organizations, the IMF and the World Bank, to meet the challenges of short-term balance-of-payments disruptions and long-term financing of economic reconstruction and growth. Critically, a country could change its IMF exchange parity (with IMF notification) in circumstances of long-term "fundamental disequilibrium" – such as that which bedevilled Britain on gold after 1925. In such cases, an overvalued currency, if not devalued, would condemn the economy to a long period of unemployment and deflation. In Keynes's mind, having the option to change an exchange rate in cases of fundamental disequilibrium would enable national currencies to adjust consistently with requirements of domestic macro stability. This would be much preferable to having prices, output, and employment adjust to the requirements of an immutable exchange rate. Through a compromise made possible by the IMF's capacities, its rules squarely addressed the dilemma between exchange rate stability and price level stability that Keynes had identified in his *Tract*. IMF lending, if necessary, would help countries maintain stable exchange rates in the face of *temporary* balance-of-payments disturbances (thereby promoting a less volatile international trade environment). However, in the face of hopefully less frequent *permanent* balance-of-payments disturbances – those requiring long-term adjustment of the domestic price level through deflation in order to maintain full employment – the pegged exchange rate would instead be adjustable to avoid protracted recessions.

Critical to the viability of this compromise was the absence of speculative capital movements. If private investors were free to move funds across borders and even suspected that an exchange rate might be devalued, they would perceive a "one-way bet" and would shift their investments in such a high volume that central banks, even with the aid of IMF resources, might be overwhelmed. Keynes's and Nurkse's critiques of such destabilizing "hot money" flows during the inter-war period were central to the Bretton Woods system's design (Clavin 2013). Thus, while the IMF Articles of Agreement aimed to restore currency convertibility for current account transactions quickly, and thereby to promote international trade, they did not intend to promote convertibility for *financial account* transactions, even as an implicit goal. By excluding free private capital mobility, the IMF rules aimed to operate a regime of deliberate infrequent exchange rate changes, thereby gaining most of the assumed benefits of fixed exchange rates for trade, while guarding against protracted disequilibria in labour markets. Restrictions on international finance would match the widespread restrictions on domestic finance that prevailed following the post-1929 financial instability and wartime controls.

As it turned out, the final shape of the Bretton Woods agreement adhered more closely to the US blueprint than to Keynes's, and more closely reflected American economic interests than those of Britain. Nonetheless, the agreement addressed, if imperfectly, several of Keynes's key objectives, and he lent it his strong public support. Keynes personally made the case for the agreement in the House of Lords while gravely ill. Approval of the IMF and the World Bank by both Congress and Parliament marked a strong contrast with Keynes's fruitless attempts to influence the financial outcome of the Versailles treaty in 1919, and his public attacks on it after afterward. As James and Koger point out in their chapter, Keynes's relative inexperience of diplomacy in 1919 may have been counterproductive; his much greater capacity as of 1945 may have been decisive.

What had changed? For one thing, Keynes's own role was different. Unlike in 1919, in 1945 Keynes was completely committed to the war against Germany, and its Axis associates, that he had helped the Allies to win. In addition, unlike in 1919, he had a much greater degree of personal responsibility for the actual negotiations and outcomes, so the option of resigning and writing a flaming denunciation of a difficult compromise settlement was less attractive. The changing context between 1919 and 1945 went well beyond Keynes as an individual.

British radical liberal opinion more generally was at odds with World War I. And the place of experts such as Keynes in the structure of the state was still quite marginal in 1919. The emergence of "big government" and modern expertise in the inter-war period changed all of that in terms of both professional participation in policymaking and the degree of political engagement to which the experts as functionaries were now committed.

But Keynes as an individual also made a critical difference by creating an intellectual apparatus that justified government economic initiative on a large scale. This apparatus related to the state's approach to both macroeconomic stabilization and economic development. His life's work – as an economist, policy practitioner, and public intellectual – demonstrated that international economic relations must support, rather than thwart, the public pursuit of inclusive domestic prosperity. Keynesianism offered a solution to the mid-century dilemma of western capitalism: how to balance the market against the need for governmental domestic policy space to support and protect democracy. In Keynes's vision, international institutions were essential to addressing this core challenge.[30]

The Unstable Dynamics of Bretton Woods

As originally conceived, the Bretton Woods system – with its controls over international finance and its provisions for exchange rate adjustment – embodied a philosophy of the relation between market and state quite different from the classical liberalism that ruled before World War I. As Ruggie (1982, p. 393) put it, famously characterizing the underlying philosophy as "embedded liberalism,"

[U]nlike the economic nationalism of the thirties, it would be multilateral in character; unlike the liberalism of the gold standard and free trade, its multilateralism would be predicated upon domestic interventionism.

---

[30] Viner's (1947) verdict was that "[I]n the third phase of his career, from Munich to his death, [Keynes] rose to the highest levels of maturity, balance of judgment, and responsible and world-oriented statesmanship. If there is a successful outcome of the present effort of the great Western democracies to find a common platform from which to promote a postwar world in which peace, freedom, and plenty can all prevail, to Keynes will be due a significant fraction of the credit."

On its own terms, the Bretton Woods system, buttressed by the Marshall Plan and associated institution building in Europe, successfully promoted post-war reconstruction, international trade, and the achievement of full employment and growth. But the very success of the system generated internal contradictions that led to centrifugal economic and political strains Even as the scars of war healed over in the quarter century following 1945, several major destabilizing trends emerged as results of the Bretton Woods system's economic success.

First, the international mobility of financial capital rose as international trade expanded and the "international division of labour" Keynes had referred to in the *General Theory* became more efficient, through specialization along lines of comparative advantage as well as through increasing returns to scale and economies of multinational production. These developments raised the demand for global financial services, but they also provided ample opportunities for hidden or disguised capital movements. The result was greater turbulence in foreign exchange markets as cross-border funds moved with increasing violence in anticipation of exchange rate adjustments.

Second, the growing export success of Western Europe and Japan raised the competitive bar for US industries. The latter had been overwhelmingly dominant in the early years after the war. Thereafter, rising levels of US imports from lower-wage countries put pressure on US wages, while the manufacturing share of US employment levelled off in the 1960s, and then began a rapid descent at the decade's end. In contrast, manufacturing employment was still growing in Germany and Japan (Obstfeld 1985, p. 380). US organised labour supported the Kennedy Round of GATT negotiations that Congress authorized in 1962, but subsequently switched to opposing trade liberalization, a sign of pessimism that export promotion could benefit US workers enough to offset the impact of higher imports.[31]

Third, and in line with these developments, the US balance-of-payments position weakened as the post-war period of global "dollar shortage" ended. The United States, uniquely within the Bretton Woods system, had no need to use foreign exchange reserves to defend dollar exchange rates because the dollar served as a numeraire within the system: other

---

[31] Alden (2017, p. 80). The Trade Expansion Act of 1962, which authorized the Kennedy Round, also set up Trade Adjustment Assistance programs that are widely judged to have been ineffective in countering trade-induced disruptions of US labour markets.

countries bought and sold dollars to keep their currencies in line at the official par values. However, the United States had promised to keep foreign governments' dollar reserves convertible into gold at an exchange rate of $35 per ounce – making gold the bedrock of the system, despite Keynes's warnings. As foreign dollar reserves grew, the US ability to fulfil this pledge given the limits of its gold stocks came into question.[32] By the end of the 1960s, the United States relied upon the forbearance of its trade partners and allies, who had accumulated reserve holdings of paper dollars far in excess of the value of US gold. But these countries were becoming increasingly sceptical of US political and economic leadership in light of US economic policies, US policies in Vietnam, and the response the latter provoked on their own streets. US inflation rose markedly. In a world pegged to the dollar, the inflation spilled abroad.

Following the establishment of the European Economic Community in 1957, cooperation among its members increasingly intensified. In 1970, the Werner Report recommended the establishment of a single European currency. These developments were in line with the hopes Keynes expressed in the *Economic Consequences* for a free trade zone radiating from continental Europe, but they also nurtured a new economic and political power centre independent of the United States. The report clearly signalled that Europe's willingness to sustain the Bretton Woods currency system was fraying.

These tensions came to a head under US President Richard Nixon's administration. Anticipating attitudes that President Trump would take much further five decades later, in 1969 the president put forward his "Guam Doctrine" in 1969, denoting that nations of non-Communist Asia, including South Vietnam, Taiwan, and South Korea, should increasingly bear the burden of their own defence. The doctrine rationalized increased US arms sales to Iran, Saudi Arabia, and Israel, with welcome collateral benefits for the US balance of payments. In August 1971, with unemployment and inflation both having risen substantially, Nixon imposed an import surcharge on US trade partners, forcing them to revalue their currencies against the US dollar, while also mandating wage and price controls and discontinuing the US government's commitment to redeem official dollars in terms of gold.

---

[32] The Belgian economist Robert Triffin, then a professor at Yale, raised this problem at the start of the 1960s shortly after Europe attained current account convertibility for its currencies under IMF rules.

The "Nixon shock" highlights that by the later 1960s, a clear trade-off had emerged, in which Americans would increasingly evaluate the US global leadership role in terms of its economic costs at home. This trade-off was also an element of the US position in 1919, as Keynes pointed out: the implications for American policy of Wilson's Fourteen Points, including the commitment to a new League of Nations, had neither been thought through nor been tested with Congress and the US electorate. After the Wall Street crash, US internationalism was deeply tainted, with isolationists ascendant. While America embraced its leadership of a hegemonic multilateralist system in the first quarter century after World War II, Nixon's actions in 1971 were a sharp turn toward nationalism – launched without consulting allies (Garten 2021). The motivating trends in the US global economic position would only accelerate in future decades, partly because of another of Nixon's foreign policy moves, and arguably his signal foreign policy achievement, US opening to China.

This history is well known, but a less-noticed development of 1971 was economist Robert Mundell's publication of a meandering pamphlet, remembered today mostly for setting out an intellectual basis for what would later be called supply-side economics (Mundell 1971). Mundell's concern was to set out a mix of monetary and fiscal policies that could resolve the United States' simultaneous internal and external balance problems – a topic that, in a general sense, had preoccupied Keynes over the years and was fundamental to the IMF's raison d'être. Stripped of the political valence that some assign to it, Mundell's core point was important and economists of all stripes acknowledge it. Fiscal policies are diverse and can operate, not only in terms of Keynesian aggregate demand effects, but also in terms of how they change the economy's underlying productive potential.

The complete and permanent collapse of the Bretton Woods fixed exchange rates early in 1973, under the pressure of massive speculation, provided countries with welcome room for monetary policy manoeuvre. But it did not (and could not) alter the long-term direction of real structural transformation in the world economy.

Global Finance, the Market, and the State after Bretton Woods

Floating exchange rates were a sharp departure from the original Bretton Woods vision, but the dismantling of its "embedded

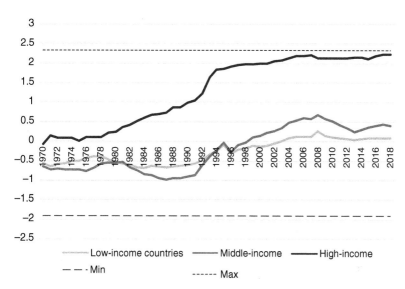

Figure 1.4 Index of capital account openness, 1970–2018
Source: Chinn and Ito (2006) de jure index updated July 13, 2020, http://
web.pdx.edu/~ito/Chinn-Ito_website.htm. The index ranges from –1.92 (most
closed) to 2.33 (most open). The figure shows simple unweighted averages
over countries. China enters the index in 1984. Russia and other former Soviet
states enter in 1996.

liberalism" was due primarily to another factor: the progressive
removal of restrictions on financial activity, particularly international
financial activity. Figure 1.4 displays the evolution of a well-known
measure of de jure openness to international capital mobility, taken
from Chinn and Ito (2006). From the mid-1970s, the industrial countries' financial openness rose markedly, accelerating in the early 1990s
and reaching a peak approximating maximal openness by the start of
the millennium. Lower- and middle-income countries begin to open
their financial accounts around 1990. To date their opening falls far
short of what the richer economies have chosen.

Freed of the need to defend fixed dollar exchange rates using their
monetary tools, countries could in principle deploy monetary policy
in pursuit of domestic price and employment objectives. Their ability
to do so resolved Keynes's policy dilemma, even for countries that
were highly financially interdependent with the rest of the world.
But this does not explain why countries would *choose* to open their

financial markets to global forces (Obstfeld and Taylor 2017). The process of financial liberalization was complex and gradual, involving the interplay of domestic and cross-border relaxation. It reflected a confluence of government objectives, changing global economic conditions, financial innovation, and the lobbying power of domestic financial interests (Helleiner 1994). In turn, the latter became richer and therefore gained political influence with each successive victory, in a snowballing process. By the 2000s, advanced economies had become extensively financialized in an environment of weak financial oversight (Krippner 2011), with momentous negative consequences. Compared with the vision of Keynes and other participants at Bretton Woods, this outcome represented a marked shift in the primacy of state power in the arrangement of states, markets, and civil society.

One irony of this process is its background in initiatives pursued by America and Britain, the same partners who in 1944 chose to make embedded liberalism the foundation of Bretton Woods. Hoping to regain some of the past financial glory of London, the UK government (already from the 1950s) promoted the London Eurodollar market as an offshore playground for global finance, finally starting in 1979 to pull down any boundaries between the domestic and international financial systems. In the early 1970s, the United States favoured financial liberalization both to cement its own standing as a financial centre and in the belief that relaxing outflow controls would further weaken the dollar, benefiting US exports. By the latter 1980s, the European Community, pursuing internal financial integration (and with the support of Britain, now a member), hopped on board the train.[33]

Ideology played a role in these developments, as well as in broader changes in economic policy. Again, the Anglo-American axis dominated the changing orientation of economic policymaking.[34] Neoliberal economists associated with the University of Chicago school (including George Shultz at Treasury and external advisers

---

[33] Accounts of the political dynamics driving financial liberalization include, along with Helleiner (1994), Abdelal (2009), Ghosh, Kim, and Qureshi (2020), and Obstfeld (2021).

[34] See Fourcade (2009) on the recent Anglo-American dominance of professional economics. It is worth noting that strong elements in neoliberal thinking originated in continental European centres, notably Vienna, Geneva, and Freiburg (Slobodian 2018). Many of the continental scholars, including economists like Hayek, Mises, Haberler, Bonn, and Schumpeter, worked closely with Britons and Americans in the EFO of the League of Nations, connections

such as Milton Friedman and Alan Greenspan) played important roles in the Nixon administration. But as in 1919, the policy outcomes – such as price administration and tariffs – tended to reflect political imperatives rather than economic theories. Nevertheless, in academia, economic models based on the rational expectations and the efficient markets hypothesis dominated the professional literature and generated arguments against discretionary macroeconomic policy and financial regulation. By the time Ronald Reagan was elected US president in 1980 – after the economic shocks and inflation of the 1970s – these ideas had set the stage for a frontal effort to scale back the reach of government policy. The conservative agenda also sought to transfer resources to wealthier groups within American society based on the unproven claim of self-styled supply-side economists that this would jump-start economic growth, which in turn would "trickle down" to lower-income households.

The public discussion of changing economic paradigms was, if anything, more visible in Britain, where the press played an important role in promoting Friedman's doctrine of monetarism as a counterpoint to Keynesianism. In an important article in the *Daily Telegraph* in 1974, Friedrich von Hayek, a founder of neoliberalism in the 1930s who had just shared that year's Nobel memorial prize in economics, airily declared: "What we are experiencing are simply economic consequences, of Lord Keynes."[35] High inflation coupled with high

that helped them flee Europe for the United States after the rise of Nazism (Clavin 2013). This history reinforced their connections to and influence on the Anglo-American scene. Of course, Swedish economists also played an outsized role both in theoretical and policy discussions before World War II (see the chapter by Carlson and Jonung). It is not just the debate between Keynes and Ohlin (who also worked at the League) that shows their influence. Also relevant are Cassel's critique of the gold standard, the Heckscher-Ohlin trade theory (which illuminates the redistributive effects of trade globalization), and Wicksell's work on monetary economics and inflation (which remains fundamental to modern central bank operations). The Freiburg school birthed ordoliberalism, which retains influence in Germany and helped to shape the design of the euro and the policy approaches of euro area policymakers. In his chapter, Clarke highlights that even in 1919, Wilson and Lloyd George approached the Paris negotiations with a shared "liberal moralism."

[35] Some early neoliberals, alarmed by the broader Keynesian project, had eagerly seized on flaws in the *Economic Consequences* as an ad hominem adjunct to their broader critique of Keynes's economics. For example, Rappard's (1946) blistering endorsement of Mantoux (1946) argues that Keynes was as much eloquent moralist as economist and adds the aside, "It is not in his *Economic*

unemployment, he said, were the product of two decades in which policies accommodated inflationary pressures while governments falsely assured voters that Keynesian tools could and should maintain high employment.[36] A pivotal point came in September 1976, when Labour Prime Minister James Callaghan, speaking at his party's annual conference, echoed Hayek, warning: "The cozy world we were told would go on forever, where full employment would be guaranteed by a stroke of the Chancellor's pen, cutting taxes, deficit spending – that world is gone." On the same day that Keynesian countercyclical policies were being questioned in Blackpool, Callaghan's government announced that it was applying for financial support from Keynes's creation, the IMF.[37] Less than three years later, running on pledges to control inflation, rein in labour unions, and address voters' concerns over immigration, Margaret Thatcher entered 10 Downing Street and administered monetarist medicine to the UK economy. Throughout these turbulent times, Keynes, now dead for three decades, remained a touchstone.[38]

Consequences alone that the pen of Keynes has often persuaded where his brain has failed to convince." Rappard was not a disinterested reviewer. In 1927, he and the historian Paul Mantoux, Étienne Mantoux's father and Clemenceau's interpreter at the 1919 peace conference, joined forces to found the Graduate Institute of International Studies in Geneva. Rappard was an ardent proponent of laissez-faire, including fully free trade, and delivered the opening address at the first meeting of the Mont Pèlerin society. Hayek organized the latter to build support for private free enterprise, and many distinguished economists participated – though not Viner, who thought people might view the group as "political" (Clavin 2013, p. 351). Some would argue that the neoliberal denial of a moral dimension in economics has intensely political implications, and in ways that have proved problematic for democratic societies (Brown 2019).

[36] The article is adapted for a US audience as Hayek (1974). For a modern retrospective on the inflation of the 1970s and its consequences, see Bordo and Orphanides (2013).

[37] For interesting background on this episode, see Sandbrook (2012, pp. 477–481). Journalist Peter Jay, the prime minister's son-in-law and an avid proponent of monetarism at *The Times*, wrote the key portion of the speech repudiating deficit spending. Milton Friedman quoted it approvingly in his own Nobel acceptance speech in December 1976.

[38] Harry G. Johnson, professor at the LSE and Chicago (where he was a colleague of Friedman and Mundell), offered a candid and perceptive analysis of the growing academic influence of monetarism, even before its broader acceptance as a basis for economic policy. In Johnson (1971, p. 13), he reached the prescient judgment that "[monetarism's] success is likely

Under the neoliberal approach promoted by both Thatcher and Reagan, the pendulum swung to an opposite extreme from the vision Keynes had accepted of government's proper role in the economy, based on its need to maintain a certain social contract. Later events would show that the pendulum had swung too far. In some ways, as the term "neoliberalism" suggested, this shift of the late 1970s was a purposeful return closer to pre–World War I economic liberalism. As Thatcher famously remarked in 1987, "[W]ho is society? There is no such thing! There are individual men and women and there are families and no government can do anything except through people and people look to themselves first."

Figure 1.5 shows one of several possible measures of income inequality for the United States and the United Kingdom, the pre-tax income share of the top 1 percent in the national income distribution. For both countries, this measure of inequality reaches its low point around the mid-1970s, having fallen from levels near 20 percent around 1919. A striking reversal begins, however, around 1980, with the US measure approaching levels that prevailed before World War I and in the inter-war period. The sharp rise in inequality starts with the specific policies Reagan and Thatcher adopted with respect to taxation, regulation, and workers' rights. But these and subsequent structural policy changes also presented an environment in which the rich were much better positioned to profit from other inequality-promoting trends in globalization, technological change, and financialization.

Close to when Thatcher and Reagan came to power, a far-reaching economic regime change was taking place elsewhere: in China. Following Deng Xiaoping's December 1978 speech to the Chinese Communist Party (CCP) central committee, China embarked on a multi-decade programme of pro-market reforms, starting with agricultural reforms, encouragement of private entrepreneurship, and

to be transitory, precisely because it has relied on the same mechanisms of intellectual conquest as the [Keynesian] revolution itself, but has been forced by the nature of the case to choose a less important political issue – inflation – to stand on than the unemployment that provided the Keynesian revolution with its political talking point." (One spectacularly wrong judgment of Johnson's was to dismiss imperfect competition in economic theorizing. Although dormant when he wrote, imperfect competition now underlies wide swaths of economics, including growth theory, the analysis of income inequality, the theory of international trade – and the New Keynesian approach to macroeconomics.)

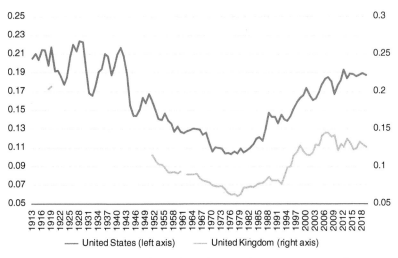

Figure 1.5 Pre-tax national income shares of top 1 percent of earners, 1913–2019
Source: World Inequality Database. https://wid.world/data/, accessed September 22, 2021.

some openness to foreign direct investment. Nixon's Sino diplomacy culminated in the formal establishment of diplomatic relations with the United States on January 1, 1979. In the years that followed, China's standard of living improved markedly. Its economy became more sophisticated, export levels surged, and it grew more economically interdependent with higher-income countries. China's growth, along with that of the many developing countries whose economic reforms started about a decade later, would have important impacts on the nature and distribution of production abroad, as well on international and intranational distributions of income.

The Cold War's End and Aftermath

The years around 1990 were a key hinge point, and not just because numerous emerging markets, including China and India, embarked on economic reforms and trade opening. On November 9, 1989, perhaps the most potent symbol of the Cold War and the long-standing division of Germany, the Berlin Wall, fell to popular protest. Over the next two years the Soviet grip on Eastern Europe melted away, with the Soviet Union itself breaking up and repudiating the political monopoly of the Communist Party in 1991. Europe fortunately was spared violent repression on the model of the CCP's Tiananmen actions, which ensured that there would be no comparable political opening in China.

In April 1990 the European Council (the grouping of the European Community's heads of state or government) approved rapid unification of the two Germanies, a decision supported by French President Mitterrand after German Chancellor Kohl promised strongly to support ambitious European economic unification. That promise led to the Maastricht Treaty of 1992, which set out the roadmap toward a common currency, the euro, and transformed the European Community into the European Union.[39] Keynes would have understood Mitterrand's strategy well: in the *Economic Consequences*, he stressed the need to embed Germany in a broad trade partnership of equals in order to avoid fears of the country "realising the former German dream of Mittel-Europa" (Keynes 1919, p. 250). In July 1990, Germany and the USSR agreed on Germany's reunification within the existing borders of the East and West (including a unified Berlin) and on the formal end of the country's 45-year occupation by the four World War II allies.[40] Eastern Europe and eventually the former Soviet Union began a process of transition to market allocation, economic integration, and, in many cases, democratic governance.

By the early 1990s, these developments led many to conclude that the capitalist system had triumphed; some asserted the world had reached the end of *economic* history. But the *form* of capitalism that prevailed in advanced economies, even in Europe to a degree, was far from the embedded liberalism Keynes had espoused. It was a global capitalism dominated by the political legacy of Reagan and Thatcher, which pushed even leaders of nominally left-wing parties to "triangulate" toward the right during the 1990s. Not only did this form of capitalism harbour inherent financial instabilities, as shown by the increasing frequency and severity of economic crises: turbulence was

---

[39] Sarotte (2011, pp. 145–148).

[40] In an ironic echo of reparations, Germany had to pay the Soviets to get them to leave – DM 3 billion in the form of an interest-free loan and DM 12 billion as a grant, ostensibly to build housing in the USSR for returning Soviet troops (Sarotte 2011, pp. 192–193). This sum was important, especially in view of the impending cost of absorbing East Germany.

an innate feature. In retrospect, it also became clear how ill equipped this form of capitalism was to meet the labour-market challenges of skill-biased technical change and a surge of developing-country exports. Both of those forces played out as the entry of newly freed and reformed economies into global trade effectively doubled the world's supply of low-skilled labour. In the United States, the populist electoral appeals of Patrick Buchanan and H. Ross Perot were leading indicators of developments that propelled Donald Trump to the White House twenty-five years later.

The year 1989, like 1919 seven decades earlier, appeared to offer the opportunity for systematic transformation in Europe. The events of that year created a single Germany as well as several nations, nascent at the Paris Peace Conference but absorbed by Stalin into a Soviet eastern bloc after 1945. An especially consequential recasting was the expansion of the NATO Alliance and EU membership eastward. As Sarotte (2011, p. 201) observes of American and European policymakers, "Rather than bringing an end to the history that had culminated in the Cold War, they had perpetuated key parts of it instead." The ramifications included later east-to-west migration pressures within Europe, the rapid absorption of young and (as it turned out) fragile democracies into an EU that required unanimity for key decisions, and a toxic Russian suspicion of the expanded western alliance now extended to its very borders.[41]

Despite high hopes in 1989, subsequent history would show that the dissolution of the Soviet empire, like that of the Habsburg and Ottoman empires earlier, could revive "the ancient conflicts now inherent in the tangled structure of Europe" (Keynes 1922, p. 13). Moreover, even the merger of the two parts of Germany has not resulted in full economic convergence. Its political and economic legacy has made the former East Germany an epicentre of right-wing extremism. Subsequent decades would show that economic history did *not* end in the years 1989–1991, and that there would be no clean break from the drawn-out sequel to World War I and the peace of Versailles. Turbulence, driven in part by new challenges, continued.

---

[41] George Kennan predicted NATO expansion would be "the most fateful error of American policy in the entire post-Cold War era" (Kennan 1997).

Keynes and the World a Century after 1919

Little over a century since Keynes wrote *The Economic Consequences of the Peace*, the world confronts existential problems raised by decades of rapid global growth. Because those problems are solvable only by national governments working in concert, the moment is perilous indeed. The multilateral institutions that a hegemonic United States sponsored after World War II remain important, but they have so far proven unequal to the immense challenges at hand. Meanwhile, politics in many places are increasingly polarizing, driven by a toxic informational ecosystem.

As in 1919, the world suffered the grip of a contagious virus, this time SARS-CoV-2 rather than H1N1, which killed millions and was more deadly than necessary due to the failure of governments to cooperate. The immediate stresses of economic reopening after COVID-19 are somewhat like those of realigning a wartime economy. The pandemic raised a larger issue, though: How can the community of nations strengthen cross-border modes of public health cooperation to forestall or manage future pathogenic outbreaks? Increasing human encroachment on nature makes future pandemics and their associated economic shocks inevitable.

Even more dangerous than pandemic disease is the closely related crisis of anthropogenic climate change. Its aspects range from extreme weather events to polar melting to ocean acidification to disease proliferation to collapsing biodiversity. Humankind is testing the planetary boundaries within which it evolved, with likely disastrous results (Rockström et al. 2009). Yet there is no agreed approach on how to change course.

The settlement of 1919 did not yield a sustainable solution to the problems left by the war. Consistent with Keynes's fears, the world slid into depression, political instability, and a new global war, despite the attempt at Versailles to re-establish international relations based on a visionary multilateral construct, the League of Nations. A resemblance between today's conditions and those of 1919 therefore bodes ill for unified global action to address humanity's most pressing challenges.

In one echo of 1919, the preponderance of US power and influence that existed in 1945 has been superseded by a multipolar world in which the United States and China will increasingly vie for global primacy in ways that unsettle established relations regionally – as in

Europe and the Pacific – and globally. Both countries have to share the benefits of any global public goods they provide, but agreement on sharing the costs appears increasingly difficult. Moreover, the inward "America First" shift of the Trump administration garnered considerable domestic political support, and elements of that approach persist under President Biden. These changes recall the inter-war position of the United States, coexisting with European empires and an ambitious Japan, but neither being a global hegemon nor aspiring to a hegemonic role. As in 1919, ethnic and racial tensions and political polarization within the United States undermine any aspiration toward global leadership. The words one of us wrote about the US position then can be paraphrased for today's United States with little modification (compare with Tooze 2014, p. 334): What recent experience has underscored is not only the central role of the United States in world politics, but also the frailty of the American state as the pivot of the international order. American history is not a purely domestic drama. Its political and economic crises have global ramifications.

As in 1919, nationalism continues to rise, mobilized to support authoritarianism in Eastern Europe, Russia, India, Brazil, Turkey, and elsewhere. It underpinned Brexit and motivated the Johnson, Truss, and Sunak governments' norm bending, both domestically and with respect to the United Kingdom's withdrawal treaty with the EU. In the United States, a domestic nationalist movement has outlived the Trump presidency and only grown more visible since, driven by new sources of grievance and increasingly anti-democratic inclinations.

Consistent with this geopolitical configuration, multilateralism remains under stress. Many of the global multilateral institutions, however useful their potential roles may be, now lie in the cross hairs of conflicts among major states. The United States has stopped threatening to withdraw from institutions it helped create, as during the Trump years. For now. But despite the need for cooperation to address global health and climate, as well as areas like trade and technology, multilateral institutions and initiatives remain peripheral to the larger countries' main policy concerns.

Nowhere is this more evident than in the area of international migration. In the past decade, increased refugee pressures due to civil conflict and climate change have fed nationalism, populism, and ethnic hostility in potential recipient countries, undermining the chances of any globally cooperative approach to this challenge (as well as to others). As in the aftermaths of both world wars, the problem is massive and may well be destabilizing for the future. Yet, absent an effective international response to contain and reverse greenhouse gas emissions, refugee flows directly or indirectly driven by climate collapse will only intensify over time.[42]

Finally, the operations of the capitalist system are being vigorously questioned, as they were after 1918. Then, socialist ideas were still gaining traction and Russia was engaged in the first experiment of socialist rule. In Europe – if not in its overseas empires – a widespread extension of the franchise was underway. The labour movement was gaining political power, a trend harder for business interests to resist after wartime sacrifices. This history begs a critical, open question before the world today: Can capitalism be reshaped in an orderly way through established political processes within nations, without damaging the necessary cooperation *between* nations?

The roots of the current malaise are complex. In essence, they all relate to the turbulence generated by economic, technological, demographic, and cultural interdependence in a globalized environment that lacks adequate social guardrails. As Ikenberry (2020, p. 6) puts it, the liberal internationalist system that superseded embedded liberalism and that reached its full extent after the Cold War "effectively overran its political foundations and undermined its social purposes."

Punctuating recent decades are key events that accelerated the emerging political impasse. Perhaps the most important was the Global Financial Crisis of 2008–2009, a direct outgrowth of the deregulation and globalization of finance. Apart from causing widespread economic misery, the crisis undermined further people's faith in government and in the economy's fairness, at the same time increasing scepticism of financial and economic expertise (Tooze 2018). The euro zone crisis which followed immediately, and advanced economies' drawn out recovery, led to further voter disaffection. Prior economic thinking was also challenged, particularly neoliberal notions that markets (including financial markets) function best without intervention,

---

[42] As of late 2021, the office of the United Nations High Commissioner for Refugees estimated the number of forcibly displaced people at 82.4 million (see www.unhcr.org/en-us/figures-at-a-glance.html, accessed December 4, 2021).

and that households and firms have sophisticated expectations of the future. In the crises of 2008–2012, Keynesian economic assumptions and policy prescriptions proved their relevance, as they did again during the later COVID-19 crisis.

The 9/11 attack on the United States in 2001 and the events that followed were, likewise, key elements on the road to the current polarization. The attack and its aftermath raised people's sense of vulnerability to global forces. At the same time, it undermined their faith in governments' ability to protect them. As Richard Haass has put it, "[W]e can now see that 9/11 was a harbinger of what was to come: less the globalization of terrorism than the terrors of globalization" (Haass 2021). The Iraq War, launched under an unfounded pretext, sapped faith in political leaders in much the same way as the Vietnam War had a generation earlier. The same was true of the troubled two-decade-long efforts to create stable functional democracies in Afghanistan and Iraq. The effects have been particularly corrosive in the United States and the United Kingdom, where the Bush–Blair partnership to promote the Iraq War represents yet another instance of the "special relationship" gone awry. Throughout the West, the 9/11 attack and its *sequelae* have shaped attitudes toward Muslim citizens and immigrants in politically polarizing directions.

Missed opportunities have had devastating effects. In 2003, the international community contained the virus now known as SARS-CoV-1, but not without public WHO criticism of China's initial secretiveness about the outbreak's early stages. That criticism and China's reaction ultimately helped countries to stop the disease with only 8,098 infections and 774 deaths worldwide. In 2005, aware of the near miss, the WHO's World Health Assembly voted unanimously to strengthen its International Health Regulations, but these enhancements clearly proved inadequate in 2020. Additionally, after 2003 there was no publicly funded push to develop a SARS-CoV-1 vaccine, which might have allowed an even faster vaccine response to SARS-CoV-2.

Were Keynes here today, he would certainly recommend a reformed capitalism, believing reform and redistribution would go some way to heal our political climate. In 1926, he wrote in the prematurely titled *The End of Laissez-Faire* (Keynes 1926, pp. 52–53):

I think that Capitalism, wisely managed, can probably be made more efficient for attaining economic ends than any alternative system yet in sight, but that in itself it is in many ways extremely objectionable. Our problem is to work out a social organisation which shall be as efficient as possible without offending our notions of a satisfactory way of life.

Keynes issued this relatively mild verdict in ignorance of the future ravages of the Great Depression, World War II, and the Cold War. Had he seen them, and observed the accelerating democratic recession in progress today even in America and Britain, he might well agree with Judt (2010) that without again reconceiving government's role in the economy, "The choice will no longer be between the state and the market, but between two sorts of state."[43]

Keynes would no doubt challenge policymakers to think big on climate. As he said in a 1942 BBC address:

Anything we can actually do we can afford. Once done, it is there. Nothing can take it from us. We are immeasurably richer than our predecessors.

Noting how much wealthier we are now than in 1942, he would be astounded to see governments disregard the economic prospects of citizens' children and grandchildren by hesitating to take vigorous action to save the planet. He would denounce the tragedy of the commons inherent in each country's unwillingness to act with sufficient purpose, and would seek to solve it through a public investment compact involving all major greenhouse gas emitters. But Keynes would also recognize that the burden of climate policy would fall disproportionately on lower-income groups, thereby creating a political backlash with attendant political risks for everyone. He would urge governments to offset these losses by some combination of taxes on the rich and borrowing, borrowing justified by the benefits of "green" investments for future generations.

Finally, Keynes would have been shocked at the discrepancy between the rapid speed of COVID-19 vaccine development and the uneven pace of vaccine distribution throughout the global population. Keynes himself may have come close to death in 1919 during the last global pandemic, when influenza vaccines were still years away. He would have challenged rich countries to invest the relatively small amounts of money needed to produce and distribute vaccines for the

---

[43] The term "democratic recession" is from Diamond (2015); the recession is threatening to become a depression.

entire world. He would surely argue, as vigorously as he railed against the self-interestedness of reparations, that globally coordinated vaccine production and comprehensive distribution would benefit vaccine donors as much as recipients. He would no doubt urge every effort to build stronger international surveillance mechanisms against future emergent threats – a function that neither the private sector nor one government can perform on its own, but which benefits all.

A final passage from the *Economic Consequences* makes this point more generally, and expresses the hopefulness that motivated Keynes's consequential efforts throughout his life (Keynes 1919, p. 251):

Even though the result disappoint us, must we not base our actions on better expectations, and believe that the prosperity and happiness of one country promotes that of others, that the solidarity of man is not a fiction, and that nations can still afford to treat other nations as fellow creatures?

This may be the key lesson for our time of *The Economic Consequences of the Peace.*

References

Abdelal, Rawi. *Capital Rules: The Construction of Global Finance.* Cambridge, MA: Harvard University Press, 2009.

Alden, Edward. *Failure to Adjust: How Americans Got Left behind in the Global Economy.* Lanham, MD: Rowman & Littlefield, 2017.

Backhouse, Roger E. and Bradley W. Bateman. "Inside Out: Keynes's Use of the Public Sphere." *History of Political Economy* 45 (Supplement 1, 2013): 68–91.

Bainville, Jacques. *Les conséquences politiques de la paix.* Paris: Librairie Arthème Fayard, 1920.

Bairoch, Paul. "European Trade Policy, 1815–1914." In Peter Mathias and Sidney Pollard, eds., *Cambridge Economic History of Europe, vol. VIII, The Industrial Economies: The Development of Economic and Social Policies.* Cambridge: Cambridge University Press, 1989.

Bell, Archibald C. *A History of the Blockade of Germany and of the Countries Associated with Her in the Great War, Austria-Hungary, Bulgaria, and Turkey, 1914–1918.* London: Her Majesty's Stationery Office, 1937.

Berger, Helge and Albrecht Ritschl. "Germany and the Political Economy of the Marshall Plan, 1947–52: A Revisionist View." In Barry Eichengreen, ed., *Europe's Post-War Recovery.* Cambridge: Cambridge University Press, 1995.

Blickle, Kristian S. "Pandemics Change Cities: Municipal Spending and Voter Extremism in Germany, 1918–1933." Staff Report 922, Federal Reserve Bank of New York, May 2020.

Bordo, Michael D. and Athanasios Orphanides, eds. *The Great Inflation: The Rebirth of Modern Central Banking.* Chicago: University of Chicago Press, 2013.

Brown, Wendy. *In the Ruins of Neoliberalism: The Rise of Antidemocratic Politics in the West.* New York: Columbia University Press, 2019.

Carroll, Sean B. "Mission: Save the Environment." *Project Syndicate,* July 15, 2016. www.project-syndicate.org/commentary/smallpox-eradication-global-cooperation-by-sean-b--carroll-2016-07, accessed September 26, 2021.

Carter, Zachary D. *The Price of Peace: Money, Democracy, and the Life of John Maynard Keynes.* New York: Random House, 2020.

Chinn, Menzie D. and Hiro Ito. "What Matters for Financial Development? Capital Controls, Institutions, and Interactions." *Journal of Development Economics* 81 (October 2006): 163–192.

Clavin, Patricia. "The Ben Pimlott Memorial Lecture 2019 – Britain and the Making of Global Order after 1919." *Twentieth Century British History* 31 (September 2020): 340–359.

Clavin, Patricia. *Securing the World Economy: The Reinvention of the League of Nations, 1920–1946.* Oxford: Oxford University Press, 2013.

Clavin, Patricia and Jens-Wilhelm Wessels. "Another Golden Idol? The League of Nations' Gold Delegation and the Great Depression, 1929–1932." *International History Review* 26 (December 2004): 765–795.

Coogan, John W. "The Short-War Illusion Resurrected: The Myth of Economic Warfare as the British Schlieffen Plan." *Journal of Strategic Studies* 38 (7, 2015): 1045–1064.

Cooper, Richard N. "International Cooperation in Public Health as a Prologue to Macroeconomic Cooperation." In Richard N. Cooper, Barry Eichengreen, Gerald Holtham, Robert D. Putnam, and C. Randall Henning, eds., *Can Nations Agree? Issues in International Economic Cooperation.* Washington, DC: Brookings Institution, 1989.

Corsetti, Giancarlo, Philippe Martin, and Paolo Pesenti. "Varieties and the Transfer Problem." *Journal of International Economics* 89 (January 2013): 1–12.

Cox, Mary Elizabeth. *Hunger in War and Peace: Women and Children in Germany, 1914–1924.* Oxford Historical Monographs. Oxford: Oxford University Press, 2019.

Deardorff, Alan V. "Review of *Essays in International Economic Theory: Jagdish Bhagwati.*" *Journal of International Economics* 22 (February 1987): 183–188.

Diamond, Larry. "Facing Up to the Democratic Recession." *Journal of Democracy* 26 (January 2015): 141–155.

Dietzel, Heinrich. "The German Tariff Controversy." *Quarterly Journal of Economics* 3 (May 1903): 365–416.

Dimand, Robert W. "Emily Greene Balch, Political Economist." *American Journal of Economics and Sociology* 70 (April 2011): 464–479.

Dimand, Robert W. "'Perhaps I'm a Don Quixote but I'm Trying to Be a Paul Revere': Irving Fisher as a Public Intellectual." *History of Political Economy* 45 (Supplement 1, 2013): 20–37.

Duffy, Gavan. "The British Empire's Southern Dominions and the Emergence of the League of Nations 'C' Mandates, 1914–1926: Origins, Administration, and International Oversight." Ph.D. Dissertation, National University of Ireland, Galway, 2019.

Eichengreen, Barry. *The European Economy since 1945: Coordinated Capitalism and Beyond*. Princeton, NJ: Princeton University Press, 2007.

Eichengreen, Barry. "Lessons from the Marshall Plan." World Development Report 2011 Background Case Note. World Bank, April 2010.

Eichengreen, Barry. "Versailles: The Economic Legacy." *International Affairs* 95 (January 2019): 7–24.

Fidler, David P. "The Globalization of Public Health: The First 100 Years of International Health Diplomacy." *Bulletin of the World Health Organization* 79 (9, 2001): 842–849. www.who.int/bulletin/archives/79(9)842.pdf, accessed September 26, 2021.

Fourcade, Marion. *Economists and Societies: Discipline and Profession in the United States, Britain, and France, 1890s to 1990s*. Princeton, NJ: Princeton University Press, 2009.

Gaddis, John Lewis. *George F. Kennan: An American Life*. New York: Penguin Press, 2011.

Galofré-Vilà, Gregori, Christopher M. Meissner, Martin McKee, and David Stuckler. "The Economic Consequences of the 1953 London Debt Agreement." *European Review of Economic History* 23 (February 2019): 1–29.

Garten, Jeffrey E. *Three Days at Camp David: How a Secret Meeting in 1971 Transformed the Global Economy*. New York: Harper, 2021.

Gatrell, Peter. *The Making of the Modern Refugee*. Oxford: Oxford University Press, 2013.

Gerwarth, Robert and John Horne, eds. *War in Peace: Paramilitary Violence after the Great War*. Oxford: Oxford University Press, 2012.

Ghosh, Atish R., Jun I. Kim, and Mahvash S. Qureshi. "What's in a Name? That Which We Call Capital Controls." *Economic Policy* 35 (January 2020): 147–208.

Guinnane, Timothy W. "Financial Vergangenheitsbewältigung: The 1953 London Debt Agreement." Economic Growth Center Discussion Paper 880, Yale University, July 2015 (revised).

Haass, Richard. "The World 9/11 Made." *Project Syndicate*, September 9, 2021. www.project-syndicate.org/onpoint/how-9-11-remade-the-world-order-by-richard-haass-2021-09, accessed September 26, 2021.

Hayek, Friedrich A. von. "Inflation and Unemployment." *New York Times*, November 15, 1974.

Helleiner, Eric. *States and the Reemergence of Global Finance*. Ithaca, NY: Cornell University Press, 1994.

Ikenberry, G. John. "A World Economy Restored: Expert Consensus and the Anglo-American Postwar Settlement." *International Organization* 46 (Winter 1992): 289–321.

Ikenberry, G. John. *A World Safe for Democracy*. New Haven, CT: Yale University Press, 2020.

Irwin, Douglas A. "Anticipating the Great Depression? Gustav Cassel's Analysis of the Interwar Gold Standard." *Journal of Money, Credit, and Banking* 46 (February 2014): 199–227.

James, Harold. *The End of Globalization: Lessons from the Great Depression*. Cambridge, MA: Harvard University Press, 2001.

Johnson, Elizabeth and Donald Moggridge, eds. *The Collected Writings of John Maynard Keynes, vol. 16: Activities 1914–1919: The Treasury and Versailles*. Cambridge: Cambridge University Press, 1978.

Johnson, Harry G. "The Keynesian Revolution and the Monetarist Counter-Revolution." *American Economic Review (Papers and Proceedings)* 61 (May 1971): 1–14.

Jonung, Lars. "Why Was Keynes Not Awarded the Nobel Peace Prize after Writing *The Economic Consequences of the Peace*?" *Scandinavian Journal of Economics* 124 (April 2022): 396–419.

Jordà, Òscar, Moritz Schularick, and Alan M. Taylor. "Macrofinancial History and the New Business Cycle Facts." In Martin S. Eichenbaum and Jonathan A. Parker, eds., *NBER Macroeconomics Annual 2016*, vol. 31. Chicago: University of Chicago Press, 2017.

Judt, Tony. *Ill Fares the Land*. New York: Penguin Books, 2010.

Kennan, George F. *Memoirs: 1925–1950*. Boston, MA: Little, Brown, 1967.

Kennan, George F. "A Fateful Error." *New York Times*, February 5, 1997.

Kennan, George F. "A Letter on Germany." *New York Review of Books*, December 3, 1998.

Keynes, John Maynard. *The Economic Consequences of the Peace*. London: Macmillan, 1919.

Keynes, John Maynard. *A Revision of the Treaty*. London: Macmillan, 1922.

Keynes, John Maynard. *A Tract on Monetary Reform*. London: Macmillan, 1923.

Keynes, John Maynard. *The End of Laissez-Faire*. London: Hogarth Press, 1926.

Keynes, John Maynard. *The General Theory of Employment, Interest, and Money*. London: Macmillan, 1936.

Kindleberger, Charles P. *The World in Depression 1929–1939*. Berkeley and Los Angeles: University of California Press, 1973.

Krippner, Greta R. *Capitalizing on Crisis: The Political Origins of the Rise of Finance*. Cambridge, MA: Harvard University Press, 2011.

Krugman, Paul R. "Differences in Income Elasticities and Trends in Real Exchange Rates." *European Economic Review* 33 (May 1989): 1031–1046.

Krugman, Paul R. *Has the Adjustment Process Worked? Policy Analyses in International Economics 34*. Washington, D.C.: Institute for International Economics, 1991.

Lambert, Nicholas A. *Planning Armageddon: British Economic Warfare and the First World War*. Cambridge, MA: Harvard University Press, 2012.

Lemmen, Sarah. "Beyond the League of Nations: Public Debates on International Relations in Czechoslovakia during the Interwar Period." In Peter Becker and Natasha Wheatley, eds., *Remaking Central Europe. The League of Nations and the Former Habsburg Lands*. Oxford: Oxford University Press, 2021.

MacMillan, Margaret. "Keynes and the Cost of Peace." *New Statesman*, October 31, 2018.

Maier, Charles S. "Economic Consequences of the Peace ... Social Consequences of the War" (translation of "Conseguenze economiche della guerra, conseguenze sociali della pace"). *Contemporanea* 12 (1, 2009): 157–163. https://dash.harvard.edu/handle/1/33085712, accessed October 1, 2021.

Mantoux, Étienne. *The Carthaginian Peace; or The Economic Consequences of Mr. Keynes*. London: Oxford University Press, 1946.

Marder, Arthur J. *From the Dreadnought to Scapa Flow*. London: Oxford University Press, 1961.

Meissner, Christopher M. "A New World Order: Explaining the International Diffusion of the Gold Standard, 1870–1913." *Journal of International Economics* 66 (July 2005): 385–406.

Mulder, Nicholas. *The Economic Weapon: The Rise of Sanctions as a Tool of Modern War*. New Haven, CT: Yale University Press, 2022.

Mundell, Robert A. *The Dollar and the Policy Mix: 1971*. Princeton Essays in International Finance 85, May 1971.

Mundell, Robert A. "Keynes and Ohlin on the Transfer Problem." In Ronald Findlay, Lars Jonung, and Mats Lundahl, eds., *Bertil Ohlin: A Centennial Celebration, 1899–1999*. Cambridge, MA: MIT Press, 2002.

Nurkse, Ragnar. *International Currency Experience: Lessons of the Inter-War Period.* Geneva: Economic, Financial and Transit Department, League of Nations, 1944.

Obstfeld, Maurice. "Floating Exchange Rates: Experience and Prospects." *Brookings Papers on Economic Activity* 16 (2, 1985): 369–450.

Obstfeld, Maurice. "Globalization and Nationalism: Retrospect and Prospect." *Contemporary Economic Policy* 39 (October 2021): 675–690.

Obstfeld, Maurice. "The Global Capital Market Reconsidered." *Oxford Review of Economic Policy* 37 (Winter 2021): 690–706.

Obstfeld, Maurice and Alan M. Taylor. "International Monetary Relations: Taking Finance Seriously." *Journal of Economic Perspectives* 31 (Summer 2017): 3–28.

Papadia, Francesco and Tuomas Välimäki. *Central Banking in Turbulent Times.* Oxford: Oxford University Press, 2018.

Pedersen, Susan. *The Guardians: The League of Nations and the Crisis of Empire.* Oxford: Oxford University Press, 2015.

Peter, Matthias. *John Maynard Keynes und die britische Deutschlandpolitik: Machtanspruch und ökonomische Realität im Zeitalter der Weltkriege 1919–1946. Studien zur Zeitgeschichte.* Berlin: De Gruyter, 2015.

Rappard, William E. "Review of The Carthaginian Peace; or The Economic Consequences of Mr. Keynes." *American Political Science Review* 40 (October 1946): 983–985.

Reinhart, Carmen M., Vincent Reinhart, and Christoph Trebesch. "Global Cycles: Capital Flows, Commodities, and Sovereign Defaults, 1815–2016." *American Economic Review (Papers and Proceedings)* 106 (May 2016): 574–580.

Reinisch, Jessica and Elizabeth White, eds. *The Disentanglement of Populations: Migration, Expulsion and Displacement in Post-War Europe, 1944–9.* London: Palgrave Macmillan, 2011.

Riley, Barry. *The Political History of American Food Aid: An Uneasy Benevolence.* New York: Oxford University Press, 2017.

Rockström, Johan, et al. "A Safe Operating Space for Humanity." *Nature* 461 (2009): 472–475.

Rosenfeld, Siegfried. "Volkszählung und Volksgesundheit (I)." *Volksgesundheit* 5 (1931): 97–115.

Ruggie, John Gerard. "International Regimes, Transactions, and Change: Embedded Liberalism in the Postwar Economic Order." *International Organization* 36 (Spring 1982): 379–415.

Ruggie, John Gerard. "Multilateralism: The Anatomy of an Institution." In John Gerard Ruggie, ed., *Multilateralism Matters: The Theory and Praxis of an Institutional Form.* New York: Columbia University Press, 1993.

Samuelson, Paul A. "Lord Keynes and the General Theory." *Econometrica* 14 (July 1946): 187–200.

Sandbrook, Dominic. *Seasons in the Sun: The Battle for Britain, 1974–1979*. London: Penguin Books, 2012.

Sarotte, Mary Elise. *1989: The Struggle to Create Post-Cold War Europe*. Princeton, NJ: Princeton University Press, 2011.

Skidelsky, Robert. *John Maynard Keynes: The Economist as Savior, 1920–1937*. New York: Penguin Press, 1992.

Slobodian, Quinn. *Globalists: The End of Empire and the Birth of Neoliberalism*. Cambridge, MA: Harvard University Press, 2018.

Temin, Peter G. *Lessons from the Great Depression*. Cambridge, MA: MIT Press, 1989.

Tooze, Adam. "Reassessing the Moral Economy of Post-war Reconstruction: The Terms of the West German Settlement in 1952." *Past and Present* 210 (Issue suppl_6, 2011): 47–70.

Tooze, Adam. *The Deluge: The Great War, America and the Remaking of the Global Order, 1916–1931*. New York: Viking, 2014.

Tooze, Adam. *Crashed: How a Decade of Financial Crises Changed the World*. New York: Viking, 2018.

Tooze, Adam and Ted Fertik. "The World Economy and the Great War." *Geschichte und Gesellschaft* 40 (April–June 2014): 214–238.

Viner, Jacob. "Review of *The Carthaginian Peace – Or the Economic Consequences of Mr. Keynes*." *Journal of Modern History* 19 (March 1947): 69–70.

Williamson, John. "Comment on Robert A. Mundell, 'The Great Exchange Rate Controversy: Trade Balances and the International Monetary System'." In C. Fred Bergsten, ed., *International Adjustment and Financing: The Lessons of 1985–1991*. Washington, D.C.: Institute for International Economics, 1991.

2 | The Making of a Classic: Keynes and the Origins of The Economic Consequences of the Peace*

MICHAEL COX

Introduction

Few short books have had such a big impact as John Maynard Keynes's *The Economic Consequences of the Peace*. Composed in just under six months, it is a volume that has been disputed and refuted, praised and celebrated in equal measure ever since it first appeared in December 1919. Brought out in double quick time by a man in a hurry, it soon caused a stir in the United States and across the Channel, an inexpensive edition was also published by the Labour Research Department in the UK (total sales of which nearly topped 10,000), and within a year or two it had been translated into nearly a dozen languages, including Russian. In fact, so successful was the book that its publisher Macmillan could happily report that within two months it had sold 70,000 copies in the UK and the United States alone and by 1922 well over a 100,000 copies worldwide. It may not have changed the course of history. But as Adam Tooze has reminded us, no single volume did more to contribute to the 'mood of disillusionment' following Versailles than *The Economic Consequences of the Peace* (Tooze, 2015: 295).

The book also had an impact on international relations, contributing to a further souring of Britain's relations with France while causing major problems across the Atlantic, where it was used by the Republican Party to attack Woodrow Wilson. It was even deployed by the Bolsheviks in their propaganda war against the West. A few have even gone so far as to claim (wrongly) that his attack on the peace helped Hitler come to power fourteen years later (Tampke, 2017).

---

* Much of the material here is drawn from the author's much longer Introduction to the centennial edition of J. M. Keynes's *The Economic Consequences of the Peace*, published by Palgrave Macmillan, 2019.

There is little doubt, however, that his earlier plea on behalf of Germany did help create a climate of opinion in which Germany's demands for a revision of borders after 1933 met with a sympathetic response in some western circles. Unlike many in the British establishment Keynes was no apologist for Nazi Germany. On the other hand, he did believe that the injustices inflicted on Germany in 1919 needed to be addressed. As he admitted to the editor of *The New Statesman* – a publication in which he had more than a passing interest – conceding something to Germany in 1938 was the only way of ending the 'injustices of Versailles' and preventing a war for which Britain was not prepared (Martin, 1968: 242).

As has often been remarked, *The Economic Consequences of the Peace* is almost certainly Keynes's most accessible book, read for pleasure by non-economists as much as by economists themselves.[1] The same cannot be said so readily of all his books. Thus his earlier work on *Indian Currency and Finance* only appeals to the specialist (Keynes, 1913), his studies on probability theory (Keynes, 1921) and money (Keynes, 1930) have only been of interest to theoretical economists, while even his groundbreaking study, *The General Theory of Employment, Interest and Money*, can hardly be characterized as an easy read! (Keynes, 1936). In many ways *The Economic Consequences of the Peace* is a standout volume in Keynes's wider oeuvre. It has also been one of his most hotly disputed books, and nobody took Keynes to task more critically than the brilliant French writer Etienne Mantoux. Educated at the LSE in the 1930s where he came under the influence of Keynes's main free market rivals, Hayek and Lionel Robbins, Mantoux was in little doubt about the problem posed by Keynes's book. Keynes, he argued, had written an influential, but dangerously inaccurate, account of what had gone on in Paris in 1919. Yet even Mantoux had to accept that *The Economic Consequences of the Peace* was a truly remarkable work, even comparing it at one point to Edmund Burke's much earlier attack on the French revolution. 'Perhaps only Edmund Burke's *Reflections on the Revolution in France*', Mantoux argued, 'may be said to have wielded

---

[1] The then Director of the LSE, William Beveridge, calculated in 1924 that 'by – at a moderate computation – half a million who never read an economics work before and probably will not read one again' had read *The Economic Consequences of The Peace, Economica*, Vol. IV (1924): 2.

over the destinies of Europe such a widespread and immediate influence' (Mantoux, 1946: 6).

Others have been a little less generous, including a whole phalanx of modern historians who, with some notable exceptions, have been generally quite critical of Keynes. Indeed, in their view Keynes just got a lot wrong. Thus he was far too unsympathetic to the French and the Belgians, said little about what was achieved in Paris (including the creation of the League of Nations), was far too understanding of Germany, and was plainly unfair on the main statesmen trying to do their best in the most difficult of circumstances (Cox, 2019: 36–41). He even got some of his economic facts wrong as well. Yet in spite of this extended broadside (which has shown no sign of dissipating even over the past few years) his latter-day opponents have never quite managed to deliver the coup de grace. As one of the great doyens of international history has confessed, the book has been regularly attacked from several different angles, but sadly, it continues to seduce people into thinking that Versailles was a total failure (Steiner, in Dockrill and Fisher, 2001: 13–33). Margaret Macmillan expressed this sense of frustration vividly in a piece she wrote for the *New Statesman* in 2018. Keynes, she argues, 'dashed off' an insubstantial volume 'with a very dry title' without much evidence to back up his claims. Yet this 'little book' (as she refers to it) authored by a 'self-assured young economist' – as she characterized Keynes – continues to mesmerize the unsuspecting (Macmillan, 31 October 2018).

A great deal has already been written about *The Economic Consequences of the Peace*. Symposia have been organized to discuss its merits (Holscher and Klaes, 2014), historians continue to debate its argument concerning reparations (Gomes, 2010), and in the debate about the future of Europe the name of Keynes is frequently invoked (Temin and Vines, 2016: 36–49). Some believe that it was perhaps his best book; others his worse. One writer has even claimed that Keynes himself later wished he had never written the volume in the first place (Wiskemann, 1968: 53). And so the debate goes on. But there is a consensus on at least one thing: that the book which came to define the way a generation thought about Versailles launched his long career as a major public figure. Before the publication of the volume Keynes was very much the insider's insider, admired for his brilliance in Cambridge and highly regarded by the English political class, but virtually unknown outside the very narrow circles in which he moved. *The Economic Consequences of the Peace* changed all that almost overnight. Indeed, not only did the book make him a substantial amount of money – a good deal of which he then went on to lose in currency speculation; after its publication he could in the words of his principal biographer lay 'claim' to a great deal of 'attention' (Skidelsky, 2004: 249). There are very few people who become household names by virtue of writing one short book. But *The Economic Consequences of the Peace* did precisely that by bringing the young economist (he was only in his mid-thirties at the time) 'fame, brief affluence, much correspondence, public involvement and new opportunity in equal measure'. Keynes had finally arrived having composed what his first serious biographer called 'a work of art' (Harrod, 1972: 298–299) and his latest, 'the most emotionally compelling works of economic literature ever written' (Carter, 2020: 95).

Saying something new or original about a book which has been picked over in almost painstaking detail right from the day it was first published is no easy task. However, recounting the story of why he wrote the volume, and with what purpose in mind, is one that never loses in the retelling. Certainly, the story that Keynes tells himself never lacks for drama with its extraordinary cast of characters making huge decisions that would go on to define the rest of the twentieth century. It also shines a light on Keynes himself. Indeed, one of the more intriguing questions is why did this hitherto well-connected young man, with his feet very well planted in the English establishment, decide to take the risk of writing such a controversial book? After all, others had their doubts about Versailles; but none went public; and if or when they did, it was certainly not to criticize the peace settlement or the peacemakers in such a vitriolic fashion. So what led Keynes to write a book like *The Economic Consequences of the Peace*? What was his goal in doing so? Who did he think he was writing it for? And was it his last word on the subject or was it – as Keynes believed at the time – merely the first step in a longer struggle to effectively render the economic parts of the Treaty invalid? (Keynes, 1922). All these questions may seem hypothetical. But they are of more than just of scholastic interest. After all, Keynes did not have to write the book in the way in which he did: but he did. In fact, he did not have to write the book at all, but felt compelled to do so. The question then becomes: why?

The Road to Paris

Let us look first at the immediate background to the writing of the book. Keynes, as we know, arrived in Paris in January 1919 after having authored two large memorandums in late 1918 dealing with the issue of Indemnities (Moggridge, D. E., 1992: 288–297). These were in-house documents which aimed to present the official Treasury view written by someone who was then considered to be the expert on the subject. Empirically dense and informed by a genuine knowledge of the subject, what they reveal, quite clearly, is the profound division which existed on the UK side between those in the Treasury like Keynes who argued for the lowest possible figure when it came to reparations, and those, including the Committee tasked to deal with the issue, who were insisting on a very much higher figure. Significantly, his work here formed the basis of the detailed economic material that finally found its way into *The Economic Consequences of the Peace* a year or so later (which in part might explain how Keynes was able to write the volume so quickly). They also make one thing abundantly clear: that long before Keynes arrived in Paris he had concluded that reparations paid by Germany to other countries would not only do little to help these countries; if it was set too high, it would make economic recovery in Germany itself nigh impossible. This did not mean that German should pay nothing at all. But any figure set had to take account of what he termed Germany's 'capacity to pay', and its capacity to pay, Keynes insisted, was limited. Indeed, any claim made by the allies 'for the general costs of the war, in addition to reparations' would not be able to be met by Germany, 'even in part'. As Keynes put it in unambiguously clear terms: 'It is not practicable both to impoverish Germany … and also to extract tribute on the basis of her pre-war productive capacity.' Moreover, if the allies were to attempt to extract such tribute, the economic, not to mention the political, consequences of having to pay such an indemnity, could lead to untold problems (Johnson, 1971: 369, 381–383).

The other big economic question for Keynes was what to do about inter-allied debt. Here the problem of course was Wilson and the Americans. Wilson may have been the hero of the European masses yearning for the New World to solve the problems of the Old. But by 1919 he was categorically refusing to cancel the debt owed to the United States because of the war. Keynes pleaded with the Americans arguing that until the debt question was sorted there could be no solution to the reparations issue (Johnson, 1971: 418–428). Wilson though was adamant. In fact not only did he oppose cancellation; there was 'violent opposition' to the very idea back in Washington as well (Johnson, 1971: 438). Nor was he any the less uncompromising when it came to reparations. He was insistent: Germany must pay the price – and a high one at that – for having destroyed the peace of the world. This was certainly how Jan Smuts understood the American leader's position. As he explained in a letter to a colleague, Wilson 'thinks the Germans deserve a hard peace' (Hancock and Van Der Poel, 1966: 166). The Treaty may have been punitive; but in Wilson's view it served the cause of divine justice. Keynes was quite literally appalled. He was also deeply concerned about the consequences. As he prophetically warned, a failure to arrive at a decent and workable settlement on the main economic questions would very soon become 'a menace to financial stability everywhere' (Johnson, 1971: 423).

But if Keynes was appalled by the American attitude, he could hardly have been surprised. After all, his contacts with American officials during the war had never been especially easy. Americans, it seems, did not appear to like this arrogant young Englishman, and he did not care for them or indeed the United States itself. This was in part cultural. But there was also a real fear on the British side, a fear which Keynes shared, that England was fast becoming dependent on what his Cambridge friends regarded (and once referred to) as this 'barbarous country', a 'philistine and mechanized hell hole ... where size, speed and money were fetishized', and in which 'competition and strife' appeared to be the 'only life worth living' (Davenport-Hines, 2015: 91). Thus when he arrived in Paris at the start of 1919 his hopes for some kind of understanding from the United States could hardly be described as being high. Nor did he find much comfort more generally when he arrived in the French capital. As he made clear in a letter sent to a friend in late January, 'this is a shocking place'. One nightmare called the war may have come to an end; but as Skidelsky has pithily observed, another called the peace 'was about to start' (Skidelsky, 2004: 215).

And what a nightmare it turned out to be with Keynes finding himself being marginalized or ignored altogether. Yet he did not give up, and throughout the first four months in Paris continued to write memorandum after detailed memorandum making the case for what he saw as being a sane peace. Finally, in what looks to have been one last try, he proposed what he called a grand scheme for the economic rehabilitation of Europe. The Chancellor of the Exchequer, Austen Chamberlain, strongly supported it and in a letter to Lloyd George 'commended the scheme' arguing that it was 'marked by all Mr Keynes's characteristic ability and fertility of resources'. But all to no avail. By the 4th May Keynes was reporting that he and 'most of us here are exceedingly pessimistic'; the 'conference', he continued, 'has led us into a bog which it will take more statesmanship to lead us out of than it has taken adroitness to lead us in' (Johnson, 1971: 456).

Clearly Keynes had reached the end of his proverbial 'tether' and by 14 May was already confiding to Mrs Keynes (his mother) that he was 'utterly worn out, partly by work, partly by depression at the evil round me'. His course of action now seemed to be set. Five days later he informed his immediate superior that he would soon be resigning. But not before his close ally, Austen Chamberlain, made one final bid to persuade him otherwise and 'consent to continue for a time'. Keynes, however, was determined, and, in a forthright letter of reply written the same day on 19 May, asked how could he stay on given that his own Prime Minister, Lloyd George, was leading us into a 'morass of destruction' by supporting a 'settlement' which would not only disrupt the life of Europe economically, but which might even lead to Europe being depopulated 'by millions of people'. There was no turning back therefore. He would resign in protest and so leave his hands 'quite free' to carry on his opposition to a treaty which in his view contained 'much' that was 'unjust' and 'much more' that was 'inexpedient'. His letter to Lloyd George sent on 5 June made his position clear. 'I am slipping away from this scene of nightmare,' he told the Prime Minister. 'I can do no more good here ... the battle is lost ... I will leave it to the twins[2] to gloat over the devastation of Europe and to assess to taste what remains for the British taxpayer' (Johnson, 1971: 458, 459–460, 469).

The Origins of *The Consequences*

But when, then, did he begin thinking about writing *The Consequences of the Peace*, a book (he confessed) which had been born out of 'deep and violent shame'? We can never be entirely sure. Perhaps the germ

---

[2] The 'twins' in question were Judge Lord Sumner and the British banker Lord Cunliffe who set what Keynes believed were impossibly harsh economic terms on Germany.

of the idea began to form in his mind in March when Keynes already seemed close to a crisis. As he put it in a letter to his close friend, the artist Vanessa Bell – sister of Virginia Woolf – 'he was absolutely absorbed' in what he called 'this extraordinary' but 'miserable game' of convincing, or failing to convince, policymakers of coming up with a reasonable deal for Germany (Davenport-Hines, 2015: 102). But it was clear he was getting nowhere, and he wondered aloud whether he could come down to stay at Charleston (where he wrote most of the book) where he could recover his 'health and sanity' (Spalding, 2016: 183). Two months later he wrote yet another revealing note to another member of his inner circle – Duncan Grant – one of his former lovers and for some years now Vanessa's partner (Spalding, 1998). He made no effort to conceal his state of mind. He confessed wearily: 'I've been as miserable for the last two or three weeks as a fellow could be. The Peace is outrageous and impossible and can bring nothing but misfortune ... no one in England yet has any conception of the iniquities contained in it'. He added that if he were a German he'd rather 'die than sign such a Peace'. Two weeks on, and now close to collapse, Keynes even admitted that he was 'near breaking point' and was in need of somewhere where he might recover his equilibrium. On 7 June he left Paris for England (Davenport-Hines, 2015: 105–106).

But at what stage did he actually contemplate writing a book about his experiences? It was one thing to be disillusioned and angry; it was quite another to translate this anger into words on a page. The most convincing answer to the question is possibly to be found in a letter he wrote to J. C. Smuts, the South African leader who was Keynes's closest confidante in Paris. Smuts was, of course, one of the great diplomatic figures of his age who whilst drafting important statements on the League of Nations (which Wilson appeared to take over wholesale) also found time to try and settle the Irish question while taking further time out to try and fix the problems of Central Europe! Smuts is often credited with planting the idea of the book in Keynes's mind. But as their letters show, this is not the case. In fact, it was Keynes himself who initiated the discussion with Smuts on 8 June 1918, three days after his letter to Lloyd George letting the Prime Minister know he was resigning. 'I have burned my boats,' he wrote to Smuts; however, he hoped 'immensely' that Smuts 'may come to the conclusion that some public explanation of what is really happening and a protest against it is now the right course of action'. Smuts was encouraging but cautious.

Don't act under 'impulse', he warned, no doubt fearing that Keynes might do precisely that and go too far. He also suggested, tellingly, that Keynes should definitely write something 'as soon as soon as possible', but only dealing with the 'financial and economic clauses of the Treaty' (Hancock and Van Der Poel, 1966: 222–223). Keynes would certainly be capable of doing that given his unique knowledge of the subject. But as we know – and as Smuts found out to his discomfort – Keynes had no intention of simply writing a treatise on economics and finance. He had something far more explosive in mind.

Smuts's role in the making of *The Economic Consequences of the Peace* was thus a central, but complex, one. Smuts's own letters of the time clearly show how close he was to Keynes, and how much Keynes himself admired the one time Boer leader who, having been defeated by the British in South Africa, had made his peace with the victors and they with him. Smuts indeed drew on this South African experience when it came to thinking about how to deal with another defeated enemy in the shape of Germany. Smuts obviously had a very high opinion of Keynes's economic talents; he also came to know Keynes very well in Paris. Indeed, he records several occasions when he and Keynes would sit down together in private and bemoan what was going on around them. As he remarked in a diary entry of 7 May: 'Poor Keynes often sits with me at night after a good dinner and we rail against the world and the coming flood.' A week later he went on to register his own disillusion with the proposed Treaty. This 'damned thing' (by which meant the Treaty) is a 'Porcupine' of a deal; together both Lloyd George and Wilson should do their best to make it a 'more moderate and reasonable document'. But he held out a little hope of them doing so. In fact, like Keynes, he came to believe that both leaders were deeply flawed. Wilson, he concluded, was not 'really a great man', whilst Lloyd George, he felt, was 'mercurial' and 'tricky'; and neither alone nor together were a match for the determined Clemenceau. Unlike Keynes, however, Smuts was constrained by his official position. Thus even though he was to compare the Treaty with 'a tin of poisonous gas' that could well easily 'asphyxiate' his great project the League of Nations, he did in the end sign the Treaty, albeit with great reluctance. However, to make clear his position he issued a statement on the afternoon of 28 June saying that the Treaty had not 'achieved a real peace', and that what he called 'the real work of making peace' would only begin after the Treaty had been signed (Hancock and Van Der Poel, 1966: 152, 163, 171, 247).

The case of Smuts also raises the intriguing question of how many other diplomats and experts in Paris shared both Smuts's and Keynes's opinion about the proposed Treaty. The answer would seem to be a very great number. Keynes may have been the one who went on to make the public case against the Treaty in his own inimitable style. But he was by no means alone in thinking the Treaty flawed. One such dissenter was Harold Nicolson, the famous British diplomat and equally famous husband of the novelist Vita Sackville-West. Though not uncritical of Keynes's attack on Versailles – Keynes, he felt, forgot that British public opinion at the time made a peace of 'moderation and righteousness' most unlikely – he was nevertheless deeply disturbed by what had gone in in Paris itself (Nicolson, 1933). As he complained in a letter written to Vita in early May 1919, the peace was being put together badly by 'three ignorant and irresponsible men' who were 'sitting there and partitioning continents with only a child to take notes' (Nicolson, 1992: 83, 84). A little while later (just two weeks before the Treaty was signed) he made his feelings known to his father about what he had earlier termed this 'humbug peace' (ibid.: 86) 'There is not a single person among the younger people here' in Paris – including Keynes 'who is first class' – 'who is not unhappy and disappointed at the terms'. 'We can only hope', he went on, that Lloyd George, 'who is fighting like a Welsh terrier, will succeed in the face of everybody in introducing some modifications in the terms imposed upon Germany' (Nicolson, 2004: 23).

James Headlam-Morley, a senior diplomat on the British side, was another insider critic. An early admirer of Keynes – 'an extremely sensible and open-minded' young man he noted just after Keynes had arrived to take up his post – he was in no doubt that the Treaty was little short of disastrous. Indeed, on 11 May he was berating it in no uncertain terms to another British colleague, stating that it would be impossible for the Germans to accept it. The economic terms in particular were deeply problematic (Headlam-Morley et al., 1972: 103–105). He then wrote privately to Smuts on 19 May 1918 thanking the South African for saying 'what many of us here in Paris' have been 'thinking in private'. The Treaty, he went on, was 'indefensible and cannot in fact be carried out', though did concede that the territorial parts of the Treaty should stand (Hancock and Van Der Poel, 1966: 169–171). Unlike Keynes, however, he decided to keep his views in-house. Indeed, as we know from his diaries, he was appalled when Keynes's broadside was finally published, believing his account to be 'a travesty of the facts'. He even wondered whether he should write a refutation himself. 'This was approved of by Lord Curzon. But official caution prevailed and nothing came of it.' However, he was in a sense rewarded, and was then 'instructed to write an official history of the Peace Conference', though ironically his first (confidential) memorandum written in 1922, though 'more moderate and detached than Keynes's book', turned out to be 'an even stronger indictment' (Headlam-Morley et al., 1972: xxxii).

Into the Storm

Keynes began work on *The Economic Consequences of the Peace* three days before the Versailles Treaty was finally signed on 28 June. However, like any author setting out to write a book – this would be Keynes's second – he did wonder initially whether it would be worth the bother. As he remarked in one of his many letters to his mother at the time, he 'might not persevere with it'. Three weeks later on 17 July he was even asking himself whether such a book was 'really beyond' his 'powers'. Yet, typically, he persevered, encouraged along the way no doubt by his many admirers and supporters, including, interestingly, Sidney and Beatrice Webb, who were then desperately trying to recruit Keynes to the LSE.[3] Others too egged him on. Several of them even read early versions of some of the chapters, including those of his inner circle such as Duncan Grant, Goldsworthy Lowes Dickinson and Leonard Woolf, husband of Virginia. They all loved the book. Woolf, who had already made his views about this 'vindictive' peace public, was fully supportive (Glendinning, 2006: 213). Others, however, advised Keynes to tone down some of the purpler passages, particularly those relating to Lloyd George (the complete version of his portrait of Lloyd George only appeared a few years later) (Keynes, 1933: 32–39). His mother agreed. I would modify the attacks on the 'Chief' (Lloyd George) she advised. Even the acerbic Lytton Strachey

---

[3] In the spring of 1919, when still in Paris, Keynes wrote to his mother that he had just received a letter from Sidney Webb of the LSE asking him whether he wished to be considered as a 'candidate for the Directorship of the London School of Economics'. He declined the offer. See Elizabeth Johnson ed., *The Collected Writings of John Maynard Keynes: Volume XVI. Activities 1914–1919. The Treasury and Versailles*, London, Macmillan, 1971: 458.

thought it wise to lower the temperature; indeed, later, after having read the final manuscript, which he had 'gulped down' in one, he congratulated Keynes for having done so. 'I don't see how anybody can stand up against it,' he concluded (Holroyd, 2005: 464, 465).

But Keynes did not just rely on his Bloomsbury friends for feedback. He also decided to test out his ideas in public and gave a series of lectures on the 'economic consequences' of the Treaty up in Cambridge, where Austin Robinson recalls there was standing room only! (Robinson, 1947: 1–68). He also shared his early written thoughts with friends in the wider liberal establishment including, amongst others, Margot Asquith, Robert Cecil and Austen Chamberlain. Keynes may have written the book at high speed. But he took enormous care in ironing out any possible glitches before final publication. He also took great care in making sure that anybody of importance – and he was acquainted with lots of very important people – knew a book of some significance was on its way. Impact is what Keynes was looking for, and as we know, that is precisely what the book had when it was finally published by his old Etonian and Cambridge friend, Daniel Macmillan, in December 1919 (Moggridge, 2002: 220–221).

But who exactly did Keynes think he was writing the book for? It is easy to say the powerful and the influential: people like Keynes himself in other words. One of his more modern American admirers even insists that Keynes wrote the work for a 'narrow audience of British experts' (Carter, 2020: 94). But the book aimed at a much wider audience. Influencing the 'experts' was one thing; but it was equally, if not more important, to shape the ideas of the wider thinking public. This is why Keynes made every effort to ensure that book got into the hands of as many people as possible; he even sent out several copies to colleagues and friends himself. He was also active in making sure the book got translated into as many foreign languages as possible; and, just as important, received reviews from as many quarters as possible, many of which turned out to be decidedly positive.[4] Harold Laski, for instance, called it a 'very great book'; R. W. Seton Watson thought the picture Keynes painted of the 'fetid intrigue' in Paris absolutely spot on; while yet another reviewer called it a very good book

---

[4] Some of the very early reviews of the book (twenty-four in all) can be found in the section 'Press Notices' in Keynes's, *A Revision of the Treaty* (1922): 2–5. Also look at Charles Robert McCann ed., *John Maynard Keynes: Critical Responses, Volume 1*, London, Routledge, 1996. Here one can find over thirty reviews.

which showed that Keynes was a 'hard-headed but benevolent realist'. Others were altogether less impressed. Thus one critic attacked Keynes for having written a 'very angry book'; another that Keynes appeared to know about everything except the art of politics and yet one more claimed that he had slurred all those who had helped the allies 'win this war'. Nor did the reviews end there. They just kept pouring in – some decidedly hostile (especially if they were written in France) (Crouzet, Janvier-Mars, 1972: 6–26) and others extraordinarily laudatory. Apparently even the young Friedrich Hayek – then serving in the Austrian army – praised the book. Certainly, if Keynes had intended his book to cause a stir – which he clearly had – then he had succeeded quite brilliantly. As the great Austrian economist Joseph Schumpeter later remarked, the immediate reception afforded *The Economic Consequences of the Peace* made the 'word success sound commonplace and insipid' (Schumpeter, 1946: 499).

Success

But what was it about the book itself which made it such a huge, immediate success? There were several possible reasons. One, ironically, was that in spite of its title, it did not read like a treatise on economics at all. As Churchill later remarked, there was nothing stodgy or technical about the book. As he put it, it was as easy to read as 'the best novel'. It also happened to be mercifully brief. It also had an 'I was there immediacy' about it combined with 'magisterial detachment and compelling plausibility' (Clarke, 2009: 2) Moreover, in spite of its serious subject matter, it was in the end a rather uplifting read guided by Keynes's sense of fair play and insistence that one should not kick a man (in this case Germany) when he was down. Indeed, what appealed to many about the book, one suspects, was not its detailed discussion of finance or economics but its humanity and high moral purpose.

That said, Keynes still took very great care in getting his (many) economic facts right. Indeed, for a volume often described as an angry polemic, it is worth recalling that it contains page after somewhat tedious page on such nitty-gritty questions as 'transport and tariff systems' in Germany, coal and iron ore production in Upper Silesia, and of course 'reparation' (the very long chapter, Chapter 6). But this was crucial in helping Keynes make his key points: namely, that by demanding the economically impossible of Germany the allies would not only be hurting themselves – Britain in particular which had once had close economic relations with Germany – but would make any kind of European recovery impossible. To add political insult to economic injury, by then focusing on the territorial settlement while promoting the idea of self-determination (something for which he held Wilson responsible) the Treaty made economic recovery even less likely. As Keynes argued three years later, 'The Wilsonian dogma' which 'exalts and dignifies the divisions of race and nationality above the bonds of trade and culture, and guarantees frontiers but not happiness, is deeply embedded in the conception of the League of Nations as at present constituted. It yields us the paradox that the first experiment in international government should exert its influence in the direction of intensifying nationalism' (Keynes, 1922: 11).

But it was, in the end, Keynes's insider 'tell all' story of the conference and its key personae (interestingly he more or less ignored the Italian Prime Minister Orlando) that really helped sell the book. As Austen Chamberlain put it in a note to Keynes only a few days after having read it, Keynes's book may create all manner of problems for 'our international course'; nonetheless he had still managed to read his 'description of the conference with malicious pleasure'. Others agreed, and even though the section on the conference may have been the shortest chapter in the book (a mere twenty-eight pages) it was Keynes's description of what went on behind closed doors that readers seemed to delight in.

Keynes, of course, took some care not to reveal any secrets and, as we know, pulled his punches when it came to Lloyd George. However, he pulled few when it came to the French leader Clemenceau, though even here Keynes never let his criticism of Clemenceau cloud his assessment of the man himself. Clemenceau was, of course, the true villain of the piece, the mordant Carthaginian sitting round the table working out how to render Germany incapable. Yet in spite of that, Clemenceau was, in his view, 'by far the most eminent member of the Council of Four', who by virtue of 'his age, his character, his wit and his appearance' had the clearest idea of what needed to be done, at least in the interests of France. Wilson, on the other hand, is presented as being both confused and inadequate. Not only did he betray his own liberal principles in Paris; this naïve and uncultured product of the New World quite simply did not have the 'intellectual equipment' to deal with that spellbinder Lloyd George or that 'Pericles' of Paris, George Clemenceau! Little wonder that Wilson's enemies back in the United States lapped up Keynes's book while his supporters berated him for having stabbed the only hope for liberalism worldwide in the back.[5]

One section of the *Consequences* which has perhaps received less attention than it deserves – apart from what many regard as the weakest section at the end where he deals with 'remedies' – is that where Keynes reflects on the structure of Europe more generally. Here in bold imaginative brush-strokes Keynes outlines the conditions of Europe's success and the fragile basis on which that success rested. It is a brilliant piece of synthesis in which he asks whether the working class would any longer be prepared to accept its lot in life (it would not he believed), the extent to which its economic stability rested on the continued existence of its three land-based empires (all of which collapsed in 1918) and the degree to which the transformation in the relationship between the Old and the New World would work to the advantage of Europe or not (it would not). He also went on to analyse the issue of population and why Europe post-war would be facing a major challenge caused in the last analysis by what one of his intellectual heroes, Thomas Malthus, had anticipated would happen: that the continent's population would increase geometrically while its capacity to grow food would only grow arithmetically. Keynes agreed (Keynes, 1933: 81–124). As he himself put it, Europe faced a crisis caused by 'the disruptive powers of fecundity' that over the longer term would prove to be just as disruptive of the established order than 'either the power of ideas or the errors of autocracy'.

Whether or not Keynes was right to locate one of the causes of the post-war crisis in an unsustainable growth in Europe's population remains a moot and controversial point (Toye, 1997: 1–26). But the more general thesis he was advancing seemed incontrovertible: that 'too much of what had emerged from the war rested on long-standing, underappreciated and elaborately enmeshed networks and foundations' and that these foundations had now been kicked away

[5] For a discussion of the American responses to *The Economic Consequences of the Peace*, as well as Keynes's lengthy response to US critics, see the relevant sections in Elizabeth Johnson ed., *The Collected Writings of John Maynard Keynes: Volume XVII. Activities, 1920–1922*, London, Macmillan, 1977: 24–50.

by the war (Kirshner, 7 December 2019). All the more critical therefore to get the peace right. But as Keynes made clear in no uncertain terms, the peacemakers failed completely. If anything, they made the situation far worse by failing even to understand that there was a problem to be addressed. As he put it in a way that only he could, the Treaty included 'no provisions for the economic rehabilitation of Europe – nothing to make the defeated Central empires into good neighbours, nothing to stabilize the new states of Europe', and nothing to restore 'the disordered finances of France and Italy'. Moreover, forcing Germany into servitude, he continued, would only 'sow the decay of the whole of civilized life of Europe'. A disaster awaited if nothing were done.

The German Question

But this was not all that the peacemakers had got wrong in Paris according to Keynes. They also displayed ignorance and self-interest when it came to looking at the deeper causes of the war itself. Germany, they insisted, was solely to blame for the war, and this is why Germany would have to 'pay'. Indeed, this was the whole point of the much disputed Article 231 which was not only designed to assign guilt to one country and 'its allies', but on the basis of this compel them to pay reparations as well. Keynes was not naïve. Germany in his view bore a very heavy responsibility for what happened in 1914. But the war, he implied, was not simply caused by Germany but was rather the result of a series of accumulated tensions that finally blew the 'European family' apart leading to what Keynes tellingly called a 'European Civil War'. No doubt influenced by the work of one of his close friends – Goldsworthy Lowes Dickinson – whose 1916 book on the origins of the war argued that the conflict was the result of an anarchic system and not the ambitions of just one power, Keynes was not just indulging in history for its own sake; he was also challenging the very basis on which reparations was justified. After all, if Germany alone was not the basic cause of the war, as Dickinson believed, then there was no justification in demanding that it pay the full costs of a war for which it alone was not responsible (Dickinson, 1916).

Nor should we forget how much Germany as an idea, and even an ideal, continued to shape the attitudes of intellectuals like Keynes and his circle. Hatred of the 'Hun' may have played to the gallery and helped newspaper owners like Northcliffe sell their tabloid papers. But amongst a certain layer of the British elite 'views of Germany were by no means predominantly negative' (Ruger, 2011: 588). Indeed, Germany was seen by liberal reformers as having pioneered the welfare state while its higher education system was regarded by many in Britain as being second-to-none. Economists too understood how important Germany was. Indeed, the dominant view amongst them – one which Keynes would no doubt have shared – was that the two countries were not only central to the stability of the international economy, but that their economic interests together were so deeply entangled that war between them was unthinkable.[6] Furthermore, if there was to be any kind of economic recovery after the war, let alone some degree of political stability in Europe, it was absolutely vital to help Germany recover. This moreover was not just Keynes's view (one shared by the Treasury) but also that of the majority of liberals, including Lloyd George whose strong belief was that 'the peace terms must not destroy Germany' (Macmillan, 2003: 207). Concerned that a harsh peace might open the way to Bolshevism and 'probably lead to another war' in the future – a punitive peace he warned will only force Germany to exact 'retribution' from her 'conquerors' when she has recovered – he was more than willing to accept Keynes's lower figure when it came to Germany's capacity to pay (Lentin, 1984: 46–53) In the end, however, he proved unwilling to confront Tory hardliners at home. Not for the first time during the negotiations domestic politics trumped rational decision-making (Morgan, 1996: 755–766).

---

[6] Writing in July 1914, a British economist noted the importance of both Britain and Germany in the international economy and their shared interests in each other's prosperity. He noted that 'The British and German Empires together transact approximately 39% of the international trade of the world ... they own 53% of the merchant shipping of the world, and their credit institutions play an enormous and indispensable part in the conduct of the trade of the world. It is inevitable, therefore, that the commercial and financial relations of the two Empires should be of vast magnitude, both directly and indirectly'. He also added poignantly (this only one month before the outbreak of the war), 'so far as the existing relations of the two Empires with each other are concerned, we may look to the future with confidence. At the present time it may be affirmed that their true economic interests are reciprocal rather than antagonistic'. See Edgar Crammond, 'The Economic Relations of the British and German Empires', *Journal of the Royal Statistical Society*, Vol. LXXLVII, Part VIII, July 1914: 777, 806.

War in Bloomsbury

This in turn raises the question about the deeper reasons for Keynes writing *The Economic Consequences of the Peace*. The book was in the short term occasioned by what Keynes saw as the failure of the peacemakers to make a serious peace in Paris. Yet this was clearly a work that had been in gestation for a long time. It may have only been written in 1919. But it is clear that Keynes had been in a state of high anxiety ever since the start of a war of which he fundamentally disapproved, whose costs he saw as being disastrously high (already in 1916 he was looking for a peace without victory), and which was fast rendering Great Britain – a country he loved – increasingly reliant on a country across the Atlantic for which he had little time. As Charles Maier once observed, Keynes authored a very great book in 1919: 'brilliant, unfair, wrong-headed' and 'destructive in its consequences'. However, as he went on to point out, even though Keynes had written a book which was ostensibly about the peace, basically it was about 'a topic that he did not acknowledge in his title': namely the impact which the First World War had had on the world (Maier, 2009: 157–163).

The war also influenced the writing of *The Economic Consequences of the Peace* in another important way: namely by driving something of a wedge between Keynes and his close circle of intimates in Bloomsbury. Nearly all of them were vociferous critics of the war; several in fact went on to become conscientious objectors, and, in Bertrand Russell's case, to serve a prison term for opposing the war.[7] It was hardly surprising therefore that many of them – almost all old Cambridge friends of very long standing – could never quite come to terms with Keynes being involved in the war effort. He may have done his best to protect his friends. However, his role at the Treasury still caused a stir. Indeed, Strachey himself had famously once asked as early as 1916 why he, 'Dear Maynard', was still working for the war while 'still at the Treasury?' Keynes wondered why too, and at one point was even contemplating resignation from a government which he despised and whose 'ends' he believed to be 'criminal'. No doubt he had other more

---

[7] Bertrand Russell, who thought Keynes's intellect the 'sharpest' and 'clearest' he had ever known, nonetheless observed that there was always 'a certain hard, glittering inhuman quality in most of his writing'. But there 'was one great exception, *The Economic Consequences of the Peace*' which 'roused the earnest moralist in him that he forgot to be clever – without however ceasing to be so' (Russell, 2000: 68).

important reasons for writing *The Economic Consequences of the Peace*. But by so doing he helped repair relations with a group of intimates upon whom he had hitherto depended emotionally and whose disapproval had hurt him grievously (Holroyd, 2005: 343).

The book, however, was not just some bridge-building exercise. It also bore all the hallmarks of Bloomsbury, and indeed of Keynes's own philosophy of life that had been forged when an undergraduate and an 'Apostle' in Cambridge. Nobody else in his circle could have written *The Economic Consequences of the Peace*. But it was from that circle that he drew inspiration. Though hardly radical in their outlook – the poet Stephen Spender later termed Keynes and his wider group as representing the 'last kick of an enlightened aristocracy' – they were in turn critical, honest and opposed to anything they deemed to be conventionally bourgeois (Spender, 1951: 141). As Keynes admitted in a short autobiographical paper outlining his 'early beliefs', he and his group 'had no respect for traditional wisdom or the restraints of custom. We lacked reverence' (Keynes, 1949: 99). They also thought life was lived through individuals and therefore that individuals (like the peacemakers in Paris) had to be held personally responsible for their actions. Keynes clearly took all this on board. Indeed, his book was composed very much in the shadow of the work of his long-standing friend, Lytton Strachey. Strachey knew little about economics, but his earlier work of biography, *Eminent Victorians*, with its less than heroic pen portraits of significant figures like Cardinal Manning and Florence Nightingale, seems to have influenced the way Keynes wrote about statesmen like Wilson and Lloyd George. It has even been suggested that Strachey's critical and iconoclastic approach to the famous may have made Keynes 'more indiscreet than he was by nature', giving him the 'courage to print' what previously 'he would have' only 'said in conversation' (Holroyd, 1994: 428).

But if the book bore the very strong imprint of Bloomsbury (indeed much of it was written while Keynes was enjoying the company of his old friends down in Charleston where had his own bedroom),[8]

---

[8] In her diary, Keynes's close Bloomsbury friend Virginia Woolf recalls 'Maynard' down at Charleston in Sussex in early July 1919 expressing his deep disillusionment with 'the dismal and degrading spectacle of the Peace Congress where men played shamelessly, not for Europe, or even England, but for their own return to Parliament at the next election'. Cited in Anne Olivier Bell, *The Diary of Virginia Woolf: Volume One, 1915–1919*, New York and London, Harcourt Brace Jovanovich, 1977: 288.

it also carried with it a very clear warning from Keynes: that what he had written in 1919 should not be taken as his final word on the subject. It was the first approximate shot in what Keynes always felt would be a long war. Thus even though the question of reparations may have been debated in almost painful detail during 1919, no figure in the end was agreed upon. Nor was the toxic and punitive atmosphere which then prevailed in Paris likely to last for ever. Again it was Smuts who probably understood this better than most. As he made clear to Keynes at the time, he would not, and in fact could not, openly agitate against the Treaty given his official position. On the other hand, he was fairly certain that as the world settled and the mood began to change (if not in France, then at least in the rest of Europe) punishing Germany would increasingly look a less attractive option. History in other words was on the side of the economic moderates. Keynes could not have agreed more. As he had made clear in *The Economic Consequences of the Peace* itself, reparations were not merely ethically questionable, but economically 'impossible' and the chances of reparations ever being collected in any significant amount were slim to say the least. Best therefore to wait and keep up the public agitation against the treaty in the knowledge that Germany would not – as he had earlier predicted – have the 'capacity to pay' (Johnson, 1978).

Conclusion

Finally, in thinking about *The Economic Consequences of the Peace* one is bound to ask how it has fared when compared to all the other books written by those who happened to be 'present at creation' in 1919. The answer very much depends on what one thinks of Keynes's original intervention. As we have already indicated, Keynes clearly had his admirers and camp followers. On the other hand, there were an equally vociferous group of influential people – a large number of whom had been present in Paris – who regarded the book as being at best one-sided and at worst propaganda. Yet in spite of the best efforts of some fairly distinguished people to present what they believed to be a more balanced account of what went on in Paris, in the vast majority of cases their various attempts to present a different picture not only failed to find a mass audience (quite unlike Keynes) but tended to sink without trace soon after publication. Everybody came to hear of, possibly even read, *The Economic Consequences of the Peace*. But few one suspect have ever read (or still read) the works of other senior officials who put pen to paper. This may be unfair; and it may well have led to Keynes's version of events being accepted far too easily. And it has certainly annoyed many of his critics in the history profession. But a hundred years after the publication of his original book, people are still discussing it, whereas few today (except the specialist scholar) read the works of Bernard Baruch, James Shotwell, Andre Tardieu, Jacques Bainville or David Hunter Miller.[9]

There are many reasons why this might be so, perhaps the most important being that Keynes himself went on to become the most famous economist of the twentieth century with a worldwide following. His book moreover was in its own way a literary masterpiece which captured the 'readers imagination' by a 'clever' use of 'metaphors, analogies and allusions' which alerted them in ways that a more conventional approach might not have done 'to the gravity of the situation facing Europe' (Holscher and Klaes, 2014: 35). Keynes also turned out to be extraordinarily prescient. He was clearly naive about Germany and its war aims. Nor did he have anything to say about the balance of power in 1919 and how the world may have looked from the point of view of France. But he did at least ask the right questions and come up with important answers, even if some of what he was proposing did not find a receptive audience amongst policymakers at Versailles. Nor was it ever likely to. After all, when the First World War came to an end, nationalism was on the rise and the urge to punish the defeated overwhelming. A quarter century later after an even more brutal war, the world had moved on, and much, if not all, of what Keynes had had to say in a previous time about treating enemies fairly and looking forward to a new Europe now found a much more receptive audience. No doubt the onset of the wider struggle against the USSR had much to do with this; and the United States was clearly a very different country with a different outlook after the

---

[9] For a sample of the American and French memoirs which present a very different picture to that painted Keynes, see Bernard M. Baruch. *The Making of the Reparation and Economic Sections of the Treaty* (1920); Jacques Bainville, *Les Conséquences Politiques de la Paix* (1920); Andre Tardieu, *The Truth about the Treaty* (1921); David Hunter Miller, *My Diary at the Conference* (1924); and James T. Shotwell, *At The Paris Peace Conference* (1937).

Second World War than it had been back in 1919 when it quite literally crawled back into its shell. Still, Keynes had earlier shown the way. As often proved to be the case, he turned out – yet again – to be a man ahead of his times.

References

Bainville, Jacques, *Les Conséquences Politiques de la Paix*, Paris, Nouvelle Librarie Nationale, 1920.

Baruch, Bernard M, *The Making of the Reparation and Economic Sections of the Treaty*, New York, Harper and Bros, 1920.

Bell, Anne Olivier, *The Diary of Virginia Woolf: Volume One, 1915–1919*, New York and London, Harcourt Brace Jovanovich, 1977.

Beveridge, William, Economica, Vol. IV (1924).

Carter, Zachary D., *The Price of Peace: Money, Democracy and the Life of John Maynard Keynes*, New York, Random House, 2020.

Clarke, Peter, *Keynes: The Twentieth Century's Most Influential Economist*, London, Bloomsbury, 2009.

Cox, Michael ed, *John Maynard Keynes, The Economic Consequences of the Peace*, Palgrave, Macmillan, 2019.

Crammond, Edgar, 'The Economic Relations of the British and German Empires', *Journal of the Royal Statistical Society*, Vol. LXXLVII, Part VIII, July 1914.

Crouzet, Francois, 'Reflections francaises devant "Les consequences economiques de la paix" in *Revue d'histoire modern et contemporaine*', Tome 19, No. 1 (Janvier-Mars) 1972.

Davenport-Hines, Richard, *Universal Man: The Seven Lives of John Maynard Keynes,* London, William Collins, 2015.

Dickinson, Goldsworthy Lowes, *The European Anarchy*, London, G. Allen & Unwin, 1916.

Glindinning, Victoria, *Leonard Woolf: A Life*, London, Pocket Books, 2006.

Gomes, Leonard, *German Reparations: A Historical Survey*, London, Macmillan, 2010.

Hancock, W. K. and Jan Van Der Poel, *Selections from the Smuts Papers. Volume IV. November 1918–August 1919*, Cambridge, Cambridge University Press, 1966.

Harrod, R. F., *The Life of John Maynard Keynes*, Penguin Books, 1972.

Headlam-Morley, Agnes, Russell Bryant and Anna Cienciala eds, *Sir James Headlam-Morley, A Memoir of the Paris Peace Conference 1919*, London, Methuen & Co., 1972.

Holroyd, Michael, *Lytton Strachey: The New Biography*, New York, London, W.W. Norton & Company, 1994.

Holroyd, Michael, *Lytton Strachey: The New Biography*, New York and London, W.W. Norton, 2005.

Holscher, Jens and Matthias Klaes, eds, *Keynes's Economic Consequences of the Peace: A Reappraisal*, London, Pickering & Chatto, 2014.

Johnson, Elizabeth ed, *The Collected Writings of John Maynard Keynes: Volume XVI. Activities 1914–1919. The Treasury and Versailles*, Macmillan, St Martin's Press, 1971.

Johnson, Elizabeth ed, *The Collected Writings of John Maynard Keynes: Volume XVII. Activities, 1920–1922: Treaty Revision and Reconstruction*, Macmillan, Cambridge University Press, 1977.

Johnson, Elizabeth ed, *The Collected Writings of John Maynard Keynes: Volume XVIII. Activities, 1922–1932: The End of Reparations*, Macmillan, Cambridge University Press, 1978.

Keynes, J. M., *Indian Currency and Finance*, London, Macmillan, 1913.

Keynes, J. M., *A Treatise on Probability*, London, Macmillan, 1921.

Keynes, J. M., *A Revision of The Treaty – Being a Sequel to The Economic Consequences of the Peace*, London, Macmillan, 1922.

Keynes, J. M., *A Treatise on Money*, London, Macmillan, 1930.

Keynes, J. M., 'Mr Lloyd George' in *Essays in Biography*, London, Mercury Books, 1933.

Keynes, J. M., 'Robert Malthus' in *Essays in Biography*, London, Mercury Books, 1933.

Keynes, J. M., *The General Theory of Employment, Interest and Money*, London, Macmillan, 1936.

Keynes, J. M., *Two Memoirs*, London, Rupert Hart-Davis, 1949.

Kirshner, Jonathan, 'The Man Who Predicted Nazi Germany', *The New York Times*, December 7, 2019.

Lentin, A., *Lloyd George, Woodrow Wilson and the Guilt of Germany*, Il Mulino, Leicester University Press, 1984.

Macmillan, Margaret, *Peacemakers: The Paris Conference of 1919 and Its Attempt to End War*, London, John Murray, 2003.

Macmillan, Margaret, 'Keynes and the Cost of Peace', *New Statesman*, 31 October, 2018.

Maier, Charles, 'Economic Consequences of the Peace, Social Consequences of the War'. *Contemporanea*, 12(1) 2009.

Mantoux, Etienne, *The Carthaginian Peace or The Economic Consequences of Mr. Keynes*, London, Oxford University Press, 1946.

Martin, Kingsley, *Editor: A Volume of Autobiography, 1931–1945*, London, Hutchinson, 1968.

McCann, Charles Robert ed, *John Maynard Keynes: Critical Responses, Volume 1*, London, Routledge, 1996.

Miller, David Hunter, *My Diary at the Conference*, 2 Vols, New York, Appeal Printing Company, 1924.

Moggridge, D. E., *Maynard Keynes: An Economist's Biography*, London and New York, Routledge, 1992.

Moggridge, D. E. 'A Risk-Bearing Author: Maynard Keynes and His Publishers', in Elizabeth James ed, *Macmillan: A Publishing Tradition*, Palgrave Macmillan, Houndmills, 2002.

Morgan, Kenneth O., 'Lloyd George and Germany', *The Historical Journal*, 39(3), September 1996.

Nicolson, Harold, *Peacemaking 1919*, London, Constable, 1933.

Nicolson, Nigel ed, *Vita and Harold: The Letters of Vita Sackville-West and Harold Nicolson*, New York, G.P. Putnam's Sones, 1992.

Nicolson, Nigel ed, *The Harold Nicolson Diaries, 1907–1963*, London, Weidenfeld & Nicolson, 2004.

Robinson, Austin, 'John Maynard Keynes: 1883–1946', *The Economic Journal*, 57(225), 1 March 1947.

Rugger, Jan, 'Revisiting the Anglo-German Antagonism', *The Journal of Modern History*, 83(3), September 2011.

Russell, Bertrand, *Autobiography*, Routledge, London and New York, 2000.

Schumpeter, Joseph, 'John Maynard Keynes, 1883–1946', *American Economic Review*, 36(4), September 1946.

Shotwell, James T., *At The Paris Peace Conference*, New York, Macmillan Company, 1937.

Skidelsky, Robert, *John Maynard Keynes, 1883–1946: Economist, Philosopher, Statesman*, London, Pan Books, 2004.

Spalding, Francis, *Duncan Grant: A Biography*, London, Pimlico, 1997.

Spalding, Frances, *Duncan Grant*, London, Pimlico, 1998.

Spalding, Francis, *Vanessa Bell: Portrait of the Bloomsbury Artist*, London, Tauris Parke, 2016.

Spender, Stephen, *Stephen World within World: The Autobiography of Stephen Spender*, London, Hamish Hamilton, 1951.

Steiner, Zara, 'The Treaty of Versailles Revisited' in Michael Dockrill and John Fisher eds, *The Paris Peace Conference 1919: Peace without Victory*, Houndmills, Palgrave, 2001.

Tampke, Jurgen, *A Perfidious Distortion of History: The Versailles Peace Treaty and the Success of the Nazis*, Melbourne, London, Scribe, 2017.

Tardieu, Andre, *The Truth about The Treaty*, Indianapolis, BobbsMerrill, 1921.

Temin, Peter and David Vines, 'Keynes and the European Economy', *Review of Keynesian Economics*, 4(1), Edward Elgar Publishing, January 2016.

Tooze, Adam, *The Deluge: The Great War and the Remaking of Global Order, 1916–1931*, London: Penguin Books, 2015.

Toye, John, 'Keynes on Population and Economic Growth', *Cambridge Journal of Economics*, 21(1), January 1997.

Wiskemann, Elizabeth, *The Europe I Saw*, London, Collins, 1968.

3 Keynes's Economic Consequences *(1919)*
The Book and Its Critics

PETER CLARKE

The Economic Consequences of the Peace has never been out of print since its publication in December 1919. It has continued to set the terms of ongoing debates about the impact of the First World War, about the nature of the peace imposed through the Treaty of Versailles, about the post-war economic settlement in Europe, about the signifi-cance of reparations and 'war guilt', and thus about the rise of the Nazis and the origins of the Second World War. I will suggest that we need to add a further concern to this list: about the moral ambit of the case for intervention in the war as perceived by Anglo-American liber-als, and its consequent implications in making peace.

Keynes's book was a bestseller not only in Britain, where it had sold 18,500 copies by April 1920, but also in the United States, where the American edition sold 70,000 copies within a year. *The New York Times* had given it a prominent, but hostile, full-page review declar-ing: 'in the English-speaking countries it is capable of doing immense mischief by still further clouding the issues of an epoch already suf-ficiently turbid' [28 March 1920]. This was, in short, the book that made Keynes's name, years before he had acquired eminence as an economist. The relevant digital databases show that in *The Times* (London) Keynes was mentioned about 100 times in the 1930s when the two volumes of his *Treatise on Money* (1929) and his *General Theory* (1936) conclusively established his professional status; but before that, in the 1920s, his name had already appeared about 60 times. Likewise in *The New York Times*, where his 400 mentions in the 1930s only slightly exceeded the 300 already notched up in the 1920s. It was the *Economic Consequences*, rather than his academic publications, that had first propelled him to this kind of fame.

I am grateful to Stefan Collini, John Thompson and Maria Tippett for their acute criticisms of an earlier draft.

Moreover, it remains remarkable that a polemic published so long ago – and so near the events that it described and analysed – should still be accorded so much notice. We can all benefit today from some groundbreaking books published by historians during the last twenty-five years, with the names of Niall Ferguson (1998), Margaret MacMillan (2001), Zara Steiner (2005), Patricia Clavin (2013) and Adam Tooze (2014) particularly prominent. And more recently, although a publication by Jürgen Tamke (2017) is hardly of comparable distinction, its focus on Keynes's supposed influence remains unrelenting. The reception literature thus extends over a whole century, during which Keynes's status has become almost totemic, whether the views and the influence attributed to him provoke reverence or dissent.

As a historian, I am naturally concerned with establishing the context in which Keynes's arguments were conceived at the time of writing. There are some things known to us that he could not possibly have known at the time, hence giving rise to subsequent arguments into which he should not properly be conscripted. Conversely, we may need to recapture some of the assumptions behind his work, which were commonplace at the time but may now be easily overlooked.

I suggest that there was a common Anglo-American discourse in which liberal moralism informed judgment about interlocking issues of war and peace – a set of assumptions on which Woodrow Wilson drew as much as Lloyd George, both of them indebted to a Gladstonian paradigm. In this mindset, it was natural to infuse the big decisions, whether about waging war or making peace, with notions of guilt. The fact that a Liberal government had taken the British Empire into war over the German violation of Belgian neutrality in 1914 was thus crucial; this was what made a European war into a world war. And although Wilson kept the United States out of that war during his first term as president – indeed he fought a campaign for re-election in 1916 on this basis – the entry of the United States into hostilities was retrospectively legitimated by identifying German aggression as its cause. This Anglo-American perspective simultaneously elevated the emotional and rhetorical level of debate while generating a quest to identify and to punish those who were deemed guilty. Some of this was explicit in overt and declared ways that are easy to document; some of it was implicit, not least in the pages of the *Economic Consequences*.

It is hardly the sort of publication that would make an academic reputation, either then or now. We need to recall that its author did not have the sort of career path that we would expect of a professional economist today. His only degree was a BA in mathematics; his own formal instruction in political economy – which had recently emerged from the Moral Sciences Tripos at Cambridge – was confined to eight hours of supervision, in the informal one-to-one style conventional in Cambridge. Admittedly his mentor was Professor Alfred Marshall, co-opted into this role not least as a family friend. The young Keynes originally thought of becoming a civil servant and he sat the competitive entry examination in 1906, only to come second rather than first. 'I have done worst in the only two subjects of which I possess a solid knowledge – Mathematics and Economics,' he complained [Moggridge 1992: 5]. Coming first would have entitled him to a position in the Treasury; instead, he had had to settle for the India Office for a few years and then returned to Cambridge, elected at King's College in 1909 to a Fellowship, which he was to hold for the rest of his life – never as a 'professor' in the strict sense. In Cambridge he was already well known in these years for his outspoken liberal views, later made evident enough on both sides of the Atlantic to readers of the book that was suddenly to make him famous.

Keynes had served as a temporary Treasury official during the First World War and had seen British policy evolve, especially in relation to the United States in the external finance of the war, which became his primary responsibility. This is why, following the Armistice agreed with Germany in November 1918, he had been sent to Paris for the negotiations that ensued during the first half of 1919, acting as an adviser to the British Treasury.

In Paris Keynes was often precipitated into the heart of the decision-making, especially in relations between the British delegation led by David Lloyd George as prime minister and the American delegation led by President Woodrow Wilson, as they interacted in concerting strategy with the French premier Georges Clemenceau. These were 'the Big Three', as they became known once the Italian premier dropped out of the picture. Keynes was right to state in the *Economic Consequences* that he had been present, despite his relatively junior official status, at some crucial points in their confidential dealings (though this claim was initially challenged by Clemenceau's interpreter, Paul Mantoux).

In short, nobody was better placed than Keynes, for all his relative youth at the age of thirty-six, to provide a technical analysis of the final treaty. This was well recognized at the time. In January 1920 Bernard Shaw wrote to a friend:

A great sensation has been made here by Professor Keynes of Cambridge, who was at Versailles as an economic expert, and resigned that position and came home as a protest against the peace terms. He has now published a book in which he demonstrates that the indemnity demanded from Germany is an economic impossibility; and nobody ventures to dispute this. [Clarke 2017: 263]

For a contrasting view of the nature or character of the book, however, here is what Keynes's close friend Virginia Woolf wrote in her diary a couple of months later: 'Reading Maynard too – a book that influences the world without being in the least a work of art: a work of morality, I suppose' [Clarke 2017: 267]. Leaving aside Mrs Woolf's rather demanding artistic criteria, she was surely right to perceive what the hard-nosed Shaw characteristically missed: the moral ambit of the book. Indeed I suggest that Keynes exhibited a disjunction that was characteristic of Anglo-American liberalism, shifting in disconcerting ways between two alternative kinds of analysis and judgment: one of them indeed concerned with analysing economic consequences but the other concerned with scrutinizing moral intentions.

In which genre, then, is Keynes's tract? When someone identified as 'a Cambridge professor' publishes a book with the term 'Economic Consequences' in its title – well, he would say that, wouldn't he? But we, as his readers today, can reasonably decline to take all of this at face value; we can instead follow up on the many clues, hints and indeed forthright statements that license us to examine Keynes's underlying concern with moral intentions as his yardstick of judgment on why the peacemakers failed in Paris in 1919. And from this failure – this is, to be sure, *also* the message of the book – there flowed economic consequences for the future of Europe, storing up trouble in a scenario where, as Keynes put it, 'vengeance, I dare predict, will not limp' [JMK 2: 170]. The book indeed gives us (especially in Chapters 4–7) the sort of close economic analysis that we would expect from a professional economist, but in the service of a morality tale.

* * *

The tone has already been set in the famous third chapter, with its imperishable vignettes of Clemenceau, Lloyd George and Wilson at the conference and its eminently quotable lines on each of them. Clemenceau is conveyed with great artistry as a loveable rogue and single-minded French patriot; then Lloyd George depicted as an amoral visitor from a realm of political chicanery, alternately attempting to bamboozle and to debamboozle the hapless American president; and finally – all achieved in ten pages – the cameo of Wilson, the straitlaced Presbyterian who was, above all, the target of Keynes's satire.

Keynes had, like many British Liberals, been an admirer of President Woodrow Wilson in holding out a vision of a negotiated peace that would provide both for political stability and for economic prosperity throughout post-war Europe. Hence the bitter sense of disillusion conveyed in the *Economic Consequences*. 'The President, for me, was a fallen hero,' Keynes privately admitted to an American correspondent in April 1920. 'I describe the others as very clever and very wicked: the President as sincere, well-intentioned and determined to do what was right, but perplexed, muddleheaded and a self-deceiver' [JMK 17: 42]. Wilson pre-eminently, and Lloyd George in a more complex way, are thus depicted as the liberals who betrayed the vision of a liberal peace, above all through their demand that Germany pay for the costs of the war.

Why should Germany not pay? Hadn't it just lost the war? And didn't it have a record of imposing an indemnity on France in 1871 when France had lost the previous war? And, in 1914–18, hadn't the French and the Germans each based their own war finance on the prospect of making a defeated enemy pay? On this reading, the Versailles Treaty imposed terms that were only to be expected in a zero-sum game.

But Keynes's point was that the Germans had sued for peace with the *Americans*, accepting *American* mediation in defining terms for a temporary Armistice, during which a peace treaty would be negotiated with a democratic German government. In this context, Britain and France had been brought (albeit with some reluctance, especially on the French side) to endorse the deal that was struck. For the American position was famously defined by the Fourteen Points that Wilson had first enunciated back in January 1918. Keynes reminds us that all this had meanwhile been clarified in other official American statements as 'an express part of the contract with the enemy', with the explicit stipulations of 'no contributions' and 'no punitive damages'.

It was Wilson's obedient Secretary of State, Robert Lansing, who was formally responsible for embodying these terms in the formal agreement with the new German government on 5 November 1918, generally referred to as the 'Lansing Note', which thus became binding as the key document defining the contract for an Armistice between the Allies and Germany [JMK 2: 71–2].

But of course we all know now – what the Allies at the time soon enough discovered – how close, by November 1918, Germany had already come to outright collapse (despite the pretences of military leaders like Ludendorff and the claim that the German armies had not been defeated in the field). In which case, the terms of the Versailles Treaty, especially when compared with those recently imposed on revolutionary Russia by the victorious Germans in the Treaty of Brest-Litovsk, may appear relatively lenient. It is in this frame that Keynes's arguments have often been dismissed as misguided or at any rate unfounded, or even termed pernicious. Recent historians have certainly signed up to such judgment.

Yet Keynes, of course, was perfectly well aware of all this, as the *Economic Consequences* explicitly affirms. As he puts it, within a month of the Armistice: 'We had discovered how hopeless the German position really was, a discovery which some, though not all, had anticipated, but which no one had dared reckon as a certainty. It was evident that we could have secured unconditional surrender if we had determined to get it' [JMK 2: 85–6].

But, faithful to his mindset of liberal moralism, Keynes was quite unimpressed by this point; or rather, in his eyes, far from licensing the Allies to impose more stringent terms, it had the opposite effect. 'Germany having rendered herself helpless in reliance on the contract, the honour of the Allies was peculiarly involved in fulfilling their part and, if there were ambiguities, in not using their position to take advantage of them' [JMK 2: 37–8]. Yet the extortionate economic conditions specified in the Treaty, as signed in June 1919, had done just this.

Keynes's further charge, moreover, was that the Allies had erred, not only by betraying their purported moral intentions but also in terms that could be measured by the economic consequences of their reparations demands upon Germany. Fulfilment would require the vanquished to transfer these sums through achieving a long-term balance of payments surplus which (paradoxically) would undermine

the export trade of the victors – not a zero-sum game at all but
one in which all parts of Europe would lose simultaneously. This
was the prospect that Keynes lucidly disclosed. And it was all made
worse in 1919 by the form in which reparations were demanded,
requiring Germany to assume a burden of debt that, while intended
to be heavy, was deliberately left unspecified. Keynes offered his
own calculations of what was demanded under these provisions.
But no final sum was explicitly stated in the Treaty itself, leaving
open the question of exactly how much was implied by its various
stipulations.

This was an exercise in wishful thinking, especially on the part of
Lloyd George, in supposing that at some future point it would be easier to achieve a compromise with Germany on the final figure. This
is evidently the best historical defence that can be offered of Lloyd
George's role, shifting the responsibility for any long-term effects on
to the shoulders of subsequent leaders when they tried in vain (as the
British sometimes did) to revise the terms of the peace or tried in vain
(as the French sometimes did) to enforce the unenforceable. But such
ruminations by modern historians, while having some validity in their
own terms, are surely flawed in a fundamental respect. They ignore the
irreversible impact on German public opinion not only of the notional
financial demand made in the Treaty itself but also of the moral charge
of war guilt, upon which the claim for reparations rested.

* * *

One extraordinary aspect of the debate about 'reparations' is that
the origins of the expression and its provenance have been so little
explored. The historic term was 'indemnities' and, if you consult
either English or French dictionaries, you find that the modern usage
of 'reparations' is explicitly tied to the Versailles Treaty of 1919. The
Oxford English Dictionary acutely notes that, in the relevant section of the Treaty, the heading is 'reparation' in English but uses the
plural *réparations* in French. How the usage 'reparations' came to
displace the term 'indemnities' is not only a largely untold story but
a largely unacknowledged problem; yet it is crucial to understanding
what happened in 1918–19, if only because both Wilson and Lloyd
George had publicly and explicitly ruled out imposing indemnities
on Germany.

I dealt with this at some length in my book *The Locomotive of War* since I was unable to cite a satisfactory literature on this point [Clarke 2017: esp. 194–6, 283–6]. I must now admit to having ignored the pioneering work of Robert E. Bunselmeyer, some forty years ago, in elucidating the relevance of the concepts of indemnity and reparation and documenting the purposeful elision of the senses in which they were applied in making peace terms in 1918–19, including the 'war guilt clause' [Bunselmeyer 1976: esp. 67, 174–6, 182–4]. I will confine myself here to some salient points that are relevant to the stance of the *Economic Consequences*.

It may, however, be helpful to supply a little more historical context, perhaps even of an anecdotal flavour, to capture the nuances with which we are faced. For the plain fact is that, for Anglo-American liberals 'indemnities' had long been considered a Bad Thing, smacking of German militarism, and thus something to be abjured in formulating peace proposals to end this world war. This assumption permeates the treatment rendered in the *Economic Consequences*. 'I do not believe that, at the date of the armistice, responsible authorities in the Allied countries expected any indemnity from Germany beyond the cost of reparation for the direct material damage which had resulted from the invasion of Allied territory and from the submarine campaign' [JMK 2: 85]. In explaining how the Germans were subsequently faced with demands to meet the costs of the war, Keynes suggests that liberals who should have known better capitulated to right-wing populist pressure, notoriously exemplified in demands to 'hang the Kaiser', to 'make Germany pay', and – in a graphic phrase that the *Economic Consequences* rescued from the obscurity of an election campaign meeting in Cambridge – to 'squeeze her until you can hear the pips squeak' [JMK 2: 87–90].

Yet this account, whether by accident or design, virtually ignores the implications for making peace of the fact that Anglo-American liberals had so heavily moralized their own actions in making war. In this context, it seems not so much inaccurate as inadequate to identify the demand to 'make Germany pay' with a right-wing thirst for retributive indemnities. True, such demands were prominently voiced, especially in the so-called 'coupon election' that Lloyd George fought in alliance with the Conservative party in December 1918. It has always been apparent that the cry for Germany to pay the full costs of the war came naturally from many Conservative candidates;

and it is correct to think that the great pre-war fiscal controversy between Liberal free traders and Conservative advocates of 'tariff reform' or 'imperial preference' foreshadowed such a stance. It was the Liberals who had always insisted that free trade benefitted all parties and the Conservatives who were most likely to insist that 'making the foreigner pay' was a good reason to adopt tariffs. Thus protectionist economic reasoning (or instincts) indeed fuelled the demand for *indemnities*. But there was also a moral dimension to such perceptions: one that fostered notions of German guilt as a rationale for *reparations*.

We need to remember that the basis on which a Liberal Government had brought the British Empire into the war in August 1914 was crucially influenced by a moral judgment that Germany was guilty of violating Belgian neutrality: a case put to the House of Commons on Monday, 3 August 1914, with uncharacteristic eloquence by Sir Edward Grey as Foreign Secretary. And although President Wilson ostentatiously proclaimed American neutrality at this time, it is clear that, in private exchanges between himself and his close advisor Colonel House, both looked at the situation through the same kind of spectacles – framed, one might say, by Gladstonian moral imperatives. None of which escaped the keen eye of the British Ambassador in Washington, Sir Cecil Spring Rice; and the American Ambassador in London, Wilson's old friend Walter Hines Page, was similarly attuned.

It was Page who reported to Washington in September 1914, after a confidential talk with Grey: 'Any terms that England will agree to must provide for an end of militarism forever and for reparation to ruined Belgium' [Clarke 2017: 194]. Only a month into hostilities, then, and this new term 'reparation' is introduced, and quickly picked up by the Americans – all under impeccable liberal auspices. Thus 'reparation' for Belgium in particular was proposed by Grey himself, later the patron saint of the League of Nations in Britain, and put into circulation in Washington, not least through the efforts of Spring Rice (author of the lyrics of the uplifting anthem 'I vow to thee my country'). These were nothing if not high-minded antecedents for the concept of reparations, a register not conveyed in Keynes's matter-of-fact comment in the *Economic Consequences*: 'The special position occupied by Belgium in the popular mind is due, of course, to the fact that in 1914 her sacrifice was by far the greatest of any of the Allies' [JMK 2: 79].

Reparations for the Germans' spoliation of Belgian and, later, French assets were in due course built in to the Fourteen Points, as accepted by the Germans under the terms of the Armistice. Indemnities, by contrast, had been ruled out in two well-publicized speeches given within days of each other in January 1918, one by Lloyd George in London, the other by Wilson in Washington, when the 'Fourteen Points' were first unveiled. Lloyd George explicitly ruled out a 'war indemnity such as that imposed on France by Germany in 1871', and talked instead of 'the complete restoration, political and territorial and economic, of Belgium and such reparation as can be made for the devastation of its towns and provinces'. A few days later, Wilson's Point 7 not only insisted that 'Belgium, the whole world will agree, must be evacuated and restored', but his Point 8 added: 'All French territory should be freed and the invaded portions restored' [Clarke 2017: 236–8].

Thus a wholesome American process of restoration, reinforced by the archaic British term 'reparation' (which Lloyd George had appropriated from Grey), came to define, step by step, what the Germans had to accept in the Armistice ten months later, in November 1918. One step in this process was the successful British move to define the German obligation for reparation as a consequence not just of 'invasion' but instead of 'aggression' by Germany, as specified in the Lansing Note [Bunselmeyer, 81–2]. Belgium, of course, had been the most notable victim of German invasion; but the British Empire had surely suffered too from German aggression – even in faraway Australia, as its trenchantly vocal prime minister, Billy Hughes, was currently reminding British audiences while he prepared for his role as one of two prominent Dominion representatives at the forthcoming peace conference. (The other was Jan Christiaan Smuts of South Africa, as totemic an embodiment of devotion to liberal causes like the League of Nations as Hughes was of a tough-minded determination to make Germany pay.)

Here was an iterative process in which a duty to restore caused by invasion could, via 'reparations' for aggression, become an obligation on the guilty party to indemnify the innocent parties. And in this process, it was the emphasis of Anglo-American liberals upon the war as a great crime, rather than simply French insistence on *revanchiste* recompense, that set the terms of the negotiations from the outset [Trachtenberg 1980: 48–52]. The way that the Armistice was drafted was itself a significant step in this process, and it helped to set the scene for the fine semantic game that was to be played out in Paris during 1919 in further extrapolations from its terms.

When are indemnities not indemnities? When they are reparations, of course. This is one issue on which the *Economic Consequences* chooses not to dwell. 'I cannot here describe the endless controversy and intrigue between the Allies themselves, which at last after some months culminated in the presentation to Germany of the reparation chapter in its final form.' Keynes's abstention from further comment at this point is ostensibly justified by a display of general contrition: 'I doubt if anyone who took much part in that debate can look back on it without shame' [JMK 2: 95]. But the innocent reader will hardly appreciate the extent to which Keynes is engaged, in the paragraphs that follow, on a cover-up of his personal role.

For what follows is a discussion of the origin of Article 231 of the Versailles Treaty, the stipulation on which Germany's liability for paying reparations depended. Of course it is not helpfully head-lined 'War Guilt Clause' in the text of the Treaty but the import is deadly: 'The Allied and Associated governments affirm and Germany accepts the responsibility of Germany and her allies for causing all the loss and damage to which the Allied and Associated governments and their nationals have been subjected as a consequence of the war imposed upon them by the aggression of Germany and her allies.' The *Economic Consequences* describes this as 'a well and carefully drafted article' [JMK 2: 95]. But it does not disclose that this careful drafting was the work of a young American lawyer on Wilson's staff, John Foster Dulles, working with a young British economist in Lloyd George's team – Keynes himself, of course.

This omission is buttressed by further evasion. Keynes's following five pages explain how German liability for Allied war pensions, hith-erto thought of as indemnities and thus inadmissible, was redefined as reparations. This extension was transparently engineered so as to boost the proportion received by countries of the British Empire – setting Australian war pensioners alongside Belgian farmers as recipients – but its consequential effect was likewise obvious in tripling the total amount demanded from Germany. There was some talk of a thirty-year time limit to offset the total impact on Germany's liability; but this proposal soon fell by the wayside. So the effect was indeed to triple the extent of the total reparations claim upon Germany under Article 231.

Now this highly significant shift in the Allied position on reparations was achieved on the advice of Smuts: much to his subsequent chagrin. His advocacy proved uniquely influential in winning the assent of Wilson precisely because Smuts was so highly esteemed in liberal circles. It was Smuts, moreover, who first privately encouraged Keynes, on his resignation in June 1919, 'to set about writing a clear connected account of what the financial and economic clauses of the treaty actually are and mean, and what their probable results will be' [JMK 17: 3].

The fact that the origin of Keynes's tract came from Smuts in the first place is not acknowledged in the *Economic Consequences*; indeed Smuts's name never appears in its pages. Only with the publication of its far less prominent sequel in 1922, *A Revision of the Treaty*, did Keynes supply a more candid version of the episode. He now took cover by citing Smuts's memorandum on pensions, and accounts of its impact upon Wilson, taken from American sources, including Dulles. Keynes claimed that this justified him to 'set forth, for the inspection of Englishmen and our Allies, the moral basis on which two-thirds of our claims against Germany rest' [JMK 3: 104]. Whether this should be read as an apology to readers of the *Economic Consequences* for not telling the full story is perhaps a matter of judgment. But it is a story in which nobody has clean hands: not Wilson, to be sure, but also not Dulles nor Smuts – and certainly not Keynes, the joint author of the War Guilt Clause.

* * *

We are now stumbling into a thicket of subsequent controversy stretching over a full century; but two specific points still need clarification in defining some outstanding issues at stake. The first is that, whatever conclusion is drawn about Keynes's claim about the burden of reparations, it must refer to what is specified in the Treaty as signed in June 1919, with its deliberately open-ended principles about what was due and for how long. It is obviously nonsense to assess the claims in the book as though they referred to subsequent modifications of these terms, notably the revision made in the 1921 London Schedule – which Keynes himself reluctantly endorsed.

Secondly, still less does it invalidate the claims in a book published in 1919 to point out that in fact Germany never paid any substantial amount of the reparations demanded in the Treaty. It was, rather, the demand itself that became the problem, in political terms as much as economic. Hence the centrality of the War Guilt Clause, right from the first week of May 1919 when it was presented to the German representatives in Paris. This is a point amply demonstrated by Isabel Hull in a book that deserves more attention than it has so far received [Hull 2014]. The fact that German propaganda did not limp should hardly have come as a surprise to Keynes.

To adapt an old joke, when six economic historians are gathered to assess the impact of the reparations demanded under the Versailles Treaty, there will be seven opinions – two of them held by Niall Ferguson. I do not propose to treat him as a straw man in yet another disputation over the financial scale and economic impact of the reparations demanded under the Treaty; but the element of subjectivity involved in these ostensibly dry exercises in quantification is perhaps worth noting. For in 1995 Ferguson published a formidable scholarly volume, derived from his doctoral dissertation, on German financial issues in the 1920s, including the impact of reparations, duly detailed in a table in an appendix. This served as the authority for his claim in the text: 'Reparations, as envisaged in 1921, *were* therefore excessive – as the German government claimed' [Ferguson 1995: 315; emphasis in original]. Now this is surely more Keynesian than Keynes himself (who had grudgingly commended the 1921 London schedule), though Ferguson appears to settle the matter with all the technical apparatus of modern econometric scholarship.

But in 1998 Ferguson published another big book, *The Pity of War*, for a wider readership. Quite legitimately, it reproduced at one relevant point, this time as a graph, exactly the same calculations that the author had published three years previously; and, also quite understandably, the author offered the conclusion that he drew from this evidence – this time, however, phrased rather differently: 'Nor can it credibly be maintained that the reparations total set in 1921 constituted an intolerable burden' [Ferguson 1998: 414]. Exactly the same evidence, then, but a diametrically opposite conclusion.

We all need to walk warily if we venture into this minefield of historic controversy. Let me simply note that in 1871 the total indemnity imposed by Germany was less than 25 per cent of French national income; the demands in the 1921 schedule are variously computed as around 100 per cent of German national income. I am not competent to adjudicate on the technical differences here beyond noting that, however the calculation goes, starkly different orders of magnitude seem evident. To put it another way, it was evidently not open to the Germans to pay off reparations quickly, even had the will to do so been more evident. And if this applies to the specified schedule of 1921, how much more is it true of the (unspecified but much heavier) demands in the Treaty as signed in 1919.

Certainly, perspectives change over time. In many ways the classic critique of Keynes's contentions on the economic potential of reparations is the volume published in 1946, *The Carthaginian Peace: The Economic Consequences of Mr Keynes*. The author, Étienne Mantoux, was the son of Paul Mantoux, not only Clemenceau's interpreter during the Paris conference but also Keynes's subsequent critic in writing about it. The young Mantoux was naturally imbued with filial and patriotic passions that gave him a different perspective from that of Anglo-American liberalism. By the time of his own book's publication, alas, the author had died in combat in the last phase of the Second World War.

The Carthaginian Peace honourably conceded (twice over) the correctness of Keynes's calculations of the reparations demanded in the 1919 Treaty [Mantoux 1946: 107, 160]. But Mantoux argued that the London Schedule of 1921 was perfectly feasible and that if Germany *did not* comply it was no proof that it *could not* have done so [Mantoux 1946: 87, 119]. This contention is fair enough in its own terms, though I think that these days we are more impressed by 'willingness-to-pay' constraints rather than notional 'capacity-to-pay' arguments, a point well put by Albrecht Ritschl [Broadberry and Harrison (ed) 2005: 71].

And here, admittedly, the *Economic Consequences* is open to criticism for much the same reason as is Keynes's advice to the Treasury on British economic capacity during the First World War. Thus it has long been recognized that as a wartime civil servant he had failed to appreciate the impact of the war in expanding the capacity of the British economy [Skidelsky 1983: 305]. Likewise, as a polemical author in 1919, Keynes sought to identify post-war German economic resources in static and finite ways. So he dealt with the transfer problem without allowing for those knock-on effects of stimulus or leakages in a dynamic process that a modern Keynesian economist would naturally look for (and about which the Swedish economist

Bertil Ohlin tried unavailingly to educate Keynes in the 1920s, as we
have been reminded at this conference).

Mantoux sometimes hints at this missing dimension, with its theoretical implications [Mantoux 1946: 124–5]. But the significant point
is, I think, practical and experiential: that Mantoux was a child of
his time. He had lived through the Nazi era, which had demonstrated
through brute force the fragility of the bien-pensant assumptions of
1919. Not only did Mantoux point to the economic power of the Nazi
war machine in stimulating the economy but then went one step further. He pointed, often with mordant sarcasm, to the success of Nazi
methods in extracting wealth from countries under occupation – on a
scale far greater than any estimates of what was possible in Keynes's
scenario. Mantoux appealed to the object lesson of the Nazi occupation of France, showing that nothing was 'impossible' when the jack-
boot was on the other foot.

It was only in 1922, in his (little read) sequel *A Revision of the
Treaty*, that Keynes had explicitly addressed this alternative, dismiss-
ing the 'project of extracting at the point of a bayonet – for that is
what it would mean – a payment so heavy that it would never be paid
voluntarily' as 'neither good nor sensible' [JMK 3: 129]. Was this later
clarification because of a hitherto undisclosed gap, lacuna or weakness
in the argument that the *Economic Consequences* had presented two
years earlier? Surely not; the idea of military occupation of Germany,
or continued conscription in Britain, was never on Lloyd George's
agenda. And in studying the outcome of the First World War as much
as in studying its origins, we often need to recapture the unspoken
assumptions. For Anglo-American liberals who aimed at bringing a
permanent peace by *reconciling* Germany to a mutually agreed solution of an organic European problem, actual willingness to pay was as
much the test as notional capacity to pay.

One canard that can surely be dismissed is that Keynes was simply anti-French. Admittedly he was often identified as such by those
who saw heavy reparations from Germany as the only path to French
economic recovery from the war. Keynes's argument was that neither
nation could expect to benefit from impoverishing the other, but that
France's real hopes of prosperity would be within a revived European
economy that encompassed Germany too. Hence his insistence that
'the financial problems which were about to exercise Europe could not
be solved by greed. The possibility of *their* cure lay in magnanimity'

[JMK 2: 92; emphasis in original]. Here was a Keynesian perspective upon the vision of an integrated Europe, where the strong have not only a moral obligation in helping the weak but share a mutual benefit in doing so. The abiding relevance of the *Economic Consequences* has thus been rediscovered in a radically different context from that in which the tract was written, with insights that still have continuing relevance in the Europe of today [Holscher and Klaes 2014]. Perhaps the book will remain in print for another century.

References

Broadberry, Stephen and Harrison, Mark (ed) (2005), *The Economics of World War I* (Cambridge) for Albrecht Ritschl, 'The pity of peace: Germany's economy at war, 1914–18 and beyond'.

Bunselmeyer, Robert E. (1976), *The Cost of the War, 1914–1919: British Economic War Aims and the Origins of Reparation* (Hamden: Conn).

Clarke, Peter (2017), *The Locomotive of War: Money, Empire, Power and Guilt* (London and New York: Bloomsbury).

Clavin, Patricia (2013), *Securing the World Economy: The Reinvention of the League of Nations*, 1920–46 (Oxford: Oxford UP).

Ferguson, Niall (1990), *Paper and Iron: Hamburg Business and German Politics in the Era of Inflation, 1897–1927* (Cambridge: Cambridge UP).

Ferguson, Niall (1998), *The Pity of War* (London: Cambridge UP).

Holscher, Jens and Klaes, Matthias ed. (2014), *Keynes's Economic Consequences of the Peace: A Reappraisal* (London: Pickering and Chatto).

Hull, Isabel V. (2014), *A Scrap of Paper: Breaking and Making International Law During the Great War* (Ithaca, NY: Cornell UP).

JMK, with vol. number and page reference: The Collected Writings of John Maynard Keynes, 30 vols., Donald Moggridge and Austin Robinson (managing editors), Cambridge University Press for the Royal Economic Society, 30 vols., (1971–1989). JMK 2: *The Economic Consequences of the Peace* (1919); JMK 3: *A Revision of the Treaty* (1922); JMK 17: *Activities, 1920–1922: Treaty Revision and Reconstruction*.

MacMillan, Margaret (2001), *Peacemakers: The Paris Conference of 1919 and Its Attempts to End War* (London: John Murray).

Mantoux, Étienne (1946), *The Carthaginian Peace: Or the Economic Consequences of Mr Keynes* (Oxford: Oxford UP).

Moggridge, Donald (1992), *Maynard Keynes: An Economist's Biography* (London: Routledge).

Skidelsky, Robert (1983), *John Maynard Keynes, vol. 1, Hopes Betrayed, 1883–1920* (London: Macmillan).

Steiner, Zara (2005), *The Lights That Failed: European International History, 1919–1933* (Oxford: Oxford UP).

Tamke, Jürgen (2017), *A Perfidious Distortion of History* (London: Scribe).

Tooze, Adam (2014), *The Deluge: The Great War and the Remaking of the Global Order, 1916–31* (London: Allen Lane).

Trachtenberg, Marc (1980), *Reparation in World Politics: France and European Economic Diplomacy, 1916–1923* (New York: Columbia UP).

4 | "Too Bad to Be True": Swedish Economists on Keynes's The Economic Consequences of the Peace and German Reparations, 1919–29

BENNY CARLSON AND LARS JONUNG

1 Introduction[1]

The publication in December 1919 of John Maynard Keynes's book on *The Economic Consequences of the Peace* met an immediate response in Sweden. The volume was immediately translated into Swedish and appeared in print in the spring of 1920 (Keynes, 1920). It became a source of comments and discussion from then on, continued by his sequel *A Revision of the Treaty* (Keynes, 1922a; in Swedish as Keynes, 1922b). As a consequence, Keynes was invited to serve as a regular contributor to *Dagens Nyheter*, a leading Stockholm daily, in the period 1920–23. Keynes's criticisms of the Versailles Treaty were also the main reason for his election to the Royal Swedish Academy of Sciences.

In this chapter, we concentrate on the response of five prominent Swedish professors in economics: David Davidson (1854–1942), Knut Wicksell (1851–1926), Gustav Cassel (1866–1945), Eli F. Heckscher (1879–1952) and Bertil Ohlin (1899–1979). All five made outstanding scientific contributions. Davidson was an important transitional link between classical and neoclassical economics. Cassel's work on monetary economics, and Heckscher's research in economic history and his impact on the Heckscher-Ohlin theory have stood the test of time. In the 1920s, Cassel even rivalled Keynes for the position as the

[1] We appreciate support from Lund University Library, the National Library of Sweden, the archives of the Riksbank and of King's College, Cambridge. We have benefitted from comments by Boris Begović, Klas Fregert, Mats Lundahl, Bo Sandelin, Claes-Henric Siven, Anders Waldenström and Lars Werin.

world's most known economist (Carlson, 2009). Wicksell's monetary theory and his proposal that central banks should target the price level is presently the theoretical base for the inflation-targeting regimes adopted by leading central banks across the world. Ohlin, Nobel laureate in 1977, laid the foundation of the prevailing theory of international trade in the 1920s. In the 1930s, he presented the Stockholm school of economics (*Stockholmsskolan*) as an alternative to Keynes's *General Theory*.

Sweden was neutral during World War I. The views of the Swedish economists are thus not biased by Sweden taking part in the war. Still, they had their leanings. Davidson was an admirer of British classical economists, but nonetheless "his sympathies lay with Germany" (Heckscher, 1953, p. 305). Cassel wrote favourably on Germany during the war and was widely read in Germany. Heckscher had turned from a conservative to a liberal position in the 1910s (Carlson, 2006); his previous conservatism, however, drew inspiration from British, rather than German, sources. Wicksell detested the war, initially taking no side and holding a pacifist stance. However, as many conservatives in Sweden, including the King, hoped for German victory, he became supportive of the Entente. As a high school student when the war began, Ohlin held a positive attitude towards the Entente, probably influenced by his mother's dislike of the pro-German views held by the upper classes in Southern Sweden (Ohlin, 1972).

Our report is organized in the following way. First, we give a short description of the Swedish professors' engagement in public debate. Next, we deal with the views of the five economists. We take them in chronological order as they entered the debate on Keynes's book. We also comment on Davidson's, Cassel's, Heckscher's and Ohlin's assessments of Keynes after the publication of his *General Theory* in 1936. We conclude with a short summary.

2 Swedish Economists in Public Debate

To understand the Swedish response to Keynes, a glimpse of the strong involvement of Swedish university professors in public debate may be useful (Carlson and Jonung, 2006; Jonung, 1992). This tradition was initiated by Knut Wicksell, who once wrote to a friend that "I have always looked upon the education of the Swedish people as my chief obligation" (Gårdlund, 1958, p. 305).

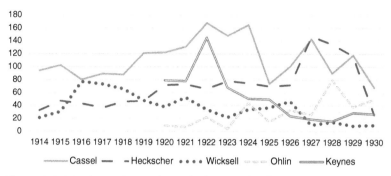

Figure 4.1 Mentions of Cassel, Heckscher, Wicksell, Ohlin and Keynes in Swedish newspapers 1914–30

Altogether Wicksell published about 440 newspaper articles, mostly in newspapers with a leftist leaning (Knudtzon, 1976). He also left about 100 unpublished manuscripts (published in Jonung et al., 2001). Cassel published about 1,500 articles, mostly Op-Eds, in *Svenska Dagbladet*, a leading conservative daily (Carlson and Jonung, 1989). Heckscher, after turning liberal, published about 300 articles in *Dagens Nyheter*, a liberal newspaper (*Eli F. Heckschers bibliografi*, 1950). Davidson did not publish much in daily newspapers – it was said that "he cannot tolerate a more journalistic posture within the economics debate" (Jacobsson, 1939, p. 9) – but wrote about 250 articles and reviews for an academic audience in *Ekonomisk Tidskrift*, a journal he himself launched and edited for forty years. The next generation of economists continued the tradition of publishing in newspapers. Here Ohlin stands out with about 2,000 articles, mostly Op-Ed pieces in *Stockholms-Tidningen* (Carlson et al., 2000). Like his predecessors, Ohlin felt an urge to inform the public about economic issues: "The most important task of the economists should be to teach the public how to think in economic terms" (Larsson, 1998, p. 40).

The media exposure of the Swedish economists as well as of Keynes in the period 1914–30 is summarized in Figure 4.1, based on the number of times their names appeared in Swedish newspapers as displayed in the National Library of Sweden digitized newspaper database. Davidson is not included since he had rather few mentions, between five and twenty a year.

3 David Davidson

Davidson wrote several articles on the economies of the belligerent nations during the war. In the first 1920 issue of *Ekonomisk Tidskrift*, he reviewed the original English edition of Keynes's book, introducing Keynes as "an eminent scholar, who gives a much needed orientation into the maze of the peace treaty" (Davidson, 1920, p. 15). Most writings dealing with the war lacked in neutrality, but this book had strong guarantees for objectivity, namely

that it is written by an Englishman, known as a conscientious scholar within this field, who as an official representative for his country has participated in the peace conference in a distinguished role, but has been convinced, that the peace conditions, which were to be put forward, would amount to such a gross and for all Europe fatal breach of promise against Germany, the enemy of his motherland, that he for pangs of conscience had to leave his position before the closure of the peace conference. (Davidson, 1920, p. 15)

Keynes's book, in short, gave an impression of "unquestionable honesty" (Davidson, 1920, p. 15). If Keynes was right in his perception that Germany could not pay the reparations, it would for all of its economic life be dependent upon the discretion of the Entente.

Davidson was particularly impressed by the third chapter in Keynes's book, which could have been headed "how Clemenceau and Lloyd George fooled Wilson," and ended his review by saying that "nobody, having to take part of the issue of his country's entry into the League [of Nations], should decide about his vote without having read Keynes's book" (Davidson, 1920, p. 21).

In the first 1921 issue of *Ekonomisk Tidskrift*, Davidson, referring to Keynes's book, pointed to the contradictions in French policy: on the one hand the ambition to squeeze as much out of Germany as possible in order to save France from financial bankruptcy; on the other hand an ambition to hurt Germany as much as possible without regard to the consequences upon Germany's ability to pay reparations (Davidson, 1921).

Davidson returned to the German reparations in a couple of articles in the latter part of the 1920s. He also commented upon Keynes's article on the transfer problem in 1929. His ambition was, however, not to treat this "very tricky international economic problem," but to show that Keynes's critique of the Dawes plan missed the target (Davidson, 1929, p. 82).[2]

Davidson's admiration for Keynes waned in the 1930s. In 1936–37 he devoted no less than four articles in *Ekonomisk Tidskrift* to Keynes's *General Theory*. He spent much energy defending his "lifetime hero" Ricardo against Keynes while declaring that his ambition was not to criticize Keynes's theory per se; it was rather to question its practical usefulness. His main objection was that Keynes proposed "not only a new perception and solution of the unemployment problem, but also a transformation of the whole problem of [wealth and income] distribution, both running in a strong socialist direction" (Davidson, 1936a, p. 88).

An experiment of this kind has only been conducted in one country, namely Russia, but how this experiment has turned out nobody outside Russia can say with any degree of certainty. The prevailing opinion outside Russia seems to be that the experiment has turned out in a way which ought to be very forbidding. (Davidson, 1936b, p. 103)

The two problems ought to be solved separately, which was the approach taken in Sweden.

4 Gustav Cassel

In early 1916, the German Minister to Stockholm invited Cassel to visit Germany and study its economic power of resistance. Cassel accepted the invitation, under a set of conditions supposed to secure his stance as a neutral observer. He spent the month of March in Germany and Belgium and had a book ready in late April. The Swedish edition was promptly translated into English and German (Cassel, 1916a, 1916b, 1916c). Cassel's main conclusion was that the Entente had underestimated Germany's economic strength. In his memoirs, he wrote that the book was widely circulated and "eagerly read in German trenches," but that it was difficult to get it circulated in Britain (Cassel, 1940, p. 186).

Already in December 1918, Cassel highlighted the contradictions in the Entente demands on Germany: on the one hand demands for huge

---

[2] There was no exchange of letters between Davidson and Keynes; at least there are no letters from Davidson at the King's College archive.

reparations which meant that Germany must achieve immense export surpluses and "totally flood the poor Western powers with its goods"; on the other hand an ambition to "as much as possible cut Germany off from trade relations with the rest of the world" (Cassel, 1918).

In the autumn of 1919, Cassel characterized the occupation of German territory as "a heritage from the same militaristic hubris as the Western powers had set out to eradicate" (Cassel, 1919). In February 1920, he stated that the Treaty of Versailles suffered, "as Keynes in his book on the economic consequences of the peace has clearly demonstrated," from the contradiction that it "on the one hand wished to crush Germany, not only politically but also economically, but at the same time figured Germany would be able to pay" (Cassel, 1920a). A few weeks later he laid down the preconditions necessary for a reconstruction of the European economy: Germany must be able to control its borders, the war amount of reparations must be fixed and the payment thereof be postponed (Cassel, 1920b).

During the summer of 1920, Cassel repeated that the amount of reparations must be fixed before a planned international economic conference could be held in Brussels (Cassel, 1920c, 1920d). In the early autumn he issued a warning:

But what will result [...] if Germany's insolvency becomes definite and if the whole German national economy tumbles down? [...] The rest of Europe would never be able to immure itself from such a terrible collapse; it does not matter if one counts oneself as friend or foe, the economic and social destiny of Europe is mutual [...]. [---] If Europe is to avoid an increasingly threatening disaster, its politicians must no doubt carry out a thorough revision of all concepts regarding the economic conditions needed for the restoration of peace. (Cassel, 1920e)

In the years to come, Cassel continued his relentless campaign against the war reparations policies and Keynes's and his paths crossed several times. As a matter of fact, they had met and exchanged letters even before the war.[3] In 1916, Cassel had sent his book on Germany's economic power of resistance to Keynes. In the spring of 1919, Cassel wrote to Keynes, proposing an international conference on monetary

---

[3] Keynes and Cassel exchanged letters between 1912 and 1932. There are about forty letters from Keynes to Cassel, significantly fewer copies of letters from Cassel to Keynes. Cassel's letters are available at the National Library of Sweden (EP C1a).

affairs. Keynes (25 June 1919) promised to bring the proposal to the Royal Economic Society and gave a glimpse from the Paris peace conference: "My experience in Paris has not led me to anticipate good prospects at present for a sound or wise scheme. I have a deeply pessimistic view of the prospects of Europe and I am much ashamed of the part played by my country in the settlement of the Peace."

In the summer of 1921, Cassel visited London and met Keynes at lunches and dinners on several occasions. In the autumn, he sent his second Financial Memorandum for the League of Nations to Keynes, who (in a letter dated 10 October) offered to publish it in *The Economic Journal*. However, Cassel (18 October) told Keynes that he had been offered to publish it in *The Manchester Guardian*, whereupon Keynes (26 October) responded that he would be engaged in a *Manchester Guardian* project, for which he hoped to secure Cassel's collaboration.

In early 1922, Keynes (6 January) asked Cassel to contribute an article on the Scandinavian exchange rates. Cassel (13 January) agreed – the article appeared in April (Cassel, 1922a) – and Keynes (23 January) sent him his "new book," certainly *A Revision of The Treaty* judging by Cassel's (9 February) response: "I have read it with the utmost interest and with great admiration both for the lucidity of exposition and for the moral strength which is at the bottom of it." Next, the correspondence revolved around the Genoa conference (where the two met) and Keynes (16 February, 28 March, 24 April, 18 May and 7 June) persuaded Cassel to write a summary and evaluation of the event. In June 1922, this summary appeared in Keynes's series of *Manchester Guardian Commercial* supplements on "Reconstruction in Europe." Cassel wrote of "a world of illusions" and continued:

Once it is perceived with perfect clearness that payment means the transfer year after year of real income from one people to another, and that this income is nothing else than a mass of goods and services produced by the debtor people but not consumed by it, everybody will begin to see that the payment of such sums as are here involved in the present indebtedness is impossible, both for the reason that the debtor countries cannot pay and for the reason that the countries claiming payment are not willing to receive it. (Cassel, 1922b, p. 139)

If the debtor country was to pay these sums, its consumption would be reduced below the subsistence level. That countries claiming payment were not willing to receive it might seem strange. "But the transfer of goods and services to such an extent [...] would undoubtedly cause a considerable dislocation of the economic life of the countries receiving them" (Cassel, 1922b, p. 139).

In the summer of 1922, Keynes (letter 26 July) invited Cassel, along with several other renowned economists, to contribute an article on "Reconstruction in Europe" to *The Manchester Guardian* supplements. This supplement – "Symposium by Six Professors" – appeared in late September. The professors were, in addition to Cassel, Andreas Andréadès, G. W. J. Bruins, Edwin Cannan, Luigi Einaudi and Charles Gide. Cassel denoted the policy against Germany "as an extremely costly experiment, not only for Germany but also for the Allies themselves and for the whole economy of the world." The Allied powers had been "almost hypnotised" by pre-war estimates of Germany's accumulated wealth, but the wealth of a country could only to a very limited extent be transferred to other countries. Germany's capacity to pay was a function of its economic future and "if the treatment of Germany hitherto is to be continued, it is safe to estimate the sum which can be paid in indemnity as nil" ("How Much Can the Allies," 1922, p. 511).

Cassel in a letter (8 October 1922) to Keynes praised this "Reconstruction Issue" as "the most significant work for the enlightenment of public opinion" which would do "more for a solution of this problem than any of the big international conferences." However, he added: "Perhaps I am a grade more pessimistic than you. [...] there is not the slightest possibility that the politicians will come to economic sense before it is too late."

Shortly thereafter, Cassel, Keynes, the Dutch central bank governor Gerard Vissering, the British banker Robert Brand, the American economist Jeremiah Jenks and a couple of other experts were invited to Berlin by the German government to discuss measures to arrest the decline of the German currency. In his memoirs, Cassel recalls "the most pleasant cooperation with Brand and Keynes, although I sometimes even against these two had to resist too far-reaching demands upon Germany" (Cassel, 1940, p. 401).[4] On 7 November,

---

[4] The German Chancellor Joseph Wirth had "watered" Keynes and Cassel with these other experts since he had been told that "Cassel and Keynes were both men of extreme theoretical views, and quite indifferent to what anybody else thought of their subject" (Johnson, 1978, p. 61).

the experts presented a report, demanding immediate stabilization of the German mark, which presumed a final settlement of the reparations issue and a two-year moratorium on payments.[5] However, their advice was ignored, and soon Germany was sucked down in a maelstrom of hyperinflation.

In early 1923, Cassel (13 January) sent an article on "Economic Fallacies of the Versailles Policy" to Keynes, hoping to get it published in *The Manchester Guardian* series. When he got no immediate answer, he wrote again (19 January), adding some arguments: "If France is going to take Germany's last coal resources, it seems clear to me that the rest of Germany must become so poor that its present population can no longer find subsistence." Keynes (1 February) responded by saying that Cassel's article was brilliant but that he was no longer responsible for *The Manchester Guardian* series.

In 1924, on Cassel's initiative, Keynes was elected as a member of the foreigners' section of the economic class of the Royal Swedish Academy of Sciences.[6] Cassel introduced Keynes to the public in an article and justified his election mainly with reference to his two books on the Versailles Treaty (Cassel, 1924). Cassel lauded the sound economic judgment, theoretical clarity, brilliant art of presentation and moral courage Keynes had shown by speaking on behalf of truth and common sense against the world opinion. He also praised Keynes's work on the reconstruction issue in *The Manchester Guardian*.

After this peak in the relation between the two famous economists, there was no exchange of letters for five years until Cassel submitted an article for publication in *The Economic Journal*. Now, Keynes was less enthusiastic and responded (14 and 27 February 1929) that he had a feeling that there was something wrong in the argument.

As Keynes turned into an advocate of government intervention and full employment policies, whereas Cassel was a leading

---

[5] These were the demands in the majority report, signed by Keynes, Brand, Cassel and Jenks. There was also a minority report, signed by Vissering and others, "which made everything depend on a large loan" (Johnson, 1978, p. 63).

[6] Cassel told Keynes about this in a letter dated 9 October 1924. Keynes wrote on 21 October that he was honoured to "fill the place held by my master, Alfred Marshall."

critic of state intervention, the relation between the two cooled down (Carlson, 1994).[7] When Keynes's *General Theory* appeared, Cassel's main objection was that it was not a general theory, but based on the artificial conditions prevailing in the British economy during the depression, and failed to reflect crucial features of a normal economy.

One such feature is undoubtedly progress, and even the most elementary picture of society must explain in broad outline how progress comes about. This aspect of the economy disappears in a most disquieting manner in the picture of society which we are now offered. What we are shown is instead a picture of a society falling into hopeless stagnation. However, since this stagnation seems to be mainly the result of temporary government measures, it is impossible to see in it a necessity conditioned by given economic factors. (Cassel, 1937, p. 137)

5 Eli Heckscher

In the summer of 1915, Heckscher departed on a five-week study tour to the Netherlands, England, France and Germany. The outcome was the publication of a book in November on the economics of the world war (Heckscher, 1915). Stating that he was not taking a stand for or against any of the belligerents, Heckscher wanted to analyse the general patterns created by the war – not the specific pattern in a single country.[8] According to one of Heckscher's colleagues, "his sympathies were no doubt emotionally pro-British" and it was difficult for him to see this nation in war with "the by him respected if not beloved Germany" (Brulin, 1953, p. 415).

When Keynes book was published in Swedish in early 1920, it was promptly reviewed by Heckscher in *Svensk Tidskrift* (a journal he had himself previously edited) with a quote from the book as headline: "Too Bad to Be True."

Heckscher characterized Keynes's book as a bright spot in a time of darkness. It offered what the peoples of Europe needed, "men who follow their reason, their knowledge and their sense, unaffected by even

---

[7] The extent to which Cassel's attitude towards Keynes had changed is demonstrated by the fact that in 1939 he tried to block Heckscher's proposal to have the Academy of Science award Keynes with the Söderberg Gold Medal (Arthmar and McLure, 2018).

[8] Heckscher's book is analysed in Fregert (2016).

the strongest national prejudices and party alignments" (Heckscher, 1920, p. 138). Keynes was "the spiritually free man, 'the independent gentleman', a species extinct in almost all other nations."

Such a man must be seen as more credible than most, he represents no party, no interests; he speaks to air his innermost opinion. To this are added all the gifts bestowed by his intellect and experience: exceptional insight into the motives of the actors as well as the material facts; theoretical education, powers of observation and psychological perception that are not common. And, finally, an ability to express his views with restraint and academic elegance in a way that gives them penetrating precision. (Heckscher, 1920, p. 138)

Heckscher was dismayed by the conditions set forth in the Treaty of Versailles which were to "destroy the future of a whole nation," he made a comparison with "the Inquisition's instruments of torture" and concluded that every German "can be deprived of whatever property, if it only appeals to a commission in Paris composed by the nation's enemies" (Heckscher, 1920, pp. 141–142).

Keynes had demonstrated the contradictions of the Treaty, that Germany must create a surplus in its production and trade to be able to pay draconian reparations at the same time as this was prevented through "methodic destruction" (Heckscher, 1920, p. 145). The French wished to milk the cow and at the same time cut its throat. Heckscher thus found Keynes's description of the treaty as "a Karthagian peace" very telling and argued that previously much criticized European peace treaties like the Westphalian peace and the Congress of Vienna in comparison were "monuments of far-sighted state wisdom and generosity" (Heckscher, 1920, pp. 145–146). The French Prime Minister Georges Clemenceau could perhaps realize his Karthagian objective, the destruction of Germany, but then the new Rome (France) would be drawn into the downfall of the new Karthago (Germany). The review ended with an apocalyptic and prophetic vision:

It is, however, also possible that Germany retrieves itself and gets rid of the yoke, as it did after its humiliation under Napoleon; but the consequences for Europe will in this case hardly be less devastating. [...] When the Frankfurt treaty [after the Franco-German War 1871] could induce the Treaty of Versailles, one can hardly imagine what offsprings the latter will eventually conceive. It must be seen as very unlikely that the European civilization will survive also this coming twilight of the gods. (Heckscher, 1920, p. 146)

Unlike Cassel, Heckscher did not correspond much with Keynes in the early 1920s.[9] However, he apparently sent some reviews of the Swedish edition of *The Economic Consequences* since Keynes in a letter (6 July 1920) wrote the following: "I am delighted that you should be able to write as you have done as to the success of my book in Sweden. Many thanks for the reviews which you have sent me."

During 1921, Heckscher continued to discuss the requests by the Entente, aimed at "keeping a nation of 60 million in slavery forever," or at least until 1963 (Heckscher, 1921a, p. 92). He concluded in a most pessimistic mode:

All that remains is – chaos. Nothing of practical value for the salvation of Europe has emerged out of the witch-dance created by the reparations demands. [...] The conclusion is the usual and sad one: there is no other future for Europe than the complete overhaul of the Treaty of Versailles. [...] But the future of modern culture can be lost before a decision of this kind is made. (Heckscher, 1921b, p. 148)

In 1922, Keynes's *A Revision of the Treaty* was reviewed in *Svensk Tidskrift*. The review was not signed, and although it is not listed in his bibliography, it is not improbable that Heckscher was the author. The reviewer noted that the book could not be fully compared to its predecessor, even though the "etching sharpness and stylistic design" of the verdicts had not been weakened.

The new book [...] just as the old one originates from an irresistible need to tell the truth, to display, taunt and condemn the whole fabric of half-truths and full lies which have made possible the Versailles Treaty and foremost the reparations policy. The most encouraging [...] is the belief by its author [...] that the truth is under way – in England. ("Dagens frågor," 1922, p. 145)

Two years later, Heckscher introduced Keynes in a Swedish encyclopedia. He focused on *The Economic Consequences of the Peace*, characterized by "great stylistic talent, clear economic vision and unusual command of the statistical material" and furthermore by "a strong conviction of great importance for its success." However, Heckscher found that Keynes contributions in "purely scientific matters [...] have not been equally important" (Heckscher, 1924; see also Carlson, 2016).

---

[9] Keynes and Heckscher exchanged letters between 1909 and 1939. Heckscher's letters are available at the National Library of Sweden (L 67).

In the late 1920s, Heckscher and Keynes were in touch a couple of times. In 1927, Heckscher (letter 6 November) wished for Keynes to give a lecture at the Swedish Economic Society (Keynes on 16 November declined due to lack of time); in 1928 Keynes (29 August) accepted Heckscher's article "A Plea for Theory in Economic History" (Heckscher, 1929); in 1930 Heckscher (26 March) expressed his gratitude for Keynes's kindness towards his "boy" (Gunnar Heckscher, who had visited Cambridge). In the years 1932–35, Heckscher wrote Keynes several times about the publication, distribution and review of his *Mercantilism* (Heckscher, 1934). When Keynes had read the book, he (15 May 1935) told Heckscher it was "a masterpiece" which he intended to make use of in his upcoming book (i.e., *General Theory*):

I had long had it in mind to write a chapter in my new book upon the relation between Mercantilist theory and current ideas and I was hopeful that your book would supply me with the necessary background and material. My hopes have been more than fulfilled, and I shall, if I may, draw very freely on the mine of information you have made available.

Heckscher was, hardly surprising, encouraged by this praise and (21 May 1935) asked Keynes straight out: "Would it be impossible for you to review the book in *The Economic Journal* yourself?" As it turned out, this review was not to be written by Keynes but by T. H. Marshall of the London School of Economics (Marshall, 1935).

After Keynes's visit in Stockholm and talk at the Political Economy Club in September 1936, he and Heckscher exchanged letters (8 and 13 October) of mutual satisfaction. However, they had by now drifted apart ideologically. In the same year as *General Theory* was published, a new encyclopedia entry on Keynes by Heckscher appeared (Heckscher, 1936). It was short and critical: "Having been a faithful follower of classical economics, K. has [...] increasingly challenged its basic theorems and even associated himself with mercantilist interpretations." Keynes had furthermore "deemed it necessary to introduce a to a large extent new terminology, which has often caused misunderstandings." Heckscher was not happy with the way Keynes had used his *Mercantilism* in *General Theory*. As one of his colleagues, Arthur Montgomery, said, Keynes had read *Mercantilism* in the same way as "the devil reads the Bible" (*Tre tal*, 1945, p. 9).

When Keynes passed away, Heckscher in an obituary summarized his opinion of *General Theory*. It was in "harmony with prevailing political and spiritual tendencies in almost all countries" but "Keynes's perception of the universality of the prerequisites on which he builds is a fundamental mistake"; still, Heckscher had admiration for Keynes: "[H]is ability to put thoughts in motion, to shake people out of their habits of thought, has been extraordinary, and such a vivid, intense and brilliant writer must be of enduring importance for our whole contextual perception" (Heckscher, 1946a).

What did Heckscher mean by questioning the prerequisites of Keynes's theory? The explanation is given in an extensive 1946 article by Heckscher on "'General Theory' from the standpoint of economic history" and is in line with Cassel's view. Heckscher states that the impulse of Keynes's book came from the permanently high British unemployment between the wars "which he almost seems to have been obsessed by. Never before, it seems, has a work making claims for universality in such a one-sided manner been built on one single point of view" (Heckscher, 1946b, pp. 181–182).

6 Knut Wicksell

Wicksell's writings on the German reparations have their roots in his strong Malthusian belief. In the 1880s, he had become an ardent neo-Malthusian. The objections he met from established economists made him study economics. In his academic work, he focused on other issues than the population question in order to get a university position. However, he never abandoned his Malthusian conviction; it was brought in whenever he discussed political and social issues.

When peace arrived, Wicksell presented a Malthusian interpretation of the war in a lecture at a summer course in 1919 at Uppsala University on "The War and the Population Problem." He argued that "if a population increase were to occur in all the countries of the world on the same scale as during the past century, all hopes for a world peace would be in vain. The stomach is a stern ruler, against its demands all treaties are annulled" (Wicksell, 1978, p. 119). In order to bring about peaceful conditions population growth must be reduced. Wicksell noted that prior to the war, birth rates had declined in most "civilized countries," prominently Germany. This decline could even have induced Germany to enter the war as a "cause for striking as soon as possible." Wicksell now expected the German population to stay stationary as a response to the war and "hence one should be able to depend upon the same love for peace within the German nation as within the French" (Wicksell, 1978, p. 124).

During the war, Wicksell had toured the belligerents. After visiting Germany and Austria in the autumn of 1915 to meet with economists and policymakers, he was sent by the Riksbank to England in the spring of 1916 and had the opportunity to meet with Keynes. To Wicksell, a lunch with Keynes, "their keenest theorist," was the high point of the tour as seen from the letter from Wicksell to his wife, Anna Bugge:

Then today I met Keynes and lunched with him at his club. We had a very interesting conversation. On some points he was not very well informed; for one thing he had no very clear idea of how to go about arranging a rational standard of value; [...] On the other hand he has a good mind and, as I said, I gained much from our conversation; only wished it could have been longer; [...] I walked with him to his barber's. (Gårdlund, 1958, p. 295)

The German reparations eventually attracted Wicksell's attention. His archive at the University Library of Lund contains half a dozen manuscripts on this issue, often overlapping in contents. In May 1921, he spoke out for the first time on German reparations in one of these manuscripts: "In contrast to most of my writing fellow-countrymen, I have not expressed my opinion about this subject as long as the issue has remained unsettled. As the provisions now are a fait accompli, I take the liberty to present some simple thoughts" (Jonung et al., 2001, p. 190). In Wicksell's opinion, there were two faulty arguments in the popular discussion: according to the first, Germany would be pressed down to a nation of proletarians or even slaves in order to fulfil the demands of the victorious powers. According to the second, the victors would not benefit as their industries suffered from harsh German competition when Germany tried to pay its reparations.

Wicksell rejected both arguments by the use of an example of a French worker, killed or disabled in the war, who produced luxury goods for export to Germany before the war. Germany paid by exporting consumables to this worker and his family. Due to the peace treaty, Germany is now obliged to support the family of the French worker. The production by the French worker as well as the consumption in Germany of French luxury goods has ceased. Now, wealthy Germans pay for the reparations through the export of consumables to France. The German worker receives his salary as before the war. He is not enslaved, nor is world trade disrupted.

Concerning the second argument, inspired by an article in *Dagens Nyheter* by Georg Gothein, German Minister of Finance, Wicksell turns to the savings of wealthy Germans. According to Gothein, these savings were not available for reparations since they must be used for new housing, utensils and tools for the ever-growing German population. Wicksell notes that "if this is correct even for me the reparations would appear to be an insolvable problem" (Jonung et al., 2001, p. 193). However, he can see no reason why Germany should allow its population to grow. Germany should aim at a stationary population, implying that German savings previously destined for new housing could now be used for reparations. The Malthusian message is summarized in a straightforward way: All things considered, "[t]he regulation of the population in Western Europe is our foremost guarantee of peace without which all treaties are illusory" (Jonung et al., 2001, p. 194).

As mentioned, following the publication of *The Economic Consequences*, Keynes was invited to serve as columnist in the leading daily *Dagens Nyheter*. In the years 1920–23, he regularly published articles translated into Swedish: one in 1920, ten in 1921, eight in 1922 and five in 1923. On August 18, 1921, he announced a set of columns on the international economic outlook, the first one dealing with the new agreement on German reparations (Keynes, 1921a). These articles were part of a worldwide syndication.[10]

In his first contribution, Keynes focused on the reparations agreement of 11 May 1921, welcomed by many as a definite settlement (Keynes, 1921a). In his opinion this was a faulty interpretation, although it was an improvement compared to the Versailles Treaty as the size of the indemnity was reduced. He argued that the agreement would require a revision already in 1922 as Germany would fail to pay. He validated this conclusion by analysing the implications of the total annual debt burden for Germany of 500 million dollars plus an export fee of 26 per cent of the value of German exports. Anticipating a volume of German exports of 1,500 million dollars, inducing 390

---

[10] The five articles are reprinted in chapter 12 in Johnson (1977). The articles were printed in Germany, France and the United States. Johnson does not mention the Swedish version in *Dagens Nyheter*.

million dollars in export fees, Keynes claimed that it would be impossible for Germany to pay 890 million dollars between May 1921 and May 1922. It would require a doubling of Germany's exports without any increase in its imports. Keynes seals his argument with a rhetorical question: "Would anyone believe that this is possible?"

The article by Keynes had an immediate and international impact. According to Robert Skidelsky the article heralded a series of depressing events: the German currency depreciated rapidly, German hyperinflation began and the German government asked for a moratorium on reparations before the close of 1921 (Skidelsky, 1992).

Keynes's article caught Wicksell's attention, and on 27 August he published a reply in *Dagens Nyheter*, the only case of a public exchange of views between the two economists (Wicksell, 1921). Initially, Wicksell notes that Keynes's column is convincing, but that "his calculations like those of former minister Gothein suffer from a fundamental mistake which makes the result illusory." They assumed that the enormous German reparations must represent an additional economic burden on Germany. If this view was correct, Wicksell would be "the first to agree that this requirement is an absurdity that should be abolished." Next, Wicksell presents his Malthusian solution. The German population growth rate before the war required enormous investments in housing and infrastructure like tramways and railways, financed by German savings. If this volume of savings could be used for reparations, after proper readjustment of the German economy, the consumption of Germans need not be restricted.

Wicksell's answer to Keynes's rhetorical question, whether "it would be possible for Germany to double its present exports without any increase in its imports?" was yes – with some qualifications for the immediate future. If all workers involved in housing and infrastructure could be moved to other industries Germany could most likely double its exports with only a minor increase in imports. Wicksell figured that the German population might in fact soon be stationary, and he therefore looked "much more optimistic on the solution to the problem of reparations than professor Keynes does," assuming that Germany was given some respite, preferably through a "global credit operation." In addition, Wicksell believed that Germany with a stationary population would immediately cease to be a danger for peace. If so, the Entente might even cancel a greater or lesser share of the reparations. Wicksell ends by hoping that Keynes will consider his arguments in any of his future columns in *Dagens Nyheter*.

On 28 August, Keynes published another column in *Dagens Nyheter*, in which he addressed and dismissed the fear in England for a sharp rise in German exports when Germany was trying to fulfil the new reparations agreement (Keynes, 1921b). The long duration of the reparations was a particular problem. "Who believes that the allies under one or two generations would be ready to exert such coercion on the German government or the German people so that it will be forced to slave labor at a striking extent? Nobody believes this in all honesty, not anyone."

In an unpublished manuscript on reparations and world trade, Wicksell commented on Keynes's column, agreeing with his basic arguments (Jonung et al., 2001). True to his Malthusian predilection, Wicksell ended his manuscript by claiming that the sharp growth in the German population prior to the war was the sole cause of the British complaints concerning German industrial competition.

On 15 October 1921, Wicksell wrote to Keynes with respect to his first column in *Dagens Nyheter*.[11] Wicksell's article in *Dagens Nyheter* of 27 August had apparently been forwarded to Keynes, who had responded in a letter to Wicksell. Now, Wicksell notes that Keynes had stressed that he was "dealing only with the *near future*":

> If so, there is no quarrel between us, because I am also of the meaning that for the nearest difficult years it will be next to impossible for Germany to pay the damages if she not gets assistance from other quarters, either in the form of credit or by selling its real property to foreigners. But to my understanding You were speaking of Germany's capacity of pay in general; this at any rate is the case in Your well-known book: The economic consequences of the peace.

Wicksell suggested that Keynes was too kind to Germany, "a former enemy." It would be wrong if "England and France were ruined by the war and Germany thriving." Next, he commented on Keynes's estimates of Germany's capacity to pay in *The Economic Consequences*, suggesting they were deficient.

Keynes responded in a letter of 26 October.[12] First, he stressed that his newspaper articles dealt with the near future due to limitations of space and that his book dealt with "Germany's capacity

---

[11] This letter is summarized in Johnson (1977, pp. 279–280).
[12] *In extenso* in Johnson (1977, pp. 280–281).

to pay in general." Next, he addressed Wicksell's argument that a stationary German population would release resources making the reparation payments possible:

I agree an important part of Germany's pre-war savings were required to look after the growing population and that economy in this respect would increase the surplus available for other purposes to a certain extent. But I believe I could produce a hundred reasons [...] for thinking that in practice this factor cannot be quantitatively important. Let me remind you in particular that additional house room is mainly required, not for new-born babies, but for young couples growing up and marrying. There is therefore a very material time-lag between a decrease in the birth rate and a decrease in the number of couples growing up and marrying.

Keynes did not believe that Wicksell's proposal would find acceptance: "Nor [...] do I think that it would be an argument which the world would care to approve that by largely abandoning the production of babies, who are admittedly a considerable expense to their parents, Germany could somewhat increase her surplus for reparation purposes." Although he was a neo-Malthusian and proponent of birth control, Keynes was not ready to go along Malthusian lines as far as Wicksell when analysing the reparations problem.

Keynes's reply did not dampen Wicksell's enthusiasm for Malthusian policy solutions. In three unpublished manuscripts from 1922, 1923 and 1924, he repeated his message that the German reparations were primarily a population issue.[13]

7 Bertil Ohlin

In 1922, Bertil Ohlin, at the recommendation of his supervisor Cassel, submitted to *The Economic Journal* a summary of his licentiate thesis, containing in his own words the "core of my work" on the theory of international trade. A few weeks later, he got a refusal letter from Francis Edgeworth, co-editor with Keynes of the journal. Ohlin found a small note apparently intended for Edgeworth: "This amounts to nothing and should be refused, J. M. Keynes." Ohlin remarks in his

---

[13] The relationship between Wicksell and Keynes was probably somewhat strained after Keynes in January 1924 politely rejected a manuscript by Wicksell on unemployment in Ricardo's model. Wicksell prepared a letter in response; it was apparently never posted but was eventually published; see Jonung (1981).

memoirs: "I keep this little note as a gem," suggesting that Keynes was not familiar with the theory of international trade at this time (Ohlin, 1975, pp. 107–108). Most likely, this was the first contact between Ohlin and Keynes.

In 1928, Ohlin addressed the German reparations in two articles in *Index*, a journal published by *Svenska Handelsbanken*. This analysis is of central importance as it moved into the famous Keynes–Ohlin debate one year later. Here, Ohlin gives a much more detailed description of his views of the transfer problem than in his exchange with Keynes in 1929: 44 pages in *Index* compared to 7 in *The Economic Journal*.

In March 1928, Ohlin published his first *Index* article on "The Reparations Problem" (Ohlin, 1928a). His point of departure was that the transition period of the Dawes plan for the German economy to recover from the Ruhr occupation and hyperinflation would come to an end on September 1.[14] From then on definitive reparations arrangements should be reached. Ohlin concluded that there had not been time, as the Dawes committee had imagined, to gain experience of the economic possibility of the transfer, the main reason being the large capital flow from the United States to Germany, not expected by the signers of the Dawes plan. After reviewing the performance of the German economy, Ohlin wanted to focus on "matters of principle," stating that "with the aid of the theory of international capital movements it is possible to form an opinion as to the financial policy that is best calculated to promote the reparations payments" (Ohlin, 1928a, p. 13).

The second article, in April, is a lengthy comparison between the "orthodox theory" of international capital movements and the theory promoted by Ohlin (Ohlin, 1928b). In his view, a country that wants to export capital must according to orthodox theory create an export surplus of goods by lowering its export prices, for example by a restrictive central bank policy reducing the general price level, and reducing imports as well. Lower prices will reduce the price of exportables, but it is uncertain if the volume of exports will increase enough to obtain

---

[14] The Dawes plan went into effect in 1924 in order to solve the reparations issue temporarily. It allowed for an end of the occupation of the Ruhr area and export of US capital to Germany. However, the size of the reparations was not decided.

a sufficient export of capital.[15] According to orthodox theory, international price movements are thus the key to the transfer of capital from one country to another.

Ohlin suggests that orthodox theory had influenced those who held the view that the German reparation payments are "impracticable," not least the Dawes Committee. However, "the orthodox view is not quite correct, because it fails to take into consideration one fact of great importance" (Ohlin, 1928b, p. 3).

When for some reason or other a country B exports capital to another country A, this means that B *places purchasing power at the disposal of A.* The latter's demand for goods must consequently be greater and B's demand less than before. The decisive point for the machinery of capital movements is, on the contrary, that the demand has undergone a radical change. (Ohlin, 1928b, p. 4)

Using a model of two countries and three goods, export, import and home-market goods, Ohlin explains the role of demand changes, both in the short and long run. The analysis is based on his theory of international trade as seen from a footnote in which he refers to his book on this subject "which is due to appear in the near future" (Ohlin, 1928b, p. 10).[16] Ohlin concludes that in the adjustment process the primary effects are due to demand changes and the secondary effects are driven by relative price movements. In contrast to Ohlin's model, the orthodox view ignored the effects of demand and looked only at price effects.

Next, Ohlin applies his "somewhat abstract" analysis to form "an opinion of the reparations problem and the Dawes plan." His view of Germany's capacity to pay reparations is fairly optimistic:

As far as the reparations problem is concerned, the annuities laid down in the Dawes Plan represents about 5–6% of the German national income. This is a comparatively modest figure. Payments of this size would not by any means involve a revolutionary adjustment of the economic life of Germany. (Ohlin, 1928b, p. 21)

According to Ohlin, "mercantilistic tendencies of the economically untrained person" had prevented an understanding of the

---

[15] The orthodox theory is in short the classical theory of international trade based on classical value theory as seen from the English translation of Ohlin's dissertation in Flam and Flanders (1991).

[16] The book was eventually published as Ohlin (1933).

role of changes in purchasing power and in demand. Finally, he proposed that an international conference "to discuss reparations and inter-allied debts should be put into effect as soon as possible" (Ohlin, 1928b, p. 33).

We find it remarkable that these 1928 articles have not been given any attention in the international literature on the transfer problem. Those who have assessed the debate between Keynes and Ohlin (see below) rely only on *The Economic Journal* articles by Ohlin.

In the autumn of 1928 the Young committee was organized to consider the final design of the system of reparations set up by the Dawes plan. The first meeting of the committee took place in February 1929. Inspired by this event, Keynes published in the March 1929 issue of *The Economic Journal* an article titled "The German Transfer Problem" (Keynes, 1929a). This article triggered a debate between Keynes and Ohlin that holds a prominent position in the theory of international economics. It marked a new turn in the analysis of the German reparations, away from the approach dominating during the first ten years after the publication of *The Economic Consequences of the Peace*.

In his analysis of the transfer problem, Keynes found it most likely that German wages relative to wages in the rest of the world must be reduced in order for German exports to expand. But experience gave no guide concerning the proper size of the fall in German real and money wages. Nor did the Dawes plan advice a route to reduce German wages. In short, Keynes identified a number of obstacles to the necessary adjustment process, including the assertion that world demand for German exports was inelastic.

Upon receiving *The Economic Journal*, Ohlin "sat down immediately at the typewriter to prepare a critical comment" (Ohlin, 1972, p. 154). It took him five or six hours to finish the first version. The arguments came straight from the *Index* articles from the spring of 1928. The next day he made some editing. He then wrote to Keynes on 9 April:[17]

Your article in the last issue of *The Economic Journal* has excited me so much, that I have been unable to resist the temptation to write a brief paper setting forth, why I think your conclusions are partly unfounded. I know that *The Economic Journal* is always full up and that the editors have to refuse many contributions. Yet, in view of the special interest which attaches

[17] The correspondence between Ohlin and Keynes is reprinted in Moggridge (1983, pp. 460–475).

to the reparation problem at present it does not seem quite unthinkable that you may be able to find room for my little paper in the June issue. I should of course be very grateful if you did. (Moggridge, 1983, p. 460)

Ohlin's letter set off a lively interchange between him and Keynes, written in a most respectful tone, in which they tried to clarify the issues. On 18 April, Keynes replied: "I shall be happy to print in *The Economic Journal* a comment or criticism from your pen on my recent article"; but first he wanted to discuss the effects of reparations payment on the German balance of trade. Ohlin replied and adjusted his manuscript according to Keynes's questions and comments.

A central passage in their pre-publication discussion is Ohlin's stress on the role of demand:

That is indeed my main point: the conditions of demand are changed. [...] Will you not agree that demand in both countries is changed directly through the change in capital movements? And that this makes it easier to bring about the necessary adjustment? [...] In your two letters nothing is said about the indirect effects of this change in demand conditions, except your statement about real wages [...] To make my position clear I am sending you two numbers of *Index*, where I have dealt at some length with the reparation problem. (Moggridge, 1983, p. 466)

In the final section of this letter, Ohlin refers again to the *Index* articles: "several well known economists have informed me that on the whole they share my view. So I cannot believe that it is all wrong" (Moggridge, 1983, p. 467).

Ohlin's reply was published in the June issue of *The Economic Journal* (Ohlin, 1929). Inspired by his theory of international trade, he stressed aggregate demand and price effects of transfers not considered by Keynes and stated that Keynes's approach appears to build upon classical barter theory. In short, Ohlin looked more optimistically on the possibility for Germany to pay its indemnity than Keynes.

In a rejoinder, Keynes is not at all convinced by Ohlin's analysis with the reservation that he is not sure he understands it correctly. Keynes suggests that his focus is on "the particular case of German Reparation payments," not on "the theory of international trade" (Keynes, 1929b, p. 179). Ohlin replies in the September issue, once more with a comment by Keynes. Again, they are not able to reconcile their differences. Keynes notes: "As before, I find it extremely difficult to be sure just what he (that is Ohlin) means" (Keynes, 1929c, p. 407).

The comments by Swedish economists on Keynes and the German reparations ended with the exchange between Ohlin and Keynes in 1929. The whole issue lost in attention with the arrival of the Great Depression and the Nazi takeover in Germany. The Lausanne conference of 1932 settled the issue in the sense that no more requests were made on Germany.

The Keynes–Ohlin controversy about the transfer problem continues to attract the attention of the economics profession. Judging from post–World War II evaluations, Ohlin won the debate convincingly. Comparing the "unknown David from Sweden against the world famous Goliath," Paul Samuelson sides with Ohlin (Samuelson, 1981, p. 365). By bringing in income effects, Ohlin was able to disclose the weaknesses in Keynes's analysis. Robert Mundell praises Ohlin and criticizes Keynes for ignoring income and expenditure effects: "The editor of the *Economic Journal* – Keynes himself – should have had it [his March 1929 article] properly refereed!" (Mundell, 2002, p. 245). Robert Skidelsky reaches a similar conclusion, stating that Keynes held a "pre-Keynesian" view of the transfer problem (Skidelsky, 1992). Don Patinkin also stresses "the paradoxical situation that it was Ohlin who was insisting on the necessity of taking into account the effect of an increase in 'purchasing power' on demand – and that it was Keynes who was persistently denying the validity of the principle that was to become the major one of his *General Theory*" (Patinkin, 1979, p. 9). Leonard Gomez, in a recent summary of the Keynes–Ohlin debate, also concludes that Ohlin had the strongest case (Gomez, 2010).

Ohlin held Keynes in great esteem. In his memoirs, Ohlin states that "Keynes was the most versatile, talented and interesting scholar I have met" (Ohlin, 1975, p. 110). The debate on the transfer problem in 1929 fostered their relation, and they kept close contact over the years (Trautwein, 2019).

With rising unemployment at the end of the 1920s, Ohlin as well as Keynes turned to various proposals to foster employment. They reached roughly the same conclusions concerning public works and other policy measures. When Keynes visited Sweden in the autumn of 1936, to give a lecture at the Political Economy Club, Ohlin was "reported to have told Keynes with facetious malice that the Swedish economists had read his *General Theory* 'with joy of recognition'" (Henriksson, 1991, p. 41).

In response to *General Theory*, and at the invitation by Keynes, Ohlin wrote two articles for *The Economic Journal* in 1937, comparing Keynes's approach to that of the Swedish economists – the Stockholm school of economics (Ohlin, 1937a, 1937b). Ohlin notes: "As in 1929, it became evident that entering into an academic debate with Keynes was an infallible way of attracting international attention" (Ohlin, 1975, p. 109).

8 Concluding Discussion

Keynes's book on *The Economic Consequences of the Peace,* translated into Swedish in early 1920, met with great interest in Sweden. Gustav Cassel, Eli Heckscher and Knut Wicksell, all committed "to educate the Swedish people," turned their attention to the Versailles Treaty and Keynes's views in a number of contributions. David Davidson also paid attention to Keynes's book, although addressing his colleagues rather than the general public.

Davidson was the first Swedish economist to publish a review (of the English edition) of Keynes's book. He lauded Keynes's objectivity and honesty and accused the Entente of "a fatal breach of promise against Germany." He pointed to the contradictory demands of the French government: the ambition to squeeze as much out of Germany and at the same time hurt Germany as much as possible.

Cassel had already in 1918 attacked the Entente demands on Germany for being contradictory: on the one hand demands for huge reparations which meant that Germany must achieve immense export surpluses; on the other hand an ambition to cut off Germany from trade with other countries. In early 1920, he came back to these contradictions, which "Keynes in his book on the economic consequences of the peace has clearly demonstrated," and which could end in a European disaster. Cassel continued his relentless campaign against the war reparations for years. His and Keynes's paths crossed several times, and he contributed articles to *The Manchester Guardian* supplements on reconstruction in Europe edited by Keynes.

Heckscher reviewed Keynes's book under the headline "Too Bad to Be True" as soon as it was published in Swedish. He portrayed Keynes as a "spiritually free man" equipped with extraordinary theoretical, psychological and pedagogical abilities. Heckscher used powerful words to condemn the Treaty of Versailles: bondage, Inquisition, methodic destruction and Keynes's parable of a Karthagian peace. His vision of a possible outcome of the treaty was even more apocalyptic than Cassel's: "It must be seen as very unlikely that the European civilization will survive [...] this coming twilight of the gods."

Wicksell applied a Malthusian perspective when analysing the German reparations. He suggested a solution that would make Germany able to pay without reducing its standard of living. Germany should move to a stationary population, freeing resources from investment in housing and infrastructure for a growing population and transferring them into the required reparations. In a letter to Wicksell, Keynes was unconvinced: "this factor cannot be quantitatively important." Furthermore, the time lag involved when moving to a stationary population was large.

Bertil Ohlin examined the reparations issue in 1928 in two previously overlooked articles in *Index*, a banking journal, applying his theory of international trade and capital movements. Ohlin was thus well prepared when Keynes in 1929 published an article on the German transfer problem. Using his path-breaking work on the theory of international trade, Ohlin could show that Keynes did not pay sufficient attention to aggregate income effects of reparations from Germany to the Allies. This is surprising as Keynes during the Great Depression developed a macroeconomic theory giving aggregate income and demand a major role. The Keynes–Ohlin debate turned into a classical controversy that still attracts attention.

When Keynes began to move away from classical liberalism, Davidson, Cassel and Heckscher distanced themselves from him. With the advent of *General Theory* in 1936, they definitely turned against him. The younger Swedish economists admired Keynes, but they, particularly Ohlin, were not content being his followers but claimed that they – due to the heritage from Wicksell – were on equal footing with, or even ahead of, him.

References

Arthmar, Rogério and McLure, Michael. (2018). "John Maynard Keynes and the Royal Swedish Academy." *History of European Ideas*, 44(5), 605–622.

Brulin, Herman. (1953). "Eli Heckscher och Svensk Tidskrift." *Svensk Tidskrift*, 40(8), 407–425.

Carlson, Benny. (1994). *The State as a Monster: Gustav Cassel and Eli Heckscher on the Role and Growth of the State.* Lanham, New York & London: University Press of America.

Carlson, Benny. (2006). "When Heckscher Changed Direction: from Social Conservatism to Economic Liberalism." In Ronald Findlay, Rolf G. H. Henriksson, Håkan Lindgren and Mats Lundahl eds., *Eli Heckscher, International Trade, and Economic History.* Cambridge, MA & London: MIT Press.

Carlson, Benny. (2009). "Who Was Most World-Famous – Cassel or Keynes? The *Economist* as Yardstick." *Journal of the History of Economic Thought*, 31(4), 519–530.

Carlson, Benny. (2016). "Eli Heckscher as a Portrait Maker." *Essays in Economic & Business History*, 34, 341–364.

Carlson, Benny and Jonung, Lars. (1989). "Gustav Cassels artiklar i Svenska Dagbladet 1903–1944." *Lund: Meddelande från Ekonomisk-historiska institutionen*, 62.

Carlson, Benny and Jonung, Lars. (2006). "Knut Wicksell, Gustav Cassel, Eli Heckscher, Bertil Ohlin and Gunnar Myrdal on the Role of the Economist in Public Debate." *Econ Journal Watch*, 3(3), 511–550.

Carlson, Benny, Orrje, Helena and Eskil Wadensjö. (2000). *Ohlins artiklar: Register över Bertil Ohlins artiklar i skandinaviska tidningar och tidskrifter 1919–1979.* Stockholm: Institutet för social forskning.

Cassel, Gustav. (1916a). *Tysklands ekonomiska motståndskraft.* Stockholm: Norstedt.

Cassel, Gustav. (1916b). *Germany's Economic Powers of Resistance.* Stockholm: Norstedt.

Cassel, Gustav. (1916c). *Deutschlands wirtschaftliche Wiederstandskraft.* Berlin: Ullstein.

Cassel, Gustav. (1918). "Krigsskadeersättning och slaveri." *Svenska Dagbladet*, 20 December.

Cassel, Gustav. (1919). "Ekonomi och militarism." *Svenska Dagbladet*, 20 October.

Cassel, Gustav. (1920a). "Krigsskadestånd och världsekonomi." *Svenska Dagbladet*, 14 February.

Cassel, Gustav. (1920b). "Europas ekonomiska återuppbyggande." *Svenska Dagbladet*, 12 March.

Cassel, Gustav. (1920c). "Krigsskadeersättningen." *Svenska Dagbladet*, 13 August.

Cassel, Gustav. (1920d). "Krigsskadeersättningen." *Svenska Dagbladet*, 14 August.

Cassel, Gustav. (1920e). "Tysklands ekonomiska läge." *Svenska Dagbladet*, 8 September.

Cassel, Gustav. (1922a). "The Scandinavian Exchanges." *The Manchester Guardian Commercial*, 20 April.

Cassel, Gustav. (1922b). "The Economic and Financial Decisions of the Genoa Conference." *The Manchester Guardian Commercial*, 15 June.

Cassel, Gustav. (1924). "Keynes i Vetenskapsakademien." *Svenska Dagbladet*, 9 October.

Cassel, Gustav. (1937). "En förvänd samhällsbild." *Sunt Förnuft*, May.

Cassel, Gustav. (1940). *I förnuftets tjänst: En ekonomisk självbiografi.* Stockholm: Bokförlaget Natur och kultur.

"Dagens frågor." (1922). *Svensk Tidskrift*, 12, 145–147.

Davidson, David. (1920). "Keynes, J.M., The Economic Consequences of the Peace." *Ekonomisk Tidskrift*, 22(1), 15–21.

Davidson, David. (1921). "Ententens skadeståndsanspråk mot Tyskland." *Ekonomisk Tidskrift*, 23(1), 24–25.

Davidson, David. (1929). "Problemet om det tyska skadeståndets transferering." *Ekonomisk Tidskrift*, 31(2), 82–86.

Davidson, David. (1936a). "Nationalekonomien i stöpsleven." *Ekonomisk Tidskrift*, 38(4), 87–102.

Davidson, David. (1936b). "Nationalekonomien i stöpsleven." *Ekonomisk Tidskrift*, 38(5–6), 103–124.

Eli, F. Heckschers bibliografi 1897–1949. (1950). Stockholm: Ekonomisk-historiska institutet.

Flam, Harry and Flanders, June eds. (1991). *Heckscher-Ohlin Trade Theory*. Cambridge and London: The MIT Press.

Fregert, Klas. (2016). "The Costs and Finances of World War I According to Eli F. Heckscher." *Oeconomia*, 6(4), 515–524.

Gomes, Leonard. (2010). *German Reparations, 1919–1932: A Historical Survey*. Basingstoke: Palgrave Macmillan.

Gårdlund, Torsten. (1958). *The Life of Knut Wicksell*. Stockholm: Almqvist & Wiksell.

Heckscher, Eli F. (1915). *Världskrigets ekonomi: En studie af nutidens näringslif under världskrigets inverkan*. Stockholm: Norstedt.

Heckscher, Eli F. (1920). "För illa att vara sannt." *Svensk Tidskrift*, 10(2), 138–146.

Heckscher, Eli F. (1921a). "Ententekraven och Tysklands tvångsbetalning." *Svensk Tidskrift*, 11(2), 85–92.

Heckscher, Eli F. (1921b). "Skadeståndspolitikens fortsättning." *Svensk Tidskrift*, 11(3), 143–148.

Heckscher, Eli F. (1924). "Keynes, John Maynard." *Nordisk Familjebok* (supplement) column 993–995.

Heckscher, Eli F. (1929). "A Plea for Theory in Economic History." *The Economic Journal*, 39 (Supplement 1), 525–534.

Heckscher, Eli F. (1934). *Mercantilism*, Vol. 1. London: George Allen & Unwin Ltd.

Heckscher, Eli F. (1936). "Keynes, J.M." *Nordisk Familjebok* (supplement) column 968–969.

Heckscher, Eli F. (1946a). "Lord Keynes Avliden." *Dagens Nyheter*, 23 April.

Heckscher, Eli F. (1946b). "Något om Keynes' 'General Theory' ur ekonomisk-historisk synpunkt." *Ekonomisk Tidskrift*, 48(3), 161–183.

Heckscher, Eli F. (1953). "David Davidson 1854–1942." In Joseph Schumpeter ed., *Stora nationalekonomer*. Stockholm: Natur och Kultur.

Henriksson, Rolf. (1991). "The Political Economy Club and the Stockholm School, 1917–1951." In Lars Jonung ed., *The Stockholm School of Economics Revisited*. Cambridge: Cambridge University Press.

"How Much Can the Allies Induce Germany to Pay with Advantage to Themselves? A Symposium by Six Professors." (1922). *The Manchester Guardian Commercial*, 28 September.

Jacobsson, Per. (1939). "David Davidson." *Ekonomisk Tidskrift*, 41(1), 1–10.

Johnson, Elizabeth ed. (1977). *The Collected Writings of John Maynard Keynes, Vol. XVII. Activities 1920–1922: Treaty Revision and Reconstruction*. Cambridge: Cambridge University Press.

Johnson, Elizabeth ed. (1978). *The Collected Writings of John Maynard Keynes, Vol. XVIII, Activities 1922–1932. The End of Reparations*. Cambridge: Cambridge University Press.

Jonung, Lars. (1992). "Economics the Swedish Way 1889–1989." In Lars Engwall ed., *Economics in Sweden: An Evaluation of Swedish Research in Economics*. London: Routledge.

Jonung, Lars. (1981). "Ricardo on Machinery and the Present Unemployment: An Unpublished Manuscript by Knut Wicksell." *The Economic Journal*, 91(361), 195–198.

Jonung, Lars, Hedlund-Nyström, Torun and Jonung, Christina. (2001). *Att uppfostra det svenska folket: Knut Wicksells opublicerade manuskript*. Stockholm: SNS Förlag.

Keynes, John Maynard. (1919). *The Economic Consequences of the Peace*. London: Macmillan.

Keynes, John Maynard. (1920). *Fredens ekonomiska följder*. Stockholm: Bonnier (translated by Evert Berggren).

Keynes, John Maynard. (1921a). "Den nya skadeståndsuppgörelsen." *Dagens Nyheter*, 18 August.

Keynes, John Maynard. (1921b). "Skadeståndsuppgörelsen och världshandeln." *Dagens Nyheter*, 28 August.

Keynes, John Maynard. (1922a). *A Revision of the Treaty: Being a Sequel to The Economic Consequences of the Peace*. London: Macmillan.

Keynes, John Maynard. (1922b). *En revision av freden*. Stockholm: Bonnier (translated by Evert Berggren).

Keynes, John Maynard. (1929a). "The German Transfer Problem." *The Economic Journal*, 39(153), 1–7.

Keynes, John Maynard. (1929b). "A Rejoinder." *The Economic Journal*, 39(154), 179–182.

Keynes, John Maynard. (1929c). "Mr Keynes' Views on the Transfer Problem." *The Economic Journal*, 39(155), 388–408.

Knudtzon, Erik J. (1976). *Knut Wicksells tryckta skrifter 1868–1950*. Lund: Liber/Gleerup.

Larsson, Sven-Erik. (1998). *Bertil Ohlin. Ekonom och politiker*. Stockholm: Atlantis.

Marshall, T. H. (1935). "Mercantilism." *The Economic Journal*, 45(180), 716–719.

Moggridge, Donald ed. (1983). *The Collected Writings of John Maynard Keynes, Vol. XI. Economic Articles and Correspondence*. Cambridge: Cambridge University Press.

Mundell, Robert. (2002). "Keynes and Ohlin on the Transfer Problem." In Ronald Findlay, Lars Jonung and Mats Lundahl eds., *Bertil Ohlin. A Centennial Celebration (1899–1999)*. Cambridge: MIT Press.

Ohlin, Bertil. (1928a). "The Reparations Problem. I. The Economic Development in Germany since the Stabilization and the Dawes Plan." *Index*, 27, 2–13.

Ohlin, Bertil. (1928b). "The Reparations Problem. II. General Views of International Movements of Capital." *Index*, 28, 2–33.

Ohlin, Bertil. (1929). "The Reparation Problem: A Discussion." *The Economic Journal*, 39(154), 172–178.

Ohlin, Bertil. (1933). *Interregional and International Trade*. Cambridge: Harvard University Press.

Ohlin, Bertil. (1937a). "Some Notes on the Stockholm Theory of Savings and Investment I." *The Economic Journal*, 47(185), 53–69.

Ohlin, Bertil. (1937b). "Some Notes on the Stockholm Theory of Savings and Investment II." *The Economic Journal*, 47(186), 221–240.

Ohlin, Bertil. (1972). *Bertil Ohlins memoarer: Ung man blir politiker*. Stockholm: Bonniers.

Ohlin, Bertil. (1975). *Socialistisk skördetid kom bort*. Stockholm: Bonniers.

Patinkin, Don. (1979). "On the Relation between Keynesian Economics and the 'Stockholm School'." In Steinar Ström and Björn Thalberg eds., *The Theoretical Contributions of Knut Wicksell*. London: Macmillan.

Samuelson, Paul A. (1981). "Bertil Ohlin (1899–1979)." *The Scandinavian Journal of Economics*, 83(3), 355–371.

Skidelsky, Robert. (1992). *John Maynard Keynes: The Economist as Savior 1920–1937*. London: Macmillan.

Trautwein, Hans-Michael. (2019). "Bertil Ohlin." In Robert W. Dimand and Harald Hagemann eds., *The Elgar Companion to John Maynard Keynes*. Cheltenham and Northampton: Edward Elgar.

Tre tal hållna vid den middag som ett antal kolleger och lärjungar gav för Eli F. Heckscher och hans anhöriga den 13 december 1944 på restaurangen Tre Kronor i Stockholm. (1945). Stockholm.

Wicksell, Knut. (1921). "Det tyska skadeståndet." *Dagens Nyheter*, 27 August.

Wicksell, Knut. (1978). "The World War: An Economist's View." *Scandinavian Journal of Economics*, 80(2), 233–235.

5 | Revisionism as Intellectual-Political Vindication, or the French Receptions of Consequences after the Two World Wars (1919–1946)*

GUILHERME SAMPAIO

Introduction

The French translation, by Paul Franck, was published ten months ago already. But its conclusions, Keynes's suggestions, have once again become topical as numerous writers and politicians are referring and alluding to them, discussing them indirectly and directly.[1]

Among most scholars of interwar international history, there is a consensus that *Consequences* was barely read in France and received a homogeneously hostile reception (Crouzet 1972). This argument took an unsavoury turn when a renowned historian concluded that Keynes's sexual preferences largely explained his alleged pro-German commentary on reparations (Schuker 2014).[2] Then there is the chronic claim that by recklessly exaggerating the Versailles Treaty's shortcomings, *Consequences* undermined Anglo-French relations and burdened Britain and the United States with a catastrophic sense of guilt for Germany's plight (Steiner 2001, p. 22).

Most of these assumptions have deep roots in the attitude of the French Foreign Office towards Keynes and in conservative centre-right and nationalist right-wing French critiques of *Consequences*. We see this voiced from politicians like the former President of the Republic Raymond Poincaré to Jacques Bainville, the monarchist historian and

---

* This work received funding from the CY Initiative of Excellence (grant "Investissements d'Avenir" ANR-16-IDEX-0008) and was developed during my stay at CY Advanced Studies whose support is gratefully acknowledged.
[1] "Les suggestions de M. Keynes." *L'Information financière*, January 30, 1921.
[2] For a rebuttal, see: Moggridge and Skidelsky (2015).

130

author of the aptly named anti-*Consequences* tract, *Les Conséquences politiques de la paix*. A great source of their frustration with the book was the belief that Keynes had dressed his 'pro-German' ideas in the puritanical morals of liberal internationalism and the superficial, austere quantitative rigour of economics.

However, what has been forgotten in current historical discourse is that Keynes's indictment of Versailles was in tune with previous, powerful French condemnations of the Versailles Peace and of how it was negotiated. Those criticisms were not initially shared by the French political mainstream but were voiced by politically and intellectually relevant figures throughout the interwar years – rather than a few isolated cranks.

Unsurprisingly, Keynes's supporters in 1919–20 belonged to the Socialist Party or moved within the interwoven circles of left-wing pacifists and internationalists clamouring for a strong, eventually supranational LON. But they also included two of the major French academic economists of interwar years: Charles Gide and Charles Rist. The overlapping interests and even networks of these different political and academic groups explain how and why *Consequences* was published in France in June 1920. Afterwards, the increasing openness of French centre-left politicians to Franco-German rapprochement throughout the 1920s allowed for a gradual and public recognition of the prescience of Keynes's forebodings.

Accordingly, this chapter charts the ebb and flow of French support for Keynes from the interwar years to the end of the Second World War. Firstly, I will examine how *Consequences*' publishing and initial reception reflected previous French political-intellectual opposition and critiques of the Versailles Treaty. The goal is not to dissect Keynes's arguments but to understand why they proved congenial to a part of French opinion. Secondly, I will discuss how the unfolding of the reparations saga, with the crucial contribution of Poincaré's occupation of the Ruhr in 1923, prompted a more positive reassessment by the mainstream Radical-Socialist Party's centre-left faction of *Consequences*' predictions. I will stress how it was not reparations but rather Keynes's views on monetary policy and his critique of the gold standard that ultimately separated him from the majority of French opinion in interwar years.

Finally, the chapter's third section explores how WWII provoked a radical reassessment of *Consequences*' epistemological validity in the form of Étienne Mantoux's 1946 tract, *The Carthaginian Peace or the Economic Consequences of Mr. Keynes*. I argue that Mantoux's condemnation of Keynes's arguments, particularly on reparations transfers, ultimately rested on ahistorical assumptions and a de-contextualized reading of Keynes's texts. Like *Consequences* in 1919, Mantoux's moral indictment of Keynes captured (to an extent) the zeitgeist. By being likewise dressed in quantitative objectivity, it has continued to influence how historical discourse has come to approach Keynes's involvement in reparations.

1 The Prophet Meets the Mountain: *Consequences* in 1920 France

1.1 French Opinion before Consequences

From the November 1918 armistice to the months following the signing of the Versailles Treaty in June 1919, inflamed debates took place in French politics about whether the peace settlement safeguarded France's national interests. Ten of France's richest departments had been destroyed, GDP had decreased by 30 per cent and war costs amounted to 142 billion gold francs – approximately 125 per cent of the 1913 national income. After Russia, France was the largest debtor of the United States and Britain, owing $7 billion (35 billion gold francs).[3]

Against this Dantean scenario, French politicians agreed only that the Treaty did not safeguard French security and that France had an unwavering right to German reparations to reconstruct its devastated areas. They reached those conclusions, however, by making different readings of the Treaty. Republican conservatives and the monarchists of *L'Action française* (along with most Radical-Socialists, the main French centre-left party) emphasized Germany's liability for war costs and called for the occupation of the Rhineland to permanently curtail German military-economic potential.[4] Opposing the wide-spread belief that Germany held vast, easily transferable financial and economic resources were left-wing pacifists, the Confédération générale du travail (CGT, the main French trade union), and, most

---

[3] See Hautcœur (2005, p. 169–205).
[4] See Miquel (1972, p. 401–60) and Soutou (1998, p. 182–5).

importantly, the Socialist Party (SFIO): the only party that refused to ratify the Treaty. The SFIO had lost the general elections of 1919 by a wide margin, but it remained the second most voted political formation and even increased its popular vote respective to 1914. Only a reform of the electoral system that restricted proportional representativeness prevented the SFIO from taking a larger slice of Parliamentary seats.[5]

Other than these left-leaning political spheres, only a few financial journalists and economists dared denounce the dominant 'Germany will pay' rhetoric, of whom Charles Gide and Charles Rist must be singled out. Both edited France's main economics journal, *Revue d'économie politique*, and had corresponded with Keynes since before 1914. Since 1916 they warned that by paying reparations to France in convertible currency, Germany (given its small gold reserves and its depleted economy) would have to substantially increase its exports and inevitably compete against Allied industries for Allied and neutral markets alike.[6] Their warnings that France's devastated areas would (also) be reconstructed with French taxpayers' money left barely any mark in a country traumatized by war.

Judging from contemporary scholarship on French foreign policy, Keynes's depiction of a Clemenceau cold-bloodedly bent on ruining Germany is more representative of the foreign policymaking views epitomized by Raymond Poincaré and Marshal Foch, rather than of Clemenceau's government itself.[7] After all, it was Clemenceau who, against Poincaré's and Foch's wishes, exchanged France's Rhenish ambitions for the promise of an Anglo-French tripartite security alliance.[8] Yet, some of Keynes's warnings about the hawkish impulses latent in certain strands of French foreign policymaking proved eerily prescient. Namely, his warning about the negative impact on French

---

[5] Centre-right and right-wing parties had established pre-electoral alliances; the SFIO had not, leaving the Radical-Socialists isolated: see Becker and Berstein (1990, p. 192–5) and Maier (1988, p. 91–109).

[6] See Gide (1919, p. 201–8), Rist (1919), Pénin (1997, p. 187).

[7] A point also made by Clarke (2017).

[8] To preserve Allied unity, Clemenceau reneged on separating the Rhineland from Germany but gained for France the right to reoccupy it if Germany defaulted on reparations payments (an eventuality whose occurrence he confidently predicted): see Bariéty (1977, p. 61–3).

finances and European stability of a Rhineland policy seeking to disrupt German national unity, as later demonstrated by the 1923 Ruhr occupation.[9]

The key point, however, is that Keynes's depiction of French hawkishness resonated with those political sectors endorsing appeasement – the Socialists, who faulted the Treaty for imposing unenforceable terms on Germany while leaving France's war debts unsettled and the left-wing pacifists upon whom Clemenceau had launched a crackdown during the war. Before Keynes's depiction of a Wilson bamboozled by Lloyd George and Clemenceau, the French Left had already produced a starkly similar narrative. The Left had expected Wilson to bring Russia into the LON's fold and stood aghast upon the realization that the LON would not form the basis of supranational governance. Socialists and left pacifists indeed believed, wrongly as it turned out, that Clemenceau's reparations demands had antagonized Wilson and prevented the creation of a strong LON capable of enforcing conflict arbitration and regulating post-war relations by depoliticizing the discussion of reparations. Clemenceau's intransigency, they further believed, had prevented the United States from accepting a general abatement of inter-Allied debts and proposing Germany a moderate reparations settlement.[10]

Meanwhile, economists and financial journalists endorsed two key arguments of *Consequences* that they had, if in much smoother tones, publicly articulated beforehand. The first was Keynes's warning that the Treaty's commercial clauses against German trade contradicted the declared aim of making Germany pay hefty reparations. The second was Keynes's accusation that French peacemakers like the Minister for Reconstruction Louis Loucheur and the Minister of Finance Louis-Lucien Klotz were deliberately inflating France's reparations demands and concomitantly inflating estimates of French reconstruction costs. They did so, Keynes correctly argued, partly in response to budgetary requirements and partly to comply with electoral pressures for German amends before domestic tax hikes. If the figures Keynes presented in *Consequences* to criticize Loucheur and

---

[9] Compare Keynes's forebodings (1971, p. xxi) with Fischer (2003, p. 84–5, 229); and Jeannesson (1998, p. 302–33).

[10] Miquel (1972, p. 484–6, 544–5); Gombin (1970, p. 13–6); Soutou (1998, p. 185–6).

Klotz were incorrect, his intuition was indeed accurate.[11] An unnamed French peacemaker (which could well have been Loucheur) eventually admitted some years afterwards to the political commentator Alfred Fabre-Luce that 'I could not tell the truth for they would have killed me' (1926, p. 249).

1.2 *Publishing* Consequences

Whether for political or academic reasons, economists, Socialists and pacifists thus had, a priori, strong motives to sponsor a French translation of *Consequences*. Other than a few high-ranking civil servants from the French Treasury that Keynes met during inter-Allied war finance discussions, those also happened to be the groups with which Keynes had contact in France, mainly through Bloomsbury and academia. Keynes planned to publish a translation of *Consequences* from the start and hence tapped on Bloomsbury's extensive French contacts for editorial advice. These included Socialist sympathizers moving in the Parisian artistic and literary milieus that tried to arrange for the publication of *Consequences* in *L'Humanité*, the main French Socialist daily of the time. Keynes's most fruitful French connections, however, were with the economist Charles Gide and his nephew André Gide, the founder of the avant-garde *Nouvelle Revue française* (NRF). Charles Gide promptly convinced his nephew that the NRF must publish a French translation of *Consequences* and further found Keynes a translator from among his students, Paul Franck. He was an intellectually gifted nineteen-year-old hailing from a well-to-do bourgeois Jewish family and, like Charles Gide, actively involved in pacifist politics (Sampaio 2020, p. 458ff).

The translation was published in June 1920, and its literary quality and accuracy pleased both Keynes and André Gide. Compared to the English original, its differentiating feature was a foreword tackling initial French criticisms of the book. Keynes rebuffed accusations of Germanophilia and accused Britain, rather than France, of being responsible for the Treaty's reparations terms:

Let it not be supposed that I visit on France a responsibility for this disastrous treaty, which is distributed in truth between all parties to it. England,

---

[11] Sampaio (2020, p. 455–8); Markwell (2006, p. 76–82).

it may be pointed out with justice, was not slow to secure her selfish supposed interests, and it is she who must bear the main blame for the form of the reparation chapter. (Keynes 1971, p. xxi)

Despite overturning *Consequences'* original narrative, the French preface did not discourage conservatives' claims of Keynes's German bias. Overall, the book sold about 5,000 to 8,300 copies in France. These are lesser figures than those attained in Britain and the United States. Yet, when accounting for the contemporary French editorial context, *Consequences* – which notwithstanding its polemics was an economic tract – sold well: social sciences books usually sold 5,000 copies at best. Regardless, Keynes did expect higher figures and broke relations with the NRF after becoming convinced that the NRF had purposely strangled *Consequences'* circulation due to its editors' political conservatism. In 1932, Gallimard finally acknowledged that the NRF was not at the time logistically equipped to widely distribute *Consequences* (Sampaio 2020, p. 460–2). Keynes's suspicions were, however, legitimate because to review *Consequences* in its own journal, the NRF chose the diplomat-author Paul Morand, who wrote a damning review of the 'often false' book (1920, p. 909).

1.3 Reactions to Consequences

To understand the NRF's questionable commitment to *Consequences*, we need to survey its reception. Overall, French responses essentially focused on: Keynes's figures on French reconstruction estimates; Keynes's evaluation of Germany's economic potential (his discussion of the transfer mechanism, however, was generally ignored by his critics); and Keynes's quantitative examination of the Treaty's clauses on Germany's coal and steel output. Although statistically correct, that latter analysis proved overly pessimistic as Germany compensated for its territorial losses by further exploring the Ruhr basin and relying on Swedish iron ore imports.[12] Interestingly, very little criticism was directed against *Consequences'* portrait of Clemenceau: he remained a controversial figure in French politics as proved by his defeat in the January 1920 presidential election.

Economists, financial journalists and the left were the first to engage with *Consequences*. All agreed that the successive meetings on reparations that took place in 1920 and the French government's willingness

[12] Cf. Keynes (1971, p. 51–63); with Bariéty (1977, p. 155–63).

to revise the Treaty's terms confirmed Keynes's admonishment that the Treaty, as it stood, was inapplicable. Among the economists, Gide and Rist believed that Keynes had underestimated both Germany's capacity to pay and French reconstruction costs. In private, Keynes acknowledged that his figures on France's indemnity 'may be on the low side' but doubted whether 'it would be politically expedient to endeavour to secure a greater sum' from Germany.[13] But unlike Keynes's detractors, Gide and Rist agreed that although his figures were wrong, their general order of magnitude was correct (a point Keynes himself emphasized). *Consequences'* statistical shortcomings were seen as ultimately minor points that did not detract from what Gide and Rist believed was its main message: the contradiction between the Treaty's demanding reparations terms and the Allies' protectionist fears. Like Keynes, both economists emphasized the practical difficulties involved in exacting, along a lengthy period (and, it was understood, by peaceful means), substantial yearly payments from a debtor country.[14]

Within strictly political spheres, only the Socialists and fringe pacifist groups fully and openly backed Keynes. The Socialist press was the first to discuss *Consequences*. Karl Marx's nephew, Jean Longuet, gave it a warm reception and used *Consequences* to declare the Treaty unfeasible and revengeful. *Consequences* was seen as 'the documentary illustration' of the party's views on peace (1920). Meanwhile, the Anglophile Léon Blum, the Socialist parliamentary leader, favoured establishing a fixed sum of reparations if France received priority on future payments. Inter-Allied financial solidarity would enable mobilizing Germany's debt by an international loan. To support these ideas and attack the conservative parliamentary majority, Blum and his peers frequently referred to Keynes (1920). Underlining Germany's and Russia's relevance to international economic stability, the Socialist newspapers never portrayed Keynes as a Germanophile, instead praising his and Norman Angell's conceptions of economic solidarity (Sampaio 2020, p. 474).

Significantly, *Consequences* was actively discussed by its critics, starting with Clemenceau's right-hand men: former Treaty negotiators like André Tardieu and Louis Loucheur that had been harshly

---

[13] Keynes to Charles Gide (January 1, 1920). Bibliothèque La Contemporaine/ CG/FΔRéserve 938/3/13.
[14] Gide (1920); Rist (1920).

criticized by Keynes were relegated to Parliament's opposition benches after the 1919 general elections. They regularly used *Consequences* as a proxy to attack the government of Alexandre Millerand, tasked with enforcing an unenforceable Treaty. After Millerand acknowledged that Germany's debt would not pay for French reconstruction costs, Tardieu and Loucheur defended their legacy by accusing Millerand of falling prey to Keynes's gospel. During the peace negotiations, however, Loucheur had agreed on the eventual need to settle for a low reparations figure once Allied opinion would stomach it.[15]

From November 1919 to April 1924, in the form of the *Bloc national*, conservatives formed a parliamentary majority. Their views on *Consequences* represented that of most French political opinion. The nationalist centre-right and the monarchist right of *L'Action française* saw Keynes as breaking the Anglo-French alliance by defending a reparation sum accounting for Germany's capabilities rather than full French reconstruction costs and war pensions. Keynes's Germanophilia was taken for granted and his calculation of reconstruction costs was seen as ignoring French suffering.[16]

Conservatives downplayed and ignored *Consequences*' economic argumentation, proffering instead allegations of faulty statistics or opposing Germany's latent economic potential to the magnitude of French losses. Thus, they rejected settling for a fixed reparation sum before the Reparations Commission verdict (due in May 1921), fearing that it would anticipate future rebates burdening taxpayers with reconstruction. France's yearly share of indemnities should instead absorb the maximum possible of Germany's yearly balance-of-payments surpluses. Longing for territorial gains, Poincaré and his peers refused to accept that the long-term receipt of sizable reparations was irreconcilable with the aim of guaranteeing French security by breaking Germany's unity and/or strangling its economy. That aim was rejected by both the United States and Britain. The extent to which Anglo-American economic-financial power could shape French diplomacy only became evident to conservatives after Poincaré's failure to unilaterally settle the German question by occupying the Ruhr (and supporting Rhenish autonomy) in 1923. As Keynes had predicted, this fully revealed the financial frailty of post-war France.[17]

---

[15] Skidelsky (1983, p. 364); Carls (1993, p. 173–5); Markwell (2006, p. 82).
[16] Similarly, see Lévy (1920) and Bainville (2002).
[17] On the occupation of the Ruhr, see Jeannesson (1998, p. 302–33).

2 'Perhaps the First Book Where the Spirit of Geneva Appeared': *Consequences* in Interwar Years

2.1 From Versailles to Lausanne: Keynes and French Left-Wing Internationalism

Consequences ended with Keynes's call to 'the true voice of the new generations [which have] not yet spoken' (1971, p. 189). Keynes hoped that public sentiment would shift towards support for Treaty revision, as a first step onto the eventual pacification of European political-economic life. Keynes had in mind those 'new generations' attuned to appeasement, to which his nineteen-year-old translator, Paul Franck, belonged. Franck actively spread *Consequences* within leftist university groups espousing liberal internationalism (*Jeunesses socialistes*, the *Groupement universitaire pour la Société des Nations*).[18]

Two of Franck's closest acquaintances were Jean Luchaire and Jacques Kayser who, during the 1920s, were keen promoters of internationalism and from 1924 became increasingly influential in the left-wing of the Radical-Socialist party. Luchaire favourably compared Keynes to Norman Angell and endorsed *Consequences* by guaranteeing that 'the [new generation] will speak'.[19] Kayser and Franck wrote a treatise defining the ultimate goal of those young French internationalists: a borderless United States of Europe, conceived as a group of regional blocks represented at the LON and placed under its security thanks to the enforcement of universal disarmament and conflict arbitration. Kayser and Franck presciently foresaw that the LON, by allowing the establishment of common approaches to economic and monetary policy, offered a pathway for European cooperation.[20]

Franck became Keynes's political-literary agent in France but died prematurely in 1926, shortly after starting his political career in the small, centre-left Republican-Socialist Party. Luchaire and

---

[18] Luchaire (1924). It was also within those groups that France's equal responsibility in the outbreak of the Great War was questioned: see Ingram (2019).

[19] See Luchaire, Jean. "Les économistes et le Traité de paix." *Don Quichotte*, October 1, 1920. Retrieved at Keynes's papers at King's College, Cambridge: JMK/A/61/2/86. See also Sampaio (2016, p. 69, 121).

[20] Kayser, Franck, Lemercier (1926, p. 188–99).

Kayser eventually pursued starkly contrasting political trajectories. Opportunism would lead Luchaire to collaborate with the German occupier during the Second World War and, in 1946, to the execution platoon. Kayser, on the other hand, joined the Resistance. Yet their 1920s trajectories, from fringe leftist pacifism towards the mainstream Radical-Socialist party, mirrored the latter's evolution on international matters. In 1919–20, Radical-Socialists were indistinguishable from conservatives when backing hefty reparations, German disarmament and the occupation of the left bank of the Rhine. Disillusioned by the Treaty, Radical-Socialists stood nonetheless for its integral execution, prompting their leader Édouard Herriot to condemn *Consequences*.[21] Since 1919, however, the Party's left wing rejected breaking German unity and backed Franco-German rapprochement. It also quickly perceived the rhetorical usefulness of using *Consequences* to buttress critiques of the *Bloc national*, by underlining the Treaty's unenforceability and its terms' inability to alleviate French finances (Delbos 1920).

This helps explain why 1921–23 saw the Radical-Socialists increasingly endorsing Keynes, greatly thanks to the *Bloc national*'s failure to establish a definitive reparations figure. This was particularly the case after May 1921 when the Reparations Commission settled on a nominal sum (132 billion gold marks) far below the Clemenceau government's public promises. The clincher was the ousting of Aristide Briand from power in January 1922 and the coming to power of Raymond Poincaré, known in leftist parlance as 'Poincaré-la-guerre' (de Jouvenel 1922). At this stage, Keynes's newspaper articles about reparations started being used by the Radical-Socialists as a means to attack Poincaré through publication in the most popular Parisian Radical-Socialist newspaper, *L'Œuvre*. The *Manchester Guardian Commercial* supplements on European reconstruction directed by Keynes – published since the start of the Genoa Conference in April 1922 – included articles by all the leading lights of the French (non-Communist) left, particularly the Socialist and Radical-Socialist leaders Léon Blum and Édouard Herriot.[22]

After the Ruhr occupation, the 1924 Dawes Plan and the Locarno Agreements of 1925 nurtured a short-lived stabilization that allowed

[21] Herriot (1920, p. 9); and Berstein (1980, p. 87–103).
[22] "Les Collaborations de M. Keynes." *L'Ère nouvelle*, April 12, 1922.

for political–intellectual support for Franco-German rapprochement to grow. This culminated in Briand's call for a Franco-German federal union in 1929. Thanks to this context, by 1928 Keynes was publishing in the internationalist *L'Europe nouvelle*, a weekly journal that received subventions from the French foreign office and which in 1920 had stood against *Consequences* (Keynes 1929). It was also in 1929 that the renowned French literary critic Albert Thibaudet, when discussing the post-war political literature inspired by liberal internationalism and supporting the LON, wrote that *Consequences* embodied the 'spirit of Geneva':

The spirit of Geneva is the spirit of internationalism in a world of nations, States, races. [...]. Perhaps the first book in which the spirit of Geneva appeared was *Consequences*, intersected, however, with the spirit of Manchester. (1929)

In short, by the late 1920s, *Consequences'* moral-economic indictment of a Treaty that many internationalists believed had failed to account for European economic interdependence was now in tune with France's main political formation's views on foreign policy. Unsurprisingly, the path leading from Versailles to the 1932 June–July Lausanne Conference, which effectively froze German reparations payments amid the Great Depression, was interpreted by the centre-left as confirming the validity of Keynes's predictions. To pick only one example, the Radical-Socialist *L'Œuvre* went farther than Keynes by concluding a few months before the Lausanne Conference that:

First of all, we must conclude that events have proven right Norman Angell, who since before the war, and Keynes, who right after Versailles denounced the practical impossibility of massive payments from country to country. (Clerc 1932)

Similar conclusions had been advanced in previous years by centre-left journalists, political commentators holding an internationalist outlook, financial specialists and academics seeking to historicize the reparations question. Examples are the prolific writer Alfred Fabre-Luce, who wrote extensively on post-war French foreign policy and reparations (1926, p. 267–8); and the journalist Georges Lachappelle, who examined post-war French monetary policy (1928, p. 43, 50–5). Both cited and echoed *Consequences* when concluding that French peacemakers had erred in not agreeing on a realistic reparations sum and in not settling the means for Germany to discharge it immediately.[23] Like Keynes, Fabre-Luce and Lachappelle stressed the gulf separating French peace-makers' bold public statements about German capacity to pay and their behind-the-doors avowal of its limitations. Fabre-Luce boldly concluded, unlike Lachapelle, that German unwillingness to pay reparations was predictable:

> To talk of the possibility of 'goodwill' on the part of the vanquished nation towards a Treaty such as that of Versailles is to imagine an ideal world which has never existed. Or, at any rate, if the absurd expression is to be retained, it must be made clear that 'goodwill' is only likely to be shown if the considerations of self-interest, which may determine it, are present. (1926, p. 268)

2.2 *The Exceptions That Would Resurface after the Second World War*

There were, however, two major exceptions to those respectful acknowledgements of Keynes's assessment of the Treaty, which resurfaced after the Second World War. Firstly, conservatives continued throughout the interwar years to denounce Keynes as an inveterate Germanophile. To that, they added the indictment of promoting inflationary recklessness, following Keynes's systematic condemnations of French monetary policy before and after the Great Depression. To conservatives, Keynes was 'one of the most formidable snobs of the post-war period' (Géraud 1933). Political figures as diverse as the writer Jacques Bardoux (close to Poincaré and Foch) and influential conservative journalists like André Géraud (known as Pertinax, the foreign editor of *L'Écho de Paris*) and Stéphane Lauzanne (editor of the widely circulated newspaper *Le Matin*) explained the successive revision of the reparations settlements with the blunt conclusion that:

> the capacity of payment depends on the will to pay. Once that will disappears, the capacity of payment becomes open to doubt and easily revisable. (Géraud 1929)[24]

The second exception to liberal internationalists' endorsement of Keynes consisted, partly, of academic economists, particularly at the time of the 1930 Young Plan negotiations and within the 1928–29

---

[23] See also Imbert (1935).
[24] See also: "La France et la trêve douanière." *Journal des débats*, March 9, 1930; and Bardoux (1921, p. 177ff).

Keynes–Bertil Ohlin debate on the transfer question. It is beyond the remit of this article to examine the repercussions of that debate in France. Yet it must be stressed that it represented the first time French economists – namely the Treasury civil servant Jacques Rueff and the Sorbonne professor Albert Aftalion – raised a serious theoretical challenge to Keynes's analysis of the transfer mechanism. Beforehand, economists like Charles Gide (1921) and Charles Rist (1922) had supported Keynes. When dissonant voices appeared, like Bertrand Nogaro (1922, p. 47–79) and Jean Lescure (1922, p. 5–6, 30, 38–63), they limited themselves to advance optimistic estimates of Germany's economic potential. Their theoretical analyses of the difficulties involved in transferring large sums in inconvertible currency across countries were like Keynes's.

Unlike their peers, Rueff and Aftalion bluntly concluded that the transfer problem was either inexistent or seriously overblown. Rueff argued that by simply raising a reparation levy, whose proceedings would be transferred to the Allies, Germany would both depress internal consumption and depreciate the mark in the foreign exchange market. A balance-of-payments adjustment would, in turn, occur as German goods would become cheaper and more attractive to the Allies. Rueff's case rested on his admittedly free-market belief that 'economic phenomena were best left to themselves' (Rueff 1929, p. 399).

Similarly to Ohlin, Aftalion emphasized how transfers could be triggered by comparative changes in national income. Refuting the neoclassic assumption that gold flows necessarily entailed automatic balance-of-payments equilibrium, Aftalion noted how the United States' large gold reserves did not match its internal price level. His narrative described how Germany was borrowing more than it needed to pay for reparations and using that income surplus to stimulate its domestic economy. If those loans were halted, Germany would then increase taxes and transfer the proceedings to the Allies. German income would decrease, leaving some output unpurchased and forcing industries to redirect their production towards exports. Arguably because of intellectual prudence rather than lack of understanding, Aftalion refrained from positing (like Ohlin) that increased Allied income would be necessarily spent on German goods.[25]

---

[25] Aftalion, Albert. "Le Problème des transferts. I." *L'Information financière*, January 4, 1929; and "Le Problème des transferts: II." *L'Information financière*, January 5, 1929.

Regardless, if Keynes erred in theoretically conceiving the transfer problem only in terms of supply (how the terms of trade were determined by productive factors and internal prices), Rueff and Aftalion erred in not realizing how their arguments presumed enough Allied demand elasticity for German goods in the short term. Both failed to consider predating Allied reluctance at opening its markets to German goods and the growing menace of a declining international trade environment (Rueff 1929, p. 398). By 1929, heavier protectionist clouds were on the horizon, as Ohlin himself recognized in his exchanges with Keynes:

If the policy of protection and of preference to homemade goods, which has been growing so much after the war, is intensified when German exports begin to grow and is used consistently to prevent such exports, then the reparation payments may become virtually impossible. There can be little doubt that if Great Britain turns to protection and other countries are thereby led to raise their tariffs, the chances of substantial reparation payments are considerably reduced. (1929, p. 177)

3 Second World War or the Historiographical Consequences of Étienne Mantoux

After the *Tract on Monetary Reform* (1923), Keynes's intellectual focus switched from reparations to monetary-economic theory and policy. In France, his name became associated during 1924–26 with the defence of monetary stabilization at a parity lower than that of 1914; and from 1928 onwards, with the defence of a managed currency and his unrelenting critique of France's deflationary gold standard policy. During the Great Depression, Keynes's reflationary proposals were widely rejected given societal fears of inflation and backing of the gold standard: tenets likewise shared by the French left. This started to change in 1936 after the Popular Front's coming to power and the publication of *The General Theory of Employment, Interest and Money*. Until then, support for Keynes's economics was restricted to a few isolated journalists like Georges Boris, the future right-hand of the Radical-Socialist politician Pierre Mendès-France. Afterwards, the outbreak of the Second World War saw French political commentators and economists discussing not whether *Consequences* had been proven wrong but, rather, whether *How to Pay for the War*'s anti-inflationary war finance proposals could be applied in France (Sampaio 2016, p. 293–427).

Inevitably, the humiliation of the 1940 defeat and Germany's ensuing milking of the French economy prompted several Frenchmen to read *Consequences* and Keynes's subsequent writings on German reparations in a very different light. Compare, for instance, how Keynes was framed by the CGT official newspaper *Le Peuple* in 1929 and in 1946, the year of his death:

M. Keynes was charitably treated [in 1920] like an agent of the Boches and a vulgar Socialist. I ignore whether he was pro-German, but while rereading his writings on reparations, I realise that his predictions were not off the mark.[26]

Men reputed for their perspicacity erred in their appraisals of Germany after 1919. Was it not Keynes who wrote that 'in the near-future France would not have anything to fear from Germany'? [Regarding Germany] Keynes committed errors of appreciation of considerable dimension and magnitude.[27]

Old projects for seizing the left bank of the Rhine were thus dusted off the shelves after the Liberation, to address the Franco-German economic imbalance and fuel French reconstruction and industrial modernization. Such was the aim of none other than Pierre Mendès France, Minister of the National Economy in the first post-Liberation provisional government. Mendès France was the first and perhaps the only French politician to have read the *General Theory* and genuinely admired Keynes, thanks to Georges Boris' urging.[28]

Discussions of German reparations once again became topical. This was particularly so after the posthumous publishing in 1946 of Étienne Mantoux's *The Carthaginian Peace or the Economic Consequences of Mr. Keynes*, a few months after Keynes had died of a heart attack. A former pupil of Charles Rist and an admirer of Lionel Robbins and Friedrich von Hayek, Mantoux was also one of the first Frenchmen to have read the *General Theory* – his PhD thesis used Hayek's concept of forced saving to attack Keynes's book (Mantoux 1941, p. 31–68 and 129–40; Sampaio 2016, p. 386–89). Mantoux fled from France thanks to the Rockefeller Foundation and, before returning to join Free France's army in 1944, wrote *The Carthaginian Peace* at Princeton's Institute for Advanced

---

[26] Fontanier, Henry. "Autour des réparations." *Le Peuple*, May 9, 1929.
[27] "Lu pour vous: L'éternel problème allemand." *Le Peuple*, January 19, 1946.
[28] See Wolff (1988, p. 59) and Bossuat (2000, p. 50).

Studies (Duclert 2010, p. 167–83). Patricia Clavin has shown how the League of Nations' Economic Section, exiled in Princeton during the war, provided Mantoux with both statistical data and (via the Canadian economist Jacob Viner) with networking to the US Treasury led by Henry Morgenthau Jr. The parallels between Mantoux's and the US Treasury's argumentation that Germany possessed the economic capability to pay reparations are striking. Both concluded that after the Great War the missing ingredient had been enough Allied political coercion to enforce the Versailles Treaty.[29]

Mantoux's book attempted to mobilize Allied opinion towards imposing upon Germany the 'rightful' reparations burden it had escaped two decades before. To back his case, Mantoux juxtaposed *Consequences'* statistical apparatus and economic predictions to the League of Nations' figures and two decades of historical hindsight. As *L'Action française*'s Jacques Bainville before him, Mantoux claimed that *Consequences'* wrongly emphasized economics over politics – that Keynes had underestimated German economic might and accordingly grossly exaggerated the impact of Versailles' economic clauses. In practice dusting-off conservatives' accusations, Mantoux claimed that *Consequences'* success helped foment a guilt complex in Britain and the United States that blinded Western democracies to Hitler's menace (1952, p. 6–19). Mantoux's argumentation ignored that several of Keynes's conclusions about the unfeasibility of the Treaty had been formulated beforehand by Frenchmen and members of the Allied delegations to Versailles (Skidelsky 1983, p. 364).

There were certainly valid aspects to Mantoux's critique of Keynes, like the blunders it uncovered on Keynes's estimates of how much reparations would impact German national income or Keynes's often roundabout estimates of French reconstruction costs – originally calculated, however, when precious little reliable data was available.[30] Yet, what should have been the strongest part of Mantoux's book, whether reparations could have been transferred, remains its weakest. Mantoux reproduced Rueff's thesis that the transfer question had never existed in the first place. Imposing a reparations tax on German

[29] Clavin (2013, p. 261–2, 321–4); Clavin (2005, p. 515–30).
[30] Keynes believed the reparations burden of the 1921 May Schedule of Payments would amount to 25 per cent of German national income when it probably amounted to 5–10 per cent. Cf. Mantoux (1952, p. 114–7); with Moggridge (1992, p. 372); and Sampaio (2020, p. 456–8).

citizens would have sufficed to depress German prices and wages, shifting domestic resources towards augmenting export capacity. Like Rueff, Mantoux took no account of time lags, labour friction or the scale of Allied demand elasticity for German exports at a time of rampant protectionist feelings and political instability. Mantoux even crudely argued that the productivity of the German war economy and its ability to extract resources from occupied countries disproved Keynes's emphasis on the difficulties of transferring hefty reparations. Keynes, however, had always framed relations between Allied creditors and debtor Germany against the background of the liberal democratic framework recognized by the Versailles Treaty, rather than on an illiberal context where resources were transferred by murderous, rapacious armies.[31]

If in the 1920s *Consequences'* painting of moral rhetoric onto an economic-statistical canvas proved gradually in tune with political support for Franco-German rapprochement, reactions to Mantoux's book both in France and in the United States showed how much *The Carthaginian Peace* was in the mood of the times. Economists, journalists and political scientists lauded Mantoux for exposing with scientific honesty the 'constant intermingling of economic reasoning and of eloquent ethical pleading which mar the brilliant writings of Keynes'.[32]

Nonetheless, most conceded that Mantoux had not recognized how the Treaty paradoxically imposed upon Germany strict reparations terms while allowing the Allies to raise tariffs against its exports. Raymond Aron, who prefaced the French translation, was sceptical of Mantoux's confidence about how smoothly Germany could adapt its productive structure to pay reparations, and concurrently, on whether Allied economies would willingly accept increased German competition (Aron 2002).[33] Meanwhile, Charles Rist partly endorsed Mantoux by claiming that Keynes had always been blind to Germany's penchant for military aggression (1983, p. 20). Rist, however, had enough recall of his earlier views to argue that *Consequences* was mainly a legitimate reaction against the false promises made by

---

[31] Cf. Mantoux (1952, p. 61, 117–32); with Skidelsky (1983, p. 397–400); and Moggridge (1992, p. 340–6).

[32] Rappard (1946, p. 984). See also Scelle (1940–8).

[33] See also Viner (1947).

politicians regarding Germany's capacity to pay reparations and the Treaty's contradictory terms. By stressing the 'insanity' of Allied reparations claims in 1919, Rist tacitly reiterated the validity of *Consequences*' driving argument (1947).

Ultimately, Mantoux's book failed in its short-term objective. Against the onset of the Cold War and with Europe ravished by financial weakness and economic disruption, the United States finally acted as a forward-looking hegemon. Morgenthau's project to pastoralize Germany was dropped and France had to accept resuming political-economic relations with Germany not from a position of force but of equality. However, despite its analytical shortcomings, Mantoux's book triumphed at a historiographical level, being frequently cited in historical surveys of the Versailles Peace as sound evidence that Keynes's writings on reparations were utterly misguided.[34]

Indeed, following the opening of the French diplomatic archives in 1972, *The Carthaginian Peace* was retrieved by historians of international relations who, in seeking to write a more nuanced narrative of French foreign policymaking, have inversely caricatured Keynes. By focusing on a narrow part of French political life and ignoring centre-left and left positions on the Versailles Peace, that historiography has helped to consolidate the myth of Keynes's Germanophilia.[35] Chances are that the allure of Mantoux's critique of Keynes to international historians was boosted by the backlash Keynesian economics suffered after the 1970s stagflation. Keynes's certainty that economic policy is bounded by political and social constraints made him an easy target at a time when it became popular to believe that, if left to themselves, markets would optimally allocate resources domestically and internationally, allowing for smooth balance-of-payments adjustments to external shocks. This belief aligned nicely with Rueff and Mantoux's liberal conclusion that no transfer problem existed. Hence, the allegedly swift adjustment of the global economy to the OPEC oil shock during the 1970s was at the time understood by historians critical of Keynes as discrediting his position about the difficulty of enacting large transfers (Schuker 1983, p. 757–8).

---

[34] See, for instance: Tooze (2015, p. 295).

[35] Two examples being: Gomes (2010, p. 233–4); and Marks (2009). A contrasting perspective akin to this chapter's is: Markwell (2006, p. 113–115).

In an ironic twist of fate, in 2000 Gallimard published a joint edition of Jacques Bainville's *Les Conséquences politiques de la paix* and *Consequences*. Tellingly, the critical apparatus to *Consequences* was largely based on Mantoux's book. Bainville and Mantoux were thus assumed to unequivocally represent France's response to *Consequences*. The fact that there had never been a single French stance on the Versailles Peace and hence on Keynes's book had, by then, long faded from historical memory.

Concluding Remarks

No evidence exists to suggest Keynes was an avowed Francophobe, as attested by his continuous efforts to make his writings known in France and his dealings with French economists and translators, painters and art gallerists. It is fallacious to assume that Keynes should be held accountable for seeding discord between the Allies and France when *Consequences*' axiomatic arguments against the Treaty had already been advanced by Frenchmen beforehand. In turn, although *Consequences* was widely discussed in France, there was never a homogeneous French response to it because policymakers and political opinion were divided about the Treaty's merits, which explains economists' and the left's support of *Consequences* and conservatives' overt rejection of it. Hence, Jacob Viner's remark that interwar economists refrained from publicly pinpointing flaws in Keynes's arguments for political reasons is misleading – at least regarding France. Those French economists – Gide and Rist – that supported *Consequences* did so for their own political or intellectual reasons; others like Rueff and Aftalion never refrained from criticizing Keynes.

Finally, although very different works, both *Consequences* and Mantoux's *The Carthaginian Peace* can be said to share an intricate mingling of moral-ethical judgment with statistical and economic analysis. Both works are not value-free narratives and need, therefore, to be historically tackled as the works of engaged scholars, rather than neutral works of scholarship. Yet, drawing greatly from Mantoux, current historical analyses of the Treaty overstress German unwillingness to pay when, amongst the Allies, there was never political unanimity to make Germany pay reparations by force – before or after the publishing of *Consequences*. Perhaps more realistically, Keynes's French supporters were instead convinced that Allied political unwillingness to accept German goods was an equally important factor in blocking reparations. As Fabre-Luce surmised, the notion of 'German unwillingness to pay' is, indeed, fallacious. Debtors can be expected to try escaping their obligations and need to be offered an incentive to pay, especially when they are not the individual agents of microeconomics but rather politically fragile liberal democracies of considerable demographic and economic weight. Regardless of its shortcomings, this was a realistic message that *Consequences* successfully conveyed and that is why, 100 years after its publication, it still deserves to be revisited by historians.

References

Aron, Raymond. "Préface." In Étienne Mantoux, ed., *La Paix calomnié ou les conséquences économiques de M. Keynes*. Paris: L'Harmattan, 2002: 7–12.

Bainville, Jacques. *Les Conséquences politiques de la paix*. In David Todd, ed., *Les Conséquences politiques de la paix*. Paris: Gallimard, 2002.

Bardoux, Jacques. *De Paris à Spa*. Paris: Félix Alcan, 1921.

Bariéty, Jacques. *Les Relations franco-allemandes après la Première Guerre mondiale*. Paris: Éditions Pedone, 1977.

Becker, Jean-Jacques and Serge Berstein. *Victoire et frustrations (1914–1929)*. Paris: Seuil, 1990.

Berstein, Serge. *Histoire du Parti Radical: La recherche de l'âge d'or, 1919–1926*. Paris: Fondation nationale des sciences politiques, 1980.

Blum, Léon. "L'Ardoise nette." *L'Humanité*, June 24, 1920.

Bossuat, Gérard. "Le Plan Marshall dans la modernisation en France." In Serge Berstein and Pierre Milza, eds., *L'Année 1947*. Paris: Presses de Sciences Po, 2000: 45–73.

Carls, Stephen D. *Louis Loucheur and the Shaping of Modern France, 1916–1931*. Baton Rouge, London: Louisiana State University Press, 1993.

Clarke, Peter. *The Locomotive of War: Money, Empire, Power and Guilt*. London: Bloomsbury, 2017.

Clavin, Patricia. "Reparations in the Long Run." *Diplomacy & Statecraft* 16 (3, 2005): 515–30.

Clavin, Patricia. *Securing the World Economy: The Reinvention of the League of Nations, 1920–1946*. Oxford University Press, 2013.

Clerc, Henri. "Réparations et dettes." *L'Œuvre*, April 12, 1932.

Crouzet, François. "Réactions françaises devant les Conséquences économiques de la paix de Keynes." *Revue d'histoire moderne et contemporaine* 19 (1, 1972): 6–26.

de Jouvenel, Robert. "De Cannes à Boulogne." *L'Œuvre*, February 27, 1922.

Delbos, Yvon. "Notre programme." *L'Ère nouvelle*, December 27, 1920.

Duclert, Vincent. *L'Avenir de l'histoire*. Paris: Armand Colin, 2010.

Fabre-Luce, Alfred. *The Limitations of Victory*. New York: Alfred A. Knopf, 1926.

Fischer, Conan. *The Ruhr Crisis*. Oxford: Oxford University Press, 2003.

Géraud, André (Pertinax). "La Conférence de Londres." *L'Écho de Paris*, June 22, 1933.

Géraud, André (Pertinax). "M. J.M Keynes et le plan Young." *L'Écho de Paris*, June 21, 1929.

Gide, Charles. "L'Indemnité de guerre." *La Paix par le droit* 5–6 (1919).

Gide, Charles. "Le Livre de M. Keynes et les réparations à attendre de l'Allemagne." *Cahiers des droits de l'homme* 13 (1920): 14–6.

Gide, Charles. "Les Idées de M. Keynes." *Le Progrès civique*, March 11, 1921.

Gombin, Richard. *Les Socialistes et la guerre*. Paris: Mouton, 1970.

Gomes, Leonard. *German Reparations, 1919–1932*. Basingstoke: Palgrave Macmillan, 2010.

Hautcœur, Pierre-Cyrille. "Was the Great War a Watershed?" In Stephen Broadberry and Mark Harrison, eds., *The Economics of World War I*. Cambridge: Cambridge University Press, 2005: 169–205.

Herriot, Édouard. "Une Réponse à M. Keynes." *L'Exportateur français*, October 7, 1920.

Imbert, Louis. *Le Règlement des réparations, 1919–1935*. PhD Thesis. Université de Marseille, 1935.

Ingram, Norman. *The War Guilt Problem and the Ligue des droits de l'homme, 1914–1944*. Cambridge: Cambridge University Press, 2019.

Jeannesson, Stanislas. *Poincaré, la France et la Ruhr (1922–1924)*. Strasbourg: Presses Universitaires de Strasbourg, 1998.

Kayser, Jacques, Paul Franck, Camille Lemercier. *Les États-Unis d'Europe*. Paris: Éditions du Monde Moderne, 1926.

Keynes, John Maynard. *The Economic Consequences of the Peace*. Vol. 1 of Donald Moggridge and Elizabeth Johnson, eds. *The Collected Writings of John Maynard Keynes*. Cambridge: Cambridge University Press, 1971.

Keynes, John Maynard. "Y-a-t-il assez d'or dans le monde?" *L'Europe nouvelle*, January 19, 1929: 78–80.

Lachapelle, Georges. *Les Batailles du franc*. Paris: Librairie Félix Alcan, 1928.

Lescure, Jean. *Le Problème des réparations*. Paris: Librairie Plon, 1922.

Lévy, Raphaël-Georges. *La Juste paix ou la vérité sur le traité de Versailles*. Paris: Librairie Plon, 1920.

Longuet, Jean. "La Trahison des grands 'patriotes'." *Le Populaire*, June 11, 1920.

Luchaire, Jean [Jean Florence]. "Quelques jeunes qui sont de vieux militants." *L'Ère nouvelle*, October 28, 1924.

Maier, Charles S. *Recasting Bourgeois Europe: Stabilization in France, Germany, and Italy in the Decade After World War I*. Princeton: Princeton University Press, 1988.

Mantoux, Étienne. *The Carthaginian Peace or 'The Economic Consequences' of Mr. Keynes*. Pittsburgh: University of Pittsburgh Press, 1952.

Mantoux, Étienne. *L'Épargne forcée monétaire*. Lyon: Riou Imprimeurs-Éditeurs, 1941.

Marks, Sally. "Le conseguenze politiche di Maynard Keynes." *Contemporanea* 12 (1, 2009): 190–6.

Markwell, Donald. *John Maynard and International Relations: Economic Paths to War and Peace*. Oxford: Oxford University Press, 2006.

Miquel, Pierre. *La Paix de Versailles et l'opinion publique française*. Paris: Flammarion, 1972.

Moggridge, D. E. *Maynard Keynes: An Economist's Biography*. London and New York: Routledge, 1992.

Moggridge, D. E. and Robert Skidelsky. "Comment: Critique of Schuker, 'J. M. Keynes and the Personal Politics of Reparations'." *Diplomacy and Statecraft* 26 (4, 2015): 736–44.

Morand, Paul. "Les Conséquences économiques de la paix." *La Nouvelle Revue française* 81 (1920): 905–9.

Nogaro, Bertrand. *Réparations, dettes interalliées, restauration monétaire*. Paris: Presses Universitaires de France, 1922.

Ohlin, Bertil. "The Reparation Problem: A Discussion." *The Economic Journal* 39 (154, 1929), 172–82.

Pénin, Marc. *Charles Gide, 1847–1932: L'esprit critique*. Paris: L'Harmattan, 1997.

Poincaré, Raymond. "Chronique de la quinzaine." *Revue des deux-mondes* 56 (1920): 469–80.

Rappard, William. "Book Reviews and Notices." *The American Political Science Review* 40 (5, 1946): 983–5.

Rist, Charles Rist. "Comptes-rendus critiques." *Revue d'économie politique* 35 (4, 1922): 516–17.

Rist, Charles. "Indemnité de guerre et commerce international." *L'Action nationale* 7 (1919): 26–37.

Rist, Charles. "Keynes (J.-M.), The Economic Consequences of the Peace." *Revue d'économie politique* 34 (1, 1920): 93–4.

Rist, Charles. "Notes et mémoranda – I, La Paix calomnié." *Revue d'économie politique* 57 (1, 1947): 132–6.

Rist, Charles. *Une Saison Gâtée. Journal de la guerre et de l'occupation (1939–1945)*. Paris: Fayard, 1983.

Rueff, Jacques. "Mr. Keynes's Views on the Transfer Problem. I. A Criticism by M. Jacques Rueff." *The Economic Journal*, 39 (155, 1929): 388–408.

Sampaio, Guilherme. "'This Is No Longer a Book, It Is a Political Event': The French Reception of John Maynard Keynes's Economic Consequences of the Peace (1919–1920)." *French Historical Studies* 43 (3, 2020): 451–82.

Sampaio, Guilherme. "The Translation, Diffusion, and Reception of John Maynard Keynes's Writings in France (1920s–50s)." PhD Thesis, European University Institute, 2016.

Scelle, Georges. "Mantoux (Étienne)." *L'Année sociologique* 2 (1940–8): 619–22.

Schuker, Stephen A. "J. M. Keynes and the Personal Politics of Reparations, Part I." *Diplomacy and Statecraft* 25 (3, 2014): 453–71.

Schuker, Stephen A. "Review of Trachtenberg, 'Reparation in World Politics'." *The Journal of Economic History* 43 (3, 1983): 757–8.

Skidelsky, Robert. *Hopes Betrayed, 1893–1920. Vol. 1 of John Maynard Keynes: A Biography*. London: Macmillan, 1983.

Soutou, Georges-Henri. "The French Peacemakers and Their Home Front." In Manfred F. Boemeke, Gerald D. Feldman and Elisabeth Glaser, eds., *The Treaty of Versailles: A Reassessment after Seventy-Five Years*. Cambridge: Cambridge University Press, 1998.

Steiner, Zara. "The Treaty of Versailles Revisited." In Michael Dockrill and John Fisher, eds., *The Paris Peace Conference, 1919: Peace without Victory?* Basingstoke: Palgrave Macmillan, 2001.

Thibaudet, Albert. "L'Esprit de Genève." *Les Nouvelles littéraires*, July 6, 1929.

Tooze, Adam. *The Deluge: The Great War and the Remaking of the Global Order, 1916–1931*. London: Penguin Books, 2015.

Viner, Jacob. "Reviews of Books" *The Journal of Modern History*, 19 (1, 1947): 69–70.

Wolff, Jacques. "Pierre Mendès France et J. M. Keynes: un premier repérage." In Michel Margairaz, ed., *Pierre Mendès France et l'économie*. Paris: Odile Jacob, 1988: 57–72.

6 Between Cambridge, Paris, and Amsterdam

HAROLD JAMES AND ANDREW KOGER

They sat. They stood about.
They were estranged. The air,
As water curdles from clear.
Fleshed the silence. They sat.

They were appalled. The bells
In hollowed Europe spilt
To the gods of coin and salt.
The sea creaked with worked vessels.

Geoffrey Hill, "The Apostles: Versailles 1919"
(*For the Unfallen: Poems, 1952–1958*, 1959)

The Paris Peace Conference failed fundamentally in its objective of creating a durable and just world order. The Conference's overly ambitious goals, and the flawed personalities of those pursuing them, were so obvious as to invite Keynes's lethal rebuke in a work that made his public reputation and also critically created a new model or template for the economist as polemicist.

Keynes's critique of the Paris process and its participants was devastating, and he knew it. In October and November of 1919, he attended meetings, hosted by the Dutch banker Gerard Vissering, in Amsterdam, where bankers from the United States. and various neutral powers developed a sophisticated plan for leveraging private US finance for the sustainable reconstruction of Europe. The plan showed great promise, and had many elements in common with the plans eventually adopted at the London Conference of 1924 (in the Dawes Plan). But Keynes could not associate himself with it, because his brilliant polemic had alienated the political leaders who were needed to carry it out.

This chapter depicts the different logics of policymaking in the face of enormous economic challenges: one, associated with Paris, is sophisticated multilateral diplomatic negotiation (which Keynes viewed as "sophistry and Jesuitical exegesis"); another, associated

154

with Cambridge, is clever writing as well as clear analysis; and finally, as a third and alternative approach, the vision from the neutral financial centre Amsterdam, where market-oriented people tried to devise a solution using financial products/financial engineering. Each of these logics worked – and continues to work – in a quite different way, and the interaction of the three can occasionally be productive, but may often be destructive and stymy effective and resolute action. The logics of 1919 have their counterpart in the aftermath of the 2008 financial crisis and in confronting the continuing European debt crisis.

1 Paris

The Paris Peace Conference produced the Treaty of Versailles, along with equivalent treaties of Saint-Germain, Neuilly, and Trianon. Versailles and the Paris treaties in general have come to represent (in the popular mind) the most striking example of a pointlessly vindictive peace settlement. Keynes in his polemic against the treaty used an ancient analogy when he called this a "Carthaginian peace" (victorious Rome had destroyed the city of Carthage and strewn salt over the fields to make them infertile for generations). The German nationalist campaign against the "Diktat von Versailles," and against the German politicians who signed it, was a major part of the increasingly violent language that overthrew democracy. The memory of Trianon is still vivid in Hungary, and drives Hungarian nationalism, revisionism, and the current government of Viktor Orbán. The final Paris treaty, Sèvres (August 1920), immediately provoked a violent nationalistic response of Mustafa Kemal Atatürk, who pushed for the signatories to be stripped of Turkish citizenship, and then launched a war against Greece. The whole Paris peace process is often interpreted as a reminder of how good intentions about international cooperation and the promotion of democracy turn out badly. President Woodrow Wilson's experiment in destroying autocracies as a way to establish a lasting peace looks like an initial failure of high-mindedness, of the interventionist consensus that dominated US foreign policy thinking for the past century. At a moment when both international cooperation and democracy are again under unbearable strain, it is worth asking why ideals fail so spectacularly – the question that drove Keynes's psychological examination of the mind of Woodrow Wilson.

The problem of Wilsonianism and how to respond to it is at the heart of the argument, and a key to Keynes's disgust at the process of the peace settlement. Did he "edge around the question of America's part in the disaster" (Tooze 2014, 296–297)? He clearly realized at an early stage that Wilson was not likely to proceed with a general economic accommodation with the UK that seemed to Keynes as a necessary preliminary for a viable treaty. But was there another way?

Most recent historians have a milder view of the peace, and rightly point out that the real problem was the legacy of the war that was so painful and costly that any settlement would be a disillusion and produce insoluble conflict. Historians of the reparations settlement, notably Sally Marks (1978; 1998), Mark Trachtenberg (1980), and Stephen Schuker (1988), have argued that Germany never really paid that much in reparation, and that therefore the settlement could not have been so burdensome after all, and the weight or burden fell mostly on the reparations creditors. The most obvious answer to explain the Paris failure is that expectations were too high, and were thus bound to be disappointed. That was true of the reparations debate, where the French aspirations were always destined to remain dreams as there was no economic possibility that *le boche paiera tout*. But the tale of necessarily unrealized frustrated hopes also holds true more generally in the case of the imposition of democracy and self-determination, which was at the heart of the Wilsonian project. Democracy does not necessarily lead to the fulfilment of liberal democratic wishes, particularly when the wishes of each people are cast politically in the language of national hatred and economically in terms of inflicting the cost of four and a half years of total military mobilization, and the legacy burdens of pensions for cripples and widows onto outsiders – onto other countries.

The Paris peace treaties in 1919 had not specified an amount that Germany should pay: the gap between what the Allies (and in particular France) hoped and what Germany might realistically be expected to pay was simply too wide. It was only in 1921 that a figure was set; but the reparations schedule had to be revised after the German hyperinflation, a fiscal and monetary collapse in the early 1920s. Under the 1924 Dawes Plan, reparations payments would rise as the German economy recovered. In addition, "prosperity clauses" linked specific indicators – such as the number of automobiles sold in Germany – to higher payments: a sort of early anticipation of the idea of GDP bonds. After 1924, Germany borrowed extensively. Some members of the German establishment, notably the central bank president, Hjalmar Schacht, saw the borrowing as a way of forcing a new and much lower reparations settlement, in that as the loans (mostly from the United States) built up, they would constitute a rival claim on Germany to the political payments of reparation, largely for Belgian and French reconstruction. At the same time, the need to present a united and moderate front in order to negotiate a better reparations deal kept Germany's divergent parties together. In 1924, even the anti-republican German National People's Party (DNVP) was required to support legislation that implemented a reformed reparations plan, the Dawes Plan. In 1929–30, a Grand Coalition government (including right-wing liberals and left-wing social democrats) stayed together in order to pass through the parliament laws for a new approach to reparations, the Young Plan; and almost immediately the reparations plan was passed the last fully democratic government of the Weimar Republic collapsed, and was replaced by a minority government dependent on the use of emergency powers under the constitution.

As long as there was a prospect of a favourable and supportive revision of the reparations settlement, the framework tied Germany into the international system, and obliged hard-line nationalists to adopt a realistic course. But the mechanism that German government chose to make revision more likely – the building up of private foreign claims that rivalled reparations – made for a substantial vulnerability to financial panic in the Great Depression. Arguments against TINA politics ("There Is No Alternative") helped a populist insurgency in response to the economic crisis, which proved fatal once the encompassing restrictive framework was taken away.

To realize how important the international circumstance of the reparations framework was for the establishment of Hitler's government, it is enough to conduct a simple thought experiment. Before 1930, Germany was held down by treaty obligations, and there were foreign troops on German soil (in the Rhineland). If a radical and threatening German populist had seized power before the evacuation of the Rhineland, French troops would have reacted to any attempt at military self-assertion or rearmament, and they could have dealt easily with any challenge to their authority. Even after 1930, the treaty limitations (in particular reparations) remained. Had a populist dictator come to power at any point before the Lausanne conference of

July 1932, he would have had a choice about whether to continue to pay reparations or not. If he had paid, he would have looked foolish and discredited to supporters who believed that German national reassertion involved casting off the fetters of the Versailles Treaty. But had he not paid, French troops would have had the justification for marching on Berlin. In a deep historical irony, the harsh treaty – with a possibility of revision – was thus in fact the improbable bracket that held together Germany's experiment in democracy. That, however, was not a case that it would be easy or attractive to make for either Allied politicians or policy thinkers.

It was exactly the "insecurity" of the "language and substance of the whole Treaty" (Keynes 1919, 47) that made for the possibility of revision, and hence of keeping Germany on a necessarily collaborative path as it sought that revision. A part of the logic was to show the economic benefits of cooperation, and that was the course that Keynes tried to make at the centre of his vision of how Europe might be reconstructed.

2 Cambridge

Keynes was profoundly disgusted by the Peace Conference and its politics. He resigned from the British delegation and returned to London and Cambridge. He needed to swap the "fog and filthy air" of Paris for the ethical climate of Bloomsbury and G.E. Moore's Cambridge. Virginia Woolf wrote in her diary on July 8, 1919, after Keynes had resigned from the Treasury and the text of the Versailles Treaty had been published, that Keynes was suffering from a disillusionment "forced on him by the dismal and degrading spectacle of the Peace Conference, where men played shamelessly, not for Europe, or even England, but for their own return to Parliament at the next election" (Skidelsky 1986, 376). At the end of May, Keynes had written to Duncan Grant, his former romantic partner and fellow Bloomsburyite, "I've been as miserable for the last two or three weeks as a fellow could be. The Peace is outrageous and impossible and can bring nothing but misfortune" (Skidelsky 1986, 370–371). In a few weeks, Keynes formulated his response on paper – a product of deep conviction.

Keynes saw the challenge as a structural and economic one, but the problem as psychological and personal. One of the most compelling sections of the ensuing book came with the pen portraits of the allied leaders. In particular Keynes conceived his work as a tragedy (he quotes Shakespeare's *Macbeth*), a tragedy of one man: "What a place the President held in the hearts and hopes of the world when he sailed to us in the *George Washington!*" (Keynes 1919, 34). And then the disillusion, that followed from a character flaw (the Presbyterian personality) of the President: "What had happened to the President? What weakness or what misfortune had led to so extraordinary, so unlooked-for a betrayal?" (Keynes 1919, 35). Keynes's interpretation, centred on the ideas and ideals of Wilson and their betrayal, was an outgrowth of his long-standing conviction, best articulated in the concluding passages of the *General Theory* that ideas, rather than interests, direct the course of the world.

Keynes's book became a bestseller. The first printing of 20,000 quickly sold out, and a new run of 30,000 was quickly produced. It remained almost constantly in print to the present. Austin Harrison, in *The English Review*, hailed it as "absolutely authoritative," and then popularized the message in *The Sunday Pictorial* as "Reverse the Treaty – Or Crash" (Harrison 1920, 79–90; Vogeler 2008, 234). By contrast, the devastating review in the London *Times* began with a snide comment about cleverness: "Mr. Keynes has written an extremely 'clever' book on the Peace Conference and its economic consequences. It is the work of an erudite university don who was attached as adviser to the British Treasury during the war." It ended with questioning Keynes's patriotism: "special tenderness towards Germany" and concluded that the book was "vitiated by a persistent pro-German bias" that meant that its recommendations were "seriously impaired" (Times 1920).

American academic critics were mostly sceptical. Frank Taussig was sympathetic to much of the critique, but complained about the utopianism of the vision and specifically about the pen portraits. "In regard to international loans, Mr. Keynes's proposals again are utopian. He puts forth a plan which he believes to have been feasible in 1919, and which he still favors now that the smoke of the treaty struggle has cleared away" (Taussig 1920, 385–386). Another American reviewer, Clive Day, a Yale economist and economic historian, who had served as chief of the Balkan Division of the American Commission to Negotiate Peace part of the Paris process, complained that the first chapters were "altogether theatric," "like a drawing by Gustave Dore, with its exaggerations, its heavy shadows, its implication of something horrible in the background" (Day 1920, 300).

The historical verdict on Keynes's work is patchy, and not unambiguously supportive. Kindleberger (1973, 39) thought that the *Economic*

Consequences "may have been distorting in many ways," and especially "self-confirming in its contention that if the Germans heard a reasonable argument to the effect that they could not pay, they would not," and above all "devastatingly encouraging to American isolationists." Robert Skidelsky's magisterial biography (Skidelsky 1983, 400), on the other hand, concludes that "Above all, he was absolutely right to insist that no political structure for keeping the peace would stand up if its economic foundations were rotten".

One crucial point divided Keynes from his intelligent critics (the stupid and nationalistic ones are obviously a different case). Keynes took the treaties seriously, and the harsh rhetoric of Lloyd George and Clemenceau about punishment at face value. Some of his critics, on the other hand (rightly), assumed that anything political was a subject of future negotiation, and that the critical issue was what kind of framework was to be set up for that negotiation. Taussig concluded that "No sensible man at Paris believed that the provisions could be carried out in detail to the bitter end" (Taussig 1920, 386).

The *Economic Consequences* is a less fundamental work of economic theory than the 1936 *General Theory*, and that is reflected in citations over the late twentieth century (see Figure 6.1). But strikingly in the aftermath of the 2008 financial crisis, both works seemed more relevant, and were heavily referenced (see Figure 6.2). Keynes's biographer, Robert Skidelsky (2010), now wrote of the "The Return of the Master." Above all in the European debt crisis, in its most critical years, 2012 and 2015, extraordinarily there were more press references to the *Economic Consequences* than to the 1936 work. There

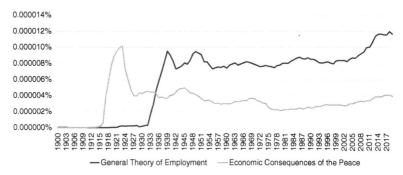

Figure 6.1 Google N-Gram book citations 1900–2008
Note: Figure created by authors using Google Books Ngram Viewer, accessed June 2021.

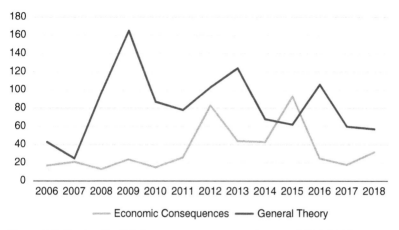

Figure 6.2 Factiva English language newspaper references 2006–2018
Note: Figure created by authors using Factiva, accessed June 2021.

was an obvious similarity to what became now a widely shared argument: that an economic nonsense could never make political sense, and was doomed to fail.

3 Amsterdam

The most concrete policy recommendation of the *Economic Consequences* was the launching of an international loan for reconstruction. Keynes thought of £200 m. That suggestion was one which could be realistic, but it needed more than a book to put it into practice. The underlying thought was to mobilize interests rather than ideas for the task of reconstruction.

Frustrated by the harsh peace terms and the dithering of politicians while the situation in Central Europe moved towards economic collapse, a secret meeting of leading financiers was held at Dr Gerard Vissering's house in Amsterdam on Monday, October 13, 1919. Along with Vissering, the chairman of the Dutch central bank, there gathered Fred Kent, Paul Warburg, Raphael Georges Levy from Paris, and three Dutch financiers, J. van Vollenhoven, P. J. C. Tetrode, G. H. M. Delprat, C.E. ter Meulen, as well as Swiss, Swedish, and Norwegian figures – and John Maynard Keynes.[1] Vissering was experienced in

---

[1] "Minutes from the Monday Oct 13, 1919 meeting in Amsterdam," Paul Moritz Warburg Papers, Sterling Memorial Library, Yale University, Group No. 535, Series No. 11, Box 7, Folder 93.

international financial mediation with American bankers dating back
to 1911 when, as director of the central bank of the Dutch East Indies
in Java, he had acted as an independent advisor to the Chinese during their loan negotiations with European and American bankers (De
Vries 1989). Kent was a leading international trade financier from
Bankers' Trust in New York, closely associated with J.P. Morgan, and
Warburg was a German-born banker transplanted to the United States
who had been one of the principal architects of the Federal Reserve
System, and had an older brother Max, who had been the chief financial adviser to the Kaiser.

Paul Warburg began the meeting by complaining that the future of
Europe was hostage in the hands of the politicians of the Reparations
Committee. He suggested as an alternative that "the bankers of
Europe ought to come together and judge the present situation like
doctors over a case" (Péteri 1992, 236). At the end of the meeting,
the group decided to write a memorandum setting out their views in
order to persuade the governments of some sense, and to meet again
in November (2–3). The document they drafted laid out the basic
principles of their business perspective for post-war settlements and
reconstruction:

> The signatories submit that, while much can be done through normal bank-
> ing channels, the working capital needed is too large in amount and is
> required too quickly for such channels to be adequate. They are of opinion
> therefore that a more comprehensive scheme is necessary. It is not a ques-
> tion of affording aid only to a single country, or even a single group of coun-
> tries which were allied in the war. The interests of the whole of Europe and
> indeed of the whole world are at stake.... The outlook at present is dark. No
> greater task is before us now, than to devise means by which some measure
> of hopefulness will reenter the minds of the masses. The reestablishment of
> a willingness to work and to save, of incentives to the highest individual
> effort and of opportunities for everyone to enjoy a reasonable share of the
> fruit of his exertions must be the aim towards which the best minds in all
> countries should cooperate. Only if we recognize that the time has now
> come when all countries must help one another, can we hope to bring about
> an atmosphere, in which we can look forward to the restoration of normal
> conditions and to the end of our present evils.

One might sum up the document as a call to the people to return to pre-
war standards of reason, an appeal to the Reparation Commission for wise
moderation as to the best business policy for all concerned; an appeal to
Governments to arrest inflation and meet inevitable burdens by increasing

their revenue rather than by further increasing their debts; an appeal to the people to work and to save; and finally, an appeal to leaders of commerce and finance to get together in order to study the problem dispassionately and take it up as a business proposition relying on independent action rather than Government intervention. Governments must be relied upon, however, to remove as rapidly as possible the obstacles that impeded such a course.

The group hoped that by submitting the report to the League of Nations and organizing a meeting of financial minds from around the world, it would be possible to sort out the mess of post-war settlements and reset the European economy on a prosperous path. They emphasized the fundamental truths of the government debt crisis where "A decrease of excessive consumption and an increase of production and taxation are recognized as the most hopeful – if not the only, – remedies."

One particular issue was at the heart of the deliberations at Amsterdam and the attempt to formulate an alternative strategy to the one adopted at Versailles. Germany – and indeed central Europe more generally – would require substantial external financing in order to make the transition from a depleted wartime economy to peacetime. But that financing could scarcely be handled by pre-war, conventional private market measures. One of the most influential backers of the Vissering memorandum was James Alexander, President of the National Bank of Commerce in New York. Already in August 1918, he had written an article in the *Banker's Magazine*: "The situation is that Europe must have from the United States immense quantities of materials to rebuild and refit for a normally productive economic life. Europe's international banking situation is such that she cannot pay as she goes. Neither is her present productivity such as to enable her to pay for what she buys with what she produces" (Alexander 1919, 196). Therefore in order to acquire goods from American firms, European purchasers needed to borrow funds from America's supply of capital, which was the world's only source of liquidity at the time. Alexander emphasized the importance of Europe as a market for surplus American production. "Our industries are committed," he wrote

to an output greater in many respects than our own domestic trade alone will consume. Unless Europe is enabled to purchase the surpluses, we will be left with them on our hands, and we will have the picture on one hand of Europe suffering physically for need of them, and, on the other, of American industries incurring great losses simply because they were unable to get their goods to market. (Alexander 1919, 196).

For instance, American pig farmers had produced a surplus of 400 million pounds of pork beyond what was needed for domestic consumption. French, Italian, and Belgian demand covered 60 per cent of the excess production, but the cancellation of Britain's order meant 140 million pounds of pork that might be stranded in American slaughterhouses. "If there should be no remedy to this situation," wrote Hoover to President Wilson, "we shall have a debacle in the American markets, and with the advances of several hundred million dollars now outstanding from the banks to the pork products industry.... The surplus is so large that there can be no absorption of it in the United States, and, being perishable, it will go to waste" (Fisk 1924, 238).

On December 24, 1919, Congress passed the Edge Act, which enabled the formation of investment trusts to be organized in the United States that could raise funds by selling equity shares to domestic investors in order to provide long-term loans to European importers of American exports. However, no Edge corporation funded a significant amount of trade. The economist Clyde Phelps summarized the reasons for its failure in 1927: "The risks presented by the uncertain political and economic situation abroad, the doubtfulness of the advisability of extending more credits when American banks and manufacturers were loaded with foreign accounts which were proving hard or impossible to collect, and the pressure for credit at home were obstacles to the success of the corporations" (Phelps 1927, 122).

As the Edge Act looked unpromising, Alexander also tried to prepare an innovative way of handling the capital inflows that were required for European reconstruction since the heavy debt burdens and instability of Europe made the prospect of lending to European nations and businesses extremely risky. In order to both reduce the risk of default and widen the scope of lending across European risk classes, Alexander advocated that all the credit needs of Europe should be pooled together, securitized, and sold to American investors. In other words, rather than having a different credit arrangement with each individual borrower in Europe, American investors would buy the rights to one share in the cash flow stream from the interest and principal payments of all European borrowers. Additionally, the debt needed to be strongly backed by high-value collateral in order to both provide the lender an asset in case of default and reduce the incentive for the borrower to default in the first place since it would sacrifice the collateral. Alexander wrote that "The individual European buyer [of American goods] must be prepared to give a general mortgage upon his entire assets. His loan should be further endorsed by a consortium of banks in his own country, reinforced, where possible, by government guarantees" (Alexander 1919, 198).

While Alexander's proposal for a securitized lending structure was quite novel, it was not entirely unprecedented as this form of securitization had been pioneered previously in the farm mortgage market in the Midwest in the 1870s–90s. As far back as 1890, approximately 10 per cent of mortgage debt was structured with *covered mortgage bonds* – meaning the underlying mortgages were bundled and held in trust with debentures backed by the overall mixed cash flows from all of the bundled mortgages (Frederiksen 1894; Brewer 1976; Snowden 2010). One of the main innovators of this financial innovation was Austin Corbin of the Corbin Banking Company in New England, but there were a number of firms active in this business until the 1893 crash shut down investor appetite for these securities (Levy 2012, 159).

However, even with innovative financial engineering, the lack of a clear outcome to the reparations and inter-Allied debt issues created massive uncertainty for the investment community. Even if European securities were backed by legitimately valuable European assets it was not clear that the average American investor would feel comfortable "going along" Europe after the continent had just fought a terrible civil war and newspapers continued to report strife across the Atlantic. In order to accumulate the level of capital needed in Europe the savings of everyday Americans across the country had to be tapped. In this case, the average American investor was the average American farmer, small-time businessman, or working professional. Because of the breadth of investors needed on the American side of the deal, European collateral, no matter how strong in theory, was fairly impracticable. Collateral is meant to be seized by a lender if a borrower defaults, such that the lender's capital can be at least partially recovered. In this way lenders are more likely to offer their capital in the first place since there is less risk of complete loss. There is an inefficiency or an obstacle to the flow of capital if the lender is comfortable and experienced in the business of lending capital and receiving a stream of monetary payments in return, but inexperienced and unfit to operate whatever collateral assets he acquires in a default. This inefficiency would be very pronounced in the case of a massive lending operation of an accumulation of thousands of Americans' savings to a wide variety of European countries and businesses. Some German politicians and business leaders were thinking of a direct involvement of foreign investors, in part also as a way of fending off socialization demands by the radical left (James 2016). If there were to be a default, Americans would not have the expertise or interest to operate a German steel mill, a French municipality, or an Austrian import-export business. Even for the major financial institutions that would organize the European security offering in America, unwinding collateral assets if a default occurred would be an incredibly messy business.

There was then a second innovative element to the scheme: it would require some commitment on the part of the creditor governments in order to convince sceptical markets. Accordingly, Kent tried to obtain a response from the US Treasury. At the same time, Keynes had misgivings about the ultimate chances for success, and suggested going forward with or without official American support. In his November 18 letter to the Dutch banker Meulen, Keynes wrote: "If the American administration takes up an unsympathetic attitude, we must nevertheless bring the issue to the bar of the public opinion of the world. And if America quite deliberately decides that she is going to leave Europe to her misfortunes, she must say so openly and in so many words" (Keynes 1978, 142). Given Keynes's time spent dealing with the Americans during the Versailles Peace Conference in the spring of 1919, he felt he had "a long experience of this practice of theirs of blowing hot and cold," and therefore thought "if we wait until the Americans actually press us to go forward, we shall wait forever" (Keynes 1978, 144). In the event, the US Treasury wrote back to Kent that no more taxpayer money should be lent to Europe. On November 26, Norman Davis, the Treasury financial adviser who represented the United States in London and Paris, wrote to Warburg that "I cannot but think it illadvised [*sic*] for American bankers – and most especially you and Kent who have so recently been in Government service – to sign any circular with international bankers advocating a plan which is not in accord with the views of those American officials who have charge of questions dealt with in the proposed circular". In addition, "While the proposed circular may state that the signers are acting purely on their own initiative, it will be most difficult to make the rest of the world think that our Government had not at least indirectly approved it."[2]

In response to this setback, the Amsterdam Group decided to have each member focus on collecting support from their respective country's prominent politicians and financiers and presenting the memorandum to each national government instead of the whole group jointly presenting to the League of Nations. Warburg believed that the memorandum itself might prohibit the League of Nations' representatives from supporting certain reform ideas laid out in the memorandum if they were too closely associated with the memorandum as a whole. If the group could individually convince each national representative that a constructive post-war policy was his own good idea, it had a better chance of coming to fruition than if the idea seemed to be presented to the diplomats from the outside.

After debating the likelihood of US support for inter-Allied debt forgiveness at the October meeting, the group decided to include a paragraph in the memorandum in favour of reducing the debts owed to the United States and Britain, the two net creditors on the Allied side. Offering a compromise between Keynes's call in October for full cancellation and Kent and Warburg's concern that American sentiment would block such a move, the memorandum proposed that the debt burden should be reduced either by cancelling a portion of the debt principal or by abandoning interest charges on the debt. "In view of the fact that a portion of these loans reacted to the benefit of the loaning countries in waging what was a common cause," then, the report goes on somewhat tentatively, "a scaling down of such loans in proper proportion might be justifiable and could be written off as a legitimate war expense by the lending-countries."[3]

On January 16, copies of the memoranda were sent to the major neutral and Allied governments except in France, where not enough signatures had yet been secured. Keynes was not optimistic about the chances of gaining governmental support, writing to Vissering on January 31, "I have no great hopes of any adequate results." "It is evident," Keynes continued, "that the Americans are determined to

---

[2] "Norman Davis to Warburg, November, 26 1919," *Warburg Papers*, Box 5, Folder 59.
[3] "Report to the Council of the League of Nations," *Kent Papers*, Box 35, Folder 1.

do nothing, and this, combined with the very unsatisfactory situation in France, makes it look a very burdensome task for any other country to enter on a course of action [to help reconstruct the European economy]." And in one of Keynes's many prophetic statements, he concluded that "All this makes it increasingly probable that things will have to get worse before they can get better" (Keynes 1978, 150).

The Amsterdam proposal gained widespread support in the international business community and among neutral European governments. Included in the list of American signees were the heads of all the major financial institutions in the country: Frank Vanderlip, Chairman of the Banking Committee for the New York Chamber of Commerce and former President of the National City Bank of New York; James A. Stillman, Vanderlip's successor as President of the National City Bank of New York; A. Barton Hepburn, Chairman of Chase National Bank; Charles Sabin, President of Guaranty Trust Co.; James Forgan, President of Kent's old employer, the First National Bank in Chicago; A.W. Mellon, President of the Mellon National Bank in Pittsburgh; and Jacob Schiff, a senior partner at Kuhn Loeb & Co. There were also signatures from a couple railroad industrialists, such as Samuel Rea, President of the Pennsylvania Railroad Company, and Louis Hill, Chairman of the Great Northern Railroad Company. Perhaps tellingly, most of the politicians who signed the document did not actively hold political positions when they signed, which may have given them greater freedom to take a stand against government policies. William Howard Taft, former President of the United States; Elihu Root, former Senator and former Secretary of State; and Myron Herrick, the former Ambassador to France, all signed the memorandum.

There was also considerable support from Britain, the Netherlands, Norway, Sweden, and Switzerland, with a noticeably small collection of signatures from France. Notable in the list of British signees was Sir Richard Vassar-Smith, Chairman of Lloyds' Bank; Reginald McKenna, former Chancellor of the Exchequer and Chairman of the London Joint City and Midland Bank; Robert Brand, Partner at Lazard Bros. & Co.; Lord Robert Cecil, former Chairman of the Supreme Economic Council of the Allies and a former Assistant Secretary of State for Foreign Affairs; and H.H. Asquith, Prime Minister of Britain from 1908 to 1916 (Warburg 1930, vol. 2, 659–665). These names represent the foremost experts in international financial matters anywhere in the world. Their support demonstrated both the importance of the Amsterdam document in particular and the robust degree to which the international financial community believed in the essential need for a reconstructive post-war agreement.

Despite the Amsterdam Group's intentions to keep their initiative outside of the political arena, as they believed that it was their business experience that accounted for the strength of their memorandum, they were rather quickly sucked into the political whirlpool. In early November, Kent began to worry about the political optics of having Warburg sign the memorandum because of Paul's relationship with his brother Max, who was a leading financier in Germany. While Paul and his brother had cut off communications during the war and, despite a strong affection for one another, were both loyal to their respective countries, Kent worried about how the public might view a proposal to support German reconstruction led by a German-American with close family ties to power circles in Germany. As Kent explained in a letter to Warburg, "the fact that your brother had such a principal part in Germany, and that you have just returned from visiting him, as has been largely advertised, might lead those who do not know you to feel that the memorandum was undertaken solely on German account."[4]

Kent also succumbed to the logic of his own political situation. In addition to his background as a banker, he had travelled to Europe in part on behalf of the US government. He felt that he had to ask the US Treasury for an official opinion regarding the Amsterdam Group's plans before the memorandum could be publicized.[5] Given the isolationist political climate in the United States, Kent was adamant that presenting a public proposal for further American involvement might create more harm than good. Aware of the sustained emotional impact of the war's violence, Kent wrote to Warburg that

There is a large portion of the public whose hurts during the war have been so severe that for a time they are going to be resentful of anything seemingly done for Germany's account. If their opposition is stirred up to too high a pitch, it is going to retard reconstruction in Europe, whereas working quietly where one can be effective, and letting opposition gradually die down, is going to accomplish more good.[6]

---

[4] "Kent to Warburg, 10 November 1919," *Kent Papers*, Box 6, Folder 4.
[5] "Kent to Vissering, 18 November 1919," *Kent Papers*, Box 6 Folder 4.
[6] "Kent to Warburg, 10 November 1919," *Kent Papers*, Box 6, Folder 4.

Indeed, the US Treasury wrote to Kent that they did not want to lend any more taxpayer money to Europe.[7]

Keynes quickly found himself in a similar political predicament, in the aftermath of the December 12, 1919 publication of *The Economic Consequences of the Peace*. Keynes wrote to Lord Robert Cecil, a leading British representative to the League of Nations, for advice as to whether Keynes should sign his group's memorandum. Cecil was particularly concerned about the reaction in Washington to Keynes's book. "I admit I am a little afraid of the result [of *The Economic Consequences of the Peace*]," Cecil wrote to Keynes,

> on the mind of President Wilson and his entourage. He is a vain man and the picture you draw of him in the book is not likely to minister to his vanity. He is said to be very "rancunier." As you point out we must appeal to American generosity and if we had the administration against us obviously we should fail.

Because Keynes had already made his position more than clear in his book, Cecil felt it was not necessary to also sign the memorandum, especially since it might preclude the support of important British and American officials. However, Cecil, who principally supported plans for a constructive European policy, wrote, "I fully admit that there is something very incongruous in your not being openly connected with the first step in carrying out your policy."

In a January 6, 1920, letter to Keynes, Cecil reiterated his position, writing, "we are out on an almost forlorn hope for a very big result and must not throw away any chances." Keynes's signature "might antagonize powerful influences" (Keynes 1978, 148). Cecil continued to worry about Wilson and his government as the main obstacles. President Wilson's "entourage have always been personal adherents," wrote Cecil, "and it is beyond human nature to expect that they will read your brilliant sketch of him with pleasure – Its very moderation makes it the more stinging. Most people would rather be thought villains than dupes" (Keynes 1978, 148–149). So Keynes had to rule himself out from what was unambiguously the most promising solution to the dilemma of managing reconstruction, and of bringing in the New World to rescue the Old.

---

[7] "Norman Davis to Warburg, November, 26 1919," *Warburg Papers*, Box 5, Folder 59.

4 The Dawes Plan and a Financial Solution

As the German government financed its deficits with the printing press, the price level in Germany increased from thirty-five times the pre-war level in December 1921, to 1,475 times the pre-war level a year later, and at the peak of the inflation in the second half of 1923, domestic prices rose to an astronomical 1,382,000,000,000 times the pre-war level (November 27); prices of imported goods rose even more rapidly, as the Mark depreciated rapidly on the foreign exchanges (Bresciani-Turroni 1937, 36). It was not until the beginning of January 1924 that an American-led international conference, which would quickly become known as the Dawes Commission, was arranged to negotiate a working plan for German economic reconstruction. Finally, after four years of unprecedented financial and economic crisis in Germany and Central Europe, that could clearly only be resolved through help from the outside, the American government was willing to put their weight behind the reconstruction effort. The key was a private sector reconstruction loan of the type envisaged in the 1919 Amsterdam meeting. Secretary of State Charles Evan Hughes wrote back to the J.P. Morgan partners that without a loan there would be "chaotic conditions abroad," and "a feeling of deep despair." Hughes reported that the State Department hoped that J.P. Morgan & Co. and the financial community would "see their way clear to undertake the participation which the world expects and that is essential to the success of the Dawes Plan" (Rosenberg 2003, 169). It was, according to Morrow, "as good as we can expect," from the American government (Costigliola 1976, 70). While still only offering a cagey and half-hearted show of support, it was enough for the Morgan partners, who had had a generally strong working relationship with the government for decades, to read between the lines and feel that the loan, and its repayment, would be backed by the US government (Wiebe 1959). That sentiment, backed by a powerful financial house, convinced markets. The Morgan partners also demanded, and received, official letters from the Allied governments requesting that the firm arrange a loan to Germany. The Morgan loan operations were the key to bringing France into line, an operation that Stephen Schuker (1976) interpreted as "The End of French Predominance in Europe."

While the members of the Amsterdam Group had deliberately tried to keep their actions outside of the political maelstrom they saw around them, in the end they could not escape. Each of the leading figures eventually ran into inescapable political concerns and constraints. Kent and Keynes in the end could not even sign their own memorandum because of political stumbling blocks. For Germany, too, the issue was fundamentally political: there was the need to find a framework that constrained policy in order to limit the wild political fantasies of unreconstructed nationalists. The experience demonstrates the limits of technocracy. In an international crisis environment, debates over policies that will impact entire populations inevitably include politics, and cannot be handled by technocrats on their own. Experts ridiculing politics is as foolish and as counterproductive as politicians ridiculing experts.

The lesson from the 1919 episode is also about the limits of trenchant polemic: about how an overwritten public critique may be counterproductive. Setting political leaders on the right course of action requires persuasion, not polemic. Hence, when the time came to remake the world in 1944–45, Keynes adopted a very different approach. There had in the meantime been repeated failures of multilateralism. There was no new polemic, but a realization of how effective policy could be made. After the Second World War, while Keynes was critical of large parts of the decisions being made at the international financial conference at Bretton Woods (the predication of trade opening and the restoration of convertibility that followed from the Atlantic Charter and seemed to unilaterally advantage the United States; the politicization of the International Monetary Fund through abandoning the principle of automaticity in terms of access to credit support), he chose not to write another public diatribe against the proceedings analogous to the *Economic Consequences* of 1919. In 1933, Keynes had commented on the abortive London World Economic Conference that a powwow of sixty-six nations could never be expected to agree. A workable plan could only be realized at the insistence of "a single power or like-minded group of powers" (Skidelsky 1992, 482). That was how the vision of a new world order was realized after the Second World War. Keynes in the Second World War elaborated a complex reconstruction plan over an extended period of negotiation with the US Treasury, but this time he operated behind the scenes, and he kept his disdainful comments about his American counterparts mostly to private letters. In *The Economic Consequences*, Keynes (1919, 268) had written,

But if America recalls for a moment what Europe has meant to her and still means to her, what Europe, the mother of art and knowledge, in spite of everything, still is and still will be, will she not reject these counsels of indifference and isolation, and interest herself in what may be decisive issues for the progress and civilisation of all mankind?

In 1944 that moment had arrived.

5 The Euro Crisis

The clash of 1919 was about creditors and debtors, with creditors apparently demanding the impossible, and debtors radicalized politically in consequence. It is tempting to see almost exact parallels in the European debt crisis, with Germany (and perhaps France) taking on the role of the inflexible creditor powers, with substantial differences in their negotiating positions, analogous to those that separated France and Great Britain in 1919. Southern or peripheral Europe now took the place of the debtor with a politically imposed burden. The Euro crisis can be treated as a clash of interests between creditors and debtors, but it was also a clash of ideas about collective action problems might be resolved.

But by the twenty-first century, the balance of the logics analysed in this chapter for the 1919 Peace Conference had shifted. All the components of what we have called Paris, Amsterdam, and Cambridge now looked rather different. Politicians in the major countries in the early twenty-first century were less rhetorically connected with popular sentiment, less capable of inspiring, and perhaps less gifted, but also more experienced in international diplomacy and international compromises, than Clemenceau or Lloyd George. The international framework – embedded in the institutions of the European Union and the Euro – was much more robust, and substantially limited the chances for populist politicians. It is striking that the most conspicuous success of a populist party in the Eurozone, the Syriza victory of 2015, within six months turned Syriza into a much more conventional centre-left party; while a populist party outside the Eurozone, Nigel Farage's UKIP, prompted the British government into a promise of a referendum on EU membership, the aftermath of which led to a spectacular disintegration of the UK's political system.

Financiers were for the most part very short-sighted in their vision, and many felt more drawn to the lucrative prospects of shorting

European government debt than to long-term reconstruction visions (though there may be a parallel to the Amsterdam meeting in the attempt in 2012 and afterwards by George Soros to put together a vision of how to rescue Europe). The most ingenious technical solutions – for synthetic Europeanized bonds (ESBIes) or for bonds with different levels of multilateral guarantee (the red and blue bonds proposals) – went nowhere.

But there were among economists many would-be Keynes figures dispensing policy advice. And they wanted to be as flamboyant as possible: after all no one remembers Clive Day's arguments about 1919, but everyone knows Keynes. The problem lies now, as then, in the mix of economic argumentation and non-economic emotional or rhetorical presentation (what Keynes's critics thought of as unnecessary polemic). In the Euro crisis, the multilateral approach was highly complex, with the involvement of many governments and institutions, and often lent itself to destructive games of chicken. Might there be a way in which financial common sense might prevail – in the creation for instance of new European financial instruments? As in 1919, it was plausible to think that a better financial engineering could provide the solution, yet much of the commentary around the Euro crisis has been consistently distracted by personal attacks that poisoned the atmosphere for cooperative discussion, analysis, and negotiation necessary to achieve a workable solution.

In the Euro crisis, it also looked attractive to many economically sophisticated commentators to imitate the famous pen portraits of the 1919 book and to ridicule the leading political figures who were failing to deal with the problems. German surpluses were a source of the structural problems and imbalances of the Eurozone, but they were often explained in a particular and peculiar way. Economics was now psychologized, with more drama and more vulgarity and less style than in Keynes's refined writing of 1919. Angela Merkel could easily be portrayed as economically naïve. Her occasional reference to the virtues of the prudent Swabian housewife offered clear evidence of her ignorance of the paradox of thrift (Blyth 2013, 115). Many commentators thought they could spice up their commentary by attempting a psychological explanation – along the lines offered in the *Economic Consequences*. Joseph Stiglitz complained about Merkel's "deficit fetishism" (Stiglitz 2016). Paul Krugman (2013) thought about the phenomenon of sado-monetarism as applied by the Bundesbank (as well as by American monetary hawks). Journalists and second-rate academics went further – much, much further. Thus the *Guardian*'s Larry Elliott (2012): "The language of S&M is also now part of the eurozone discourse. [...] There's plenty of raw material here, given a tweak or two, for a modern version of Leopold von Sacher-Masoch' *Venus in Furs.*" Detailed biographies of the officials of the IMF and the other members of the troika tried to explain their activity in terms of social or religious roots ("Calvinist" became a frequent term of abuse). The dilemma such arguments posed is a simple repetition of that of 1919. They read like fun, but it is difficult to see the psychologizing polemic as the most effective way of convincing the people whose decisions mattered – Woodrow Wilson or Angela Merkel – to take an all-encompassing view of a solution that transcends national interest and builds and reinforces a common good.

That is a pity, because there is a clear case to be made in terms of the economic logic of how surplus and deficit positions are two sides of the same coin, and how adjustment by the surplus countries is an essential element to the solution of a fundamental problem. Underpinning the German or North European position in the Euro debt crisis, on the other hand, was the belief that resolving debt problems is the sole responsibility of the debtor. Keynes, by contrast, held that both creditors and debtors should share the task of getting economies out of holes they had jointly dug (Miller and Skidelsky 2012).

The economist and political scientist Mancur Olson (1965) identified what he termed a logic of collective action, in which powerful sectoral groups frustrate attempts to find an overall collective solution that corresponds to a general or overarching interest. His analysis offers a helpful way to understand Europe's contemporary stasis. Obviously the complex political construction of a mechanism for integrating and coordinating the positions of twenty-eight national governments lends itself to blockage by particular interests. In modern Europe, there is really at least as yet no clear way of articulating and politically representing the general interest of Europeans. There are immediate financial reasons why a crisis makes people look more at the national political framework. Managing the aftermath of major financial crises, as opposed to trying to prevent them developing, always involves the mobilization of substantial fiscal resources. That task inevitably at present remains in the hands of national governments, since the EU has only a very small fiscal capacity of its own.

So inevitably, when it comes to demands for state action, people focus on the national states, and these are the wrong framework for dealing with many of today's problems.

There is in other words a need for a mechanism for seeing the big picture: for zooming out from the obsession with the national and onto the aggregate, to Europe considered as a whole. But how can Europeans get this larger picture, and how can they stop seeing the world primarily in terms of national interest, national advantage, and national egotism? How can the overall framework be seen in a way that is not just fundamentally a constraint or restraint? It may be that aggregating problems, rather than making them more intricate and less easy to solve, allows the negotiation of a grand bargain. Big crises – and even more the concatenation of big crises (the Euro debt crisis, Crimea, energy problems, migration from civil wars and failed states, Brexit, Trump) – prompt a rethinking, that may give birth to big or encompassing solutions. As long as there is a deep commitment to keeping the institutional framework, alternatives are simply too complex to be realized without great cost, at least in the national framework. The Europe of the future might think of common goods – in security policy, in handling the practical and political causes and consequences of migration, in energy policy – as a way of establishing a general overarching interest. Specifying how those schemes might work is surely better and more productively done without individualizing polemic.

References

Alexander, J. (1919). *Meeting the Credit Needs of Europe*. Banker's Magazine, August 1919.

Blyth, M. (2013). *Austerity: The History of a Dangerous Idea*. Oxford University Press.

Bresciani-Turroni, C. (1937). *The Economics of Inflation: A Study of Currency Depreciation in Post-War Germany*. Allen and Unwin.

Brewer, H.P. (1976). Eastern Money and Western Mortgages in the 1870s, *The Business History Review*, 50/3, 356–380.

Costigliola, F. (1976). The United States and the Reconstruction of Germany in the 1920s, *The Business History Review*, 50/4, 477–502.

Day, C. (1920). Keynes'sEconomic Consequences of the Peace, *The American Economic Review*, 10/2, 299–312.

De Vries, J. (1989). Vissering, Gerard (1865–1937), in, Biografisch Woordenboek van Nederland. www.historici.nl/Onderzoek/Projecten/BWN/lemmata/bwn3/vissering

Elliott, L. (2012). Angela Merkel Has the Whip Hand in an Orgy of Austerity, *The Guardian*, January 12, 2012, www.theguardian.com/business/economics-blog/2012/jan/08/eurozone-crisis-angela-merkel-whip-hand

Fisk, H. (1924). *The Inter-Ally Debts: An Analysis of War and Post-war Public Finance, 1914–1923.* Bankers Trust Company.

Frederiksen, D.M. (1894). Mortgage Banking in America, *Journal of Political Economy*, 2/2, 203–234.

Harrison, A. (1920). The Work of Old Men, *The English Review*, 30 (January 1920), 79–90.

James, H. (2016). Das Reichswirtschaftsministerium und die Aussenwirtschaftspolitik: "Wir deutschen Pleitokraten, wir sitzen und beraten." In Carl-Ludwig Holtfrerich ed., *Das Reichswirtschaftsministerium der Weimarer Republik und Seine Vorläufer*, De Gruyter, 517–578.

Keynes, J.M. (1919). *The Economic Consequences of the Peace.* Macmillan.

Keynes, J.M. (1978). The Collected Writings of John Maynard Keynes. In Elizabeth Johnson, Donald Moggridge eds., *Activities 1920–1922: Treaty Revision and Reconstruction*, vol. 17. Royal Economic Society.

Kindleberger, C.P. (1973). *The World in Depression 1929–1939.* Allen Lane.

Krugman, P. (2013). The Intellectual Contradictions of Sado-Monetarism, *The New York Times* blog April 8, 2012.

Levy, J. (2012). *Freaks of Fortune: The Emerging World of Capitalism and Risk in America.* Harvard University Press.

Marks, S. (1978). The Myths of Reparations. *Central European History*, 11/3, 231–255.

Marks, S. (1998). Smoke and Mirrors. In Smoke-Filled Rooms and the Galerie des Glaces. In M. Boemeke. G. Feldman and E. Glaser eds., *The Treaty of Versailles: A Reassessment After 75 Years.* Cambridge University Press, 337–370.

Miller, M. and Skidelsky, R. (2012). How Keynes Would Solve the Eurozone Crisis, *The Financial Times*, 16 May 2012.

Olson, M. (1965). *The Logic of Collective Action; Public Goods and the Theory of Groups.* Harvard University Press.

Péteri, G. (1992). Central Bank Diplomacy: Montagu Norman and Central Europe' Monetary Reconstruction after World War I, *Contemporary European History*, 1/3, 233–258.

Phelps, C. (1927). *The Foreign Expansion of American Banks: American Branch Banking Abroad.* The Ronald Press Company.

Rosenberg, E.S. (2003). *Financial Missionaries to the World: The Politics and Culture of Dollar Diplomacy, 1900–1930*. Harvard University Press.

Schuker, S.A. (1976). *The End of French Predominance in Europe: The Financial Crisis of 1924 and the Adoption of the Dawes Plan*. The University of North Carolina Press.

Schuker, S.A. (1988). *American "Reparations" to Germany, 1919–33: Implications for the Third-World Debt Crisis*. International Finance Section, Department of Economics, Princeton University.

Skidelsky, R. (1983). *John Maynard Keynes Volume One: Hopes Betrayed 1883–1920*. Macmillan.

Skidelsky, R. (1992). *John Maynard Keynes Volume Two: The Economist as Saviour 1920–1937*. Macmillan.

Skidelsky, R. (2010). *Keynes: The Return of the Master*. Penguin.

Snowden, K.A. (2010). Covered Farm Mortgage Bonds in the Late Nineteenth Century U.S. NBER Working Paper No. 16242.

Stiglitz, J.E. (2016). *The Euro: How a Common Currency Threatens the Future of Europe*. Norton.

Taussig, F.W. (1920). The Economic Consequences of the Peace by John Maynard Keynes, *The Quarterly Journal of Economics*, 34/2, 381–387.

Times (1920). A Critic of the Peace. January 5, 1920, 42299, 17.

Tooze, J.A. (2014). *The Deluge: The Great War, America and the Remaking of the Global Order*. Viking Penguin.

Trachtenberg, M. (1980). *Reparation and World Politics: France and European Economic Diplomacy, 1916–1923*. Columbia University Press.

Vogeler, M.S. (2008) *Austin Harrison and the English Review*. University of Missouri Press.

Warburg, P. (1930). *The Federal Reserve System, Its Origin and Growth; Reflections and Recollections*. Macmillan.

Wiebe, R. (1959). The House of Morgan and the Executive, 1905–1913, *The American Historical Review*, 65/1, 49–60.

7 | Keynes, the Transfer Problem, and Reparations

SIMON HINRICHSEN

Keynes (1919) wrote in *The Economic Consequences of the Peace* that the peace settlement reached at Versailles to end World War I would have terrible consequences. He predicted the disintegration of Europe through protectionism, argued that Germany had little capacity to pay reparations, and that debt forgiveness of inter-Allied loans should be given. The 1920s interwar period, which saw both German hyperinflation and deflation, (re)ignited a debate about war reparations and the role they played in fuelling economic crises. Keynes played a pivotal role in the original debate on German reparations, he contributed in later writings to the debate on the transfer problem, and he was a key architect in the economic system that emerged after World War II. He saw two problems for Germany in paying reparations. The first was a budgetary problem in generating enough cash to cover the transfer. The second was the transfer problem, where he feared a deterioration of the terms of trade because Germany would not run large enough trade surpluses because of low import and export elasticities. He was, of course, neither alone in thinking about these topics, nor was he right in every prediction he made. This chapter is an attempt to find out where the debate Keynes started is now, by looking at the largest war reparations in recent history and discuss how they were actually paid.

War reparations have been a common feature in peace settlements for thousands of years. Following the First Punic War in 241 BC, Rome imposed reparations on Carthage in the form of 3,200 talents of silver (see e.g., Oosterlinck 2008). The peace settlement would later be used as an example by Keynes to describe the Treaty of Versailles because of its harsh conditions. The practice of extracting reparations simply for winning a war was common until around the seventeenth century, after which reparations and indemnities were mostly specified as compensation for the expenditures and destruction of war. The nineteenth century saw large French reparations following the Napoleonic Wars (in 1815) and the Franco-Prussian War (in 1871), where reparations were specified in terms of damages and written down in treaties. The transfers were enforced by military occupation and paid for in large parts by sovereign debt. The nineteenth century saw several large reparations paid, as will be discussed later in the chapter, but the French reparations were important because they would serve as an inspiration for the reparations imposed on Germany after World War I. German reparations would partly, although not completely, end the practice of reparations, in large part because of the influence of John M. Keynes.

Reparations transfers can take many forms but are most commonly in hard currency or precious metals. Less common are the transfer of intellectual properties, industrial assets, natural resources, or goods. Money, precious metals, or goods as payment are easier to trace because they are usually specified in treaties. The transfer of intellectual properties, patents, or industrial assets can be harder to track, regardless of whether they are legal or illegal. Paying money is a direct cost of money now, which can be smoothed by borrowing. Transferring assets is a longer-term cost because it lowers the country's income from those assets. Both direct transfers of money and indirect transfer or assets affect trade flows and future income. Regardless of the type of the transfer, it is a direct cost either in the short or the long term. Financing a transfer is a budgetary problem, as Keynes suggested. The country has a budgetary problem if it does not have the capacity to raise the money, which can be done either through taxes, by borrowing, or by increasing the money supply. Some of Keynes' critics suggested that he underestimated Germany's capacity to pay when he suggested that it only had the capacity to two billion pounds. Most prominent was Mantoux (1946), who showed that Germany would go on to spend many times the amount on rearmament from 1933 to 1937. Mantoux instead suggested studying reparations as a question of willingness to pay, rather than a capacity to pay issue. An argument for his case is provided by Occhino, Oosterlinck, and White (2008), who show that Germany extracted more than one year's worth of output from Vichy France between 1940 and 1944. If a country can borrow the money, it is the willingness to pay that is the constraint, not the capacity to pay.[1]

---

[1] Ritschl (2012) made this argument for German reparations. He showed that a sovereign debt approach was identical to a willingness to pay approach.

The second cost to reparations is through second-order effects, or what is commonly called the transfer problem. A transfer can have second-order effects on savings, investments, consumption, and output, because interest rates or the terms of trade might mitigate or exacerbate the economic costs of the transfer. If, say, France had to pay two billion francs in reparations to Germany, the question is if the actual economic costs are more or less than those two billion francs. Here it is harder to infer causality from terms of trade or interest rate movements without a counterfactual. A full exercise of reparations in the context of the transfer problem would require more space than a chapter. It is, however, possible to understand how the budgetary problem was solved and if the terms of trade improved or worsened. The rest of the chapter will therefore provide an overview of how reparations were actually paid, and then an overview of the literature on the transfer problem a hundred years after Keynes started the debate. I will show that the terms of trade, for the most part, improved in the years following the announcement of reparations, and that sovereign debt markets allowed countries to finance reparations by borrowing.

A Brief History of Recent War Reparations

The first issue that Keynes highlighted was the budgetary problem of how to actually pay reparations. As with other government expenditures, reparations can be financed through taxes, by borrowing, or by increasing the money supply. If countries have any foreign assets that can be sold, it is also a possibility, but most countries coming out of war had few, if any, foreign assets left, because they have been sold to finance military expenditures.[2] Because reparations are mostly paid in foreign currency, sovereign debt and taxes have been the most common way of financing transfers. The reason is that increasing the money supply is likely to put pressure on the exchange rate. A devaluation of the exchange rate will increase the cost of paying reparations. Since 1800, there have been at least 15 episodes in which war reparations have been enforced, which are shown in Table 7.1.

Another argument is that the list of repaid reparations includes several cases where the transfers were larger than GDP.

[2] France following the Franco-Prussian War is an exception.

Table 7.1 *War reparations and indemnities since 1800*

Reparation related to	Percentage of output	Who paid?	Repaid?
1815–1819: Napoleonic Wars	22	France	Yes
1825–1947: Haiti independence	300	Haiti	Yes
1848–1881: Mexican-American War	<1	US	Yes
1871–1873: Franco-Prussian War	25	France	Yes
1895–1901: Sino-Japanese War	–	China	Yes
1897–1898: Greco-Turkish War	–	Greece	Yes
1901–1939: Boxer Rebellion		China	Yes
1918–1918: WWI (Russia)	37	Russia	No
1919–1964: WWI (Bulgaria)	>150	Bulgaria	Yes
1923–1933: WWI (Germany)	100	Germany	No
1945–1952: WWII (Finland)	20	Finland	Yes
1947–1965: WWII (Italy)	1	Italy	Yes
1953–1965: WWII (Germany)	3	Germany	No
1955–1965: WWII (Japan)	4	Japan	Yes
1994– : Gulf War	>400	Iraq	Yes

Sources: Hinrichsen (2023) and see the text for details.

All episodes in the table had a treaty governing the transfer that followed war between two states.[3]

The table shows the war each reparation relates to, the approximate value in terms of the paying country's output, who paid, and whether it was repaid in full. The straightforward way of comparing the size of each reparation has several drawbacks. First, it does not account for how long it took to repay. A reparation worth a quarter of GDP is harder to pay back in three years than in thirty unless the country has access to borrowing. Second, the denominator (output) is the year of the first payment, but it can be difficult to estimate. Third, not all countries have available GDP estimates (China and Greece), even though reparations following the Sino-Japanese War, the Greco-Turkish War, and the Boxer Rebellion were significant. With these caveats, the table is an overview of the major reparations paid in the

---

[3] As a result, no civil war or other intra-state conflict reparations are included. Reparations under negotiation, such as German reparations to Namibia for massacres during the colonial era of 1904 to 1908, have also been left out.

last 200 years. They constitute the history leading up to when Keynes wrote, and the aftermath. A full history of each episode requires more than one chapter, but I will go through the most important parts of each to allow for an overview.

Napoleonic Wars Reparations

After the Napoleonic Wars ended in 1815, France had to pay reparations worth 22 per cent of output (White 2001). Initial negotiations for peace failed when Napoleon escaped his exile on Elba and tried to launch an attack on Britain (the Hundred Days War). The result was Napoleon's default at Waterloo. The other Great Powers of Europe at the time were Austria, Prussia, Russia, and Britain, which imposed harsh reparations on France with the Second Treaty of Paris as a result. Reparations had a dual purpose: to slowly reintroduce France into the power structure of Europe and to prevent any further attempt of war (see, e.g., Chapman 1998). Reparations, indemnities, and occupation costs would total two billion francs and were to be paid in five years. The incentives to repay quickly were considerable, as France was occupied from Calais to the Swiss border for as long as payment was outstanding (Veve 1989, p. 99). France did not initially have access to international capital markets as its credit reputation had been squandered during the revolution, and the war was mostly financed by taxes (Bordo and White 1991). Initial payments were made almost exclusively from taxes, which meant France ran an austere budget balance. Market access was restored in 1817 when France tried and was successful in borrowing with the help of international banks, Barings Brothers in London and Hope & Company in Amsterdam. After the first successful loan, France quickly borrowed the entire amount due in reparations and repaid the transfer ahead of time (Oosterlinck et al. 2014; Greenfield 2016). Reparations amounting to 1.9 billion francs were paid in the end, which is slightly lower than the agreed figure. The reason was that the swift repayment lowered occupation costs.

Haiti Independence Reparations

France imposed a reparation on Haiti in 1825 after the former colony gained its independence in 1804 (James 1938; Blackburn 2006).

The reparation was justified as compensation for loss of slaves and land, with France conditioning the recognition of Haiti as a sovereign state only against such payments. The imposed indemnity was 150 million gold francs in 1825. The amount is significant compared to the Haitian economy at any point in time, and Piketty (2020, p. 473) estimates it being equivalent to 300 per cent of 1825 GDP. The outstanding reparation was reduced to 90 million francs in 1938, but it was not until 1947, over a century after the initial settlement, that all loans related to the indemnity were paid off (Munro 1969, p. 25). In the end, Haiti paid the equivalent of 21 billion in 2015 US dollars to France (Sommers 2015, p. 124).

Mexican-American War Reparations

The United States paid indemnities to Mexico from 1848 to 1881, after the Mexican-American War.[4] In national income terms, this reparation was minor. The Treaty of Guadalupe Hidalgo of 1848 stipulated the United States pay 18 million US dollars, of which 15 million were indemnities and 3.25 million were transferred debts. Using data from the Federal Reserve to convert the indemnity to 2011-equivalent dollars, and comparing that to the chained real GDP per capita multiplied by the population at the time (Bolt et al. 2018), I find it is the equivalent of less than 1 per cent of GDP.

Franco-Prussian War Indemnity

Fifty years after the Napoleonic Wars reparations, France was again forced to pay indemnities after losing the Franco-Prussian War. The total size of the indemnity imposed by Prussian Chancellor Otto von Bismarck was five billion francs, or around 25 per cent of GDP (Monroe 1919, p. 269). The indemnity was to be paid over three years and was mainly financed by sovereign debt (Kindleberger 1993, p. 241–50). The French had a large stock of foreign assets and were able to issue debt at low interest rates (Taussig 1927, p. 266–68). The indemnity was considered too big to pay by many at the time, but easy and fast issuance of loans and asset sales meant the indemnity was

---

[4] The war ended in 1848. I am indebted to Eugene White for pointing out that it contained reparations.

repaid quickly (Gavin 1992, p. 175). Output and consumption fell in the lead-up to the transfer but rebounded during and after (Devereux and Smith 2007, p. 2381). Both French nineteenth-century reparations were paid quickly, despite significant distortions to the economy, with pivotal roles in both cases for sovereign debt markets. Enforcement of the transfers was binding by creditors who militarily occupied France until repayment was ensured.

The reparations had long-term consequences beyond the direct economic costs, as the structure of international trade and factor mobility shifted. One example is Dedinger (2012), who found that Franco-German trade specializations changed dramatically in the aftermath of the Franco-Prussian War indemnity in the 1870s. The change could have been affected by the idiosyncratic economic shock that caused Bismarck to impose tariffs in 1879, but a more likely explanation were structural changes stemming from the indemnity (Zussman 2008). France had been accumulating foreign assets at a rapid pace before the war. It changed during the repayment as export receipts went to pay the indemnity, but the current account reversed to be positive after the indemnity was paid.

Sino-Japanese War and Boxer Rebellion Reparations

Between 1895 and 1901 China paid 230 million taels of silver to Japan following the Sino-Japanese War (Dong and Guo 2018, p. 17–18). Between 1901 and 1939, it paid another 669 million taels of silver as reparation for the Boxer Rebellion (Hsu 2000, p. 477–91). The Treaty of Shimonoseki of 1895 stated that China owed indemnities to both Japan and Britain. The payment was too large to finance without a loan, which China obtained from Russia, France, Britain, and Germany (Dong and Guo 2018, p. 18). The loss of the Boxer Rebellion in 1901 doubled indemnity payments, as all eight invaders had to be compensated.[5] China was thus shackled with significant indemnity payments for the next thirty years, which it financed with European loans.

Neither China nor Greece has reliable nominal GDP figures to compare the size of the indemnities. In context, however, they were undoubtedly large, and required significant sovereign debt issuance (in the form

---

[5] The Eight-Nation Alliance: Austria-Hungary, Britain, France, Germany, Italy, Japan, Russia, and the United States.

of bilateral loans) to finance. But with no dependable output number, is it difficult to put in perspective and they are left blank in Table 7.1.

Greco-Turkish War Reparations

In 1897, Greece lost the Cretan War to the Ottoman Empire. Greece had been overrun and asked the Great Powers of Europe to broker an armistice, which they did just before Athens was invaded. Greece was at the time highly indebted and defaulted on some of its outstanding sovereign bonds. In the negotiations that followed, sovereign debt payments were directly linked to indemnities by creditors. The Ottomans had required 10 million lira but were negotiated down to 4 million and loss of some territory (Waibel 2015, p. 14–16). The amount was considered so high as Greek capacity to pay was in question, but with no reliable GDP figures it is not possible to quantify directly. Creditors forced an intervention in Greek fiscal decisions, to make sure there was capacity to pay. The final agreement included a loan of 6.8 million pounds from the UK, France, and Russia to Greece (ibid., p. 16). The loan was thus larger than the indemnity but ensured Greece could repay existing private creditors too. Greece did not have much choice in the matter: enforcement of sovereign debt happened under the threat of invasion. The terms included the de facto takeover of fiscal affairs (ibid., p. 17), and made indemnities and existing creditors pari passu (meaning equal ranking of claims), ensuring repayment. In the end, Greece paid the equivalent of 94 million francs in indemnities.

World War I Reparations

German interwar reparation is well documented in the literature because of its importance in the lead-up to World War II, and for its role in the Great Depression. But Germany' interwar reparation was not the only one.

The Bolshevik government in Russia ended their involvement in World War I with the auxiliary Treaty of Brest-Litovsk on 3 March 1918. Russia gave up territorial control over the Baltic states and defaulted on previously incurred debts to the Allies. A subsequent financial appendix was agreed on 27 August 1918, which set out financial terms of the Treaty. Soviet Russia was to pay six billion marks to Germany in five instalments from 1918 to 1920, with parts of the transfers consisting of commodities and gold.[6] Russian pre-war output was 16 billion Russian roubles (Markevich and Harrison 2011, p. 680),[7] which at the prevailing exchange rates in 1918 meant the reparation was around 37 per cent of GDP.[8] Only the first two instalment were paid in September 1918, according to Smele (1994, p. 1319) who investigates the flow of Imperial Russian gold reserves. The later transfers were not made because the Treaty was subsequently annulled by the Armistice of 11 November 1918 that ended fighting between Germany and the Allies.

Bulgaria was initially given a bill of 2.25 billion gold francs to France, which took its debt-to-GNP to over 200 per cent (Tooze and Ivanov 2011, p. 37–43). Bulgaria's reparations burden cannot be easily untangled from its war debts, but assuming the increase in foreign public debt from 1919 to 1921 was entirely reparations, the initial imposed transfer was over 150 per cent of output (Dimitrova and Ivanov 2014, p. 239). After the first payment was missed in 1921, the French forced the Bulgarian government to prioritize debt payments. Under great strain, reparations payments were made through 1923. The League of Nations mediated a deal, which postponed most reparations. Of the 2.25 billion, 550 million was extended to 1935 with the additional 1.7 billion postponed to 1953. From 1923 to 1935, only 28 million was paid (ibid., p. 221). No explicit default happened, outside of the missed initial payment. It was a story of extreme economic hardship and repayment under duress and diplomacy, albeit more the former.

German reparations had a different ending. As a share of output, the combined A- and B-bonds, which covered reparations and inter-Allied war debts, were around 100 per cent of German GDP (Ritschl 2012, p. 945–46). If the entire proposed reparation is included, the bill represented 300 per cent of pre-war GNP. The further 200 percentage points of debts included C-bonds, a debt that was added for political reasons to maintain a grip on Germany and avoid further aggression. However, there was no real expectation of repayment of the C-bonds, at least according to diplomatic cables from the time. The reparations (A-bonds) were around 24 per cent of output, which is

---

[6] Memorandum Appendix XXI (Russian-German Financial Agreement) to The Treaty of Brest-Litovsk, signed on 27 August 1918, published in *Izvestia* on 4 September 4 1918 [accessed 13 February 2021].

[7] The GDP number is for Soviet interwar territory in 1913.

[8] Rouble and mark exchange rates are found in Mixon (2011).

close to the value of the indemnity France paid in 1871. There is reason to think that the size of the reparation was negotiated with the same size in mind. According to Marks (2013), who surveys the literature on the negotiations of the Versailles Treaty, diplomats and politicians made numerous references to the Franco-Prussian War indemnity. The French would be intimately aware of the cost they bore which shows up in discussions from French archives at the time. The German business cycle was extremely volatile from 1921 to 1923 and was characterized by hyperinflation. Initial German resistance to pay the higher-than-anticipated reparations bill meant that military force was needed to enforce payment. As a result, the Allies occupied the Ruhr in January 1923, which forced Germany back to the negotiations table.

Given the level of repayment and debt servicing required, foreign investors demanded protections if they were to finance the increased level of debt that Germany needed to pay reparations. Investors received protections in the form of seniority claims on the foreign exchange reserves at the Reichsbank (Ritschl 1995, p. 2–4). The Dawes Plan was agreed in 1924 to formalize the payment schedule, as Germany had been in default since 1922 (Yee 2020, p. 49). The Dawes Plan gave commercial creditors preferential treatment to reparations. It set a fixed exchange rate, resulting in high real wages in Germany, and a resulting uncompetitive export sector. Capital outflows from Germany during the 1920s were significant, but were matched by external investments, which allowed Germany to keep rolling over debt at reasonable interest rates (Farquet 2019). Germany issued bonds to repay reparations in the form of 'Dawes' and 'Young' bonds, which were a significant share of the overall debt burden in Germany until the early 1930s. Once capital flows reversed in the late 1920s, Germany could no longer finance transfer payments and had an unsustainable debt burden. The Young Plan was agreed in 1929 which reversed the seniority and set a new payment schedule, but without capital inflows Germany had to finance the transfers without additional external debt. The subsequent austerity politics and global depression resulted in deflation and a collapse in growth.

In 1931, US President Hoover had initiated a moratorium on payments after pressure from Germany, which was followed by a negotiated end to reparations at the Lausanne Conference 1932. The German sovereign debt default had wider implications for the issue of inter-Allied war debt following World War I. Italy had significant external debt to the United States and the UK as it had borrowed money from the Allies. Italy received reparations from Germany, and it was understood the two were linked (Astore and Fratianni 2019, p. 200–10). Italy managed to get significant debt relief in 1926 but nonetheless defaulted in 1934 (Reinhart and Trebesch 2016; Astore and Fratianni 2019). Until then, loans had been forthcoming – as they had been for Greece or China. War debts were only defaulted on when credit markets shut. Germany first defaulted in 1932 and continued defaulting on other state liabilities in the following years (Clement 2004, p. 37–38). Full capital controls were introduced in 1934 (Schuker 1988, p. 47–82). The role sovereign debt played in the initial payment is paramount, as without it Germany would not have been able to pay reparations.

World War II Reparations

Four countries paid reparations after World War II: Finland to the Soviets; Germany, Japan, and Italy to the Allies.[9] These ranged from 1 per cent (Italy) to 4 per cent (Japan) but were largely offset by American economic assistance (DeLong and Eichengreen 1993). The reconstruction policy after World War II absorbed some of the lessons of Keynes (1919, 1929a). The focus was thus on industrial disarmament to ensure the peace rather than punishment (Cohen 1967, p. 270). German reparations were in the form of explicit payments to Israel, indemnities to prisoners, indemnities for expropriated property, other restitutions, and the dismantling of German factories. All payments amounted to 5.2 billion US dollars between 1953 and 1965, around 3 per cent of 1960 output (ibid., pp. 282–88).[10] Italian reparations were paid in kind to Yugoslavia (125 million), Greece (105 million), the Soviet Union (100 million), Ethiopia (25 million), and

---

[9] The Peace Treaties of Paris of 1947 also specified reparations should be paid by Hungary, Romania, and Bulgaria, mainly to the Soviet Union. The payments were meant to be paid in kind (i.e., in non-monetary goods), but no country was able to produce any goods of value. As the countries fell under the Soviet umbrella, reparations were cancelled (Nevakivi 1996, p. 95–97). However, Kramer (2009) notes there was a large flow of money from the periphery to the centre in the years following World War II, regardless of whether the transfers were regarded as reparations.

[10] GDP data is from World Bank Indicators. Germany also paid significant restitutions, largely domestically, under the Restitution Act, so the amounts here are specific to the period before 1965. East Germany is not included but paid substantial amounts.

Albania (5 million). An additional payment of 6 million in interest brought the total to 366 million US dollars, with some minor payments to other countries (ibid., pp. 272–73).

Japan was, like Germany, forced to dismantle its war industries in order not to pose a threat. The Japanese Peace Treaty of 1951 considered that Japan did not have the capacity to pay reparations and only minor transfers to Burma, Cambodia, Indonesia, Laos, Philippines, South Korea, Vietnam, and Thailand were made (ibid., p. 273). In total, Japanese reparations in goods and money came to 1.5 billion US dollars, or about four per cent of GDP.

Finnish reparations were paid in kind (mainly in goods and timber) and were by far the largest as a share of the economy. They were paid primarily to the Soviet Union and the money-equivalent was around 20 per cent of GDP (Pihkala 1999, p. 32). Finland had easy access to credit and most of the goods were produced thanks to loans from the United States.

The post-war period included significant non-monetary transfers. Gimbel (1990) argues that the United States took reparations from Germany in the form of intellectual property. Patents and scientific know-how were transferred from Germany to the Allies, which included visits to Germany and the migration of scientists to especially the United States. The value of the transfer is hard to estimate because it consisted of both people and information. O'Reagan (2019) shows the flow of information from Germany to the Allies in the post-war period was significant and had an impact on diplomacy, as well as industry and science. Fisch (1992) argues that the inability to obtain large reparations meant that the Soviet Union did so indirectly through Eastern Germany, although it does not show up as war reparations in the national account.[11] Finland alone followed the example of previous reparations and issued sizable amounts of sovereign debt to finance the payment.

The smaller World War II reparations were the only reparations not funded by debt. The reason was that sovereign debt was not needed to finance relatively minor liabilities. Reparations following World War II

---

[11] One curious side note is that in 1946, the United States offered France debt relief but with conditions: In three of every four weeks, French cinemas had to show American movies. They were allies, as such this is not considered reparations, but a condition for loans. After two years, the French reneged (Ulff-Møller 2001, p. 144).

were modelled to not follow the issues of World War I. They were small in value and targeted specifically to deter industrialization.

Gulf War Reparations

Reparations were uncommon during the Cold War because there were no peace settlements in which reparations were negotiated. The one exception is Iraqi reparations after the Gulf War, imposed by the UN after its invasion of Kuwait. The reparation is governed by UN resolutions and state that reparations are to be paid out of Iraqi oil exports, although they should not exceed 30 per cent of oil revenues (Resolution 705). It is the longest lasting and most complicated transfer, and it is covered in detail in Hinrichsen (2022, 2021, 2023). Iraqi reparations are the largest ever repaid, as a share of output. The reparations-to-GDP of over 400 per cent in 1991 alone testifies to a total output collapse, but even in absolute terms the Iraqi reparation is large, at 52 billion US dollars.[12] Following the award of the reparations and the creation of the United Nations Compensation Commission (which oversee payments), Iraq was effectively shut out from the global economy. No new external debt was possible and very limited commercial trade. Total Iraqi debt as a share of GDP exploded, making it the most indebted nation in the world. Reparations were, of course, not a direct cause of the collapse, but merely reflected another avenue of punishment. Iraq lost a war, was not welcome in any geopolitical alliance, which resulted in a spectacular societal collapse in the wake of imposed reparations.

The Transfer Problem

In the international finance literature, reparations have mostly been studied as a transfer problem. The transfer problem originates with Mill (1844) and seeks to understand what, if any, consequences unilateral fiscal transfers have on savings and the current account (Obstfeld and Rogoff 1995, p. 1755–59). Reparations are one such transfer. The transmission mechanism is the level of interest rates and terms of trade, where the latter is defined as the price of exports in terms

---

[12] As of the writing, USD 2 billion of awarded reparations is outstanding, with USD 50 billion paid.

of imports. If the terms of trade improve, a country can buy more imports for the same amounts of exports.

In several papers, Keynes (1929a, 1929b, 1929c) stated that reparations would have negative second-order effects. He suggested the debtor would experience a worsening of the terms of trade, due to low import and export elasticities. A large transfer of capital abroad puts downward pressure on the real exchange rate, as the reparation is paid. If import and export elasticities are low and not adjusting, the lower real exchange rate means that imports become relatively more expensive in terms of exports. On the contrary, Ohlin (1929a, 1929b) posited that a reparation would improve the terms of trade, because the debtor would have lower purchasing power. The lower purchasing power means less money spent on imports, which lowers their relative price. The adjustment in the relative price of nontraded goods means the debtor's terms of trade will improve to offset the capital flow, and the cost of the reparation would be the stipulated sum. The Keynes–Ohlin debate about German reparations thus came down to discussions about how the terms of trade reacted to a fiscal transfer. Keynes' (1919) critique of Versailles ended up as the theoretical framework for much of the debate.

The problem of transfers in high capital mobile economies was formalized in models in the same tradition as a standard part of open economy macroeconomics (Metzler 1942; Johnson 1955, 1956). Samuelson (1952, 1954) showed how Keynes' insights held *in theory*. In a competitive two-good, two-country model, the terms of trade will deteriorate if the debtor's marginal propensity to consume its export goods is larger than the recipient's. In other words, if the debtor's consumption basket, that is no longer purchased, is the same as what the creditor chooses to purchase, there is no transfer problem. But in any instances where preferences differ, the terms of trade of the debtor will deteriorate. As Keynes' views were formalized, the assumption underlying Samuelson's original analysis was that the current account balance would remain unchanged, that is, that the trade balance would match the capital flow.[13] He was wrong. Machlup (1964) and Gavin (1992) noted that this did not match the evidence from French reparations after the Napoleonic Wars or the Franco-Prussian War indemnity; nor the German World War I reparation.

---

[13] Meaning that if the reparations payment is one billion, the capital account will see an outflow of one billion which will be matched by an inflow of one billion through the trade balance.

The problem was that the prevalent static models did not incorporate the importance of the political economy in explaining economic performance, with full employment simply assumed to occur (Brakman and van Marrewijk 1998). Balogh and Graham (1979) first noted that if there was no active aggregate demand policy in the receiving country, the paying country would have to incur unemployment. Similarly, by changing preferences of substitution, the sign on the terms of trade adjustment could change (Djajic et al. 1998). The literature evolved towards more dynamic models of small open economies with Obstfeld and Rogoff (1995, 1996) using an intertemporal approach to the current account to show that a wealth transfer causes deterioration in the terms of trade. It happens because households in the recipient country choose to spend some of the financial gains on leisure, which lowers total output and raises prices. Brock (1996) viewed the transfer problem as fundamentally one of adjustments in the relative price of nontraded goods, allowing for borrowing in a small open economy setting. Building on the resource discovery literature (the 'Dutch disease'), he considered the transfer as a permanent increase in income in an economy facing fixed terms of trade. Cremers and Sen (2009) showed how impacts from an increase in world net wealth affect the terms of trade, but also raise welfare in both countries. Corsetti et al. (2013) accounted for product varieties in their study of the transfer in the context of the US current account deficit. Most dynamic models of the terms of trade, such as Uribe and Schmitt-Grohé (2017), emphasize the difference between a permanent and temporary shock, with no long-run effect from the latter. The reason is that if an improvement in the terms of trade is permanent, then households will save less of it because it will raise their permanent income. If the shock is transitory, they are more likely to save the windfall.[14] Trionfetti (2018) finds that the effects crucially depend on the assumptions of the economy, such as trade costs and comparative advantage, but that the effects of a transfer are real, both for the debtor and creditor, and for world welfare because of productivity changes from the transfer.

Some scholars have addressed the original empirical question of whether war reparations are worsened or mitigated through the terms of trade, but the studies are few and far between. Gavin (1992) and

---

[14] The effect is called the Obstfeld-Svensson-Razin Effect, based on Obstfeld (1982) and Svensson and Razin (1983).

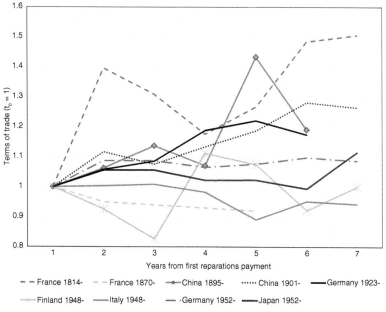

Figure 7.1 Terms of trade changes (after first transfer)
Sources: Napoleonic Wars estimated based on Esteban (1987); Franco-Prussian War is from Levy-Leboyer and Bourguignon (1990, table A-VI); Chinese data from Dong and Guo (2018). Rest is from the UN Archive. Finland and Italy data for 1949 is an extrapolation between 1948 (where data starts) and 1950. Replication file, *plot_tot.m* available on personal website.

Devereux and Smith (2007) studied the Franco-Prussian War indemnity and found no permanent impact from the transfer on consumption. The investment response was significantly depressed in the decade after, but financing was easier due to France's stock of net foreign assets. In Devereux and Smith's model, the predicted effect of the reparation depends on the degree of home bias in consumption and international borrowing and lending, but results in terms of trade deterioration.[15] It is a problem of data limitations for older episodes, where prices and volumes of imports and exports are not available for certain periods. It is possible to obtain aggregate terms of trade data for the main reparations since 1800, which are shown in Figure 7.1.

---

[15] Results are like those of Brakman and van Marrewijk (2007).

It shows the terms of trade in the years following the first reparations payment for nine historical reparations.

It is worth nothing that while the data shows an improvement in the terms of trade, it does not tell us anything about the transfer problem per se. To make inferences about the transfer problem would require counterfactuals and granular data, which is not available.[16] What the data does say is that, if the terms of trade improved (the line in the figure goes up), then there was an economic windfall. In only three cases did the terms of trade deteriorate: France after Franco-Prussian Wars, and in Italy and Finland after World War II. In each case, reparations were repaid successfully. The aftermath of the other reparations shown in Figure 7.1 saw improved terms of trade, including Germany in the interwar years, albeit a brief improvement followed by stability in the terms of trade and a structural current account deficit because of capital inflows. Given the sparse data, it is difficult to assign causality and significance in general, though I can observe the positive direction of the historical terms of trade, no clear trend is evident given the difference in repayment schedules.[17] The literature has therefore focused more on how reparations were financed and the role of sovereign debt.

Concluding Remarks

Keynes saw the dangers of reparations when he first wrote about them in 1919. He wrote that they had the potential to destabilize European trade and were not in the interest of any nation. As we have seen in this chapter, reparations much bigger and smaller than the German ones Keynes objected to have been repaid. He might have underestimated the capacity of nations to transfer large amounts of money, especially when they have access to loans. The theoretical transfer problem debate remains unsettled, except to say that it depends a lot on your assumptions. But reading the *Economic*

---

[16] For some cases, it is possible to get GDP and trade balances, but not for all. The set of reparations in Figure 7.1 is already a subset of total reparations because terms of trade data are not continuous for the other episodes discussed in the next section.

[17] Terms of trade data is not available for Bulgaria, but data is available for its total exports and imports. Its trade balance was volatile but positive throughout the 1920s (Dimitrova and Ivanov 2014, p. 225).

Consequences of the Peace a hundred years after it was first released, Keynes was right on the big picture. Countries have enormous capacity to pay, but it comes with the risk of political upheaval. It is hard to look at the large reparations of Haiti or Iraq and say that they did much good. Keynes was a writer who could look beyond the initial impact and judge the bigger picture. That is why he is more important than ever, even to this day.

References

Astore, Marianna, and Michele Fratianni. 2019. '"We Can't Pay": How Italy Dealt with War Debts after World War I'. *Financial History Review* 26 (2): 197–222.

Balogh, Thomas, and Andrew Graham. 1979. 'The Transfer Problem Revisited: Analogies Between the Reparations Payments of the 1920s and the Problems of the OPEC Surpluses'. *Oxford Bulletin of Economics and Statistics* 41 (3): 183–91.

Blackburn, Robin. 2006. 'Haiti, Slavery, and the Age of the Democratic Revolution'. *The William and Mary Quarterly* 63 (4): 643–74.

Bolt, Jutta, Robert Inklaar, Herman de Jong, and Jan Luiten van Zanden. 2018. 'Rebasing "Maddison": New Income Comparison and the Shape of Long-Run Economic Development'. *Maddison Project Database*, Online Working Paper Version 2018 10.

Bordo, Michael D., and Eugene N. White. 1991. 'A Tale of Two Currencies: British and French Finance During the Napoleonic Wars'. *Journal of Economic History* 51 (2): 303–16.

Brakman, Steven, and Charles van Marrewijk. 1998. *The Economics of International Transfers*. New York: Cambridge University Press.

——— 2007. 'Transfers, Nontraded Goods, and Unemployment: An Analysis of the Keynes-Ohlin Debate'. *History of Political Economy* 39 (1): 121–43.

Brock, Philip L. 1996. 'International Transfers, the Relative Price of Non-Traded Goods, and the Current Account'. *The Canadian Journal of Economics* 29 (1): 163–80.

Chapman, Tim. 1998. *The Congress of Vienna: Origins, Processes, and Results*. London: Routledge.

Clement, Piet. 2004. '"The Touchstone of German Credit": Nazi Germany and the Service of the Dawes and Young Loans'. *Financial History Review* 11 (1): 33–50.

Cohen, Benjamin J. 1967. 'Reparations in the Postwar Period: A Survey'. *Banca Nazionale Del Lavoro Quarterly Review* 20 (82): 268–88.

Corsetti, Giancarlo, Philippe Martin, and Paolo Pesenti. 2013. 'Varieties and the Transfer Problem'. *Journal of International Economics* 89 (1): 1–12.

Cremers, Emily T., and Partha Sen. 2009. 'Transfers, the Terms of Trade, and Capital Accumulation'. *The Canadian Journal of Economics* 42 (4): 1599–616.

Dedinger, Béatrice. 2012. 'The Franco-German Trade Puzzle: An Analysis of the Economic Consequences of the Franco-Prussian War'. *Economic History Review* 65 (3): 1029–54.

DeLong, J. Bradford, and Barry Eichengreen. 1993. 'The Marshall Plan: History's Most Successful Structural Adjustment Program'. In *Post-War Economic Reconstruction and Lessons for the East Today, 190–230.* Cambridge, Massachusetts: MIT Press.

Devereux, Michael B., and Gregor W. Smith. 2007. 'Transfer Problem Dynamics: Macroeconomics of the Franco-Prussian War Indemnity'. *Journal of Monetary Economics* 54 (8): 2375–98.

Dimitrova, Kalina, and Martin Ivanov. 2014. 'Bulgaria: From 1879 to 1947'. In *South-Eastern European Monetary and Economic Statistics from the Nineteenth Century to World War II*, 199–242. Greece: Bank of Greece.

Djajic, Slobodan, Sajal Lahiri, and Pascalis Raimondos-Moller. 1998. 'The Transfer Problem and the Intertemporal Terms of Trade'. *The Canadian Journal of Economics* 31 (2): 427–36.

Dong, Baomin, and Yibei Guo. 2018. 'The Impact of the First Sino-Japanese War Indemnity: Transfer Problem Re-examined'. *International Review of Economics & Finance* 56 (July): 15–26.

Esteban, Javier C. 1987. 'Fundamentos para una interpretacion de las estadisticas comerciales Francesas, De 1787–1821 con referencia espacial al comercia Franco-Espanol'. *Hacienda Publica Espanol* 108 (9): 221–51.

Farquet, Christophe. 2019. 'Quantification and Revolution: An Investigation of German Capital Flight after the First World War'. EHES Working Paper 149.

Fisch, J. 1992. *Reparationen Nach Dem Zweiten Weltkrieg.* Munich: Verlag C. H. Beck.

Gavin, Michael. 1992. 'Intertemporal Dimensions of International Economic Adjustment: Evidence from the Franco-Prussian War Indemnity'. *American Economic Review* 82 (2): 174–79.

Gimbel, John. 1990. *Science, Technology, and Reparations: Exploration and Plunder in Postwar Germany.* Stanford: Stanford University Press.

Greenfield, Jerome. 2016. 'Financing a New Order: The Payment of Reparations by Restoration France, 1817–18'. *French History* 30 (3): 376–400.

Hinrichsen, Simon. 2022. 'The Rise of Iraqi indebtedness, 1979–2003'. *Middle Eastern Studies* 58 (5), pp. 782–796.

2021. 'The Iraq Sovereign Debt Restructuring'. *Capital Markets Law Journal* 16 (1): 95–114.

2023. *When Nations Can't Default: A History of War Reparations and Sovereign Debt.* Cambridge: Cambridge University Press.

Hsu, Immanuel Chung-Yueh. 2000. *The Rise of Modern China.* Oxford: Oxford University Press.

James, Cyril L. R. 1938. *The Black Jacobins.* London: Secker & Warburg Ltd.

Johnson, Harry G. 1955. 'The Transfer Problem: A Note on Criteria for Changes in the Terms of Trade'. *Economica* 22 (86): 113–21.

1956. 'The Transfer Problem and Exchange Stability'. *Journal of Political Economy* 64 (3): 212–25.

Keynes, John M. 1919. *The Economic Consequences of the Peace.* New York: Harcourt, Brace, and Hove.

1929a. 'The German Transfer Problem'. *The Economic Journal* 39 (153): 1–7.

1929b. 'The Reparation Problem: A Discussion'. *The Economic Journal* 39 (154): 172–82.

1929c. 'Mr. Keynes' Views on the Transfer Problem'. *The Economic Journal* 39 (155): 388–408.

Kindleberger, C. P. 1993. *A Financial History of Western Europe.* Second edition. New York: Oxford University Press.

Kramer, Mark. 2009. 'The Soviet Bloc and the Cold War in Europe'. In *A Companion to Europe since 1945, Europe and the Cold War World,* edited by Klaus Larres, 67–94. Oxford: Wiley-Blackwell.

Levy-Leboyer, Maurice, and François Bourguignon. 1990. *The French Economy in the Nineteenth Century: An Essay in Econometric Analysis.* Cambridge: Cambridge University Press.

Machlup, Fritz. 1964. *International Payments, Debts and Gold.* New York: Charles Scribner Sons.

Mantoux, Étienne. 1946. *The Carthaginian Peace; or the Economic Consequences of Mr Keynes.* London: Oxford University Press.

Markevich, Andrei, and Mark Harrison. 2011. 'Great War, Civil War, and Recovery: Russia's National Income, 1913 to 1928'. *Journal of Economic History* 71 (3): 672–703.

Marks, Sally. 2013. 'Mistakes and Myths: The Allies, Germany, and the Versailles Treaty, 1918–1921'. *Journal of Modern History* 85 (3): 632–59.

Metzler, Lloyd A. 1942. 'The Transfer Problem Reconsidered'. *Journal of Political Economy* 50 (3): 397–414.

Mill, John S. 1844. *Essays on Some Unsettled Questions of Political Economy*. Second edition. London: Longmans, Green, Reader, and Dyer.

Mixon, Scott. 2011. 'The Foreign Exchange Option Market, 1917–1921'. Unpublished working paper.

Monroe, Arthur E. 1919. 'The French Indemnity of 1871 and Its Effects'. *The Review of Economics and Statistics* 1 (4): 269–81.

Munro, Dana G. 1969. 'The American Withdrawal from Haiti, 1929–1934'. *The Hispanic American Historical Review* 49 (1): 1–26.

Nevakivi, Jukka. 1996. 'The Soviet Union and Finland after the War, 1944–53'. In *The Soviet Union and Europe in the Cold War, 1943–53*, edited by Francesca Gori and Silvio Pons. First edition. London: Palgrave Macmillan.

O'Reagan, Douglas. 2019. *Taking Nazi Technology: Allied Exploitation of German Science after the Second World War*. Baltimore: John's Hopkins University Press.

Obstfeld, Maurice. 1982. 'Aggregate Spending and the Terms of Trade: Is There a Laursen-Metzler Effect?' *The Quarterly Journal of Economics* 97 (2): 251–70.

Obstfeld, Maurice, and Kenneth Rogoff. 1995. 'The Intertemporal Approach to the Current Account'. In *Handbook of International Economics*, edited by Gene M. Grossman and Kenneth Rogoff, 1731–99, volume 3. Amsterdam: Elsevier.

——— 1996. *Foundations of International Macroeconomics*. Cambridge, MA: MIT Press.

Occhino, Filippo, Kim Oosterlinck, and Eugene N. White. 2008. 'How Much Can a Victor Force the Vanquished to Pay? France under the Nazi Boot'. *Journal of Economic History* 68 (1): 1–45.

Ohlin, Bertil. 1929a. 'The Reparations Problem: A Discussion, Transfer Difficulties Real and Imagined'. *The Economic Journal* 39 (154): 172–83.

——— 1929b. 'Mr. Keynes' Views on the Transfer Problem. Sec. 2, A Rejoinder from Professor Ohlin'. *The Economic Journal* 39 (155): 400–04.

Oosterlinck, Kim. 2008. 'Reparations'. In *The New Palgrave Dictionary of Economics*, edited by Palgrave Macmillan, 1–5. London: Palgrave Macmillan UK.

Oosterlinck, Kim, Loredana Ureche-Rangau, and Jacques-Marie Vaslin. 2014. 'Baring, Wellington and the Resurrection of French Public Finances Following Waterloo'. *Journal of Economic History* 74 (4): 1072–102.

Pihkala, Erkki. 1999. 'The Political Economy of Post-War Finland, 1945–1952'. *Scandinavian Economic History Review* 47 (3): 26–48.

Piketty, Thomas. 2020. *Capital and Ideology*. Cambridge, MA: Harvard University Press.

Reinhart, Carmen, and Christoph Trebesch. 2016. 'Sovereign Debt Relief and Its Aftermath'. *Journal of the European Economic Association* 14 (1): 215–51.

Ritschl, Albrecht. 1995. 'Was Schacht Right? Reparations, the Young Plan, and the Great Depression in Germany'. Unpublished working paper.

——— 2012. 'The German Transfer Problem, 1920–33: A Sovereign-Debt Perspective'. *European Review of History* 19 (6): 943–64.

Samuelson, Paul A. 1952. 'The Transfer Problem and Transport Costs: The Terms of Trade When Impediments Are Absent'. *The Economic Journal* 62 (246): 278–304.

——— 1954. 'The Transfer Problem and Transport Costs, II: Analysis of Effects of Trade Impediments'. *The Economic Journal* 64 (254): 264–89.

Schuker, Stephen A. 1988. *American 'Reparations' to Germany, 1919–33: Implications for the Third-World Debt Crisis*. Princeton: Princeton University Press.

Smele, J. D. 1994. 'White Gold: The Imperial Russian Gold Reserve in the Anti-Bolshevik East, 1918–? (An Unconcluded Chapter in the History of the Russian Civil War)'. *Europe-Asia Studies* 46 (8): 1317–47.

Sommers, Jeffrey. 2015. *Race, Reality, and Realpolitik: U.S.–Haiti Relations in the Lead Up to the 1915 Occupation*. Lanham, MD: Lexington Books.

Svensson, Lars E. O. and Assaf Razin. 1983. 'The Terms of Trade and the Current Account: The Harberger-Laursen-Metzler Effect'. *Journal of Political Economy* 91 (1): 97–125.

Taussig, Frank. W. 1927. *International Trade*. New York: Macmillan.

Tooze, Adam, and Martin Ivanov. 2011. 'Disciplining the "Black Sheep of the Balkans": Financial Supervision and Sovereignty in Bulgaria, 1902–38'. *Economic History Review* 64 (1): 30–51.

Trionfetti, Federico. 2018. 'Firm Heterogeneity, Comparative Advantage and the Transfer Problem'. *European Economic Review* 108 (September): 246–58.

Ulff-Møller, Jens. 2001. *Hollywood's Film Wars with France: Film-Trade Diplomacy and the Emergence of the French Film Quota Policy*. Rochester: University of Rochester Press.

Uribe, Martin, and Stephanie Schmitt-Grohé. 2017. *Open Economy Macroeconomics*. Princeton: Princeton University Press.

Veve, Thomas D. 1989. 'Wellington and the Army of Occupation in France, 1815–1818'. *International History Review* 11 (1): 98–108.

Waibel, Michael. 2015. 'Echoes of History: The International Financial Commission in Greece'. In *Sovereign Default – Do We Need a Legal Procedure?*, edited by Christoph G. Paulus (2014), 3–19. Berlin: Bloomsbury Publishing.

White, Eugene N. 2001. 'Making the French Pay: The Costs and Consequences of the Napoleonic Reparations'. *European Review of Economic History* 5 (3): 337–65.

Yee, Robert. 2020. 'Reparations Revisited: The Role of Economic Advisers in Reforming German Central Banking and Public Finance'. *Financial History Review* 27 (1): 45–72.

Zussman, Asaf. 2008. 'The Rise of German Protectionism in the 1870s: A Macroeconomic Perspective'. Stanford Institute for Economic Policy Research Working Paper.

8 | The Speculative Consequences of the Peace

OLIVIER ACCOMINOTTI, DAVID CHAMBERS,
AND JAMES ASHLEY MORRISON

1 Introduction

Thomas Carlyle once cast economics as the "dismal science." Few works better fit that characterization than does John Maynard Keynes's *Economic Consequences of the Peace*. Beyond his general Malthusian pessimism, Keynes specifically warned that the Treaty of Versailles would render European life *"inefficient, unemployed, disorganised"* and *"torn by internal strife and international hate, fighting, starving, pillaging, and lying."*[1]

The Economic Consequences provoked debate on everything from normative questions of international justice to the technical analysis of the "transfer problem." And it attracted criticism on every front. Mantoux (1946), for instance, highlighted inaccuracies in Keynes's assessment of Germany's capacity to pay reparations, while Ohlin (1929) challenged Keynes's underlying theoretical model. Yet, the controversies only further elevated the bestselling book. By 1921, it had become, the *Wall Street Journal* noted, *"the text book which the German economic experts used in basing their objections to the reparations clauses of the Treaty of Versailles."*[2]

But while Keynes's detractors questioned his empirics, his theory, and even his patriotism, no serious critic questioned his integrity. Yet, Keynes's publication of *The Economic Consequences* coincided with his first great foray into the realm of market speculation. From the summer of 1921 through 1927, Keynes continuously traded major European currencies and the US dollar against the pound sterling, variously going short and long as he thought circumstances warranted.

---

[1] Keynes, *Collected Writings*, 2:157.
[2] *Wall Street Journal*, April 30th, 1921, "Keynes to Blame for Hun Reparations Tactics", p. 6.

Previous writers have described Keynes's speculative activities and analysed his performance as a currency trader (Moggridge, 1983; 1992; Skidelsky, 1992; Accominotti and Chambers, 2016), but there remains little perspective on the interaction between his activities as a speculator and his theoretical and policy work as an economist. More broadly, Keynes is a particularly fascinating case given that he developed a revolutionary perspective on the gold standard, that he had almost peerless insight into the policymaking process at the time, and that he held the ear – and commanded the respect – of the most powerful policymakers in London.

This chapter explores how Keynes's ideas in *The Economic Consequences* related to his activities as a foreign exchange trader. We address two questions. First, how did Keynes's understanding of the post-war international economic and political situation influence his foreign exchange speculation strategy? Second, how did Keynes's experience as a speculator influence his political-economic theory in the years following the publication of his book?

To answer these questions, we utilize a dataset of all Keynes's currency trades developed by Accominotti and Chambers (2016). We then construct a day-to-day narrative exploring the interaction between Keynes's trades on the foreign exchange market and his work as an economist and public figure in the months from August 1919 to February 1920. Finally, we present some of our own speculations on how Keynes's experience in currency trading influenced his theories and views on financial markets over the years following.

2 The London Forward Exchange Market and Keynes's Speculation

Throughout the First World War, the risk of losing gold shipments to submarine attacks disrupted international gold movements. At the same time, the belligerents propped up their currencies through a mix of formal capital controls, informal moral suasion, and direct foreign exchange intervention. In early 1919, the UK government ceased propping up the pound–dollar exchange rate in the market and commenced liberalizing the UK's capital controls – well before it had wrung out the wartime currency inflation.[3] This sent sterling sliding;

---

[3] Morrison (2021), Ch 8.

but it also brought a dramatic resumption of foreign exchange activity in London. Indeed, the surge in exchange trading volumes – and exchange rate volatility – dwarfed anything seen in the pre-war years.[4] Many traders used the nascent forward currency market to hedge their foreign exchange exposure, but others, like Keynes, simply speculated in the pursuit of profit.

Keynes began currency speculation in the summer of 1919, just after the Treaty of Versailles was signed and just as he completed drafting *The Economic Consequences*. Using his friend Oswald Falk's brokerage firm, he sold/bought currencies against the pound sterling on the forward market (for future delivery). He also alternated between long and short positions on the US dollar (Accominotti and Chambers, 2016). Because of the dollar's unmatched link to gold at the time, this was partly a bet about the trajectory of the dollar but also partly a bet about the trajectory of the European currencies – including the pound – relative to gold. Typically, Keynes closed his positions a few days before the forward contract's maturity by buying/selling (on the spot market) the notional amount of foreign currency specified in the forward contract.

Accominotti and Chambers (2016) describe Keynes's foreign exchange speculation strategy during his two periods of active trading, 1919–1927 and 1932–1939. Drawing on Keynes's personal ledgers in the archives of King's College, Cambridge, the authors reconstitute his positions and assess his performance. It is clear from his positions and his correspondence that Keynes was a *fundamentals-based* trader. Simply put, Keynes tried to leverage his understanding of political economy (broadly construed) to out predict the market on the trajectory of particular exchange rates.

In general, Keynes's currency positions in the early 1920s followed from his pessimistic analysis of macroeconomic fundamentals in *The Economic Consequences*. There, Keynes warned that the (unavoidable) post-war adjustments would combine with the (unnecessary) burdens of inter-allied war debts and reparations to perpetuate the "menace of inflationism."[5] Keynes thus shorted the French franc, German mark, and Italian lira across the majority of the 1919–1927

---

[4] London remained the leading foreign exchange market in the interwar period (Einzig, 1937) and over the rest of the twentieth century (Atkin, 2005).
[5] Keynes, *Collected Writings*, 2:157.

period. Yet, he varied these positions based on his perceptions of the shifting political and economic winds.

In the long run, Keynes earned substantial profits from his currency speculation, but his returns were extremely volatile. In May 1920, huge losses on several short positions of European currencies against sterling brought him to the brink of personal bankruptcy. However, with a loan from Ernest Cassel, Keynes maintained the same short positions and eventually made an overall profit. When comparing his returns to the risks he took, his performance as a currency trader during the 1920s can be judged as quite modest (Accominotti and Chambers, 2016).

3 The Political Economy of Keynes's Earliest Speculation: A Narrative

How did Keynes translate his analysis of the post-war economic order in *The Economic Consequences* into precise currency forecasts? Keynes's interchanges with Falk offer insights into his approach to some of his trades (Accominotti and Chambers, 2016). However, this information is far from exhaustive. In this chapter, therefore, we systematically situate his most important individual currency trades from August 1919 to February 1920 in the context of his political writings, remarks, and activities.[6] While one cannot read Keynes's mind, this contextualization enriches our understanding of how a prominent – and politically well-connected – economist converted his analysis of the complex post-war economic and political order into an actual trading strategy.

Learning from the Treaty

As Keynes drafted *The Economic Consequences*, he hit upon several of the Treaty's most immediate, practical consequences for UK finances. He was no longer formally attached to the UK Treasury, but, in late July, he wrote to his former colleague, John Bradbury, one of the two Permanent Secretaries to the Treasury. The Treaty, Keynes explained,

---

[6] We draw on Keynes's materials in both *The Collected Writings of John Maynard Keynes* and in the John Maynard Keynes Papers collection in the archives at King's College, Cambridge. We also use materials from various collections in the National Archives and the Bank of England.

would require the UK to pay to the Reparation Commission the value of whatever warships it received from Germany. But this, Keynes feared, was likely to happen well before the Commission had settled most of the UK's own claims, leaving the UK "hav[ing] to pay over actual cash to Belgium" upfront.[7] The short-term effects were clear: such a significant capital outflow would put downward pressure on the exchange rate.

Before the war, 1 pound sterling traded at, or near, $4.86. Following the war, sterling was artificially supported at about $4.76 – 2.3% below the pre-war exchange rate parity. This lasted until late March 1919, when the UK ceased official foreign exchange market support. Within a week, sterling had dropped below $4.60. It then stabilized, and traded at around 5% below the pre-war rate into the spring. In June, however, the slide resumed. By mid-July, sterling had fallen to $4.26 – 12.4% below the pre-war exchange rate.[8]

Keynes knew that Bradbury was committed to a strong pound. Arguably, Bradbury's was the single most influential voice on the Cunliffe Committee, which famously recommended (in 1918) that the UK return to the gold standard through orthodox fiscal and monetary policies.[9] So, even as the pound fell, Bradbury waged a principled attack on the UK's remaining wartime capital controls. A week after Keynes wrote, Bradbury persuaded Lloyd George's Cabinet to significantly liberalize the gold export restrictions.[10] At the same time, he lobbied the Bank to begin implementing one of the most important – and painful – provisions of the Cunliffe Committee recommendations: all new currency note issues would be matched by earmarking gold within the Bank.[11] It was a crucial step on the road back to the gold standard. Nevertheless, sterling continued its descent. On 20 August, the pound fetched just $4.12 in the exchange market – its lowest point since the Napoleonic Wars.[12]

---

[7] Keynes, *Collected Writings*, 17:115.
[8] Unless otherwise indicated, all exchange rate data is from *Global Financial Data*.
[9] Morrison 2021, 31.
[10] "Cabinet Minutes" (National Archives; CAB 27/71, July 24, 1919).
[11] Henry Clay, *Lord Norman* (New York: Macmillan, 1957), 120.
[12] Global Financial Data, "British Pound to US Dollar Exchange Rate (GBPUSD)."

The next day, Keynes began speculating with two key ideas at the forefront of his mind. Firstly, he was certain that the disastrous economic consequences of the peace would preclude most of Europe from driving their currencies back to their pre-war gold values in the immediate future. Secondly, he doubted the pound's prospects. His insight into the particular economic circumstances of the UK–and, crucially, his familiarity with its leading policymakers–gave him the confidence to bet heavily against sterling.

Keynes's First Trades

Keynes's first trade was a short sale of French francs. On 21 August, he sold 500,000 French francs on the forward market at the price of 34.06 francs to the pound. The delivery date was late November, and Keynes bet that the franc would continue to fall in the meantime. The next day, he bet that sterling would continue its slide against the dollar, meaning gold.[13] The average market rate that day was $4.18; and Keynes entered into two forward contracts – each for $25,000 – at the prices of $4.12 and $4.15 respectively. With delivery dates in mid-November, Keynes was betting that sterling would still not have recovered by then. He followed this three days later with a $40,000 bet that sterling would still be below $4.18 at the end of September. At the same time, Keynes also went long on the Dutch guilder, betting £5,300 that it would appreciate (relative to sterling) within a month. All told, Keynes had wagered more than £27,000 against sterling.[14]

At this point, sterling climbed back north of $4.20 and was becoming increasingly volatile. Yet, Keynes was undeterred. At the time, he was being courted by Henry Strakosch, one of the leading figures in the international gold market, to jointly form a bank. Keynes bowed out

---

[13] At this time, the dollar was the major currency most easily converted into gold. Also, the United States had the world's largest gold reserves. Morrison (2021, Ch. 11) traces the shift from a fixation on the London gold price to the pound–dollar exchange rate in the years following the First World War.

[14] Keynes's trades are recorded in ledgers among his papers at Kings College, Cambridge. They have been transcribed and compiled into a dataset described in Olivier Accominotti and David Chambers, "If You're So Smart: John Maynard Keynes and Currency Speculation in the Interwar Years," *The Journal of Economic History* 76, no. 2 (2016): 342–386.

of the scheme to focus on his speculating.[15] On the 3rd of September, he bet another $50,000, this time at $4.18 with a delivery date at the end of November.

Keynes made his boldest move yet just a few days later. On 8 September, he contracted to sell an even $100,000 in four weeks' time at an exchange rate of just $4.14. This was a supremely bearish move. The rate was sterling's lowest dollar (and thus gold) value in more than a century; but Keynes was confident that it would fall still further. The move effectively doubled down on that hunch, bringing his initial total in dollar speculation to nearly a quarter of a million dollars.

Keynes's first contract – on dollars – was scheduled to come due on the 30th of September. As the date approached, he expanded his bearish positions against the European currencies. On the 16th, he halved his short position against the franc. This gave him the space to take out a short position (of one month's duration) on £12,100 worth of Italian lire. The following week, he re-expanded his short on the franc. On the 25th, he went long again on the dollar, betting nearly £18,000.

By this point, Keynes had committed £75,000 on his dollar bets. It was unlikely that the dollar would sink and the pound rise so much that he could be wiped out; and, as was typical, he only had to put down a margin of 10% of the total.[16] But the sum is still enormous – more than thirty times Keynes's annual income.[17] In addition, he had also shorted £33,000 worth of francs and lire.[18] His potential losses in this case were theoretically unlimited.

Keynes's years in the Treasury ensured that he knew better than most the weakness of the UK's financial position. There were now vastly too

---

[15] Keynes's rationale is explained in a draft letter. Keynes, *Collected Writings*, 17:125–127.

[16] Donald Edward Moggridge, *Maynard Keynes: An Economist's Biography* (New York: Routledge, 1992), 349n.

[17] Accominotti and Chambers, "If You're So Smart," 368.

[18] Throughout, we estimate the pound value of Keynes's positions at various points using the spot rates (listed in *Global Financial Data*) at those times. In reality, closing a position early meant accepting whatever *forward* rate (for the original contract date) prevailed at the time. In this discussion, it would be simpler and more accurate to just describe the nominal positions themselves (e.g. "a short of 500,000 French franc with a delivery of 21 November"). But translating the position into pound terms grants the reader some (albeit imperfect) sense of the magnitudes of Keynes's various trades.

many pounds and too little gold to keep the pound at its pre-war gold value.[19] Moreover, the investment prospects in the UK were less than rosy: there was too much inflation, too little real growth, and the public debt remained extraordinary. Keynes bet that these economic "fundamentals" would drive sterling's market value to new lows. Of course, he was right about the long-term trajectory of the pound. However, he underestimated the political power of the gold standard orthodoxy.

During the war, the Treasury had relied upon ever-larger "Ways and Means Advances" from the Bank of England. This practice continued into 1919, but the new (Conservative) Chancellor of the Exchequer Austen Chamberlain was determined to restore the principles of sound finance. So when the autumn budget prompted him to make the now customary request of the Bank, he and Bank Governor Brien Cokayne agreed that the Bank would file a formal objection.[20] The two drafted the letter together, and then Cokayne steered it through the Bank's Committee of Treasury and its Court of Directors on the 24th–25th of September.[21] As this strong, unified stance became more widely known, sterling rallied against the dollar. By the 27th of September, it had gone up several per cent to $4.25 – its strongest position since Keynes had begun speculating.

Keynes had not counted on this. His first dollar position was meant to close on 30 September. Having contracted for the dollars at the price of $4.18, he closed it on the 26th at $4.24, losing £150 on the trade. This was just the beginning. He had another $100,000 that was due to close on 10 October. That contract had the pound valued at just $4.14. On 6 October, however, Chamberlain raised the Treasury Bill rates a full 1%, bringing them in line with the Bank's interest rate. Sterling went from $4.19 to $4.22. Yet, Keynes was undeterred. The next day, he rolled over that contract, buying himself another month, and bought another £17,900 worth of dollars at $4.21. He closed his previous short of the lire due to close on 19 October. This dealt him a £39 loss, but it freed up betting capacity of £12,150. He gambled that much and more – £12,866 – going long on Danish krone, further shortening his position on the pound.

[19] See further discussion below.
[20] Court of Directors, "Minutes" (Bank of England; G4/142, September 18 and 25, 1919).
[21] ibid. Committee of Treasury, "Minutes" (Bank of England; G8/54, September 17 and 24, 1919).

A few days later, Keynes closed out a prior dollar position with a loss of £25. The pound was at $4.20, and most of Keynes's bets were now below this level.

Insights in Amsterdam

The same day – 11 October – Keynes travelled to Amsterdam, at the invitation of Dr Vissering, the Governor of the Bank of the Netherlands. There, Vissering mooted a bold proposal for an international loan to Europe. It would be "furnished mainly by America, but … the neutrals also were to contribute on a generous scale." Tellingly, he "put down Holland for as large a contribution as the United Kingdom, viz. $200 million." But, Keynes noted, "all those present, took an exceedingly pessimistic view of the whole situation and evidently regarded any attempt to carry out the treaty in any literal way as spelling disaster for Europe."[22]

In the final stages of completing the *Economic Consequences*, he solicited feedback from two of Vissering's guests: Dr Carl Melchior and Paul Warburg. The former had been a part of Germany's delegation to the post-war negotiations and thus had sat opposite Keynes on prior occasions.[23] The latter had helped to create the US Federal Reserve and then served on its board (1914–1918) and as a Vice-Governor (1916–1918). He was, as Keynes described, "formerly the chief spirit of the Federal Reserve Board." With great pride, Keynes later recounted how his scathing portrait of Woodrow Wilson drew both laughter and tears.[24]

The trip reassured Keynes that his book would prove provocative. But it also unsettled his confidence in his speculations. Melchior and Warburg were two of the best connected, and most powerful, financiers in the world. Keynes shared their devotion to mitigating the economic disaster that he knew would follow from the Treaty's implementation.[25] If their reform efforts gained momentum, European currencies – including sterling – would appreciate against the dollar.

---

[22] John Maynard Keynes, "Diary" (Kings College; PP/41/15, October 11, 1919). Keynes, *Collected Writings*, 17:128–129.

[23] Moggridge, *Maynard Keynes,* pp. 300–301.

[24] Keynes, *Collected Writings*, 10:427–429.

[25] Warburg subsequently created the International Acceptance Bank (IAB) in 1921. The IAB specialized in providing short-term trade credits (bankers' acceptances) to foreign, especially German, firms.

At the time, Keynes had shorted more than £21,000 worth of French francs. He had sold the first two thirds of the francs in August when it took just 34 francs to buy a pound. It was a long-term bet, with a delivery more than a month in the future; and with the exchange rate at 36.1 francs to the pound, it looked to be a winning one. Prior to the visit, Keynes had expanded this franc short position by £6,986 at a rate of 35.75 francs to the pound. But now he considered the franc might not fall all that much further – particularly if the actions of he and his colleagues increased the prospects of a major international loan. Keynes wasted no time. On the 13th – even before he had returned from Amsterdam – he closed out the most recent franc forward position, locking in a £54 profit.[26]

Initially, Keynes took no action on the dollar position, but insights from Warburg changed his mind. Warburg, Keynes later suggested, "hated" President Wilson "for personal reasons." So, at the previous reading of Keynes's *Economic Consequences* in Amsterdam, Warburg had a "a chuckling delight" at the thought of Wilson's "discomfiture" during the Paris peace negotiations.[27] Warburg, however, was privy to one of the most important political secrets of the time. On the 3rd of October, Wilson had suffered a massive, debilitating stroke. Few people outside of the White House knew this; but, on the 17th of October, Warburg informed Keynes that Wilson was "pretty critically ill."[28]

Warburg only intended that Keynes should curb some of his sharpest criticisms. Keynes did follow that advice, and softened the manuscript. He also, it appears, incorporated this information into his currency trades. The same day, Keynes closed out a $75,000 long

---

[26] Keynes, "Diary." Keynes's appointment book reports that he left for Amsterdam on the 11th. It is unclear from that book precisely when he returned from Amsterdam. But Keynes notes in his "biography" of Melchior that they met three days after he arrived in Holland (on the 12th). Keynes, *Collected Writings*, 10:427–429. The appointment book does not mention this or the other meetings in Amsterdam. Instead, it lists several of Keynes's usual commitments in England: his weekly lecture on Monday and the Wednesday National Mutual meeting, along with a (mistaken?) entry for a Tuesday National Mutual meeting. These entries, however, may have been written in advance and then simply rescheduled. Moggridge (1992, 356) also specifies the 15th as the date for the meeting.

[27] Keynes, *Collected Writings*, 10:429.   [28] Keynes, *Collected Writings*, 17:6.

position on the dollar – a position initiated only ten days previously.[29] During that time, the pound had declined from $4.21 to $4.17. But now Keynes reconsidered whether the dollar would continue to rise across the remaining four weeks of the contract. So, several weeks early, he happily took a profit of £151 and reduced his overall sterling short position against the dollar (and the Danish krone).

Keynes distilled the insights from his Amsterdam discussions into a series of short "notes which he put to use in his private dealings." He described the "extraordinary scale" of speculation: "foreign holdings of marks [have] now reached the prodigious figure of 20 milliards [billion]." With the gold mark valued at 45 times that of the paper mark, Keynes thought that "a very disastrous collapse of the [exchange] rate might easily occur." This was a ripe opportunity for shorting the currency. But, at this point, Keynes held off. His other notes detailed the ambiguities in the Treaty, particularly concerning the title to property in Germany, in its overseas possessions, and beyond. Keynes recognized that the value of the mark in the coming weeks depended on how these largely political questions were resolved by the Reparation Commission and the Allied powers themselves. At the same time, law and order within Germany, "which was formerly quite incorruptible" was "getting down to the Russian level." Altogether, there was just too much uncertainty in Germany. But, in another note, Keynes warned of the growing American investment in Germany – and of the "good deal of criticism of America" when these contracts "come to be generally known."[30]

So, instead of speculating against the mark, Keynes made a simpler, but more surprising, trade: he shorted the dollar for the first time. The next day – 21 October – Keynes sold $150,000 at the rate of $4.18 to the pound. The first $50,000 was to be delivered on 9 November. The next $100,000 was to be delivered six days after that.

Thus, following this first visit to Amsterdam, Keynes became convinced that the dollar was going to plunge. He was horrified by the spectacle of special interests – like Standard Oil – capturing the apparatus of American foreign policy to secure monopoly privileges. Still

---

[29] As discussed above, Moggridge's suggestion that he was still in Amsterdam on the 15th increases the likelihood that he was there on the 17th. If so, he might have received Warburg's letter the same day.

[30] Keynes, *Collected Writings*, 17:130–136.

a congregant in the church of laissez-faire, he was certain that such mercantilism would prove costly. Inspired by his discussions, he was filled with hope that the United States would make a serious financial and political commitment to European stability. At the same time, he knew that Wilson's health was fading. Having construed Wilson as his principal impediment, he naively believed that a British-led European initiative could be foisted onto the Americans. This would save European civilization even as it exacted a momentary depreciation in the dollar. Yet, Keynes's position was a short-term one, and he expected the dollar to fall quickly.[31] One week later, he adopted a long position on the dollar, buying a two-month forward of $100,000 at the price of $4.16.

Fighting for International Cooperation

On 2 November, Keynes returned to Amsterdam. Together with Warburg, he crafted an ambitious programme "to heal the unprecedented economic evils from which all Europe is now suffering."[32] The "very grave" problem was just as he had warned in the *Economic Consequences*. War debts and reparations – including "some...fictitious items" – had grossly inflated the public obligations, "lead[ing] to fear or despair on the part of some, and to recklessness on the part of others." The conventional means to redress the problem were a "decrease of excessive consumption and an increase of production and taxation." Without it, "the depreciation of money ... [would] continue, wiping out the savings of the past and leading to a gradual but persistent spreading of bankruptcy and anarchy in Europe."[33]

Even this, however, would prove insufficient. This was a collective problem, and so Keynes and Warburg called for "a great international act of co-operative assistance." Most ambitiously, they pressed "the United States and England [to] consider how far they can ease the burden of their Entente debtors either by abandoning interest charges

---

[31] On the 23rd, Keynes bought £18,150 in a long position on the Dutch guilder with a contract date of 13 November. This was implicitly a short of the pound over the same period. Taken together, we can infer that Keynes expected the dollar to fall (generally) rather than the pound to rise (generally).

[32] The editors of Keynes's *Collected Writings* (17:136n) suggest that this work was drafted largely by Warburg and Keynes.

[33] Keynes, *Collected Writings*, 17:136–141.

or by cancelling a portion of the claims they hold." They contended that this was "justifiable and could be written off as a legitimate war expense by the lending countries." After all, "a portion of these loans reacted to the benefit of the loaning countries, in waging what was a common cause."[34]

The proposal was immensely practical and eminently reasonable. Yet, it was hardly politically feasible. In the weeks that followed, the US representative in Amsterdam (Fred Kent) withdrew his signature from the proposal, effectively stopping it in its tracks. At the time, the US Senate had been considering the Treaty of Versailles for months. The following week, the Senate invoked cloture for the first time in its history. On the 19th, they voted overwhelmingly to reject the Treaty in its entirety.[35]

It was a crushing defeat of the very internationalism that Keynes had championed. Whereas he had attacked the Treaty for doing too little to bind together the leading countries of the world, the US Senate was vociferous in asserting it would do too much. "Americanism shall not, cannot, die," Senator Henry Cabot Lodge proclaimed.[36]

Yet, somehow, Keynes remained optimistic. Closely following the debates, he nevertheless wrote to his Dutch colleagues, "it does not follow that America may not be prepared to do voluntarily a good deal to which she is not willing to bind herself in advance." In retrospect, the view was out of touch. Keynes was riding high following positive developments in his rather extensive conversations with colleagues in the French Treasury and Embassy. He may have assumed that leading individuals like Warburg could – and would – overrule the American public's zeal for disengagement. He thus resolved that they should "go forward boldly" "bring[ing] the issue to the bar of the public opinion of the world." "[I]f America quite deliberately decides that she is going to leave Europe to her misfortunes," he quipped, "she must say so openly and in so many words."[37]

---

[34] Keynes, *Collected Writings*, 17:136–141.
[35] So far from securing two-thirds of the Senate in favour, nearly two-thirds voted against it. They voted 53–38 against ratification without reservation. And they even voted (55–39) against Henry Cabot Lodge's resolution of ratification, which included more than a dozen reservations to the Treaty.
[36] Record, 66 Cong., I Sess., pp. 8777–8778; 8768–8769, 8781–8784. www .mtholyoke.edu/acad/intrel/doc41.htm.
[37] Keynes, *Collected Writings*, 17:142–143.

Less Hope, More Big Shorts

The hopefulness expressed in Keynes's correspondence did not match the bearishness of his speculation. Increasingly, his trades reflected his recognition that the United States would not come to Europe's assistance.

It was clear by the first week of November that Keynes had been wrong about a short-term decline in the dollar. So far from coming to Europe's assistance, the United States moved to strengthen the dollar. On 3 November, the Federal Reserve raised interest rates from 4% to 4.75%. In response, the Bank of England raised its discount rate a full 1% to 6%. The next day, UK Treasury bills were raised 0.5%. This proved inadequate, and the pound began a one-month slide that would eventually take it to as low as $3.65.

It was a painful lesson for Keynes. The dollar had not appreciated enough over the past few months to do him any good on his long bets; but it was appreciating fast enough now to do a good deal of damage on his short-term short positions. On the 6th, Keynes closed out a three-month long position on the dollar at $4.17, one penny below his original purchase price. At the same time, he closed the first ($50,000) position on 6 November at $4.16 to the pound. This cost him £92.20. He ought to have closed the remaining $100,000 at the same time. Instead, he waited another week, closing it only after the pound had sunk to just $4.12. Altogether, these 20-day shorts lost him £540–more than £27,000 in 2019 terms.

Bitten by his having misread the US trajectory, Keynes reeled in his bets and reassessed his position. Across the second week of November, he had less than £45,000 worth of contracts. This was down from his high of £118,000 just one month earlier. Indeed, he had not had so little money on the table since the end of August.

In late November, Keynes despaired, "so far as finance is concerned, everything depends on the U.S. Without her we can do nothing effective. And at present the U.S. Treasury has vetoed even the discussion of the European financial problem."[38] He wrote to another colleague, "I … feel that if we wait until the Americans actually press us to go forward, we shall wait for ever."[39]

At the same time, Keynes contemplated the profound market consequences of continued US isolationism. The currencies of the

---

[38] Keynes, *Collected Writings*, 17:8.   [39] Keynes, *Collected Writings*, 17:144.

Continental European belligerents – Germany, France, and Italy – would bear the brunt of it. Without the United States to referee their political squabbles and buoy their economies, they would all sink together. The UK could try to distance itself from this internecine conflict; but the pound, too, would suffer relative to the currencies of the neutral powers. Attending so dutifully to their own narrow interests, the Americans would ensure that the dollar would reign supreme. Across these next several months, Keynes's trades were all predicated upon the expectation that this Hobbesian world would be realised.

On the 11th of November, Keynes took a massive profit on his first speculation: the short against the French franc from 21 August. Keynes had sold 500,000 francs at the price of 34.06 francs to the pound. Since then, the franc had fallen nearly 12%. Closing this trade ten days early, it netted £1,487.[40] Yet even this windfall could not prepare Keynes for the boom and the bust in the months to come.

The next day, Keynes speculated against the German mark for the first time. In less than a week, the mark fell from 149.5 to 165 marks to the pound. Keynes made £462 in just five days.

Keynes then poured these profits into further ambitious shorts of the continental belligerents' currencies. First, he shorted nearly £10,000 worth of Italian lire. The next day, he shorted £11,721 worth of French francs. He then expanded this by another £11,579 worth of French francs. More shorts followed along the same lines across the next week.

In October, Keynes had bought £12,866 worth of Danish krone and £18,205 worth of Dutch florins. Into November, neither was appreciating much against the pound, contrary to his expectations. When aggressive rate hikes by the Bank of England and the UK Treasury did not stop sterling's slide into November, Keynes renewed his bets on the currencies of these two neutral powers, extending the delivery dates for each into December. In mid-November, he again extended both positions by another month.

Keynes's position on the neutral powers was less about their value and more about his expectations for the value of the pound. Because he was beginning and ending his trades with his local currency – the pound sterling – his shorts of these other currencies were relative to

---

[40] This is equivalent to £75,422 in 2019 pounds.

the pound in the first instance. At this time, he thought that the pound was also likely to depreciate relative to gold, so he simultaneously shorted the pound by going long on both the US dollar and the currencies of the European neutrals.

By late November, Keynes's total speculation approached £110,000. Of that, roughly half was in the form of shorts against the mark, the lire, and the franc. The other half was in the form of long positions on the dollar (£25,000) and on the Dutch florin and the Danish krone (£18,262 and £12,833 respectively).

These latter bets were proving disappointing. The pound was still sliding – now dipping toward the $4.00 threshold – but the currencies of the European neutrals were not behaving as he had expected. The Dutch florin was up, and so Keynes was able to take a profit of £498 at the end of November. But he lost more than this amount (£549) a few days later when he closed out the long position on the Danish krone.

In retrospect, Keynes might have known better. Even the neutral economies were inextricably tied to those of the belligerents. But their trajectories were unknowable ex ante. After all, the policies depended as much on politics. Even if those countries' monetary authorities had the economic means to appreciate their currencies, they may have also wanted the requisite political will.

At the same time, the lessons of the franc, the lira, and the mark appeared clear. On the 18th and 19th of November, he shorted more than £25,000 worth of French francs.

Both contracts had one-month delivery dates; but the franc fell so fast that within a few weeks Keynes closed out these trades with an incredible profit of more than £2,400. He took £753 profit on the mark across the same period. He might have realized large profits on the lire as well; but, instead, he expanded this position as he wound down his position on the neutral powers.

This became the new theme of Keynes's trades. He shorted the franc and the lire, took some profits, and expanded his bets against them. By the end of the year, more than £89,000 of the £116,600 that he had bet were in the form of short positions against these two economies' currencies.

Given his success, it is not surprising that Keynes was pleased to continue betting against the French and the Italians. But this does not fully explain his trading position. After all, every currency trade was necessarily a bet about two different things. Correctly predicting that the franc would fall relative to gold could still prove unprofitable if the pound simultaneously depreciated (relative to gold) by even more. Also, because Keynes was operating in the forward market, he was betting on his expectations relative to those of the market consensus.

Previously, Keynes had bet overtly against the belligerents *and* implicitly against the pound by betting on the dollar and the neutral powers at a ratio of about 1:1. He bet almost as much on the pound's trajectory relative to the dollar as he did on European belligerent currency trajectories relative to the pound. Across the last six weeks of 1919, however, Keynes had three times as much money riding on the depreciation of the franc and the lira (relative to the pound) as on the pound (relative to the dollar). We will see that, according to his own analysis at the time, this had less to do with his views about the dollar than with his views about the pound.

Securing the Pound?

At the beginning of December, the Cunliffe Committee published its *Final Report*. For Bradbury, this was an opportunity to further pressure the government to continue the fiscal austerity and monetary contraction that he hoped would drive sterling back up to its pre-war gold value.[41]

The gambit proved successful. A few weeks later, Chancellor of the Exchequer Austen Chamberlain declared in Parliament that the government "agree with the [Cunliffe] Committee's view that increased production, cessation of Government borrowings, and decreased expenditure both public and private are the first essentials to recovery."[42]

At this point, Chamberlain held the keys to sterling's future. First and foremost, the Chancellor was preeminent in setting fiscal policy. With a public debt of nearly £7.8 billion – more than ten times its pre-war level – the government's budget and its approach to debt

---

[41] Cunliffe Committee, "Discussion Following Wright Testimony" (National Archives; T185/2, July 23, 1919), 664. As Permanent Joint-Secretary to the Treasury, Bradbury had already pressed this course vigorously onto the Cabinet. "Cabinet Minutes." 4.

[42] Hansard vol 123, cc 43–46.

management would have a huge effect on the real value of sterling.[43] This is to say nothing of war debts and reparations, the approach to which was increasingly dictated by the government in general and the Treasury in particular.[44]

Throughout the war, the Treasury had massively expanded the money supply by printing its own "Currency Notes." By 1918, the Cunliffe Committee estimated that two-thirds (£259 million) of the £388 million in circulation took the form of such Treasury notes. Only 12% of these notes were backed by gold. Yet, the notes themselves were designated legal tender, and they were treated as such in the market.[45]

Naturally, the Bank disclaimed all responsibility for the Treasury notes. It was a private institution, after all; and it certainly did not relish sullying its standing by taking the government's paper notes (liabilities) onto its balance sheet. To avoid that "awkwardness," the Cunliffe Committee recommended:

during the transitional period, the issue should remain a Government issue, but ... such post-war expansion (if any) as may take place should be covered, not by the investment of the proceeds of the new Notes in Government securities, as at present, but by taking Bank of England Notes from the Bank and holding them in the Currency Note reserve.[46]

This joined the Treasury and the Bank at the hip, with the Treasury responsible for driving the currency notes out of circulation and the Bank with recourse to interest rate hikes to discipline the government.

Thus, the Bank *could* dictate fiscal policy since the Chancellor would have to keep the interest rate on Treasury bills in line with the Bank's market rate to consolidate its wartime borrowing, let alone to issue fresh debt. In this early phase, however, the Bank's Governors

---

[43] Prior to the war, the public debt was just £706 million. In his first year as Chancellor, Chamberlain was able to reduce the debt by 3.2% to £7.6 billion. Global Financial Data, "UK National Debt (GVGBRDEBT)."

[44] During the war, sometime Bank of England Governor Cunliffe had proven instrumental in organizing the first wartime Anglo-American loan; and he was one of the UK's representatives at the Paris Peace Conference on reparations. But this authority had been transferred (implicitly) to the Treasury that autumn, when Bradbury (from the Treasury) was appointed as the principal British delegate to the Reparation Commission.

[45] Cunliffe Committee, *First Interim Report*, 5. Currency and Bank Notes Act, 1914 (4 & 5 Geo. 5, c. 14).

[46] Cunliffe Committee, *First Interim Report*, p. 10.

chose not to exercise this control over the Treasury. Some within the Bank questioned this surrender of its prerogative. In 1917, Governor-in-waiting Montagu Norman bitterly denounced Governor Cunliffe's deference to the Treasury.[47] The assertion of the Bank's autonomy – some would say supremacy – came to define Norman's 24-year reign as Bank of England Governor. At this point, however, even Norman followed the party line.[48]

For these reasons, Chancellor Chamberlain's public embrace of the Cunliffe Committee recommendations was massively important. Since April, when the government began liberalizing the wartime capital controls, sterling had fallen from $4.76 to just $3.67. Following Chamberlain's announcement, the pound rose 17 cents (nearly 5%) against the dollar.

In the midst of this, Keynes released the *Economic Consequences* into the world. He sent the better part of a hundred copies of the book to colleagues, friends, and anyone he thought might influence the course of events. Of course, he was sure to include Chamberlain among them. In the first instance, Keynes pressed the Chancellor so as to shape the realm of international finance. But when Chamberlain replied with some substantive thoughts, Keynes used the opportunity to encourage him to pursue orthodoxy in the UK's macroeconomic policy. "I was immensely glad to read of your decision about [removing the Treasury's] currency notes," Keynes wrote at the end of December. Keynes did warn him that the "drastic" policy "will have far-reaching consequences": "if it is maintained, [it] must logically end in a very high bank rate and corresponding rates for Treasury bills." Yet, Keynes endorsed it fully. "I was nearly moved to write to *The*

---

[47] Montagu Norman, "Diary" (Bank of England; ADM34/5, August 2, 1917).
[48] In January 1920, Danish representatives approached the Bank about issuing debt. Governor Cokayne refused to see them outright. Norman met with their representative from Hambros bank and explained the Bank's decision-making, as he recorded in his diary: "H Hambro – after failing to get appt with G[overnor]– came with 3 Danes to see me. Saw him alone – on subject of short or long Danish issue in [?] – but refused to hear the Danes or see them. Confirmed … our opposition to issue here by any Neutral, long or short: said such issue w[oul]d justify or require rise in B[ank] R[ate]: Said we sh[oul]d so advise Treasury, with object of preventing it, even if favoured by F[oreign] O[ffice]…He said issue w[oul]d probably be made by Barclays. I said Danes sh[oul]d go to N[ew] Y[ork]. (His position generally unpleasing)." Montagu Norman, "Diary" (Bank of England; ADM34/9, January 29, 1920).

Times in defence of the new policy; but decided that it had better work its remedy in silence for the present," he recounted. Nonetheless, Keynes did give some talks praising the austerity advocated by the Cunliffe Committee. Yet, he was under no illusion: "it is a very drastic policy and one which cannot be pursued half-heartedly."[49]

A few days after writing to Chamberlain, Keynes closed his long US dollar position (from the end of October). The pound had depreciated so much that he realized £2,300 of profit in just two months' time. This trade alone accounted for more than a third of his total profit to date. It finally tipped his dollar trading into a cumulative profit.

At this point, Keynes opted not to renew this position, and a two-month-long hiatus in any dollar-based speculation followed. Moreover, at the same time as closing his dollar position, he opened a £33,000 short position (with a delivery in late March) on the Indian rupee. Shifting from going long on the dollar to short on the rupee put Keynes firmly in the most bullish position he had yet taken on the pound. Just what was Keynes thinking?

Intellectualizing Exchange Rates

In mid-January, Keynes spoke to the Manchester and District Bankers' Institute on the subject of the foreign exchanges. His remarks offer unparalleled insight into his thinking about the determinants of exchange rates in general. They reflect an early step on the road to his revolutionary critique of the gold standard. However, when it came to discussing the trajectory of specific currencies, Keynes was obtuse and appears to have pushed in the direction opposite to that of the speculative positions he held at the time.

Keynes's speculation had taught him that key elements of the pre-war system no longer operated. He denigrated "the popular delusion that the exchanges had a tendency always to swing back to par." Of course, the decline of the franc since the autumn was proof enough of this; and Keynes's (correct) predictions on that account had paid him handsomely. Keynes, nearing the crest of his first speculative wave, could not help but condescend. "Many ignorant people," he informed the bankers, "often spoke of the exchanges as though some psychological or psychical influence were at work determining the rates, whereas

[49] Keynes, *Collected Writings*, 17:179–184.

nothing moved the exchanges except the demand for a particular currency." He went so far as to question the cornerstone of the gold standard orthodoxy itself: "it was an elementary fact that gold could only affect the exchanges if the existence of the gold affected people's demands for the currency concerned."[50]

The traditional view – encapsulated in Hume's price-specie-flow mechanism – was that exchange rate movements triggered gold flows which, in turn, necessitated adjustments in the money supply. Over the ensuing century and a half, this system became intermediated by central banks and treasuries adjusting monetary and fiscal policy in response to exchange rate movements. But, by following these so-called "rules of the game," the international gold standard system would operate, as the Cunliffe Committee had put it, "automatically."[51] Yet, there were still limitations on the free movement of gold in the UK and abroad. These capital controls insulated governments from some of the market pressures, propping up their currencies' nominal gold values. More important, few governments were implementing the fiscal and monetary austerity necessary to appreciate their currencies. Thus, despite his overt remarks to the contrary, Keynes did recognize that the supply side was also crucial. Indeed, this became the main thrust of his critique of the gold standard in the years that followed.[52] At this early stage, however, Keynes fixated on reconceptualizing the demand side of the equation.

Keynes explained that there were three types of demand: the "trade" demand, "arising out of commerce," the "investment" "demand of people who are going to make permanent investments in the currency in question," and the "speculative" demand, "a sort of gamble" on the direction of exchange rate movements. The real gamble, Keynes

---

[50] Keynes, *Collected Writings*, 17:172.

[51] Cunliffe Committee, *First Interim Report*, p 9.

[52] Obviously, macroeconomic policies affect the money supply and thus the real value of a currency. So, the commitment to maintain the gold value of a currency means that changes in reserve levels lead to changes in those all-important macroeconomic policies. At this point, however, Keynes was at pains to stress that both mattered *exclusively* in terms of their effect on speculators' psychology. "Again," he said, "if there were a large gold reserve in the country, that fact might create in the minds of speculators the idea that the gold reserve could be used to advantage some day, so that the gold reserve to that extent would be an inducement to speculation on the exchanges." "Just in the same [way], in a country like France, when the budget did not balance, that factor might deter people from investing in francs." Keynes, *Collected Writings*, 17:175.

asserted, actually existed on the trade side as "trading profits [were] frequently ... swallowed up by changes in the rate of exchange." To allow traders to offload this risk onto those willing to bear it – that is currency speculators – Keynes championed the active development of the forward market "in London and other parts of the country."[53]

Yet, Keynes's application of this framework to the currencies of Germany, France, and the UK all cut against the speculative positions he held at that time. In each of his discussions, he was honest but less than fully forthcoming. He largely confined his remarks to the economic dimension, while the trajectory of each exchange rate turned crucially on the *policies* adopted by that currency's monetary and fiscal authorities. His large speculative positions suggest that he held private opinions about this other dimension, but he did not share those opinions with the bankers.

Germany

As early as October 1919, Keynes had concluded that the German position was untenable. The war-weary Germans had an inelastic demand for vital imports but relatively few exports. This ought to have depreciated the exchange rate, and Keynes bet that it would, wagering about £5,000 against the mark that autumn. When these shorts proved disappointing, Keynes revised his theory and reversed his position.

As he later explained to the Manchester bankers, "Immediately after the armistice, speculators in other countries ... purchased mark notes, with the result that ... Germany had practically paid for her imports out of the proceeds of this speculation." Of course, this was not entirely sufficient, and so the mark's gold value did decline. Keynes calculated that prices would have to rise "thirty times" above their pre-war level just to "keep pace with the fall in the exchange" rate. "[B]ut this was an absurd state of affairs." In the heady days of early 1920, Keynes could hardly imagine the hyperinflation to come. Instead, "the future value of the German mark" depended on "what credit Germany would obtain from other countries," and "what the vast army of speculators were going to do."[54]

---

[53] Keynes, *Collected Writings*, 17:171–179.
[54] Keynes, *Collected Writings*, 17:176–177.

Keynes was unconventional in challenging the "automaticity" that was central to orthodox gold standard theory. But for the speculators, Keynes posited, the mark's exchange rate would have fallen even more than it had, and the prices in Germany would have fallen *much* more than they had done. In other words, the policymakers did not follow the rules of the game, and the speculators did not play the game the way it was meant to be played.

Just prior to this talk in Manchester, Keynes went long on the mark for the first time, entering into a six-week contract worth nearly £10,300. He ought not to have done so. When the forward rate on the mark plunged, Keynes quickly liquidated his position – but not before he had lost £1,230 in less than a week. It dwarfed the £448 he had lost trying to short the dollar. By the end of 1920, Keynes had lost nearly £6,500 on the mark. Even as he clawed back some of his speculations over the next several years, he still lost £4,354 (net) in his bets on the mark. Keynes the speaker appreciated what Keynes the speculator did not: "the situation [in Germany] was perplexing, as the elements determining it were very complicated."[55]

France

Keynes's remarks implied that France's position had much in common with that of Germany. For France, "The trade demand was the determining factor of the situation." And, like Germany, France was likely to run a negative balance of trade. Similarly, "prices had risen in France more than in this country, but not sufficiently to correspond with the fall in the exchange." Keynes offered a rough calculation from a "logarithmic table," which "showed a fall in the exchange of 4 per cent per month." But, as ever, "there was the question as to how far France would be able to borrow in this country and America."

Keynes significantly understated his position. At the time, he had about £73,000 worth of short positions against the franc. Here again, there was much that Keynes thought about this currency that he chose not to divulge to his audience.[56]

Why was Keynes so pessimistic about the franc? We can glean his perspective from a letter to a French critic of the *Economic*

[55] Keynes, *Collected Writings*, 17:177.   [56] Keynes, *Collected Writings*, 17:177.

Consequences. For Keynes, it came down to politics. The French government refused to grasp the logic of his book. Keynes "recognise[d] fully the necessity of a generous attitude...towards France," and he restated his commitment to forgiving France's external war debt. Furthermore, "[France] and Belgium should have first claim upon all payments made by Germany." Yet, "Frenchmen," Keynes lamented, still "refuse to consider...the general European situation" and, in particular, "Germany's real capacity to pay."

Time would prove that Keynes was not wrong. The conviction that Germany could – and would – be made to pay might deflect temporarily blame from French policymakers. But this "obstinate illusion" would lead to "economic and financial catastrophe."[57] Just as predicted, the franc did fall. And Keynes did profit – on the franc, at least.

The UK

Yet, Keynes's bets were not strictly about the gold value of the franc. He had eliminated his bets on the dollar and the currencies of the neutrals and thus bet that the pound would not continue to follow the franc down. He held this position because he was confident that the UK policymakers would drive the pound back onto gold.

Keynes, however, hesitated to broadcast this view. In his Manchester lecture, Keynes invoked the "very optimistic trade forecast ... recently made by the Board of Trade," but he quickly deflated expectations. Such a positive "forecast ... was probably a little too premature." Beyond this, Keynes just gave the standard caution against foreign lending. Instead, the UK needed to use its purchasing power abroad to cover its foreign trade.

It is peculiar that Keynes, who pressed the Chancellor with such clarity and conviction to strengthen the pound, was so tepid – and unhelpful – in his comments on this occasion. In fact, he was more confident than ever about the trajectory of the pound. By this point, Keynes had reduced his bets on the dollar and the strong currencies of the neutrals to just £13,100 in total.

Evidently, Keynes's audience too were surprised by his remarks. The question of South African gold came up. Keynes conceded that the UK "obtained from South Africa about 3 million sterling of gold

[57] Keynes, *Collected Writings*, 17:22–23.

per month." At the time, this annual inflow was more than 20% of the UK's total gold holdings.[58] This, of course, ought to strengthen the pound and grant the UK more opportunities to consume and invest abroad. But, Keynes insisted, "This gold had been taken to a fairly large extent for the arts. A certain amount had gone to New York as exchange transactions, but by far the greater part had gone to India."[59] This last remark is particularly surprising given that, two weeks prior, Keynes had shorted about £33,210 worth of rupees. If Keynes thought this trend were going to reverse, he did not say so to this group of bankers. Here, again, was evidence that Keynes thought – in private, at least – that the pound would fare well.

Safeguarding His Biggest Gamble

Three days after his lecture in Manchester, Keynes stretched further than he ever had done or would do in this period. He added another million (each) French francs and Italian lire to his short positions. For two brief days, Keynes had more than £173,000 on the table. When one of his franc positions closed – paying him a massive £1,982 profit – he went into late January with nearly £146,000 in contracts. Of this, £133,000 was in the form of short positions, principally against France.

On the 23rd, however, the Federal Reserve raised interest rates 1.25% to 6%. This was on a Friday. Typically, the Bank of England's powerful Committee of Treasury decided on rate adjustments at their Wednesday meeting.[60] But on Wednesday, the 28th, the Bank decided not to raise its interest rate. That day, Keynes bought 500,000 French francs on the spot market to close out a short position he had on the franc. This was two weeks before the maturity date of the corresponding forward contract.

Although he was shaken, Keynes retained outward confidence that the pound would follow the dollar. On 2 February, he gave a public

---

[58] Estimating the UK's gold supply was difficult and fraught. The Cunliffe Committee put it at around £165 million, but their *First Interim Report* was (deliberately) vague. Cunliffe Committee, *First Interim Report*, p. 5. Morrison 2021, 54–57.

[59] Keynes, *Collected Writings*, 17:177.

[60] Technically, the adjustments needed to be approved by the Bank's Court of Directors (which met the following day). This was largely perfunctory, however. Committee of Treasury, "Minutes." April 14, 1920.

lecture at Cambridge on "The Future of the Rate of Interest." His notes suggest a certain conclusion: "Fact must prevail in the long run. In the near, future interest rates must rise."[61] Certainly, Keynes's speculative position had assumed as much.

That same day, however, Chamberlain finally replied to Keynes's previous calls for further rate increases. "I am being strongly pressed to lower the [Treasury Bill] rate again," the Chancellor wrote to Keynes. He then challenged Keynes to reply "to [those] who argue that in the [current] special circumstances ... the raising of the Bank or Treasury Bill rate has no effect upon borrowing or upon the exchanges except to raise the price of money against Government itself[.]" He hoped to discuss it with Keynes in person. Barring that, "I hope you can find time to write pretty fully," he wrote.[62]

Such wavering was not what Keynes wanted – or expected – to hear. Had not Chamberlain promised Parliament that he would implement the requisite austerity? Deviating now would doom the pound to fall. Keynes would make his case for austerity both in person and in writing. But, first, he closed out another short position by buying 500,000 French francs on the spot market that very day.

Keynes met with the Chancellor two days later. He was emphatic that the UK needed to raise interest rates. Following the Fed's action two weeks before, "rates for money in New York [were] 2 to 3 per cent in excess of the London rate."[63] Thus, "The danger of our exchanges now lies ... in ... [London] lending money she has not got to borrowers of unexceptional character at a rate far below the real value of new capital." To defend the exchange rate, "it is above all necessary that money in London should be a little dearer than in New York."[64]

"Dear money," Keynes argued in highly orthodox fashion, "will do good by checking bankers' loans, diminishing foreign loans and ... bringing the mind of the business world to a better realisation of the true position." "A continuance of inflationism and high prices will not

---

[61] Keynes, *Collected Writings*, 17:180. [62] Keynes, *Collected Writings*, 17:180.
[63] In the meeting, Chamberlain noted an even larger difference: the "New York [interest] rate for good commercial borrowers is 8 or 9%." "Can't keep London steady if it is 3 or 4% below New York rate," Keynes is reported to have said. [Austen Chamberlain], "Note of Interview with Keynes" (National Archives; T172–1384, February 4, 1920).
[64] Keynes, *Collected Writings*, 17:180–184.

only depress the exchanges," Keynes insisted, "but by their effect on prices will strike at the whole basis of contract, of security, and of the capitalist system generally."[65]

Naturally, the Conservative Chancellor wanted none of that; but he also did not want to trigger a national economic contraction. He was under pressure from Lloyd George to finance an ambitious housing scheme; and his predecessor (Reginald McKenna) had suggested that raising interest rates would do little to appreciate sterling but much to hinder government borrowing. Chamberlain wanted to be certain that the orthodoxy still applied "in the special circumstances of the time."[66]

Keynes conceded, "The old arguments in favour of dear money no longer hold in their entirety because a high bank rate has no immediate effect on the exchanges either by influencing the volume of bills offered for discount in London or by influencing the flow of gold." "It is also true," Keynes further admitted, "that a moderate increase of the bank rate may have very little salutary effect indeed and may merely make Government borrowing dearer without deterring other borrowers."[67]

But this really just meant that the old medicine had to be administered in stronger doses. An increase today of "1% perhaps only equals 0.25% pre-war." So, the rate hikes must be substantial: "a rate of even 10% must be contemplated." Sensing Chamberlain's misgivings, Keynes agreed that it did not need to come all at once. "Such a very high rate may produce a crisis," but, Keynes assured him, such a crisis would "be only financial and not commercial ... [I]t would not ... cause any serious amount of unemployment."[68]

Keynes was hardly alone in clamouring for austerity. Prominent bankers and virtually all of Chamberlain's advisors echoed Keynes's recommendations. Among them, Bank Governor Cokayne followed a memorandum with a strongly worded letter to Chamberlain. "[T]here are obviously limits to the accommodation which the Bank can

---

[65] Keynes, *Collected Writings*, 17:182–184.
[66] Keynes, *Collected Writings*, 17:180.   [67] Keynes, *Collected Writings*, 17:180.
[68] Chamberlain noted, "Mr. K. agrees dear money must come but not yet. Presses not to check trade now. But K. thinks you must check development" [Chamberlain], "Note of Interview with Keynes"; Keynes, *Collected Writings*, 17:183.

continue to grant without applying the proper corrective of higher rates," Cokayne warned Chamberlain.[69]

The day that Keynes met with Chamberlain, sterling traded at $3.18 – its lowest point in a century and the lowest point it would reach until the end of 1932. It was nearly a full dollar less valuable than it had been in August, when Keynes began speculating. But, contrary to all of Keynes's hopes and orthodox expectations, the Chancellor demurred. He deferred the hikes until April, when the Bank of France took their rate from 5 to 6% and Montagu Norman had taken the helm of the Bank. Chamberlain finally raised the Treasury Bill rate to 6.5%, and the Bank raised its rate to 7% the next day. This was the highest Bank rate had been in peacetime since 1907. It would not go this high again until 1967.[70]

Keynes must have known by the end of the meeting that the Chancellor was not going to raise interest rates. So, once again, he engaged in damage control by fully closing his lira position – netting a profit of £3,373.

By the next day – February 5th – Keynes had reduced his total position to £80,504. It was still a massive sum but only half of what it had been a fortnight prior. He ought to have gone further. As the United States, and then France and the UK, raised interest rates, inflation gave way to deflation, which spread globally (Tooze, 2015, pp. 344–373). Whether due to "fundamental" or "sentimental" reasons, continental currencies recovered that spring.[71] It was only temporary; and they would resume their slide that summer. But, in the short run, it nearly broke Keynes. Indeed, Keynes only scraped by with a £5,000 loan from the City financier Ernest Cassel.

Yet, Keynes was undeterred. Continuing to focus on the long run, he returned to his fundamentals-based strategy in June 1920.[72] Progressively, he recovered his losses and eventually earned substantial profits through to 1925 (Accominotti and Chambers, 2016, Figure 5).

---

[69] Brien Cokayne, "To Chancellor of the Exchequer" (National Archives; T172-1384, February 25, 1920).

[70] *Financial Times*, April 9, 1920, "Bank of France Discount Rate Raised", p. 1. *Financial Times*, April 16, 1920, "Bank Rate Raised", p. 1. Committee of Treasury, "Minutes." April 14, 1920. Global Financial Data, "British Pound to US Dollar Exchange Rate (GBPUSD)." Even leaving the gold standard unexpectedly in 1931 did not take sterling this low.

[71] *Financial Times*, May 27, 1920, "The Rise in Exchanges", p. 4.

[72] Moggridge (1983, p. 7).

Moreover, most of the general predictions about European economies in *The Economic Consequences* also proved to be correct in the end. Thus, Keynes did prove successful as a currency speculator – despite that his strategy saw him taking substantial risks again and again. Perhaps more important, Keynes's practical experience likely proved invaluable intellectually.

4 Conclusion: Keynes's Lessons

Keynes's incomparable indictment of the Paris Peace Conference and his castigation of the Treaty of Versailles turned on an orthodox analysis of the economic consequences that would follow this "peace." As the years wore on after 1919, his dire predictions proved true again and again. The "Carthaginian peace" was utterly unsustainable and broadly self-defeating to whomever attempted to impose it.

At first blush, Keynes appears to have been perfectly positioned to profit personally from this prescience. He had a virtually incomparable combination of academic training and practical experience. His decades in Cambridge combined with his years in Westminster to ensure that he was thoroughly versed both in orthodox theory and in how it played out in practice. Similarly, he remained intimately familiar with many of the most important policymakers of the day. As we have seen, he repeatedly made moves in the markets within hours of consulting the fiscal and monetary authorities in the UK, the United States, and several continental powers.

And, yet, in light of these advantages, Keynes's speculative performance proves underwhelming. Why?

The answer appears to be that which comprised one of Keynes's greatest intellectual contributions: the all-important distinction between the short run and the long run. Keynes was right in 1919 that the Treaty would prove disastrous, just as he was right in 1920 that the mark would collapse. In both cases, however, Keynes learned that "obstinate illusion[s]" could persist far longer than a frank reading of the plain facts would have allowed. And so it was possible to be right but broken, or even "dead," "in the long run" – particularly if the "tempestuous" short-run proves particularly "violent."[73]

---

[73] Keynes, *Collected Writings*, 4:65, 118.

Keynes deepened these insights over the decades that followed. Reportedly, he warned, "nothing is more suicidal than a rational investment policy in an irrational world" (Friedman and Schwartz, 1963, 810). In the *General Theory*, Keynes concluded, "Investment based on genuine long-term expectations is so difficult to-day as to be scarcely practicable...Furthermore, an investor who proposes to ignore near-term market fluctuations needs greater resources for safety and must not operate on so large a scale, if at all, with borrowed money."[74] As we have seen, Keynes had learned this himself in the summer of 1920. Such lessons were costly – at times, literally. But they were also indispensable in propelling Keynes towards his world-shaping apostasy. In the longest run, this has proved to be the most valuable of the speculative consequences of the peace.

References

Archival References

Bradbury. "Future Dimensions of the Fiduciary Issue." National Archives; T185/1, March 9, 1918.

"Cabinet Minutes." National Archives; CAB 27/71, July 24, 1919.

Chamberlain, Austen. "Note of Interview with Keynes." National Archives; T172–1384, February 4, 1920.

Cokayne, Brien. "To Chancellor of the Exchequer." National Archives; T172–1384, February 25, 1920.

Committee of Treasury. "Minutes." Bank of England; G8/54, various dates.

Court of Directors. "Minutes." Bank of England; G4/142, various dates.

Committee on Currency and Foreign Exchanges after the War [Cunliffe Committee]. *First Interim Report*. Cd. 9182, August 15, 1918.

Committee on Currency and Foreign Exchanges After the War [Cunliffe Committee]. "Discussion Following Wright Testimony." National Archives; T185/2, July 23, 1919.

Keynes, John Maynard. "Note on Interview with Chancellor of the Exchequer on 4 Feb." National Archives; T172–1384, February 15, 1920.

Keynes, John Maynard. "Diary." Kings College; PP/41/15, 1919.

Keynes, John Maynard. "Diary." Kings College; PP/41/16, 1920.

Norman, Montagu. "Diary." Bank of England; ADM34/5, 1917.

Norman, Montagu. "Diary." Bank of England; ADM34/9, 1920.

---

[74] Keynes (1973 [1936]), p. 157.

Secondary Literature

Accominotti, Olivier, and David Chambers (2016). "If You're So Smart: John Maynard Keynes and Currency Speculation in the Interwar Years." *The Journal of Economic History*, vol. 76, pp. 342–386.

Atkin, John (2005). *The Foreign Exchange Market of London*. New York: Routledge.

Bateman, Bradley W. (1987). "Keynes' Changing Conception of Probability". *Economics and Philiosophy*, vol. 3, pp. 97–120.

Clay, Henry (1957). *Lord Norman*. New York: Macmillan.

Eichengreen, Barry (1992). *Golden Fetters: The Gold Standard and the Great Depression, 1919–1939*. Oxford: Oxford University Press.

Einzig, Paul (1937). *The Theory of Forward Exchange*. London: Macmillan.

Financial Times, various dates.

Friedman, Milton, and Anna J. Schwartz (1963). *A Monetary History of the United States, 1867–1960*. Princeton: Princeton University Press. "Director's Comment. Albert J. Hettinger Jr.", pp. 809–814.

Global Financial Data. "Bank of England Base Lending Rate (IDGBRD)."

Global Financial Data. "British Pound to US Dollar Exchange Rate (GBPUSD)."

Global Financial Data. "UK National Debt (GVGBRDEBT)."

Keynes, John Maynard. *The Collected Writings of John Maynard Keynes*. 30 Volumes. Edited by Elizabeth Johnson and Donald Moggridge. London: Macmillan, 1971–1989.

Mantoux, Etienne (1946). *The Carthaginian Peace: or, The Economic consequences of Mr Keynes*. Oxford: Oxford University Press.

Mini, Piero V. (1995). "Keynes' Investments: Their Relation to the General Theory." *The American Journal of Economics and Sociology*, vol. 54, pp. 47–56.

Mixon, Scott (2011). "The Foreign Exchange Options Market, 1917–1921", unpublished manuscript, Lyxor Asset Management Inc.

Moggridge, Donald E., ed (1983). *The Collected Writings of John Maynard Keynes*, vol. XII. Cambridge: Cambridge University Press.

Moggridge, Donald Edward (1992). *Maynard Keynes: An Economist's Biography*. New York: Routledge.

Morrison, James Ashley (2021). *England's Cross of Gold: Keynes, Churchill, and the Governance of Economic Beliefs*. Ithaca: Cornell University Press.

Ohlin, Bertil (1929). "Mr Keynes' View on the Transfer Problem II: A Rejoinder from Professor Ohlin". *The Economic Journal*, vol. 39, pp. 400–404.

Phillips, H. W. (1926). *Modern Foreign Exchange and Foreign Banking*. London: Macdonald and Evans.

Skidelsky, Robert (1992). *John Maynard Keynes: The Economist as Saviour, 1920–1937*. London: Macmillan.

Tooze, Adam (2015). *The Deluge: The Great War and the Remaking of Global Order, 1916–1931*. London: Penguin Books.

Wall Street Journal, various dates.

9 Why Was Keynes Opposed to Reparations and a Carthaginian Peace?

ELISE S. BREZIS*

I Introduction

The Economic Consequences of the Peace was first published in 1919 and, since then, changed the economic discourse surrounding reparations and Carthaginian peace. The entire book is a thoughtful plea against the peace treaty signed in Versailles. It contains some 180 pages of data, calculations, and projections, reshuffling the data as a deck of cards in the hands of a virtuoso player. Keynes's conclusion is cut and dried: Reparations are bad.

The book begins in another sphere altogether. The first two chapters do not even mention reparations. Why? Recall the movies based on the books of Agatha Christie: The movie begins with one or two frames that appear unrelated to the rest of the story. It is these frames that hold the solution to the mystery: a seeming digression, that contains the explanation for what happens at the end. If you missed this first frame, you missed the entire plot of the movie. Likewise, if you seek to understand why Keynes claims that 'the purpose of [his] book is to show that Carthaginian peace is not practically right or possible' (p. 18), then focus on the first two chapters of his book.

What ideas do we find in the first two chapters, which are essential for understanding reparations and Carthaginian peace? Three main subjects are developed in these two chapters; subjects that are hinted at in the introduction and that are essential to understanding reparations and Carthaginian peace: (i) the 'International Political system', (ii) the notions of 'social identity' and 'national sovereignty', and

* I wish to thank Lord Skidelsky, Stanley Fischer, Michael Bordo, Patricia Clavin, Giancarlo Corsetti, Harold James, Maurice Obstfeld, and Albrecht Ritschl, for their comments and insights, as well as Warren Young and Moshe Keshet. I thank Sarah Wertheimer for excellent research assistance.

(iii) the fact that 'social identities' differ for the various social classes, that is, the elite versus the working class.

About the international political system, Keynes made a clear dichotomy between periods of rivalries and periods of international-ization.[1] About national sovereignty and power, Keynes stressed that the notion of nation and nationalism enter the economic realm:[2]

Finally, the difference between social classes is crucial in Keynes writings. The first page of the introduction begins with this statement: 'All classes alike thus build their plans, the rich to spend more and save less, the poor to spend more and work less' (p. 2), and there-after, 'Thus the bluff is discovered; the laboring classes may be no longer willing to forgo so largely and the capitalists classes no longer confident of the future, may seek to enjoy more fully their liberties of consumption so long as they last, and thus precipitate the hour of their confiscation' (p. 11).

These three elements – the international political system, national sovereignty, and the differences between the elite and the working class are the hints given by Keynes in the introduction and which enable understanding of his position on reparations.

This chapter's purpose is to indicate how these three elements can explain Keynes's assessment on Carthaginian peace. About the inter-national political system, and the differences between social classes, I show that when there is a hegemonic state, it is optimal for all classes to ask for no reparations: the working class as well as the elite find free trade to be optimal, and there is no need for harsh reparations.

However, when countries are in a 'balance-of-power' period, then the elite and the working class have differing optimal policies. While, for the working class, it is optimal to claim for harsh reparations, the transnational elite find it optimal to reduce reparations.

---

[1] He wrote: 'The projects and politics of militarism and imperialism, of racial and cultural rivalries, of monopolies, restrictions, and exclusion, which were to play the serpent to this paradise, were little more than the amusements of his daily newspaper, and appeared to exercise almost no influence at all on the ordinary course of social and economic life, the internationalization of which was nearly complete in practice' (p. 6).

[2] 'Nations are real things, of whom you love one and feel for the rest indifference – or hatred. The glory of the nation you love is a desirable end – but generally to be obtained at your neighbour's expense. The politics of power are inevitable.... the balance of power in one's own interests' (p. 17).

Is Keynes on the side of the working class or of the elite? Keynes exhibits in his writing a 'transnational elite' assessment, and he chooses to reduce reparations since identity and nationalistic values are for him no more than 'nonsense' despite his having lived during a period of balance of power.[3]

The reasons for the difference between the view of the elites and the working class about reparations are their difference in social identity. The working class cares about national sovereignty, because it gives them a national identity, while the elite are part of the transnational elite, and do not need a national identity. So, Keynes, who is part of the intellectual transnational elite, chooses to reduce reparations since identity and nationalistic values are not important for him.

It is interesting to note that in France, Clemenceau takes the view of the working class, which cares about national sovereignty and therefore claims harsh reparations. Keynes believed in a top-down flow of ideas, while Clemenceau understood that the rage of the working class burst from the bottom-up. And indeed Keynes's remarks about Clemenceau and the French are harsh:

He [Clemenceau] had one illusion – France, and one disillusion – mankind... His principle for the peace can be expressed simply. In the first place, he was a foremost believer in the view of German psychology that the German understands and can understand nothing but intimidation (p. 16).... The future life of Europe was not their concern; its means of livelihood was not their anxiety. Their preoccupations related to frontiers, nationalities, to the balance of power, to imperial aggrandisements, to the future enfeeblement of a strong and dangerous enemy. (p. 27)

Therefore, Keynes' views differ from those of Clemenceau and of the working class of France that cares about national sovereignty. Thus, the main differences between Keynes and Clemenceau are in their identification either with the elite, or to the working class. Keynes feels part of the elite, while Clemenceau is close to the working class and cares about reparations, which are linked to nationalism and national sovereignty.

But why do the workers care so much about national sovereignty? Because it gives them a national identity, while the elite are part of the transnational elite, and do not need a national identity. This is the topic of the next section.

---

[3] See also Mantoux (1946), Katiforis (2004), and Binkley (1929).

II National Sovereignty and National Identity

One of the main shifts in the history of economic theory lay in the introduction of Behavioural Economics in mainstream theory, which opened the floodgates to many other innovative lines of thinking. In consequence, it not only became 'kosher' to speak of culture and psychology in the economic realm, it became 'in'.[4]

Sociology also slowly penetrated the field of economic theory. In 2000, Akerloff and Kranton introduced 'identity' as an element affecting economic choices. In the field of social psychology, Tajfel developed the 'theory of social identity'. He contended that individuals have an inherent tendency to categorize themselves into one or more 'in-groups', building a part of their identity based on membership in that group and enforcing boundaries with other groups.

The social identity theory posits the fact that a person's self-concept and self-esteem derive not only from personal identity and accomplishments, but from the status and accomplishment of the groups to which s/he belongs (Tajnel and Turner, 1979). In their experiments, they have shown that humans have a need for 'us/them' distinctions. Thus, social identity theory suggests that people identify with groups in such a way as to *maximize positive distinctiveness*.

Tajnel and Turner (1979) have shown that social identity leads to discrimination. When being divided into two groups, and asked to split budgets between the two groups, individuals had the choice of giving $100 to each member of both groups, or receiving $50 for each person in their group, but only $10 to the other group. Most individuals chose the second option. Making the other group worse off is more important than making your group better.[5]

In some of their experiments, group selection was chosen along random traits, and in some of the experiments, it was chosen randomly by tossing a coin. Yet, all the experiments have shown that human beings have a tendency to identify with a group.

These results were for a random selection of groups, so what happens when the group has some sort of common trait or culture, such as being white? Or being French?

---

[4] In reference to Temin (1997): 'Is it Kosher to talk about Culture?'

[5] Moreover, it was shown that those who had been allowed to engage in intergroup discrimination had higher self-esteem than those who had not been given the opportunity to discriminate (Lemyre and Smith 1985; Oakes and Turner 1980).

Metzl (2019) discussed discrimination between whites and non-whites. He shows that individuals belonging to a given group can make decisions that are not 'rationally' productive for them, just to feel part of the group and to separate themselves from the other group. An example he gives is that young white individuals belonging to the working class who were sick and in need of Medicare chose 'to be broke, but not to let the other group get it for free'.[6] They are willing to make choices that harm themselves in order to maintain their class identity.

Another clear grouping is the nation itself. One speaks today about the identity of being American: While 'Being an American is an element of the self-concept of most Americans', it leads to discrimination and to in-group favouritism.

What are the 'markers' of social identity of a nation? Following Metzl (2019), the main elements defining working-class identity are the symbols of nationalism, which, alongside sovereignty, are always part of the identity of the working class. Thus national sovereignty and power influence the sense of well-being of the working class.

However, social identity is not a value assimilated across society in a one-size-fits-all manner. Within each nation-state, the various in-groups – especially the working class and the elite – do not share the same identity.

The literature on twentieth-century elites pinpoints the interconnection of all elites, and their transnational values.[7] Weber (2008) showed that at the beginning of the twentieth century, the elites of Germany and England had connections between them, and shared the same values despite tensions between the countries, and acted to improve Anglo-German relations: 'The British and German ruling elites tried to ease the tensions between the two empires' (p. 49).[8]

---

[6] Medicare might improve life for all groups, but as it would improve the well-being of the non-white group more, working-class 'white' Americans actively oppose it.

[7] See Brezis and Temin (1999, 2008).

[8] Indeed Weber brings Britain and Germany's preeminent universities and playgrounds for political and social elites back to life to reconsider whether any truth is left in the old contrast between British liberalism and German illiberalism.

Ciampani and Tolomeo (2015) follow a similar reasoning about the elite: 'In effect, the research avenue that focuses on the meetings of the European elites aims to account for the progressive 'amalgam' of the European elites' national

Plate 1 John Maynard Keynes. A rare image of John Maynard Keynes at work from the King's College Archive, Cambridge University. Reproduced by kind permission of the King's College Archive.

Plate 2 John Maynard Keynes and Jan Christiaan Smuts. Smuts attended the Paris Peace Conference and played a "central but complex" role in the making of the *Economic Consequences*. Reproduced by permission of the National Portrait Gallery.

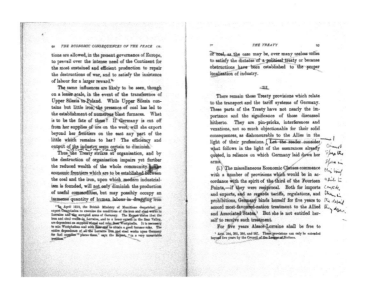

Plate 3 Original proofreading copy of the *Economic Consequences*, with Keynes's notes. Keynes reduced the length of the manuscript through extensive cuts as he revised. One key motivation was to make sure that the book could be produced at reduced cost and thus sold at an accessible price for the widest audience. Reproduced by kind permission of the Marshall Librarian.

Plate 4 Keynes's mother, Florence Ada Keynes. Maynard's friends affectionately referred to her as "the good mother Keynes," and although she was committed to so many important causes, her family always came first and she was immensely proud of her elder son. Reproduced by permission of the National Portrait Gallery.

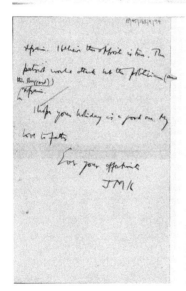

Plate 5 A letter by John Maynard Keynes to his mother Florence, written during the negotiations at Versailles in 1918. "Everything is always decided for some reason other than the real merits of the case [...] Still and even more confidently I attribute all our misfortunes to George. We are governed by a crook [...] In the meantime old Asquith who I believe might yet save us is more and more of a student and lover of slack country life and less and less inclined for the turmoil. Here he is extremely well in health and full of wisdom and fit for anything in the world - except controversy. He finds, therefore, in patriotism an easy excuse for his naked disinclination to attack the Gov[ernment]. People say that the politician would attack, but the patriot repair. I believe the opposite is true." Reproduced by kind permission of the King's College Archive.

Plate 6 John Maynard Keynes with Carl Melchior (left) and Dudley Ward (center) in Trèves (Trier), Germany, in 1919. Dr. Melchior, a prominent German banker, was part of a German delegation that met with French, British, and American financial officials in January 1919 to negotiate German payment for food imports in the light of potential reparations. Ward was a member of Keynes's Treasury staff and a former student at Cambridge. Reproduced by kind permission of the King's College Archive, Cambridge University.

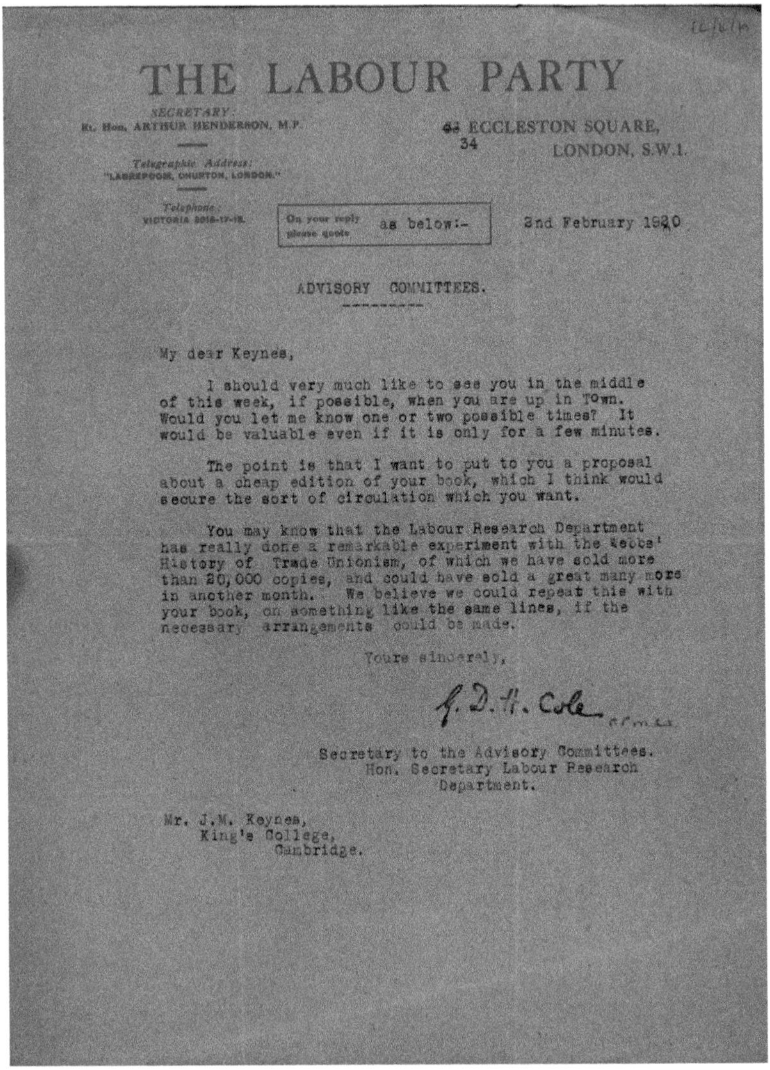

Plate 7 Letter to Keynes from G. D. H. Cole, proposing the publication of a cheaper Labour Research Department edition of Keynes's book. The very great success of *The Economic Consequences of the Peace* in the United Kingdom was in no small part due to a publishing deal Keynes had with the Labour Research Department, who brought out and sold a cheap version of the book. Total sales of this edition nearly topped 10,000 copies. Reproduced by kind permission of the Labour Party.

Plate 8 Ali Fethi Okyar, translator of the *Economic Consequences* into Turkish and later Prime Minister of Turkey, in the company of Kemal Atatürk. Ali Fethi translated Keynes's book in 1920 while imprisoned by the British in Malta. The translation appeared in print in 1922. Courtesy of the Okyar family.

Plate 9 The 1922 Turkish edition of *The Economic Consequences of the Peace*. This image is reproduced from the personal copy of the translator, Ali Fethi Okyar. Courtesy of the Okyar family.

Plate 10 Keynes with US Secretary of the Treasury Henry Morgenthau. Keynes led the UK delegation to the 1944 Bretton Woods Conference that designed the International Monetary Fund and World Bank. Reproduced by permission of Alamy.

Plate 11 Keynes in 1918. Under enormous strain owing to his wartime duties at the Treasury, Keynes relaxed in the countryside on weekends with Blooms-bury friends or at the home of the former prime minister, Herbert Asquith. Reproduced by kind permission of the King's College Archive.

Plate 12 Keynes circa 1911. This portrait was taken after Keynes had returned to King's from the India Office. Reproduced by kind permission of the King's College Archive. A high resolution image was obtained from Charleston.

Plate 13 John Maynard Keynes and Bertil Ohlin in Antwerp, 1935. Keynes's 1929 exchange with Ohlin over the "German transfer problem," published in the *Economic Journal*, raised fundamental questions for future research in international macroeconomics. Reproduced by kind permission of Tomas Ohlin, son of Bertil.

Plate 14 Participants at the September 2019 *Economic Consequences* centenary conference, King's College, Cambridge. Courtesy of Julian Peters.

Plate 15 Lord Skidelsky during the conference, leaning on the black government despatch box found at Keynes's brother Geoffrey's home, Lammas House, Brinkley, Suffolk. The box carries the cypher of King George V and was presumably issued to Maynard while he was working at the Treasury from 1915. One of his friends tells the story that he used to come to their support, when attending tribunals in connection with conscription, carrying an official black box with the royal cypher on it, in order to intimidate the panel. Presumably this is the same box! Courtesy of Julian Peters.

Weber showed that militarist nationalism and European transnationalism were not mutually exclusive concepts: militarist nationalism appealed to the working class and transnationalism to the elites. He stressed that the elite of various countries feel related by their culture, and feel themselves to be part of the same group – the transnational elite of Europe. They emphasize humanistic, universal values and do not relate to values such as militarism, power, and nationalism.

Therefore, we obtain a dual social identity.[9] On the one hand, the working class of each country cares about national sovereignty and power. On the other, the elite in each country want a globalized economy with interdependence between countries. The transnational elite identity values internationalism, humanism, and universalism.

And to which group did Keynes belong? Did his feelings pull towards the working class? or towards the elite? As he mentioned in *Essays in Persuasion*, commenting about Marxism (1931):

How can I adopt a creed which, preferring the mud to the fish, exalts the boorish proletariat above the bourgeois and the intelligentsia who, with whatever faults, are the quality in life and surely carry the seeds of all human advancement? Even if we need a religion, how can we find it in the turbid rubbish of the Red bookshops? It is hard for an educated, decent, intelligent son of Western Europe to find his ideals here, unless he has first suffered some strange and horrid process of conversion which has changed all his values. (p. 298)

This dual social identity leads to a dual view on trade policy and reparations. On the one hand, the working class of each country care about national sovereignty and power. On the other, the elite in each country want a globalized economy with interdependence between countries. In the next section, we analyse the relationship between reparations and national sovereignty in the perspective of the international political system. We analyse why in periods of hegemony, the elites as well as the working class have common views on trade policy and reparations, while in periods of balance of power, their views differ. We start with a historical perspective on these relationships.

---

groups, their coming together both to initiate the processes to form new generations of élites, and to broaden (or restrict) the means of access to decision-making' (pp. 10–11).

[9] See also Brezis and Hellier (2018).

III Reparations and the International Political System

The historical record of the past 350 years shows cycles in which there are periods of 'hegemony', in which one nation-state has leadership, while there are periods of 'balance of power' in which there is no dominant state, and many nations have similar power.

We should, of course, first ask if in 1919, at the time of the Treaty of Versailles, is the international system in a hegemonic or a 'balance of power' period?

The data are presented in Figures 9.1–9.3. From 1850 to 1910, the Western world lives in a system of *Pax Britannica* – the UK is the leader of the world. The UK has leapfrogged the Dutch, and is the hegemonic power. However, after 1910, the UK is not anymore a leader country (see Figure 9.1).

After 1945, we are in a period of *Pax Americana*, the United States is the leader of the world, and the United States has leapfrogged the UK. From 1945 until 2008, the United States is the hegemonic power of the world (see Figure 9.2).[10]

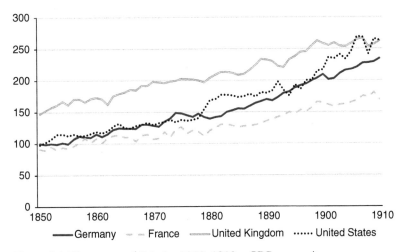

Figure 9.1 Hegemony of Britain: 1850–1910 – GDP per capita
Notes: The GDP per capita index is set at 100 for 1850. The UK is in yellow, Germany is in blue, France in red, and the United States is the green line.
Source: Maddison.

[10] Brezis, Krugman, and Tsiddon (1993) present a model explaining endogenously the changes in hegemony, and about the data on the balance of payments; see Brezis (1995).

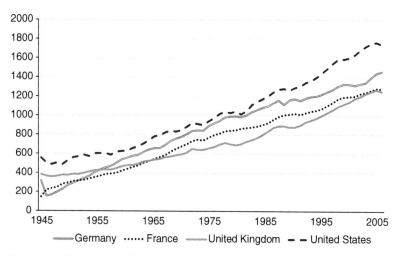

Figure 9.2 Hegemony of the United States: 1945–2008

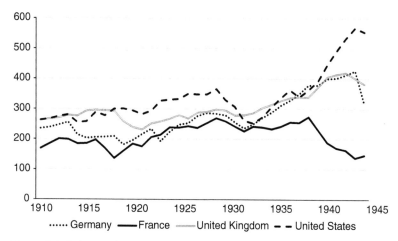

Figure 9.3 Balance of Power: 1910–1945

But, during the period 1910–1919, the data display that GDP per capita among the main powers are similar (although Germany has higher GDP than France from 1900 and on). This is a typical 'balance of power' period. There are no leader countries, and this situation will stay so until 1945, the end of World War II (see Figure 9.3). thus, the international system shows cycles in power leadership.

In almost complete correlation with the cycles in leadership, the historical record of the past 350 years shows cycles in trade policy. These two cycles are correlated: Hegemony is related to periods of free trade, while protectionism occurs in periods of balance of power.

To give some examples, the most notable change in policy is the Navigation Act of 1651, which is widely held to have represented the end of effective Dutch commercial hegemony in Europe and to have marked the beginning of the British challenge.

By the end of the second decade of the nineteenth century, Britain had set about dismantling its own protectionist apparatus and had initiated an era of free trade which lasted as long as the *Pax Britannica* endured.[11]

And as a last example, in the twentieth century, the rise of American power in the pre–World War II years was associated with a succession of protectionist measures, whereas the establishment of American hegemony after the war led to the pursuit of free trade.[12]

Why is there a relationship between trade policy and the international system? The relationships between protectionist commercial policy, nationalism, and balance of power have been explored in the works of a number of political scientists. One of the most widely accepted paradigms linking the structure of the international political system with protectionism is the theory of 'hegemonic stability'.[13]

Kindleberger (1973), following in the footsteps of Frohlich, Oppenheimer, and Young (1971), argues that international security is a collective good. Since free trade can arise only in a climate of international security, it is only when a national power is dominant enough to enforce security that a regime of free trade will arise. Given the inevitable tendency of weaker states to free-ride on the provision of the collective good by a hegemonic power, the absence of a hegemonic state leads to the erosion of free trade and to the growth of protectionism. Gilpin (1975) writes that 'a liberal international economy cannot come into existence and be maintained unless it has behind it the most powerful state(s) in the system. ... A liberal economic system is not

---

[11] Gilpin (1975) writes that 'Britain's interest lay in universal free trade and the removal of all barriers to the exchange of goods' (p. 84).

[12] About the end of the American hegemony and 'neomercantilism' at the end of the twentieth century, see Calleo and Rowland (1973), Cline (1980), and Malmgren (1970).

[13] A precursor is Hirschman (1945); see also Kindleberger (1975), Whitman (1975), Krasner (1976), Keohane and Nye (1977), MacEwan (1978), Keohane (1980), Wallerstein (1980), and Gilpin (1977, 1981).

self-sustaining, but is maintained only through the actions – initiatives, bargaining, and sanctions of the dominant power(s)'.[14]

Another paradigm linking these cycles is the theory of 'imperialism of free trade'.[15] It purports to explain the development of the world trading system in the presence of a hegemonic power. This theory argues that 'the hegemonic power is expected to extend its control – and the open international trading order – over local economies by informal or indirect means whenever possible, since this constitutes the cheapest way to create and maintain its predominant position in the world'. The link between the international political system and economic policy was also emphasized by Skidelsky (2010, 1976).

In conclusion, the literature relating trade policy to the international political system is vast. But the theories of 'imperialism of free trade', 'hegemonic stability', or 'collective good' are too broadly stated. There is a need to pinpoint the essential elements which are the thread between trade policy and the international system. Some political scientists stress that during a period of balance of power, maintaining power necessitate to increase foreign reserves.

Already in 1776, Adam Smith has laid out the reasons for increasing foreign reserves during periods of balance of power:

The real wealth or poverty of the country ... would depend altogether upon the abundance or scarcity of those consumable goods. But ... they are obliged to carry on foreign wars, and to maintain fleets and armies in distant countries. This, cannot be done, but by sending abroad money to pay them with; and a nation cannot send much money abroad, unless it has a good deal at home, Every such nation, therefore, must endeavour in time of peace to accumulate gold and silver, that when occasion requires, it may have wherewithal to carry on foreign wars.[16]

Wallerstein (1980) also emphasized the importance of foreign reserves: 'control of an adequate bullion stock was ... a crucial variable in the struggle between core powers'.[17] Much earlier, Colbert also claimed: 'trade is the source of public finance and public finance is the vital nerve of war'. With more foreign reserves available in the economy, the nation-state could increase its success at war, and even in 'balance of power' system refrain from war. Moreover,

---

[14] Gilpin (1975), p. 85. See also Coleman (1969), and Brezis (2003).
[15] See Gallagher and Robinson (1953), MacDonagh (1962), Moore (1964), Mathew (1968), and Platt (1968, 1973).
[16] Smith (1937), p. 399.   [17] Wallerstein (1980), p. 277.

Kinder and Hilgemann (1964) note that 'the duration of campaigns depended on finances'.[18]

In this vein, this chapter asserts that the main reason for asking for reparations is the desire to increase foreign reserves in periods of balance of power, in order to increase 'national sovereignty' and thus national power. Requesting reparations is one of these means in the hands of a nation to maintain its national sovereignty, especially when the other country is slightly more developed. In periods of hegemony, then, reparations are not necessary, as countries can free-ride on the power of the hegemonic nation-state.

This is the idea developed in the following framework. We focus on periods of balance of power, as it was the case in 1919, when Keynes published *The Economic Consequences of the Peace* exploring the effects of reparations. We show that the optimal policy for the elite is different than for the working class, due to the fact that their social identities differ. In order to analyse the effects of reparations, we incorporate in the model these following elements: social identity theory, the concept of national sovereignty for the working class, and the concept of humanism for the transnational elite.

IV The Framework

4.1 Introduction

The Economic Consequences of the Peace was published in 1919, a period of balance of power. In consequence, we will only analyse the case of balance of power, wherein no single actor on the international scene possesses hegemonic status.

We focus on the case of France and Germany for describing the model. In Table 9.1, it is shown that the GDP of Germany is higher than that of France.

This very simple framework will permit to explain why during a period of balance of power, as it was the case in 1919, the working class (and Clemenceau) will choose harsh reparations, while the elite (and Keynes) will not. And the main reason I emphasize in this chapter is that it is due to social identity. The social identity of the working class is national identity and national sovereignty. The social identity of the elite is humanism, and internationalism, and they

---

[18] Kinder and Hilgemann (1964), p. 253.

Table 9.1 *Data on leader countries – 1850–1950*

Year	Germany	France	United Kingdom	United States
GDP per capita in 2011 US$				
1860	3,312	3,113	4,988	3,425
1870	3,715	3,086	5,716	3,736
1880	4,023	3,488	5,879	4,866
1890	4,904	3,909	6,711	5,184
1900	6,029	4,731	7,446	6,252
1910	6,763	4,878	7,567	7,586
1920	5,647	5,309	6,881	8,485
1930	8,027	7,455	8,504	9,490
1940	10,914	6,650	10,716	11,307
1950	7,840	8,531	10,846	15,241
Population, in thousands				
1850	33,746	36,350	27,181	23,580
1860	36,049	37,300	28,888	31,839
1870	39,231	38,440	31,400	40,241
1880	43,500	39,045	34,623	50,458
1890	47,607	40,014	37,485	63,302
1900	54,388	40,598	41,155	76,391
1910	62,884	41,224	44,916	92,767
1920	60,894	39,000	46,821	106,881
1930	65,084	41,610	45,866	123,668
1940	69,835	41,000	48,226	132,637
1950	68,375	42,518	50,127	152,271

Source: Maddison.

want a globalized economy with interdependence between countries. Therefore, we obtain a dual social identity.

Then, as already hinted in the previous section, we show that the 'markers' of national sovereignty and power are related to foreign reserves, while the 'markers' of internationalism are just increasing investments. Let us start by modelling social identity.

4.2 Social Identity of the Working Class

This model is assuming a duality of social identity: There are two social classes, and each class has its own identity, which has an impact on the individual's utility. We start with the working class.

One of the main elements defining the working class is its attachment to symbols of nationalism, as 'national sovereignty' and power. (We use these two notions as equivalent.) How national sovereignty and power affects the utility of the working class? We could, of course, introduce national sovereignty directly into the utility function. In this chapter, I try a more 'subtle' line of modelling.

Following the research presented above, I assume that the working class does not have utility from the size of national sovereignty per se; it is the comparison with the other country which affects utility. If power is less than a required amount in competition with another country, then the utility is affected.

We focus on the case of France and Germany for describing the model. France is country 1, and Germany is country 2. Thus, the country with higher output is country 2. Moreover, France could ask for reparations, since it was a winner at war.

Each country is represented by an individual of the working class, and which faces the following payoffs:

$$V_1 = \begin{cases} c_1 & PW1 \geq PW2 \\ c_1 - K & PW1 < PW2 \end{cases} \tag{1}$$

Equation (1) presents the utility of a worker in France (country 1). For country 2, it is the same equation, with the suffixes inverted. We define c_i as the output allocated to consumption. Equation (1) emphasizes that the utility/payoff of a citizen is equal to its utility from consumption (assuming that $U(C) = C$).

The workers care about consumption, but the workers care also about national sovereignty and power (this is their social identity). In other words, the French working class feel 'insulted' by an equivalent quantity of size K when the power of Germany is greater than the one of France, as it was shown above in the works of Tajnel and Metzl that people feel insulted when the other group gets some more than their own group.

What is the definition of power, PW? In Appendix 1, I show that the power of a nation can take the following form:

$$PW_i = \text{Min}(c_i, R_i + y_i - c_i) \tag{2}$$

where R_i represents the reparations paid by a foreign country (only a country having won a war can ask for reparations), and y_i is output (see the exact definitions in the appendix).

4.3 Objectives and Payoffs for the Transnational Elite

The transnational elite put the emphasis on humanism, that is consumption and economic growth of the world. Moreover, recall that the elite are the individuals who are investing (as underlined by Keynes in the introduction). So the utility function of the elite in country 1 is:

$$V_{E,1} = U(C_E, I) \qquad (3)$$

where C_E is the consumption of the elite, and I are investments, since the savings of the elite finance the investment of the nation. In their utility, there is no national sovereignty and power.

4.4 Equilibrium

In equilibrium, the workers choose c and R as to maximize (1). The elite maximize equation (3). Remember that we assume $y_2 \geq y_1$ (Germany has higher output than France). We get the following proposition.

Proposition 1

When countries are in a balance-of-power regime, with output quite similar, then in the unique equilibrium, the working class (and the politicians listening to the working class) will choose to increase their national power by hoarding foreign reserves until they attain maximum power. In case, one country can ask for reparations, then, the optimal size of reparations is:

$$R_1^* = -R_2^* = (y_2 - y_1)/2 \qquad (4)$$

and

$$c_1^* = c_2^* = (y_1 + y_2)/4 \qquad (5)$$

The proof is presented in Appendix 2.

Proposition 2

In a balance-of-power system, the transnational elite choose not to hoard foreign reserves and not to ask for reparations.

In their utility, there is no national sovereignty so that hoarding foreign reserves are not important, and therefore reparations are not necessary. And since we have:[19]

$$S = I + NX \qquad (6)$$

Then, they are better off, when hoarding foreign reserves and reparations are zero.

To conclude, in case of balance of power, and when one takes into consideration the aspirations of the working class, then it is optimal to ask for harsh reparations. This was the point of view of Clemenceau, in the name of the 'people of France'. The optimal size of reparations is given by equation (4). It is interesting to note that the optimal amount of consumption and reparations is such that all countries have equal consumption.

The transnational elite put the emphasis on humanism, that is, consumption and economic growth of the world. Moreover, recall that the elite are the individuals who are investing. Hoarding foreign reserves is not optimal, and therefore the amount of optimal reparations is zero.

V Conclusion

There is no better conclusion of Keynes's *Economic Consequences of the Peace* than to quote Skidelsky:

Keynes was also a product of the old Europe, of which Britain was an integral part. He was brought up by a German governess, married a Russian ballerina, and was at home in France and Italy. He looked forward to an era of small political and cultural units combined into 'larger, and more or less closely knit economic units (2010, 191–192).... Keynes was staking the claim of the economist to be Prince. All other forms of rule were bankrupt. The economist's vision of welfare, conjoined to a new standard of technical excellence, were the last barriers to chaos, madness and retrogression. (1983, p. 384).

---

[19] Government expenditures are included in the maximization of the working class.

This chapter seeks to explain the disagreements between Keynes and Clemenceau. I have shown that the differences in national identities of the working class and the elite explain their opposing views on reparations. For the working class, national sovereignty is essential, despite 'the apparent inability of the intelligentsia to understand and appreciate power-problems'. This difference in identity can explain why the optimal policy for the working class differs from that of the elite.

This chapter has stressed that in the context of a hegemonic country, both classes, the working class and the elite, opt for no reparations. But, in a 'balance of power' situation, wherein no single actor on the international scene possesses hegemonic status, the working class will choose harsh reparations, while the elite will not.

What, then, does this chapter teach us? There are two main conclusions: The first is that if we ask why 1945 is so different from 1918; and why the peace treaties after 1945 differ from those of the 1919 Treaty of Versailles, the answer is obvious.

Because in 1945, there was a hegemonic state – the United States – while in 1919, the world was in a balance-of-power period. As this chapter has shown, this fact changes the entire perspective of countries on reparations and free trade. Under a hegemonic system, there is no 'Clemenceau' to ask for harsh reparations 'in the name of the people', in order to enhance national identity. In periods of hegemony, there is room for coordination, for the UN, for the GATT, for the Marshall plan; there is no room for harsh reparations.

Being part of the intellectual transnational elite, Keynes understood this already in 1919. He fought for a treaty of reconciliation. But Clemenceau could not accept this. On behalf of the French working class, Clemenceau cared about national sovereignty and national identity, for which the French were willing to pay the price. They did not know that the price will be so high.

The second conclusion of this chapter is that the small framework presented in the previous section helps us understand the present. Indeed, the hegemony of the United States extended from 1945 until 2008. Since then, we are back in a balance of power between the United States and China. From 2008 and on, the world has entered a new balance-of-power system. Therefore, the working class in many countries oppose free trade.

I hope this chapter shed new light on Keynes' view on reparations and Carthaginian peace. Let me conclude this overview on Keynes with a practical quote:

It is our duty to prolong peace, hour by hour, day by day, for as long as we can. We do not know what the future will bring, except that it will be quite different from anything we could predict. I have said in another context that it is a disadvantage of the 'long run' that in the long run we are all dead. But I could have said equally well that it is a great advantage of the 'short run' that in the short run we are still alive. Life and history are made up of short runs. (Keynes, *New Statesman,* July 1937)

Appendix 1

The debates over the definition and measurement of national sovereignty and power are endless. Despite the lack of consensus on precise definitions, most scholars of the 'realist' school agree that economic as well as military factors are crucial. We thus begin with the premise that the national sovereignty, that is power of a nation depends both on its economic and on its military power. Mathematically, we express this assumption as:

$$NS_i = PW_i = F\left(\text{EPW}_i, \text{MPW}_i\right) \qquad (A1)$$

where $NS_i, PW_i, \text{EPW}_i, \text{MPW}_i$ are national sovereignty, total, economic and military power respectively. Without loss of generality, we take a Leontief form of relationship between both powers:[20]

$$NS_i = PW_i = \text{Min}\left(\text{EPW}_i, \text{MPW}_i\right) \qquad (A2)$$

All suggested measures of economic power are intrinsically ad hoc. The proxy we adopt for economic power is total consumption – private and public. A priori, a more natural choice might be output. This choice has the inconvenience that in the case where a country decides to allocate its output to exports and leave very little for consumption, this country would be said to have economic power. Consumption is therefore a more appropriate proxy in the context of our model. Thus:

$$\text{EPW}_i = C_i + G_i = c_i \qquad (A3)$$

Where C_i is consumption of citizen, G_i government expenditures, and c_i is then the output allocated to consumption.

---

[20] I choose this discontinuous functional form for convenience, and in order to ensure transparency of the results, but any functional form in the class of the CES function yields the same results.

Military power, MPW_i is a function of the stock of military equipment and infrastructure of war owned by the country (planes, missiles, artillery, warships...), but also of the possibility of immediately purchasing ammunition and financing the soldiers. The stock of military equipment, as well as the stock of foreign reserves hoarded in the past, M_i is given exogenously at the start of the period and there is no depreciation of materials during periods of peace. The possibility of being ready for war is then a function of the stock of foreign reserves.

Therefore the increase in foreign reserves, denoted by O_i is a factor influencing the military power of a country. (Note that the accumulation of foreign reserves in the past is included in M_i.)

We therefore have the specification

$$MPW_i = O_i + M_i \qquad (A4)$$

Therefore the power of a nation, PW is:

$$NS_i = PW_i = \mathrm{Min}\left(c_i, O_i + M_i\right) \qquad (A5)$$

From the national income identity, we have that:[21]

$$Y_i = C_i + G_i + NX_i \qquad (A6)$$

The flow of foreign reserves and the trade balance are linked by the simple expression:

$$O_i = R_i + NX_i \qquad (A7)$$

where O_i is the increase in foreign reserves, NX_i is the current account surplus, and R_i represents the reparations paid by a foreign country (only a country having won a war can ask for reparations).

In consequence we have:

$$NS_i = PW_i = \mathrm{Min}\left(c_i, R_i + y_i - c_i\right) \qquad (2)$$

where $y_i = Y_i + M_i$.

---

[21] Recall that investments are equal to the savings of the elite, a small group of size 0 not included in this part.

Appendix 2

In order to prove Proposition 1, we first show two lemmas. Note that we assume that K is such that $K \gg y_1 / 2$.

Lemma 1

Given reparation of size R, consumption which lead to maximum power is:

$$c_i^* = (y_i + R_i) / 2 \tag{A8}$$

Proof

Equate the two elements of equation (2). See also Figure 9.4.

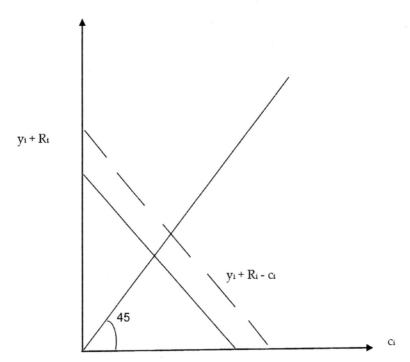

Figure 9.4 Equilibrium

Lemma 2

Given that $K \gg y_1 / 2$ then the optimal amount of reparations is:

$$R_1^* = -R_2^* = (y_2 - y_1) / 2 \qquad (4)$$

And therefore we get:

$$c_1{}^* = c_2{}^* = (y_1 + y_2) / 4 \qquad (5)$$

$$\mathrm{NX}_1{}^* = (3y_1 - y_2) / 4 - M_1 \qquad O_1{}^* = (y_1 + y_2) / 4 - M_1 \qquad (\mathrm{A9})$$

$$\mathrm{NX}_2{}^* = (3y_2 - y_1) / 4 - M_2 \qquad O_2{}^* = (y_1 + y_2) / 4 - M_2 \qquad (\mathrm{A10})$$

Proof

The equilibrium is a perfect Nash equilibrium of a one period decision game. In the case of balance of power, then the Nash equilibrium necessitates that $PW_2 = PW_1$.

In consequence, given equation (A8), we get the equations (4) and (5) and especially that $c_1{}^* = c_2{}^* = (y_1 + y_2) / 4$. QED

References

Akerlof, G. A. and R. Kranton. (2000). "Economics and Identity," *The Quarterly Journal of Economics,* 115(3): 715–753.

Akerlof, G. A. and R. Kranton. (2010). *Identity Economics.* Princeton University Press.

Bar-Siman Tov, Y. (2004). *From Conflict Resolution to Reconciliation.* Oxford University Press.

Binkley, R. C. (1929). "Ten Years of Peace Conference History," *The Journal of Modern History,* 4: 607–629.

Brezis, E. S. (1995). "Foreign Capital Flows in the Century of Britain's Industrial Revolution: New Estimates, Controlled Conjectures," *Economic History Review,* February, pp. 46–67.

Brezis, E.S. (2003). "Mercantilism", Oxford Encyclopedia of Economic History.

Brezis, E. S. and J. Hellier. (2018). "Social Mobility at the Top and the Higher Education System," *European Journal of Political Economy,* 52: 36–54.

Brezis, E. S. and P. Temin. (2008). "Elites and Economic Outcomes," In S. Durlauf and L. Blume, eds., *New Palgrave Dictionary of Economics*, Macmillan.

Brezis, E. S. and P. Temin, eds. (1999). *Elites, Minorities and Economic Growth*, North Holland: Elsevier.

Brezis, E. S., P. Krugman and D. Tsiddon. (1993). "Leapfrogging in International Competition," *American Economic Review*, December, pp. 211–19.

Brito, D. and M. Intriligator (1976). "Strategic Weapons and the Allocation of International Rights," In John V. Gillespie and Dino A. Zinnes, eds., *Mathematical Systems in International Relations Research*, New York: Praeger.

Calleo, D. P. and B. M. Rowland (1973). *America and the World Political Economy*, Bloomington: Indiana UP.

Ciampani, A. and R. Tolomeo. (2015). "The Need for an Interpretive Framework in the History of European Élites." In A. Ciampani and R. Tolomeo, eds., *National Identities and Transnational European Élites*, 5–13, Soveria Mannelli: Rubbettino Editore.

Cline, R. S. (1980). *World Power Trends and US Foreign Policy for the 1980s*, Routledge.

Coleman, J. S. (1986). "Social Theory, Social Research and a Theory of Action," *American Journal of Sociology*, 91(6), 1309–1335.

Gallagher, J. and R. Robinson (1953). "The Imperialism of Free Trade," *Economic History Review*, 6(1), 1–15.

Gilpin, R. (1975). US Power and the Multinational Corporation.

Gilpin, R. (1977). "Economic Interdependence and National Security in Historical Perspective." In K. Klaus and F.N. Trager, eds., *Economic Issues and National Security*, Kansas: Regents Press.

Gilpin, R. (1981). *War and Change in World Politics*, New York: CUP.

Heckscher, E. F. (1965). *Mercantilism*, 2nd edition, ed. E. F. Söderlund.

Hirschman, A. O. (1945). *National Power and the Structure of Foreign Trade*, Berkeley: Univesity of CP.

Katiforis, G. (2004). "Keynes as a Bourgeois Marxist." In Philip Arestis and Malcolm C. Sawyer, eds., *The Rise of the Market: Critical Essays on the Political Economy of Neo-liberalism*, 181–224. Northampton: Edward Elgar Publishing, Inc.

Keohane, R. (1980). "The Theory of Hegemonic Stability and Changes in International Economic Regimes, 1967–1977," In Ole R. Holsti, Randolph M. Siverson, and Alexander L. George, eds., *Change in the International System*, Boulder: Westview.

Keohane, R. and J. S. Nye (1977). *Power and Interdependence: World Politics in Transition*, Boston: Little Brown.

Keynes, J. M. (1919). The Economic Consequences of the Peace.

Keynes, J. M. (1931). *Essays in Persuasion*. London: Macmillian and Co. Limited.

Keynes, J. M. (1936). The General Theory of Employment, Interest and Money.

Kinder, H., and Hilgemann, W. (1964). *The Anchor Atlas of World History*, New York: Anchor.

Kindleberger, C. (1973). *The World in Depression, 1929–1939*, Berkeley: UCP.

Kindleberger, C. (1975). "The Rise of Free Trade in Western Europe, 1820–1875," *Journal of Economic History*, XXXV, 20–55.

Krasner, S. D. (1976). "State Power and the Structure of International Trade," *World Politics* 28 (April 1976).

Lake, D. (1983). "International Economic Structures and American Foreign Economic Policy, 1887–1934," *World Politics*, 35: 517–543.

Lawson, F. H. (1983). "Hegemony and the Structure of International Trade Reassessed: A View from Arabia," *International Organization*, 37: 317–339.

Lemyre, L. and P. Smith. (1985). "Intergroup Discrimination and Self-esteem in the Minimal Group Paradigm" *Journal of Personality and Social Psychology*, 49: 660–670.

MacDonagh, O. (1962). "The Anti-Imperialism of Free Trade," *Economic History Review*, 2d series, 14 (August).

MacEwan, A. (1978). "The Development of the Crisis in the World Economy," In B. Steinberg et al., eds., *US Capitalism in Crisis*, New York.

Malmgren, H. (1970). "Coming Trade Wars? Neo-Mercantilism and Foreign Policy," *Foreign Policy*, 1(1): 115–143.

Mantoux, E. (1946). *The Carthaginian Peace: Or the Economic Consequences of Mr. Keynes*, New York: Oxford University Press.

Mathew, W. M. (1968). "The Imperialism of Free Trade: Peru, 1820–70," *Economic History Review*, 2d series, 21 (December).

Metzl, J. (2019). *Dying of Whiteness: How the Politics of Racial Resentment is Killing America's Heartland*, Hachette.

Moore, R. J. (1964–5). "Imperialism and 'Free Trade' Policy in India, 1853–4," *Economic History Review*, 2d series, 17(1): 135–145.

Oakes, P. J. and J. C. Turner. (1989). "Social Categorisation and Intergroup behaviour," *European Journal of Social Psychology* 10: 295–301.

Organsky, A. F. K. (1968). *World Politics*, New York: Knopf.

Platt, D. C. M. (1968). "The Imperialism of Free Trade: Some Reservations," *Economic History Review*, 2d series, 21 (August).

Platt, D. C. M. (1973). "Further Objections to an 'Imperialism of Free Trade,' 1830–1860," *Economic History Review*, 2d series, 26 (February).

Skidelsky, R. (1976). "Balance of Power or Hegemony" In B. M. Rowland ed., *The Interwar Monetary System*, New York: New York University Press.

Skidelsky, R. (2003). *John Maynard Keynes 1883–1946, Economist, Philosopher, Statesman*, London: Macmillan.

Skidelsky, R. (2010). Keynes: The Return of the Master, PublicAffairs.

Smith, A. (1937). *The Wealth of Nations*, New York: Modern Press.

Tajfel, H. and J. Turner. (1979). "An Integrative Theory of Inter-Group Conflict," In W. G. Austin and S. Worchel eds., *The Social Psychology of Intergroup Relations,* Monterey.

Taussig, F. (1892). *The Tariff History of the United States*, New York: Capricorn Books, 1964 edition.

Temin, P. (1997). "Is it Kosher to Talk about Culture?" *The Journal of Economic History*, 57(2): 267–287.

Trachtenberg, M. (1979). "Reparations at the Paris Peace Conference," *The Journal of Modern History*, 51: 24–55.

Veblen, T. (1899). *The Theory of the Leisure Class*, New York: Macmillan.

Viner, J. (1930). "English Theories of Foregn Trade Before Adam Smith," *Journal of Political Economy,* XXXVIII, 239–310 and 404–457.

Viner, J. (1955). *Studies in the Theory of International Trade*, London: Allen and Unwin.

Viotti, P. and Kauppi, M. (1987). *International Relations Theory*, New York: Macmillan.

Wallerstein, I. (1980). *The Modern World System, vol.2: Mercantilism and the Consolidation of the European World Economy, 1670–1750*, New York: Academic Press.

Weber, T. (2008). *Our Friend "The Enemy": Elite Education in Britain and Germany before World War I*, Stanford: Stanford University Press.

Whitman, M. v. N. (1975). "Leadership without Hegemony," *Foreign Policy*, 20: 138–160.

Wilson, C. (1949). "Treasure and Trade Balances: The Mercantilist Problem" *Economic History Review*, 2(2).

10 | One Case Where The Economic Consequences of the Peace *Mattered*
The Reshaping of Economic Mindset in Early Republican Turkey

EYÜP ÖZVEREN

[*The Economic Consequences of the Peace*] met with a reception that makes the word Success sound commonplace and insipid. [...]

Primarily the feat was one of moral courage. But the book is a masterpiece – packed with practical wisdom that never lacks depth; pitilessly logical yet never cold; genuinely humane but nowhere sentimental; meeting all facts without vain regret but also without hopelessness; it is sound advice added to sound analysis. And it is a work of art. Form and matter fit each other to perfection. Everything is to the point, and there is nothing in it that is not to the point. No idle adornment disfigures its wise economy of means. The very polish of the exposition – never again was he to write so well – brings out its simplicity. In the passage in which Keynes tries to explain, in terms of the *dramatis personae*, the tragic failure of purpose that produced the Peace, he rises to heights that have been trodden by few.

The economics of the book, [...] is of the simplest and did not call for any refined technique.

–Joseph A. Schumpeter (1946), 'John Maynard Keynes, 1883–1946,' Obituary.

Parable and Paradox as a Point of Departure

Cahit Kayra (1917–2021) was a technocrat in public service, a political figure, and a prolific writer who wrote his memoirs, a monumental insider's account of Turkish economic history and policy in some 700 pages of easy read that made three successive editions (1995, 2002, 2012). Having been deeply impacted by the Great Depression, he was trained as an economist in *Mülkiye*, the Ottoman-Turkish version of the *célèbre* French Science Po set up in imperial Istanbul and relocated to Ankara in the 1930s. Kayra recounts how he had accidentally heard of John Maynard Keynes, and, in one of his mischievous moments, seized the opportunity to test one of his professors by asking his opinion of Keynes, only to find out that he did not know of him (Kayra, 2012: 57). This, in his view, was representative of economics in Turkey at a time when university education was being reformed to catch up with Europe. This is paradoxical and begs for an explanation. But it may also be true that Kayra was misled to think that Keynes was not yet known. Before we proceed further, a brief evaluation of economic thought and history in the Ottoman Empire (hereafter OE) is necessary.

As of the eighteenth century it became increasingly obvious that OE was losing ground in terms of its relative military power vis-à-vis the rival Russian and Austrian empires. This triggered higher military expenditure and higher imports of technology and equipment. The British were called in to protect the OE from the Russian threat. Their protection was extended in return for the adoption by the OE of the free-trade principle. The OE would integrate with the world-market as a producer of primary goods, while opening up its internal trade to foreigners. Ottoman imports would increase drastically while traditional manufactures were badly hit by the competition. The Ottoman ruling class would also adjust its tastes and preferences and become addicted to consumption of European imports of manufactures and luxury goods. This would aggravate the balance of payments and lead to increasing foreign indebtedness (Pamuk, 1994: 124–150).

It soon became clear that at least some 'transitional' protection was needed for the survival through readjustment of domestic manufactures. However this was practically impossible. The new trade regime had not replaced the traditional one but was superimposed upon it. During the sixteenth century, the OE at the height of its power had unilaterally extended commercial privileges known as 'capitulations' to France and later to other European trading partners in order to keep the eastern trade across its territories alive in the face of competition from oceanic routes. These privileges included customs exemptions as well as legal 'extraterritoriality'. Now they could not be revoked by a powerless OE and remained in effect until the First World War. Moreover, by the so-called Great Depression of the nineteenth century, the OE had become bankrupt and conceded to the imposition of a Public Debts

Administration to improve its credibility and defer its loan payments and be able to borrow abroad. This was a temporary solution that could save the day but not the patient. Thus meaningful economic policy-making had become more and more impossible. After the Young Turk Revolution of 1908, a chain of wars best described as the 'Long War' or 'Turkey's Great War' (Mango, 2000: 99–101), starting with the Italian War in Libya (1911–1912), running through the Balkan Wars (1912–1913) and culminating in the First World War (1914–1918), only to be succeeded by the War of Independence (1919–1922) meant spiralling military expenditure and foreign debt (Parvus Efendi, 1977). This put enormous strains on resources, decimated the population, and physically destroyed the country and damaged the economy.

It was but natural that economic thought would turn to attaining development, at least as an intellectual exercise for finding a way out from the cul-de-sac within which the OE was caught. Whereas the free-trade programme had been inaugurated with an orchestrated strong wave of international and indigenous 'cosmopolitan' fanfare and propaganda as of the 1830s, the autochthone protectionist reaction emerged, in much the same way as Karl Polanyi put it in a more general context, 'spontaneously' within few decades (Polanyi, 1944: 141 and 149).

Already by 1908, 'The National Economy Thesis' was probably more popular than the 'Classical Liberal Approach' among the reading public. The former nevertheless exercised a monopoly over economic policy until the First World War. Even after the disruptive Young Turk Revolution, economic policy remained virtually untouched and was invested in the safe hands of Mehmed Cavid Bey, the powerful Minister of Finance, who represented the very best of Ottoman mainstream economics with his book *İktisat İlmi* (The Science of Economics, in Turkish, 1913). Because the alternative was never tested, it became a self-reinforcing legacy, if not a sell-fulfilling legend, within an insulated intellectual domain. The only evidence in its favour was the exemplary unification and economic rise of Germany. The war context allowed the Young Turks to experiment with certain national economic policies (Toprak, 1982: 56–73 and 267–312). By all accounts, if only the prevailing trends continued, the post-war economic thought and policy would finally be emancipated from the fetters of mainstream economics and be shaped by the developmental national political economy perspective. Yet this did not happen. Germany lost the war along with her allies including the OE. The defeat discredited the German model as a lodestar as well as Germany as a leading economic partner.

The success of the national liberation movement could have encouraged the new rulers of Turkey to embrace the untested economic approach and adopt a new economic course. Yet they refrained. Something else must have interfered to change the minds of the leading cadres before the Great Depression. It is the identification of this interfering factor that deserves our attention in this paper. We have seen above how Kayra's memoires indicate that Keynes was unknown to his professors in the mid-1930s. Yet we deduce here that some important factor must have intervened to change the predicted course of things in the development of economic thinking and policy. If it were to be an economist with a book, can one think of anyone but Keynes who could have played such a role? So, can it be that perhaps Kayra's observation and inference were not true after all?

The Adventures of a Book

Only a few books could have had as extraordinary a career as the one we recount here. Keynes wrote *The Economic Consequences of the Peace* in a haste during the months of July and August because he considered it a timely warning against an unjust and unsustainable peace that could bring a further round of escalating disorder, destruction, and possibly warfare to Europe. First published in December 1919 in London, the book gained wide recognition after it came out in the United States. By April 22, 1920, 70,000 copies of the book were sold in the United States in addition to the 18,500 in UK, and by August 1920, total sales worldwide had surpassed 100,000 when the book had become available through translations into German, Dutch, Danish, Swedish, Italian, Spanish, Romanian, Russian, Japanese, and Chinese (Skidelsky, 1986: 394).

The Turkish translation was not yet in sight. Hardly anyone knew that Ali Fethi had just translated the book, in a haste comparable to that of the author, into Turkish during the very same year, though the publication had to await 1922. He attached to the Preface a note clarifying the peculiar circumstances of his role as the translator:

This book has been translated from English while being a prisoner in the Polverista barracks in Malta.

He undersigned the note as Ali Fethi and dated it as April 29–May 14, 1920. This was unusual for that time. The observation of intellectual property rights as we understand it now did not then carry the day. Translators were condemned to invisibility unless exceptional circumstances obtained. The decision to translate a book was taken on a personal basis and usually the author and/or his original publisher did not know of the translation except by chance. Royalty payment under such circumstances was a rarity. Ali Fethi, while choosing to limit himself consciously to being a faithful translator in the modern sense, opted to insert himself in the Preface in an equal status with the author by revealing his where and when in comparable terms.

Ali Fethi (1880–1943) was only three years senior to Keynes (1883–1946), and died three years before him. He was among the many potentially dangerous Ottoman statesmen, politicians, and intellectuals who were forcefully exiled to Malta. Sixty-seven such people were transported by the British occupation authorities on May 28, 1919, from Istanbul, to Malta where they arrived on June 1. Ali Fethi was thus confined as the political prisoner with the assigned number of '2689' in the Fort Salvatore Castle, sharing a room with four others. He would have to shift again until he would be relocated to Polverista Castle, his final destination in Malta, by February 1920 (Okyar, 2014: 80–97). The prisoners were kept under close surveillance from the beginning. Their mails were searched and censored.[1] At first, they were not allowed to have access to books or newspapers. After a while, some freedom of communication was introduced. They could then follow the news through the British newspapers. We know Ali Fethi followed *The Times* (Okyar, 2014: 97; Balkaya, 2005: 43–49) after having learned English. No incriminating evidence was found against him, and he, along with the other prisoners, was not brought to trial. He remained in prison until May 30, 1921 when he was finally released. Ali Fethi arrived first in Taranto, the port of Italy, and then went to Munich to see his children after about two years of exile, before returning to Istanbul (Toker, 2006: 140).

His letter of May 6, 1920 to his wife is one of the very rare instances, if not the only, where Ali Fethi touches upon his translation of *The Economic Consequences of the Peace*. He tells her that for about twenty days, he had been occupied with his translation, has about

---

[1] He wrote to his wife that he shifted to French in a letter because the French-proficient censor was more lenient (Okyar, 2014: 172).

200 pages completed, and expected to finish the rest in about 10 days
(Okyar, 2014: 118). The timing was almost perfect. At this point, the
book traversed the difficult inter-linguistic border across English to
Ottoman Turkish. It was available for publication.

The publication itself proved even more difficult than the translation. It came out with a substantial – but given the circumstances,
understandable – delay in 1922. It was nevertheless made available at
a time when the attention of the limited, but influential, reading public
in Ankara was concentrated in how the peace talks would take shape
in the forthcoming international conference. It was one of the very few
relevant books available in Ankara noted for its shortage of books and
lack of a public library (Vurkaç, 1987: 38). This made *The Economic
Consequences of the Peace* far more important than its author per
se. We know that Kemal Salih Sel, a journalist who would cover the
Lausanne peace conference, possessed a copy. The copy at the Library
of Ege Üniversity in İzmir belonged to Refik Şevket İnce, the Minister
of Justice (1921) of the Ankara government. Last but not least, Ahmet
Ağaoğlu, who had also been a prisoner in Malta, owned a personal
copy of the translation. He responded to the nationalist calling and was
appointed as head of the *Matbuat ve İstihbarat Matbaası* (Publication
and Intelligence Press). This unit was created by law on June 7, 1920
and published only a few (3) books (Emiroğlu and Karaduman, 2018).
The contemporary relevance of the topic in this example gives a good
indication as to why limited resources were assigned to Ali Fethi's
translation of Keynes. Given that Mustafa Kemal was 'above all a
man of the Enlightenment' (Mango, 2000: 528), a bibliophile with a
personal library of some 4000 books, it would be unthinkable if he
had not been presented a copy, as the book was printed in the very
publishing house he had formed with a specific purpose.[2]

When the book finally came out in 1922, it was called *Versay
Barışı'nın Netâyic-i İktisadiyesi* (Plate 9). The choice in favour of a
slight modification of the title must have been deliberately made to
avoid any confusion on part of the potential reader about what 'the

---

[2] Atatürk's books have been preserved in two museum collections. He also
donated some books to a public library as well as lending regularly to
his entourage. We have not been able to track down his copy. His library
contained 145 books about economics out of a total number of 1108 in the
social sciences; social sciences constituting slightly more than a quarter of the
collection, and history another equal proportion (Vurkaç, 1987: 68–9).

Peace' in Keynes's original title referred to. Ali Fethi's translation of the title of Keynes's book is representative of the translation in general. With the exception of 'Versay' (Versailles), virtually every word contained in the Turkish title is of Arabic origin, and the book was printed in Arabic letters. With the Reform of Alphabet (1928) that introduced a modified Latin alphabet, this translation would become obsolete. Only a few among the generation of Kayra could be able to read this version. It was only too normal that it disappeared from sight, but its memory lingered on. As late as the Second World War, Keynes's position was alluded to as part of a common heritage. It found its expression from time to time in the articles of prominent newspaper columnists as well as in history books.

A reprint in Latin alphabet of Ali Fethi Bey's translation had to await until 2018 and the collaboration of Kudret Emiroğlu and Erman Harun Karaduman. With this reprint now available, we know that the 1922 edition had one important difference from Keynes's original. The whole section on Soviet Regime and its prospects entitled 'The Relations of Central Europe to Russia'[3] had been left out and is only restored by the translation of Emiroğlu and Karaduman (231–235). Keynes, unable to follow the narrative in an impossible script, could not have noticed this omission either.[4] It is highly likely that the section was censored at the stage of publication and not of translation. Ahmet Ağaoğlu, with his Azerbaijani background and proficiency in Russian, must have been fully aware that this would have irritated the Russians who supported the Turkish national liberation movement, and thereby jeopardize ongoing cooperation between the two governments.[5] Both shared, at least for the time being, an ideological conception of their own vocations, and Soviet Russians would not welcome a down-to-earth interpretation of what was in store for

---

[3] Keynes had already complained that the Treaty included 'nothing to reclaim Russia' in introducing his Chapter VI (Keynes, 1971: 226). The omitted section was conceived in this spirit.

[4] Keynes himself facilitated this omission by the very way in which he introduced the section on the 288th page of a 298 page book: 'I have said very little of Russia in this book. The broad character of the situation there needs no emphasis, and of the details we know almost nothing authentic' (Keynes, 1971: 288).

[5] Ahmet Ağaoğlu travelled together with the newly appointed Soviet Ambassador Aralov with specific instructions from Lenin. He was well informed of how the official Soviet position was articulated as anti-imperialist alliance with the progressive nationalist Turkish forces (Arolov, 2007: 33).

them. Ağaoğlu must have warned the translator of the pending danger, and convinced him to cut the section out. Ali Fethi would bow to such reasoning given his sensible and moderate character and diplomatic tact. In any case, this was not the only instance of censorship the book had ever been subject to until then. Keynes himself had taken out his vindictive characterization of Lloyd George[6] in a 'deadlier sketch' than the 'mordant character sketches of' George Clemenceau and Woodrow Wilson (Lekachman, 1971: xxxvi), only to publish it much later as a separate piece in his *Essays in Biography* (1933). Hence the original was itself already truncated when first published.

At least for the translator Ali Fethi, the book with its immediate relevance overshadowed by a wide margin the author. Soon after his arrival in Ankara, Ali Fethi started working on another translation, this time from German: *Das Türkische Reich* (1854) by Alfred von Besse (Tevetoğlu, 1987: 127). This was a book about economic statistics of the mid-nineteenth century OE. The statistical content of this otherwise outdated book makes one think of a possible resonance of *The Economic Consequences of the Peace* in the choice. Anyway, he abandoned the project. It would only be in 1932 that his translation from English into Turkish of Sir Arthur Salter's conventional assessment of the Great Depression, *The World's Economic Crisis and the Way of Escape* (1932), as *İktisadi Hastalıktan Kurtuluş* would be published. This very last choice confirms the thesis that Ali Fethi was attracted by the book *The Economic Consequences of the Peace* rather than by the author Keynes who was yet to make his original theoretical breakthrough. The memory of the content of the book was preserved indirectly via both the name of its author to which it was increasingly attached and its association with the Treaty of Lausanne. However, the fact that this book was translated by Ali Fethi was forgotten until recently by even the educated. There is one exception that makes one ponder: Lord Kinross, in his book on Kemal Atatürk and Modern Turkey, first published in 1964:

Above all, [Ali Fethi Okyar] had from his youth made a serious study of economics. During his exile in Malta he had translated into Turkish a work by Maynard Keynes. He believed profoundly in the principles of a free economy. (Kinross, 1995: 451)

---

[6] The international politics image of Lloyd George abroad contradicted sharply with his domestic legacy as the architect of the foundations of the British welfare state.

Unfortunately he revealed no further information about how he came to know of it.

We do not know for sure if the Turkish version of the book ever completed the full circle and reached Keynes's hand. There is good reason to think it did. The translator served as the Turkish ambassador to London (1934–1939). During this period he might have met Keynes and mentioned his translation, and even presented him a copy. In any case, his son Osman Okyar (1917–2002) studied economics at Cambridge after 1936 and obtained his bachelor's degree in 1940.[7] This may have prompted his father to meet Keynes just as the son might by himself have brought up the translation in a conversation with his professor.[8] In all likelihood, a copy of the translation would be presented to Keynes that may still be lying somewhere. If it can be found, this would bring the extraordinary adventures of this book to a full circle.

An Unintended Consequence of *The Economic Consequences of the Peace*

Keynes improvised the title of his own book when he published his piece targeting the return of Britain to the Gold Standard, with the title *The Economic Consequences of Mr. Churchill* (1925). In turn, a strong criticism his book met was by Étienne Mantoux (1913–1945), who resorted to the same game in his choice of subtitle: *La paix*

---

[7] Osman Okyar, upon his return, pursued a PhD in the University of Istanbul and was the first to write a thesis in Keynesian economics to get his degree in 1947 (Özveren, 2012: 235). As such, he became one of the three economists who diffused Keynesian economics in Turkey. He joined Hacettepe University in Ankara in 1967 and set up the department of economics.

[8] One of his colleagues mentions Osman Okyar being introduced to Keynes and his wife in a social event (Türkkan, 1985: 9). I interviewed his colleagues and descendants. Mehmet Seyitdanlıoğlu, who co-authored a book on the memoirs of Fethi Okyar, told me he was sure he heard from Osman Okyar that his father knew Keynes and Keynes knew of the Turkish translation. The grandson of Ali Fethi and the son of Osman Okyar, bearing the name Ali Fethi Okyar, informed me that such an acquaintance was likely, because he was told by his father that Keynes talked him into majoring in economics rather than in politics and international relations as he originally intended, and Osman Okyar suspected that this Keynes might have done upon the request of his father who wanted likewise. Another colleague sounded sure that Keynes knew Ali Fethi well before meeting his son and had no doubt that he also knew of the translation.

calomniée: ou les conséquences économiques de M. Keynes (*The Carthaginian Peace or the Economic Consequences of Mr. Keynes* in English translation, 1946). Here we join the line by our choice for the section-heading, to approach the boomerang effect of the book in an international conflict that involved Great Britain and Turkey that ultimately led to a non-Carthaginian Peace, the first of its kind, after the First World War. The book became a weapon in peacemaking at the Conference of Lausanne that sanctioned the international recognition of the Republic of Turkey. To resume our narrative, we return to the point where we left the story of Ali Fethi.

Once freed from prison on April 30, 1921, Ali Fethi returned to Ankara via Munich, where he wished to see his children first. He was in Munich on May 20. From Munich he travelled to Rome and from Rome he took a boat to Istanbul. At the end of July he left Istanbul by boat for İnebolu on the Black Sea coast. He reached İnebolu on August 3, 1921. On August 5, he set out for Ankara. He arrived in Ankara on August 8. On the same evening he was received by Mustafa Kemal in the parliament where they had a long conversation as he noted in his diary (Tevetoğlu, 1987: 121). They had first met in War College (*Harbiye*), where Ali Fethi was three years senior to him. They fought together against the Italians in Tripoli in 1911. Ali Fethi was then appointed as Ottoman Ambassador to Sofia, where Mustafa Kemal served with him as the military attaché. Between November 1 and December 21, 1918, together they published the newspaper, *Minber*, in Istanbul. Mustafa Kemal saw him in Bekirağa Prison before Ali Fethi's deportation to Malta on May 14, 1919. He told him he would be leaving for Samsun the next day to start the struggle for liberation and that Ali Fethi should be relieved of his sufferings and sorrows once he heard that they have reached their destination. He was thus to remain as 'Mustafa Kemal's close collaborator' (Mango, 2000: 313; see Plate 8). Within their conversation in Ankara after a long interval, it is but natural that the two officers addressed how the war of national liberation progressed. Mustafa Kemal must have briefed him of the details of ongoing warfare. But as two statesmen, they also exchanged views about the international context and Ali Fethi shared with him whatever he surmised from Keynes's book (Çavdar, 1992: 196).

We do not know for sure what prompted Ali Fethi's interest in Keynes's book in the first instance (Okyar and Seyildanlıoğlu, 2005: 22–3; Toprak, 2014: xv). *The Times* reacted very strongly against

Keynes's *The Economic Consequences of the Peace* entirely for the sake of, not economic, but 'international' political reasons:

Indeed one of the striking features of Mr. Keynes' book is the political inexperience, not to say ingeniousness, which it reveals. Yet he sits in judgment upon and condemns severely, as statesmen and as men, the French and British Prime Ministers and the American President. He draws portraits of them in which only those who know his subjects more intimately can distinguish the true from the false [...] Mr. Keynes may be a 'clever' economist. He may have been a successful Treasury official. But in writing this book, he has rendered the Allies a disservice for which their enemies will, doubtless, be grateful. (Unsigned, The Times, 5, January, 1920, p. 17)[9]

This allegation alone would have sufficed to provoke Ali Fethi's curiosity. Despite his pro-British sympathies and liberal bent placing him among the Anglophile exiles (Şimşir, 1976: 324), when seen from the British viewpoint, he belonged to the 'enemy' camp. He would be inclined to find out what exactly was the inherently promising 'service' available to him and his likes in the book. We do not know how he laid his hand on the book, but we know that by November 1919, he was already able to receive from London the book orders he placed (Okyar, 2014: 56). Moreover, despite this furore, even *The Times* conceded that Keynes could be a 'clever' economist. As a matter of fact, the economic reactions to Keynes's book were far more favourable as we saw above, even in Schumpeter's obituary. Keynes's economic analysis was classical (in the Marshallian sense) as well as original, professional, matter-of-factly, and thought-provoking. Hence it generated a broad-based alliance of the initiated across the spectrum. This is precisely why also learned people of various economic persuasions in Turkey could readily welcome it, and consider it instructive for responding to the international politicking in wait for them. Ali Fethi himself also had no problems with endorsing it and launching its national success in Turkey whereas he was going to shy away from the emergent Keynesian economics in the eventful 1930s. In short, *The Economic Consequences of the Peace* united rather than dividing in Turkey and helped shape the public opinion.

The possible Turkish readings of Keynes's *Economic Consequences of the Peace* have been explored in two studies (Ağır and Özveren,

---

[9] The article is by the then editor of the newspaper, Wickam Steed (1998).

2014, 2016), where two major topics were addressed: (1) What the potential Ottoman-Turkish reader found in the book, and (2) how the effect of the book over the reading public changed over time. In relation with the first, we identified one by one the likely 'consequences' of Keynes's direct references to Turkey, and the indirect inferences an Ottoman-Turkish reader could have drawn from the work. With respect to the second topic, we traced immediate as well as long-term effects of the reception through newspaper articles and references by content analysis. There is no point in repeating in detail those previous findings here. In relation with the theme of this paper, it is more important to emphasize the broader connections. Firstly, Keynes's book, by way of its characterization of the leading figures, by bringing gods down to earth, demonstrated their potential weaknesses and vulnerability. Secondly, and more importantly, the Turks drew a lesson concerning the nature of the peacemaking process in Versailles, the description of which they found in Keynes's work. The peace was negotiated among the winners and imposed upon the losers. The winners were inside the room, and the losers were left out (Keynes, 1971: 54). Hence the peace process was hierarchical and unipolar. The Turkish side inferred that a repetition of this scenario would deliver similar results, that is, another undesirable Carthaginian peace.[10] Faced with this 'Versailles Syndrome' (Ağır and Özveren, 2014: 74), they drew their red line as agreeing to nothing less than being one of the two equal sides when a peace treaty concerning their future was to be drawn. Finally, Keynes expressed his view that the treaty of Versailles had to be thoroughly revised to be viable but thought this was impossible because of the powerful actors on the scene and the manipulated populace.[11] In relation with this last point, what if they altered significantly the on-the-ground configuration of *rapports des forces*? In this respect, a battlefield victory would modify

---

[10] Keynes put the purpose of his book succinctly: 'My purpose in this book is to show that a Carthaginian Peace is not *practically* right or possible.' And 'I am mainly concerned in what follows, not with the justice of the Treaty,—neither with the demand for penal justice against the enemy, nor with the obligation of contractual justice on the victor,—but with its wisdom and with its consequences' (Keynes, 1971: 36, 65).

[11] 'A great change is necessary in public opinion before the [remedy] proposals of this chapter can enter the region of practical politics' (Keynes, 1971: 288). For his conviction that the Treaty needed a thorough revision, see also (Keynes, 1971: 256–61).

the reality significantly enough to force the winners to reconsider their positions. With this insight, Turks sought to replace the Treaty of Sèvres (August 10, 1920), worse than the Paris Conference Treaties of Versailles, Saint-Germain, and Neuilly in terms of the treatment of the losers (Meray and Olcay, 2019: xl), and imposed upon them a dictated peace, with a new and fair peace, namely, the Treaty of Lausanne signed on July 24 1923, that would be viable and lasting.

The Treaty of Lausanne as the First Non-Carthaginian Peace

The Turkish side had already gained some experience in diplomatic negotiation within the contexts of the Turkish-French Treaty of Ankara (1921) and the Armistice of Mudanya following the ultimate military victory (1922). When it came to choosing a head of delegation for the Lausanne talks, Mustafa Kemal endorsed İsmet Pasha among the several names considered because he could also question and alter the rules of the game when needed by combining tactics and strategy. He could easily shift back and forth between the two roles, that of an amateur diplomat and that of a military commander, as befitting his purpose. Just in case he came under extreme pressure, he could count on Dr Rıza Nur who was notorious for his strong temper, rapidly shifting moods, and occasional outbursts. The third member of the negotiating team was Hasan Saka, better known for his mastery of economic and financial matters. The Turkish team was assisted by a number of advisors with a strength in economic and financial matters. On the way to the talks, İsmet Pasha met Cavit Bey, the leading economist and former Ottoman Minister of Finance. He was impressed by Cavit Bey's knowledge and experience, and decided to have him in the delegation as an advisor (Tunçer, 2010: 238). Şükrü Kaya was in the delegation (Toker, 2006: 142) and was concerned with the customs policy, and economic and fiscal matters. Hence economics was relatively well represented in the Turkish delegation.

İsmet Pasha was to face Lord Curzon,[12] a seasoned diplomat and politician with a long track record[13]. The talks continued much

[12] For the David-versus-Goliath resonances of journalistic reports and Turkish nationalist historiographical accounts, see Karacan (1943).
[13] He was desperate to win big, as otherwise he would spoil his chances for becoming Prime Minister (Demirci, 2011: 236).

longer than originally expected, were suspended once, and then resumed, and consisted of two rounds. İsmet Pasha, originally taken as an inexperienced diplomat[14] by his rivals, proved himself as a born diplomat by the end. To understand why the talks lasted unusually long, we need to identify the rival strategies and tactics of the two sides. Lord Curzon, to realize his political ambition, could return to London with nothing less than another Carthaginian peace.[15] To this end, he pretended as if nothing had changed in the meantime, that is, the national liberation struggle of the Turks had not modified the *rapports des forces* on the ground,[16] and the Russian Revolution next door had not occurred. He was determined to bring the British allies under his yoke because he feared they could betray him otherwise. Lord Curzon wanted to assume the role of a master of ceremonies who would deliver a soliloquy, or better still, a sermon, and come out of the talks with a slightly revised version of the Treaty of Sèvres. In conformity with the diplomatic tradition of the nineteenth century, he had at his disposal the advantage of being the President of the Conference (Ryan, 1951: 175).

In contrast, İsmet Pasha's strategy was to ensure that nothing less than an equal status should be extended to his delegation. The observance of the principle of equality was tantamount to acknowledging that the Turkish side represented not the defunct OE but an emergent state that demanded international recognition of its sovereignty and independence. At the end of the road, this was the objective, and nothing less than a negotiated peace could serve the purpose. Attention to details was important because the cumulative effect of unequal treatments built into the ritualistic and ceremonial repertoire of traditional diplomacy would jeopardize the realization of his objective.

---

[14] Lord Curzon saw İsmet Pasha as a second-rate military commander, not even a diplomat (Benoist-Méchin, 1954: 304), and the Allies 'tried to treat him as representative of a defeated nation' (Shaw and Kural Shaw, 1977: 365).

[15] Treaty of Sèvres set the standard: 'What [Lloyd George] wanted, and got, was a treaty described by Keynes as Carthaginian' (Kinross, 1995: 231).

[16] Curzon insisted that the Turks had defeated, not the Allies but the Greeks, but Lausanne was about settling the account of the world war. This formulation played down Turkish victory. İsmet Pasha objected by arguing that the British had encouraged Greeks to occupy Anatolia and fight a proxy war on their behalf with their full support. Moreover, now that there was no longer the OE, the talks were taking place between those who defeated and relinquished it and an entirely new state that emerged from the national liberation struggle. So the game had changed.

A comparison of the opening and closing ceremonies helps one see how the conference changed shape. Originally, the opening public ceremony to be held on November 20, 1922 was designed in the traditional format. Some 250 press members had come to Lausanne to cover the ceremony where, in addition to Lord Curzon, the Minister of Foreign Affairs, celebrities like the French Premier Raymond Poincaré, Italian Prime Minister Benito Mussolini, and the Greek Representative Eleftherios Venizelos were to attend this symbolic event taking place in *Casino de Montbenon*. Firstly the President of the Swiss Confederation as host would speak and then Lord Curzon would take the floor and thank him on behalf of the participants. When İsmet Pasha heard this programme, he objected by saying that if Lord Curzon spoke in the opening ceremony he would also take the floor and deliver a speech. Once Curzon spoke, İsmet Pasha took the floor and read his brief but-to-the-point speech. This was very unusual as tradition of diplomacy in Old Europe was concerned, but it was symbolic of the fact that equality of status was a must from the viewpoint of the Turkish delegation.[17] He also objected to the seating arrangement for the talks when it became apparent that around one table would sit the delegates and consultants of Britain, France, Italy, and Japan, and in a second table would be seated the Turkish team along with those of Bulgaria, Romania, and Serbia. Upon İsmet Pasha's insistence, this arrangement was revised and the Turkish delegates were invited to share a table with the British, French, and Italian delegates. The revised seating plan was recognizant of the fact that the peace process was bilateral with the Turks an equal player. Secondly, the original name for the conference was drafted as 'Conference on the Eastern Question'. İsmet Pasha objected because this put the conference into the context of the nineteenth-century Eastern Question when the OE was characterized as the Sick Man of Europe. He suggested instead that it should be referred simply as the Conference of Lausanne. A compromise was made to redefine it as the Lausanne Conference on the Near Eastern Problems. When a negotiated peace was finally achieved on July 24, 1923, İsmet Pasha was extended the symbolic honour of signing the treaty first. The Allies were somewhat weary of their losses and wished

---

[17] After İsmet Pasha, the Swiss President came back to thank both for their opening speeches, thereby extending recognition to İsmet Pasha's out-of-the-programme statement of purpose.

to downplay the historic event hence opted for a low-key ceremony. An independent-minded conservative[18] Turkish journalist, Velid Ebuzziya, as an eyewitness attributed this simple and short ceremony to the fact that the Allies saw themselves as those who had lost comparatively (Temiz, 2007: 654–60).

İsmet Pasha's strategy for achieving his goal underwent a fundamental change in the course of negotiations. Unlike Curzon who stuck to the same strategy, İsmet Pasha was flexible enough to modify his own in accordance with the way the process unfolded. Lord Curzon had all along handled Britain's allies heavy-handedly and forced them into orchestrated action so that he could isolate the Turks. İsmet Pasha's original strategy was to develop good relations with each country independently and advance informal talks. After a while, İsmet Pasha saw that the French and Italians were saying one thing when they talked with the Turks separately and another in the conference talks orchestrated by Lord Curzon. In reaction, İsmet Pasha decided to move forward on issues that were of utmost priority for the British such as the determination of the future of Istanbul and the Straits, and the fate of Mosul province rich in oil resources and under British occupation. Once considerable progress was made on these issues, he anticipated, Britain would have a stake in securing a peace treaty, and it would be easier for the Turks to deal with the French and Italians. This new approach helped resolve the problem of the Straits and future of navigation in the Black Sea, and some progress was also made on the question of Mosul. If the talks faltered because of the problem of Mosul, the blame would be put on Britain, as this priority was of the least concern for her allies. On the issue of capitulations that concerned the French interests most, however, all stood fast against the Turks because of the importance they gave to the principle. The Americans and the Japanese joined this chorus because they feared the abolishment of the capitulations would set a dangerous precedent for the colonial world (Ryan, 1951: 185). As the first round of talks came thus towards deadlock, Lord Curzon made an important calculation mistake. He forced upon the Turks a take-it-or-leave-it option. This was his last chance to dictate a Carthaginian peace. He bet that the Turks needed peace urgently and would yield to pressure in the very last moment. He announced he was going to

---

[18] A contemporary conservative journalist also chose to give the final word in his recent book about Lausanne to Ebuzziya (Akyol, 2014: 326).

leave Lausanne for London by a certain deadline, and before his departure he would dissolve the talks. İsmet Pasha retaliated by making an unexpected counter offer. As the majority of the more important issues were resolved, he proposed that a partial interim peace treaty could be signed. This was seen as a 'clever move' by the American diplomat Joseph Grew (1952: 550). However Curzon did not consider this offer seriously because he was sure of his bet. He insisted on his own proposal. İsmet Pasha refused, and the talks collapsed. Curzon could hardly believe that his scheme to secure a Carthaginian peace and return to London as a victorious politician had failed so miserably.

When the talks resumed, Lord Curzon stepped back and left his seat to Sir Horace Rumbold, the High Commissioner in Istanbul during the occupation. The downgrading of the level of British representation indicated that İsmet Pasha's strategic move had proven productive. When the talks were about to stumble because of a disagreement on whether the Turkish share of Ottoman debt and interest payments would be made in terms of gold, pounds sterling or French francs, Rumbold wrote to London stating that, after all the efforts spent, a failure of the conference because of intransigence on such a silly detail would be most unfortunate (Coşkun, 2019: 345). Britain's allies also felt free to deal with the Turks separately.[19] İsmet Pasha was successful in turning the talks into a win-win game that was beneficial to both sides, the British because of the relative gains in the Straits navigation regime and the control over the oil-rich province of Mosul, and the Turkish side because of the international recognition they gained as a new sovereign state, and they rid themselves of the Ottoman economic and legal capitulations. As the intended sermon of Lord Curzon gave way to the unfolding of a game of chess, Versailles was not re-enacted, and a Carthaginian Peace was avoided. No wonder why, future historians singled out the Treaty of Lausanne among the offshoots of Versailles as the only one that survived the test of time (Kinross, 1995: 373) and 'a signal success for Turkish diplomacy' (Mango, 2000: 387).

---

[19] When the peace talks were suspended, Venizelos approached İsmet Pasha, who was planning to reach Istanbul by a stopover in Romania, and invited him to consider travelling through Salonica with the guarantee of safe passage by the Greek government. During the second round of talks, Rumbold noted that Venizelos informed the Allies that Greece could no longer afford to keep an army of 200,000 men mobilized and wished to sign a treaty with Turkey (Coşkun, 2019: 346).

Conclusion

The use of the metaphors of 'sermon' and 'chess' may have invoked in the mind of the careful reader, 'The Fire Sermon' and 'A Game of Chess' as the titles of two successive parts in T.S. Eliot's *The Waste Land* (1922). Written two years after *The Economic Consequences of the Peace*, Eliot's poem echoed Keynes's book as reaction to Europe's self-destructive war. By allusions to a trans-historical chain of civilizational experiences that include going back and forth between London, Europe and a Carthage caught on fire, Eliot's poem only touched obliquely the effects of the recent war, but this sufficed to make the damage all the more visible. The connection between the two texts has already been noted (Cook, 1979). Keynes and Eliot knew each other as both were linked to the Bloomsbury Circus, a hub of artists and intellectuals. Eliot read Keynes's *The Economic Consequences of the Peace* to have been at least in part inspired by it:

Keynes' vision of a derelict Europe, the hot, dry atmosphere in the chamber where the negotiations were conducted, the destruction of industry and the exhaustion of the soil all feed Eliot's vision of the European wasteland. Noting Keynes' influence, we can see that at least sporadically in the poem, Eliot offers a subtle liberal humanist vision of the European wreckage. (Paulin, 2007)

Eliot confessed, in his obituary for Keynes, this was his only book that he read. He continued:

He foresaw the consequences of bad economics corrupted further by political passion and expediency, and the consequences were realized. Disdainful aloofness would have been the natural resort [...] and certainly, he had at command a cynical wit which sometimes expressed itself in conversation, when public affairs or economic doctrines were touched upon in private company. (Eliot, 1946: 47–8)[20]

Schumpeter, the author of another obituary for Keynes, an excerpt of which served as the epigraph, emphasized a number of points that recapitulate our arguments. Just as Eliot read *The Economic Consequences*

---

[20] Keynes loved reading poetry and Sir Roy Harrod wrote how he remembered 'coming into his rooms in the autumn of 1922, to find that he was reading aloud *The Waste Land* by T.S. Eliot, a poet of whom [he] had so far not heard' (Harrod, 1951: 29).

of the Peace as an outsider, so did the Turks. They picked up what was useful for them and used it to their ends. In this respect, most useful were, first, the description of the diplomatic process at Versailles, and secondly, the so-called 'German Transfer Problem' to do with reparations. In the case of Turks, this problem was even more complicated as they were faced with, not only a likely demand for reparations, but also the obligation to pay back the Ottoman foreign debt and its interest.[21] Borrowing terms from Schumpeter, the book provided them with plentiful 'practical wisdom' useful for both, but also with 'hope' to come to terms with what awaited them. Simply put, it was political-economically relevant for the immediate agenda. For the diplomatic peace-making process, Turks turned to 'the passage in which Keynes tries to explain, in terms of the *dramatis personae*, the tragic failure of purpose that produced the Peace, [where] he rises to heights that have been trodden by few'. They discovered it was not only masterful but also didactic. Thanks to this specific application, the immediate impact of the book was blown out of proportion.[22] Last but not least, the 'economics of the book,' which Schumpeter characterized as 'of the simplest and did not call for any refined technique', was what everyone could make sense of. Hence it made sense to Eliot, the poet, just as it did to the Turkish delegation on the way to Lausanne peace talks, but also to its translator, Ali Fethi who would assume political power as Prime Minister. Precisely because its economics was simple and straightforward, it made sense, and united, rather than dividing,

[21] This was one of the most thorny issues brought to table at Lausanne. The Turkish starting-point was that Greece should be compelled to share the Ottoman debt and pay reparations for the destruction it inflicted on Asia Minor after the armistice (Coşkun, 2019: 95). The Allies saw that Greece could not afford to pay the claimed sum and therefore they would have to foot the bill. An agreement was thus reached relatively easily. Turkey undertook the payment of 2/3 of the Ottoman debt calculated in accordance to time-weighted territorial percentage of the successor states. This amounted to some 85 million gold liras with about 6 million gold lira payments per year. Debt payments were, however, deferred with a successive agreement until 1929 when the first payment would be 15 million liras (Boratav, 2003: 43–44). Turkey fulfilled its payment obligations by 1954.

[22] This does not mean to belittle other factors exerting a parallel force in the same direction. During the occupation in Istanbul, various publications, in journals as well as in the press, of Prof Ahmet Selâhattin Bey (1878–1920), a specialist in international law, helped shape public opinion concerning international affairs, and served as a foundation for the Turkish position at the Lausanne talks (Meray, 1976).

the otherwise disparate readers. In the long term the lasting legacy of
the book is the touch and turn it gave to economic thinking in Turkey.
Before the book, Ottoman-Turkish intelligentsia in general, and economists in particular were divided into rival camps. Irrespectively of the
choice, across the spectrum there existed a strong belief that being liberal, pro-Allies, and politically 'conservative' was synonymous. On the
opposite side, progressive nationalists by definition had to be unlib-
eral, economically *dirigiste*, sympathetic to Germany and later the
Soviet Union. Keynes, with his eccentric combination (liberal but also
not dogmatic about market economics yet free-tradist and pragmatic
in approaching Germany and Soviet Russia), defied the conventional
clusterings, demonstrated that hitherto unthought new combinations
(market-friendly policy at home combined with free-tradism, but also
cooperation with Soviet Russia in a way prefiguring post-war international nonalignment politics) could be worked out to the benefit of
Turkey.

   In his posthumously published magnum opus, *History of Economic
Analysis* (1954), Schumpeter adopted a progress-ridden view of economic thought. He was nevertheless well-read enough in the subject
to qualify his position by emphasizing the numerous instances of lost
knowledge as a result of which further progress was occasionally
arrested for considerable periods of time. Returning to our introductory parable and paradox, we can characterize the peculiarity of the
Turkish case as one such instance of actual loss of knowledge that
disrupts continuity. Keynes was, albeit in the shadow of his *The
Economic Consequences of the Peace*, known in Turkey because his
book played a considerable role in helping shape the Turkish position
in the Conference of Lausanne. Independently of Keynes's original
intent, the book responded to the very needs of the Turks desperately in search of a fair and lasting peace that would significantly
depart from the Versailles paradigm. Thanks to success in this respect,
despite the prior strength of the German-inspired 'national political
economy' approach, liberal economic policy was reinvigorated in the
1920s when the country was faced with economic reconstruction.
Had it not been for the Great Depression, this momentum might have
continued well into the thirties. On the other hand, had it not been
for the economic lessons learned from *The Economic Consequences
of the Peace*, this critical turn may not have come about in the first
instance. Ali Fethi, the translator of Keynes's book, played a major

role as prime minister in adopting pro-market policies in general, and removing the traditional agricultural tax (*aşar*) to give incentive to self-interested farmers, in particular. Hence, the book helped reshape Turkish economic mindset that would survive the avalanche ushered by the Great Depression, and would be resurrected as the backbone of a mixed-economy model that combined markets with public and private enterprises within the context of moderate planning in the 1960s.

References

Ağır, Seven and Eyüp Özveren (2014) "The Reception and Impact of Keynes's *Economic Consequences of the Peace* in Turkey," In Jens Hölscher and Matthias Klaes, eds., *Keynes's Economic Consequences of the Peace: A Reappraisal*. London: Pickering & Chatto, 63–81.

Ağır, Seven and Eyüp Özveren (2016) "Türkiye'ye Özgü bir Keynes Etkisi: Versay Sulhu'nun Netayic-i İktisadiyyesi," In Deniz Taner Kılınçoğlu ve Emre Özçelik, eds., *John Maynard Keynes... Yine, Yeniden*. Istanbul: İletişim, 205–34.

Akyol, Taha (2014) *Bilinmeyen Lozan*. Istanbul: Doğan Kitap.

Arolov, Semyov Ivanoviç (2007) *Bir Sovyet Diplomatının Türkiye Anıları, 1922–1923*. Istanbul: Türkiye İş Bankası Yayınları.

Balkaya, İhsan Sabri (2005) "Ali Fethi Okyar'ın Bekirağa'dan Malta'ya Uzanan Hapis Hayatına Kendi Kaleminden ve Hatıralarından Bir Bakış," *Atatürk Dergisi*, 4,3: 41–57.

Benoist-Méchin, Jacques (1954) *Le Loup et le Léopard: Mustapha Kémal, ou La mort d'un empire*. Paris: Éditions Albin Michel.

Besse, Alfred von (1854) *Das Türkische Reich*. Leipzig: Remmelmann.

Boratav, Korkut (2003) *Türkiye İktisat Tarihi: 1908–2002*. Ankara: İmge Kitabevi.

Çavdar, Tevfik (1992) *Türkiye'de Liberalizm (1860–1990)*. Ankara: İmge.

Cavid Bey, Mehmed (1913[2001]) *İktisat İlmi*. Istanbul: Liberte.

Cook, Eleanor (1979) "T. S. Eliot and the Carthaginian Peace," *ELH (English Literary History)*, 46, 2: 341–55.

Coşkun, Alev (2019) *1922–1923: Diplomat İnönü: Lozan*. Istanbul: Kırmızı Kedi.

Demirci, Sevtap (2011) *Belgelerle Lozan: Taktik – Stratejik – Diplomatik Mücadele, 1922–1923*. Istanbul: Alfa.

Eliot, T.S. (1946) "John Maynard Keynes," *New English Weekly*, 16 May, 47–8.

Eliot, T.S. (1922) *The Waste Land*. London: Faber.

Emiroğlu, Kudret and Erman Harun Karaduman (2018) "Sunuş: Keynes, Fethi Okyar, Türkiye Cumhuriyeti ve Ekonomik Bunalım ve Kapitalizm…" *Introduction, John Maynard Keynes, Versay Sulhu'nun Netâyic-i İktisadiyesi, 9–27.*

Grew, Joseph C. (1952) *Turbulent Era: A Diplomatic Record of Forty Years, 1904–1945.* Boston: Houghton Mifflin.

Harrod, Roy (1951) *The Life of John Maynard Keynes.* London: Macmillan.

Karacan, Ali Naci (1943) *Lozan Konferansı ve İsmet Paşa.* Istanbul: Maarif Matbaası.

Kayra, Cahit (2012) *'38 Kuşağı: Cumhuriyet'le Yetişenler.* Istanbul: Türkiye İş Bankası Kültür Yayınları.

Keynes, John Maynard (1925) *The Economic Consequences of Mr. Churchill.* London: The Hogart Press.

Keynes, John Maynard (1971) *The Economic Consequences of the Peace.* New York: Harper Torchbooks.

Keynes, John Maynard (2018) *Versay Sulhu'nun Netâyic-i İktisadiyesi. Versay Barışı'nın İktisadi Sonuçları.* Translated into Turkish by Ali Fethi Okyar, Kudret Emiroğlu and Erman Harun Karaduman, eds., Istanbul: Islık Yayınları.

Kinross, Patrick (1995[1964]) *Atatürk: The Rebirth of a Nation.* London: Phoenix.

Lekachman, Robert (1971) "Introduction to the Torchbook Edition," In John Maynard Keynes, ed., *The Economic Consequences of the Peace.* New York: Harper Torchbooks, ix–xxxvii.

Mango, Andrew (2000) *Atatürk: The Biography of the Founder of Modern Turkey.* Woodstock, NY : The Overlook Press.

Mantoux, Étienne (1946) *La paix calomniée, ou les conséquences économiques de M. Keynes,* Paris: Gallimard.

Meray, Seha L. (1976) *Lozan'ın Öncüsü: Prof. Ahmet Selâhattin Bey, 1878–1920.* Ankara: Türk Tarih Kurumu Yayınları.

Meray, Seha L. and Osman Olcay (2019) *Osmanlı İmparatorluğu'nun Çöküş Belgeleri.* Istanbul: Türkiye İş Bankası Kültür Yayınları.

Okyar, Fethi (2014) *İki Gözüm Galibem: Malta Sürgününden Mektuplar.* Istanbul: Türkiye İş Bankası Yayınları.

Okyar, Osman and Mehmet Seyildanlıoğlu (2005) *Atatürk, Okyar, ve Çok Partili Türkiye: Fethi Okyar'ın Anıları.* Istanbul: Türkiye İş Bankası Yayınları.

Özveren, Eyüp (2012) "The Great Depression as a Stimulus for Turkish Economic Thought: The Kadro Movement from within and Keynesianism from without," In Michalis Psalidopoulos, ed., *The Great Depression in Europe: Economic Thought and Policy in a National Context.* Athens: Alpha Bank Historical Archives, 215–40.

Pamuk, Şevket (1994) *Osmanlı Ekonomisinde Bağımlılık ve Büyüme (1820–1913).* Istanbul: Tarih Vakfı Yayınları.

Parvus Efendi (1977) *Türkiye'nin Mali Tutsaklığı.* Muammer Sencer ed. Istanbul: May Yayınları.

Paulin, Tom (2007) "All at sea in the Waste Land," Book Review of T.S. Eliot by Craig Raine, *The Observer,* Sunday 7 January 2007.

Polanyi, Karl (1944) *The Great Transformation: the Political and Economic Origins of Our Time.* Boston: Beacon Press.

Ryan, Andrew (1951) *The Last of the Dragomans.* London: Geoffrey Bles.

Salter, Arthur (1932) *The World's Economic Crisis and the Way of Escape.* New York: Century.

Schumpeter, Joseph A. (1954) *History of Economic Analysis.* New York: Oxford University Press.

Schumpeter, Joseph A. (1946) "John Maynard Keynes, 1883–1946," *Obituary. The American Economic Review,* XXXVI, 4 (September 1946), 495–518.

Shaw, Stanford J. and Ezel Kural Shaw (1977) *History of the Ottoman Empire and Modern Turkey. Vol II: Reform, Revolution and Republic: The Rise of Modern Turkey, 1808–1975.* Cambridge: Cambridge University Press.

Şimşir, Bilal N. (1976) *Malta Sürgünleri.* Istanbul: Milliyet Yayınları.

Skidelsky, Robert (1986) *John Maynard Keynes. Vol I: Hopes Betrayed (1883–1920).* New York: Elisabeth Sifton Books.

Steed, Wickam (1998) "A Critique of the Peace, the Candid Friend at Versailles, Comfort of Germany," In McCann Jr, ed., *John Maynard Keynes: Critical Responses.* London, Routledge, 51–9.

Temiz, Ahmet (2007) *Velid Ebuzziya'nın Lozan Mektupları.* Istanbul: IQ Kültür Sanat Yayıncılık.

Tevetoğlu, Fethi (1987) "Ali Fethi Okyar'ın Günlük Hâtıraları (30 Nisan 1921–16 Ekim 1921)," *Belgeler,* Türk Tarih Belgeleri Dergisi, XII, 16: 113–30.

Toker, Yalçın (2006) *Malta Sürgünlerinden Portreler.* Istanbul: Toker Yayınları.

Toprak, Zafer (2014) "Malta Sürgünü Fethi Bey ve Çevirisi," In Fethi Okyar, ed., *İki Gözüm Galibem.* Istanbul: Türkiye İş Bankası Yayınları.

Toprak, Zafer (1982) *Türkiye'de 'Milli İktisat' (1908–1918).* Ankara: Yurt Yayınları.

Tunçer, Polat (2010) *İttihatçı Cavit Bey.* Istanbul: Yeditepe.

Türkkan, Erdal (1985) "Batılı Anlamda Bir Bilim Adamı: Osman Okyar," *H.Ü. İktisadi ve İdari Bilimler Fakültesi Dergisi,* III, 1–2, 9–15.

Vurkaç, Yılmaz (1987) *Atatürk ve Kitap.* Istanbul: Milliyet Yayınları.

11 | Keynes and International Trade Politics after the First World War

MADELEINE LYNCH DUNGY

John Maynard Keynes's intervention in favour of multilateral organization after the Second World War is well known, when he proposed an International Clearing Union which helped lay the groundwork for the Bretton Woods settlement (Clarke, 2009, pp. 86–93; Keynes, 1980, pp. 1–144; Skidelsky, 1990, pp. 179–232). It was, however, after the First World War that Keynes – and the world – made the initial leap towards institutionalized international cooperation. As a representative of the British Treasury at the 1919 Paris Peace Conference, he called for a sweeping multilateral programme that would link together the complex moving parts of the world economy:

> only a scheme of large and broad dimensions, which can be announced to and understood by the whole world, can inspire that sentiment of hope which is the greatest need of Europe at this moment. A proposal which unfolds future prospects and shows the peoples of Europe a road by which food and employment and orderly existence can once again come their way, will be a more powerful weapon than any other for the preservation from the dangers of Bolshevism of that order of human society which we believe to be the best starting point for future improvement and greater well-being. (Keynes, 1971, p. 436)

Recent scholarship on the legacy of the First World War has emphasized that the massive overhang of war debts and reparations politicized international economic relations in ways that could only be managed through sustained and deliberate multilateral coordination (Boyce, 2009; Tooze, 2014). Historians of the League of Nations have revealed the extensive technical apparatus that it spawned to promote economic diplomacy (notably, Decorzant, 2011; Clavin, 2013). Although this activity never assumed the all-encompassing scope that Keynes recommended in 1919, it did gradually take over the League, establishing a durable regime of global governance dominated by questions of money and trade (Clavin, 2013).

In 1919, Keynes made a distinction between finance – which he believed required immediate and thorough multilateral action – and trade – which he believed could be managed with a lighter touch. He predicted that once wartime trade restrictions related to the blockade were removed 'private enterprise may be safely entrusted with the task of finding the solution'. By contrast, 'in the financial sphere, the problem of restoring Europe is almost certainly too great for private enterprise alone' (Keynes, 1971, p. 434). Thus, Keynes concentrated his innovative energies on devising mechanisms for international lending to reduce the burden of war debts and reparations on the world economy. Historical scholarship on the economic consequences of the war has also focused on international efforts to manage political debts and rebuild the gold standard and has accorded limited consideration to international trade. The 1920s did, however, bring important changes in the legal and institutional tools of trade policy and, more importantly, in the kinds of questions that those tools were used to address. Interwar economic leaders attempted to apply the new multilateral capacity offered by the League of Nations to geopolitical problems on a grand scale – notably problems tied to Europe's external marginalization in global markets and its internal fragmentation, as continental empires were divided into nation-states.

Although in 1919 Keynes and most other international economic leaders demanded relatively limited international trade cooperation in order to restore the pre-war status quo, this modest goal was in fact quite radical. In the 1920s returning to the comparatively integrated markets of 1913 was a big leap because the surrounding political context had changed so much. The war had greatly expanded the role of private commerce as a tool of military power; it precipitated the collapse of the German, Russian, Austro-Hungarian, and Ottoman Empires; and it de-centred Europe in the world economy by fuelling the rise of the United States and other overseas trading powers (Tooze & Fertik, 2014). This chapter shows that in 1919, Keynes had already identified many of the new points of tension and drivers for change that propelled multilateral trade cooperation during the coming decades. It will begin by briefly summarizing Keynes's response to the actual trade terms of the 1919 Peace Settlement and then discuss his alternative proposal for a 'Free Trade Union'. This scheme highlighted two important and related issues – Germany's role in Europe and Britain's relationship to Europe – which remained at the centre of subsequent trade debates in the League of Nations.

Keynes described the core trade clauses in the Treaty of Versailles as 'pin-pricks', as affronts to German sovereignty with limited practical significance (Keynes, 1919, p. 93). He was referring primarily to a provision that required Germany to grant the Allies most-favoured-nation (MFN) status unilaterally for a period of five years.[1] This allowed Allied governments to introduce targeted restrictions against German exports without fear of reprisal until 1925. Above and beyond any practical macroeconomic impact, these restrictions held great political significance because they concerned an elemental principle of international trade law.[2] MFN had become a central pillar of the trade treaty system in the nineteenth century, and, crucially, it was norm of non-discrimination. MFN status entitled a state to claim any trade concessions accorded to third parties. Thus, in 1919 Germany committed to treat the Allies at least as well as all of its other trading partners but did not receive the same assurance. Keynes rightly understood that this provision was a source of international tension not simply because it was one-sided but also because it was set against the universalist backdrop of the new League of Nations. Wilson's initial sketch for the League in his famed Fourteen Points included a commitment to 'equality of trade conditions' (*Woodrow Wilson's Fourteen Points*, 1918). This principle was subsequently qualified and incorporated into the League Covenant as Article 23(e), a pledge to secure 'equitable treatment of commerce for all Members' (*Covenant of the League of Nations*, 1920).

It was significant that the League's economic mission was defined as promoting 'equitable treatment' rather than free trade. Many of the League's economic initiatives were concerned less with reducing trade restrictions and more with ensuring that those restrictions were applied evenly without discrimination. The fact that League trade policy was

---

[1] For a fuller analysis of trade law in the context of the 1919 Peace Settlement, see Clavin & Dungy (2020).

[2] Research by Matthias Schulz suggests that the Allies' treaty-based restrictions on German trade may have had a sizeable practical impact. Compared against the baseline of 1913, by 1925 a substantially lower share of German exports went to Allied markets, while a substantially higher share went to neutral countries that continued to grant Germany MFN rights after the war. However, this shift may have also reflected the general reorientation of the belligerents' supply chains towards neutral states for strategic reasons (Schulz, 1997, pp. 57–58).

formulated as a battle against discrimination made the lopsided aspects of the 1919 Peace Settlement stand out in starker relief. The phrase 'equitable treatment' continued to be invoked frequently in League trade debates and became a durable reminder of the unilateral character of the obligations imposed on the defeated states in the peace treaties, even after those obligations lapsed.[3] In 1919, Keynes argued that 'if they were reciprocal' the MFN obligations imposed on Germany and the other defeated states would have been fully consistent with the League Covenant (Keynes, 1919, p. 93). He proposed to achieve this equivalence through the formation of a general 'Free Trade Union', a multilateral pact to eliminate protective tariffs 'under the auspices of the League of Nations' (Keynes, 1919, pp. 248–250). This arrangement would not have been fully reciprocal because participation would have been mandatory for the defeated states but voluntary for the victors. Keynes hoped, however, that Britain would be a leading participant. That was a significant assumption to make at a time when Britain's future position in the world economy was uncertain.

A more modest MFN pact prepared by Britain's Board of Trade for the Paris Peace Conference highlights the constraints on British international leadership (Miller, 1928, pp. 16–22). Unlike Keynes, the Board of Trade did not include the defeated states in its plan, and it focused on preventing discrimination and not preventing tariff protection, as such. It also explicitly allowed for imperial preference, a policy that Keynes opposed in this period (Skidelsky, 1992, p. 485). Many Dominion governments had already begun to apply preferential tariff reductions on imports from the empire before 1914, and the UK government responded by introducing a margin of imperial preference into its own limited tariffs in 1919 (Drummond, 1972, pp. 51–70). This made colonial trade an active issue at the peace conference and a central point of conflict between the United States and Britain. It was one of the main reasons why the two governments abandoned efforts to achieve comprehensive trade cooperation at the conference. In 1919, US leaders drew up their own proposal for an agreement on equality of trade conditions that would have explicitly prohibited imperial preference, or at least made it subject to League oversight.

---

[3] From 1921 to 1927 the League's trade agenda was set in a standing Sub-Committee on the Equitable Treatment of Commerce. The minutes are in the Archives of the League of Nations, Geneva, R307-R308.

Neither side was willing to compromise on this point, and so they decided to include a vague placeholder trade clause in the League Covenant, Article 23 (e), transferring unresolved tensions over international and imperial economic order to Geneva (Mezes, 1918; Miller, 1928, pp. 16–22, 1918).

In the 1920s imperial preference remained a key point of contention in League trade debates, but it was discussed less in relation to US global ambitions and more in relation to European unity. In 1919, Keynes identified European solidarity as a top priority, affirming 'the intense need of the Continent for the most sustained and efficient production to repair the destructions of war, and to satisfy the insistence of labour for a larger reward' (Keynes, 1919, p. 92). He placed Britain on the sidelines of Europe, however, because it did not suffer from the same level of material destruction and geopolitical turmoil as the Continental states, and because it did not face the same danger of Bolshevik revolution (Keynes, 1919, p. 237; Skidelsky, 1992, p. 485). He nevertheless argued that Britain needed a prosperous and united Europe and should subordinate its own trade policy to multilateral rules that would restore order to the Continent. A commitment to imperial preference prevented Britain from doing this in 1919 and remained an important constraint on British engagement with Europe for the rest of the interwar period.

The next crucial moment of decision came in spring 1931, when some leaders in Britain's Foreign Office supported a pan-European alternative to a proposed Austro-German customs union. The most ambitious among them suggested that Britain lock Europeans into a multilateral programme of tariff reduction by agreeing to freeze its own low rates. The Cabinet rejected these plans, with advocates of imperial preference and universal free trade joining forces to oppose tariff cooperation on a limited regional scale (Anonymous, 1931; Boyce, 1987). At this juncture, Keynes responded to mounting unemployment and fiscal strain in Britain by demanding a national tariff, diverging from his earlier calls for League-backed free trade. Keynes's shift towards protection can be read against the backdrop of Britain's lacklustre economic performance after it re-joined the gold standard in 1925 at the pre-war parity of $4.86 – a decision that Keynes had stridently opposed. A strong pound led to a sustained pattern of low growth and high unemployment that worsened with the onset of the Great Depression. Starting in 1930, Keynes began to call for a tariff in order to create jobs and revive business confidence in Britain (Boyce, 1987, pp. 71–75; Eichengreen, 1984, pp. 364–366; Skidelsky, 1992, pp. 200–207, 369–372).

Historians disagree about how to interpret Keynes's embrace of trade protection in the early 1930s. Barry Eichengreen argues that Keynes advocated tariffs only reluctantly and contingently as a 'second-best solution' when monetary constraints left few other options (Eichengreen, 1984). Peter Clarke notes, however, that Keynes continued to contemplate a tariff response to the depression even after Britain gained more latitude in monetary policy with its departure from the gold standard in 1931 (Clarke, 2009, p. 71). Robert Skidelsky similarly observes that although 'national self-sufficiency' was not Keynes's uppermost policy commitment, it did stem from heartfelt economic patriotism and genuine theoretical scepticism about the continued relevance of comparative advantage in older industrial economies (Skidelsky, 1992, pp. 476–479). On the latter point Keynes observed that 'experience accumulates to prove that most modern processes of mass production can be performed in most countries and climates with almost equal efficiency' (Keynes, 1982, p. 238). He also challenged the political rationale for free trade, by questioning the nineteenth-century assumption that 'economic entanglement' would lead to peace. Keynes suggested that concentrating production and investment within national borders might better reduce the risk of war by minimizing economic threats to military security and social stability. He advised: 'let goods be homespun whenever it is reasonably and conveniently possible, and, above all, let finance be primarily national' (Keynes, 1982, p. 236).

Yet, Keynes also urged caution in tariff policy. He found little to praise in contemporary fascist and communist experiments or more conventional 'protectionism of the old-fashioned type', observing that 'in those countries where the advocates of national self-sufficiency have attained power, it appears to my judgment that, without exception, many foolish things are being done' (Keynes, 1982, pp. 243–244). He supported League-led efforts to reduce tariffs at the World Economic and Financial Conference in 1933 but suggested that trade was not a top priority for that gathering. Rather, the conference's main goal should be to construct a system of international financial and monetary cooperation that would allow governments to undertake expansionary national investment and tax policies to boost domestic production. Once those measures began to reverse global deflationary trends, concerted tariff reduction would become more feasible (Keynes, 1982, pp. 214–215, 267–269; Skidelsky, 1992, pp. 467–472).[4] Thus, it seems that Keynes neither wholeheartedly condemned nor endorsed tariff protection in response to the Great Depression; he was genuinely ambivalent (Clarke, 2009, p. 71). When presenting his case for 'national self-sufficiency', he reflected:

The decadent international but individualistic capitalism, in the hands of which we found ourselves after the war, is not a success. It is not intelligent, it is not beautiful, it is not just, it is not virtuous – and it doesn't deliver the goods. In short, we dislike it, and we are beginning to despise it. But when we wonder what to put in its place, we are extremely perplexed. (Keynes, 1982, p. 239)[5]

British policymakers in the Board of Trade spent the 1920s in a similar muddle, and this position fundamentally constrained their engagement with the League of Nations.

After 1918, the Board of Trade preserved a range of wartime duties and also introduced new measures to protect Britain's 'key industries' in the interest of national security. Alongside this targeted protection, Britain continued to promote a general policy of open markets through the League (Boyce, 1987, pp. 79–100; Varian, 2019). The tension between Britain's traditional commitment to free trade and the new post-war ethos of economic security was prominently on display in debates over the League's Convention on Prohibitions in the 1920s.[6] This was an attempt to roll back the quantitative restrictions that European governments had placed on foreign trade during and after the war as they sought to conserve raw materials and hard currency and to shelter strategic industries. Firms could usually apply to import and export prohibited goods within a quota, but the approval process for these licenses was often opaque and influenced by geopolitical considerations. Britain's Board of Trade enthusiastically supported a League

---

[4] On the fraught politics that impeded this kind of concerted engagement at the 1933 World Economic and Financial Conference, see Clavin, 1996.

[5] Keynes laid out the reasons for his indecision concerning protection and free trade more systematically in his article on 'Pros and Cons of Tariffs' (Keynes, XXI, pp. 204–208).

[6] For a fuller analysis of the significance of the Prohibitions Convention for British trade policy see Dungy (2023, pp. 134–136).

convention to eliminate prohibitions in order to reduce the scope for trade discrimination, while also demanding latitude to protect the country's own 'vital' national interests (League of Nations Economic Committee, 1925).

A British prohibition on synthetic dyes quickly emerged as a crucial sticking-point in negotiations. Britain had been heavily reliant on German dye imports before 1914, and this had impeded wartime production of textiles and TNT (the latter depended on chemical processes linked to dye-making). Consequently, the Board of Trade singled out dyes for special protection after the war. It 'safeguarded' other strategic industries using tariffs, but placed a firmer prohibition on trade in synthetic dyes (*History of the Ministry of Munitions*, 1922, Vol. 7, Part 5, pp. 5,58; Part 4, pp. 11–12; Högselius et al., 2015, p. 147; Jones, 2005, p. 204; President of the Board of Trade, 1920; War Cabinet, 1918). The Board of Trade insisted on preserving this one prohibition, while supporting the broader League plan to end such policies. The Germans responded by demanding to keep their own quantitative restrictions on coal, a key source of leverage in trade relations with France and Poland. British and German exemptions for highly politicized restrictions on dyes and coal opened the floodgates for special requests from other European governments (Boyce, 1987, pp. 126–127; Serruys, 1927). The Convention on Prohibitions went through prolonged negotiations from 1927 to 1929 but ultimately failed to attain sufficient ratifications to have any real effect (Clavin, 2013, pp. 102–103; League of Nations Economic, Financial and Transit Department, 1942).

The Prohibitions Convention highlighted the tension between British efforts to de-couple strategically valuable domestic industries from Germany while facilitating the country's reintegration into international markets, more generally. The broad British commitment to restoring German commercial influence in Europe can be seen in the relatively favourable responses to the Austro-German customs union proposed in 1931. Officials in the Board of Trade argued that this arrangement should be allowed to proceed on a bilateral basis, while their counterparts in the Foreign Office wanted to extend it to include Britain and the major Continental powers (Boyce, 1987, pp. 314–317). It is noteworthy that the alternatives on offer in 1931 were general pan-European cooperation with British support or narrow Austro-German union. Keynes had already sketched those alternatives in 1919. When discussing his proposed Free Trade Union in *The Economic Consequences of the Peace*, he wrote:

> It would be objected, I suppose, by some critics that such an arrangement might go some way in effect towards realizing the former German dream of Mittel-Europa. If other countries were so foolish as to remain outside the Union and to leave to Germany all its advantages, there might be some truth in this. (Keynes, 1919, p. 250)

Thus, it was partly to counterbalance German influence in Europe that Keynes urged British participation in his proposed Free Trade Union. At the same time, he suggested that some restoration of German economic power within Europe was desirable because the country had been the central engine of European prosperity before 1914. He argued that Germany's neighbours, especially to the East, depended on its market, but also on its capital and 'organization' (i.e., rules, expertise, company structures, physical infrastructure, and networks of supply and distribution) (Carabelli & Cedrini, 2010, pp. 1013–1014; Keynes, 1919, pp. 13–14, 275–276; Skidelsky, 1983, p. 391). Keynes's Free Trade Union was in part a bid to reverse the transition from empires to nation-states in Central and Eastern Europe. He commented that 'economic frontiers were tolerable so long as an immense territory was included in a few great Empires; but they will not be tolerable when the Empires of Germany, Austria-Hungary, Russia, and Turkey have been partitioned between some twenty independent authorities' (Keynes, 1919, p. 249). Keynes proposed to use the multilateral architecture of the League of Nations to restore the 'organization' previously provided by these empires by curtailing the regulatory authority of 'greedy, jealous, immature, and economically incomplete nationalist states' (Keynes, 1919, p. 249).[7] He did want to support the new states materially – he actually proposed to give them Britain's share of German reparations – but he also sought to place firm legal constraints on their economic development (Keynes, 1971, p. 418).

Keynes thus hit upon an important tension between the League's commitment to promote economic prosperity, enshrined in Article 23

---

[7] A recent study suggests that interwar commentators assigned undue weight post-war territorial changes as the source for commercial fragmentation in Central and Eastern Europe. Interwar trade flows in the region generally followed patterns of segregation that had already begun to emerge in the nineteenth century (Wolf et al., 2011).

(e) of the Covenant, and its ethnically derived conception national sovereignty. During the League era, territorial claims were asserted by demonstrating a population's cultural cohesion and its political commitment to a particular state. This happened at the Paris Peace Conference through ethnographic surveys and continued in the League through plebiscites (Payk & Pergher, 2019; Smith, 2018; Weitz, 2008). Keynes fundamentally rejected this approach to international order. In discussing planned plebiscites to determine the disposition of economically valuable territory, he wrote:

> The Wilsonian dogma, which exalts and dignifies the divisions of race and nationality above the bonds of trade and culture, and guarantees frontiers but not happiness, is deeply embedded in the conception of the League of Nations as at present constituted. It yields us to the paradox that the first experiment in international government should exert its influence in the direction of intensifying nationalism. (Keynes, 1922, p. 11)

The principle of Wilsonian 'national self-determination' was applied only selectively in 1919 (Manela, 2009). It nevertheless established a firm link between population and sovereignty that aligned awkwardly with the technical work of the League, which promoted integrated markets.[8] The League tried to bridge this gap through heavy international oversight of commercial policy in the young states of Central and Eastern Europe, in a vain attempt to keep 'nationalism' in the political sphere.

To a large extent, League trade policy in the 1920s focused on managing the young successor states' economic sovereignty and in particular their relations with former imperial overlords in Germany and Austria. Tellingly, an Austrian German nationalist named Richard Riedl emerged as one of the most influential advocates of European unity in League trade debates.[9] During the Paris Peace Conference,

---

[8] Susan Pedersen highlights the complex functions that the League of Nations fulfilled as a framework for managing different forms of attenuated sovereignty resulting from the gradual end of empire and as a system for technical cooperation buttressing world markets (Pedersen, 2015). I analyse the tension between these functions in League trade policy in Dungy (2021b). Jamie Martin shows how the League's financial interventions posed a novel challenge to sovereignty in post-imperial Central and Eastern Europe in Martin (2022).

[9] Quinn Slobodian also emphasizes Riedl's influence as an advocate of multilateralism in the 1920s but does not assess how German nationalism shaped his international engagement (Slobodian, 2018, p. 37, 40, 42). I examine this linkage in more detail in Dungy (2021a, 2023). See also Brettner-Messler (1998).

Riedl had travelled to Berlin to help negotiate an abortive union between the new Austrian and German republics (Brettner-Messler, 1998, pp. 297–298). He remained committed to *Anschluss* as a long-term goal even after the peace treaties barred this path, but he later sought to embed Austro-German integration in the framework of the League of Nations. Like Keynes, Riedl fundamentally rejected the economic transition from empires to nation-states in Central and Eastern Europe. On the topic of 'national self-determination', he wrote:

> with this idealistic phrase, he [Wilson] hides the eminently materialistic aspiration to place more than a third of the inhabited world in a condition of permanent economic atomization, perhaps in such an advanced condition fragmentation, confusion, and conflict that it will be possible for the more organized political and economic bodies of the world to dominate here without using the force of arms. (Riedl, 2020)

Riedl proposed to reverse this process of economic disintegration through a sequence of multilateral treaties regulating a wide range of issues, from tariffs to port duties to consular appointments (Riedl, 1926).[10] Germany and Austria would pursue deeper bilateral integration along the same lines, gradually forming a small nucleus within a wider multilateral structure. Riedl's commitment to *Anschluss* was not unusual in the Austrian economic and political elite in the 1920s; what distinguished him was his determination to use the League to pursue this goal.[11] Indeed, Riedl became an enthusiastic and influential advocate of trade liberalization in both the League and the International Chamber of Commerce, a testament to pro-Austrian sympathies in both bodies.[12]

---

[10] This report for the International Chamber of Commerce is a sanitized version of a long-term 'Action Plan' for Austro-German union that Riedl prepared for his colleagues in the Vienna Chamber of Commerce (Riedl, 1926, April).

[11] Support for *Anschluss* in interwar Austrian business circles was broad but far from unanimous. On the relevant debates, see Fischer (1977); Nautz (1991); Suppan (1994).

[12] The League's main trade official, Pietro Stoppani, developed a close relationship with Riedl, whose dry technical style he preferred over the flamboyance of the more famous Pan-European based in Vienna, Richard Coudenhove-Kalergi. Stoppani and Riedl's relationship is documented in several hundred pages of letters and working papers in the League of Nations Archive in Geneva in R2727 10C/2968/578, R2728, 10 C /7560/578, R2729, 10C/20810/578, R 2732, 10 C/1149/1149, R2868, 10D/15378/14711.

Riedl was able to spread his ideas in Geneva partly because he worked in tandem with a French counterpart, Lucien Coquet, who was pushing a very similar plan for European economic unity but with quite different motives. Riedl was a fairly straightforward German nationalist. As a prominent figure in the Viennese fraternity scene, he believed in German economic and cultural superiority. In his view, Europe needed a regional hierarchy with Germans at the top in order to survive over the long-term (Brettner-Messler, 1998, p. 217). In contrast, Coquet had a complex attitude towards Germany. He had been an enthusiastic proponent of Franco-German rapprochement before 1914. During the war, he inverted his position and became a leading advocate for Rhineland separatism and then went on to support the 1923 Ruhr occupation. When Germany regained its commercial sovereignty in 1925, Coquet shifted his footing again and began to call for European unity (Badel, 1998; Poidevin, 1969, p. 455). His goal was to prevent Germany from dominating its neighbours by channelling its economic dynamism through multilateral structures. Riedl and Coquet both proposed a system of progressive percentage-based tariff reductions set within a framework of regulatory standardization. Keynes's own 1919 plan for a Free Trade Union had included a somewhat similar provision for gradual tariff reduction as a path towards the full elimination of protection (Keynes, 1919; Service Français de la Société des Nations, 1929; Union Douanière Européenne, 1928). Whether such an arrangement produced Riedl's vision – German domination of Europe – or Coquet's vision – collective European control of the German economy – depended partly on which other large commercial powers were in the mix. In 1919, Keynes called upon Britain to hold the balance in his Free Trade Union. Significantly, Coquet worked hard to secure British participation in a European customs union, whereas Riedl was more inclined to see the British Empire as a separate multilateral system (Dunford House (Cobden Memorial) Association, 1930; Riedl, 1926).

In 1919, Keynes's call for British leadership also highlighted a central dilemma concerning the mechanics of multilateralism: Should international cooperation aim for wide application or deep integration? This question remained at the heart of the League's economic work through the 1930s, but it had greater relevance for trade policy – which was based on a universal commitment to 'equitable treatment' – than for financial cooperation – which proceeded through a series of targeted interventions in specific countries. In 1919, Keynes identified the League's unanimity requirement as 'a disastrous blot on the covenant'. He predicted that this rule would transform the Assembly into 'an unwieldy polyglot debating society in which the greatest resolution and the best management may fail altogether to bring issues to a head against an opposition in favour of the status quo' (Keynes, 1919, p. 243). When Keynes revived his proposal for institutionalized free trade in the context of the Genoa Conference of 1922, he argued that such arrangements need not be universal: 'let those who like them come in, and those who don't, stay out' (Keynes, 1977, p. 371). Over time, the League's Economic and Financial Organization gradually moved towards this selective approach, shifting away from its initial commitment to unanimity.

After struggling in the 1920s to negotiate multilateral treaties that were both universal and binding, League collaborators began to advocate more flexible forms of economic cooperation which could be applied gradually and selectively by a small vanguard of leading states (Clavin, 2013, p. 141). For example, in the 1920s, the League's Fiscal Committee produced a series of model texts on double taxation to be implemented through bilateral treaties and national legislation. These models formed the basis for dozens of bilateral tax treaties, creating an initial framework for international tax law (Jogarajan, 2018). In 1938 Alexander Loveday, a long-serving economic official in the League Secretariat, cited this example when he observed:

> We are in fact gradually moving from a system of general conventions to the system of applying to each problem the procedure which seems most likely to result in business being done – in business being done, not universally, not even between or as regards all Member States, but between those States where there is a desire to do business. (Loveday, 1938, p. 789)

One crucial advantage offered by a more flexible negotiating procedure was to facilitate the association of non-member states with the economic work of the League, most notably the United States.

In *The Economic Consequences of the Peace*, Keynes defined Europe's relationship to the United States primarily in terms of financial dependence while also highlighting related tensions in trade policy. The financial shift in gravity from Europe to the United States as a result of the First World War meant that Europe had become more reliant on export revenues. Keynes noted that France had paid most of its indemnity from the Franco-Prussian War by diverting foreign investments. Because Europeans sold off a large share of their securities in order to pay for the First World War, this was no longer an option in the 1920s. The only sustainable way to fund the cycle of reparations and war debts was through exports, and in particular through German exports. Yet Keynes concluded that the sums were simply too large to be paid in this way. Even if the United States could be persuaded to accept a significant increase in transatlantic imports, ramping up German export production on the scale required would entail a severe disruption of economic and social life there, which he thought could lead to civilizational collapse and revolution (Keynes, 1919, pp. 211–234, 1971, pp. 315–317, 325–326, 376–380).

Moreover, Keynes argued that even if Germany proved able to fund a large reparations bill through exports without deep social and economic dislocation at home, it would severely undercut British industry in international markets. Although Keynes saw healthy German trade as an essential component of European economic stabilization, he did not want to give German exports added stimulus through reparations policy. He concluded that this would be a losing bargain for Britain, which competed directly with German industry in many third markets. In the 1920s, Keynes continued to argue that a high reparations bill was fundamentally incompatible with the British government's ongoing efforts to bolster the country's flagging manufacturing sector. In an assessment of the 1929 Young Plan, which fixed the final payment schedule for German reparations, Keynes observed: 'it is a question of how far we want to force down German wages in order that she may steal our export industries from us, and how much pressure we are prepared to put upon her in order to achieve that result' (Keynes's response to Brand, 1929, p. 219). He considered all elements of this formula to be highly problematic from both a political and an economic standpoint.

In 1919, Keynes had advocated directly breaking the cycle of war debts and reparations through financial cooperation. He predicted that if the United States would not agree to an international programme of debt-forgiveness, it would either have to loan Europeans the money to pay their debts or allow them to earn that money by buying more of their exports. The US government opted for the former course, raising tariffs and funnelling extensive private loans into Europe in the 1920s. In 1929, Keynes concluded that Germany had not yet been asked to fund reparations on a sustainable basis through export revenues: 'it is only when this process of borrowing comes to an end that we shall begin to gather experience of what figure Germany can safely be asked to pay' (Keynes's response to Brand, 1929, p. 216). In 1928, the US government did begin to dial down foreign lending, as it also prepared for a further tariff hike. This double-squeeze on the European economy – the loss of foreign lending and reduced access to the US market – gave a boost to regionalist projects like those of Coquet and Riedl at the end of the 1920s (Salter, 1929). It also compelled Germany to adopt a draconian programme of fiscal austerity. Demands for belt-tightening came just as the Young Plan fixed reparations payments at rates that German public deemed shamefully high. This combination stoked hostility to the Weimar Republic, energizing the National Socialists and pushing the ruling conservatives towards a more aggressive commercial policy in Central and Eastern Europe as a sop to nationalists (Rödder, 1996, pp. 199–201; Tooze, 2006, pp. 13–19). This was the context for the Austro-German customs union plan in 1931.

One could argue that in the 1920s, international economic cooperation had some of the basic structural features that Keynes outlined in 1919 but in a highly distorted form. The United States did participate in various multilateral financial schemes, but this activity proceeded through private channels and added new debts to old. Britain used the League of Nations to promote trade liberalization in Europe but did so through a series of narrowly circumscribed treaty projects rather than a comprehensive free-trade pact. Any provisional stability provided by these arrangements collapsed with the onset of the Great Depression. US foreign lending dried up. Britain moved towards imperial preference and started to disengage from Europe. Germans and Austrians grew more assertive in their regional ambitions. These different crisis trajectories began to converge in 1931, with disastrous economic and political effects.

This can be interpreted as a narrative of failure, as it usually is when discussing the League of Nations. Looking back from the standpoint of a rather troubled present, it arguably makes more sense to say simply that the 1919 Peace Settlement framed a new set of institutional and geopolitical problems. While it is true that the League of Nations and broader interwar international politics did not solve those problems, many of them have not yet been solved today. Keynes, and the world, did embrace a more comprehensive multilateralism after

1945. In Keynes's plan for an International Clearing Union, and in the subsequent institutional settlement that he helped craft, there was a much deeper integration between trade and finance than there had been in 1919. The United States also agreed to play a leading role in both spheres, for a time. Yet, the conflict over international constraints on national commercial sovereignty, the problem of German regional power, the question of Britain's commitment to Europe, and the vulnerabilities associated with transatlantic economic and political dependence all remained central issues in international politics well after 1945. The Paris Peace Settlement and the League of Nations that sprang from it helped define those issues in intellectual and institutional terms, and Keynes's *Economic Consequences of the Peace* was an important contribution to that process.

References

Anonymous. (1931, April 18). [Memorandum, 'Proposals for a possible solution of the present conflict concerning the Austro-German Union']. *The National Archives of the United Kingdom (T188/19)*, Kew, United Kingdom.

Badel, L. (1998). "Les promoteurs français d'une union économique et douanière de l'Europe dans l'entre-deux-guerres." In A. Fleury & L. Jílek eds., *The Briand Plan of European federal union: National and transnational perspectives, with documents* (pp. 17–30). Peter Lang.

Boyce, R. (1987). *British capitalism at the crossroads, 1919–1932: A study in politics, economics, and international relations.* Cambridge University Press.

Boyce, R. (2009). *The great interwar crisis and the collapse of globalization.* Palgrave Macmillan.

Brand, R. H. (1929). The reparation problem. *International Affairs, 8*(3), 203–226.

Brettner-Messler, G. H. (1998). *Richard Riedl – ein liberaler Imperialist: Biographische Studie zu Handelspolitik und 'Mitteleuropa'-Gedanken in Monarchie und Erster Republik [PhD].* University of Vienna.

Carabelli, A. M., & Cedrini, M. A. (2010). Keynes and the complexity of international economic relations in the aftermath of World War I. *Journal of Economic Issues, 44*(4), 1009–1028.

Clarke, P. (2009). *Keynes: The rise, fall, and return of the twentieth century's most influential economist (1st U.S. ed).* Bloomsbury Press.

Clavin, P. (1996). *The failure of economic diplomacy: Britain, Germany, France and the United States, 1931–36.* Macmillan Press.

Clavin, P. (2013). *Securing the world economy: The reinvention of the League of Nations, 1920–1946.* Oxford University Press.

Clavin, P., & Dungy, M. (2020). Trade, law, and the global order of 1919, *Diplomatic History, 44 (4)*, 554–579.

Decorzant, Y. (2011). *La Société des Nations et la naissance d'une conception de la régulation économique internationale*. Peter Lang.

Drummond, I. M. (1972). *British economic policy and the empire, 1919–1939*. Allen and Unwin.

Dunford House (Cobden Memorial) Association. (1930, 12 February). [Letter]. *Archives du Ministère des Affaires Étrangères de France* (SDN/2495), La Courneuve, France.

Dungy, M. L. (2021a). International commerce in the wake of empire: Central European economic integration between national and imperial sovereignty. In P. Becker & N. Wheatley eds., *Remaking Central Europe: The League of Nations and the former Habsburg lands* (pp. 213–240). Oxford University Press.

Dungy, M. L. (2021b). Writing multilateral trade rules in the League of Nations. *Contemporary European History*, *30*(1), 60–75.

Dungy, M. L. (2023). *Order and rivalry: Rewriting the rules of international trade after the First World War*. Cambridge University Press.

Eichengreen, B. (1984). Keynes and protection. *The Journal of Economic History*, *44*(2), 363–373.

Fischer, P. (1977). Die österreichischen Handelskammern und der Anschluß an Deutschland. Zur Strategie der 'Politik der kleinen Mittel' 1925 bis 1934. In Wissenschaftliche Kommission des Theodor-Körner-Stiftungsfonds und des Leopold-Kunschak-Preises, eds., *Das Juliabkommen von 1936: Vorgeschichte, Hintergründe und Folgen* (pp. 299–314). Oldenbourg.

History of the Ministry of Munitions (Vol. 7). (1922). HMG Stationery Office.

Högselius, P., Kaijser, A., & Vleuten, E. van der. (2015). *Europe's infrastructure transition: Economy, war, nature*. Palgrave Macmillan.

Jogarajan, S. (2018). *Double taxation and the League of Nations*. Cambridge University Press.

Jones, G. (2005). *Multinationals and global capitalism: From the nineteenth to the twenty-first century*. Oxford University Press.

Keynes, J. M. (1919). *The economic consequences of the peace*. Macmillan and Co.

Keynes, J. M. (1922). *A revision of the treaty: Being a sequel to the economic consequences of the peace*. Macmillan and Co.

Keynes, J. M. (1971). *The collected writings of John Maynard Keynes: Vol. XVI*, E. Johnson, ed., Macmillan Press for the Royal Economic Society.

Keynes, J. M. (1977). *The collected writings of John Maynard Keynes: Vol. XVII*, E. Johnson, ed. Macmillan Press for the Royal Economic Society.

Keynes, J. M. (1980). *The collected writings of John Maynard Keynes: Vol. XXV*, D. Moggridge, ed. Macmillan Press for the Royal Economic Society.

Keynes, J. M. (1982). *The collected writings of John Maynard Keynes: Vol. XXI*, D. Moggridge ed. Macmillan Press for the Royal Economic Society.

League of Nations Economic Committee. (1925, March 1–5). [Minutes: Sub-Committee on the Equitable Treatment of Commerce: 13th Session]. *League of Nations Archive* (R/308, 10/50616/6105), Geneva, Switzerland.

League of Nations Economic, Financial and Transit Department. (1942). *Commercial policy in the interwar period: International proposals and national policies.* League of Nations.

Loveday, A. (1938). The economic and financial activities of the league. *International Affairs, 17*(6), 788–808.

Manela, E. (2009). *The Wilsonian moment: Self-determination and the international origins of anticolonial nationalism.* Oxford University Press.

Martin, Jamie. (2022). *The meddlers: Sovereignty, empire, and the birth of global economic governance.* Harvard University Press.

Mezes, S. (1918, January 19). [Letter to David Hunter Miller, 'Dr. Young's memorandum. "Possible international action with respect to tariffs"']. *United States National Archives, RG 256: American Commission to Negotiate Peace, Economic Division* (Box 112, Folder 321), College Park, Maryland, United States.

Miller, D. H. (1928). *The drafting of the Covenant* (Vol. 2). G.P. Putnam's Sons.

Miller, D. H. "Letter to E. M. House." (December 1, 1918), In *Foreign relations of the United States, 1919, vol. 1, The Paris Peace Conference,* Joseph V. Fuller ed., (Doc. 387). Government Printing Office, 1942.

Nautz, J. (1991). Tarifvertragsrecht und 'Anschluß.' Das Projekt einer gemeinsamen Tarifrechtsreform in Deutschland und Österreich 1919–1931. *Archiv Für Sozialgeschichte, 31*, 123–135.

Payk, M. M., & Pergher, R. eds. (2019). *Beyond Versailles: Sovereignty, legitimacy, and the formation of new polities after the Great War.* Indiana University Press.

Pedersen, S. (2015). *The guardians: The League of Nations and the crisis of empire.* Oxford University Press.

Poidevin, R. (1969). *Les relations économiques et financières entre la France et l'Allemagne de 1898 à 1914.* Armand Colin.

President of the Board of Trade. (1920, November 29). [Memorandum, 'Position of the dye-making industry']. *The National Archives of the United Kingdom* (CAB 24/115/92), Kew, United Kingdom.

President of the Board of Trade. (1928, 10 October). [Memorandum, 'Convention for the Abolition of Import and Export Prohibitions and Restrictions']. *The National Archives of the United Kingdom* (CAB 24/297/45), Kew, United Kingdom.

President Woodrow Wilson's Fourteen Points. (1918). *Avalon Project at Yale Law School*. Lillian Goldman Law Library. https://avalon.law.yale.edu/20th_century/wilson14.asp

Riedl, R. (1920). Die Wirtschaftspolitik der Entente und Wilsons vor dem Frieden. *Deutsche Review, 45*(1), 97–117.

Riedl, R. (1926). *Collective treaties facilitating international commerce in Europe: Report of the Austrian national committee to the committee on trade barriers.* Vernay.

Riedl, R. (1926, April) [Memorandum, 'Aktionsprogramm vom April 1926']. *Österreichisches Staatsarchiv, Allgemeines Verwaltungsarchiv* (Nachlass Richard Riedl/80), Vienna, Austria.

Rödder, A. (1996). *Stresemanns Erbe: Julius Curtius und die deutsche Aussenpolitik, 1929–1931.* Ferdinand Schöningh.

Salter, A. (1929, September 2). [Memorandum, 'The "United States of Europe" idea']. *League of Nations Archive* (R2868 10D/14711/14711), Geneva, Switzerland.

Schulz, M. (1997). *Deutschland, der Völkerbund und die Frage der europäischen Wirtschaftsordnung, 1925–1933.* Krämer.

Serruys, D. (1927, October 29). [Letter to Commerce, Travaux Publics and Relations Commerciales], *Archives du Ministère des Affaires Étrangères de France* (Y/629), La Courneuve, France.

Service Français de la Société des Nations. (1929, December 2). [Note, 'Entente douanière européenne. Visite de M. Riedl']. *Archives du Ministère des Affaires Étrangères de France* (SDN/2495), La Courneuve, France.

Skidelsky, R. (1983). *John Maynard Keynes: Hopes betrayed, 1883–1920.* Macmillan.

Skidelsky, R. (1990). *John Maynard Keynes: Fighting for Britain, 1937–1946.* Macmillan.

Skidelsky, R. (1992). *John Maynard Keynes: The economist as saviour, 1920–1937.* Macmillan.

Slobodian, Q. (2018). *Globalists: The end of empire and the birth of neoliberalism.* Harvard University Press.

Smith, L. V. (2018). *Sovereignty at the Paris Peace Conference of 1919.* Oxford University Press.

Suppan, A. (1994). "Mitteleuropa Konzeptionen zwischen Restauration und Anschluss." In R. G. Plaschka, H. Haselsteiner, A. Suppan, A. M. Drabek, & Zaar, Birgitta eds., *Mitteleuropa-Konzeptionen in der ersten Hälfte des 20. Jahrhunderts* (pp. 171–197). Verl. der Österr. Akad. der Wiss.

The Covenant of the League of Nations. (1920). *Avalon Project at Yale Law School*. Lillian Goldman Law Library. http://avalon.law.yale.edu/20th_century/leagcov.asp

Tooze, A. (2006). *The wages of destruction: The making and breaking of the Nazi economy*. Allen Lane.

Tooze, A. (2014). *The deluge: The Great War and the remaking of the global order, 1916–1931*. Allen Lane.

Tooze, A., & Fertik, T. (2014). The world economy and the Great War. *Geschichte und Gesellschaft, 40*(2), 214–238.

Union douanière européenne. (1928). *[Report, 'Comité français d'études. Rapports des Commissions']. Archives Nationales de France* (F 12/9416), Pierrefitte sur Seine, France.

Varian, B. D. (2019). The growth of manufacturing protection in 1920s Britain. *Scottish Journal of Political Economy, 66*(5), 703–711.

War Cabinet. (1918, January 8). [Memorandum, 'Scheme for the development of the British dye industry']. *The National Archives of the United Kingdom* (CAB 24/4/38), Kew, United Kingdom.

Weitz, E. D. (2008). From the Vienna to the Paris system: International politics and the entangled histories of human rights, forced deportations, and civilizing missions. *The American Historical Review, 113*(5), 1313–1343.

Wolf, N., Schulze, M.-S., & Heinemeyer, H.-C. (2011). On the economic consequences of the peace: Trade and borders after Versailles. *The Journal of Economic History, 71*(4), 915–949.

12 | Gold, International Monetary Cooperation, and the Tripartite Agreement of 1936

MAX HARRIS*

The economic war of the 1930s played out on many fronts. There was the battle over trade barriers. There was the struggle surrounding debts, reparations, and defaults. And there was the conflict over monetary policy.[1] Each was vicious on its own; combined, they tore the world economy apart. The centrifugal forces were too strong, the centripetal ones nearly non-existent. Some thought that the World Economic Conference in the summer of 1933 offered the chance for a grand bargain, but its unceremonious collapse "dispelled whatever hopes were still nurtured about multilateral coordination in general and on monetary matters in particular" (Toniolo 2005, 136).

Indeed, while all of the conflicts were destructive, the monetary war was especially so. It was not merely an issue of the value of one currency in terms of another: it involved questions about the very foundation of the monetary system. Should currencies remain on the gold standard? If not, should they remain fixed with one another? What role should gold play? Through the first half of the decade, France believed morality and economic theory dictated staying on gold in its most orthodox form; Britain, after suspending gold convertibility in 1931, felt the gold standard impinged too much on domestic policy and favoured a managed currency; and the United States thought a middle way, exemplified by its devaluation of the dollar and installation of a heavily modified gold standard in 1934, was best.[2] These

---

* I thank Amaan Mitha and Mike Wong for comments on this draft. All errors are my own.
[1] Key works on this period include Eichengreen (1992), Clavin (1996), and Kindleberger (2013).
[2] See Mouré (2002) for an overview of French monetary policy, Howson (1980) and Sayers (1976) for British, and Edwards (2018) and Meltzer (2003) for American.

three countries argued bitterly over the optimal setup of the international monetary system (IMS). At times, the ill-will was such that they simply stopped discussing the matter with one another at all. Anglo-American monetary relations were so strained that, as late as May 1936, US Secretary of the Treasury Henry Morgenthau, Jr., scolded the British financial attaché, "If we were at war with each other we could not be acting any differently."[3]

Given this state of affairs, the world was stunned when, shortly after midnight Paris time on September 26, 1936, Britain, France, and the United States announced the Tripartite Agreement (TA).[4] In this agreement – issued concurrently with France's long-needed devaluation – the countries renounced competitive exchange depreciations, declared the importance of a well-functioning IMS, and endorsed liberalizing the world economy. They did not peg their exchange rates, but they expressed their intent to work toward more stable ones. Belgium, the Netherlands, and Switzerland joined the "currency club" in November.[5]

The TA was a turning point, ushering in a new era of monetary cooperation. The parties recognized that the IMS was not zero-sum. To be sure, the agreement was not universal (notably, Germany, Italy, Japan, and Russia were not parties to it), and it did not formally bind any country to anything.[6] It by no means reversed all of the damage that had been done in previous years. Nevertheless, in a decade of rising nationalism, it represented a remarkable effort among the Western democracies to restore some order to the world economy and unite amid the growing fascist threat.

The TA served as the backdrop to just about every issue of international monetary policy during the twilight years before the Second World War. But as the agreement was concerned principally with exchange stability, its greatest influence was on exchange intervention. Officials considered intervention crucial to prevent excessive swings in exchange rates since rates were no longer pinned down by

---

[3] Morgenthau conversation with Bewley, May 18, 1936, MD 24 (193).

[4] The United States released its statement during the evening of September 25 Washington time, so that both days have been used in dating the TA.

[5] Belgium announced its support for the TA's principles on September 26, but it was not considered part of the club until November. "Text of Belgian Note to Hull," *New York Times*, September 27, 1936.

[6] There were some minor discussions in 1937 about including Japan and Russia, but they were not serious and did not progress.

gold parities. But because currencies were no longer tied to gold, policymakers did not want to hold foreign exchange on their balance sheets for fear of valuation losses: they insisted on holding gold.[7] The TA members therefore created a system of reciprocal gold facilities, whereby they exchanged their currency for gold with one another on a daily basis. For example, when country A purchased country B's currency in the market, country B would give gold in exchange for its currency. This gold-clearing mechanism stitched the TA members' disparate monetary systems together, providing a coherent basis for the IMS.

The TA in general, and the gold facilities in particular, have received little attention in the literature. Many studies on interwar monetary policy end in 1936 with the disintegration of the gold bloc. Drummond (1981, 223) argues that the agreement brought "a shadow of international monetary cooperation but not its substance," and claims that "little need be said about central bank cooperation, important though this may have been in giving the general public a new impression of orderliness."[8] Others have found merit in the TA's principles of multilateral cooperation but have not delved into its execution.[9] As a result, our understanding of how the IMS actually operated during these years is far from complete.

Examining the mechanics underlying exchange intervention helps fill this gap, offering new insight into the evolution of the IMS and the history of monetary cooperation. I argue that gold clearing provided a means for monetary authorities to cooperate with one another and allowed them to put to the side larger and more contested issues for the time being; it was a modus vivendi that served the parties well during those tumultuous years. Empirical evidence suggests that transactions between TA central banks increased dramatically, so that collaboration grew increasingly routine. Moreover, these technical arrangements established a foundation for cooperation more generally that helped policymakers avoid relapsing into the antagonisms of earlier

---

[7] This refusal to hold foreign exchange was not universal and applied only to countries in charge of key currencies in the system. Smaller countries often held these key currencies as reserves; for example, members of the sterling area – comprising the Empire, much of the Commonwealth, and some of Britain's biggest trading partners – tied their exchange rates to sterling and maintained balances in London as reserves.

[8] See also Drummond (1979).   [9] For instance, Dam (1982).

years. Though the IMS no longer revolves around gold, the experience under the Tripartite system underscores the importance of continued technical cooperation today.

This paper proceeds in four sections. Section I provides background on monetary developments, from Britain's suspension of convertibility in 1931 to the negotiation of the TA in 1936. Section II details the creation and operation of the reciprocal gold facilities. Section III discusses the facilities' role in building trust and aiding cooperation. Section IV concludes.

Section I From War to Peace

Britain's suspension of gold convertibility in September 1931 marked the "end of an epoch," in the words of *The Economist*.[10] Gold convertibility – the right to present domestic currency at the central bank and receive gold in exchange at a fixed price – was the core of the gold standard and the mechanism by which arbitrageurs kept exchange rates in narrow bands. By suspending it, Britain freed the pound from the metal, and within a couple of months, the pound fell 30% against gold currencies. Though the government insisted that returning to a modified gold standard was its North Star, it in fact had little intention of doing so. Rather, sterling's value would be determined by a combination of market forces and the actions of Britain's Exchange Equalisation Account (EEA), a massive fund created in 1932.[11] The EEA had the seemingly innocuous statutory mandate of "checking undue fluctuations in the exchange value of sterling," but to the rest of the world, the fund, which operated in secrecy, appeared to be a weapon to weaken the pound.[12] Adding to the anger, the central banks of France, Belgium, and the Netherlands had held substantial amounts of sterling that plunged in value with Britain's suspension. All three central banks required government support to handle the loss after Britain refused to compensate them, and thereafter the monetary authorities concluded that Britain could not be trusted and that gold was the only safe reserve asset.[13] Figure 12.1 depicts the precipitous

---

[10] "The End of an Epoch," *The Economist*, September 26, 1931.
[11] See Howson (1980) and Harris (2021) for histories of the EEA.
[12] Finance Act, 1932, 22 & 23 Geo. 5, c. 25.
[13] Mouré (1991, 70–73) and Straumann (2010, 100–103).

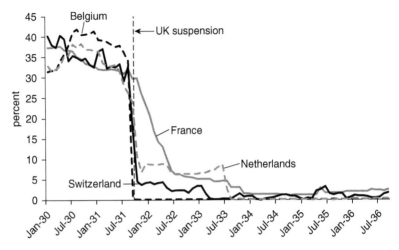

Figure 12.1 Gold bloc foreign exchange holdings, 1930–36 (per cent of total reserves)
Source: Board of Governors of the Federal Reserve System (various issues).

decline in foreign exchange holdings after Britain's suspension for the central banks of France, Belgium, the Netherlands, and Switzerland.

Hostility intensified in 1933 when Franklin Roosevelt became US president and liberated the dollar from the gold standard.[14] He infamously condemned efforts at exchange stabilization during the World Economic Conference and then engaged in a controversial programme of gold purchases to force the dollar price of gold up; central bankers and finance officials in Europe looked on with a mixture of outrage, fear, puzzlement, and Old World condescension. At the beginning of 1934, Roosevelt decided to put US monetary policy on a firmer basis. Using the powers granted him by the just-passed Gold Reserve Act, he officially devalued the dollar, raising the price of gold from $20.67 to $35 per ounce. The United States would buy gold at this price from anybody, but it would sell gold only to central banks that remained on the gold standard, so that the Bank of England (BoE) was not eligible to turn dollars into gold. Moreover, Roosevelt retained the power to alter the official price of gold at any time to a level between $34.45

---

[14] See Harris (2021, ch. 4) for a summary of the regulations surrounding the dollar.

and \$41.34. The legislation also established the Exchange Stabilization Fund (ESF) as a direct counter to the EEA. Moving forward, the dollar was more stable than it had been in 1933, though, as the administration constantly warned, it remained on a "24-hour basis."[15]

While the British and US depreciations enraged the countries of the gold bloc (Belgium, France, Italy, the Netherlands, Poland, and Switzerland), relations were actually worst between Britain and America. Both countries understood the motives of the gold bloc – remain on gold at the current parity – and could eventually work with its members to some extent, but the mutual incomprehension about each other's policies and the apparent competition between the two currencies was corrosive. They both had large exchange funds about which they provided no information. It did not help that Britain's exchange fund had held over \$190 million in dollar assets when Roosevelt began depreciating the dollar, causing a substantial loss and teaching the British what holders of sterling had already learned: only gold seemed safe.[16] From 1934 to the spring of 1936, there was little communication between the two Treasuries, let alone cooperation, and the central banks mostly exchanged pleasantries. One BoE official recalled decades later that during these years, "there was a complete break in relations on the technical level with the Americans."[17] The British found Roosevelt untrustworthy, while the Americans were insecure, fretting that the British were always a step ahead. Though neither side was actively depreciating its currency as in 1931–34 – the dollar-sterling rate had essentially returned to its pre-1931 par as shown in Figure 12.2 – both remained armed and on alert.

As British and American policymakers stared each other down, the gold bloc countries struggled to maintain their parities. Belgium devalued in 1935, and the combination of economic distress, social

---

[15] For example, on May 5, 1936, Roosevelt, in response to a question of whether the administration was "taking any steps to fore-arm itself against possible monetary action in Europe," replied, "Yes, on a 24-hour basis. We re-arm ourselves every morning." Press conference, May 5, 1936, RPC 292.

[16] "A review of the Exchange Equalisation Account," April 11, 1934, BoE C43/23.

[17] Sayers interview with Bolton, January 20, 1971, BoE ADM33/25. In fact, technical cooperation restarted in the autumn of 1935 when the United States authorized the BoE to purchase gold on its behalf to be held in London in an effort to reduce shipments across the Atlantic, but Bolton's sentiment is surely correct. Bordo et al. (2015, 77–80).

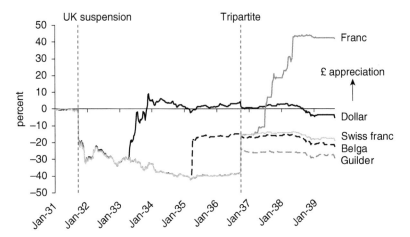

Figure 12.2 Sterling exchange rate, 1931–39 (per cent deviation from pre-1931 parity)
Source: *Financial Times.*

disruption, and political uncertainty in France made pressure on the franc unbearable by the summer of 1936.[18] The French, however, were loath to devalue. Morally, many in the country considered it dishonourable; economically, they worried that Britain and America would retaliate and render the action useless.[19] The French government insisted on reaching an agreement with the two countries to frame the move as an international realignment of currencies, rather than a franc devaluation, and to secure their promise not to counterattack. For their part, Britain and America were less concerned about the direct effects of a French devaluation, which they thought had been necessary for some time, than how each other would respond. They were content with their recoveries and did not want to return to the chaos of previous years but would react if necessary. As a US Treasury memorandum in May 1936 argued, if the British responded to a French move by letting sterling decline "below the level we feel is reasonable, the situation, so far as we are concerned, represents a

---

[18] The Bank of France's reserves fell from 83 billion francs in October 1934 to 58 billion in May 1936 and 51 billion in September 1936. Federal Reserve Bulletin (various issues).

[19] See Jackson (1985, ch. 8) and Mouré (1991, chs. 6–7).

state of monetary 'war'."[20] Spurred by the dangers of such a conflict, as well as the precarious situation in France and ever-more concerning international developments, Morgenthau pushed for an understanding with the British. The Anglo-Americans agreed between themselves not to retaliate to a franc devaluation and then worked with the French to craft an accord.[21]

The resulting TA – three nearly identical, five-paragraph statements released on September 26 – set forth principles for a more stable IMS.[22] Britain and America "welcomed" France's decision to devalue. The countries did not agree on any specific exchange rates, but they promised to use their exchange funds in pursuit of the "greatest possible equilibrium in the system of international exchange" and to "arrange for such consultation ... as may prove necessary." They would "of course ... take into full account the requirements of internal prosperity," so that depreciation was not forbidden. But seeking "unreasonable competitive exchange advantage" was verboten. And they emphasized the importance of "relax[ing] progressively the present system of quotas and exchange controls." The hope was that working together in this way would help "safeguard peace," "promote prosperity in the world," and "improve the standard of living," language that was no doubt extravagant but underscored the perceived interconnection between exchange rates, politics, and international relations. As for the franc's devaluation, the French announced separately that they would hold the currency's value between 43 and 49 milligrams of gold, corresponding to a mean devaluation of 30% from the old parity of 65.5 milligrams, but would not repeg right away.[23]

The press hailed the TA. The *New York Times* praised the "three great democracies" for giving "evidence of their ability to work together in behalf of economic peace, recovery and order."[24] Observers understood that the TA did not bind the countries, but after years of failed conferences and going-it-alonism, this unexpected declaration offered

[20] Haas, "French Devaluation," May 8, 1936, HDWP B49F7.
[21] Clarke (1977) is the seminal work on the negotiations leading up to the TA.
[22] Full text of the statements is in Bank for International Settlements (1937).
[23] The gold reserves were revalued based on the franc being worth 49 milligrams, and 10 billion francs of the 17 billion profit went toward endowing a stabilization fund. Mouré (2002, 228–229).
[24] "Toward Stabilization," *New York Times*, September 26, 1936.

reason for optimism.[25] The TA evinced, to friend and foe alike, that the democracies still had the capacity to work together. And as public interest in the TA grew, the governments and central banks invested it with greater importance in a positive feedback loop that further boosted its role.

In November, Belgium, the Netherlands, and Switzerland joined the TA, the latter two having devalued their currencies in the days after the French move.[26] There was an implicit hierarchy: the Big Three thought of the new members as junior partners, and Britain and the United States thought of themselves as the "two big boys at the table," with France as the "little fellow," given its political and financial difficulties.[27] Indeed, Anglo-American cooperation was the most significant development of the TA: the two countries went from a war footing on monetary matters to a remarkably collaborative relationship. This is not to say that there were not intense disagreements on policy and even on exactly what the TA meant. The British – "the least enthusiastic party" according to Howson (1980) – thought Morgenthau overhyped the TA and the French too often confined themselves to paying lip service to its principles; the smaller members, for their part, felt that they were excluded from too many discussions. Despite these differences, until the outbreak of war, issues of international monetary policy were overwhelmingly considered – by both the public and governments – through the prism of the TA.

Section II Reciprocal Gold Facilities

The TA's principles were all well and good, but their realization required proactive policy. The 1930s was a decade of immense capital flows, driven by investor skittishness over economic and political

---

[25] There were certainly skeptical voices. In November, Columbia economics professor Walter E. Spahr ridiculed the TA as "a collection of vagaries and pious platitudes" and "a collection of affable nothings." Some considered the TA a dangerous move back towards the gold standard, others a dangerous move further away from the gold standard. "International Currency Stabilization Discussed at Meeting of American Statistical Association," *The Commercial and Financial Chronicle*, November 21, 1936.

[26] Straumann (2010) provides an excellent monetary history of these and other small European countries.

[27] Meeting re exchange of views with British on French situation, September 21, 1937, MD 89 (132).

developments; officials believed exchange intervention to be indispensable to counteract these flows and reduce uncertainty.[28] The
problem was that club members insisted on holding their reserves in
gold, but none of them were willing to convert their currencies into
gold.[29] Britain had stopped doing so in 1931; France had just stopped
doing so; and the United States would only do so for central banks
on the gold standard, which excluded Britain and now France. With
exchange intervention essential but holding foreign exchange anath-
ema, the prospects of fulfilling the TA's aims were slim.

For this reason, the question of who would be able to get gold
from whom was key. This was particularly true for the British, given
that, of the three currencies, sterling was the least connected to gold
and so policymakers worried the most about their ability to manage it. They had controlled the pound vis-à-vis the franc from 1934
to 1936, immediately converting franc purchases into gold, but with
France no longer on the gold standard, this method was no longer
possible. During the TA negotiations, the British Treasury expressed
the importance of gold convertibility in an internal memorandum:
"One of the things we won't stand is an arrangement by which the
French and Americans would buy and sell gold from each other, but
not from us. If that is proposed there is no chance of British cooperation."[30] While there was considerable discussion of the matter in the
weeks leading up to the TA, the whirl of events meant that it was not
yet solved when the governments issued the accord. A British official
met with counterparts at the Bank of France on Sunday, September
27, and over the next two weeks the three countries devised a mechanism to square the circle.[31]

In simultaneous announcements on October 12, each country
promised to buy and sell gold for its currency with one another –
through central banks operating on behalf of the exchange funds – at

---

[28] In November 1936, Roosevelt employed the term "hot money," which had
previously referred to illegal gold movements, to characterize capital seeking
refuge. This use of the term became standard thereafter. Rauchway (2015, 127).
[29] Of the junior members, Belgium had returned to the gold standard and
reinstalled convertibility in April 1936, but the Big Three did not consider the
belga a suitable vehicle currency for their interventions.
[30] Phillips to Waley, September 18, 1936, T 160/840/F4.
[31] Cobbold, "Note of conversations at Bank of France," September 28, 1936,
BoE OV48/10.

prices set each day.[32] For the United States, the price was $35 per ounce (plus or minus ¼% handling charges), though the government retained the right to change it with 24 hours' notice; the British and French provided new prices each day to the United States and often multiple prices throughout the day to each other (which was feasible given the comparative ease of communication and large overlap of market hours). The British price quoted to the United States, for example, was the price at the daily fixing in the London gold market; its price to the French was a function of the prevailing sterling-dollar rate and the US statutory price of $35.[33] These prices were for official transactions only and, except for the US price, were not made public. In order to limit the potential drain on gold holdings, the agreement to sell gold applied only to balances obtained that day through exchange intervention, so that convertibility was not nearly as universal as under the prototypical gold standard. Nonetheless, this "24-hour gold standard" gave countries the confidence to intervene in exchange markets without needing to accumulate foreign exchange balances and risking capital losses. Figure 12.3 illustrates the mechanism, demonstrating the relationship between foreign exchange intervention and gold conversion for the BoE and Federal Reserve Bank of New York (FRBNY).

When the three junior members joined in November, they set up similar facilities, though the specifics between each pair of countries differed slightly depending on location and the precise statutory relationship between currencies and gold.[34] As *The Economist* noted after their accession, "the world is now passing under a form of quasi-gold standard, the key to which lies in semi-rigid parities maintained by official international transfers of gold."[35] To be sure, countries continued to disagree on issues such as the optimal relationship between currencies and gold – some favouring fixed prices and others not – but

---

[32] Bank for International Settlements (1937).
[33] "Exchange: Terms of day-to-day working arrangements with Central Banks," November 2, 1936, BoE G1/473. The British added a spread of two pence on either side of the fixing price for the price quoted to the United States beginning in March 1937. Bolton conversation with Knoke, March 16, 1937, BoE C43/327.
[34] Belgium was the only member that did not use an exchange fund, having gotten rid of it when returning to gold in April 1936.
[35] "Financial Notes," *The Economist*, November 28, 1936.

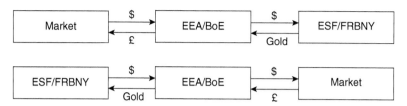

Figure 12.3 Reciprocal gold facilities
(a) BoE converting dollars purchased in the market into gold at FRBNY
(b) BoE obtaining dollars from FRBNY to sell in the market
Source: Harris (2021).

the agreement for daily convertibility allowed these differences to exist without the countries once again segregating into different camps.

Further insight into the main principles underlying these arrangements comes from a BoE note given to the National Bank of Belgium during negotiations in October 1936. The memo set forth nine key points underlying the system:

1. Bilateral.
2. Tacit.
3. Day to day.
4. To be applied in practice as may be agreed, according to circumstances.
5. Positions resulting from exchange intervention to be cleared in terms of gold delivery two days ahead.
6. Bank of England's operations move gold in Brussels, National Bank's operations move gold in London.
7. National Bank's statutory prices apply to any dealings in Belgas for account of the E.E.A.
8. Belgian intervention in sterling is cleared at the Bank of England through a special account, at prices to be agreed as required, on the basis of the exchange rates.
9. Paris gold may be used to clear whenever mutually agreed.[36]

Many of these points highlighted the informal nature of the arrangement. As the French had likewise characterized to the British, the arrangement was "ni accord, ni entente, uniquement co-opération

---

[36] "Arrangement," October 22, 1936, NBB Y190/3.

journalière" (neither an agreement, nor an understanding, only daily cooperation).[37] The points also articulated the mechanisms for clearing in gold: when the British purchased belgas, they would obtain gold in Brussels; when the Belgians purchased sterling, they would obtain gold in London. This was the general rule: when country A bought or sold currency B in the market, the corresponding gold transaction would occur in country B, though as suggested in point 9, the parties could modify this rule when mutually agreeable.

The upshot was frequent foreign exchange intervention and corresponding official gold transactions. The FRBNY's Arthur Bloomfield concluded in a 1943 report on the TA that

Currencies acquired by each fund in the course of its daily operations were invariably liquidated within the specified 24-hour period by conversion into gold, unless, of course, pressure on the foreign exchange rates reversed itself within this period, in which case the various funds would simply take the opportunity of instead selling these balances in exchange for their respective domestic currencies.[38]

Assessing the reliance on convertibility depends to a large measure on such qualitative reports given the dearth of surviving information on intervention and gold holdings.[39]

Perhaps the most interesting evidence that convertibility was the default comes from the reaction to Switzerland's bucking of the practice in 1937.[40] During the spring of that year, fears overtook markets that the price of gold would fall; there appeared to be too much of the metal for the United States and Britain – the two major buyers – to continue purchasing it at the prevailing price. This "Gold Scare" tested whether gold would remain the ultimate reserve asset for the Tripartite countries and daily convertibility the method for dealing with one another. In the end, the Anglo-Americans, believing they had

---

[37] Cobbold, "Note of conversations at Bank of France," September 28, 1936, BoE OV48/10.
[38] Bloomfield, "The Tripartite Agreement of 1936 as an Alternative to the Keynes and White Plans," May 8, 1943, FRBNY FF4608.
[39] For instance, while British archives contain data on daily gold transactions, data on daily exchange interventions during the Tripartite years does not appear to be available. Data on the US ESF is sparse.
[40] See Harris (2018) and Harris (2021, ch. 7) for a fuller discussion of this episode.

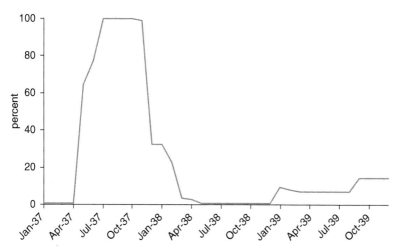

Figure 12.4 Swiss fund holdings of foreign exchange, 1937–39 (foreign exchange as per cent of total reserves)
Source: SNB 231.5.

to act in concert to uphold the TA and determined to maintain gold's role, committed to buying the metal as necessary to support its price. The British believed "our obligations under the Tripartite Agreement make it obligatory upon us to accept gold freely," and they vastly increased the EEA's size to permit further gold purchases.[41] The Swiss, however, had quickly gotten cold feet, and, as Figure 12.4 depicts, rapidly converted their exchange fund from gold to foreign exchange (almost exclusively dollars). One implication of this decision was that they were no longer clearing their interventions in gold.

Morgenthau was incandescent at the Swiss manoeuvres and instructed his financial emissary to inform the Swiss National Bank that he felt it was not "living up to the spirit of the tripartite agreement."[42] Similarly, the President of the Netherlands Bank was "very annoyed with the Swiss, whose gold sales he thinks contrary to the spirit of Tripartite Agreement."[43] With British and French concurrence, the United States presented an informal letter to the Swiss (as

[41] "Reasons for holding so much gold," undated, T 160/660. The British government obtained Parliamentary approval for an increase in the EEA's capital from £350 million to £550 million. Howson (1980).
[42] Butterworth telegram to Morgenthau, June 12, 1937, MD 72 (310).
[43] "Note of conversation with De Jong," June 14, 1937, BoE OV48/11.

well as the Belgians and Dutch) in July that articulated principles for TA countries to adhere to:[44]

At the present time, we who have joined in the tripartite accord are engaged together in an attempt to bring a greater measure of stability and of genuine equilibrium into the market for foreign exchanges.... In our opinion, the normal function of international gold movements is to liquidate international balances of payments arising from the natural flow of international commercial and financial transactions. Governments and central banks should, we believe, in their own operations conform as closely as possible to this general principle. We believe that this principle makes it incumbent upon the adherents of the tripartite declaration to hold their reserves in the form of gold either at home or earmarked abroad, and where a central bank deems it desirable to maintain foreign balances, such balances should in the main be kept with the Central Bank of the selected country and should, furthermore, be maintained essentially as working balances.[45]

Members of the club were to hold their reserves in gold. Doing so necessarily required clearing exchange interventions in the metal (save for minor actions that working balances could cover). As Figure 12.4 shows, Switzerland eventually turned its exchange fund back into gold, though it is admittedly unclear how much of this represented a desire to conform and how much reflected developments in the gold market.[46] The point of this episode is that when the system experienced great strain – a potential collapse in the price of gold that threatened the metal's role as the reserve asset *par excellence* – most of the members committed to sticking with it and sought to bring Switzerland into line. They believed that gold clearing provided the best means for enabling intervention and managing reserves in the current environment and that all members should follow this practice.

The significance of gold clearing should neither be inflated nor trivialized. Daily conversion of foreign exchange into gold meant that there

---

[44] The British and French agreed with the principles but were wary of formalizing the TA; for this reason, Morgenthau kept the letter informal.

[45] Morgenthau telegram to Butterworth, July 14, 1937, MD 78 (329–331).

[46] The Swiss expressed agreement to the principles. Cochran telegram to Morgenthau, September 20, 1937, MD 89 (47). At the same time, new rumors took hold in the autumn that the United States would depreciate the dollar in response to the worsening recession; rebalancing the exchange fund toward gold might have resulted from fears of a loss on the dollar holdings rather than a desire to get into line.

was no long-term support to weak currencies. In Bloomfield's words, there was no "genuine mutual currency support."[47] Policymakers were not oblivious to this shortcoming: at times they considered holding currencies for longer periods to provide aid, but the scars of the decade's early years held them back.[48] At the same time, these facilities were not merely a bare minimum that would have inevitably occurred even had there been no TA. The monetary authorities in Britain and the United States had had almost no technical relationship for years, and it was not foreordained that they would suddenly work together once the gold bloc collapsed. Without these facilities, it is likely that the countries would have continued to operate independently and potentially at cross-purposes, further heightening tensions. Gold convertibility was thus a significant step forward and, as discussed in the following section, provided a foundation for collaboration.

Section III Cooperation and Trust

A comprehensive account of the evolution of international monetary relations during the Tripartite years is not possible in this present paper. Exchange rates were the most visible indicator for judging the success of cooperation, with policymakers favouring stable rates – though not at the expense of domestic growth. As shown in Figure 12.2, exchange rates were relatively stable, save for the glaring depreciations of the franc. French political and financial instability repeatedly tested the TA, but countries now approached these difficulties from a desire to work together. The counterfactual of how officials would have handled the many troubles of these years had there been no reconciliation in 1936 is unknowable, but recrimination and retaliation certainly seem more likely than not. What is striking is not that the franc continued to depreciate but that the other countries refrained from using that as an excuse to revert to the practices of earlier years. Of course, stabilization of nominal exchange rates is not necessarily optimal, and critics, such as Meltzer (2003, 543–544), have argued that governments were misguided in their attempts to that end. But

[47] Bloomfield, "The Tripartite Agreement of 1936 as an Alternative to the Keynes and White Plans," May 8, 1943, FRBNY FF4608.
[48] The United States came close to building up a long position in francs during the summer of 1938. See MD 135, in particular Cochran to Morgenthau, August 25, 1938, MD 135 (260–291).

what concerns us presently is how the IMS functioned and the degree to which TA members made common cause, not the perennial debate as to the appropriateness of managed versus freely floating rates.

The aim of this section is to give a sense, through a series of snapshots, of how technical cooperation helped to ease tensions. Gold convertibility served as the price of membership, available by invitation only, to the currency club. By promising to provide gold in exchange for their currencies, members materially demonstrated their interest in upholding the system. Dealings between central banks skyrocketed, leading to more frequent discussion and collaboration. The Big Three began managing exchange markets jointly, with control passing from Europe to America as markets closed in the east and opened in the west. Though the IMS was far from perfect, the new practice of sharing information and consulting on policy issues attested to a dramatic turnaround from the non-cooperation that characterized the first half of the decade.

Examining the gold facilities from a quantitative perspective, it is evident that the frequency of dealings between central banks surged after the TA. Using the gold ledgers of Britain's EEA, which document every gold transaction beginning in 1936, we can compare transactions between Britain and other countries before and after the TA, as shown in Table 12.1 (Period 1 is pre-TA and Period 2 is post-TA).

It is clear that central bank transactions – and the interventions in markets underlying these transactions – became much more frequent under the reciprocal facilities. For example, the frequency of dealings between Britain and the United States increased by an order of magnitude, from 3% to almost 30%. Those between Britain and other members likewise increased by several multiples.

The increase in transaction frequency is not necessarily due entirely to the TA; in the absence of the TA, dealings could perhaps have risen for other reasons during these years. Contemporaries, however, certainly viewed the TA as integral. The BoE's Harry Siepmann, who was instinctively sceptical of the more grandiose language associated with the TA, noted that "the continuous dealings between the different controls leads inevitably to an intimacy of contact and a continuous exchange of market information which would have been impossible without the Agreement."[49]

---

[49] Siepmann, "Tripartite Agreement," September 3, 1937, BoE G1/304.

Table 12.1 *BoE gold transactions with Tripartite central banks*

	Period 1 Before Tripartite 1/1/36–9/25/36	Period 2 After Tripartite 11/24/36–12/31/38
United States		
Transaction frequency (per cent of market days)	3%	29%
Average transaction size (thousand £)	227	1,180
France		
Transaction frequency (per cent of market days)	37%	67%
Average transaction size (thousand £)	1,675	1,478
Switzerland		
Transaction frequency (per cent of market days)	6%	20%
Average transaction size (thousand £)	134	365
Belgium		
Transaction frequency (per cent of market days)	0%	30%
Average transaction size (thousand £)	N/A	263
Netherlands		
Transaction frequency (per cent of market days)	11%	43%
Average transaction size (thousand £)	168	448

Note: transaction frequency refers to the per cent of market days when the BoE transacted in gold with the listed central bank.
Source: Harris (2021).

The most important piece of information shared was the extent of intervention. Prior to the TA, exchange fund operations had been a state secret. The British generally did not tell the Americans about their interventions and vice versa (information flow with France was somewhat better for each country). With the TA's reciprocal facilities and the restriction to daily convertibility, members necessarily had to inform one another of their intervention amounts. If the United States purchased sterling and did not tell the British about it that day, there was no guarantee that they could later convert that sterling into gold at the BoE. Daily telegrams and frequent conversations detailing interventions thus became the norm. Siepmann described the importance of exchanging information in 1938:

As currency relationships are reciprocal, it is evidently possible that two "controls" [exchange funds] differing (even though only slightly) in their policies and objectives, might find themselves pulling at opposite ends of the same rope. The question is sometimes asked, how cooperation succeeds in avoiding such a situation. The answer is: by constant exchange of information and views, by mutual give and take, and by understanding and sharing one another's difficulties which are apt to be those of one "control" to-day and of another to-morrow.[50]

How much things had changed from 1935, when the BoE's governor, Montagu Norman, had "shudder[ed]" at just the thought of sharing information on the EEA's operations with the Americans.[51]

These central bank conversations, which covered not only intervention numbers but market tactics and developments as well, filtered up to the Treasuries. This was particularly consequential in the United States, where monetary policy and diplomacy were far more personal and less bureaucratic than in other countries. The FRBNY's foreign exchange manager, L. Werner Knoke, was in constant contact with the Treasury; he frequently relayed his talks with TA members directly to Morgenthau. For his part, Morgenthau often reached out to Knoke and requested he discuss certain issues with his counterparts: central banks were able to communicate more quickly with one another than Treasuries, which usually had to work through cumbersome diplomatic protocols. When a given currency was weakening, the other parties now knew what actions the country was taking in response; as a result, they did not automatically

---

[50] "Mr. Siepmann's Memorandum for the Treasury," February 14, 1938, BoE C43/65.
[51] Norman to Hopkins, May 27, 1935, BoE G1/140.

attribute competitive intentions as in earlier years. For instance, when sterling fell from nearly $5 in the spring of 1938 to under $4.75 in the month after Munich, leading to political pressure on the US Treasury to take some countervailing action, Morgenthau, fully up to speed on British interventions, told his subordinates, "I am personally entirely satisfied that the British Treasury has done everything possible to hold sterling in line."[52]

In addition to detailing their interventions, the parties jointly oversaw the markets. Britain and France were responsible for intervening when the European markets were open; once those markets closed, the United States would take over. Bloomfield summarized the practice:

A general principle of interfund cooperation which emerged was for each fund to undertake all official operations in its own market and to delegate the task of controlling the exchange value of its currency in foreign markets to the funds in those markets. Moreover, those funds whose currencies were relatively weak would generally take the initiative in deciding the day-to-day level at which their currencies were to be supported, while the other funds would assume the role of passive agents in helping to support the currencies at these levels in the respective centers.[53]

Matters were not quite so simple, as countries often disagreed on the extent of support provided: the constant discussions made them much more than "passive." Nevertheless, in practice, this method of market control helped to keep everyone on the same page.

Further confirmation of the value invested in gold reciprocity – both for enabling exchange operations and as a demonstration to the public that real action backed up the TA – comes from the June 1937 monetary crisis in France, which led to the removal of the gold bounds within which the franc had been held. In the run-up to the move, there was concern in London and Washington that the French might not continue to quote a gold price. Chancellor of the Exchequer John Simon wrote to Morgenthau:

I do not know whether we shall have any quotations or if so whether the French authorities will be ready to continue arrangement to turn daily surpluses of francs into gold. I am completely in the dark as to how we can

---

[52] Conference on sterling exchange rate, October 21, 1938, MD 147 (91).
[53] Bloomfield, "The Tripartite Agreement of 1936 as an Alternative to the Keynes and White Plan," May 8, 1943, FRBNY FF4608.

operate. It is no doubt true that the French Government can continue to express concurrence in the very general declarations which were embodied in the Tripartite Agreement itself but I cannot help feeling that what has especially attracted notice and especially been approved by public opinion everywhere was the general character of the administrative arrangements concerted at the time of that declaration and continued since to give practical effect to the desire to maintain the greatest possible stability in exchanges.[54]

Nonstop conversations between the Big Three on the French plans followed, and the French made clear that they fully intended to maintain reciprocity. With this guarantee, the Anglo-Americans informed the French that their depreciation would fall within the TA, which, after all, did not forbid all depreciations but only competitive ones (interpretation being up to the members). Morgenthau and Simon worried that the French situation would continue to deteriorate and the franc would continue to weaken, but the French promise on convertibility demonstrated their good faith. It was just enough to move forward as a group. As Morgenthau told Simon, "In the present juncture of world affairs, I trust you will agree with me that it is of prime importance to preserve the beneficial effects which resulted from the Tripartite Declaration and its ensuing arrangement. It was thus demonstrated that great democratic nations could, with mutual confidence, create and carry out co-operative measures."[55]

Just because officials were now talking and dealing with one another does not mean that they agreed on all issues at all times. Frustration between the members was common, debate intense. But as demonstrated in Harris (2021), it was through argument and discussion that the members were able to keep disputes within the clubhouse and achieve a far greater degree of solidarity than was imaginable just a few short months earlier.

Section IV Conclusion

The TA, too long dismissed by economic historians, was in fact a watershed. The Western democracies banded together in the belief that cooperation, and not competition, offered the best chance for

---

[54] Simon to Morgenthau, June 29, 1937, T 160/689.
[55] Morgenthau to Simon, July 1, 1937, T 160/689.

progress. There were many dimensions to the TA, some of which clearly succeeded (consultation became the norm), others which were more mixed (exchange rates were relatively stable save for the franc), and a few which largely failed (there was no grand reduction of trade barriers). While the TA did not develop into a more formalized system as some hoped it would, it nevertheless made collaboration possible by providing a foundation based on what all the members could agree on, putting to the side the longer-term issues on which they disagreed.

On a day-to-day basis, the currency club worked because members were willing to convert their currencies into gold. The irony of the gold standard's collapse was that the metal thereafter became more important as an international reserve. As *The Economist* commented, "the utility of gold has never been so apparent as to-day, when the whole world is off the gold standard ... the degree of exchange stability which the Tripartite agreement provides depends wholly on gold for its functioning."[56] It is too simplistic, then, to view the 1930s as the breakdown of the gold standard without understanding that the metal itself remained paramount. Each member of the club treated gold differently: the United States had a parity that was alterable, the British had no parity, and the French for much of the time had to maintain the franc within a range of gold values. But gold convertibility connected them all. In many ways, this system of official convertibility, coupled with the principles espoused in the TA for stable, but not ironclad, exchange rates and the primacy of domestic policy, served as a basis for the Bretton Woods agreements.

The IMS no longer revolves around a metal. That does not mean, however, that there are not general lessons to be drawn from the TA and reciprocal gold facilities. The first is how the exchange of information – particularly on reserve holdings – can build trust. The British and Americans attributed competitive motivations to each other's funds when they were not sharing information prior to 1936; all of this changed with the TA. Today, exchange intervention continues to draw much attention and sow mistrust, especially when it is not disclosed frequently. Greater disclosure, not necessarily to the public but between governments and central banks, could help reduce suspicion. Secondly, the benefits of technical cooperation are not

---

[56] "America's Gold Policy," *The Economist*, May 27, 1939.

limited to the technocratic sphere. When monetary authorities work together on everyday matters, it makes it easier for them to cooperate in times of stress.

"Exchange Stabilization Funds," Nurkse (1944, 159) reminds us, "are instruments of control and cooperation, but they may equally be used for attack and currency warfare."[57] With the TA, policymakers realized that it was to their long-term advantage for the funds to be used for the former rather than the latter. The line dividing the two – not just for exchange funds but a whole array of policy instruments – can be subtle and difficult to discern, leading to confusion, misunderstanding, and hostility. All the more reason, then, to push for cooperation and transparency so that the line becomes clear and underlying intentions evident.

References

Archival Sources

Bank of England (BoE)
Federal Reserve Bank of New York (FRBNY)
Harry Dexter White Papers at Princeton University (HDWP)
Morgenthau Diaries (MD)
National Bank of Belgium (NBB)
Roosevelt Press Conferences (RPC)
Swiss National Bank (SNB)
Treasury Papers at the National Archives of the United Kingdom (T)

Contemporary Reports

Bank for International Settlements. 1937. *The Tripartite Agreement of September 25, 1936 and Subsequent Monetary Arrangements*. Basle: Bank for International Settlements.

Newspapers

The Commercial and Financial Chronicle
The Economist
The New York Times

---

[57] The chapter on exchange funds, from which this quotation comes, was written by William Adams Brown, Jr.

Secondary Sources

Bordo, Michael D., Owen F. Humpage, and Anna J. Schwartz. 2015. *Strained Relations: US Foreign-Exchange Operations and Monetary Policy in the Twentieth Century*. Chicago: University of Chicago Press.

Clarke, Stephen V. O. 1977. "Exchange-Rate Stabilization in the Mid-1930s: Negotiating the Tripartite Agreement." *Princeton Studies in International Finance* no. 41.

Clavin, Patricia. 1996. *The Failure of Economic Diplomacy: Britain, Germany, France and the United States, 1931–36*. New York: St. Martin's Press.

Dam, Kenneth W. 1982. *The Rules of the Game: Reform and Evolution in the International Monetary System*. Chicago: University of Chicago Press.

Drummond, Ian M. 1979. "London, Washington, and the Management of the Franc, 1936–1939." *Princeton Studies in International Finance* no. 45.

1981. *The Floating Pound and the Sterling Area, 1931–1939*. New York: Cambridge University Press.

Edwards, Sebastian. 2018. *American Default: The Untold Story of FDR, the Supreme Court, and the Battle over Gold*. Princeton: Princeton University Press.

Eichengreen, Barry. 1992. *Golden Fetters: The Gold Standard and the Great Depression, 1919–1939*. New York: Oxford University Press.

Harris, Max. 2018. "Glut of Gold: The Tripartite Agreement and the Gold Scare of 1937." Unpublished manuscript.

2021. *Monetary War and Peace: London, Washington, Paris, and the Tripartite Agreement of 1936*. New York: Cambridge University Press.

Howson, Susan. 1980. "Sterling's Managed Float: The Operations of the Exchange Equalisation Account, 1932–39." *Princeton Studies in International Finance* no. 46.

Jackson, Julian. 1985. *The Politics of Depression in France, 1932–1936*. New York: Cambridge University Press.

Kindleberger, Charles Poor. 2013. *The World in Depression, 1929–1939*. Berkeley: University of California Press.

Meltzer, Allan H. 2003. *A History of the Federal Reserve, Volume 1: 1913–1951*. Chicago: University of Chicago Press.

Mouré, Kenneth. 1991. *Managing the Franc Poincaré: Economic Understanding and Political Constraint in French Monetary Policy, 1928–1936*. New York: Cambridge University Press.

2002. *The Gold Standard Illusion: France, the Bank of France, and the International Gold Standard, 1914–1939*. New York: Oxford University Press.

Nurkse, Ragnar. 1944. *International Currency Experience: Lessons of the Inter-War Period*. Geneva: League of Nations.

Rauchway, Eric. 2015. *The Money Makers: How Roosevelt and Keynes Ended the Depression, Defeated Fascism, and Secured a Prosperous Peace*. New York: Basic Books.

Sayers, R. S. 1976. *The Bank of England, 1891–1944*. New York: Cambridge University Press.

Straumann, Tobias. 2010. *Fixed Ideas of Money: Small States and Exchange Rate Regimes in Twentieth-Century Europe*. New York: Cambridge University Press.

Toniolo, Gianni. 2005. *Central Bank Cooperation at the Bank for International Settlements, 1930–1973*. New York: Cambridge University Press.

13 Exchange Rates, Tariffs and Prices in 1930s Britain

JAGJIT S. CHADHA, JASON LENNARD,
SOLOMOS SOLOMOU, AND RYLAND THOMAS[*]

We are today in the middle of the greatest economic catastrophe [...] of the modern world.

– John Maynard Keynes (1931)[1]

The "economic catastrophe" of the Great Depression led to a slump in output, prices and jobs. As Figure 13.1 shows, economic activity contracted by 5.8 per cent, retail prices dropped by 11.6 per cent and the unemployment rate doubled to more than 15 per cent in the United Kingdom between 1929 and 1931. After signs of revival in 1932, growth returned, deflation ended and unemployment subsided in 1933. This expansion continued into the Second World War.

What sparked the recovery? Central to some accounts is that raising prices was a pre-condition of the return to growth by restoring firm's mark-ups, which had been eroded by deflation and downward nominal wage rigidity, and boosting demand as a result of lower real interest rates. Internal correspondence from HM Treasury, for example, stated that "at the root of everything lies the question whether we are going to secure an increase of the wholesale price level. If we are well and good: if not the future is gloomy in the extreme" (Howson, 1975, p. 91). Dimsdale (1981) argues, "a low exchange rate was a way of promoting economic recovery from the depression through raising wholesale prices." Booth (1987) writes that policymakers

This research has been financed by the Leverhulme Trust (Grant: RPG-2018–428). For help and comments, we would like to thank Alan de Bromhead, Alan Fernihough, Brian Varian, James Ashley Morrison, Sean Holly, Seán Kenny and participants at the Centenary Conference on Keynes's Economic Consequences of the Peace at King's College, University of Cambridge and Queen's University Centre for Economic History. For excellent research assistance, we would like to thank Nathaniel Butler-Blondel and Patricia Sanchez Juanino.
[*] The views expressed here are those of the authors and do not represent the views of the Bank of England or its policy committees.
[1] Quoted in Crafts and Fearon (2013, p. 1).

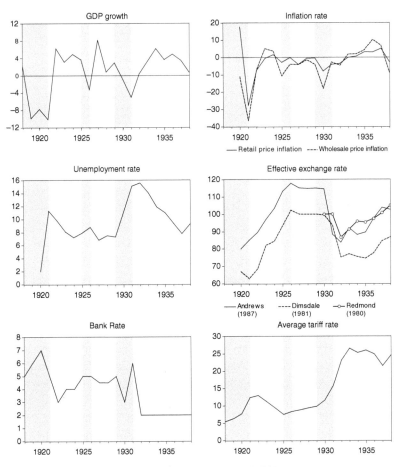

Figure 13.1 Macroeconomic indicators, 1918–38 (%)

Notes: GDP growth is calculated from Mitchell's (1988, p. 836) compromise estimate of GDP at factor cost in constant prices and Sefton and Weale's (1995, p. 188) balanced estimate of GDP at factor cost in constant prices. The inflation rates are calculated from the retail and wholesale price indices (Capie and Collins, 1983, pp. 31–2). The unemployment rate is from Feinstein (1972, T126). The effective exchange rates are from Andrews (1987, pp. 81–4), Dimsdale (1981) and Redmond (1980). Bank Rate is from Capie and Webber (2010, p. 515–8). The average tariff rate is calculated by dividing customs revenue by imports from Mitchell (1988, pp. 453, 583–4). The shaded areas represent recessions (Broadberry et al., forthcoming).

"sought recovery through reflation of the price level to raise profit margins." Eichengreen (2004, p. 338) states that "most observers agree that the tariff pushed up prices, which was helpful in a period when worldwide prices were collapsing. Higher prices stimulated aggregate supply and were good for profitability." Crafts (2013) suggests that "cheap money, a weak pound, tariffs, and encouraging firms to exploit their (enhanced) market power" promoted expected and actual inflation, which helped to revive growth.

To this end, there were a number of major shifts in economic policy in the early 1930s. First was the departure from the gold standard in September 1931.[2] In the following quarter, sterling depreciated by 22 per cent in effective terms (Andrews, 1987, p. 83). Second was the "cheap money policy," which saw Bank Rate cut in steps from 6 per cent in mid-February 1932 to 2 per cent by the end of June. Third was the Import Duties Act, which marked the onset of Britain's turn inwards (Capie, 1981; de Bromhead et al., 2019a), levying a 10 per cent tariff on many imported goods from March 1932. Fourth was the Chancellor's declaration to raise prices at the British Empire Economic Conference that began in July 1932 (*Financial Times*, 13 August 1932, p. 5). The effective exchange rate, Bank Rate and the average tariff rate are also plotted in Figure 13.1.

How successful were these policies in ending deflation? In this chapter, we investigate how changes in import prices – a function of world prices and exchange rates – and tariffs "passed-through" into changes in wholesale prices.[3] In order to do so, we construct a new monthly data set of item-level import prices, tariff barriers and wholesale prices for the imported items included in the official wholesale price index. The data set has more than 2,000 observations covering 27 imported varieties between January 1930 and December 1938. We use this micro data in panel regressions of wholesale prices on import prices and tariffs for each product variety. In terms of identification, we assume that import prices are set exogenously with respect to British wholesale prices but that tariffs are potentially endogenous. We therefore use narrative methods to distinguish between tariff changes that were motivated by changes in domestic wholesale prices and those for more exogenous reasons.

There are a number of interesting results. First, changes in import prices and tariffs were positively associated with changes in wholesale prices, although the degree of pass-through was not complete. Second,

---

[2] The extent to which the devaluation was discretionary or enforced has been debated. See, for example, Worswick (1984).

[3] As discussed later, we are limited to wholesale prices because of a scarcity of data for consumer or retail prices. However, as demonstrated by the Treasury letter above, wholesale prices were of great interest in interwar Britain.

the deflation of the early 1930s was partly caused by falling import prices, as a result of the drop in global commodity prices. The depreciation following the break from the gold standard slowed, but did not reverse, this decline. Third, rising protection exerted upward pressure on prices, contributing to the shift from deflation to inflation in 1933.

This chapter is organized as follows. Section I reviews the relevant literature. Second II introduces the data. Section III covers the methodology. Section IV presents the results. Section V concludes.

I Previous Literature

Exchange rate and tariff pass-through can be split into three stages. In many studies of exchange rate pass-through the focus is on the first stage of pass-through from exchange rates to import prices, reflecting the pricing behaviour of overseas producers and whether they adjust the price of goods in foreign currency.[4] Others focus on the other end of the supply chain, looking at how retailers pass on changes in the cost of imported goods to their customers. This chapter focuses on the second or intermediate stage of pass-through from sterling import prices to the price charged for imported goods by wholesalers. As we discuss later, this is in part due to data limitations. But this second stage of pass-through may more generally act as an indicator of pass-through by retailers.

Despite the importance of pass-through in the historiography, quantitative estimates are scarce for interwar Britain. Moggridge (1972, p. 110) conjectured that a "10 per cent appreciation of the exchange rate would, *ceteris paribus*, probably have no more than a 4 per cent effect on the cost of living" in 1925, which equates to a pass-through coefficient from exchange rates to consumer prices of 0.4. Broadberry (1986, p. 129) assumes that the 13 per cent depreciation of the effective exchange rate between 1931 and 1932 led to a rise in the sterling price of imports of 9 per cent, which translates into a pass-through coefficient from exchange rates to import prices of 0.69. Downs (1986, p. 15) suggests that "the domestic [wholesale] price level was rather sticky when it should have increased the most from the impact of the tariffs" in 1932, which implies a pass-through coefficient from tariffs to wholesale prices of close to zero.

---

[4] See, for example, Feenstra (1989) and Gopinath et al. (2010).

Keynes speculated how a fall in the exchange rate and a rise in tariffs might affect inflation. On devaluation, he wrote (Keynes, 1931, p. 290):

For less than a quarter of our total consumption is represented by imports; so that sterling would have to depreciate by much more than 25 per cent before I should expect the cost of living to rise by as much as 10 per cent. This would cause serious hardship to no one, for it would only put things back where they were two years ago. Meanwhile there will be a great stimulus to employment.

On protection, he forecasted that (Keynes, 1931, p. 278):

There might be import duties of 15 per cent on all manufactured and semi-manufactured goods without exception, and of 5 per cent on all foodstuffs and certain raw materials, whilst other raw materials would be exempt. I am prepared to maintain that the effect of such duties on the cost of living would be insignificant – no greater than the existing fluctuation between one month and another. Moreover, any conceivable remedy for unemployment will have the effect, and, indeed, will be intended, to raise prices.

These historical best guesses of incomplete pass-through are consistent with estimates for modern economies.[5] One branch of the literature is based on micro data. Nakamura and Zerom (2010), for example, find a long-run pass-through coefficient of 0.26 from costs into wholesale prices in the US coffee industry between 2000 and 2005. Hellerstein (2008) reports a short-run pass-through coefficient of 0.11 from exchange rates to retail prices in the Chicago beer industry in the 1990s. Breinlich et al. (2019) calculate a long-run pass-through coefficient of 0.29 from exchange rates to consumer prices in the aftermath of the 2016 referendum in the United Kingdom. Another branch of the literature is based on macro data. Savoie-Chabot and Khan (2015) estimate that the long-run pass-through of exchange rates to the consumer price index was 0.06 in Canada between 1995 and 2013. Forbes et al. (2017) document an average rate of pass-through from exchange rates to consumer prices of 0.05 in advanced economies between 1990 and 2015.[6]

II Data

In order to investigate pass-through in interwar Britain, we construct a new monthly data set of goods-level import prices, tariff barriers and

---

[5] Here we focus on recent estimates of pass-through into consumer, retail and wholesale prices.

[6] For a survey of earlier work, see Goldberg and Knetter (1997).

wholesale prices for imported goods included in the official wholesale price index.

The dependent variable in the analysis is the wholesale price. Monthly micro data on wholesale prices was published in the *Board of Trade Journal* (various dates).[7] The Board of Trade collected the prices of around 200 goods, falling under the categories of cereals; meat, fish and eggs; other food and tobacco; coal; iron and steel; non-ferrous metals; cotton; wool; other textiles; chemicals and oils; and other articles. These prices were aggregated to form the Board of Trade wholesale price index. Identifying which goods in the index were imported was straightforward as the origin was included in the description. Eggs from Denmark, for example, were described as "eggs: Danish" and tea from India as "tea: Indian." These prices are inclusive of duty.

As less attention is paid to wholesale prices today than in the interwar period, it is useful to clarify what a wholesale price is. This is the price of a good in a business-to-business, as opposed to a business-to-consumer, exchange. As a first approximation, it is the price paid by retailers to producers, whereas the consumer or retail price is the price paid by consumers to retailers. For example, the Board of Trade's wholesale price index included oatmeal prices from the London Corn Exchange, fish prices from Billingsgate Market and prices from specialist trade publications such as *The Builder*, *The Grocer* and *The World's Paper Trade Review* (*Board of Trade Journal*, 24 January 1935, pp. viii–xi). The wholesale price will contain duties, wholesalers' labour and capital costs, plus any mark-up. So the wholesale price will reflect many elements over and above the cost of primary goods either produced domestically or overseas. If the import price it pays at the dock is not passed on to the retailer, the wholesaler must either reduce costs or absorb it in profit margins.

One of the main independent variables in the analysis is import prices. Monthly micro data on the price of imported goods is calculated from the *Trade and Navigation Accounts* (Parliamentary Papers, various dates). This source published the imported value and quantity of individual goods by country, from which the average price or unit value can be calculated as the ratio of the two (de Bromhead et al., 2019a). To return to the previous example, the *Trade and Navigation Accounts* include "eggs in shell [...] from Denmark" and "Tea from

---

[7] Details of the collection of prices and the construction of the index are available in *Board of Trade Journal* (24 January 1935).

British India." These prices are exclusive of duty, as well as the whole-saler's costs and mark-up (National Institute of Economic and Social Research, 1943, pp. 57–8).

Another key independent variable is tariff barriers. Monthly goods-level data is constructed from the *Report of the Commissioners of His Majesty's Customs and Excise* (Parliamentary Papers, various dates). Many goods in the sample were levied an ad valorem duty. However, some goods were subject to specific duties, such as the 3/4*d*. per lb. for beef (chilled) from the Argentine Republic under the Beef and Veal Customs Duties Act 1937. In order to convert to an ad valorem equiv-alent, we divide the specific duty by the import price in the month prior to the tariff change to isolate changes in legislation from changes in import prices (Irwin, 1998). Appendix I details the methods and sources used.

The wholesale price of imported good *g* from country *c* was matched to the import price and tariff of good *g* from country *c*. As in de Bromhead et al. (2019a), we refer to a good from a particular country as a variety. The matched prices are shown in Table 13.1. Prices that could not be uniquely linked are listed in appendix II. Overall, we have 27 varieties in our sample, which represent 78.2 per cent of all imported goods, and 25.8 per cent of all goods, domestic and imported, in the wholesale price index in 1935 (*Board of Trade Journal*, 24 January 1935, p. iv).

The sample period is January 1930 to December 1938. The start date is determined by the availability of the micro data reported in the *Board of Trade Journal*. The end date represents the last full year of peace before the outbreak of war and the imposition of price controls (Mills and Rockoff, 1987). In total, we have an unbalanced sample of 2,001 variety-month observations.

An interesting extension would be to include consumer or retail prices as dependent variables to assess the degree of pass-through fur-ther up the supply chain. However, we were not able to uncover micro data on consumer or retail prices that was as rich in the cross sectional or time-series dimensions as that for wholesale prices. There is some evidence in modern data that suggests retail prices adjust immediately and fully to changes in wholesale prices, but that wholesale prices respond less than proportionately to changes in costs, which suggests that incomplete pass-through occurs at the wholesale level (Nakamura and Zerom, 2010). However, whether that applies to interwar Britain is an open question for future research.

Table 13.1 *Matched prices*

Good	Matched Sample	Wholesale Variety	Import Variety
Cereals			
Barley	1935:1–1938:12	Californian malting	United States of America
Maize	1930:1–1938:12	Yellow La Plata, spot	Argentine Republic
Rice	1930:1–1938:12	No. 2 Rangoon	Whole, British India
Wheat	1930:1–1938:12	No. 2 Northern Manitoba, ex ship	Canada
Wheat	1935:1–1936:2	Rosafé	Argentine Republic
Flour	1935:1–1938:12	Imported, average of Spring Patent and American Winter	United States of America
Meat, Fish and Eggs			
Bacon	1930:1–1938:12	Irish green, 1st	Irish Free State
Bacon	1930:1–1938:12	Danish green, 1st	Denmark
Hams	1935:1–1938:12	American green, short cut, 1st	United States of America
Beef	1930:1–1938:12	Argentine chilled, average of fores and hinds, 1st	Chilled, Argentine Republic
Beef	1930:1–1931:8	Argentine frozen, average of fores and hinds, 1st	Frozen, in quarters and sides, Argentine Republic
Beef	1931:12–1938:12	Australian frozen, average of crops and hinds, 1st	Frozen, in quarters and sides, Australia
Lamb	1930:1–1938:12	New Zealand, 1st	Frozen, New Zealand
Eggs	1935:1–1938:12	Danish, average	In shell, poultry, Denmark
Other Food and Tobacco			
Butter	1930:1–1938:12	Danish, 1st	Denmark
Butter	1930:1–1938:12	New Zealand, 1st	New Zealand
Cheese	1935:1–1938:12	New Zealand, 1st	New Zealand
Cocoa	1930:1–1931:12	Trinidad	British West India Islands

Table 13.1 *(cont.)*

Good	Matched Sample	Wholesale Variety	Import Variety
Cocoa	1932:1–1938:12	West African	British West Africa
Coffee	1930:1–1938:12	Costa Rica, good to fine	Costa Rica
Tea	1930:1–1938:12	Indian, average	British India
Tobacco	1934:12–1938:12	American Western, good to fine	Unmanufactured, if unstripped, United States of America
Cotton			
Cotton	1930:1–1938:12	American, middling	Raw (except linters), United States of America
Cotton	1930:1–1938:12	Egyptian, Sakellaridis, fully good fair	Raw (except linters), Egypt
Other Articles			
Goatskin	1934:12–1938:12	High standard selections, dry salted Patnas, 35/45/20	Dry and salted, British India
Paper-making materials	1934:12–1938:12	Esparto, Oran, 1st quality, c.i.f.	Esparto, including waste, from Algeria

III Methodology

In order to estimate the degree of pass-through, we estimate two models. One is a model in log levels:

$$\log p_{i,t} = \alpha_i + \sum_{k=0}^{4} \beta_k \log m_{i,t-k} + \sum_{k=0}^{4} \gamma_k \tau_{i,t-k} + \sum_{k=1}^{4} \varphi_k q_k + \varepsilon_{i,t} \quad (1)$$

where $\log p_{i,t}$ is the log wholesale price of imported variety i at time t, α_i is a variety fixed effect, $\log m_{i,t-k}$ is the log import price, $\tau_{i,t-k}$ is the ad valorem equivalent tariff rate and q_k is a quarter of the year dummy.

The other is a model in log differences. Following the convention in the literature (Gopinath et al., 2010; Nakamura and Zerom, 2010; Savoie-Chabot and Khan, 2015), we estimate this standard pass-through regression as the baseline model:

$$\Delta\log p_{i,t} = \sum_{k=0}^{4} \beta_k \Delta\log m_{i,t-k} + \sum_{k=0}^{4} \gamma_k \Delta\tau_{i,t-k} + \sum_{k=1}^{4} \varphi_k q_k + \varepsilon_{i,t} \quad (2)$$

where Δ is the difference operator. As a result of differencing, the variety fixed effect cancels out.

In these models, β_k measures the approximate percentage change in wholesale prices associated with a 1 per cent change in import prices at $t-k$. γ_k can be interpreted as the approximate percentage change in wholesale prices associated with a 1 percentage point change in the ad valorem equivalent tariff rate at $t-k$. The standard errors are clustered by variety.

Notice that both models include the import price as opposed to the relevant bilateral exchange rate. As the import price can be expressed as $m_{i,t-k} = \dfrac{m^*_{i,t-k}}{e_{t-k}}$, where $m^*_{i,t-k}$ is the import price in foreign currency and e_{t-k} is the relevant bilateral nominal exchange rate (foreign currency per pound), β_k therefore measures the pass-through of world prices *and* exchange rates to wholesale prices of imported goods.

For each variety, the import price, $m_{i,t-k}$, is calculated as the imported value divided by the imported quantity. As the unit value is quite volatile, perhaps because of differentiation within varieties, we use quarterly averages of the monthly data for $p_{i,t}$, $m_{i,t-k}$ and $\tau_{i,t-k}$.

The quarter of the year dummies are included to model the seasonality in prices (Nakamura and Zerom, 2010). As the Board of Trade recognized, there was significant variation in wholesale prices from month to month:

For all articles the variation in prices through-out the year is from 0.8 per cent. below the average in May to 1.1 per cent. above the average in November. Prices as a whole are shown as falling steadily by an aggregate of 1.5 per cent. between January and May, rising slightly in June and July, falling in August and then rising by 1.75 per cent. in the course of the next three months, with a fall of 0.5 per cent. in December to about the January level (*Board of Trade Journal*, 24 January 1935, p. vii).

In Section IV.B, we investigate the sensitivity of the results to variations of the baseline model, such as changing the number of lags included, using an alternative measure of the ad valorem equivalent tariff rate and including time fixed effects.

A Identification

The identification of β_k and γ_k depends on some assumptions. In the case of β_k, there are two identifying assumptions. Recall that $m_{i,t-k} = \dfrac{m^*_{i,t-k}}{e_{t-k}}$, where $m^*_{i,t-k}$ is the import price in foreign currency and e_{t-k} is the relevant exchange rate. The first assumption is that the domestic wholesale price does not affect the foreign price, which is determined globally. This standard assumption is also used by de Bromhead et al. (2019a), who provide supporting evidence that the United Kingdom did not have sufficient market power to influence world prices in the interwar period. The second identifying assumption is that the domestic wholesale price does not affect the exchange rate at the level of the individual good. Using micro-level outcomes to identify the causal impact of macroeconomic shocks has been used by Boneva et al. (2016). In the case of γ_k, the identifying assumption is that the domestic wholesale price does not affect tariffs.

The assumptions behind identification of β_k are not controversial. However, the assumption underpinning γ_k is more contestable because tariffs might be implemented to affect domestic wholesale prices. For example, if the domestic price of a British product has fallen due to foreign competition, a tariff might be imposed on the competing import to raise British prices. Fortunately, this assumption can be verified using narrative evidence.

B Narrative Analysis

"Narrative methods involve constructing a series from historical documents to identify the reason and/or the quantities associated with a particular change in a variable" (Ramey, 2016, p. 78). The narrative approach has been used to estimate the causal effects of monetary policy (Romer and Romer, 2004; Cloyne and Hürtgen, 2016; Lennard, 2018), fiscal policy (Romer and Romer, 2010; Ramey, 2011; Cloyne, 2013; Crafts and Mills, 2013, 2015; Ramey and Zubairy, 2018) and financial crises (Jalil, 2015; Esteves et al., 2021; Kenny et al., 2021). However, narrative methods have not been used to estimate the economic effects

Table 13.2 *Classifying tariffs*

Tariff	Classification
Import Duties Act 1932	Exogenous
Irish Free State (Special Duties) Act 1932	Exogenous
Ottawa Agreements Act 1932	Exogenous
Beef and Veal Customs Duties Act 1937	Endogenous
Tea 1932, 1936 and 1938	Exogenous
Tobacco 1931	Exogenous

of tariffs. In order to do so, we read the parliamentary debates and legislation related to the changes in tariff policy that affected our sample of imported goods to determine the principal motivation. We define an endogenous tariff as one that is motivated by domestic prices and an exogenous tariff as one that is implemented for other reasons.

Table 13.2 summarizes the tariffs and classifications. Appendix III contains supporting evidence. The narrative analysis suggests that of the 8 tariffs that affected the 27 varieties in our sample, 7 were exogenous, while 1 was endogenous, which could bias γ_k if ignored. We repeated this exercise for non-tariff barriers but found that all changes were endogenous. This suggests that non-tariff barriers, such as licenses, were used to manipulate prices whereas tariff barriers were used to achieve other objectives. As a result, we exclude non-tariff barriers from the analysis.

An example of a tariff that we classify as endogenous is the Beef and Veal Customs Duties Act 1937:

The Government are of opinion that if adequate provision is to be made in one form or another for the needs of the United Kingdom cattle industry, the aggregate financial assistance now given to it must be increased until such time as the conditions prevailing in the industry improve. They propose to seek the authority of Parliament to apply to the assistance of the industry such sums not exceeding £5,000,000 per annum as may from time to time be needed. Parliament will be asked annually to make provision for a sum not exceeding this amount. As an offset to this liability, the Exchequer will benefit to the extent of the revenue from the import duties to which I have referred.[8]

---

[8] Hansard, HC Deb 6 July 1936, vol 314 c842.

The principal reason was to fund a subsidy to the ailing British cattle industry. An example of a tariff that we classify as exogenous is the change in tea duty in 1938. The Chancellor of the Exchequer, John Simon, explained in the budget speech to the House of Commons:

I propose to raise the duty on all tea, Empire and foreign, by 2*d.* per pound [...] I well understand that even an extra halfpenny per week is a material and appreciable addition to the expenses of those with the smallest incomes. Why do I do it? I believe that there is a willingness and even a pride in the humblest homes to take a share in this rearmament outlay, for defending those homes from peril, just as much as in the homes of more comfortable and wealthy people.[9]

The main motivation was not to increase the wholesale price of tea but to raise government revenue in order to fund defence spending.

A potential concern is that by conducting the narrative analysis at the level of the legislation, as opposed to the variety, our results may be biased if there was endogenous selection of varieties to receive a tariff change, despite the overarching legislation being plausibly exogenous. We focus on the legislation as it was debated openly in the Houses of Parliament. How individual varieties were selected to receive legislated tariff changes, however, was a more private matter settled by civil servants and ministers. Therefore, we have more qualitative information to determine the motivation for tariff changes at the level of the legislation than we do at the level of the variety.

IV Results

A Baseline Results

The degree of import price and tariff pass-through is shown in Table 13.3. The first and second columns are based on a model in first differences. The first column shows the pass-through from import prices to wholesale prices. The impact coefficient suggests that a 1 per cent change in import prices was associated with a rise of approximately 0.62 per cent in wholesale prices. This effect is highly significant with a *t*-statistic in excess of 9. Thereafter, there are minor gyrations that bump the long-run pass-through (LRPT) coefficient ($\sum_{k=0}^{4} \beta_k$) down to 0.61. The second column shows the extent of pass-through from tariffs to wholesale

---

[9] Hansard, HC Deb 26 April 1938, vol 335 c66.

Table 13.3 *Exchange rate and tariff pass-through*

k	Differences		Levels	
	β_k	γ_k	β_k	γ_k
0	0.62	0.31	0.81	0.49
	(0.06)***	(0.11)***	(0.07)***	(0.07)***
1	0.00	0.13	–0.01	0.24
	(0.03)	(0.03)***	(0.04)	(0.04)***
2	–0.03	–0.01	0.02	–0.05
	(0.04)	(0.13)	(0.04)	(0.16)
3	0.04	0.43	0.03	0.34
	(0.02)	(0.11)***	(0.03)	(0.20)
4	–0.02	–0.08	–0.05	–0.06
	(0.04)	(0.10)	(0.04)	(0.17)
LRPT	0.61	0.79	0.82	0.95
	(0.06)***	(0.20)***	(0.05)***	(0.13)***
Observations	587		615	
R^2	0.52		0.28	

Notes: This table shows the approximate response of wholesale prices to a 1 per cent change in import prices and a 1 percentage point change in the ad valorem equivalent tariff rate based on estimation of equations (1) and (2). $\tau_{i,\,t-k}$ includes exogenous tariff changes only. Standard errors are clustered by variety and are shown in parentheses. ***, ** and * indicate statistical significance at the 1%, 5% and 10% levels respectively.

prices. The impact multiplier implies that a 1 percentage point change in the ad valorem equivalent tariff rate was associated with an increase in wholesale prices of roughly 0.31 per cent. This estimate is statistically significant at the 1 per cent level. At more distant horizons, pass-through continues, raising the LRPT coefficient ($\sum_{k=0}^{4}\gamma_k$) to 0.79. The third and fourth columns are based on a model in levels. The stylized facts remain but the economic and statistical significance is greater.

How do the results compare to estimates in the literature? As reported in Section I, previous studies estimate pass-through coefficients from exchange rates to consumer, retail or wholesale prices of approximately zero to 0.4. Therefore, our results are consistent with existing evidence of incomplete pass-through. However, our estimates are somewhat higher than those found in the literature. Why? One important reason is that we are focusing on imported goods in the wholesale price index, whereas most other studies focus on all goods, domestic and imported, in an index. As pass-through is known to be higher for imported goods (with high import shares) than for domestic goods (with low import shares) (Breinlich et al., 2019), it is unsurprising that we find higher pass-through. Differences in pass-through may also be indicative of variations in the curvature of demand and market structure or price rigidities (Corsetti et al., 2008; Nakamura and Zerom, 2010).

B Robustness

We now turn to the robustness of our estimates. We consider five alternative specifications of the baseline model. The first specification is a more parsimonious model that includes 2, as opposed to 4, lags of import price and tariff changes. The second is a richer model that allows for a longer pass-through by including 6 lags of these terms. The third includes all tariff changes, whereas the baseline model only included exogenous variation. The fourth includes year fixed effects to account for omitted variables that vary over time but are constant across varieties. The fifth specification excludes observations with extreme import price changes, defined as changes below the 10th and above the 90th percentile, to assess the importance of potential measurement error.

The results are shown in Table 13.4. The long-run pass-through from a change in import prices is in the interval of 0.41 and 0.63, which includes the baseline coefficient of 0.61. The long-run pass-through from a change in the ad valorem equivalent tariff rate ranges from 0.58 to 0.87, which includes the baseline estimate of 0.79. The standard errors of the LRPT coefficients are not constant across specifications but the effects remain statistically significant at the 5 per cent level. In summary, alternative econometric specifications consistently suggest an economically and statistically significant degree of pass-through in interwar Britain.

C Pass-Through Heterogeneity

An interesting question is whether there is heterogeneity in the degree of pass-through across varieties. In theory, this may be due to product- or industry-level differences in the curvature of demand and market structure, local costs or price rigidities. To investigate this possibility, we interact import price changes, $\Delta \log m_{i,t-k}$, and ad valorem

Table 13.4 *Robustness*

k	2 Lags (1) β_k	γ_k	6 Lags (2) β_k	γ_k	All Tariff Changes (3) β_k	γ_k	Time Fixed Effects (4) β_k	γ_k	Outliers Excluded (5) β_k	γ_k
0	0.64	0.34	0.59	0.29	0.62	0.25	0.61	0.33	0.64	0.18
	(0.06)***	(0.11)***	(0.06)***	(0.12)**	(0.06)***	(0.12)**	(0.06)***	(0.10)***	(0.04)***	(0.20)
1	0.00	0.14	−0.02	0.04	−0.00	0.20	−0.01	0.13	−0.06	0.24
	(0.03)	(0.03)***	(0.04)	(0.04)	(0.03)	(0.05)***	(0.03)	(0.04)***	(0.03)*	(0.22)
2	−0.01	0.11	−0.04	−0.03	−0.03	−0.05	−0.04	0.01	0.01	0.00
	(0.04)	(0.14)***	(0.03)	(0.14)	(0.04)	(0.10)	(0.04)	(0.13)	(0.03)	(0.21)
3			0.01	0.40	0.04	0.27	0.03	0.46	0.05	0.49
			(0.03)	(0.09)***	(0.02)	(0.12)**	(0.02)	(0.12)***	(0.03)*	(0.29)*
4			−0.06	−0.05	−0.02	−0.00	−0.03	−0.07	−0.07	−0.04
			(0.04)	(0.14)	(0.04)	(0.11)	(0.04)	(0.12)	(0.03)*	(0.23)
5			0.01	−0.25						
			(0.03)	(0.07)***						
6			−0.07	0.47						
			(0.03)**	(0.12)***						
LRPT	0.63	0.58	0.41	0.86	0.61	0.66	0.56	0.87	0.57	0.87
	(0.05)***	(0.06)***	(0.10)***	(0.18)***	(0.06)***	(0.18)***	(0.07)***	(0.24)***	(0.07)***	(0.39)**
Observations	617		557		587		587		490	
R^2	0.52		0.52		0.52		0.52		0.37	

Notes: This table shows the approximate response of wholesale prices to a 1 per cent change in import prices and a 1 percentage point change in the ad valorem equivalent tariff rate based on estimation of variants of equation (2). Standard errors are clustered by variety and are shown in parentheses. ***, **, and * indicate statistical significance at the 1%, 5%, and 10% level respectively.

equivalent tariff rate changes, $\Delta\tau_{i,\,t-k}$, with dummies. The dummies are for the groups included in the Board of Trade's wholesale price index that apply to our sample: cereals; meat, fish and eggs; other food and tobacco; cotton; and other articles. To be clear, we estimate the following model:

$$\Delta\log p_{i,t} = \sum_{j=1}^{5}\sum_{k=0}^{4} \beta_{j,k}\left(d_j\Delta\log m_{i,t-k}\right)$$

$$+ \sum_{j=1}^{5}\sum_{k=0}^{4} \gamma_{j,k}\left(d_j\Delta\tau_{i,t-k}\right) + \sum_{k=1}^{4}\varphi_k q_k + \varepsilon_{i,t} \qquad (3)$$

where each of the d_js represent one of the five groups.

Figure 13.2 plots the long-run pass-through coefficients on import price changes for the various groups. The estimates for cereals; meat, fish and eggs; and other articles (goatskin and paper-making materials) are very similar, between 0.51 and 0.56. The coefficients for the more manufactured goods (cotton and other articles) are somewhat higher, between 0.65 and 0.67. However, the confidence intervals overlap and the only difference that is statistically significant at the 10 per cent level is between meat, fish and eggs and cotton.

Figure 13.3 shows the long-run pass-through coefficients on ad valorem equivalent tariff rate changes for three groups: cereals; meat, fish and eggs; and other food and tobacco. Cotton and other articles are omitted because there were no tariff changes on the varieties that are included in our sample for these groups. The pass-through estimates range from 0.53 for meat, fish and eggs to 0.87 for cereals and 1.04 for other food and tobacco. However, the confidence bands overlap, and the differences are not statistically significant at conventional levels.

Overall, there is not compelling evidence that there was significant heterogeneity in import price or tariff pass-through across groups, although a larger sample may help to reduce some of the uncertainty around the point estimates.

D Qualitative Evidence

Fluctuations in the Board of Trade's wholesale price index were newsworthy in 1930s Britain. If, as our results suggest, pass-through was substantial (albeit incomplete), then one would expect to see

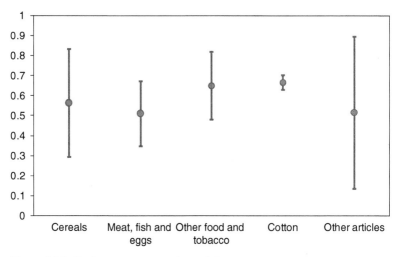

Figure 13.2 Exchange rate pass-through by group

Notes: This figure shows the approximate long-run response of wholesale prices to a 1 per cent change in import prices by group based on estimation of equation (3). The 95 per cent confidence intervals are shown by the bars.

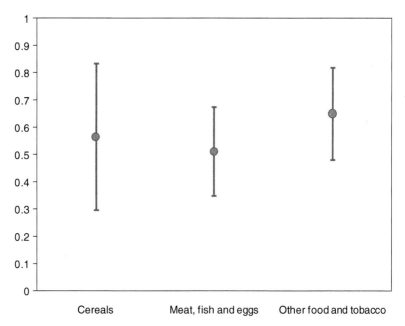

Figure 13.3 Tariff pass-through by group

Notes: This figure shows the approximate long-run response of wholesale prices to a 1 percentage point change in the ad valorem equivalent tariff rate by group based on estimation of equation (3). The 95 per cent confidence intervals are shown by the bars.

references to the impact of depreciation and protection in contemporary accounts. We therefore turn from quantitative to qualitative evidence relating to exchange rate and tariff pass-through to wholesale prices.

On the subject of exchange rate pass-through, there were numerous references in the aftermath of the devaluation. In October, the *Financial Times* (8 October 1931, p. 4) reported that "prices of imported commodities reacted at once to the depreciation of sterling, while those of home-produced commodities were only indirectly affected [...] even prices of imported goods have not yet fully adjusted themselves to the depreciation of sterling." The *FT* (9 November 1931, p. 4) reiterated this in November:

The immediate effect of the suspension of the gold standard has been to bring about a moderate rise in sterling prices [...] confined mainly to imported commodities [...] So far the depreciation of the pound sterling against gold currencies has not exercised its full effect upon home prices. At the same time, there is already some tendency for prices even of home-produced goods to rise in sympathy with the depreciation of sterling and the enhanced price of equivalent foreign goods [...] As stocks of goods imported before the suspension of the gold standard are exhausted, it is natural to look for a further increase in sterling prices, but in the absence of any increase in home production costs or further depreciation of sterling this upward movement should not go very far.

The *Financial Times* referred to this pattern time and again in the autumn of 1931.[10]

The Board of Trade Journal (24 January 1935, p. vi), reflecting on changes in its wholesale price index, also attributed a causal effect to devaluation: "following the suspension of the gold standard in September, 1931, a recovery in prices took place in the last quarter of 1931, prices of basic materials rising by 14 per cent., of intermediate products by 5 per cent., and of manufactured articles by 3 per cent."

On the topic of tariff pass-through, the Chancellor, Phillip Snowden forecasted that the increase in tobacco duty in 1931 would lead to a less-than-proportionate change in prices: "I have no reason to anticipate that the whole of this increase will be passed on to the consumer."[11]

---

[10] See, for example, *Financial Times* (22 September 1931, p. 5; 28 September 1931, p. 4; 1 October 1931, p. 4; 2 November 1931, p. 4).
[11] Hansard, HC Deb 10 September 1931, vol 256 c308.

Similarly, the *Guardian* (22 August 1932, p. 9) expected a moderate increase in prices in the wake of the Ottawa Agreements Act:

Sober consideration indicates that the rise should be small, since on certain articles such as butter and cheese, the proportion of imports from the Empire is already so high that the preservation of free entry for Empire produce is an adequate guarantee that the price will not rise by anything like the full extent of duty.

Some of these statements are covering broader aspects of the supply chain pass-through from exchange rates through to retail prices but are in line with our findings of pass-through that is greater than zero but less than 1.

In summary, the quantitative and qualitative evidence are consistent and point to pass-through from exchange rates and tariffs to prices.

E Aggregate Implications

We now investigate the macroeconomic implications of our microeconomic results. As inflation is ultimately pinned down by monetary policy, upward pressure on the price level arising from import prices or tariffs can be accommodated by monetary policy and allowed to work its way through the supply chain, or policy can attempt to weigh down on domestic prices and costs and offset the influences of import prices and tariffs on the general price level. However, much depends on the policy regime. Under the gold standard up to September 1931, policy was geared to maintaining the sterling exchange rate, so downward pressure on world prices reflecting world monetary conditions would need to be met with tight monetary policy that exerted downward pressure on domestic wages and prices to maintain competitiveness. Once Britain left the gold standard, monetary policy was free to follow domestic growth and inflation objectives. As a result, policymakers could choose whether to accommodate factors that shifted relative prices in the economy such as import prices and tariffs.

To shed light on these issues, we consider a very simple accounting decomposition of inflation (Downs, 1986, p. 49):

$$\pi_t = \omega^m \Delta \log p_t^m + \varepsilon_t \tag{4}$$

where π_t is the log difference of the wholesale price index, ω^m is the share of imported goods in the wholesale price index, $\Delta \log p_t^m$ is the average log difference in the wholesale price of imported goods and ε_t is a residual. The first term, $\omega^m \Delta \log p_t^m$, accounts for the contribution of imported goods to aggregate inflation, while the second term, ε_t, is a residual that measures the contribution of domestic goods, including domestic goods that: use imported inputs, are substitutes for imports, are exported and are non-tradable. The residual will therefore capture all the factors affecting inflation including the effects of monetary policy on domestic wages and prices.

A macro pass-through decomposition for the wholesale price of imported goods can be expressed as:

$$\Delta \log p_t^m = \beta \Delta \log m_t + \gamma \Delta \tau_t \qquad (5)$$

where $\Delta \log m_t$ is the average log difference in the import price of imported goods included in the wholesale price index, β is the pass-through coefficient on $\Delta \log m_t$, $\Delta \tau_t$ is the average difference in the average tariff rate and γ is the pass-through coefficient on $\Delta \tau_t$.

Inserting (5) into (4):

$$\pi_t = \omega^m \left(\beta \Delta \log m_t + \gamma \Delta \tau_t \right) + \varepsilon_t \qquad (6)$$

which can be re-written as:

$$\pi_t = \omega^m \beta \Delta \log m_t + \omega^m \gamma \Delta \tau_t + \varepsilon_t \qquad (7)$$

The first term, $\omega^m \beta \Delta \log m_t$, is the direct effect of changes in import prices on aggregate wholesale price inflation. The second term, $\omega^m \gamma \Delta \tau_t$, is the direct effect of changes in the average tariff rate on aggregate wholesale price inflation. The third term, ε_t, is a residual that captures all other influences on inflation.

The calibration of the model is shown in Table 13.5. The log difference of the wholesale price index, π_t, is from Capie and Collins (1983, p. 32). The share of imported goods in the wholesale price index, $\omega^m = 0.26$, is gathered from the Board of Trade's description of how the index was constructed (*Board of Trade Journal*, 24 January 1935, p. iv). The pass-through coefficients, β and γ, are estimated from equation (2). As we are focusing on annual data, we use the long-run coefficients, $\sum_{k=0}^{4} \beta_k = 0.61$ and $\sum_{k=0}^{4} \gamma_k = 0.79$ respectively. The average log annual difference in the import price of imported goods included in the wholesale price index, $\Delta \log m_t$, is approximated by the log annual difference in the import price index, which is measured as the ratio of imports at current and constant prices (Sefton and Weale,

Table 13.5 *Calibration*

Parameters	Value	Source
ω^m	0.26	*Board of Trade Journal* (24 January 1935, p. iv)
β	0.61	$\sum_{k=0}^{4} \beta_k$ in Table 13.3
γ	0.79	$\sum_{k=0}^{4} \gamma_k$ in Table 13.3

Variables	Source
π_t	Capie and Collins (1983, p. 32)
$\Delta \log m_t$	Sefton and Weale (1995, pp. 184, 188)
$\Delta \tau_t$	Mitchell (1988, pp. 453, 583–4)
ε_t	$\pi_t - \omega^m \beta \Delta m_t - \omega^m \gamma \Delta \tau$

1995, pp. 184, 188). The annual difference in the average tariff rate, $\Delta \tau_t$, is proxied by the annual difference in the ratio of customs revenue to imports (Mitchell, 1988, pp. 453, 583–4).

Figure 13.4 plots the results of the decomposition. A number of interesting results stand out. The first is that cheaper import prices were passed through into lower wholesale prices during the global slump in commodity prices in the early 1930s (Jacks, 2019; Jacks and Stuermer, 2020), which added to deflationary pressure. The downward spiral of global commodity prices meant that despite the departure from the gold standard, which caused a large devaluation, import prices *fell* by 19 per cent in 1931, reducing the aggregate inflation rate by 3.3 percentage points. Import prices decreased by another 8 per cent in 1932, lowering inflation by 1.2 percentage points. This is consistent with Howson's (1975, p. 109) interpretation:

In the case of the 1931 "devaluation", U.K. food and materials wholesale prices rose in the last quarter of 1931 and then declined through the rest of the first post-"devaluation" year, so that by the fourth quarter of 1932 they were back to the pre-depreciation levels. The initial rise in the price of imported manufacturers was also to a certain extent undone by the continuing depression in the exporting countries.

However, when considering the impact of devaluation, the correct counterfactual is what would have happened in the absence of the break from the gold standard. In this case, import prices in sterling

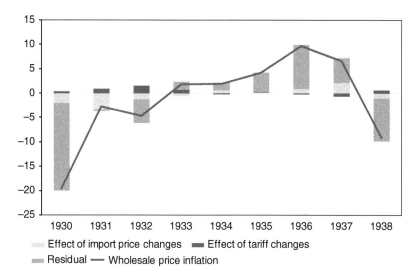

Figure 13.4 Decomposing inflation, 1930–8 (%)

Notes: This figure shows a decomposition of wholesale price inflation based on equation (7).

would have slumped to a greater degree, which would have surely led to an even larger bout of deflation.

The second is that the rise of protection contributed to inflation. Following the implementation of multiple duties, tariff changes were associated with an increase in aggregate inflation of 1.5 percentage points in 1932, which is consistent with Downs (1986, p. 15). The return to inflation in 1933 was partly driven by a further increase in protection, contributing 0.7 percentage points to the inflation rate of 1.8 per cent.

The third result is that when the United States devalued in 1933 (Bernanke and James, 1991), the sterling effective exchange rate appreciated by roughly 5 per cent (Redmond, 1980; Dimsdale, 1981; Andrews, 1987), which was associated with lower import prices of 3.4 per cent and overall deflation of 0.6 percentage points, despite a recovery in world commodity prices (Jacks, 2019; Jacks and Stuermer, 2020).

The final result is what the decomposition implies about other influences on inflation. It shows that the reflation from 1933 onwards is largely due to the residual, suggesting cheap money may well have been the main influence working to push up prices. In both 1931 and 1932, however, the residual is negative, which is suggestive of the deflationary influence of the immediate tightening of monetary policy after the

Table 13.6 *Decomposing inflation variance*

	Share of Variance (%)
Import price changes	3.4
Tariff changes	0.6
Residual	83.4
Covariances	12.6
Wholesale price inflation	100.0

Notes: This table shows a decomposition of the variance of wholesale price inflation based on equation (8) and dividing by *Var(π_t)*.

devaluation in September 1931 and the double dip recession it created in 1932, although our crude decomposition cannot be anything other than suggestive of this. The fact that the residual is correlated with what is currently known about the stance of monetary policy in the period is supportive of the results on import price pass-through from the micro data.

Our simple decomposition can be used to summarize the determinants of inflation volatility in the 1930s. The variance of wholesale price inflation is the sum of the variances and covariances of the terms in equation (7):

$$\text{Var}(\pi_t) = \text{Var}\left(\omega^m \beta \Delta \log m_t\right) + \text{Var}\left(\omega^m \gamma \Delta \tau_t\right) + \text{Var}\left(\varepsilon_t\right)$$
$$+ 2\text{Cov}\left(\omega^m \beta \Delta \log m_t, \omega^m \gamma \Delta \tau_t\right) + 2\text{Cov}\left(\omega^m \beta \Delta \log m_t, \varepsilon_t\right)$$
$$+ 2\text{Cov}\left(\omega^m \gamma \Delta \tau_t, \varepsilon_t\right) \tag{8}$$

The results are shown in Table 13.6. The residual accounted for 83.4 per cent of the total variance, import price changes accounted for 3.4 per cent, tariff changes added 0.6 per cent and the covariance terms explained the remaining 12.6 per cent.

Our extrapolation from the micro to the macro level is, however, subject to a number of significant caveats. On one hand, there could have been a greater impact on aggregate wholesale price inflation for three reasons. One, the wholesale price of domestic goods that used imported inputs may have been affected. Two, the wholesale price of domestic goods that were substitutes for imports or domestic goods that were exported may have changed in response to variations in demand. Downs (1986, pp. 100–1) finds that the price of domestic substitutes rose in line with that of competing imports following the

General Tariff. Three, the share of imported goods included in the wholesale price index is from 1935, after the depreciation and turn to protection. As these events might have lowered imports (de Bromhead et al., 2019b), the share of imported goods in the wholesale price index in the early 1930s may have been higher. These channels, which would strengthen the effect of the exchange rate and tariffs on wholesale prices, are not accounted for in our analysis.

On the other hand, we have only focused on one link in the supply chain, from import prices to wholesale prices. However, there is a link down the chain from exchange rates to import prices and a link up from wholesale prices to consumer or retail prices. If there was less-than-complete pass-through at the other stages in the supply chain, then this would diminish the impact of exchange rates and tariffs on the pound in people's pockets.

V Conclusion

How Britain escaped from deflation and contraction to inflation and expansion during the 1930s is poorly understood. An important strand of literature emphasizes two major macroeconomic shifts: the break from the gold standard in 1931 and the turn to protection in 1932, which led to a drop in the exchange rate and a spike in the average tariff rate. In this chapter, we explore how import prices and tariffs passed-through to wholesale prices. Our results suggest that pass-through was relatively high, albeit incomplete. In terms of import prices – a combination of world export prices and exchange rates – significant pass-through meant that deflation was intensified as devaluation did not overturn the slump of world export prices. In terms of tariffs, high pass-through meant that deflation was weaker than the counterfactual of constant protection. However, given the degree of duties and the share of imported goods in the wholesale price index, the direct effect of tariffs was relatively mild. Overall, our simple model suggests that price fluctuations in the United Kingdom during the 1930s remain largely unexplained.

Beyond the direct effects of pass-through from import prices and tariffs to wholesale prices, there are many interesting avenues for future research. First, there may have been indirect effects of pass-through from import prices and tariffs to wholesale prices. One indirect effect could be on the prices of domestic goods that used imported inputs, that were substitutes for imports or that were exported. Another indirect effect could be on inflation expectations. It could be that devaluation and protection raised expected inflation, which in turn, stimulated actual inflation. Second, pass-through from exchange rates to import prices and from wholesale prices to consumer or retail prices may have been other important channels through which devaluation and protection affected the macroeconomy.

Appendix I: Tariff Barriers

To identify the tariff barriers that applied during the interwar period, we consult Parliamentary Papers (1938, pp. 208–15) that summarized the specific and general tariffs that prevailed in 1914 and subsequent changes up to 1937 and Parliamentary Papers (1938, pp. 8–9, 187–91; 1939, pp. 8–9, 185–90) that outlined changes between 1937 and 1939.

Import Duties Act 1932

Effective from: 1 March 1932
Tariff: 10 per cent
Applies to: Barley from the United States of America, butter from Denmark, eggs from Denmark, flour from the United States of America
Source: Parliamentary Papers (1932, p. 189)

Irish Free State (Special Duties) Act 1932

Effective from: 15 July 1932, 9 November 1932, 13 November 1933, 19 February 1936, 19 May 1938
Tariff: 20 per cent, 30 per cent, 40 per cent, 30 per cent, 0 per cent
Applies to: Bacon from the Irish Free State
Sources: Parliamentary Papers (1939, p. 153), Parliamentary Papers (1938, pp. 157–8), National Institute of Economic and Social Research (1943, pp. 27–8)

Ottawa Agreements Act 1932

Effective from: 17 November 1932
Tariff: 15s. per cwt., 1s./1s. 6d./1s. 9d per 120, 10 per cent, 2s. per qtr.

Applies to: Butter from Denmark, Eggs from Denmark, maize from the Argentine Republic, wheat from the Argentine Republic
Source: Parliamentary Papers (1933, pp. 150–3)

Beef and Veal Customs Duties Act 1937

Effective from: 16 December 1936
Tariff: 3/4*d*. per lb., 2/3*d*. per lb.
Applies to: Beef (chilled) from Argentine Republic, Beef (frozen) from Argentine Republic
Source: Parliamentary Papers (1938, p. 152)

Other

Effective from: 1924
Tariff: 11*s*. 8*d*. per cwt.
Applies to: Cocoa from British West Africa and British West India Islands
Source: Parliamentary Papers (1939, p. 57)

Effective from: 1924
Tariff: 14*s*. per cwt.
Applies to: Coffee from Costa Rica
Source: Parliamentary Papers (1939, p. 59)

Effective from: 20 April 1932, 22 April 1936, 27 April 1938
Tariff: 2*d*. per lb., 4*d*. per lb., 6*d*. per lb.
Applies to: Tea from British India
Sources: Parliamentary Papers (1936, p. 58; 1939, p. 55)

Effective from: 1927, 11 September 1931
Tariff: 8*s*. 10*d*. per lb., 9*s*. 6*d*. per lb.
Applies to: Tobacco from the United States of America
Sources: Parliamentary Papers (1938, p. 209; 1939, p. 77)

Notes

There were other legislative changes, such as to the Key Industry Duty and to the McKenna Duty, Abnormal Importations Duty and Horticultural Products Duty, but these did not apply to the goods in the sample.

The Import Duties Act 1932 laid the ground for an:

"Import Duties Advisory Committee" to advise and assist the Treasury in the discharge of their functions under the Act, and empowered the Committee to recommend (a) additions to the free list, and (b) the imposition of "additional duties," over and above the general ad valorem duty, in respect of any goods which are "either articles of luxury or articles of a kind which are being produced or are likely within a reasonable time to be produced in the United Kingdom in quantities which are substantial in relation to United Kingdom consumption." (Parliamentary Papers, 1932, p. 121)

In order to identify which additional duties applied to the varieties of goods in our sample, we follow Albers (2020) and search the House of Commons Parliamentary Papers for "Import duties recommendations of the Import Duties Advisory Committee" and "Order." However, while hundreds of additional duties were recommended in the 1930s, none were identifiably applicable to the goods in the sample.

When tariff barriers were changed within the month, we apply the barrier that prevailed at the end of the month.

The Ottawa Agreements Act 1932 levied tariffs on eggs proportional to weight. The duty on eggs in shell were: 1s. not exceeding 14 lbs. in weight per great hundred, 1s. 6d. over 14 lbs. but not exceeding 17 lbs. in weight per great hundred and 1s. 9d. over 17lbs. in weight per great hundred. As the *Trade and Navigation Accounts* did not distinguish the quantity and value of eggs in shell by weight, we use the middle tariff of 1s. 6d.

The Ottawa Agreements Act 1932 applied to butter and eggs from Denmark, which were already subject to duty under the Import Duties Act 1932. As the National Institute of Economic and Social Research (1943, p. 47) explains, "General ad valorem duty [Import Duties Act 1932] is not chargeable on goods chargeable under this part [Ottawa Agreements Act 1932]." Therefore, the Ottawa Duties were instead of, not in addition to, the Import Duties.

Appendix II: Unmatched Prices

The wholesale prices of several imported goods were reported in the *Board of Trade Journal* but could not be uniquely matched to the relevant import prices in the *Trade and Navigation Accounts*. The goods and the explanations are:

The *Board of Trade Journal* reported prices for "Iron Ore: Best Bilbao rubio 50 per cent." However, this couldn't be matched to the *Trade and Navigation Accounts* as only values, and not quantities, of iron ore were reported.

The *Board of Trade Journal* reported prices for "Tin: Straits." However, this couldn't be matched to the *Trade and Navigation Accounts* as imported quantities and values of tin from British Malaya were not separately reported.

The *Board of Trade Journal* reported prices for cotton "Yarns: American, 32's twist," "Yarns: American, 42's weft" and "Yarns: Egyptian, 80's weft." However, these couldn't be matched to the *Trade and Navigation Accounts* as imported quantities from the United States of America and Egypt were not separately reported.

The *Board of Trade Journal* reported prices for wool "Noils: Botany, noble combed, 64's average, clear." However, this couldn't be matched to the *Trade and Navigation Accounts* as imported quantities and values from Australia were not separately reported.

The *Board of Trade Journal* reported prices for "Hemp: Raw, Manila fair." However, this couldn't be matched to the *Trade and Navigation Accounts* as imported quantities and values from the Philippine Islands were not separately reported.

The *Board of Trade Journal* reported prices for "Timber: American figured oak." However, this couldn't be matched to the *Trade and Navigation Accounts* as imported quantities from the United States of America were not separately reported.

Appendix III: A Narrative Analysis of Changes to Tariff Barriers

Import Duties Act 1932

Motivation: On the introduction of the bill in the House of Commons on 4 February 1932, the Chancellor of the Exchequer, Neville Chamberlain, summarized the aims of the Import Duties Act:

Before I come to the details of the Government' intended Measures, I think perhaps it would be convenient if I were to try to give to the Committee a very brief summary of the objects at which we are aiming, in order that they may perhaps get a better picture of the general scope and range of our intentions. First of all, we desire to correct the balance of payments by diminishing our imports and stimulating our exports. Then we desire to fortify the finances of the country by raising fresh revenue by methods which will put no undue burden upon any section of the community. We wish to affect an insurance against a rise in the cost of living which might easily follow upon an unchecked depreciation of our currency. We propose, by a system of moderate Protection, scientifically adjusted to the needs of industry and agriculture, to transfer to our own factories and our own fields work which is now done elsewhere, and thereby decrease unemployment in the only satisfactory way in which it can be diminished.[12]

Classification: As the primary aims of the Import Duties Act were to correct a balance of payments deficit and to improve the fiscal position, and because the tariff was relatively general, it is unlikely that changes in the wholesale prices of individual imported goods were a factor in the legislation. As a result, we classify this Act as *exogenous.*

Irish Free State (Special Duties) Act 1932

Motivation: Reflecting on the Irish Free State (Special Duties) Act 1932, the Secretary of State for Dominion Affairs, James Thomas, explained to the House of Commons:

When it was necessary some few months ago to ask Parliament to give us the necessary powers and authority to impose these restrictions, I said, speaking on behalf of the Government, that we would welcome any and every opportunity that might present itself for discussion or negotiation that would bring this unfortunate dispute to an end. [...] Therefore, having entered into that agreement, and the British Government being entitled to a sum of about £5,000,000 per annum, which was due to the British tax-payer, it was, as I have indicated, somewhat of a shock to find the Irish Free State repudiating their obligation.

The Government faced the situation quite frankly. They said, "If there are any just or valid reasons why this money should be withheld, we are prepared to consider them." We examined every aspect of the question; we turned up every agreement that was made; we examined every document; and we came to the conclusion that this money was due. The money was withheld, and Mr. de Valera said quite frankly, without any attempt either to disguise his feelings or his intentions, "So far as we are concerned, we not only intend to withhold this money, but we believe that there is money due

[12] Hansard, HC Deb 4 February 1932, vol 261 c287.

to us." That was a quite clear and straightforward explanation of his side of the case, and, having said that, he did not hesitate to express his views and give his reasons. We examined his side of the case, and we came to the conclusion that he could not justify that position. Therefore, having decided that we were entitled to this sum of money, having budgeted in our own national balance sheet for this money, and having ourselves undertaken the responsibility and liability of paying those who had loaned the money, we said, "We intend to take all the steps that are open to us to obtain what we believe is due to us."

We were then faced with [the] question of the ways and means of doing it, and we came, very reluctantly, I repeat, to the conclusion that the only means open to us was to impose a tax upon certain imports coming into this country. When I introduced the Bill to the House, I explained that it was not intended as a vindictive policy. I explained to the House that, the moment we secured the amounts due to us, we would take off the duty. But I also made it perfectly clear that we would shirk no task, however unpleasant it might be, in obtaining the money. I made that absolutely clear to the House when introducing the Bill. As a result of the Order of the 12th July, we imposed a 20 per cent. duty on live animals for food, animals not for food, butter, eggs, cream, bacon, pork, poultry and game, and other meat of all kinds.[13]

Classification: As the Irish Free State (Special Duties) Act 1932 was a response to a dispute over debt, we classify this Act as *exogenous*.

Ottawa Agreements Act 1932

Motivation: On the third reading of the Ottawa Agreements Bill in the House of Commons on 3 November 1932, the Financial Secretary to the Treasury, Leslie Hore-Belisha, clearly explained the motivation for the legislation:

What does the Bill do? It endeavours to complete the superstructure, the foundations of which were laid in the Import Duties Act. It was necessary to lay these foundations, not in order to satisfy any political nostrums, but in order to meet a practical necessity; in other words, to fulfil the mandate which had been imposed upon us by the electorate – to secure the Budget, and redress the adverse balance of trade.[14]

---

[13] Hansard, HC Deb 8 November 1932, vol 270 c266–8.
[14] Hansard, HC Deb 3 November 1932, vol 269 c1991.

Classification: As the key motivations for the act were to strengthen the trade and budget balances, we classify this legislation as *exogenous*.

Beef and Veal Customs Duties Act 1937

Motivation: The legislation was drafted based on the policy set out by the Minister of Agriculture, Walter Elliot, in the House of Commons on 6 July 1936:

> As the House will be aware, my right hon. Friend the President of the Board of Trade is at present in negotiation with the Argentine Government on the terms of a trade agreement to take the place of that now in force. I cannot forecast the terms of any settlement that may be reached, but I am able to say that in any event Parliament will be invited, immediately after the Summer Recess, to pass legislation providing for the collection of Customs duties on imports of chilled, frozen and other descriptions of beef and veal from foreign countries.
>
> The Government are of opinion that if adequate provision is to be made in one form or another for the needs of the United Kingdom cattle industry, the aggregate financial assistance now given to it must be increased until such time as the conditions prevailing in the industry improve. They propose to seek the authority of Parliament to apply to the assistance of the industry such sums not exceeding £5,000,000 per annum as may from time to time be needed. Parliament will be asked annually to make provision for a sum not exceeding this amount. As an offset to this liability, the Exchequer will benefit to the extent of the revenue from the import duties to which I have referred.[15]

Classification: The legislation levied a tariff on non-Empire meat to finance a subsidy to the British livestock industry, which was subject to intense competition from overseas. As a result, we classify this Act as *endogenous*.

Other

Tea 1932, 1936 and 1938

Motivation: In the budget of 1932 the Chancellor of the Exchequer, Neville Chamberlain, re-imposed the tariff on tea, explaining:

---

[15] Hansard, HC Deb 6 July 1936, vol 314 c842.

I propose to revive the duty upon foreign tea at the old rate, but the old preference of two-thirds of a penny per lb. seems to me to be totally inadequate to the present circumstances, and I propose to increase that to 50 per cent. making the duty on Empire tea 2*d*. a lb. This new preference will be the same as the preference originally was in the first years after the introduction of the system of preference, and it is notable that, whilst the preference was subsequently reduced in 1922 to 1⅓ pence, and then again in 1924 to two-thirds of a penny, the proportion of Empire tea to the total consumption of the country fell, first from 90 per cent. to 84 per cent., and since the preference was abolished with the removal of the duty it has gone down to 81 per cent. I am hoping that with a 50 per cent. preference we shall see the proportion of Empire tea regain its former figure in the process of time, and that meanwhile some help may be afforded to the hard-pressed tea industries of India and Ceylon.[16]

The principal objective of the Chancellor in the budget of 1936 was to raise revenue to finance the additional costs of rearmament. On the increase in tea duty, Chamberlain simply stated that:

I propose, also, to raise the duty on tea by 2*d*. a pound. That increase in the tea duty, which will operate as from tomorrow, will apply both to Empire and to foreign tea, thus preserving the existing preferential margin of 2*d*. a pound. I anticipate that the increased duty will give me this year £3,500,000.[17]

Under similar pressures in 1938, Chamberlain's successor, John Simon, also turned to the Tea Duty to raise revenue:

I still have nearly £3,000,000 to find and a small contribution drawn from practically every home in the land will produce what is needed. I propose to raise the duty on all tea, Empire and foreign, by 2*d*. per pound. This will maintain intact the existing margin of preference of 2*d*. per pound and it is estimated that the extra yield this year will be £2,750,000, and in a full year £3,250,000. I well understand that even an extra halfpenny per week is a material and appreciable addition to the expenses of those with the smallest incomes. Why do I do it? I believe that there is a willingness and even a pride in the humblest homes to take a share in this rearmament outlay, for defending those homes from peril, just as much as in the homes of more comfortable and wealthy people.[18]

---

[16] Hansard, HC Deb 19 April 1932, vol 264 c1437.
[17] Hansard, HC Deb 21 April 1936, vol 311 c56.
[18] Hansard, HC Deb 26 April 1938, vol 335 c66.

Classification: As the main reasons for raising the duty on tea were to raise the share of tea from the British Empire and to finance rearmament, we classify these tariff changes as *exogenous*.

Tobacco 1931

Motivation: Phillip Snowden summarised the grave economic situation in the second budget of 1931:

It is undoubtedly a fact that nationally we have, for some time past, been living beyond our means, and living to a considerable extent upon our capital. The trade depression of the last 10 years has reduced the yield of taxes and at the same time increased expenditure. Seven years ago the Unemployment Insurance Fund was paying its way. It was paying off debt. This year it is costing the Exchequer about £100,000,000. The national income has been falling rapidly. There are something like 3,000,000 persons, one-time producers, now inactive. Profits, upon which national revenue must largely depend, have fallen 20 per cent during the last two years, and in many industries wages are being paid out of capital. Now this is the problem that I have to solve, and it can be solved only in two ways, either by reducing expenditure or by increasing taxation – or by a combination of both. We have been under the delusion during the last few years, in these times of unparalleled depression, that we can maintain the expenditure of prosperous times. Our total national and local taxation is now very nearly one-third of the total national income. Now whatever measures you may take to restore solvency in our national finances, the country must face up to the position, and I am going to do it this afternoon.[19]

One of the goods to receive an increase in taxation was tobacco. The Chancellor explained:

I have also selected tobacco as a suitable article to bear an increased duty in the present circumstances, and I propose that as from tomorrow the Customs Duty on imported leaf, that is the unmanufactured form of tobacco, shall be raised from 8s. 10d. per lb. to 9s. 6d. per lb. That is an increase of 8d. The rates of duty on other forms of tobacco will be increased in the same proportion. I estimate this addition will yield £4,000,000 in a full year, and £2,100,000 this year. I have no reason to anticipate that the whole of this increase will be passed on to the consumer.[20]

[19] Hansard, HC Deb 10 September 1931, vol 256 c298.
[20] Hansard, HC Deb 10 September 1931, vol 256 c308.

Classification: As the increase in tobacco duty was not influenced by changes in the wholesale price of tobacco but as a means of raising revenue, we classify this tariff change as *exogenous.*

References

Albers, Thilo N. H. 2020. "Currency Devaluations and Beggar-my-neighbour Penalties: Evidence from the 1930s." *Economic History Review* 73 (1): 233–57.

Andrews, B. P. A. 1987. "Exchange Rate Appreciation, Competitiveness and Export Performance: The UK Experience in the Inter-war Period." PhD dissertation, University of Oxford.

Bernanke, Ben, and Harold James. 1991. "The Gold Standard, Deflation, and Financial Crisis in the Great Depression: An International Comparison." In *Financial Markets and Financial Crises*, edited by R. Glenn Hubbard, 33–68. Chicago: University of Chicago Press.

Board of Trade Journal. *Various Dates.* London: H. M. Stationery Office.

Booth, Alan. 1987. "Britain in the 1930s: A Managed Economy?" *Economic History Review* 40 (4): 499–522.

Boneva, Lena, James Cloyne, Martin Weale, and Tomasz Wieladek. 2016. "The Effect of Unconventional Monetary Policy on Inflation Expectations: Evidence from Firms in the United Kingdom." *International Journal of Central Banking* 12 (3): 161–95.

Breinlich, Holger, Elsa Leromain, Dennis Novy, and Thomas Sampson. 2019. "Exchange Rates and Consumer Prices: Evidence from Brexit." CEPR Discussion Paper No. 14176.

Broadberry, S. N. 1986. *The British Economy Between the Wars: A Macroeconomic Survey.* Oxford: Basil Blackwell.

Broadberry, Stephen, Jagjit S. Chadha, Jason Lennard, and Ryland Thomas. Forthcoming. "Dating Business Cycles in the United Kingdom, 1700–2000." *Economic History Review.*

Capie, Forrest. 1981. "Shaping the British Tariff Structure in the 1930s." *Explorations in Economic History* 18 (2): 155–73.

Capie, Forrest, and Alan Webber. 2010. *A Monetary History of the United Kingdom, 1870–1982: Data, Sources and Methods.* Abingdon: Routledge.

Capie, Forrest, and Michael Collins. 1983. *The Inter-war British Economy: A Statistical Abstract.* Manchester: Manchester University Press.

Cloyne, James. 2013. "Discretionary Tax Changes and the Macroeconomy: New Narrative Evidence from the United Kingdom." *American Economic Review* 103 (4): 1507–28.

Cloyne, James, and Patrick Hürtgen. 2016. "The Macroeconomic Effects of Monetary Policy: A New Measure for the United Kingdom." *American Economic Journal: Macroeconomics* 8 (4): 75–102.

Corsetti, Giancarlo, Luca Dedola, and Sylvain Leduc. 2008. "High Exchange-rate Volatility and Low Pass-through." *Journal of Monetary Economics* 55 (6): 1133–28.

Crafts, Nicholas. 2013. "Returning to Growth: Policy Lessons from History." *Fiscal Studies* 34 (2): 255–82.

Crafts, Nicholas, and Peter Fearon. 2013. "Depression and Recovery in the 1930s: An Overview." In *The Great Depression of the 1930s: Lessons for Today*, edited by Nicholas Crafts and Peter Fearon, 1–44. Oxford: Oxford University Press.

Crafts, Nicholas, and Terence C. Mills. 2013. "Rearmament to the Rescue? New Estimates of the Impact of 'Keynesian' Policies in 1930s' Britain." *Journal of Economic History* 73 (4): 1077–104.

Crafts, Nicholas, and Terence C. Mills. 2015. "Self-defeating Austerity? Evidence from 1930s' Britain." *European Review of Economic History* 19 (2): 109–27.

de Bromhead, Alan, Alan Fernihough, Markus Lampe, and Kevin Hjortshøj O'Rourke. 2019a. "When Britain Turned Inward: The Impact of Interwar British Protection." *American Economic Review* 109 (2): 325–52.

de Bromhead, Alan, Alan Fernihough, Markus Lampe, and Kevin Hjortshøj O'Rourke. 2019b. "The Anatomy of a Trade Collapse: The UK, 1929–1933." *European Review of Economic History* 23 (2): 123–44.

Dimsdale, Nicholas. 1981. "British Monetary Policy and the Exchange Rate, 1920–1938." *Oxford Economic Papers* 33: 306–49.

Downs, André. 1986. "General Import Restrictions and the Behaviour of Domestic Prices and Wages: The Case of the British General Tariff of 1932." PhD dissertation, London School of Economics.

Eichengreen, Barry. 2004. "The British Economy Between the Wars." In *The Cambridge Economic History of Modern Britain: Volume II: Economic Maturity, 1860–1939*, edited by Roderick Floud and Paul Johnson, 314–43. Cambridge: Cambridge University Press.

Esteves, Rui, Seán Kenny, and Jason Lennard. 2021. "The Aftermath of Sovereign Debt Crises: A Narrative Approach." CEPR Discussion Paper No. 16166.

Feenstra, Robert C. 1989. "Symmetric Pass-through of Tariffs and Exchange Rates under Imperfect Competition: An Empirical Test." *Journal of International Economics* 27 (1–2): 25–45.

Feinstein, C. H. 1972. *National Income, Expenditure and Output of the United Kingdom 1855–1965*. Cambridge: Cambridge University Press.

Forbes, Kristin, Ida Hjortsoe, and Tsvetelina Nenova. 2017. "Shocks versus Structure: Explaining Differences in Exchange Rate Pass-through across Countries and Time." Bank of England External MPC Unit Discussion Paper No. 50.

Goldberg, Pinelopi Koujianou, and Michael M. Knetter. 1997. "Goods Prices and Exchange Rates: What Have We Learned?" *Journal of Economic Literature* 35 (3): 1243–72.

Gopinath, Gita, Oleg Itskhoki, and Roberto Rigobon. 2010. "Currency Choice and Exchange Rate Pass-Through." *American Economic Review* 100 (1): 304–36.

Hansard (The Official Report). Various dates. UK Parliament.

Hellerstein, Rebecca. 2008. "Who Bears the Cost of a Change in the Exchange Rate? Pass-through Accounting for the Case of Beer." *Journal of International Economics* 76 (1): 14–32.

Howson, Susan. 1975. *Domestic Monetary Management in Britain, 1919–38*. Cambridge: Cambridge University Press.

Irwin, Douglas A. 1998. "Change in US Tariffs: The Role of Import Prices and Commercial Policies." *American Economic Review* 88 (4): 1015–26.

Jacks, David S. 2019. "From Boom to Bust: A Typology of Real Commodity Prices in the Long Run." *Cliometrica* 13 (2): 201–20.

Jacks, David S., and Martin Stuermer. 2020. "What Drives Commodity Price Booms and Busts?" *Energy Economics* 85: 1–8.

Jalil, Andrew J. 2015. "A New History of Banking Panics in the United States, 1825–1929: Construction and Implications." *American Economic Journal: Macroeconomics* 7 (3): 295–330.

Kenny, Seán, Jason Lennard, and John Turner. 2021. "The Macroeconomic Effects of Banking Crises: Evidence from the United Kingdom, 1750–1938." *Explorations in Economic History* 79.

Keynes, John Maynard. 1931. *Essays in Persuasion*. London: Macmillan and Co.

Lennard, Jason. 2018. "Did Monetary Policy Matter? Narrative Evidence from the Classical Gold Standard." *Explorations in Economic History* 68 (1): 16–36.

Mills, Geofrey, and Hugh Rockoff. 1987. "Compliance with Price Controls in the United States and the United Kingdom During World War II." *Journal of Economic History* 47 (1): 197–213.

Mitchell, B. R. 1988. *British Historical Statistics*. Cambridge: Cambridge University Press.

Moggridge, D. E. 1972. *British Monetary Policy, 1924–1931: The Norman Conquest of $4.86*. Cambridge. Cambridge University Press.

Nakamura, Emi, and Dawit Zerom. 2010. "Accounting for Incomplete Pass-Through." *Review of Economic Studies* 77 (3): 1192–230.

National Institute of Economic and Social Research. 1943. *Trade Regulations and Commercial Policy of the United Kingdom*. Cambridge: Cambridge University Press.

Parliamentary Papers. 1930. *Accounts Relating to Trade and Navigation of the United Kingdom for Each Month during the Year 1930.* London: H. M. Stationery Office.

Parliamentary Papers. 1931. *Accounts Relating to Trade and Navigation of the United Kingdom for Each Month during the Year 1931.* London: H. M. Stationery Office.

Parliamentary Papers. 1932a. *Accounts Relating to Trade and Navigation of the United Kingdom for Each Month during the Year 1932.* London: H. M. Stationery Office.

Parliamentary Papers. 1932b. *Twenty-Third Report of the Commissioners of His Majesty's Customs and Excise for the Year Ended 31st March 1932.* London: H. M. Stationery Office.

Parliamentary Papers. 1933a. *Accounts Relating to Trade and Navigation of the United Kingdom for Each Month during the Year 1933.* London: H. M. Stationery Office.

Parliamentary Papers. 1933b. *Twenty-Fourth Report of the Commissioners of His Majesty's Customs and Excise for the Year Ended 31st March 1933.* London: H. M. Stationery Office.

Parliamentary Papers. 1934. *Accounts Relating to Trade and Navigation of the United Kingdom for Each Month during the Year 1934.* London: H. M. Stationery Office.

Parliamentary Papers. 1935. *Accounts Relating to Trade and Navigation of the United Kingdom for Each Month during the Year 1935.* London: H. M. Stationery Office.

Parliamentary Papers. 1936a. *Accounts Relating to Trade and Navigation of the United Kingdom for Each Month during the Year 1936.* London: H. M. Stationery Office.

Parliamentary Papers. 1936b. *Twenty-Seventh Report of the Commissioners of His Majesty's Customs and Excise for the Year Ended 31st March 1936.* London: H. M. Stationery Office.

Parliamentary Papers. 1937. *Accounts Relating to Trade and Navigation of the United Kingdom for Each Month during the Year 1937.* London: H. M. Stationery Office.

Parliamentary Papers. 1938a. *Accounts Relating to Trade and Navigation of the United Kingdom for Each Month during the Year 1938.* London: H. M. Stationery Office.

Parliamentary Papers. 1938b. *Twenty-Ninth Report of the Commissioners of His Majesty's Customs and Excise for the Year Ended 31st March 1938.* London: H. M. Stationery Office.

Parliamentary Papers. 1939. *Thirtieth Report of the Commissioners of His Majesty's Customs and Excise for the Year Ended 31st March 1939.* London: H. M. Stationery Office.

Ramey, Valerie A. 2011. "Identifying Government Spending Shocks: It's all in the Timing." *Quarterly Journal of Economics* 126 (1): 1–50.

Ramey, Valerie A. 2016. "Macroeconomic Shocks and Their Propagation." In *Handbook of Macroeconomics*, Vol. 2A, edited by John B. Taylor and Harold Uhlig, 71–162. Amsterdam: North-Holland.

Ramey, Valerie A., and Sarah Zubairy. 2018. "Government Spending Multipliers in Good Times and in Bad: Evidence from U.S. Historical Data." *Journal of Political Economy* 162 (2): 850–901.

Redmond, John. 1980. "An Indicator of the Effective Exchange Rate of the Pound in the Nineteen-Thirties." *Economic History Review* 33 (1): 83–91.

Romer, Christina D., and David H. Romer. 2004. "A New Measure of Monetary Shocks: Derivation and Implications." *American Economic Review* 94 (4): 1055–84.

Romer, Christina D., and David H. Romer. 2010. "The Macroeconomic Effects of Tax Changes: Estimates Based on a New Measure of Fiscal Shocks." *American Economic Review* 100 (3): 763–801.

Savoie-Chabot, Laurence, and Mikael Khan. 2015. "Exchange Rate Pass-Through to Consumer Prices: Theory and Recent Evidence." Bank of Canada Discussion Paper No. 2015–9.

Sefton, James, and Martin Weale. 1995. *Reconciliation of National Income and Expenditure. Balanced Estimates of National Income for the United Kingdom, 1920–1990*. Cambridge: Cambridge University Press.

Worswick, G. D. N. 1984. "The Sources of Recovery in UK in the 1930s." *National Institute Economic Review* 110: 85–93.

14 | "Unusual, Unstable, Complicated, Unreliable and Temporary": Reinterpreting the Ebb and Flow of Globalization

MICHAEL D. BORDO AND CATHERINE R. SCHENK[1]

The power to become habituated to his surroundings is a marked characteristic of mankind. Very few of us realize with conviction the intensely unusual, unstable, complicated, unreliable, temporary nature of the economic organization by which Western Europe has lived for the last half century. We assume some of the most peculiar and temporary of our late advantages as natural, permanent, and to be depended on, and we lay our plans accordingly. (Keynes 1919)

Introduction

The opening sentences of Keynes' influential 1919 *cri de coeur*, *The Economic Consequences of the Peace*, anticipated the collapse of the structures of the international economy that had prevailed from the later nineteenth century. Unprecedented flows of people, goods and capital to a wide geographical area during the first era of globalization had created expectations of growth and emphasized the importance of open international economic relations for creating that growth and opportunity. Keynes admonished the short-sighted assumption that these years of relative peace and economic prosperity for many was a permanent norm, interrupted only briefly by the Great War. He foresaw in the Versailles Treaty the suspension of globalization as more prolonged or even perhaps permanent. Keynes was writing at the defining moment of the twentieth century, in the middle of what came to be viewed by some as a thirty-year war. The diplomatic

---

[1] For helpful comments we thank Harold James, Chris Meissner and Robert N. McCauley.

failures, lapses in leadership and promotion of narrow interests and vision outlined by Keynes in *Economic Consequences of the Peace* underpinned his predictions of a backlash of economic nationalism, trade protectionism and recession.

This chapter revisits the turning points in the evolution of the global economic system in the century since 1919 by focusing on the evolution of the international monetary system and policy cooperation/ coordination. While there is but a fleeting reference to the international monetary system in Keynes' 1919 treatise, this focus is justified by how Keynes interacted with the ensuing efforts to restore the pre-war system that he criticized in *Economic Consequences of the Peace*. This includes his 1925 sequel, *The Economic Consequences of Mr. Churchill*, and his direct role in the design of the post-1945 international monetary system. We identify three disruptions and examine how each prompted changes in the underlying ideology about how the international monetary system should be organized. Each turning point was characterized by different forms of and motivations for cooperation, how rules (either implicit or explicit) were designed and implemented, and the crucial importance of the historical context. Finally, the chapter explores how dominant interpretations of the past shaped policy reactions in the present and concludes with some lessons for today.

Turning Point I: World War I and the End of the First Era of Globalization

Keynes started *The Economic Consequences of the Peace* with a description of how the world before 1914 marked the apogee of the first era of globalization.

What an extraordinary episode... the internationalization of which was nearly complete in practice ... The inhabitant of London could order by telephone, sipping his morning tea in bed, the various products of the whole earth, in such quantity as he might see fit, and reasonably expect their early delivery upon his doorstep; he could at the same moment and by the same means adventure his wealth in the natural resources and new enterprises of any quarter of the world, and share, without exertion or even trouble, in their respective fruits and advantages; ... But, most important of all, he regarded this state of affairs as normal, certain, and permanent, except in the direction of further improvement, and any deviation from it as aberrant, scandalous, and avoidable. (pages 4–5)

In retrospect, Keynes' description of the gold standard era as "unusual, unstable, complicated, unreliable and temporary" seems remarkably perceptive. The system worked best for countries (like Britain) at its core, and it was supported by the geographic breadth of the British empire and by the persistence of Britain's open trade policy despite rising protectionism in Europe and the North America. Already by the end of the nineteenth century restrictions on trade and migration were undermining the key sources of economic prosperity of the "golden age" of the first globalization. This retreat from globalization was accompanied by rising political and strategic hostility in Europe that brought an abrupt end to this period of relative global prosperity. In 1914 the first era of globalization crashed to a close with World War I and then the Great Depression, but many of the seeds of its destruction were planted beforehand. In turn, globalization may have contributed to the wave of nationalism that led to World War I and even the second part of the Thirty Years war (Temin 1989). O'Rourke and Williamson (1999) argued that the process of globalization planted the seeds of its own destruction (see also James 2001) through the convergence of prices and wages that challenged incumbents.

By the end of the century, the era of mass migration gave way to a wave of restrictions on the movement of people. The May 1882 US Chinese Exclusion Act was the culmination of decades of social and political lobbying against Chinese immigrants, in particular. Soon afterwards, the US Immigration Act of August 1882 introduced the concept of "inadmissible aliens" who were deemed to undermine the living standards of previous, mainly white, settlers. At the end of 1901, Australia, with a much shorter history of immigration than the United States, passed its own Immigration Restriction Act aimed at stopping non-white immigration.[2] The political and social limits to globalization through migration had therefore already been reached in the decades before 1914. The most potent symbol of the era of mass migration, the Statue of Liberty in New York harbour, was finally completed in 1886, four years after the immigration backlash made it into the US law book. Emma Lazarus' poem referring to the "huddled masses" coming to the United States (written in 1886 *after* the Immigration Act) was added in 1901. In many ways the Statue of

---

[2] Other countries introduced similar restrictions after 1919.

Liberty marked a symbolic end of an era rather than a celebration of the enduring spirit of migration building the American state.

Financial globalization also experienced a backlash. Open capital accounts were associated with private investment booms and busts leading to financial crises (both currency and banking crises). Capital flowed from the capital-rich countries of Western Europe to the capital scarce countries across the Atlantic in North and South America or to former colonies, mainly in Australasia or Eastern Europe. But many lacked the institutional development to fully convert the new funds into productive investments and hence the capital inflow fuelled asset price booms (Bordo and Meissner 2017). In the absence of central banks (e.g., in the United States, Canada, Australia) or in the case of countries which had them but were unable to adhere to the gold standard (in Southern Europe, Latin America) currency crises and banking panics could lead to severe economic distress and sovereign debt crises. Moreover, under the classical gold standard, the world price level went through long swings of deflation and inflation reflecting the growth of the real economy relative to the glacially slow growing world gold stock. Gold shortages (deflation) would ultimately, via the Commodity Theory of Money, lead to technical innovation in gold mining and new discoveries (Bordo 1981; Rockoff 1984). But the timing of these events was adventitious (Keynes 1925) rather than synchronized with the needs of the global economy. In the United States and elsewhere the Great Deflation of 1873 to 1896 led to a populist outcry against gold and in favour of free silver and bimetallism (Eichengreen 2018).

The first era of globalization and the gold standard that underpinned it were clearly complex and unstable and already appeared temporary to Keynes by 1919. But this was a view that did not gain traction among policymakers. They sought to return to the relatively rapid growth of the mid-late nineteenth century by recreating the stable exchange rates and gold anchor after 1919. There was less public or political enthusiasm, however, for the free trade, open capital markets and migration that had been fundamental to the early successes of this era.

The eruption of the First World War in 1914 confirmed the end of the first era of globalization. Virtually all countries left the gold standard, de jure or de facto, once Britain suspended convertibility of sterling to gold after the 1914 financial crisis (Roberts 2013). The British and other belligerents sold most of their outstanding investments in the United States (and other emerging countries) to pay for the war (Silber

2007). Both exchange controls and capital controls were widely imposed (Eichengreen 1992). Free trade turned into managed trade, and tariffs were raised further (e.g., the Fordney McCumber Act in the US in 1922). Free long-distance migration all but ceased. Moreover, the balance of economic power was permanently shifted from the UK to the United States as leading global creditor, which posed huge political challenges for an American population distant from the hostilities that had ravaged Europe and living in a country built on a sense of individual and national ambition above internationalism. As Keynes emphasized, the potential to restore what appeared to be "normal" conditions of open trade and payments after the war was further hampered by the way the war was financed through the accumulation of debt among allied nations that depended on reparations from the defeated powers to be repaid.

The interwar gold standard was a deliberately constructed system arising from a series of international congresses after 1919 (Lausanne in 1920, Genoa in 1922, Tripartite Agreement of 1936). The need for cooperation was increasingly recognized as the German economy floun-dered, the Bolshevik Revolution brought a violent end to the Russian Empire and war debts strained the global financial system. The ambi-tious League of Nations provided a bureaucratic locus for gathering intelligence, identifying problems and seeking cooperative solutions, but the lack of engagement by the US administration was a major handicap to its effectiveness in promoting international cooperation despite the passionate efforts of many bureaucrats (Clavin 2013). Schisms within the League led to the creation of the Bank for International Settlements in 1931 as an alternative venue for European central bank cooperation (Toniolo 2005). Nevertheless, there were some lasting legacies, includ-ing new central banks in a range of emerging market economies in South America and Australasia, which were set up based on the British (Niemeier) or US (Kemmerer) models to help to manage the interna-tional monetary system (Singleton 2011). Bureaucrats and researchers also formed a cohort that re-emerged in the post-1945 era to rebuild international economic relations (e.g., Jean Monnet, Jacques Pollak, Robert Triffin) and left an intellectual legacy that Pauly (1996) argued foreshadowed the Bretton Woods institutions.

Holding large gold reserves was out of reach for most countries. In the pre-war period, this challenge had been partly overcome by the use of sterling as the dominant global currency and trust in the ability of the Bank of England to sustain the gold value of the pound. After

1919, this could no longer be assumed. The interwar system formally accepted the use of sterling and the dollar (and, to a lesser extent, the franc) as foreign exchange reserves in a gold exchange standard, but faith in the ability of the Bank of England to protect the parity was ephemeral. The new US Federal Reserve made a short-lived effort to promote the dollar as the key international currency (Eichengreen and Flandreau 2009) after successfully returning to the gold standard in 1919 at the pre-war parity, but sterling remained the main currency of settlement and unit of account for international trade.

In the end, the interwar gold exchange standard also proved "unstable, temporary and unreliable". Nominal exchange rate pegs, that did not reflect underlying economic realities or relative price competitiveness, became caught in the turmoil of the tangle of war debts and reparations. Thus, France returned to gold at an undervalued parity with a central bank law that sterilized gold flows (Moure 1996), while Britain returned to sterling at a rate that Keynes considered damagingly overvalued (Keynes 1925). The weakness of the British economy (and therefore sterling) and the inability to resolve the war debts-reparations tangle created by the Treaty of Versailles brought the unstable and fragile system crashing down in 1931. This time even Britain abandoned free trade and the world lurched into economic nationalism. For the British, the concept of nationalism extended to the Empire, which sustained global trade for many developing economies through imperial preference. But the depression in agricultural prices and protectionism elsewhere created a downward spiral of trade that left no country untouched (Kindleberger 1975; Albers 2020; de Bromhead et al. 2019). The unresolved peace settlement of 1919 was exposed, as economic nationalism fed into political populism and renewed conflict in 1939. Within months of the onset of World War II, the next phase of international economic cooperation was underway in bilateral negotiations between Britain and the United States over the next post-war settlement.

The Second Turning Point: World War II and the Bretton Woods System

The complex multilateral structures of the League of Nations and the technocratic turn in economic diplomacy found their echoes in the planning for a post-war international economic system. Both the

United States and UK sought to establish more powerful collective institutions that would have the financial as well as bureaucratic resources to govern a refreshed multilateral global economy. By this time, the predictions in Keynes' 1919 treatise seemed to have come true, except for his claim that Britain would remain immune and separate from the devastating impact on the European continent (p. xx). The prevalence of unemployment, political extremism and nationalism that characterized the 1930s was the main target for post-war planners (Arndt 1944). In West European states these imperatives led to elaborate welfare states that required substantial public funding and taxation that strengthened the nation state (Milward 1999). On both sides of the Atlantic there was also a commitment to integrate Germany back into the European economy to ensure a more sustained recovery for both Germany and its European trading partners.

What followed was a high point of international economic cooperation designed to overcome the failures of the inter-war period. The Cold War circumscribed the extent of this cooperation, but also made it more urgent among the capitalist western powers, first as a defence against creeping communism and then later as evidence of the success of the capitalist system vis-à-vis the communist system of the Eastern Bloc. As in the classic gold standard era, most participants of the international monetary system from 1950 to 1970 experienced rising incomes, economic growth and a rapid increase in international trade, particularly in manufactures. But, like Keynes' verdict on the nineteenth-century globalization, this era of relative exchange rate stability also proved "unusual, unstable, complicated, unreliable and temporary". These characteristics arose from flaws in the structure of the international monetary system which was designed for an imagined restoration of the global order that did not in the end emerge after 1945.

There were three main points of general consensus among planners for the post-war. First, ambitious plans were made for a carefully managed global monetary system by planners who still assumed that stable exchange rates for convertible currencies were needed to allow the maximum gains from multilateral trade. The second area of consensus was in the faith in freer trade to promote growth and employment as well as sustaining a more lasting peace.[3] Finally,

---

[3] Although Keynes (1933) had been quite protectionist.

after the financial crises of the 1930s there was distrust of short-term capital flows as destabilizing influences that would undermine stable exchange rates. These areas of consensus were recognized in particular by Keynes and reflected in his early writings on the organization of the international monetary system such as *The Economic Consequences of Mr. Churchill* (1925).

The design of the Bretton Woods system was heavily influenced by interpretations of the causes of the Great Depression of the 1930s (Gardner 1956; Steil 2013). The main lessons for the international monetary system were that unstable exchange rates were damaging, competitive devaluations and "hot money" had to be prevented, and the system should be freed from the depressive effect of "Golden Fetters" (Nurkse 1944; Eichengreen 1992; Albers 2020).

The lessons from Versailles meant that even before the United States joined the Second World War, the WWI system of war debts was avoided between the United States and the Allied powers as part of the expression of common commitment to freer trade after the war. Thus the avoidance of debts in return for support from the United States was enshrined in formal agreements with Britain (Atlantic Charter 1941; Mutual Aid Agreement 1942). Nevertheless, British war debts to the Empire and Commonwealth still featured as defining elements in the post-war settlement since they increased Britain's overseas liabilities well beyond their ability to repay them in foreign exchange or to supply goods to redeem them through trade (Pressnell 1987; Schenk 2010;). These so-called Sterling Balances became a symbol of the decline of Britain's post-war international economic position and the focus of multilateral cooperation after the war.

The design of the international system aimed to ensure the freer flow of goods while using exchange controls to prevent "hot money" movements in short-term capital. It was also crucial that Europe was united economically (if not politically) through freer trade. The United States did not advocate free trade, but a "freer" trade regime that eliminated discrimination (against the United States) and bilateralism. The British imperial preference system was gradually eroded in the 1950s, setting the stage for constitutional decolonization in the decade that followed (Schenk 2010). Meanwhile, Keynes' ideas of fiscal dominance and demand management policies fitted well with the moral and political imperative of Western governments to deliver welfare states, full employment and prosperity to their populations.

The contrast between the British (Keynes) and American (White) plans for the post-war institutional structure emphasizes each nation's priorities, but they also had many similarities (Gardner 1956; Horsefield 1969; Pressnell 1987). Among the most fundamental areas of agreement was that the international monetary system required a formalized, inclusive institutional structure that would reflect the US predominance as the world's largest creditor. Despite the failure of the League of Nations to sustain international economic cooperation in the interwar period, the faith in formal multilateral economic institutions was imbedded in the wartime planning for peace. Both plans aimed to avoid the economic nationalism that had plagued the 1930s by providing short-term finance for short-term balance-of-payments problems. Keynes devised a much larger pool of liquidity with more symmetric treatment of surplus and deficit countries to benefit countries like the UK, which would emerge from the war substantially weakened. Harry D. White, in contrast, proposed a more limited contributory fund with the United States dominating its governance as the world's largest creditor and able to apply pressure on deficit countries to adjust their domestic economies. Both plans also had mechanisms to deal with the debts to the Empire and Commonwealth that the UK had built up during the war, although in the end both governments insisted that the sterling balances be treated separately (Schenk 2010: 40–42). Ultimately White's vision dominated as a more politically manageable solution, especially for an American population exhausted and frustrated by the European wars (Steil 2013).

The framework was hammered out in a series of meetings that increased in scope between 1942 and 1944. This triumph of economic diplomacy ultimately brought representatives of forty-four countries together at Bretton Woods New Hampshire in July 1944. The process was in stark contrast to the 1919 economic settlement described by Keynes, which took place *after* the cessation of hostilities, where only four major powers were represented, the Americans were underprepared and the details were delegated to a reparations commission that took two more years to set the amount, by which time the reparations were inextricably intertwined with the ability of the victorious powers to repay war debts. It was also in stark contrast to the restoration of the interwar gold exchange standard, which (despite several summits) lapsed into ad hoc, politically inspired choices of currency pegs to gold. A key goal of the post-war period was therefore to create a framework for cooperation and coordination underpinned by credible rules to ensure a lasting and prosperous peace (Giovannini 1993).

Nevertheless, the system designed at Bretton Woods never operated as planned (Gardner 1956). The task of reconstruction after the war was delegated to an International Bank for Reconstruction and Development. This had the advantage of insulating the key international monetary institution, the International Monetary Fund (IMF) from the burdens of post-war reconstruction but also left the financing of this crucial transition period largely in limbo. There was an open and rolling deadline for countries to adhere to the convertibility at pegged exchange rates, which was required to restore multilateral trade and payments. This ended up lasting for twelve years in the case of Western Europe. Thirdly, the IMF was the framework for the multilateral payments system, designed to support the more liberal, non-discriminatory trade system announced in the 1941 Atlantic Charter. But completion of the International Trade Organisation (ITO) foundered on the waning enthusiasm for international compromise by 1946 and the realities of the challenges of post-war national recovery. Unlike the monetary institutions of Bretton Woods, the ITO was never ratified.

The 1946 Anglo-American Loan Agreement was Keynes' final intervention in global political economy. The negotiations in Washington exhausted him, and the outcome was a disappointment. In echoes of his verdict on Versailles, in May 1945 Keynes identified three options for Britain after the war: "Starvation Corner", "Temptation" or "Justice". The first would see Britain retreat into austerity and repudiate its debts; the second would add to the debt by borrowing too heavily from the United States. "Justice" would entail cancelling a quarter of Britain's wartime debt, funding half, a grant from the United States to reimburse British expenditure before the Lend-Lease Act had become operable and a smaller US loan on generous terms (Pressnell 1987). Neither the Bank of England nor the UK Labour government wanted publicly to be seen to be considering repudiating its wartime debts, while the Americans sought some cancellation as a condition of the loan. Keynes continued to seek a "Justice" solution, albeit reduced in scale, including cancelling a proportion of Britain's wartime debt in return for making sterling more convertible and a large US loan, but he did not find support from London

(Skidelsky 2000; Schenk 2010: 47–53). After three months of negotiations led by Keynes, Sir Edward Bridges arrived in Washington from London to take over. A week later, Britain had fallen into "Temptation" with a large loan, no settlement of war debts and a commitment to introduce convertibility on current account within a year.

Keynes died just over four months later from a heart attack at his home in Sussex aged 63. He did not live to see the run on the pound in July–August 1947 that prompted the reintroduction of exchange controls after only a few weeks. The lesson drawn across Western Europe from the sterling crisis of 1947 was that the convertibility required to adhere to the core articles of the Fund had to be postponed indefinitely. Instead, regional solutions like the European Payments Union and the Sterling Area facilitated multilateral payments and the rapid liberalization of trade. While this ad hoc system did not align fully with the vision of Bretton Woods, it did provide the foundations for freer trade for Western Europe, the British Empire and Commonwealth and North America.

There followed two decades of sustained economic growth, driven by the reduction in quotas and tariffs on international trade, the spread of technological innovation from the United States, and Japanese and European technological catching up to the United States. With the help of cooperative efforts like Marshall Aid, European integration, the IMF and regional payments systems, the perils of a repeat of Keynes' 1919 scenario seemed to have been avoided. But the international monetary system was ultimately torpedoed by the failure of the United States, at the system's core, to follow credible, sound financial policies during the 1960s.

In 1919 Keynes had identified the start of an enduring asymmetry between the United States and Europe and the periodic failure of American leadership commensurate with its economic power. The pegged exchange rate era from 1959 to 1971 proved to be "unstable, complicated, unreliable and temporary" primarily because of the inability of countries to subordinate their national interests to collective efforts to stabilize exchange rate rates. Thus, there were periodic adjustments to pegged rates, but they tended to come only after a build-up of market expectations with disruptive effects. The conflict between national and international interest was reflected in the persistent dispute between Germany (often with the Netherlands, Switzerland, France) on one side and the United States on the other over which side should adjust its policies to stabilize exchanges (Germany to inflate or the United States to deflate). The identification of an "exorbitant privilege" (Rueff 1967; McCauley 2015) provided by the dollar's dominant place in foreign exchange reserves seemed to many European observers to allow the United States to escape the constraints of the pegged exchange rate system. This had been foreseen by Keynes in his proposal for a "neutral" international unit of account (Bancor, with a fixed gold value) in his 1942 International Clearing Union scheme. Ultimately, the United States took unilateral action in August 1971 by suspending gold convertibility, threatening tariffs and a retreat to economic nationalism if other countries did not adjust their exchange rates to take pressure off the dollar (Bordo 2018).

But the end of the Bretton Woods system arguably started soon after it began operating as planned. By 1961, within two years of European states meeting the convertibility terms of the IMF Articles of Agreement, discussions were already under way for how to reform the system as it revealed its instability (Triffin 1960). For the international monetary system, the pegged exchange rate framework based on the dollar that emerged after European countries declared current account convertibility in late 1958, was faulty and required fresh cooperative efforts to prop it up. But instead of the IMF, the G10 and the Bank for International Settlements became the locus of plumbing solutions to the strains caused by the dollar's link to gold, the shifting balance of economic power between the United States, Germany and Japan and the retreat of sterling as an international currency.

The most effective solutions came from the G10 central bank governors at the Bank for International Settlements (BIS). It was here that the Gold Pool was formed in 1962 for G10 central banks to intervene in a coordinated way in the London gold market to sustain the official dollar price of gold, which was the foundation of the Bretton Woods system. In this sense, during most of the years of its operation the gold–dollar exchange rate regime did not function as planned at Bretton Woods. After six years the market finally toppled the Gold Pool in March 1968, and the fixed gold price was limited to transactions between central banks and through the IMF while the rest of the world operated with a market-determined gold price for the dollar. (Toniolo 2005; Bordo et al. 2019). The BIS also provided the meeting place for central bank governors to arrange bilateral currency swaps and multilateral lines of credit to help the retreat of sterling as an international currency without destroying the international monetary system as a whole.[4] Britain and other European states drew on their quotas at the IMF, but often as a backstop to the less conditional support arranged quietly in Basel (Toniolo 2005; Schenk 2010). In terms of scale, the support in November 1964 for sterling amounted to the equivalent of $31.7 billion in 1997 dollars which can be compared to the $40 billion bailout of Mexico by the IMF, the BIS, the World Bank and swaps in that year. From the early 1960s, the Federal Reserve arranged central bank swap facilities, and in the early 1970s these bilateral swap facilities amounted to the equivalent of over 20 per cent of global foreign exchange reserves and then declined (McCauley and Schenk 2020; Bordo et al. 2015).

The efforts of G10 finance ministers to reform the international monetary system in more permanent ways was much less successful than those of central bankers. They delegated technical matters to deputies but were still unable to resolve the fundamental problems in the global system (Solomon 1982; James 1996). Their main contribution was to launch the Special Drawing Right (SDR) just as the pegged exchange rate system fell apart and the inflation took hold. The political compromises in the design of the SDR meant that it was not as useful as had been hoped and did not relieve the system of its reliance on the US dollar with all the challenges and asymmetries this imposed (Schenk 2010). Had the United States been able to commit to a policy of price stability during the 1960s, the system could probably have survived longer with these adaptations (Despres et al. 1966; McKinnon 2015; Bordo 2018). This serves to highlight the "unstable and complicated" nature of the Bretton Woods compromise, which relied on reconciling the domestic priorities of the US policymakers with the needs of the global economy. Recognizing the asymmetry in the global system from the time of the Versailles Treaty in 1919, when the United States had power but failed to provide effective leadership, Keynes had sought to introduce a more balanced structure that avoided relying so heavily on the United States, but his innovative approach was in the end not feasible in the post-war political and economic climate.

---

[4] This cooperation extended well beyond the Bretton Woods era: the final support arrangement for sterling was launched in February 1977 (Schenk 2010).

The Third Turning Point: The 1970s Great Inflation and Managed Floating

The collapse of the Bretton Woods System in 1971–73 was in part brought about by the US shift to an inflationary stance in the mid-1960s and neglecting the rules as the centre country in the pegged exchange rate system. The end of the gold anchor in March 1968, realignment of the DM in 1969 and the float of sterling in 1972 all pulled the system apart. The US administration's effort to force other countries to adjust to US inflation did not convince the markets, and the new, more flexible pegs set under the Smithsonian Agreement in December 1971 quickly unwound. There is an extensive literature on the Great inflation that followed through the 1970s (Bordo and Orphanides 2013). Candidates for blame include flawed monetary policy by central banks trying to manipulate the Phillips curve trade-off to achieve full employment or the accommodation of supply shocks, in particular the sixfold increase in the price of oil in 1973–74.

The Great Inflation marked the abandonment of the Keynesian consensus in policymaking that had spread from the 1950s (Clarke 1990). Keynes, himself, put little emphasis on exchange rate policy in *The General Theory* (1939), but his contribution to the design of the Bretton Woods system concurred with the assumption that stable or pegged exchange rates was the most desirable framework. This premise had been fundamental to economic orthodoxy since the 1850s, but it disappeared quickly in the 1970s. The new orthodoxy of capital account liberalization was quick to catch hold partly because it merely recognized the status quo, in which the Eurocurrency market had already risen above the regulatory reach of national monetary authorities (Schenk 2010b).

The Keynesian world of pegged exchange rates, capital controls and international cooperation had disappeared by the 1980s. But the consensus during the 1970s can be overstated. The United States moved resolutely to a managed float, albeit with periods of intense intervention (e.g., 1975–78) (Bordo et al. 2015). But Western Europe drew closer to monetary union (an irrevocably fixed exchange rate system) among European Community members from 1969. Other countries caught in the middle sought compromise strategies, such as retaining a peg to the dollar or, when that became unstable, to a trade-weighted basket of currencies (Schenk and Singleton 2011).

During the 1970s, policymakers were unsuccessful in reducing inflation in part from following doctrine, later deemed to be flawed (Meltzer 2010) that is the Phillips curve and the belief that cost push forces were the key cause of inflation, to be dealt with by wage and price controls. In the UK, policymakers followed Nicholas Kaldor's (1971) view that expansionary money financed fiscal policy could raise the growth rate while inflation could be suppressed by controls. More fundamentally the Great Inflation persisted so long because of the unwillingness of monetary authorities to follow the tight monetary (and fiscal) policies needed to break the back of rising inflationary expectations for fear of the recession and unemployment that would occur. This led to a ratcheting up in inflation and inflationary expectations as the Federal Reserve (and other central banks) tightened when facing a rise in inflation and then loosened too soon when the economy soured.

On the international scene, high and variable inflation made exchange rates volatile too. This reflected Milton Friedman's (1953) view that floating exchange rates only work if they are accompanied by stable domestic macroeconomic policies. Deliberations at the IMF in the early 1970s to restore the par value system as well as exchange market intervention were doomed to failure in the face of divergent national economic policies. In 1971, the IMF formed the Committee of 20 to broaden the discussions on reforming the international monetary system beyond the G10. Its deliberations became bogged down in technical details and internal dissention during the collapse of the pegged exchange rate system, but its proposals to reinvigorate the SDR came to partial fruition (Schenk 2017). In 1974 the valuation of the SDR was changed from a weight in gold to a basket of 16 currencies (reduced to 5 in 1981) and with a market interest rate attached to make it more appealing. On the other hand, the C20's proposal to create a substitution account to help the SDR take over more of a role as a global reserve currency from the dollar was debated throughout the 1970s but ultimately lost traction in the early 1980s as the dollar exchange rate strengthened (McCauley and Schenk 2015).

The upward spiral in inflation and the downward spiral in the dollar exchange rate ended with the Volcker shock of October 1979. As chair of the Federal Reserve, Paul Volcker followed a tight monetarist monetary policy by cutting the monetary base and allowing interest rates to rise to above 20 per cent. This created serious recession between

1979 and 1982 which led to double-digit unemployment rates and prompted the largest sovereign debt crisis in history among developing economies, but it did succeed in drastically reducing inflation by the mid-1980s (Schenk 2017). Similar policies were followed by Margaret Thatcher and Alan Walters in the UK in 1980 and in Canada and other countries. By the end of the 1980s virtually all advanced countries had returned to low inflation. These actions ushered in the era of monetarism, which then spread in amended forms from the United States to the rest of the world. During this period, the success of the credibility of low inflation policies was buttressed by a new paradigm for monetary policy based on central bank independence (CBI), inflation targeting (IT) and floating exchange rates.

Despite Friedman's views that the pursuit of stable rule-like domestic policies obviated the need for international monetary policy coordination, the G7 continued its efforts to coordinate fiscal and monetary policies to stabilize exchange rates in the Plaza and Louvre Accords in the 1980s. This attested to the enduring attraction of international monetary cooperation to stabilize exchange rates. In both cases, the effects were less than were hoped. It proved easier to talk the dollar down in the Plaza Accord (1985) than to convince markets that it was undervalued in the Louvre Accord in 1987 (Schenk 2017). The impact of the G7 pressure on Japan to forgo its national economic interest in the pursuit of an appreciation of the yen against the dollar prompted a financial crisis that left the Japanese economy in the doldrums for over a decade.

The emerging market crises of the 1990s confirmed that the international economic system imagined by Keynes had disappeared. Where countries persisted with pegged exchange rates in the 1990s (such as in Russia, East and Southeast Asia, South America) a series of damaging currency crises ensued as the dollar strengthened on the basis of the Fed following domestic policy priorities, leaving emerging market currencies overvalued. Their efforts to hold on to pegged rates with open capital markets failed. By the 2000s (after the euro finally eliminated most of the national currencies of the EU), floating or managed floating exchange rates had spread further (Bordo and Schenk 2017).

It is important to recognize that the crises of the 1990s and 2000s were mainly through the capital account due to the liberalization of capital markets rather than Keynesian shocks through the current account. The inexorable financialization of the global economy made the Keynesian world of capital controls and international cooperation seem a mere historic relic. Indeed, the IMF began to see its role as having shifted from financing current account shortfalls to stemming capital account crises. The 2007–08 financial crisis was fundamentally not an international monetary issue, although there were substantial global imbalances in the 2000s.

Conclusions

Keynes' *The Economic Consequences of the Peace* has resonated with policymakers and the public ever since its publication. It continues to be implicitly or explicitly referenced in the efforts to promote international economic cooperation in the aftermath of crises through the century. The accuracy of its prediction that an irrational promotion of conflicting national interests would result in economic disaster for the people of Europe has weighed heavily on policymakers ever since. The history of the twentieth century demonstrates that international economic cooperation itself is not unusual, but it does tend to be "unstable, complicated, unreliable and temporary" because tensions inevitably arise between national and international objectives. While these interests might correspond in the wake of a crisis or emergency (partly due to the lessons learned from Keynes' critique of the 1919 settlement), domestic political as well as economic objectives will ultimately dominate despite the construction of elaborate international institutions to overcome or to mediate these conflicts.

An exception is the more functional, but limited form of cooperation evident in the Bank for International Settlements, particularly in the 1960s when central bankers from the G10 deliberately tried to insulate themselves from political influence by focusing on technical rather than systemic cooperation and by restricting the public (and political) transparency of their deliberations. This is in marked contrast, for example, to the G10 finance ministers' deliberations in the 1960s to reform the international monetary system, which were prolonged, expensive and ultimately unproductive.

A further theme of Keynes' treatise is the peril of making economic policy without reference to the underlying economic realities. His book therefore sets out detailed data to demonstrate the potential for Germany to meet its reparations payments. For him, this use of evidence is important because it shows how divorced from a rational perspective the settlement had become. The belief in the power of data-driven economic policymaking was subsequently reflected in the extremely complex structures of the League of Nations with its many technical committees collecting a bewildering amount of data from its member countries to serve as a rational basis for policymaking.

Keynes was critical of all four leaders at Versailles and of their advisors. He identified the vulnerability of political leaders to extremes of public opinion, particularly the emotional desire for a punitive peace settlement after such a painful wartime experience and the continuation of the myth that the debts accumulated during wartime could be repaid. But he gave most space to criticizing US President Wilson and his advisers, claiming that he was underprepared and therefore lacked decisiveness. He was even critical of his physical appearance; his description of Wilson as being more impressive when he was sitting down rather than standing was a metaphor for the position of the United States in the global system – seeming important when at rest, but not very impressive when it came to taking action. His portrayal of Wilson, on the one hand, as a sophisticate in terms of his dress but, on the other hand, the body beneath this façade "lacking in fineness" might also reflect a view of the United States as seeming to have become modern and as sophisticated as Europeans, but not having fully made this transformation from rougher stock. In the UK in 2016, it seemed that Keynes' observation in 1919 that "Europe is apart and England is not of her flesh and body" was emerging as a defining ideology in debates over BREXIT.

In sum, the pendulum has swung from the gold standard and the first era of globalization, through the bleak Thirty Years' War and its aftermath, back to the Great Moderation and the second era of globalization. This pattern has resonance to Keynes' views on international monetary relations. The gold standard was buttressed by a rule that subsumed internal (domestic) balance to external balance. That helped foster the first era of globalization. Tensions from this arrangement became manifest in the nationalist backlash in the first half of the twentieth century and the shift of focus to domestic considerations and autarky (tariffs and capital controls). Keynes' contribution to the post-1945 era was a rules-based arrangement to reconcile internal with external balance. With extensive international cooperation and tinkering it worked for two decades, but it broke down primarily because of the failure of the centre country, the

United States, to follow the basic rule of maintaining price stability. In subsequent decades, after the failure of wealthy countries to follow domestic macroeconomic policy rules to maintain price and exchange rate stability which created the Great Inflation, the advanced countries returned to a rules-based system under floating exchange rates based on central bank independence, inflation targeting and credibility for low inflation. These features characterized the Great Moderation, but also allowed a complacency about the governance of international financial markets that sowed the seeds for the next great global crisis in 2007–08. There is considerable resonance to the pre-1914 gold standard that fostered the first era of globalization. Then just like the first era, a backlash emerged against the adverse effects of trade integration and financial globalization following the GFC. It in turn reflected failures in financial regulation, monetary policy and global imbalances. After the global pandemic and renewed war in Europe, we are back to viewing the second era of globalization as fitting Keynes' description of the first era as "Unusual, Unstable, Complicated and Temporary". Will the world get back on the track of the pre-crisis era or go in a similar direction Keynes prophesized in 1919 for the post–World War I era? The fourth turning point in the international system is still incomplete, but following from Keynes, history reminds us that nostalgia for an earlier period needs to be tempered by a realistic understanding of how "unstable, temporary, complex and unreliable" were the golden ages of international economic cooperation.

References

Albers, Thilo N.H. (2020) "Currency Devaluations and Beggar-my-Neighbour Penalties" *Economic History Review* 73(1), pp. 233–257.

Arndt, H.W. (1944) *Economic Lessons of the Nineteen Thirties*, London: Frank Cass.

Benn Steil (2018) *The Marshall Plan: Dawn of the Cold War*, New York: Simon and Schuster.

Bernanke, Ben S. (2015) *The Courage to Act: A Memoir of a Crisis and Its Aftermath*, New York: W.W. Norton.

Bordo, Michael, Eric Monnet and Alain Naif (2019) "The Gold Pool (1961–1968) and the Fall of the Bretton Woods System. Lessons for Central Bank Cooperation" *Journal of Economic History* 79(4), pp. 1027–1059.

Bordo, Michael (2018) "The Imbalances of the Bretton Woods System 1965 to 1973 : US Inflation, The Elephant in the Room" NBER Working Paper 25409. December.

Bordo, Michael (2017) "The Second Era of Globalization Is Not Yet Over: An Historical Perspective" NBER Working Paper.

Bordo, Michael and Christopher Meissner (2015) "Growing Up to Stability? Financial Globalization, Financial Development and Crisis" NBER Working Paper 21710 (June).

Bordo, Michael and Pierre Siklos (2015) "Central Bank Credibility: An Historical and Quantitative Evolution" Chapter 3 in *Central Banks at a Crossroads: What Can We Learn from History?*

Bordo, Michael, Owen Humpage and Anna Schwartz (2015) *Strained Relations: US Foreign Exchange Operations and Monetary Policy in the Twentieth Century.* Chicago: University of Chicago Press.

Bordo, Michael and John Landon Lane (2013) "Does Expansionary Monetary Policy Cause Asset Price Booms: Some Historical and Empirical Evidence" NBER Working paper 19585, October.

Bordo, Michael and Athanasios Orphanides (2013) *The Great Inflation.* Chicago: University of Chicago Press.

Bordo, Michael and Harold James (2002) "The Adam Klug Memorial Lecture: Haberler versus Nurkse. The Case for Floating Exchange Rates as an Alternate to Bretton Woods" in Arie Arnon and Warren L. Young (eds) *The Open Economy Macromodel: Past, Present and Future,* Boston: Kluwer Academic Publishers, pp. 161–182.

Bordo, Michael (1981) "The Classical Gold Standard: Some Lessons for Today" *Federal Reserve Bank of St. Louis Review* 63(6), May.

Boughton, James M. (2011) *Silent Revolution: The International Monetary Fund 1979–1989*, Washington: International Monetary Fund.

Clavin, Patricia (2013) *Securing the World Economy: The Reinvention of the League of Nations 1920–1946*, Oxford: Oxford University Press.

Clarke, Peter (1990) *The Keynesian Revolution in the Making, 1924–1936*, Oxford: Oxford University Press.

Davidson, Paul (2009) *The Keynes Solution: The Path to Global Economic Prosperity.* Palgrave Macmillan.

De Bromhead, Alan, Alan Fernihough, Markus Lampe, and Kevin H. O'Rourke (2019) "When Britain Turned Inward: The Impact of Interwar British Protection" *American Economic Review* 109(2), pp. 325–352.

Despres, Emil, Charles Kindleberger and William Salant (1966) "The Dollar and World Liquidity: A Minority View" *Economist* 5 February, pp. 526–529.

Eichengreen, Barry (2018) *The Populist Temptation: Economic Grievances and Political Reaction in the Modern Era*, New York: Oxford University Press.

Eichengreen, Barry (2015) *Hall of Mirrors: The Great Depression, the Great Recession, and the Uses – And misuses – Of History*, Oxford: Oxford University Press.

Eichengreen, Barry and Marc Flandreau (2009) "The Rise and Fall of the Dollar (Or When Did the Dollar Replace Sterling as the Leading Reserve Currency?" *European Review of Economic History* 13(3), pp. 377–414.

Eichengreen, Barry (1992) *Golden Fetters*, New York: Oxford University Press.

Eichengreen, Barry and Timothy Hatton (1988) "Interwar unemployment in International perspective: An Overview" in Barry Eichengreen and Timothy Hatton (eds) *Interwar Unemployment in International Perspective. NATO ASI Series (Series D: Behavioral and Social Sciences) Vol43*, Dordrecht: Springer.

Fogleman, Aaron S. (1998) "From Slaves, Convicts and Servants to Free Passengers: The Transformation of Immigration in the Era of the American Revolution" *Journal of American History*, 85(1), pp. 43–78.

Friedman, Milton (1953) "The Case for Floating Exchange Rates" in Milton Friedman (ed) *Essays in Positive Economics*, Chicago: University of Chicago Press, pp. 461–494.

Gardner, Richard N. (1956) *Sterling-Dollar Diplomacy*, Oxford: Oxford University Press.

Giovannini, Alberto (1993) "Bretton Woods and Its Precursors: Rules versus Discretion in the History of International Monetary Regimes" in Michael Bordo and Barry Eichengreen (eds) *A Retrospective on the Bretton Woods System: Lessons for International Monetary Reform*, Chicago: University of Chicago Press.

Goldberg, Linda, Craig Kennedy and Jason Miu (2011) "Central Bank Dollar Swap Lines and Overseas Dollar Funding Costs" *Economic Policy Review*, May, pp. 3–20.

Goodhart, Charles (2011) *The Basel Committee on Banking Supervision: A History of the Early Years*, Cambridge: Cambridge University Press.

Horsefield, J. Keith (1969) *The International Monetary Fund 1945–1965: Twenty Years of International Monetary Cooperation*, Washington: International Monetary Fund.

International Monetary Fund (2012) The Liberalization and Management of Capital Flows – An Institutional View, November 14. www.imf.org/external/np/pp/eng/2012/111412.pdf (accessed 9 October 2019).

Irwin, Douglas (2012) *Trade Policy Disasters: Lessons from the 1930s*, Cambridge : MIT Press.

James, Harold (2001) *The End of Globalization: Lessons from the Great Depression*, Cambridge: Harvard University Press.

James, Harold (1996) *International Monetary Cooperation since Bretton Woods*, Washington: International Monetary Fund.

Kaldor, Nicholas (1971) "Conflicts in National Economic Objectives" *Economic Journal* 81(321), pp. 1–16.

Keynes, John Maynard (1944) Proposals for an International Clearing Union.

Keynes, John Maynard (1933) *National Self Sufficiency*, Dublin: Educational Company of Ireland.

Keynes, John Maynard (1930) *A Treatise on Money*, London: Macmillan.

Keynes, John Maynard (1925) *The Economic Consequences of Mr. Churchill*, London: Macmillan.

Keynes, John Maynard (1919) *The Economic Consequences of the Peace*, London: Macmillan.

Kindleberger, Charles (1975) *The World in Depression 1929–1939*, Berkeley: University of California Press.

McCauley, Robert N. and Catherine R. Schenk (2020) "Central Bank Swaps Then and Now: Swaps and Dollar Liquidity in the 1960s" *BIS Working Paper*, 851.

McCauley, Robert N. and Catherine R. Schenk (2015) "Reforming the International Monetary System in the 1970s and 2000s: Would an SDR Substitution Account Have Worked" *International Finance*, 18(2), pp. 187–206.

McCauley, Robert N. (2016) "Does the Dollar Confer an Exorbitant Privilege?" *Journal of International Money and Finance* 57, pp. 1–14.

McKinnon, Ronald (2015) *The Unloved Dollar Standard*, New York: Oxford University Press.

Meltzer, Allan (2010) *A History of the Federal Reserve, Volume 2*, Chicago: University of Chicago Press.

Milward, Alan (1999) *The European Rescue of the Nation State Routledge*, Berkeley: University of California Press.

Moure, Kenneth (1996) "Undervaluing the Franc Poincare" *Economic History Review*, 49(1).

Nurkse, Ragnar (1944) *International Currency Experience*, League of Nations.

O'Rourke, Kevin H. and Jeffrey G. Williamson (1999) *Globalization and History: The Evolution of a Nineteenth-Century Atlantic Economy*, Cambridge, MA: MIT Press.

Ostry, Jonathan D., Atish R. Ghosh, Karl Habermeier, Marcos Chamon, Mahvash Qureshi and Dennis Reinhardt (2010) Capital Inflows: The Role of Controls, IMF Staff Position Note, February 19 (accessed 9 October 2019)

Pauly, Louis W. (1996) "The League of Nations and the Foreshadowing of the International Monetary Fund" *Essays in International Finance*, 201, December.

Pressnell, L.S. (1987) *External Economic Policy Since the War Vol. 1: the Post-War Financial Settlement*, London: HMSO.

Roberts, Richard (2013) *Saving the City: The Great Financial Crisis of 1914*, Oxford: Oxford University Press.

Rockoff, Hugh (1984) "Some Evidence on the Real Price of Gold, Its Costs of Production and Commodity Prices" in Michael D. Bordo and Anna J. Schwartz (eds) *A Retrospective on the Classical Gold Standard*, Chicago: University of Chicago Press.

Rueff, Jacques (1967) "Increase the Price of Gold" in Lawrence H. Officer and Thomas D. Willett (eds) *The International Monetary System: Problems and Proposals*, Englewood Cliffs, NJ: Prentice Hall.

Schenk, Catherine R. (2019) "International Monetary Cooperation since the Global Financial Crisis" in C.R. Schenk and M. Klein (eds), *IMF's Work on Encouraging International Policy Cooperation*, International Monetary Fund, BP/19-01/06.

Schenk, Catherine R. (2017) "Coordination failures during and after Bretton Woods" in M. Qureshi, A. Ghosh (ed), *From Great Depression to Great Recession: The Elusive Quest for International Policy Cooperation*, Washington: International Monetary Fund.

Schenk, Catherine R. (2014) "Summer in the City: Banking Scandals of 1974 and the Development of International Banking Supervision", *English Historical Review*, 2014, pp. 1129–1156.

Schenk, Catherine R. and John Singleton (2011) "Basket Pegs and Exchange Rate Regime Change: Australia and New Zealand in the mid-1970s" *Australian Economic History Review* 51(2) pp. 120–149.

Schenk, Catherine R. (2010) *The Decline of Sterling: Managing the Retreat of An International Currency 1945–92*, Cambridge: Cambridge University Press.

Skidelsky, Robert (2000) *John Maynard Keynes: Fighting for Britain 1937–1946*, London: Macmillan.

Skidelsky, Robert (2009) *Keynes: The Return of the Master*, London: Penguin Press.

Silber, William (2007) *When Washington Shut Down Wall Street: The Great Financial Crisis of 1914 and the Origins of America's Monetary Supremacy*, Princeton: Princeton University Press.

Singleton, J. (2011) *Central Banking in the Twentieth Century*, Cambridge: Cambridge University Press.

Solomon, Robert (1982) *The International Monetary System 1945–1981*, New York: Harper and Row.

Steil, Benn (2013) *The Battle of Bretton Woods: John Maynard Keynes, Harry Dexter White, and the Making of a New World Order*, Princeton, Princeton University Press.

Taylor, John B. (2007) "Housing and Monetary Policy" in *Remarks at the Federal Reserve Bank of Kansas City, Jackson Hole Economic Policy*

Symposium: Housing, Housing Finance, and Monetary Policy. Kansas City, MO: Federal Reserve Bank of Kansas City, August.

Temin, Peter (1989) *Lessons from the Great Depression*, Cambridge, MA: MIT Press.

Toniolo, Gianni (2005) *Central Bank Cooperation at the Bank for International Settlements*, Cambridge: Cambridge University Press.

Triffin, Robert (1960) *Gold and the Dollar Crisis*, New Haven: Yale University Press.

Wheatley, Jonathan and Peter Garnham (2010) "Brazil in 'Currency War' Alert", *Financial Times*, September.

15 | Keynes's Arc of Discovery
From The Economic Consequences to Bretton Woods

DAVID VINES

1 Tracing Keynes's Arc of Discovery

The *Economic Consequences of the Peace* is known for its devastating criticism of the reparations burden which the Versailles peace settlement imposed on Germany after World War I. But it does much more than this. The extraordinary second chapter of this book first sets out to explain how, and why, the global system had worked so well in the late Victorian age. It is only after this preliminary chapter that Keynes turns to the main purpose of his book – which is to describe the potential damage which the imposition of reparations on Germany was likely to cause. But Keynes does this – in the rest of his book – by referring back to Chapter 2 and showing the way in which reparations were in danger of destabilizing the system which he had described there.

This chapter is also important for a deeper reason. It clearly establishes how, in order to safeguard the global economic order, one would need to solve the transfer problem, a problem to which Keynes turned his attention in 1929. More than this one can see that the world would need to solve the global unemployment problem, something on which Keynes focused in his *General Theory* of 1936. But, most fundamentally, one can see that one would need to create a new international monetary system – and the Bretton Woods agreement, which Keynes spearheaded, attempted to do just that. It is thus my view that, by studying this chapter, one can begin to visualize the arc of Keynes's creativity, which stretched from the time this chapter was written to his death in 1946.

In this chapter I first present the astonishing twelve pages of theoretical analysis which Keynes sets out in Chapter 2. Most strikingly of all I show that this remarkable piece of analysis is built upon a foundation which is – in effect – the Ramsey model of economic growth. I then go on to show that this theoretical account prefigures much of Keynes's later work – on the transfer problem, on unemployment, and on international monetary reform.

This is not the conventional view of Chapter Two of the *Economic Consequences*. That view sees this chapter as a *descriptive* exercise, one which merely sets the scene for the tragic drama of reparations which is to follow. Joseph Schumpeter set out this conventional view in his obituary of Keynes, published in the *American Economic Review* in September 1946 (Schumpeter, 1946).

It is interesting to consider, at the beginning of this chapter, just why Schumpeter's view was so mistaken. Schumpeter writes:

"[T]he book is a masterpiece....[T]he economics of the book.... is of the simplest and did not call for any refined technique .... Before embarking on his great venture in persuasion, [in Chapter 2] Keynes drew a sketch of the economic and social background of the political events he was about to survey. .... [T]his sketch may be summed up like this: Laissez-faire capitalism, that 'extraordinary episode,' had come to an end in August, 1914. The conditions were rapidly passing in which entrepreneurial leadership was able to secure success after success, propelled as it had been by rapid growth of populations and by abundant opportunities to invest that were incessantly recreated by technological improvements and by a series of conquests of new sources of food and raw materials. Under these conditions, there had been no difficulty about absorbing the savings of a bourgeoisie that kept on baking cakes 'in order not to eat them.' But now (1920) those impulses were giving out, the spirit of private enterprise was flagging, investment opportunities were vanishing, and bourgeois saving habits had, therefore, lost their social function; their persistence actually made things worse than they need have been.

"Here, then, we have the origin of the modern stagnation thesis-as distinguished from the one which we may, if we choose, find in Ricardo. And here we also have the embryo of the *General Theory*. Every comprehensive 'theory' of an economic state of society consists of two complementary but essentially distinct elements. There is, first, the theorist' view about the basic features of that state of society, about what is and what is not important in order to understand its life at a given time. Let us call this his vision. And there is, second, the theorist' technique, an apparatus by which he conceptualizes his vision and which turns the latter into concrete propositions or 'theories.' In those pages [in Chapter Two] of the *Economic Consequences of the Peace* we find nothing of the theoretical apparatus of the General Theory. But we find the whole of the vision of things social and economic of which that apparatus is the technical complement. The *General Theory i*s the final result of a long struggle to make that vision of our age analytically operative." (Schumpeter, 1946, p. 501)

I will never forget the effect that these words had on me when I first read them, sitting in my room in Oxford. I was already in my forties and had been working closely with James Meade in Cambridge for more than ten years. Meade had collaborated with Keynes in the 1930s and 1940s and had told me much about their work together. It was clear to me, from what I had learned from Meade, that Schumpeter simply did not grasp Keynes's essential purpose.

Let me explain in more detail.

Chapter Two of the *Economic Consequences* contains a vivid description, *and analysis*, of the pre–World War I global economic order. As Keynes shows, the late nineteenth and early twentieth centuries was an era in which the global economic order – despite its faults – had functioned well. It had enabled the Victorian golden age to flourish, not just in the British Empire but worldwide. But the *Economic Consequences* was written in 1919 when, thanks to World War I, that global order had completely collapsed. In my view, we should think of Keynes's theoretical work as a long struggle in which he made "analytically operative" (Schumpeter's words) his vision of how to recreate a properly functioning global economic order.

It is *not* true that, as Schumpeter says, the *General Theory* is the "final result" of that long theoretical struggle. The *General Theory* was – I think – merely a way-station – even if a vitally important one – on Keynes's theoretical journey. The destination of that journey was an understanding of how to reconstruct a properly functioning global economic order. And that understanding was implemented at the Bretton Woods Conference in 1944. That conference was extraordinary: a gathering at the Mount Washington Hotel in New Hampshire of 730 delegates from 44 nations, chaired by US Treasury Secretary Henry Morgenthau, and lasting for nearly three weeks. The outcome of the meeting was the establishment of the International Monetary Fund and the World Bank, which together created an international financial system which was better than the gold standard. Discussing their accomplishments, Keynes said:

We have had to perform at one and the same time the tasks appropriate to the economist, to the financier, to the politician, to the journalist, to the propagandist, to the lawyer, to the statesman-even, I think, to the prophet and to the soothsayer. (IMF, 2004, p. 1)

In what follows I will show the way in which that conference, inspired by Keynes, was the fulfilment of ideas which he had first begun to articulate in Chapter Two of the *Economic Consequences*.

Keynes was to die less than two years later, on 21 April 1946, just five weeks after the inaugural meetings of the Boards of Governors of the International Monetary Fund and the World Bank in Savannah, Georgia. This meant that he was not able to write a great book about what had been achieved at Bretton Woods. Nevertheless, I have no doubt that he would have done this, and that it would have occupied the same sort of position in international macroeconomics that the *General Theory* has come to occupy in closed economy macroeconomics. As a result, the key ideas needed to be written down by other people: by James Meade, in his *Theory of the Balance of Payments*, published in 1951 (Meade, 1951), and then by Trevor Swan, who made Meade's ideas universally accessible by means of the "Swan Diagram" (Swan, 1963). In the Preface to his book, for which he won the Nobel Prize, Meade writes, "my indebtedness to the ideas of Lord Keynes is, I imagine, too obvious to need any emphasis" (Meade, 1951, p. ix). Meade was a modest man, but nevertheless this statement is important.

My view of Keynes's analytical achievement is unconventional. I first articulated this view nearly twenty years ago in a long review article about the third volume of Robert Skidelsky's magisterial biography of Keynes. Skidelsky's book was published in the year 2000, and my article appeared three years after that (Vines, 2003). About ten years later, Peter Temin and I laid out this view in somewhat more detail (Temin and Vines, 2013, 2014). I provided some further elements of the story in a paper published about five years ago (Vines, 2017). I will refer to all of those publications in below. The new purpose of this present article is to take my account of Keynes's analytical achievements right back to the *Economic Consequences*, in a way which I have not done before. My purpose here is to present a picture of what I call Keynes's "arc of discovery". One end of this arc is located right back in 1919, in Chapter Two of the *Economic Consequences*, when he was still a young man, only thirty-four years old. The other end is to be found at Bretton Woods, at the end of his life, twenty-five years later.

However, it *is* true that Schumpeter, in his obituary, got one important thing right about the Chapter Two of the *Economic Consequences*. In this chapter we find nothing of the theoretical apparatus of the *General Theory*. But this does not mean that the chapter is devoid of theory. Instead, it means that Schumpeter missed what is there, because he was looking for the wrong thing.

I have recently re-read that obituary, nearly thirty years after I first read it, and I am struck by what a wonderful piece of work it is. It locates the *General Theory* at the top of a theoretical mountain and it describes Keynes's life as a heroic battle to climb that mountain. Schumpeter's description of the moves in that battle is worth re-reading today as an inspiration in how to think about economic theory. But the account of what happened after Keynes climbed the mountain is simply missing.

Instead, the obituary concludes with the following revealing paragraph

At this I will leave it. Everyone knows the stupendous fight the valiant warrior put up for the work [the General Theory] that was to be his last.

There is a footnote at this point which adds that after this last work Keynes "wrote many minor pieces almost to his dying day". Schumpeter then continues:

Everyone knows that, during the war he entered the Treasury again (1940) and that his influence grew, along with that of Churchill until nobody thought of challenging it. Everyone knows of the honor [sic] that has been conferred upon the House of Lords. And, of course, the Keynes Plan, Bretton Woods and the English loan. But these things will have to engage some scholarly biographer who has all the materials at his disposal. (op. cit., p. 518)

I am not the scholarly biographer of which Schumpeter speaks. But my own work has shown me that Keynes's analytical journey went well beyond the *General Theory*. And it has shown me just how important Chapter Two is in showing how that journey began and where it would end. Schumpeter was only interested in Keynes's journey to the top of the *General Theory* mountain, and so he did not notice many important things in Chapter Two. My view is that Bretton Woods was at the end of the rainbow and that the rainbow began right back in Chapter Two of the *Economic Consequences*.

2 Chapter Two of Keynes's *Economic Consequences*: A Model of Global Economic Growth

Keynes begins Chapter Two by prefacing his analysis with a remarkable paragraph that has been widely quoted[1] ever since:

> The inhabitant of London could order by telephone, sipping his morning tea in bed, the various products of the whole earth, in such quantity as he might see fit, and reasonably expect their early delivery upon his doorstep; he could at the same moment and by the same means adventure his wealth in the natural resources and new enterprises of any quarter of the world, and share, without exertion or even trouble, in their prospective fruits and advantages; or he could decide to couple the security of his fortunes with the good faith of the townspeople of any substantial municipality in any continent that fancy or information might recommend. (Economic Consequences, p. 6)

Wonderful though this paragraph is, it is merely the kind of description to which Schumpeter drew attention. But in the remarkable pages which follow, Keynes provides a macroeconomic model of the world economy, showing how such a set of circumstances could have actually come about.

Armed with this model, Keynes analyses the process of economic growth that was happening in the pre-WWI era, and identifies the international interactions that were part of that process. He then draws attention to the fragility of both the growth process and the international interactions. In what follows I show how Keynes does this.

But first it is worth noticing that the model which Keynes presents is a real model, and not a monetary one. That is to say, there is not within it anything about the kinds of disturbances that can be caused by the financial system – or indeed by a demand by the private sector for more liquidity. That would not come until later, first in his *Tract on Monetary Reform* (Keynes, 1923), then in the *Treatise on Money* (Keynes, 1930), and finally in the *General Theory* (Keynes, 1936). Schumpeter was right about this.

---

[1] The page numbers which accompany the quotations which follow refer to the 1971 edition of the *Economic Consequences*.

2.1 The Ramsey Growth Model

The pre–World War I period was an era in which – in historical terms – growth was extremely rapid. There were, says Keynes, two reasons for this.

First, there was a very rapid increase in what we would now call the effective labour force. There had been a huge increase in the population. Keynes notes that from 1870 to 1914 German population increased by about 70 per cent – immediately before the war it was increasing by well over 1 per cent per year – and he notes that something similar was happening in the Austro-Hungarian Empire (ibid., pp. 7 and 8). There was also, says Keynes, particularly rapid growth in the industrial labour force because of the movement of very large numbers of people from the countryside into rapidly growing cities, with increasing numbers of workers available at very low wages. That is to say, the growth process went hand in hand with a transformation of the economic system from an agricultural one into an industrial one. Here are the ideas formalized much later in the Lewis model of economic growth.[2] In addition, there was also, according to Keynes, very rapid labour-saving technical progress happening at the same time, coming from the increasing division of labour as a result of the new machines that were invented as part of the industrial revolution.

Second, along with the growth in the effective labour force there was very rapid accumulation of capital. This happened because a large proportion of national output income was saved.

This accumulation of capital was "to the great benefit of mankind". If this accumulation had not happened "the world would have found the regime intolerable". Lurking here is an idea which appeared much later in the Swan–Solow model of economic growth: if labour force growth and technical progress are both rapid, then the rate of growth in steady state will rapid, but the steady-state level of capital per worker will only be high if the savings rate is also high, and only then can output per person, and so the standard of living, be high. Otherwise, not enough will be accumulated to keep pace with the growing number of

---

[2] As Keynes knew all too well, Ricardo had discussed this transformation in his Principles. But it was not until the Lewis model of the 1950s that this process of agriculture-industry transfer was studied in a fully specified growth model (Lewis, 1954).

workers, and the steady state level of output per worker will be low.[3] That is what Keynes means by an "intolerable regime".

Why, according to Keynes, did this accumulation of capital actually happen?

Europe was so organized socially and economically as to secure the maximum accumulation of capital. While there was some continuous improvement in the daily conditions of life of the mass of the population, society was so framed as to throw a great part of the increased income into the control of the class least likely to consume it. The new rich of the nineteenth century were not brought up to large expenditures and preferred the power which investment gave them to the pleasures of immediate consumption. In fact, it was precisely the *inequality* of the distribution of wealth which made possible those vast accumulations of fixed wealth and of capital improvements which distinguished that age from all others. Herein lay, in fact, the main justification of the capitalist system. If the rich had spent their new wealth on their own enjoyments the world would long ago have found such a regime intolerable. But like bees they saved and accumulated, not less to the advantage of the whole community because they themselves held narrower ends in prospect.

The immense accumulations of fixed capital which, to the great benefit of mankind, were built up during the half-century before the war, could never have come about in a society in which wealth was divided equally. The railways of the world, which that age built as a monument to posterity, were, not less than the pyramids of Egypt, the work of labour which was not free to consume in immediate enjoyment the full equivalent of its efforts.

Thus this remarkable system depended for its growth on a double bluff or deception. On the one hand the labouring classes accepted from ignorance or powerlessness, or were compelled, persuaded, or cajoled by custom, convention, authority, and the well-established order of society, into accepting a situation in which they could call their own very little of the cake that they and nature and the capitalists were co-operating to produce. And on the other hand the capitalist class were allowed to call the best part of their cake theirs and were theoretically free to consume it, on the tacit underlying condition that they consumed very little of it in practice. The duty of 'saving' became nine-tenths of virtue and the growth of the cake the object of true religion. There grew around the non-consumption of the cake all those instincts of puritanism which in other ages has withdrawn itself from the

---

[3] This is the way in which Trevor Swan motivated his version of the Solow–Swan growth model which appeared in 1956, the same year in which Solow's version appeared (Solow, 1956; Swan, 1956).

world and has neglected the arts of production as well as those of enjoyment. And so the cake increased; but to what end was not clearly contemplated. Individuals would be exhorted not so much to abstain and as to defer, and to cultivate the practice of security and anticipation. Saving was for old age or for your children; but this was only in theory – the virtue of the cake was that it was never to be consumed, neither by you nor by your children after you.

[...] The cake was really very small in proportion to the appetites of consumption, and no one, if it were shared all round, would be much the better off by the cutting of it. If only the cake were not cut but was allowed to grow in the geometrical proportion predicted by Malthus of population, but not less true of compound interest, perhaps a day might come when there would at last be enough to go around and posterity could enter into the enjoyment of our labours.... One geometrical ratio might cancel another, and the nineteenth century was able to forget the fertility of the species in the dizzy virtues of compound interest. (ibid., pp. 11–12)

The ideas in these paragraphs are, in fact, none other than the Ramsey model of economic growth. Of course, if one were to formalize these ideas mathematically they would lead to a setup different in detail from the Ramsey model as we actually know it. That is because, in the Keynes story, workers are poor and save nothing and so only capitalists are able to have the choice between consuming and saving, choices which Ramsey would formalize by means of an Euler equation. But a mathematical model formulated in that different manner has properties very similar to those of the standard model.[4]

Everyone knows that Keynes was involved in helping give birth to the Ramsey model nearly ten years later in 1928. We know this because Ramsey thanks Keynes for producing the Keynes–Ramsey rule, as a way of articulating the findings of the model. Ramsey writes as follows:

Enough must therefore be saved to reach or approach bliss some time, but this does not mean that our whole income should be saved. The more we save the sooner we shall reach bliss, but the less enjoyment we shall have now, and we have to set the one against the other. Mr. Keynes has shown me that the rule governing the amount to be saved can be determined at once from these considerations. (Ramsey, 1928, p. 545)

---

[4] Notice that this is not a representative agent model of economic growth but class-based model of the kind to which Thomas Piketty has been urging us to return (Piketty, 2014).

What is not widely known is that it was a dinner-time conversation between Keynes and Ramsey that led Keynes to suggest to Ramsey that he should go away, write down these ideas in a formal mathematical model, and then send the resulting paper to Keynes for publication in the *Economic Journal*. Unfortunately, I do not have written evidence for this claim, an important one about the origins of a model which has become such a vital part of economists' mental equipment.[5] *Nevertheless*, both William Janeway and I believe that we heard Nicholas Kaldor make this claim during his course of lectures on the theory of economic growth in the early 1970s.

What is also not widely recognized is that Keynes himself had presented the ideas in this model, right back in 1919, in Chapter Two of the *Economic Consequences of the Peace*. It is this fact which, I believe, made it possible for Keynes to have the conversation with Ramsey, nearly ten years later, which led Ramsey to produce his model.[6]

2.2 International Interactions

The next thing that Keynes does in Chapter 2 is to set out what, in effect, is a model of an international economic system. This system is seen as including the whole of Europe:

[5] There is no evidence of this conversation in the relevant part of Moggridge's edition of the Keynes Collected Works. Keynes's correspondence with Ramsey about the article, which occurred by virtue of the fact that Keynes was Editor of the *Economic Journal*, is presented on pages 784–789 of *Volume XII of the Collected Works* (Keynes, 1983). And it is true that the relevant few pages begin with a printing of the letter that Ramsey wrote to Keynes submitting the article for publication. But there is no mention in that letter of any prior conversation. And the subsequent text is all about the analytical details of the article.

[6] A legal theorist has recently said to me that he cannot understand why everybody in economics thinks that Ramsey's idea was such a big deal. He pointed out to me that the basic ideas were already in the air. In particular, he claims that Max Weber's *Protestant Ethic and the Spirit of Capitalism* puts forward the same point of view. The only trouble with that claim is that, although the original text of much of that book was composed in 1904 and 1905, that text was in German and the book was not translated into English until much later. This was done by Talcott Parsons in 1930, and only then was the book published in English. I believe that the way in which Keynes set out these ideas, way back in 1919, in Chapter Two of *The Economic Consequences*, was extraordinarily innovative.

On the prosperity and enterprise of Germany, the prosperity of the rest of the Continent mainly depended. The increasing pace of Germany gave her neighbours an outlet for their products, in exchange for which the enterprise of the German merchant supplied them with their chief requirements at a low price.... Germany not only furnished these countries with trade, but, in the case of some of them, supplied a great part of the capital needed for their own development. (ibid., p. 10)

Within Europe, the interference of frontiers and of tariffs was reduced to a minimum. Not far short of three hundred millions of people lived within the three empires of Russia, Germany, and Austria Hungary. The various currencies, which were all maintained on a stable basis in relation to gold and to one another, facilitated the easy flow of capital and of trade....Over this whole area there was almost absolute security of property and of person. (ibid., p. 11)

But such a system also spread much further; the same process was clearly also at work within the British Empire. It was a global system, not just a European one.

[t]he accumulative habits of Europe before the war were the necessary condition [for this growth]: ... [o]f the surplus capital goods accumulated by Europe a substantial part was exported abroad, where its investment made possible the development of the new resources of food materials and transport, and enabled the Old World to stake out a claim on in the natural wealth and virgin potentialities of the New. The Old World employed with an immense prudence the annual tribute it was thus entitled to draw. The benefit of cheap and abundant supplies, resulting from the new developments which its surplus capital had made possible, was, it is true, enjoyed and not postponed. But the greater part of the money interest accruing on these foreign investments was reinvested and allowed to accumulate, as a reserve (it was then hoped) against the less happy day when the industrial labour of Europe could no longer purchase on such easy terms the produce of other continents.... The prosperity of Europe was based on the facts that, owing to the large exportable surplus of foodstuffs in America, she was able to purchase food at a cheap rate measured in terms of the labour required to produce her own exports, and that, as a result of her previous investments of capital, she was entitled to a substantial amount annually without any payment in return at all. (ibid., pp. 13–14)

Within the British Empire, and between the UK and the United States, the interference of frontiers and of tariffs was also reduced to a minimum. Keynes did not say this explicitly, but it is implicit. There too, currencies were maintained on a stable basis in relation to gold and to one another, facilitating the easy flow of capital and of trade. And there too there was almost absolute security of property and person.

2.3 Potential Instability

Finally, Keynes made clear, in these few short pages, just how fragile had been the growth process on which Europe had depended before the war. He identified two key features.

The first is the fragility of the process of accumulation which, said Keynes, "depended on a double bluff or deception".

I seek .... to point out that the principle of accumulation based on inequality was a vital part of the pre-war order of society and of progress as we then understood it, and to emphasize that this principle depended on unstable psychological conditions, which it may be impossible to re-create. It was not natural for a population, of whom so few enjoyed the comforts of life, to accumulate so hugely. The war has disclosed the possibility of consumption to all and the vanity of abstinence to many. Thus the bluff is discovered; the labouring classes maybe no longer willing to forgo so largely, and the capitalist classes, no longer confident of the future, may seek to enjoy more fully their liberties of consumption so long as they last, and thus precipitate the hour of their confiscation. (ibid., pp. 11 and 13)

The second is the fragility of the process of international equilibration. Keynes focuses on was the instability of Europe's claim, coupled with the completeness of her dependence, on the food supplies of the New World.

Even before the war, however, the equilibrium thus established between old civilizations and new resources was being threatened. The prosperity of Europe was based on the facts that, owing to the large exportable surplus of foodstuffs in America, she was able to purchase food at a cheap rate measured in terms of the labour required to produce her own exports, and that, as a result of her previous investments of capital, she was entitled to a substantial amount annually without any payment in return at all....[But by 1914], Europe's claim on the resources of the New World was becoming precarious; the law of diminishing returns was at last reasserting itself, and was making it necessary year by year for Europe to offer a greater quantity of other commodities to obtain the same amount of bread; and Europe, therefore, could by no means afford the disorganization of any of her principal sources of supply. (ibid., p. 14)

Here we see the possibility of international disequilibrium. Keynes continues:

The war had so shaken this system as to endanger the life of Europe altogether. A great part of the Continent was sick and dying; its population was greatly in excess of the numbers for which a livelihood was available; its organization was destroyed ... and its food supplies terribly impaired.... It was the task of the Peace Conference to honour engagements and to satisfy justice; but not less to re-establish life and to heal wounds. (ibid., pp. 15 and 16)

2.4 Implications for Keynes's Later Work

Harrod (1948, p. 68) suggested – and I agree with him – that what was foreshadowed in Chapter Two is Keynes's recognition of the need to bring about, by deliberate policy intervention, a satisfactory outcome for the world economy *as a whole*.

Furthermore, Keynes did not think – as Schumpeter claims – that by 1920 "those impulses [which had led to growth] were giving out, the spirit of private enterprise was flagging, investment opportunities were vanishing, and bourgeois saving habits had, therefore, lost their social function". Instead the system had an "equipoise" of rapid economic growth, what we would now call a steady-state growth rate. Keynes presented the essentials of the Ramsey model in order to demonstrate to his readers precisely what such equilibrium global growth process might look like. And his policy aim was to reinstate that global growth process.

Nevertheless this global growth process – even if reinstated – would be fragile. Herein lies the connection with Keynes's later work in the rest of his career.

First, the process of capital accumulation was fragile, resting upon "unstable psychological conditions". Because of this a private sector economy might not – on its own – be able to sustain this accumulation process. It might cease to do so – as in fact was to happen in the Great Depression. Policy action would then be required to keep the accumulation process going. The *General Theory* was written to address what might go wrong and how (fiscal) policy could be used to fix it.

Second, the process of international equilibration was fragile. Because of this the global macroeconomic system would only be able to work well if it was properly managed. By the end of his life, Keynes had come to the view that this would require two new things. It would need a new international monetary system, managed by two new international economic institutions: the IMF and the World Bank. And it would need a third new international economic institution to manage global trading relations, so as to avoid protectionism, which is what the General Agreement on Tariffs and Trade (or GATT), came into being to do.

I believe that we can see all of Keynes's life' work as a struggle to re-establish the kind of growing global system which he had sketched in this chapter. Only then might the inhabitants of London, or indeed the inhabitants of anywhere else, look out on the global world in the way which Keynes described in the passage quoted at the beginning of this section. Only then would such people be able to conduct their businesses both effectively and securely whilst moving from country to country.

Keynes did not yet have the technical apparatus needed to analyse what would actually happen to the post-war growth process if things really did go wrong. In the rest of this chapter, I describe the two pieces of analysis which Keynes needed, going beyond the discussion in the *Economic Consequences*, in order to underpin his aim of showing how to manage a growing world economy.

First, this analysis would require one to identify much more precisely how investment can become disconnected from savings, and to then carry out an analysis of *closed economy* macroeconomics to show how unemployment might emerge as a result. That analysis culminated in the *General Theory* (Keynes, 1936).

Second, that analysis would require a much clearer understanding of *international macroeconomics*. Keynes's ideas on this subject were much more scattered and took much longer to emerge. Even by 1929, he did not have the equipment necessary to understand the "transfer problem" identified in his discussion with Ohlin: what would go wrong internationally if Germany was actually forced to pay reparations without there being – at the same time – an expansion in demand for Germany's exports in other countries. And in the discussions in the early 1940s, leading up to Bretton Woods, he did not initially have the equipment needed to understand how adjustment could be made to happen in the world economy, in the face of changing patterns of technology and trade. An understanding of that process would clearly require one to use the closed-economy analysis present the *General Theory*. But it would also require the kind of international macroeconomic analysis which was developed by Keynes and others in the pre-Bretton-Woods discussions. This essentially involved under-standing how two or more countries would interact when each of the countries behaved in the manner described in the *General Theory*. However – as I have noted – Keynes died before he was able to system-atically write down these ideas, and so it fell to Meade and Swan to do that. Nevertheless, it is possible to show two things: how these ideas depend fundamentally on Keynes's work on closed economy macro-economics, and how they go beyond that work.

3 Closed Economy Macroeconomics

Macroeconomic conditions in the 1920s were worse than Keynes had predicted in the *Economic Consequences*. Germany resisted paying reparations and France invaded Germany's coal and steel regions in order to force the Germans to pay. Germany responded by inflating its currency to reduce its debt, resulting in hyperinflation. At the same time, Britain was deflating its currency in order to return to the gold standard at the old rate. The internal strife generated by Britain's defla-tion culminated in a general strike as the government strove to reduce wages. It also led to widespread unemployment. A new Labour govern-ment came to power in the election of May 1929. By October, policy-making was overwhelmed by the Wall Street crash. Soon afterward, the Prime Minister created a Committee of Enquiry which became known as the Macmillan Committee after its chairman, a Scottish judge. The Macmillan Committee was charged with carrying out a wide-ranging investigation of the options facing Britain. Keynes was the most eminent member of the committee. He had published his *Tract on Monetary Reform* some years earlier (Keynes, 1923) and his *Treatise on Money* was keenly awaited and would be published while the committee was sitting (Keynes, 1930). Keynes was central to what happened. He was asked to advance the members' thinking by presenting his ideas for five whole days in the early stages of the committee's work and for three further days when the committee was beginning to draft its report. Through the published papers of the committee, it is possible to see Keynes at work in 1930, ten years after he had written the *Economic Consequences*. We can see him examining how to restore the kind of growth process which he had analysed in that earlier book.

All that Keynes had said in the *Economic Consequences* in the pas-sage quoted above had come to pass: "Thus the bluff is discovered;

the labouring classes maybe no longer willing to forgo so largely, and the capitalist classes, no longer confident of the future, may seek to enjoy more fully their liberties of consumption so long as they last". As Schumpeter says, this passage does not yet contain the macroeconomics of the *General Theory*. And what is apparent, ten years after the publication of the *Economic Consequences,* is that it is written by someone who has still not equipped himself with the analytical tools necessary to understand why the British economy was in such a poor position, or how to correct the difficulties in which it found itself.[7]

To get to that position Keynes needed to make two further moves.

First, he had to separate the act of saving from the act of investing. In the *Economic Consequences* there is no such separation; the analysis implicitly describes those doing the saving as doing so in order to accumulate. By the time of the *Treatise*, Keynes had made this separation. But then he had to analyse what would happen if the amount which investors decided to invest was less than the amount which savers decided to save, and to consider why, if this happened, a depression might develop.

Keynes did not present a fully worked out model to the Macmillan Committee. But in the *Treatise on Money*, published at the same time as the Macmillan Committee reported, Keynes moved some of the way necessary. However, his trouble was that, in the model put forward in the *Treatise*, resources in the economy remain fully employed, and so the model did not yet do what Keynes needed. In this setup, wages are sticky but prices are flexible; a fall in investment leads to a reduction in overall demand, and thus – because resources are fully employed – results in a fall in the price level, which in turn causes a fall in the level of profits. In the *Treatise*, as in the *Economic Consequences*, Keynes still assumed that wages were consumed and profits were saved. The resulting fall in profits would thus bring about a fall in savings. There is a "price-level multiplier" at work: the price level falls until the fall in profits (and in savings) matches the fall in investment and savings are again brought into line with investment. But this is not a recession – a fall in output – of the kind which Keynes was seeking to describe.[8]

---

[7] For further details about the argument in the pages which follow,
see Temin and Vines (2013, 2014) and Vines and Wills (2020).

[8] It seems very odd to us, nearly 100 years later, to produce a model of
a depression in which it is assumed that the level of output is constant.
Hicks (1966) provides a helpful pointer to an understanding of what was going
on. Keynes's idea was that that the fall in profits just described would bring

Furthermore, in an Appendix to the Report, Keynes advocated fiscal expansion. In his model, fiscal expansion could not lead to an expansion in activity, but only to an increase in the level of prices relative to wages and so to a reduction in real wages! Moreover, he was unable to reply to the very different criticism made by members of the committee that a fiscal expansion would be crowded out by a rise in the interest rate.

Temin and Vines (2014) suggest that it was James Meade who saw what to do next. Meade said that, if investment falls and if wages are sticky, then the economy will actually move to the left along an upward-sloping short-run aggregate supply curve and output will fall, as well as there being a fall in the level of prices. The extent to which expenditure and demand falls depends partly on the size of the propensity to consume, and so on the size of the Keynesian multiplier. But how much output falls also depends on the slope of the supply curve, and so on how much prices will fall. It also depends on whether there is a fall in the interest rate which causes a moderation of the fall in investment. This was the argument which was embodied in the General Theory.[9]

It was only after he had written the *General Theory* that Keynes could properly engage with the "crowding-out" objection to fiscal expansion: that a rise in the interest rate would crowd out any fiscal expansion. If, he said, the interest rate is determined by liquidity preference then this will limit the extent to which the interest rate will rise following a fiscal expansion – or even prevent such a rise – and so will limit – or prevent – any crowding out which follows that fiscal expansion.

about a *tendency* for output to be reduced, and that was all that model of the trade cycle needed to do when analysing a depression. Similarly if, by contrast there were a rise in investment then that would, via the price level multiplier, lead to a rise in profits and that would create a *tendency* for output to increase. It is only when James Meade did what is described in the next paragraph – add an upward-sloping supply curve to the model – that one could move to set up which contained one more equation – the upward sloping supply curve – and so could solve for one more endogenous variable – which was taken to be to be the level of output. One could then show how the *tendency* for output to change would lead to an *actual change* in output. Nevertheless it took Keynes five years to get this clear in the process that led to the publication of the *General Theory* in 1936.

[9] The way in which Keynes fitted together the pieces of that argument is examined on some detail in Vines and Wills (2020).

This was what put Keynes in the position of being able to argue that the fragility of the expansion of the growing economy described in the *Economic Consequences* needed to be explicitly managed by fiscal policy.

It is worth noting the implications of my story about Keynes's arc of discovery for how one should interpret the *General Theory*. Many complained, when the *General Theory* appeared, that it was entirely confined to the short-run, and that it abstracts – possibly unhelpfully – from longer-term outcomes in the economy. As one might have expected, Schumpeter articulates these complaints very clearly in his obituary. In that spirit, many modern introductory textbooks on macroeconomics now begin with an analysis of the Solow growth model, and only turn to Keynesianism, and to short-run macro, in the second part of the book (see, for example, Jones, 2020). That wasn't true of textbooks written immediately after the Keynesian Revolution, for example that by Ackley (1961) which present the subject of macroeconomics as essentially to do with short-run issues. And that is understandable, since the Solow growth model had not yet appeared, and it was not until it did appear that macroeconomists really understood how to incorporate the Ramsey model in their macroeconomic apparatus.[10] But in the light of what I argue in this chapter, we can think of Keynes as totally modern. First he did the Ramsey growth model. And then he presented a short-run theory about how things might go wrong with the growth process analysed in that model.[11]

4 International Macroeconomics

In Chapter Two of the *Economic Consequences*, Keynes considered the need for balance between the Germany economy and the economies of southern Europe, and the need for balance between Europe, including Germany, and the rest of the world. This balance was part of what was necessary for the "equipoise" of the global growth process

---

[10] The standard way of describing the Ramsey model has become the following. Take the Solow model, in which the savings rate is exogenous. Then allow consumers to choose this savings rate. Voila – that is the Ramsey model!

[11] Some modern textbooks, for example, Blanchard (2011) and Carlin and Soskice (2015), still think that it is important to begin with the short run. But they do this in such a way as to present short-run analysis as somehow leading up to long-run analysis.

to be maintained. In the later chapters of the *Economic Consequences* he identified the danger to this balance imposed by the reparations being imposed on Germany. In particular, he saw the planned reparations as being beyond the capacity of Germany to pay. But he had not yet turned to an analysis of the implications of any attempt by Germany to actually pay the reparations to the rest of the world – in particular to the United States.

That consideration only came later in an extended discussion of the transfer problem with the Swedish economist Bertil Ohlin (Keynes, 1929; Ohlin, 1929). If Germany were to actually attempt to pay reparations, Keynes maintained, it would be required to run a current account surplus in order to make payments to foreign countries. But that requirement would lead to a "reparations transfer problem"; other countries might not be prepared to expand their demand for exports enough to enable Germany to run the required current account surplus.

What we again see, at exactly the same time as the Macmillan Committee was sitting, is someone who still did not yet completely understand what the necessary analysis of international macroeconomics would need to look like. Even if the country on which the reparations were imposed – Germany – tried to pay them, Keynes believed that the payment would only become possible if the rest of the world actually increased its demands for those exports. But it was not yet clear to him how to analyse whether the rest of the world would actually do this. Keynes would need the equipment provided by the *General Theory*, described above, in order to see how to do this.[12]

The essential idea is as follows.

As a preliminary, we note Keynes's first concern in 1929 about the "excess burden" which any transfer would involve. He effectively understood the Marshall-Lerner conditions (which were not yet widely understood). These show that a devaluation of the currency will only work – even if wages are sticky and so the real exchange rate depreciates – if trade flows are sufficiently responsive to the real exchange rate. These conditions require that the positive substitution effect, caused by the changes in relative prices which is a result of the real depreciation, is bigger in its effect on the trade balance than the

---

[12] As noted in Vines (2003), there is some discussion of interactions between countries in Keynes's *Treatise on Money*, but it is not well worked out.

negative income effect. That negative income effect is a result of the fact that a depreciation of the real exchange rate will cause the price of imports to rise relative to the price of exports (both prices being measured – for example – in domestic currency). This idea – that it will be necessary to worsen the terms of trade, causing a negative income effect, in order to improve the trade balance – is precisely what Keynes was describing in 1929 when he talked about the "excess burden". And that excess burden worried him.

But a full analysis of Keynes's concerns about the transfer problem requires more than this. The full story has two components. First, it uses the apparatus of the *General Theory* for a single country to show that a nominal devaluation of the currency will – if there is a real depreciation and if the Marshall Lerner conditions hold – not only improve the trade balance but also increase aggregate demand and output. This can be analysed using the kind of multiplier process presented in the *General Theory*. A devaluation will cause this, at the same time as it improves the trade balance. A fiscal expansion will both increase aggregate demand, working through the multiplier, and also worsen the trade balance. This means that, for any single country, like Germany, attempting to pay reparations, two instruments of policy – both a currency depreciation and a fiscal contraction – are needed in order to ensure the preservation of both internal and external balance. In particular, the payment of reparations will not only require devaluation but will also need fiscal restraint in order to release the resources necessary to make a trade surplus possible, and so enable payment of reparations. It is necessary to use the Swan diagram (Swan, 1963), building on the work of Meade (1951) to analyse this idea. As I discuss below, Keynes came to understand this analysis, but only much later, in the discussions that ran up to the Bretton Woods conference.

Second, when considering whether Germany would be able to pay its reparations internationally, it was necessary to carry out an analysis of what was happening in other countries as well as in Germany. To improve its trade balance, whilst releasing resources from home use in order that this is possible, Germany needed to both depreciate its real exchange rate (the "expenditure switching" policy) and reduce domestic demand (the expenditure changing policy). But, even if the Marshall Lerner conditions were to hold, the expenditure-switching policy might now be compromised by what was happening in the rest of the world – in Keynes's case, the United States. In such a scenario, the transfer from Germany would raise wealth and demand in the United States, which would led to an increase in aggregate demand there. At the same time, however, Germany's policy of contraction and depreciation would take demand away from the United States. Because the propensity to spend out of wealth in the United States is likely to be small, output there would be likely to fall, unless – that is – US policy stimulated domestic demand at the same time, for example by a fiscal expansion. The United States would thus be likely to go into recession. And that would mean that its demand for the exports of the home country – Germany – would fall. There would be a cumulative global response, and a world recession would emerge. As a result, Germany would not be able to improve its trade balance by as much as it would if it were acting on its own – in the way described above. This was clearly Keynes's concern in his discussion with Ohlin, but it is something which he did not yet have the equipment to understand.

The ideas about how to apply the apparatus of the *General Theory* to the international economy in this way were not clear to Keynes in 1929. This two-country story was not properly set out until it appeared in Meade's difficult book, published in 1951, for which he won the Nobel Prize. But, as I have already noted, Meade says in the Preface to his book, that the ideas in his book were formed during the War in his discussions with Keynes leading up to the Bretton Woods conference. I now briefly describe how this happened, again building on Vines (2003) and Temin and Vines (2013, 2014).

5 Putting the Ideas Together: Bretton Woods

Keynes had a heart attack soon after the General Theory was published, and nearly died. By the time he had recovered, he needed to turn to the problems which would emerge as Britain started preparing for war and – as a result – neared full employment. Of initial concern was the need to fight the war without creating inflationary or balance of payments pressures. In February of 1940, *How to Pay for the War* was published (Keynes, 1940). In it, Keynes was able to use the model of the *General Theory* to show how to conduct macroeconomic management and achieve what was desired: to ensure that demand for domestically produced goods was no greater than the supply of these goods, once the needs of war had been met.

Going beyond internal balance, the management of the British economy during World War II needed to face up to the problems of Britain's external payments – both how to pay for the war internationally and what to do after the war. It is important to remember that Keynes had been unable to deal with the problem of external adjustment when discussing the transfer problem in 1929. How would the country's external accounts now be made to add up?

Given the achievement of full employment (using the tools laid out in the *General Theory*), Keynes could think about external problems simply by asking the question: could the country export enough to pay for the imports it would need if it was operating at – or close to – full employment?

In the *short run* (during the war) there was a financing need: the level of imports (both military and non-military) required for survival needed to be paid for. As a result of the Lend-Lease programme, Britain was able to fight the war without the kind of daily threat of financial crisis which had characterized the First World War (Skidelsky, 2000, p. 100).

In the *long run*, external balance required a return to the kind of balance between regions of the world described in the *Economic Consequences*. But here the relationship with the United States came to impose an important constraint. Article VII of Lend-Lease, which became known as the "Consideration" read as follows:

The terms and conditions upon which the United Kingdom receives defense aid from the United States of America and the benefits to be received by the United States of America in return therefore, as finally determined, shall be such as not to burden commerce between the two countries but to promote mutually advantageous economic relations between them and the betterment of worldwide economic relations; they shall provide against discrimination in the United States of America or the United Kingdom against the importation of any product originating in the other country; and they shall provide for the formulation of measures for the achievement of these ends. (See Keynes, 1980a, pp. 173–173; Skidelsky, 2000, pp. 99–100)

When Keynes read this, he asked Dean Acheson (then Under-Secretary of State) whether the article referred to Imperial Preference and to the sterling payments system. Acheson said that it did. Keynes was furious and exploded (Acheson, 1969, pp. 19–30). Upon reflection he then asked himself: How might the UK deal with these American demands?

Keynes came to the following conclusion. Suppose that free trade (including the absence of trade restrictions against the United States and the unwinding of more specific imperial preference) were to be imposed on Britain along with open international finance. Then the position of the UK could only be maintained as a positive one if the trade were freed on a global basis, against a background in which international finance was adequately managed. But Britain faced the prospect of a protectionist United States, even though US rhetoric supported free trade for the world as a whole. And – as a result of Article VII of Lend-Lease – the United States had the power to require that Britain abandon the form of protectionism that it had embraced since the early 1930s with Imperial Preference.

Keynes began with international finance, producing in late summer of 1941 the first draft of his proposal for a Clearing Union. Keynes had a desired outcome in mind for the world economy as a whole: he wanted full employment of resources and he wanted this at a low level of global interest rates. Accommodating finance, at low interest rates, would provide the environment in which the world' capital – so much of which been destroyed by the war – could be rebuilt. The international movement of capital, which Keynes had analysed in the *Economic Consequences*, would need to be adequately managed. In his Clearing Union draft, we see him deploying the model of the *General Theory*. He was concerned that a shortage of global liquidity might trigger global malfunction in the form of a global recession. He thus pressed for a global 'Clearing Union' – literally something like the clearing system within a national banking process – which would enable global liquidity needs to be met without any hindrance or restraint, and without the risk of such restraint (Skidelsky, 2000, pp. 304, 310, 312). He wanted this to happen at a low level of global interest rates.

Alongside this, there needed to be a macroeconomic control mechanism, to replace that found in the Gold Standard. For Keynes, the mechanism was to be fiscal policies of demand management in individual countries, of the kind advocated on the *General Theory*. In the aggregate, these would be able to give rise to the right level of global aggregate demand. Full employment would be ensured by fiscal policy – through the full employment plans of the Treasuries of the separate countries. If expansionary policy was needed, then it should be assured by fiscal means, with cheap money in the background. If restraint was needed, it would be fiscal restraint, of the kind which Keynes had analysed in *How to Pay for the War*.

How, in addition, would international equilibrium be established between parts of the global economic system, the kind of "equipoise" analysed in the *Economic Consequences* in the passages quoted above? Keynes's first thoughts deliberately did not presume a response consistent with the requirements of Article VII of the Lend-Lease Treaty, or of the kind in place before World War I, as described in the *Economic Consequences* (Vines, 2003, 2017). Instead, there would be protectionist restrictions on foreign trade such as tariffs and quotas. These should replace the wage adjustment mechanism in the Gold Standard, as the necessary means to re-equilibrate exports with imports in response to any lack of competitiveness or any negative external shock. In addition, the financial system would need to differ from the Gold Standard by providing generous international liquidity, sufficient to allow time for the required adjustments to work, which would be brought about by protectionism. And capital controls should be used where necessary (perhaps all the time) to remove a malfunctioning of the capital-account mechanism, in that private sector capital tended to flee from countries in difficulty rather than helping to provide liquidity during periods of adjustment. At the core of these ideas was the view that a balance-of-payments constraint might stand in the way of full employment policies.

Keynes's move away from protectionism in trade towards a position consistent with the liberal global order that he had once admired is explained by Skidelsky (2000) in Chapters 7, 9, and 10, and discussed in detail in Vines (2017). Clearly, the problems which protectionism for any one country was designed to guard against are global in origin.

As already noted, Keynes was concerned with whether trade was sufficiently responsive to exchange rate change. Even if global aggregate demand was adequate, Keynes believed, external adjustment by means of relative price change by any one country would be difficult if all others were protectionist. Keynes and his disciples realized early on the prisoners' dilemma problem of trade liberalization, and, in the context of their monetary discussions, they recognized that globally freer trade was also necessary. Adjustment through relative price changes would then be in an environment of expanding trade, and so demands for goods would be much more price-elastic at the margin, enabling the Marshall–Lerner conditions to hold by a wider margin.

Meade (1990, p. 22) makes this point very clearly in a diary entry made on December 31, 1944. He emphasized

the need for flexible exchange rates to adjust balance of payments [to avoid pushing the burden of adjustment onto] rigid trade controls … in a world in which internal wage levels were not easily reduced. [Such adjustment might be] more easily acceptable if it was preceded by an international agreement to lower trade barriers, since in that case smaller movements in exchange rates would be required.

This need was why, once work was moving forward on the monetary proposals, James Meade set to work in 1944 to produce a first British draft of a proposal for an International Trade Organisation. (See Keynes, 1980b, pp. 239–327) Meade, Keynes and others on the British side saw clearly that the connection between trade and finance was circular, since a well-functioning international financial system would also ease the path to the trade liberalization which they sought.

The pages of the Keynes's "Collected Papers on Commercial Policy" (Keynes, 1980b, pp. 239–327) bear eloquent testimony to Keynes's change of view. "What Keynes wanted to recreate was a modified version of the Britain in which he had grown up – a liberal world power set in a liberal world" (Skidelsky, 2000, p. 385). In this, a liberal trading world was central. The final three pages of Keynes's last paper (Keynes, 1946), published posthumously, set out how he hoped such a system of international payments adjustment, relying on changes in relative prices, might keep balances of payments and, in particular, the US trade balance in order.

Such a system of international payments adjustment, relying on changes in relative prices as part of the process, was the kind of analysis which Keynes had needed when discussing the transfer problem with Ohlin in 1929. But it was only in the preparations for Bretton Woods that Keynes came to understand how this process might work.

Going beyond the two-target-two-instrument system outlined above, these ideas fit into an even broader overall four-by-four system. In our book on Keynes, Peter Temin and I describe how, one day in 1944, at a meeting of the Board of Trade, Keynes sketched a plan for an open liberal world economy on the back of an envelope and passed it to Meade (Vines, 2008; Temin and Vines, 2014). He remarked, as he did so, that at last he was convinced: he now knew how the world economic system should be remade. Here is what that sketch looked like (Table 15.1).

Table 15.1 *Keynes's sketch of a plan for an open liberal world economy, 1944*

Objective	Instrument(s)	Responsible Authority
Full Employment	Demand Management (mainly fiscal)	National Governments
Balance-of-Payments Adjustments	Pegged but Adjustable Exchange Rates	International Monetary Fund
Promotion of International Trade	Tariff Reductions, etc.	International Trade Organisation
Economic Development	Official International Lending	World Bank

Keynes listed four goals of international economic policies down the left side of his sketch. The first two goals were short-term; the other two were long-term. There was a policy instrument for each goal, since four instruments were needed to achieve four goals, and there were separate organizations to operate each of these instruments.

The first organization, concerned with domestic macroeconomic balance, was national; all the others were international. The first goal was full employment. This was national, representing balance within each country. The aim was to have full employment without inflation. Since the goal was national, the organizations to make policies to achieve the goal were national as well. The Full Employment White Paper in the UK, and a similar document in Australia and in many other countries, set out how this was to be done; in the US the Employment Act of 1946, revised and expanded in the Humphrey-Hawkins Full Employment Act of 1978, enjoined the US government to reach this goal.

The second goal was adjustment of the balance of payments. This, and the goals that followed, were international so the institutions to accomplish these goals had to be international as a result. Keynes anticipated a set of pegged rates that could be adjusted from time to time as needed and this became the basis of the Bretton Woods System after the war ended. The International Monetary Fund (IMF) was established as an institution that would help nations adjust their exchange rates, advise them when adjustments were needed, and deal with crises that could occur if adjustments were delayed. The IMF – an improved version of Keynes's Clearing Union – eventually became a crucial policy-making institution.

Keynes's fourth goal involved a return to his concerns in *The Economic Consequences of the Peace* for the promotion of economic growth and development. He had maintained his interest in this goal for a quarter of a century and wanted to establish an organization to promote it through international lending. He proposed that a World Bank would complement the IMF among the new institutions. The IMF would deal with short-run macroeconomic problems, while the World Bank would work to promote the international movement of capital, and investment in support of long-run growth. An institution doing this was, Keynes thought, necessary since private sector capital markets could not achieve this adequately on their own. Using today's language we would say that this institution would enable the savings which were made in the world's most advanced economy (the US) to be deployed in emerging market economies, then not just in Western European countries – where there was much war damage to repair – but further afield in the Eastern European periphery as well. The classic study of how this last set of developments might become possible, through a process of international cooperation, was the one carried out at this time by Paul Rosenstein Rodan and Heinz Arndt (Arndt, 1943; Rosenstein Rodan, 1943).[13] The Rosenstein-Rodan paper and the Arndt book both advocated export-led growth in emerging markets in the post-war world, with the capital investment necessary to make this possible funded by means of loans organized by the World Bank.

That takes us to Keynes's third goal in his sketch – the promotion of international trade: he wanted to make sure that that tariffs would be reduced after the war to promote international trade, including with emerging-market economies. I have already noted that James Meade persuaded Keynes that a liberal global trading system would be necessary in order for exchange-rate change to be able bring about the necessary adjustments of international trading patterns, as

---

[13] It is clear that Keynes will have seen the Rosenstein-Rodan paper since it was published in the *Economic Journal* and Keynes is known to have read more or less everything published in the journal. The book by Heinz Arndt was written by Arndt, whilst working for Rosenstein Rodan, as part of a Committee of Enquiry convened at Chatham House in London, to study the prospects for post-war economic cooperation.

and when that might be necessary for balance-of-payments reasons. But the need was much deeper than this. I have also noted above that the United States was determined to dismantle the preferential trading system which had been established within the British Empire in the 1930s, and that the Lend Lease Agreement put it in a position to do just that. As a result, Keynes needed to ensure that any liberalization of global trade would nevertheless provide opportunities for Britain to prosper, and for the other members of the Empire to do the same. The International Trade Organization which Meade worked to develop, and which became the GATT and ultimately the World Trade Organization, was to pursue this goal in a series of international negotiations designed to lower trade barriers. But it would manage this liberalization process in a multilateral way. As a result, Britain and the countries in its Empire would therefore not be forced to liberalise their borders unless the United States itself liberalized, and unless a global system were established in which the liberalization process would be managed in a cooperative multilateral manner.

Nevertheless, many in the United Kingdom were very concerned about the threat that the UK faced from the United States in relation to this matter. They thus questioned the strategy which Keynes had adopted in the run-up to Bretton Woods. They asked him why he had devoted so much attention to international macroeconomic management, and to the establishment of the IMF and the World Bank. Why had he not, instead, gone straight away to a discussion of how to manage international trading conditions, and immediately moved to a proposal to establish an International Trade Organisation?

I discuss this matter in some detail in Vines (2017). But it is worth ending this section of the present chapter by quoting Keynes's response to that question. Here is what he said in a speech in the House of Lords, just before the Bretton Woods conference was due to take place.

There was a logical reason for dealing with the monetary proposals first. It is extraordinarily difficult to frame any proposals about tariffs if countries are free to alter the value of their currencies without agreement and at short notice. Tariffs and currency depreciations are in many cases alternatives. Without currency arrangements you have no ground on which to discuss tariffs.... It is very difficult while you have monetary chaos to have order of any kind in other directions ... if we have a firm ground on this particular issue it will be a great deal easier to reach a satisfactory answer on other questions. It is perhaps an accident that the monetary proposals got started first ... but I am not sure that it was not a fortunate accident. (Keynes, 1944)

Soon after the Bretton Woods conference the trade negotiations got underway seriously. These led, in due course, to the General Agreement on Tariffs and Trade, or GATT, which was signed in October 1947.

6 Conclusion

In Chapter Two of the *Economic Consequences,* Keynes described the high levels of savings and investment that had enabled very rapid growth before World War I. He set out the Ramsey model of economic growth to show how equilibrium growth might be possible – what he called "equipoise". He showed how international specialization played a role in such growth. And he argued that this global growth process was fragile.

Writing in 1919, Keynes wanted to recreate the circumstances in which this fragility did not endanger the post-war global growth process. In this chapter I have argued that Keynes had already grasped what he would need to understand in order to achieve this. And I have argued that, over the course of the next twenty-five years, he obtained that understanding.

First, in order to understand how to deal with the fragility of the growth process itself, Keynes had to separate the act of saving from the act of investing. But then he had to analyse what would happen if the amount which investors wanted to invest was less than the amount which savers decided to save, and to examine why, if this happened, a depression might develop, causing widespread unemployment. Furthermore he had to understand how a fiscal expansion might help to solve such a problem. He had to show why an injection of demand by the government might not be crowded out but might – instead – help fight economic depression and enable growth to return. He achieved this in the General Theory.[14]

---

[14] And, of course, he needed to understand what needed to be done if, by contrast, savings were too low rather than too high. He did that in *How to Pay for the War* (Keynes, 1940).

Second, in order to understanding how to deal with the fragility of international interactions, Keynes had to analyse how these interactions could be incorporated into the macroeconomic framework that he had created in the *General Theory*. He then had to examine how balance-of-payments disequilibria might develop in many countries, causing problems, including unemployment. And he had to understand what would be necessary to achieve a satisfactory outcome, not just in one country, but in the world as a whole. Furthermore he had to understand how new international economic institutions might be created to help solve these problems and had to work out what rules these institutions should follow. He achieved this in the run up to the Bretton Woods conference, and the IMF and the World Bank were duly created at that conference. In addition he played a part in the establishment of the International Trade Organisation – what became the GATT and eventually the WTO – because he thought that a rules-based system of international trading relationships was also necessary.

I thus conclude that, by 1944, Keynes had obtained the understandings that, in Chapter Two of the *Economic Consequences*, he had said would be necessary in order to see how equipoise might to be regained. This takes me back to the beginning of my story.

Chapter Two of the *Economic Consequences* purports to be one thing: an introduction to a book about the effects of reparations. This is what Schumpeter took it to be. But it is actually also something else: a roadmap of Keynes's future intellectual journey, all the way to the *General Theory*, and on to Bretton Woods. Why did Keynes write something which tried to be both these things at the same time? Here – as in so many other places – we see his genius at work. The roadmap was necessary for the intellectual journey. And only when he had finished this journey would Keynes be able fully to understand the effects of reparations.

References

Acheson, D. (1969) *Present at the Creation*, New York: Norton.
Ackley, G. (1961) *Macroeconomic Theory*, New York: Macmillan.
Arndt (1943) *The Economic Lessons of the Nineteen-Thirties*, London: Chatham House.
Blanchard, O. (2011) *Macroeconomics*, Boston: Pearson.

Carlin, W. and D. Soskice (2015) *Macroeconomics: Institutions, Instability and the Financial System*, Oxford: Oxford University Press.

Dasgupta, P. (2019) "Ramsey and Intergenerational Welfare Economics", *The Stanford Encyclopedia of Philosophy (Summer 2019 Edition)*, Edward N. Zalta, ed. https://plato.stanford.edu/archives/sum2019/entries/ramsey-economics/.

Harrod, R. (1948) "Keynes, the Economist" Chapter VIII in Harris (1960).

Harris, S. (1948) *The New Economics; Keynes' Influence on Theory and Public Policy*, New York: Alfred A. Knopf.

Hicks, J. (1966) A Memoir by Sir John Hicks. Initial chapter in Robertson (1966).

IMF (2004) *The Bretton Woods Institutions Turn 60*, Washington: International Monetary Fund. Available at http://external.worldbankimflib.org/Bwf/60panel2.htm

Jones, C. (2020) *Macroeconomics*, New York: Norton.

Keynes, J. M. (1919) The Economic Consequences of the Peace. Collected Works of J. M. Keynes, vol. II.

Keynes, J. M. (1923) A Tract on Monetary Reform. Collected Works of J. M. Keynes, vol. III.

Keynes, J. M. (1929) "The German Transfer Problem", *The Economic Journal*, **39**(153), 1–7.

Keynes, J. M. (1930) A Treatise on Money, volumes 1 and 2. J. M. Keynes Collected Works, vols. V and VI.

Keynes, J. M. (1936) The General Theory of Employment, Interest and Money, J. M. Keynes Collected Works, vol. VII.

Keynes, J. M. (1940) How to Pay for the War, J. M. Keynes Collected Works, vol. VIII.

Keynes, J. M. (1944) Speech by Lord Keynes on the International Monetary Fund debate House of Lords Debates, May 16, 1944.

Keynes, J. M. (1946) "The Balance of Payments of the United States", *Economic Journal*, **56**(222), 172–187.

Keynes, J. M. (1975) Essays in Biography, J. M. Keynes Collected Works, vol. IX.

Keynes, J. M. (1980a) Activities 1940–1943: External War Finance, J. M. Keynes Collected Works, vol. XXIII.

Keynes, J. M. (1980b) Activities 1940–1944 Shaping the Post War World: The Clearing Union, J. M. Keynes Collected Works, vol. XXV.

Keynes, J. M. (1980c) Activities 1941–1946 Shaping the Post War World: Bretton Woods and Reparations, J. M. Keynes Collected Works, vol. XXVI.

Keynes, J. M. (1983) Economics Articles and Correspondence: Investment and Editorial, J. M. Keynes Collected Works, vol. XII.

Keynes, J. M. (1971) *The Collected Works of John Maynard Keynes*, London: Macmillan.

Lewis, W. A. (1954) "Economic Development with Unlimited Supplies of Labour", *The Manchester School,* 22(2) 139–191.

Meade, J. E. (1951) *The Theory of International Economic Policy*, vol. 1: The Balance of Payments, Oxford: Oxford University Press.

Meade, J. E. (1990) *The Collected Papers of James Meade*, vol. IV (S. Howson and D. Moggridge, eds.), London: Unwin Hyman.

Ohlin, B. (1929) "The Reparation Problem: A Discussion", *The Economic Journal*, 39(154), 172–182.

Picketty, T. (2014) *Capital in the Twenty-first Century*, Boston, MA: Belknap Press.

Ramsey, F. (1928) "A Mathematical Theory of Saving", *The Economic Journal*, 38(152), 543–559.

Robertson, D. (1966) *Essays in Money and Interest,* London: Collins.

Rosenstein-Rodan, Paul (1943) "Problems of Industrialization of Eastern and South Eastern Europe", *Economic Journal,* 53(210), 202–211.

Schumpeter, J. A. (1946) "John Maynard Keynes, 1883–1946", *American Economic Review,* 36(4), 495–518.

Skidelsky, R. (2000) *John Maynard Keynes: Fighting for Britain*, London: Macmillan.

Solow, R. M. (1956) "A Contribution to the Theory of Economic Growth", *The Quarterly Journal of Economics*, 70(1), 65–94.

Steil, B. (2013) *The Battle of Bretton Woods: John Maynard Keynes, Harry Dexter White, and the Making of a New World Order*, Princeton: Princeton University Press.

Swan, T. W. (1956) "Economic Growth and Capital Accumulation", *Economic Record*, 32(2), 334–361.

Swan, T. (1963) "Longer Run Problems of the Balance of Payments", Chapter 24 in the *Australian Economy: A Volume of Readings*, edited by H.W. Arndt and W. M. Corden, *Melbourne: F. W. Cheshire. Reprinted in A.E.A. Reading in International Economics,* edited by Richard E. Caves and Harry G. Johnson, Homewood: Irwin & Co.

Temin, P., and D. Vines (2013) *The Leaderless Economy: Why the World Economic System Fell Apart and How to Fix It,* Princeton: Princeton University Press.

Temin, P., and D. Vines (2014) *Keynes: Useful Economics for the World Economy,* Cambridge, MA: MIT Press.

Van Dormael, A. (1978) *Bretton Woods: Birth of a Monetary System,* London: Macmillan Press.

Vines, D. (2003) "John Maynard Keynes 1937–1946: The Creation of International Macroeconomics", Review of *John Maynard Keynes*

1937–1946: Fighting for Britain by Robert Skidelsky. *Economic Journal* 115, pp. F338–60.

Vines, D. (2008) "Meade, James Edward (1907–1995)", *The New Palgrave Dictionary of Economics*, Springer, 4079–4097.

Vines, D. (2017) "John Maynard Keynes as a Global Economic Policymaker: First Do the Macro and then Do the Rest", *Annals of the Fondazione Luigi Einaudi,* **51**(1), 123–148.

Vines, D., and S. Wills (2020) "The Rebuilding Macroeconomic Theory Project Part II: Multiple Equilibria, Toy Models, and Policy Models in a New Macroeconomic Paradigm", *Oxford Review of Economic Policy,* **36**(3), 427–497.

Weber, M. (1930) *The Protestant Ethic and the Spirit of Capitalism. (Reprinted in 1970)*, London: Routledge.

16 | Keynes, The Economic Consequences of the Peace, and Popular Perceptions of the First World War*

JONATHAN BOFF

In June 1919 Maynard Keynes resigned as Treasury adviser to the British delegation at the Paris peace talks in fury and despair at the terms dictated to Germany in the Treaty of Versailles. He spent the summer and autumn writing a mixture of statistics and satire which offered ordinary folk a peek behind the arras in Paris, indicted the inequity and economic impracticability of the treaty, and eviscerated the politicians responsible. *The Economic Consequences of the Peace* was the most famous piece of non-fiction about the First World War to be published in the decade after the Armistice. It outsold the first volume of Winston Churchill's *The World Crisis* by a factor of ten and remains in print today. This chapter reviews the ideas and reception of Keynes's *The Economic Consequences of the Peace*. The importance of the book for Keynes's subsequent career, and for the Treaty of Versailles and the interwar economy, has ensured that this story has been told before, for example by Harrod, 1951; Skidelsky, 1983; Moggridge, 1992; Clarke, 2009; Davenport-Hines, 2015; Cox, 2019; as well as Eichengreen, 1992; Feldman, 1997; MacMillan, 2001; Steiner, 2005; Tooze 2014; and Ferguson, 1998. This chapter, however, focuses on a single, as yet untold, aspect: how *Economic Consequences* fits into the context of debates about the construction of the memory of the Great War. It asks: 'What role did Keynes and *The Economic Consequences of the Peace* play in the formation of the "futility myth" which dominates British popular perception of the First World War to this day?'

* Thanks to Aimée Fox, Jonathan Gumz, Matthew Hilton, John Horne, Matt Houlbrook, Helen McCartney, Catriona Pennell, Richard Toye, and Vanda Wilcox for their comments on an earlier version of this article.

To address this question, this chapter, first, outlines the features of the futility myth itself and explores traditional explanations for its origins in the late 1920s. Second, it discusses the production and content of *Economic Consequences*, before, thirdly, tracing its influence and trying to uncover the connections between the book and myth. This exercise demonstrates three things: that the initial success of Keynes's book was predominantly concentrated with those pre-disposed to agree with it; that we still need better to understand the shift in public opinion during the 1920s which carried Keynes's views from controversial to mainstream; and that although we can see that *Economic Consequences* was highly influential in general and must have influenced the construction of the myth in some way, we have no way of either proving the connection or quantifying its impact.

I

The 'futility myth' has long dominated popular perceptions of the Great War, a war which, according to *Blackadder*, was all 'blood, noise and endless poetry' (Curtis and Elton, 1989, Episode 4 'Private Plane'). David Reynolds summarized the myth neatly: 'our overriding sense now is of a meaningless, futile bloodbath in the mud of Flanders and Picardy – a tragedy of young men whose lives were cut off in their prime for no evident purpose' (2013, p. xv). Major public events and artworks of the recent centenary, such as the Poppies at the Tower and the flashmobs of 'tommies' at railway stations on the anniversary of the first day of the Battle of the Somme, with their concentration on sacrifice and the pity of war, demonstrated its resilience (Cummins and Piper, 2014; Deller and Norris, 2016; Audoin-Rouzeau and Becker, 2002, p. 2; McCartney, 2017).

Historians have identified, and argued about the importance of, a number of important waypoints in the development of the futility myth. Candidates include the Second World War, the 1960s, the end of the Cold War, the deaths of the last veterans in the early 2000s, and the centenary itself (Bond, 1991, p. 8; Bond, 1999, p. 22; Bond, 2002, p. 51; Todman, 2005, pp. 29–35, 94–9, 118–20, 221; Audoin-Rouzeau and Becker, 2002, pp. 6–8; Danchev, 1991). The most important development, however, has traditionally been agreed to be the 'war books boom' of the late 1920s, when writers such as Erich Maria Remarque, Robert Graves, Edmund Blunden and Siegfried

Sassoon presented their soldier's eye view of the war, speaking what Paul Fussell (2000, pp. 21–2, 29) described as the language of irony, a stark contrast with the 'high diction' of Thomas Hardy and earlier poets. These war books captured the narrative, Jay Winter and Antoine Prost argue (2005, pp. 6–31, 59, 83–6; see also Grieves, 1991), because history had failed to tell the story of the war that the public needed. Attempts by John Buchan, Arthur Conan Doyle, and the official historians to tell the story of the war in top-down terms excluded ordinary soldiers. A public keen to find out 'how it was' was forced to turn to war novels and narratives to find out.

It was Fussell who identified the initial canon of 'disenchanted' literature of the late 1920s, as Blunden's *Undertones of War*, Sassoon's *Memoirs of a Fox-Hunting Man*, Graves's *Good-bye to All That*, Blunden's new edition of Wilfred Owen's war poetry, and R.C. Sherriff's play, *Journey's End*. Fussell, along with Modris Eksteins (1989, pp. 253–5), credited these 'war books' with breaking a decade of bereaved speechlessness, a silence which has become, in Max Saunders's words, 'a truism of literary history' (2010, p. xiii).[1] In fact, however, this flood of new writing did not suddenly appear from nowhere: the 1920s saw a flood of books representing a range of opinions about the war. Some of them continued the wartime trend for popular, up-beat, patriotic war novels with great success. Gilbert Frankau's *Peter Jackson, Cigar Merchant* (1919), Robert Keable's *Simon called Peter* (1921), and Ernest Raymond's *Tell England* (1922) all achieved sales in the hundreds of thousands (Bracco, 1993, pp. 65–72, 71, 29; Cecil, 1996, p. 174; Cecil, 2003).[2] Others, such as A.P. Herbert's *The Secret Battle* (1919), C.E. Montague's *Disenchantment* (1922), and Ford Madox Ford's *Parade's End* tetralogy (1924–8), were outspoken in their criticism of the war (Hynes, 1990, pp. 269–463; Winter, 1995, pp. 1–8, 204–21; Todman, 2005, pp. 17–21; Watson, 2004, pp. 185–221).

Even when the literature of disenchantment boomed in the late 1920s, it was not exclusively anti-war. Some books, such as Manning's *Her Privates We*, are impossible to categorize, and pro-war books, such as Charles Carrington's *A Subaltern's War*, were still being published (Bond, 2002, pp. 28–30, 32; Todman, 2005, pp. 21–2; Prior and Wilson, 1994, p. 79). Further, many of the authors characterized

---

[1] See also Falls, 1989, p. xv and Barnett, 1970.
[2] See also Audoin-Rouzeau and Becker, 2002, pp. 170–1.

as 'anti-war' rejected the label. Thorough-going pacifists like Max Plowman, author (anonymously) of *A Subaltern on the Somme* (1927), were rare (Ceadel, 2000, pp. 228–9). The German author Erich Maria Remarque, whose *All Quiet on the Western Front* directly inspired some of the British writers, claimed that his was a book, not about the war, but about his lost generation, adrift amid the economic and political storms of Weimar Germany. He felt so strongly that this message had been misinterpreted in *All Quiet* that in 1931 he wrote *The Way Back* specifically to make that case more directly (Eksteins, 1989, pp. 278–84). Nor did the authors form a coherent group, or even agree among themselves. Blunden described *All Quiet on the Western Front* as 'piddling, lying rubbish' (Cecil, 2003, p. 814). Robert Graves professed surprise at being taken for 'the author of a violent treatise against war' (1929, p. 13). The rage of people like Sassoon was directed, not at the war, but at the jingo civilians who ignored its costs. Tim Kendall has usefully described the attitude as 'anti-pro-war' (2013, pp. xx–xxi).[3]

These books were, on the whole, both commercial and critical successes. Sales figures are not always available, but at a time when British sales of 2,000 copies was considered respectable for a first novel, *Good-bye to All That*, for example, sold 20,000 copies in its first five days (Watson, 2004, p. 219; Bracco, 1993, p. 28). *Undertones of War* was reprinted three times within a month; *Her Privates We* four times (Bond, 2003, p. 821). A.P. Herbert's *The Secret Battle*, which had sold poorly when first published in 1919, became a success when re-issued in 1928 (Hynes, 1990, p. 306). *Journey's End* ran for 593 performances and sold 175,000 copies of the script (Eksteins, 1989, p. 277; Trott, 2017, pp. 30–43). Critical reception was also positive. Blunden received very positive reviews; Graves the same; and *Memoirs of a Fox-hunting Man* won both the Hawthornden and James Tait Black Memorial prizes (Watson, 2004, pp. 195–9, 219–20).

Why did books, seen, by the audience at least if not by their authors, as disenchanted, cut through so effectively after 1928 and help establish a lasting 'futility myth', when they had not a decade earlier? Four possible solutions have been suggested. The first idea, that this literature played a cathartic function after a decade of conscious or unconscious repression and mourning at both the individual and collective

---

[3] Thanks to Dr David Griffith for bringing Kendall's distinction to my attention.

levels, is not borne out by the chronology, as we have already seen (Audoin-Rouzeau and Becker, 2002, pp. 170–81, 225). Secondly, perhaps stories of individual experience offered 'the truth about the war', in a way which history could not, to an audience which had, as a result of the war, lost its sense of history as an uninterrupted pattern (Hynes, 1990, pp. ix–x, 433, 455; Fussell, 2000, pp. 21–4; Winter and Prost, 2005, pp. 85–6). Dan Todman makes the related point that, by concentrating on what the war had been like, these books avoided potentially divisive debates about its meaning (2005, p. 22). The third possibility is, as Jay Winter maintains, that these books captured a widely shared sense that the war was an exercise in futility, that 'older languages of grandeur and glory had to be recast in the light of what soldiers saw and felt during that war', and that these books expressed the alienation and *anomie* of returning soldiers in the years of peace and 'the failure of postwar experience to justify the war'. They thus resonated with readers who themselves felt 'disenfranchised and dispossessed' in a world which had lived up to few or none of the wartime promises made for it (2017, p. 94). Within the context of what John Horne (2005, 2009) calls 'cultural demobilisation', as different individuals, groups and societies, all at their own speed and with varying degrees of completeness, found the emotions and antagonisms of wartime unwinding, the war increasingly could be judged on its results.[4] 'Once the early economic troubles of the 1920s turned into the interwar depression, once the brotherhood of arms turned into the embitterment of the General Strike of 1926', argues Winter, 'then what possible benefit the British people had gained from their victory became a question without an answer' (2017, p. 112). One of the first and loudest to warn of this danger was Maynard Keynes.

II

Keynes, as a consequence of his work at the Treasury in 1914–18, and at the Paris Peace Conference in 1919, is an important witness for economic and financial histories of the First World War and its aftermath (Roberts, 2013; Burk, 1985; MacMillan, 2001; Mantoux, 1946; Toye, 2015; Markwell, 2006; Strachan, 2004; Broadberry and Harrison,

---

[4] Thanks to Professor Horne for reminding me of this point, and for sending me a copy of one of these articles.

2005). His biographers tend often to treat *Economic Consequences* as important primarily because it was the book which made Keynes famous. Yet the connection between *Economic Consequences* and popular perceptions of the Great War has been largely ignored. Even Samuel Hynes, who claims to see the book as important, spends just two pages discussing it in a book nearly 500 pages long (1990, pp. 291–3).

The story of how Keynes produced *The Economic Consequences of the Peace* is well known (Skidelsky, 1983, pp. 370–91). Into it he poured his disgust at the folly and wickedness of the populist politicians in Paris who had repeatedly rejected his proposals for limited reparations and inter-Allied debt forgiveness. The book also became an outlet for the strain he had endured since 1915 in a high-pressure job in His Majesty's Treasury during a war he thought futile, working 'for a government I despise for ends I think criminal' (Keynes, 1917). Important friendships, for instance with the generally pacifist members of Bloomsbury, had come under extreme stress at times. Other friends had been killed at the front. Indeed, Keynes felt that the world he loved had come to an end, as Virginia Woolf's diary (Bell, 1977, p. 288) shows:

He is disillusioned, he says. No more does he believe, that is, in the stability of the things he likes. Eton is doomed; the governing classes, perhaps Cambridge too. These conclusions were forced on him by the dismal and degrading spectacle of the Peace Conference, where men played shamelessly, not for Europe, or even England, but for their own return to Parliament at the next election.

Keynes had more worldly motivations for writing *Economic Consequences*, too. Ambitious and still in his thirties, his book staked a claim to be heard on the public stage. He was also keen not to be left behind by his Bloomsbury chums, one of the closest of whom, Lytton Strachey, had just achieved an iconoclastic sensation with his *Eminent Victorians* (1918). Keynes adopted some of Strachey's mordant irreverence for his own work. *Economic Consequences* is short, only some 60,000 words long, but intensely literary. The tone and approach are unlike almost any other economics book. They reflect the breadth of his education, as well as the artistic circles – or, in Bloomsbury's case, squares – within which he moved (Davenport-Hines, 2015, pp. 38–60, 251–60; Lepper, 2016). It opens and closes with quotations from Hardy and Shelley. The style is an attractive mix of the lucid, common-sense prose of Treasury memoranda, and the rhetoric and logic of the Cambridge Apostles' debates (Lepper, 2013). This famous extract, describing the world destroyed by the war, is a good example (1919, pp. 6–7):

> the inhabitant of London could order by telephone, sipping his morning tea in bed, the various products of the whole earth, in such quantity as he might see fit, and reasonably expect their early delivery upon his doorstep; he could at the same moment and by the same means adventure his wealth in the natural resources and new enterprises of any quarter of the world and share, without exertion or even trouble, in their prospective fruits and advantages.... He could secure forthwith, if he wished it, cheap and comfortable means of transit to any country or climate without passport or other formality, could despatch his servant to the neighbouring office of a bank for such supply of the precious metals as might seem convenient, and could then proceed abroad to foreign quarters, without knowledge of their religion, language or customs, bearing coined wealth upon his person, and would consider himself greatly aggrieved and much surprised at the least interference. But, most important of all, he regarded this state of affairs as normal, certain and permanent, except in the direction of further improvement, and any deviation from it as aberrant, scandalous and avoidable.

III

The last sentence of *Economic Consequences* dedicates the book 'to the formation of the general opinion of the future' (1919, p. 189). How successful was it? Keynes worked hard to keep himself and his ideas in the public eye. He was never in much doubt that there had been 'an immense change in public sentiment' by January 1922, with 'the desire for a quiet life, for reduced commitments, for comfortable terms with our neighbours ... now paramount. The megalomania of war has passed away, and everyone wishes to conform himself with the facts' (1922, pp. 4–5). By 1931 he argued that 'scarcely anyone in England now believes in the Treaty of Versailles or in the pre-war gold standard or in the policy of deflation. These battles have been won – mainly by the irresistible pressure of events and only secondarily by the slow undermining of old prejudices' (1931, p. xix). When Keynes appeared to deprecate himself, in the same preface to *Essays in Persuasion*, by claiming to present merely 'the croakings of a Cassandra who could never influence the course of events in time', his intention was to reassert, not undercut, how right he had been (1931, p. xvii). His biographers and historians have tended to agree. Roy Harrod maintained that 'his influence on the British public was profound and rapid' (1951, p. 254). For Robert Skidelsky, Keynes's was 'a very influential book. Of the dozens of accounts of the Treaty which appeared in the 1920s, it is the only one which has not sunk without a trace' (1983, p. 399). Richard Davenport-Hines calls it 'a bestseller which exercised a profound influence' (2015, p. 118; see also Moggridge, 1992, pp. 335–40). Indeed, Adam Tooze claims that 'no single individual did more to undermine the political legitimacy of the Versailles peace than Keynes' (Tooze, 2014, p. 295).[5] Intuitively, these claims seem plausible. The passion and wit of Keynes's writing; the clarity and conviction of his argument; and the timing of his intervention: all three seem to suggest that *Economic Consequences* must have been an important and influential book.

What evidence is there to support this intuition, however, and to help us understand what Peter Mandler calls the 'throw', the 'dissemination and influence', of *Economic Consequences* (Mandler, 2004, pp. 96–7)? Such evidence might take three forms: sales figures; the responses of critics; and the impact of its ideas both on the war poets and on elite and popular opinion more broadly. Let us take these in order.

First, *Economic Consequences* was a huge commercial and critical success. Published in December 1919, worldwide sales by the end of summer 1920 were around 100,000. Macmillan sold 21,915 copies in the United Kingdom, and 38,403 in America (Macmillan & Co., 1920; Harcourt, Brace and Howe, Inc., 1920).[6] Another nearly 10,000 copies had gone to Labour Party members in a cut-price edition (Cole, 1920; Moggridge, 1992, p. 499). The Society of Friends bookshop could not keep up with demand (*Friend*, 1920). Keynes was clearly reaching the ordinary public. *The Daily News* reported, for instance, that a progressive book shop in Glasgow sold all bar eight of 100 copies ordered in less than a fortnight: 'the purchaser in every case

---

[5] Thirlwall, 1982, made the same point: p. 105; as, indeed, had Mantoux (1946)
[6] The Liberal Party also reproduced a section of *Economic Consequences* as a leaflet: Keynes (1920). Thanks to Professor Richard Toye for bringing this to my attention.

was a working man' (1920). Sir William Beveridge later commented that 'his book has been read by – at a moderate computation – half a million people who never read an economic work before and probably will not read one again' (1924, p. 2).

Secondly, Keynes worked hard to make sure that *Economic Consequences* was widely reviewed (Beaverbrook, 1919). The progressive press was predictably enthusiastic. Norman Angell's review in the *Daily Herald* (1919), under the headline 'How Paris Betrayed the World', exhorted Labour to make 'a political event' of this book. *The Westminster Gazette* (1919)described it as 'a smashing and unanswerable indictment of the economic settlement.... It is too much to hope that the arbiters of our destinies will read it and perhaps learn wisdom, but it should do much good in informing a wide section of that public which will in its turn become the arbiter of theirs'. The *Manchester Guardian* (1919) saw it as 'not merely an act of conspicuous courage and public spirit: it is an infinitely more important event than any speech that has been made on the peace by any of its authors. He tells us what he thinks: they tell us what they force themselves to think. As a piece of literature, it is beyond praise'. *The National Review* (1920) argued that 'for the second treaty of Versailles no one except its actual authors has a good word'.

The reviewer for *The Economist*, while regarding Keynes's case as 'unanswerable' and the book as 'the most important and authoritative account of the Treaty that has yet appeared', saw the situation clearly: 'what he tells us of the origins of the Treaty, of its genesis in the peculiar psychology of Paris, and of its justice, will be judged and interpreted by every reader according to his preconceived opinions and prejudices on questions which are certainly not economic' (1919). Indeed, the conservative press was predictably more hostile, criticizing Keynes for being too academic, too pro-German, for a betrayal of trust, and most of all for forgetting who had started the war (*Spectator*, 1919 and *Morning Post*, 1919). The *Sunday Chronicle*, for instance, wrote of his 'enthroned and dehumanised intellectual point of view which regarded the war precisely as if he had arrived on November 11, 1918, from the planet Mars' with no understanding that the treaty was a consequence of Germany's actions (1920). The editor of *The Times*, Wickham Steed, thundered that 'Mr Keynes may be a "clever" economist. He may have been a useful Treasury official. But, in writing this book, he has rendered the Allies a disservice for which their enemies will, doubtless, be grateful' (*The Times*, January 1920). Reviewers, in other words, were split along predictable lines. Those who had been least enthusiastic about the war, who had been least culturally mobilized, tended to be keenest on *Economic Consequences*, and vice versa.

Thirdly, three particular ideas of Keynes's are echoed in the later war books: futility; a 'lost Golden Age' trope; and a general sense of anomie and instability. Futility, first, because he argued that the Allies had won the war but lost the peace by imposing a Treaty which was both immoral and bound to fail. It was both a crime and a mistake. By failing to consider the economic reconstruction of Europe, the peacemakers had bound the continent to further desperate hardship and political instability (Keynes, 1919, chapter 6; Clavin, 2013, pp. 12–13). The war had not only brought none of the benefits promised, but had solved nothing. All that sacrifice had been in vain. Secondly, a 'lost Golden Age', because, as we saw in the extract above, Keynes presented 1914 as the end of an era. The 'lost Golden Age' trope is echoed in the loving descriptions of pre-war life in both *Good-bye to All That* and *Memoirs of a Fox-hunting Man*, for instance, and trails down to later popular culture in, for instance, *The Go-Between*, *The Shooting Party*, and *Downton Abbey* (Hartley, 1953; Bridges, 1985; Fellowes, 2010; Marwick, 1965, p. 9). Legends of the fall were far from novel, of course. Paradise lost is, after all, one of the oldest tropes in western literature. Prophecies of Armageddon were widespread even before the war began (Neiberg, 2011; Jones and Weinreich, 2013; Mulligan, 2019). As the fighting went on, the Bloomsbury set saw war as the destruction of the civilization it held so dear (Hynes, 1990, pp. 10, 83–5, 312). Quentin Bell, Clive's son, later described *Economic Consequences* as the natural sequel to his father's 1915 book *Peace at Once* (Bell, 1980, p. 76; Davenport-Hines, 2015, p. 108). Richard Overy has built this up into a thesis of an interwar 'Morbid Age' (Overy, 2009). This sense of the end of an era, of old certainties swept away, fed directly into Keynes's third relevant idea: the general sense of rootlessness, anomie, and instability, which also carried through into the war books.

The transmission mechanism by which Keynes's ideas found their way to the war poets, however, is harder to isolate and identify. There is little evidence for much direct link. Sassoon knew Keynes, but not well, and did not like him – or much of Bloomsbury. Sassoon saw Keynes some seven times between October 1918 and November 1925

(Sassoon, 1983, p. 279; 1981, pp. 20, 61, 63; 1985, pp. 23–4, 294; Wilson, 2003, pp. 122–3). Although Sassoon and Blunden both knew the book well enough to enjoy a pun about the 'economic consequences of the piece' in 1929, and in the early 1930s Blunden wrote for Keynes's paper *The Nation*, there appears to have been no direct link at all between them all during the 1920s. None of them left any record of their impressions of *Economic Consequences* (Blunden, 1929). When Sassoon's estate sold off his library in 1975, Keynes's book was not among the lots sold (Christie's, 1975).

Further, while the vigour and wit with which Keynes wielded his pen were unprecedented, and his economic logic was devastating, the larger ideas his polemic contained were, on the whole, not original, but shared by many who had similar feelings about the Great War. Although his attitudes to the war were extremely complex, and indeed conflicted, simultaneously embracing both conscientious objection and government service, his feeling that war was immoral and futile, capable only of destroying civilization, was a central liberal (and Liberal) belief stretching back to Gladstone and Cobden. When Keynes condemned Versailles, he was expressing an opinion shared by many who were anti-war or anti-pro-war. The war poets, especially those such as Sassoon who moved in a similar milieu to Keynes, could easily have picked up such ideas from many places other than *Economic Consequences* (Ceadel, 2000, p. 240).

Keynes's impact on broader opinion is even harder to identify, much less to quantify. He distinguished between 'inside' and 'outside' opinion. The former was what politicians, journalists, and civil servants said to each other in private; the latter 'the opinion of the public voiced by the politicians and the newspapers,' which in turn can be separated into 'that which is expressed in the newspapers and that which the mass of ordinary men privately suspect to be true' (Keynes, 1922, pp. 3–4). 'Inside' opinion was quick to take notice of Keynes's book, not least because he sent copies to at least seventy-three important opinion-formers (Moggridge, 1992, p. 335). Both Unionists and Asquithian Liberals enjoyed Keynes's satire of Lloyd George. A.J. Balfour and Winston Churchill were just two among the senior politicians who read and drew on *Economic Consequences* (Bonar Law, 1919; Marsh, 1919; Asquith, 1919; McKenna, n.d.; Chamberlain, 1919; Lloyd-Greame, 1920). In the House of Commons, a February 1920 debate on the peace treaties became 'a tribute to the remarkable book of

Mr J.M. Keynes' (*Western Daily Press*, 1920; *The Times*, February 1920; *Hansard*, 12 February 1920, columns 290–302). Prominent supporters of the Treaty, such as André Tardieu and Bernard Baruch, paid *Economic Consequences* the compliment of hurrying to write book-length responses (Baruch, 1920; Tardieu, 1921). Even hostile reviewers, whatever they thought of Keynes's politics, tended not to criticize him on his economics. Perhaps, as the *Saturday Review* put it in January 1920, 'competent opinion is rapidly veering round to Mr Keynes's view of the indemnity clauses of the treaties with Germany and Austria. It is now generally recognized that the indemnities cannot, in anything like their present form, be exacted, and that if persisted in the only result will be the ruin and Bolshevisation of Europe' (*The Saturday Review*, 1920). Keynes soon repaired any damage done to his popularity with the government and wider establishment: already in 1921 he was appointed to a Royal Commission (Skidelsky, 1994, pp. 18–20, 27, 431–2; Davenport-Hines, 2015, pp. 144–5).

'Outside' opinion is harder to track in a period before Mass Observation and Gallup. There are a few clues. We have already noted Beveridge's impression. Sir Josiah Stamp claimed that, by the time of the Young Plan in 1929, 'the world came to the conclusion that Keynes was not far out', in his economic prophecy, at least (1934, p. 109). Foreign observers were noticing a shift in British opinion. In June 1920 *Le Revue Bibliographique* reported that 'the English public has been so struck by the originality of this work that its publication kicked off a genuine movement in favour of a revision of the Treaty of Versailles.' By September, the American Dr Alonzo Engelbert Taylor was arguing that

a remarkable change in attitude toward Germany has developed in the United Kingdom during the last year. Of the millions who swore never again to purchase a German-made article, nine-tenths have either forgotten all about the oath or have frankly discarded it because exclusion of Germany's products is now regarded as more harmful to the British than to the Germans. (*The Saturday Evening Post*, 1920)

How far *Economic Consequences* really penetrated the working class, however, remains doubtful. Jonathan Rose has shown that only small minorities of the adult working class were active readers, and that the communal libraries, even of the politically engaged miners of South Wales, stocked strikingly few works such as Keynes's. Of the loans from the Sengenhydd Institute Library in 1925, 93.4% were fiction, with only 0.4% economics books (Rose, 2001, pp. 121, 245–8).[7]

Another way to explore this question might be by proxy. The most popular history book published between the wars was H.G. Wells's *The Outline of History*, which sold some two million copies world-wide in five editions and multiple reprints between 1920 and 1932. Wells was a progressive broadly in sympathy with Keynes's view: he had written to congratulate him on 'a very fine book indeed' (Wells, n.d.). In early editions, Wells followed Keynes's account of the conference and directly quoted his character sketches of Wilson and the others, but said nothing about reparations or war debts. From the 1925 edition onwards, however, the burden of reparations was introduced, and by 1932 Wells included seven pages on the harm done by the failure to unwind wartime debt burdens (Wells, 1920, and further editions 1923, 1925, 1930, and 1932). Wells was highly sensitive to what interested his readers, so the changes he made may reflect evolving attitudes on their part. Roy Harrod's contention, that Keynes had 'voiced the sentiments of the civilisation to which he belonged' and that the rapidity with which public opinion caught up with Keynes's ideas demonstrated the traditional 'magnanimity of British society', may seem a romantic view, but equally might well be correct (1951, pp. 264–6).

Events and ideas interact in complex ways to change attitudes, and Keynes's, of course, were not the only ideas helping to form opinion. The growth of pacifism between the wars is an interesting and related example, as Martin Ceadel has shown (2000, pp. 239–80). It is a striking paradox, however, that the moment at which British public opinion found the futility myth most attractive, in the late 1920s, was in fact when it began to seem that peace at last had been achieved, and the Great War might have discovered some meaning. As David Reynolds argues, '1914-18 might still be justified if it did indeed prove to be the war to end wars. Ultimately the meaning of the war would depend on the persistence of the peace' and the outlook in 1928–9 on the international front was calmer than it had been for some time (2013, p. 207). The savage wars of the early 1920s had burnt themselves out; the Locarno Security Pact had gone a long way

---

[7] Thanks to Professor Richard Toye for alerting me to Rose's work and for reminding me about H.G. Wells and *The Outline of History*.

to resolving Franco-German problems; and in 1928 some thirty-three countries subscribed to the Kellogg–Briand Pact, outlawing war. The League of Nations was up and working. Weimar Germany had recovered from the crisis of 1923, and the Dawes Plan seemed, for the moment at least, to have mitigated the worst excesses of reparations. Within the United Kingdom, the picture was less clear, but overall Britain's passage had been far less storm-tossed than that of her European neighbours. The political instability of 1919–24 had settled down. Economically, normal service had apparently been resumed with the return to the 'knave-proof' gold standard. Although the country had experienced a decade of industrial unrest and stubbornly high unemployment, stock market crashes and worldwide depression remained in the future. And yet, despite what seemed like a successful international settlement, and a domestic economic and social situation which was not getting worse, even if it was not getting any better, British people turned against the war in the late 1920s. For Martin Pugh, this was largely a product of Germany seeming less of a threat to peace in the 1920s, and so more sympathetic in British eyes, than France (2009, pp. 18–19, 394). Peter Clarke argues that 'one way or another, the war and the peace alike came to be seen in terms more sympathetic to Germany than had been the case in 1918-19. The arguments to which Keynes had given canonical expression in publishing his *Economic Consequences* inevitably fed the "innocence campaign"' (2017, pp. 349–51). The shift may also suggest three other things, however. Firstly, that British public opinion was perhaps more interested in what was going on at home than abroad. Secondly, that perceptions were more important than reality. Public opinion saw the world as worse than it objectively was. In other words, ideas, including those of Keynes, mattered more than facts. Thirdly, this challenges views of Britain between the wars as being, at least compared to European nations, a relatively homogeneous, politically apathetic place, as described for example by Kevin Jefferys (2007, pp. 20–51). The debate about this has re-surfaced recently in the work of historians such as Helen McCarthy (2010 and 2012), Daniel Todman (2016), and Jonathan Fennell (2019), each of whom, in different ways, has depicted the British electorate as deeply politically engaged between the wars. This is an interesting and important historical question which deserves further research. What does seem clear, however, is that cultural demobilization was merely one among the complex set of ever-changing and intersecting currents which were carrying public opinion along.[8]

To summarize: Keynes was among the first to demobilize culturally because he had never been much mobilized in the first place. By 1919 his distress about the war, nostalgia for a lost world, anger at the Treaty, and frank ambition drove him to polemics. *Economic Consequences* proved a big hit, but its success was initially primarily limited to those whose support for the war, like that of Keynes himself, had been highly conditional. At some stage during the 1920s, messages like Keynes's became increasingly mainstream and the disenchanted literature of the war attracted an interest it had earlier struggled to achieve. Although we are left with a general sense that Keynes's eloquence, and his ideas of 1919, must have influenced the reception of the war books, we have no way of either proving a specific connection or quantifying their impact.

IV

This chapter has explored the impact of Keynes's *The Economic Consequences of the Peace* on the construction of the British 'futility myth' of the First World War. It has shown that Keynes's book and his ideas initially enjoyed greatest success among those already predisposed to agree, but that, for reasons we still do not fully understand, public opinion shifted later in the 1920s, creating a climate where disenchanted literature which picked up on some of the tropes evident in *Economic Consequences* could flourish. This suggests that perhaps we need to see that disenchanted literature less as the personal responses of a handful of aesthetes and more as representative of a longer tradition of anti-war, or perhaps better 'anti-pro-war', thinking and writing which might question existing histories of British popular engagement with politics. It has demonstrated also that there is still room to re-evaluate the influence of Keynes in particular, and non-fiction in general, on how we perceive the First World War, even if we cannot find a specific drive train connecting Keynes's ideas with the war books, and have no way of quantifying the impact of the former on the latter.

From this emerge three interesting implications for the practice of cultural history. Firstly, that there remains work to be done to

---

[8] Thanks to Dr Helen McCartney for suggesting this point.

integrate non-fiction and other cultural forms into stories of the construction of memory of the First World War. For efforts in this direction, see Walters, 2016; Napper, 2013; and Trott, 2017. Secondly,
that we need to develop new ways to assess the reception accorded to
texts by their audiences (Mandler, 2004, pp. 96–8, 107, 103; Grandy,
2019, p. 7). And, thirdly, that we need to have realistic expectations
about the ability of cultural history to prove causation (Burke, 2008,
pp. 21–3; Jackson, 2008, pp. 160–3; Arnold, Hilton and Rüger,
2018, p. 10).

These implications must await another day. What this chapter has
demonstrated, however, is how Keynes transcends economics and
economic history. He allows us to explore almost every highway and
byway of British and international history in the first half of the twentieth century. That is just one of the ways in which, a hundred years
after the publication of *The Economic Consequences of the Peace*,
Maynard Keynes remains not only fascinating, but deeply relevant to
our world today.

References

Arnold, John H., Hilton, Matthew and Rüger, Jan, 'The Challenges of History'. In Arnold, John H., Hilton, Matthew and Rüger, Jan (eds), *History
after Hobsbawm: Writing the Past for the Twenty-First Century*. Oxford:
Oxford University Press, 2018: 3–14
Asquith, Margot, letter to Keynes, 15 December 1919, King's College Cam-
bridge, Keynes Papers EC 2/1/42
Audoin-Rouzeau, Stephane and Becker, Annette, *1914–1918 Understand-
ing the Great War*. London: Profile, 2002
Barnett, Correlli, 'A Military Historian's View of the Great War', *Transac-
tions of the Royal Society of Literature* 36 (1970): 1–18
Baruch, Bernard, *The Making of the Reparation and Economic Sections of
the Treaty*. New York: Harper Brothers, 1920
Beaverbrook, Max, letter to Keynes, John Maynard, 12 December 1919,
King's College Cambridge, Keynes Papers EC 2/1/18
Bell, Anne Olivier (ed.), *The Diary of Virginia Woolf Volume I 1915–1919*.
London: Hogarth Press, 1977
Bell, Quentin, 'Recollections and Reflections on Maynard Keynes'. In Crab-
tree, Derek and Thirlwall, A.P. (eds), *Keynes and the Bloomsbury Group*.
London: Macmillan, 1980: 6986
Beveridge, William, 'Mr Keynes' Evidence for Over-Population', *Econom-
ica* 10 (1924): 1–20

Blunden, Edmund, letter to Sassoon, Siegfried, 11 May 1929. In Roth-kopf, Carol Z. (ed.), *Selected Letters of Siegfried Sassoon and Edmund Blunden, 1919–1967 Volume I Letters 1919–1931*. London: Pickering & Chatto, 2012: 222

Bonar Law, *Andrew, letter to Keynes*, 30 December 1919, King's College Cambridge, Keynes Papers EC 2/1/3–4

Bond, Brian, 'Editor's Introduction. In Bond, Brian (ed.), *The First World War and British Military History*. Oxford: Clarendon Press, 1991

Bond, Brian, 'Liddell Hart and the First World War. In *'Look to Your Front': Studies in the First World War by the British Commission for Military History*. Staplehurst: Spellmount, 1999

Bond, Brian, *The Unquiet Western Front: Britain's Role in Literature and History*. Cambridge: Cambridge University Press, 2002

Bond, Brian, 'British "anti-war" Writers and their Critics'. In Cecil, Hugh and Liddle, Peter H. (eds), *Facing Armageddon: The First World War Experienced*. Barnsley: Pen and Sword, 2003 [originally published 1996]: 817–30

Bracco, Rosa Maria, *Merchants of Hope: British Middlebrow Writers and the First World War, 1919–39*. Providence RI: Berg, 1993

Bridges, Alan, director, The Shooting Party, film (1985)

Broadberry, Stephen and Harrison, Mark (eds), *The Economics of World War I*. Cambridge: Cambridge University Press, 2005

Burk, Kathleen, *Britain, America and the Sinews of War, 1914–1918*. Boston: George Allen & Unwin, 1985

Burke, Peter, *What is Cultural History?* Cambridge: Polity, 2008

Ceadel, Martin, *Semi-Detached Idealists: The British Peace Movement and International Relations, 1854–1945*. Oxford: Oxford University Press, 2000

Cecil, Hugh, *The Flower of Battle: How Britain wrote the Great War*. South Royalton, VT: Steerforth Press, 1996

Cecil, Hugh, 'British War Novelists'. In Cecil, Hugh and Liddle, Peter H. (eds), *Facing Armageddon: The First World War Experienced*. Barnsley: Pen and Sword, 2003 [originally published 1996]

Chamberlain, Austen, letter to Keynes, 22 December 1919, King's College Cambridge, Keynes Papers EC 2/2/8–10

Christie's, auction catalogue, 'The Library of the late Siegfried Sassoon'. London 1975

Clarke, Peter, *Keynes: The Twentieth Century's Most Influential Economist*. London: Bloomsbury, 2009

Clarke, Peter, *The Locomotive of War: Money, Empire, Power and Guilt*. London: Bloomsbury, 2017

Clavin, Patricia, *Securing the World Economy: The Reinvention of the League of Nations, 1920–1946*. Oxford: Oxford University Press, 2013

Cole, G.D.H., letter to Keynes, John Maynard, 30 September 1920: King's College Cambridge, Keynes Papers, EC 4/46, 4/48

Cox, Michael, 'Introduction'. In *John Maynard Keynes, The Economic Consequences of the Peace*. Cham: Palgrave Macmillan, 2019: 1–44

Cummins, Paul and Piper, Tom, 'Bloodswept Lands and Seas of Red', art installation, Tower of London, July–November 2014

Curtis, Richard and Elton, Ben, Blackadder Goes Forth, BBC TV series, first broadcast September–November 1989

Daily Herald, newspaper, 12 December 1919, King's College Cambridge, Keynes Papers A/54/2/6–7

Daily News, newspaper, 5 February 1920, King's College Cambridge, Keynes Papers A/54/3/61

Danchev, Alex, 'Bunking and Debunking: The Controversies of the 1960s'. In Bond, Brian (ed.), *The First World War and Military History*. Oxford: Clarendon Press, 1991: 263–88

Davenport-Hines, Richard, *Universal Man: The Seven Lives of John Maynard Keynes*. London: William Collins, 2015

Deller, Jeremy and Norris, Rufus 'We're Here Because We're Here', participation event across the UK, 1 July 2016

Economist, The, 27 December 1919, King's College Cambridge, Keynes Papers A/54/2/52–4

Eichengreen, Barry, *Golden Fetters: The Gold Standard and the Great Depression, 1919–1939*. New York: Oxford University Press, 1992

Eksteins, Modris, *Rites of Spring: The Great War and the Birth of the Modern Age*. London: Bantam, 1989

Falls, Cyril, *War Books: An annotated Bibliography of Books about the Great War*. London: Greenhill, 1989 [originally published 1930]

Feldman, Gerald D., *The Great Disorder: Politics, Economics and Society in the German Inflation, 1914–24*. New York: Oxford University Press, 1997

Fellowes, Julian, creator, Downton Abbey, TV series, first broadcast 2010

Fennell, Jonathan, *Fighting the People's War: The British and Commonwealth Armies and the Second World War*. Cambridge: Cambridge University Press, 2019

Ferguson, Niall, *The Pity of War*. London: Allen Lane, 1998

Friend, newspaper, 23 January 1920, King's College Cambridge, Keynes Papers A/54/3/45

Fussell, Paul, *The Great War and Modern Memory*. Oxford: Oxford University Press, 2000 [originally published 1975]

Grandy, Christine, 'Cultural History's Absent Audience', *Cultural and Social History* 16 (No. 5, 2019): 643–63

Graves, Robert, *Good-bye to All That: An Autobiography*. London: Jonathan Cape, 1929

Grieves, Keith, 'Early Historical Responses to the Great War: Fortescue, Conan Doyle, and Buchan'. In Bond, Brian (ed.), *The First World War and British Military History*. Oxford: Clarendon Press, 1991: 15–40

Hansard, 5th Series, Volume 125, 12 February 1920

Harcourt, Brace and Howe, Inc., royalty statement for Keynes, John Maynard, to 30 June 1920, King's College Cambridge, Keynes Papers EC 5/1/50

Harrod, R.F., *The Life of John Maynard Keynes*. London: Macmillan, 1951

Hartley, L.P., *The Go-Between*. London: Hamish Hamilton, 1953

Horne, John, 'Demobilizing the Mind: France and the Legacy of the Great War, 1919–1939', *French History and Civilization*, 2 (2009): 101–19

Horne, John, 'Kulturelle Demobilmachung 1919–1939. Ein sinnvoller historischer Begriff?'. In Hardtwig, Wolfgang (ed.), *Politische Kulturgeschichte der Zwischenkriegszeit 1918–1939*. Göttingen: Vandenhoeck & Ruprecht, 2005: 129–50

Hynes, Samuel, *A War Imagined: The First World War and English Culture*. London: Bodley Head, 1990

Jackson, Peter, 'Pierre Bourdieu, the "Cultural Turn", and the Practice of International History', *Review of International Studies* 34 (2008): 155–81

Jefferys, Kevin, *Politics and the People: A History of British Democracy since 1918*. London: Atlantic Books, 2007

Jones, Heather and Weinreich, Arndt (eds), 'The Pre–1914 Period: Imagined Wars, Future Wars', *Francia: Forschungen zur westeuropäischen Geschichte XL* (2013), accessed 26 November 2021: 305–16

Kendall, Tim (ed.), *Poetry of the First World War: An Anthology*. Oxford: Oxford University Press, 2013

Keynes, John Maynard, letter to Grant, Duncan, December 1917, quoted in Skidelsky, Robert, *John Maynard Keynes Volume I Hopes Betrayed 1883–1920*. London: Macmillan, 1983: 319

Keynes, John Maynard, *Collected Writings Volume II The Economic Consequences of the Peace*. Cambridge: Cambridge University Press, 2013 [originally published 1919]

Keynes, John Maynard, *Mr Lloyd George's General Election*. London: Liberal Publication Department, 1920

Keynes, John Maynard, *Collected Writings Volume III A Revision of the Treaty*. Cambridge: Cambridge University Press, 2013 [originally published 1922]

Keynes, John Maynard, *Collected Writings Volume IX Essays in Persuasion*. Cambridge: Cambridge University Press, 2013 [originally published 1931]

Lepper, Larry, 'Rhetoric and Keynes's Use of Statistics in *The Economic Consequences of the Peace*', *Cambridge Journal of Economics* 37 (2013): 403–21

Lepper, Larry, 'What Literary Criticism tells us about Keynes's *Economic Consequences of the Peace*'. In Hölscher, Jens and Klaes, Matthias (eds), *Keynes's Economic Consequences of the Peace: A Reappraisal*. Abingdon: Routledge, 2016: 35–62

Lloyd-Greame, P., letter to The Times, 9 January 1920, King's College Cambridge, Keynes Papers A/54/3/15

MacMillan, Margaret, *Peacemakers: The Paris Conference of 1919 and Its Attempts to End War*. London: John Murray, 2001

Macmillan & Co. statement for Keynes, John Maynard, to 30 June 1920, King's College Cambridge, Keynes Papers EC 4/52

Manchester Guardian, newspaper, 24 December 1919, King's College Cambridge, Keynes Papers A/54/2/46–8

Mandler, Peter, 'The Problem with Cultural History', *Cultural and Social History*, 1 (No. 1, 2004): 94–117

Mantoux, Étienne, *The Carthaginian Peace or the Economic Consequences of Mr Keynes*. London: Oxford University Press, 1946

Markwell, Donald, *John Maynard Keynes and International Relations: Economic Paths to War and Peace*. Oxford: Oxford University Press, 2006

Marsh, Eddie (p.p. Winston S. Churchill), letter to Keynes, 15 December 1919, King's College Cambridge, Keynes Papers EC 2/1/27

Marwick, Arthur, *The Deluge: British Society and the First World War*. London: Bodley Head, 1965

McCarthy, Helen, 'Democratising British Foreign Policy: Rethinking the Peace Ballot, 1934–5', *Journal of British Studies* 49 (April 2010): 358–87

McCarthy, Helen, 'Whose Democracy? Histories of British Political Culture between the Wars', *Historical Journal* 55 (No. 1, 2012): 221–38

McCartney, Helen B., 'Commemorating the Centenary of the First World War: National and Transnational Perspectives', *War and Society* 36 (No. 4, 2017): 289–303

McKenna, Pamela, letter to Keynes, n.d. but December 1919, King's College Cambridge, Keynes Papers EC 2/1/44–45

Moggridge, Donald, *Maynard Keynes: An Economist's Biography*. London: Routledge, 1992

Morning Post, 24 December 1919, King's College Cambridge, Keynes Papers A/54/2/49

Mulligan, William, 'Armageddon: Political Elites and their Visions of a general European War before 1914', *War in History* 26 (No. 4, 2019): 448–69

Napper, Laurence, 'That Filth from which the Glamour is not even yet Departed! Adapting *Journey's End*'. In Palmer, R. Barton and Bray,

William Robert (eds), *Modern British Drama on Screen*. New York: Cambridge University Press, 2013: 12–30

National Review, The, January 1920, King's College Cambridge, Keynes Papers A 54/2/80–1

Neiberg, Michael S., *Dance of the Furies: Europe and the Outbreak of World War I*. Cambridge, MA: Belknap Press, 2011

Overy, Richard, *The Morbid Age: Britain between the Wars*. London: Allen Lane, 2009

Prior, Robin and Wilson, Trevor, 'Paul Fussell at War', *War in History* 1 (No. 1, 1994): 63–80

Pugh, Martin, *We Danced All Night: A Social History of Britain between the Wars*. London: Vintage, 2009 [originally published 2008]

Revue Bibliographique, Le, June 1920, King's College Cambridge, Keynes Papers EC 13/59

Reynolds, David, *The Long Shadow: The Great War and the Twentieth Century*. London: Simon & Schuster, 2013

Roberts, Richard, *Saving the City: The Great Financial Crisis of 1914*. Oxford: Oxford University Press, 2013

Rose, Jonathan, *The Intellectual Life of the British Working Classes*. New Haven: Yale University Press, 2001

Sassoon, Siegfried, *Diaries: 1920–1922*. London: Faber and Faber, 1981

Sassoon, Siegfried, *Diaries: 1915–1918*. London: Faber and Faber, 1983

Sassoon, Siegfried, *Diaries: 1923–1925*. London: Faber and Faber, 1985

Saturday Evening Post, The, 18 September 1920, King's College Cambridge, Keynes Papers EC 13/89–96

Saturday Review, The, 31 January 1920, King's College Cambridge, Keynes Papers EC 13/55

Saunders, Max, 'Introduction', Ford, Ford Madox, *Parade's End: Some Do Not...* Manchester: Carcanet Press, 2010 [originally published 1924]

Skidelsky, Robert, *John Maynard Keynes Volume I Hopes Betrayed 1883–1920*. London: Macmillan, 1983

Skidelsky, Robert, *John Maynard Keynes Volume II The Economist as Saviour 1920–1937*. New York: Allen Lane, 1994 [originally published in UK, 1992)

Spectator, The, 20 December 1919, King's College Cambridge, Keynes Papers A/54/2/22–4

Stamp, Josiah, 'The Economic Consequences of the Peace', *Foreign Affairs*, 13 (No. 1, October 1934): 104–12

Steiner, Zara, *The Lights that Failed: European International History 1919–1933*. Oxford: Oxford University Press, 2005

Strachan, Hew, *Financing the First World War*. Oxford: Oxford University Press, 2004

Strachey, Lytton, *Eminent Victorians*. London: Chatto & Windus, 1918

Sunday Chronicle, 21 December 1919, King's College Cambridge, Keynes Papers A 54/2/39–40

Tardieu, André, *The Truth about the Treaty*. London: Hodder & Stoughton, 1921

Thirlwall, A.P., *Keynes as a Policy Adviser*. London: Macmillan, 1982

Times, The, 5 January 1920, King's College Cambridge, Keynes Papers A/54/3/10–11 and EC 13/8

Times, The 13 February 1920, King's College Cambridge, Keynes Papers EC 13/11

Todman, Dan, *The Great War: Myth and Memory*. London: Hambledon, 2005

Todman, Daniel, *Britain's War Volume I: Into Battle 1937–41*. London: Allen Lane, 2016

Tooze, Adam, *The Deluge: The Great War and the Remaking of the Global Order*. London: Allen Lane, 2014

Toye, Richard, 'Keynes, Liberalism and "The Emancipation of the Mind", *English Historical Review* 130 (No. 546, 2015): 1156–91

Trott, Vincent, *Publishers, Readers and the Great War: Literature and Memory since 1918*. London: Bloomsbury, 2017

Walters, Emily Curtis, 'Between Entertainment and Elegy: The Unexpected Success of R.C. Sherriff's *Journey's End* (1928)', *Journal of British Studies* 55 (April 2016): 344–73

Watson, Janet S.K., *Fighting Different Wars: Experience, Memory and the First World War in Britain*. Cambridge: Cambridge University Press, 2004

Wells, H.G., letter to Keynes, John Maynard, n.d., King's College Cambridge, Keynes Papers EC 2/179

Wells, H.G., *The Outline of History*. London: Cassell, 1920

Western Daily Press, 13 February 1920, King's College Cambridge, Keynes Papers EC 13/12

Westminster Gazette, The, 'The Tower of Babel', 20 December 1919, King's College Cambridge, Keynes Papers A/54/2/33–5

Wilson, Jean Moorcroft, *Siegfried Sassoon: The Journey from the Trenches: A Biography (1918–1967)*. London, Duckworth, 2003

Winter, Jay, *Sites of Memory, Sites of Mourning: The Great War in European Cultural History*. Cambridge: Cambridge University Press, 1995

Winter, Jay, *War beyond Words: Languages of Remembrance from the Great War to the Present*. Cambridge: Cambridge University Press, 2017

Winter, Jay and Prost, Antoine, *The Great War in History: Debates and Controversies, 1914 to the Present*. Cambridge: Cambridge University Press, 2005

Index